Introduction to Political Analysis

Introduction to Political Analysis

David E. Apter

Yale University

Winthrop Publishers, Inc.
Cambridge, Massachusetts

Library of Congress Cataloging in Publication Data

Apter, David Ernest
  Introduction to political analysis.

  Includes bibliographical references.
  1. Political science. I. Title.
JA66.A59   320   77–1345
ISBN 0–87626–408–9

Cover and interior design by Designworks

© *1977 by Winthrop Publishers, Inc.*
  17 Dunster Street, Cambridge, Massachusetts 02138

10 9 8 7 6 5 4 3 2 1

For Emily and Andrew

Contents

Preface

Since *Introduction to Political Analysis* is not a typical text, a few guides to its use may prove helpful. This book is not a history of the field. Rather, it is designed to trace the evolution of political science as a discipline. It uses contributions of other fields: economics, sociology, psychology, and anthropology. It also incorporates ideas and materials developed abroad. Six dimensions of political science, representing the main analytical alternatives in the literature, bring all these together, but certain exclusions should be noted. International relations has been omitted because despite the richness of some of its theory we consider it to be an applied field (like comparative politics, or American government). Theorists who work in international politics themselves favor one or several of the approaches suggested here.

Also excluded, except for passing reference, is organizational behavior, a subject which has largely replaced public administration in political science. The field covers such a diversity of concerns, from the study of bureaucracy to the examination of work motivation, that it would require another book to trace its development. Formal modeling, set theory, and other logico-deductive mathematical applications have been left out because they represent an approach to political problems so different from those employed here that they would require learning very different scientific languages and utilizing quite other assumptions. Statistical treatments are another matter. They can facilitate virtually all of the approaches examined but because of space (and limited competency) they are not included. My purpose here is to make sense out of the different approaches to politics by selecting some of their most significant ideas, pulling together out of the diverse strands of the subject those which are not only the most representative but are accepted as the most coherent and lively in the field.

Despite the sequence of presentation there is considerable overlap among the approaches around which the book is organized: political philosophy, institutionalism, behavioralism, pluralism, structuralism, and developmentalism. These approaches represent successive emphases but several, especially the latter two, overlap greatly. And pluralism, which represents the dominant approach to the field today, incorporates crucial features of both institutionalism and behavioralism. (Pluralism also includes most of what we regard as American government and the specialized examination of the Presidency, Congress, political parties, the legislature, interest groups—in short, all of what David Truman once called the "governmental process.")

A few other assumptions ought to be made clear. Taken as a whole, political science is about the relations between rulers and ruled, and the means and the ends each employs. Despite the diversity of the material, we have tried to hold to that essentially classical model partly because it has the virtues of simplicity and clarity and also because so many of the more elaborate formulations in the field are variants of that original.

Secondly, generally speaking, political science, as it has evolved, has been about democracy—its definition, purpose, and improvement. The alternative is "totalitarianism." In practice most countries actually are somewhere in between. The "bias" of the subject is that its practitioners want to realize democracy at the expense of totalitarianism, a too facile demonism (the triumph of a political science "good" over a political science "evil") but insofar as it remains a premise of its practitioners, in one way or other, that bias is reflected in the approaches employed here.

The book is organized as follows. The first unit introduces the field as a whole. Then comes the main body of the text, which is organized in six units. The unit on political philosophy contains three chapters, the others two chapters; within each unit the first chapter is more basic, covering the main ideas of the approach, and the second more advanced. By "advanced" we mean it concentrates on the dynamics of the approach, the models employed, and summarizes their advantages and limitations for political analysis. In more elementary political science courses these second chapters ought to be used primarily by students who have a special interest or aptitude in political analysis. Chapter Sixteen, the final chapter, is very brief, suggesting how the materials in the units can be divided between two main styles of political thinking. The book as a whole is designed to stimulate discussion. It is not an encyclopedia of politics.

The units themselves are organized so that they roughly correspond to today's intellectual division of labor in political science. The book can be used in courses taught either by a single or by several instructors. For example, the first two chapters might be presented by the organizers of the course, the second three by a political theorist, the institutionalist chapters by a specialist in comparative politics, and so on. While it is by no means suggested that any instructor will fit neatly or exclusively into one of these categories, the way in which most political scientists approach the field of politics as a whole tends to fall into one or several of them.

The material can be presented on a one-semester or two-semester basis. (I have done it both ways.) I find the two-semester form better for more introductory students simply because I can provide necessary illustrative material, little of which is included in the book. This also allows more time for class discussion, special projects, papers, and so forth. As a one-semester course, however, it is possible to move along at a good pace by concentrating on the material in the book itself, without assigning much more additional reading.

The main purpose of this enterprise is to clarify for introductory and advanced students what is a bewildering but fascinating field. The confusion is a result of its exceptional liveliness. Over the past years there has been an explosion in new ideas (and of every political persuasion). In addition, the growing complexity of political problems has stimulated efforts to improve both theories and methods. All this is to the good. But for a student it presents real difficulties of selection and comprehension. Moreover, political scientists do not necessarily agree among themselves, either about what is important or how the field should be shaped. Hence, there are few good guides. This text tries to resolve that problem not by elevating one approach over another, but by showing how each evolved as a consequence of the other, both in terms of a succession of new ideas and as ways of compensating for inadequacies of emphasis or treatment. One challenge has been to cull main concerns which have stood the test of time without making the book into a museum of old ideas and stale issues. Another has been to be faithful to the internal dialogue of theories and ideas as they form "interior" arguments. Such dialogue itself is important for the way we think about politics. It is essential if we want to gain an overall grasp of the subject. Also, such ideas make a student and a citizen "political."

These, then, have been the guidelines. I have tried to limit discussion to theorists whose works continue to stimulate new thinking and interpretation and so demarcate the field itself. The work of many important political scientists is not specifically included in this text unless it serves in this way. Those represented will find many of their ideas juxtaposed in a context of philosophical alternatives.

Perhaps one more comment is in order. If one underlying theme in political science is the relations of ruler and ruled, means and ends—that is, distributions of power (social, economic, as well as the conventionally political) —another is participation. It is a common assumption that participation is the benign side of power, a view taken by proponents of all approaches described here. However, theorists differ over how much participation, what kinds are preferable, and what *instrumentalities* will secure it. That is perhaps a central concern in the literature today and the source of frequent debate among those of liberal and radical political persuasions. Participation then represents as important a theme as power.

The book itself consists of three parts. In the first, I have tried to show how the field has evolved as a subject. Second, I have described its evolution in the form of six main alternative approaches to politics, each having a substantial literature as noted in the footnote references. Third, I have suggested that there are two dominant styles of political thinking, paradigmatic and behavioral. Preferences for one or other leads students to favor either more generalized forms of theory or more empirical and descriptive treatments.

I have incurred many debts during the writing of this book, only a few of which can be acknowledged here. My students at Yale suffered through earlier versions of the manuscript and pointed out some of its most vulnerable spots with unfailing delight, grace, and good humor. Dr. Peter Ewell of the University of Chicago not only went over the manuscript in detail, but rewrote parts of Chapter Eleven.

I had three sources of assistance in writing this book. At the Institute for Advanced Study, where I was a member during the spring of 1973 and the autumn of 1974, I not only prepared most of the first draft but also benefited from the comments of Professor Clifford Geertz and his colleagues.

In the later stages of this work I received assistance from the Institution for Social and Policy Studies at Yale University, whose Director, Professor Charles E. Lindblom, provided me with support and encouragement.

Finally, I am grateful to Mr. Joseph Goldsen, Executive Director of the Concilium of International Studies at Yale, who provided funds for travel and research.

I must acknowledge particular gratitude to Jim Murray who gave me the original idea for this project; Mrs. Sylvia Korn, who patiently, cheerfully, and efficiently typed draft after draft; and to Eleanor S. Apter, who is not only a wise critic, but also did the final proofs.

D. E. Apter
March 1977

Introduction to
Political Analysis

Political Science
as a Discipline

chapter one
Why a Political Science?

The proper study of politics began when human beings came to believe that they could fashion their own government according to understood principles. The discovery occurred in ancient Greece when, for the first time, the universe was no longer the precinct of the gods. The realities of the physical world became intelligible as science. First Plato, and then Aristotle, advanced the notion that by applying certain principles of reason to the conduct of human affairs, men could govern themselves. The connection between science and reason has continued to be important in politics in one way or another ever since. Despite all the predicaments of today's world, many of which seem to defy rationality, science and reason in politics represent our only form of collective hope. Admittedly, this hope is sometimes less than apparent. You might ask how rationality can save us when maximum population growth occurs in the poorest regions of the world. How can we cope with changes that redefine property relations? Where is the individual's place when control of the means of production shifts from predominantly private ownership to the state or the workers?

Political science tries to predict the consequences of change. Problems that challenge our thinking are population growth; the transformation of industrial societies; the growing tension between poor nations and rich; the emergence on a world scale of problems once confined to particular societies; the breakdown of class differences; massive urbanization; new information technologies; the possibility of effecting a democratization of all kinds of institutions against a global backdrop of spreading nuclear capabilities. These dilemmas not only test our capacity for rational thinking, they demand that such thinking be swifter and more accurate than ever before.

As a discipline, political science confronts all these problems, but it is often unable to keep pace with them. It cannot be expected that any single method or theory will fully comprehend all the factors involved. What is at stake is the "political culture": the orientation of men's thinking, their priorities, their ideals, their conventional wisdom about normative aspects of life. A political culture centers upon the ideal and how to obtain it. Since the Industrial Revolution our—that is, American —political culture has been founded on thinking that defines rationality as growth, growth as development, and finally development as improvement. The rationality of science with its innovative power has been intellectually combined with the rationality of democracy, the synthesis supposedly allowing us to control our environment, while ameliorating and improving the quality of our lives. In fact, this belief has been carried even further, to argue that democracy should distribute its benefits according to the shared interests of all, diffusing the concentration of power. Without democracy, it is said, science would be a terrible sword in the hands of a few; with it, science becomes the means for beneficial social improvement.

Today, however, we no longer believe that the connection between science and democracy is self-evident. Too many problems, too many changes in social and economic relationships between rich and poor and among individuals and nations—too much complexity in all our relationships—have muddled the principles by which we live. As bureaucracy grows, democracy declines. Everywhere the urge to create new and better forms of democratic participation, coordination, and freedom breaks down. More and more people are angry, frustrated, and manipulated. Political scientists, hard-pressed of late to explain what has happened, have provided but few solutions for the future.

One reason for this is that people react to events in ways much more complex than anyone ever anticipated in the past. At one time it was believed that most people felt competent to handle the problems of their daily lives and that they could act on that competency in a rational way. Democracy itself is based on the idea that each person is capable of understanding his or her own predicament better than anyone else— thus the most individual of political acts: the vote. To choose, and to act collectively as it suits one's purposes, is the essential act of intelligence. It is at the basis of the notion of rights. However, since Freud at least, we have realized that there is more to human behavior than rationality. Today we ask what new political alternatives will be necessary—given the complexity of human feelings, given the boredom, anger, and frustration that accompany the stresses and strains of work and given our everyday associations. It is inevitable that imponderable "human nature" does change, and political science must find good ways to fit such changes to the needs, conditions, and circumstances of modern life. This is the political predicament.

All this does not mean, however, that we have lost faith in the connection between science and politics. The premise of political science is that moral purposes and priorities, the relations of exchange and reciprocity, and the capacities of men to perceive, and motivate their actions accordingly, coalesce in a mutually reinforcing political system. We believe that political efficacy and better understanding generate a healthier climate in which individuals can make decisions. The alternative is to rely on coercive rule, the balance of terror that seeks to restrain powerful nations and maintain equilibrium in the world at large.

If politics has as its object the survival of human society through the meshing of individual and collective intelligence, it is equally true that those who govern are never quite up to the task. Hence the common dilemma. We waver between cynicism and the hope that a clear eye will lead us out of our difficulties. We are increasingly doubtful that our problems can be solved. The urge to improvement, and the need for leaders who can uplift and provide us with moral regeneration is complicated by a certain shrewdness and distrust of politicians. On one side of the coin is the veneration of the Washingtons, Lenins, Nkrumahs, and Maos of this world. On the other side is fear and the sense of betrayal aroused by a history of tyranny and abuses of public trust.

The Bases of Power

Political science shares in some measure the ambiguities of politics as a profession. There is within the profession the same mixture of curiosity, passion, and contempt for the subject as exists among the public generally. Like sex, politics has been a subject to avoid in polite society. But, just as we need the taboos associated with the one, we need the controversy of the other.

Both political and sexual associations generate the most intense feelings: love, hatred, loyalty, pride, shame, and anger. We have created certain institutions to control and channel such passions, the one in family life and kinship, the other in organized power. Both types represent continuity, the continuity of the species and the continuity of community. Each implies cherished beliefs and conventional practices.

Both are central to organized life, and both share a certain ambiguity—a shady side. Each, as part of everyone's experience, involves substantial social learning.

Politics, specifically, requires the learning of power. Not intimate, personal, private power involving mutual relationships, but social, collective, and public power. The difference is more than one of scale. Mutual respect and concern bind the family together, but in the larger political community, the bonds of obligation are more distant. An abstract form of authority is more important. Our lives take shape and meaning within authoritative boundaries, consisting of both the familial and the political, the individual and collective, private and public. Within these are all the institutions that prepare a child for the political world—schools and universities, the occupational alternatives, our personal associations. All these institutions represent tensed boundaries of political significance. Inside them, each of us sees the world with our own eyes, observing the scene, taking its measure, feeling the way, testing the social environment as if it were a lake or a pond. Is it too cold? Is it too deep? Will we get in over our heads? Or will we be invigorated?

We are political learners. Our criteria, the private estimates of our own capacities and interests, derive from the public arena in which we perform and where, observing, we are also observed. Between the autonomous private world of our own secret hopes and doubts and the workings of the public world are the rudiments of power. Power is derived not from abstract principles but from definable relationships. It is not only a matter of rules but of roles—parent, worker, politician, doctor, patient and the like—each of which represents a public as well as a private view.

Political analysis then, like any interpretive discipline, is concerned with all such relationships. Its science consists of breaking down the compelling phenomena of our daily lives into its private and public components, then recreating them in a new way. In the same way, a chemist analyzes compounds by breaking them down into elements or constituent parts. What a chemist or a political analyst learns by recombining the elements generates hypotheses, new questions, and theories. Theory represents a better understanding of parts and wholes.

Political scientists seek to discover the ingredients of power in their concentrated and abstracted forms. Power is to the political scientist what scarcity is to the economist. Scarcity assumes that something is valued, and that there is an insufficiency of it available. People will try to get something of value for themselves or their families. How they do has stimulated theories which deal with distribution, income, price, and quantities and their indicators, interest rates, inventories, and so forth. Power is less neat and calculable than scarcity. The political scientist lacks universalized standards of measure like gold or money. There is no interest rate for power, nor can it be put in the bank for reinvestment. Political science thus draws on theories from other disciplines to show how power is formed and used. It makes use of economic theories. It looks to history. It draws on psychology to learn why people believe and act as they do. If it is a less precise discipline than some, it is more encompassing than most. It takes many of its ideas from other fields, but retains its own coherence, its own principles. And we must not lose sight of these.

Analytical Systems

Accordingly, we concentrate on themes rather than on specific analytical or theoretical problems. This is not only because the subject matter is important, but because the ideas within which the subject develops are equally so. The symposium of theories and methods of analysis gives coherence to the discipline.

In this book we shall deal separately with each of six approaches to or systems of political analysis. The purpose is threefold. First, we show how political scientists have studied politics by defining these general networks of ideas. Second, we have organized the material so that it reflects the historical development of the subject. Third, we have assumed as a basis of political science the notion that classical principles of justice offer a design to which governments should conform. The idea of development is subsumed into the tenet that people can not only contrive their politics, but constantly improve upon and strengthen them.

To show the coherence, or integrity, of political science we shall trace its evolution through six major traditions or themes that mark the emergence of political analysis as a body of thought: political philosophy, institutionalism, behavioralism, pluralism, structuralism, and developmentalism. Each of these themes is briefly defined in the following pages.

Political philosophy: **Political philosophy** is the study of reason applied to human affairs. This was the main emphasis of political science or, more properly, the science of politics for a long time. The emphasis of political philosophy was on purposes, moral ends, and intentions. These are ideas that are as old as Plato and Aristotle. As the Greeks used the precepts of this philosophy to solve the problem of justice or equity under the laws, the emphasis became more and more one of application. Certain institutions of government came to represent distinct philosophies translated into practice.

Institutionalism: Institutions realize philosophical purposes in governmental practices. Most empirical or applied political science derives from such application. Institutions "order" social life by political means. In doing so they affect the character of political ends. So "representative government" is an institutional prerequisite of democracy. But institutions do not exist in and of themselves; they are composed of people acting in accord with their own individual interpretations of the fitness of governing bodies to rule. Moreover, people do not limit their political actions to those prescribed by institutions or philosophies. Democratic institutions, for example, may fail in modern industrial societies when normal common sense beliefs about rational political action are converted into mass paranoia, hatred, fear by "insiders" of "outsiders." In Nazi Germany or Fascist Italy, for example, people gave the consensus of power over to the rule of dictators, and committed acts—in the name of a new political culture—which defied any elemental standard of civility. Such occurrences have led to concern about the *political pathology* of people in modern society, their behavioral characteristics, and their political philosophies; which brings us to the third traditional framework of study.

Behavioralism: Taking the individual as political man to be the basic unit of concern, **behavioralism** shifts the emphasis away from institutions to the study of how people behave and what motivates their behavior. It deals with many topics: people's opinions and preferences; what induces them to violence; when they abide by rules; whether they accommodate opposing views; how their views are changed; when they participate in politics (or remain aloof or apathetic) ; how they protect their interests; and how all such factors affect their membership in or affiliation with political parties, factions, and other aspects of group life in politics.

Pluralism: Incorporating the institutionalist's concern about democracy and representative government and building upon behavioral theories, political scientists have focused much attention on pluralism. **Pluralism** deals with modes of competitive and cooperative interaction among groups and the connections between diverse forms of organizational behavior. It examines the effect of this interaction on the organization of democracy in a modern, complex society. Specifically, the pluralist focus is on development or growth—how to achieve it, how to control it, what to do with it. Critics of pluralism believe that this approach to political analysis and the behavioral approach deny the consequences of political philosophy by taking the political world at face value, without accounting for the underlying relationships that connect them both to the larger purposes and meanings of government.

Structuralism: The division of social life into networks of exchange roles, classes, and regularized ways of effecting reciprocity is the province of **structuralism.** A variant of both institutionalism and behavioralism, structuralism concentrates on the connection between the individual and the community. The broad relationships, as of class affiliations, are seen to be the determinants of power.

Developmentalism: Structures, however, are affected by change. And, just as institutionalism represents the empirical application of political philosophy to the organized practice of politics, so developmentalism, a new "applied" approach to the study of politics, seeks to examine the processes of growth, industrialization, and change and their impact on governmental forms and policies. The development changes in the world include, in addition to internal problems, power conflicts occurring between the first or democratic industrial world, the second or socialist industrial world, and the third or developing world. All analytical systems can be linked to the concept of developmentalism, its patterns of change and innovation, and the impact of the more powerful and dynamic countries on weaker, peripheral, and developing nations. But ideas about how to direct change and what its purposes are also bring us back to issues of philosophy. We have ideologically come full circle. As the diagram in Figure 1-1 shows, the different forms of analysis represent different ways to view the continuum of private and public organization we call politics.

In terms of the foregoing six approaches to political analysis, perhaps the most important debates are between political philosophy and institutionalism on the one hand and behavioralism and structuralism, which represent a more "scientific" emphasis, on the other. There is a growing debate between the adherents of structuralism and those of behavioralism.

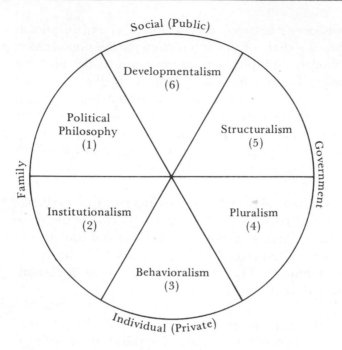

Figure 1-1. Basic Elements of Political Analysis

The most distinctive products of the behavioral mode so far have dealt with individuals—*individuals who vote, participate in politics in other ways, or express certain attitudes or beliefs. But an individual is not a political system and analysis of individual preferences cannot fully explain collective decisions, for in addition we need to understand the mechanisms by which individual decisions are aggregated and combined into collective decisions. We cannot move from a study of the attitudes of a random sample of American citizens to a reasonably full explanation of, say, the United States.*[1]

Political philosophy and institutionalism retain affinities. After all, together these systems are the foundation of the discipline. Behavioralism broke with them in theory and methods as well as in terms of the scope of inquiry. But whatever the differences, a broad evolutionary thrust connects all systems of political analysis. Political philosophy de-

1. See Robert A. Dahl, "The Behavioral Approach in Political Science: Epitaph for a Monument to a Successful Protest," reprinted in Heinz Eulau, ed., *Behavioralism in Political Science* (New York: Atherton Press, 1969), p. 84.

fines the conditions of democracy. Institutionalism provides instrumentalities by which democracy can be practiced. Behavioralism deals with the who, what, when, and how of actual political life in democracies and seeks new programmatic solutions and principles. Pluralism is concerned with participation and accountability. Structuralism raises questions of how political behavior is determined. Developmentalism focuses on change and transformation. The question of democracy is what kind of pluralism is appropriate for what levels of development.

Applications of Political Science

There are probably close to 30 thousand political scientists in the world, of whom about 28 thousand are Americans. Most, but not all, are teachers. Some are in government service, at all levels. Some are journalists or writers unaffiliated with universities; others pursue full-time careers in public or private research. They may study military strategy, arms control, the improvement of the environment, municipal reform or other topics. They apply one, or a combination, of the six themes or analytical frameworks to their studies of the different fields or specialized areas of interest.

Occasionally a "field" coincides with an approach, for instance, political philosophy. But this is rare. Some common fields are comparative politics, the study of political systems other than the American; areas studies, such as African or Latin American politics; and international relations, which is concerned with the ways in which interstate alliances, associations, and organizations work.

Some fields are delimited by culture area or geographic region (Europe, for example), by degrees of societal development (the politics of developing countries), or by a predominant type of political system (like that of the USSR and other Soviet-bloc socialist countries). One might concentrate on democracy, political parties, American government, or specific analytical or theoretical problems. Any one of the major approaches to political analysis can be brought to bear on any particular field of study.

Fields can mesh or intersect. For example, the study of political behavior leads to the field of political socialization. Inquiry is concentrated on how people learn political ideas and values and the ways these are inculcated in children. The fields of American politics and political sociology come together in a behavioral approach.

Fields also arise in response to immediate considerations. The field of urban politics is a response to such problems as racial conflicts, ghettoization, neighborhood busing, and changing ethnic composition.

In this book we concentrate on the *approaches* or themes as they can be applied to virtually any field. A college catalogue will list fields under political science or government. These change from time to time as interest and resources permit. What will be less apparent from the catalogue is what approach will be used in a certain field.

Each of the main approaches to politics has its appropriate methodological emphases and subject areas or fields. Political philosophy tends to be concerned with the establishment of moral purposes, the ethical basis of the political community, and a logic which establishes their priority or validity. The results comprise the field of normative political theory and the evolution of the moral basis of the state. Institutionalism assumes such ethical priorities as given and tries to realize them in the mechanisms of government. Hence its emphasis is on law and history, both of which describe how appropriate instruments of government evolved. In turn these provide the basis of courses on American and comparative politics and more specialized subjects like constitutions, bureaucracies, parties, and the like. Behavioralism, which focuses on both individual and aggregate, emphasizes experimental methods in group situations, how decisions are made, and organizational aspects affecting action. Courses in the field include methodology, the study of public opinion and voting, how opinions form and belief systems are established, political psychology and theories of political coalition and games. Pluralism, which combines both institutional concerns with behavioral ones, is more concerned with how social differentiation and participation broaden the political sphere. The primary emphasis is on modes of democratic participation and their effect on learning and behavior. Courses on liberal and radical modes of participation, communalism, community power, decentralization of functions, all become important. Structuralism, which is concerned with the "hidden agenda" behind political action, seeks to discover the determinants of behavior. Hence its emphasis is on class analysis, role analysis, exchange theory, and Marxist, functionalist or other ways of determining the boundaries of political behavior. Courses include the study of classes, ideologies of change and revolution, stable polities and regimes as "systems." Finally, developmentalism emphasizes problems of transition, from one type of political system to another, and how innovation occurs, its effects, distribution, who benefits, how imperialism works, problems of instability, etc. Courses include studies of new nations, revolutionary transformations, nationalism, and even the impact of the multinational corporation on "periphery" countries by "metropolitan" centers of power.

We can, somewhat arbitrarily, summarize the discussion so far in Table 1-1.

Table 1-1

Main Approaches	Emphases	Fields
Political Philosophy	Logical Analysis, Principles of the Good Society, Moral Basis of Authority	History of Ideas and Political Philosophy
Institutionalism	Legal and Historical Analysis, Descriptive and Comparative Methods, Interest Group Theory	American, Comparative, and International Politics, Parties, Constitutions
Behavioralism	Experimental Method, Psychological Analysis, Learning, Decision-making and Organizational Theory	Public Opinion, Voting, Coalitions, Violence, Ideology
Pluralism	Participation Theory, Empirical Methods, Coalition Theory, Maximizing Behavior	Political Parties, Electoral Systems, Legislative Behavior, National Government, Community Power
Structuralism	Exchange Theory, Role Analysis, Class Analysis, Marxian, Functionalist, Linguistic Analysis	Class and Elite, Change and Revolution, Ideology and Social Position, Stability and Integration
Developmentalism	Theories of Transition, Growth, Causes of Innovation, Instabilities, Political Regimes	Developing Areas, Revolution, Colonialism, and Imperialism, New Nations, Nationalism

Areas studies, like those dealing with Africa or the Middle East or the Soviet Union, bring together various combinations of approaches and fields to pinpoint a single problem or treat more than one problem from a historical or comparative viewpoint. The field of American politics may be broken into studies of parties, the presidency, Congress, committees, the administrative system or bureaucracy, local government, and so on. It can also be an "area study" in the sense that America has its own cultural tradition, is a bounded geographical space containing one of the oldest and most stable democracies in the world, and is the most industrialized nation in the world. It can be studied in terms of the politics of growth, the politics of inflation or depression, the politics of social welfare, the politics of reform, the politics of education —the list is endless.

Table 1-1, then, simply suggests points to which political scientists have given special attention in both teaching and research. No matter how much we discuss such approaches and emphasis, there can be no substitute for substantive data information. Scholars who are deeply immersed in studying some area of the world—Southeast Asia, perhaps, or France—or those who probe deeply into a particular problem like nuclear disarmament or the Middle East crisis, develop an aversion to abstract formulations. Extensive knowledge about an area or deep acquaintance with a problem elucidates its complexities and reveals the inadequacies of abstract formulas. Hence descriptive or intuitive techniques can by no means be ruled out of political science. The fact remains that political science is determined less by its method than its questions. How clearly these are stated is more important than the issue of science qua science or technique.

The American Political Heritage

Political science has been and continues to be an overwhelmingly American discipline, just as American government is overwhelmingly a lawyers' government. Not surprisingly, the American science of politics has always had connections to philosophy on the one hand and to law on the other. It has entailed the application of legal principles to governmental institutions. Americans fundamentally believe that politics fashioned out of law is a form of codified common sense.

The practical side of philosophy, as it is manifested in the writings of Harrington, Locke, and Montesquieu and in the workings of the American commonwealth, is stressed. The principles of constitutionalism are considered to be of universal application. For Americans political science is a discipline concerned with how to fashion good democracies for all people.

Why is political science such an American discipline? It began with the Constitution. Americans had great faith that not only could they design a perfect constitution for their own governance, but that they could improve its workings over time. (As Richard Hofstadter once put it, Americans are the only people who, believing that they had formed the perfect society, then proceeded to try to improve on it.) To this day, political science is first and foremost a bundle of principles and recipes for betterment. This view persists, although in a somewhat shaken or chastened form. Political science was first recognized in this way by Thomas Jefferson. In founding the University of Virginia, he created one of that institution's original eight professional chairs, the Chair of Law and Civil Policy. The first curriculum consisted of a study of the Constitution of the United States, the Constitution of Virginia, Locke's *Essay on Civil Government,* Sidney's *Discourse on Government,* the Declaration of Independence, *The Federalist Papers, The Resolutions of the General Assembly of Virginia* dealing with the Alien and Sedition laws, and the valedictory address of President Washington.[2] Not bad stuff for a beginning curriculum. It has been followed more or less faithfully in spirit and broad design in the years since.

If political science is an American discipline, its origins are both classical and European. The idea of rationality is Greek, that of law Roman, and the concern with equality, liberty, and power is taken mainly from concepts of the English and French. Preoccupation with the state as such is more German. One distinction between European and American political practice, however, is that, in the absence of traditional institutions like monarchy, and because of the connection in the American mind between the European traditions and tyranny, Americans, more than any previous peoples, associated politics with universal, reasonable, and therefore self-evident principles of government.

The founding fathers who contributed those principles and provided commentary for their interpretation were men of exceptional

2. Cited in Bernard Crick, *The American Science of Politics* (London: Routledge and Kegan Paul, 1959), pp. 14–15.

ability and education. No government had ever been formed by so well instructed an elite, so concerned with the shaping of tools for governing. Political science may have been for Americans a practitioner's art, but the practitioners were educated and civil men, lawyers, farmers, surveyors, possessors of mechanical skills, whose interests ranged from medicine to astronomy and whose sense of the well-governed society mirrored the harmony of the spheres, or the laws of physics. If the European tradition emphasized moral philosophy and jurisprudence, the American one stressed instruments and practices of popular government. It was an applied discipline, an exercise in pragmatism. (The American Political Science Association was founded in 1904, not as a purveyor of philosophy but as a way to accumulate facts.) Suspicious of large theories and grand designs, it was an investigative discipline that took democracy as its one self-evident truth.

To understand political science one also needed to know something about economics. Law regulated the political marketplace. Competition regulated the economic. The founders believed that a high proportion of political action could be explained on the basis of these. If you could find out what someone did for a living, you could predict his or her politics. Landowners and aristocrats, merchants and manufacturers, workers and farmers all could be expected to act in political factions according to their class. The problem was to keep the factions from destroying society, and to that end the founders established the Constitution as the legal framework for economic competition.[3]

It was not until the end of the nineteenth century that some of these assumptions began to break down. As new principles for explaining human conduct were sought, psychology, with its emphasis on learning, education, and public opinion formation began to kindle wide interest. Philosophers-cum-psychologists like William James and John Dewey became intrigued with the possible contributions of psychology to politics just about the time the American Political Science Association was founded. The third president of the association, A. Lawrence Lowell, became especially concerned with the increasing role of public opinion in politics, particularly as the public became less homogeneous. He foresaw some of the possible uses of statistics in political analysis to

3. See Alexander Hamilton et al., *The Federalist* (New York: Random House, n.d.) no. 10, pp. 53–62. See also Robert A. Dahl, *A Preface to Democratic Theory* (Chicago: University of Chicago Press, 1956), pp. 4–33.

show distributions of preferences, ideas, and beliefs—so-called "behavioral" considerations. While Lowell was no behavioralist (and would have rejected what it implies), he helped to establish the groundwork for what came to be an important focus in American political science.

Today political science is a truly worldwide discipline. New theoretical developments in France, Germany, and elsewhere in Europe are becoming significant in the United States as well. European structuralism represents a set of concerns not particularly congenial to a behavioral pluralism but it is slowly catching on as its potentialities as a system of thought are realized. As a discipline, today's political science is not "European" or "American" or "Russian." Neither do political scientists go around with name tags labeling them as a "behavioralist" or "developmentalist" or "structuralist." Ideas shift around continuously. Each political scientist in effect uses the components of research the way an artist uses colors on a palette. But whatever the approach or the origin of its ideas, we can say that political science as a discipline is concerned with the problem of ends: the *goals* of the good society; the *means* of governing in such a manner as to realize the good society; the *activities* of the ruled (the public), especially political actions personified in voting, public opinion, and attitude formation; and the underlying *connections* between society and government. Its key concern is with power—how it is shared through participation and representation, and how it is affected by growth and change.

The Search for Perspectives

As a discipline political science is much broader in scope than any ideology. As a science it purports to be more general than any ideology, but the history of the discipline would represent it as a particular way to understand the values of democracy. This is particularly the case in the United States and Britain where political philosophy represents the triumph of democratic ideals and institutional practices. As an American discipline political science can be said to represent the "ideology" or belief system of democracy. The preferred form may be conservative, liberal, radical, or reformist. However, in practice, American political science has been primarily reformist rather than conservative or radical. Most recently the subject has been stimulated by radical interpretations. The ideas of Karl Marx have become influential today, as a result of both European influences and the impact of developing socialist and third-world countries.

In political science, ideologies are important in several ways. They help to define major alternative political values which focus on essential questions or suggest what is important for further examination. They suggest different kinds of political "realities" by stimulating criticisms. Controversy is basic to the conduct of political affairs. It establishes criteria for intellectual discourse. It provides guidelines to the activities of politicians. Ideologies therefore affect professionals, intellectuals, and politicians alike.

The intellectual perspective: The original purpose of politics was political action. It required teaching to enlarge the sensibilities of a citizenry so that it could act. One learned the nature of people's obligations to each other by means of a civic language, which imparted a shared political culture. To act well politically, people need to learn both political principles and political arts, the values deemed important by society, how these are embodied in various institutions, and tactics and strategies of action. So one learned how power could be tamed, as fire was tamed by Prometheus, and made to serve human purposes.

Political ideas are associated with learning, but they did not, for the most part, come from thinkers who only sat back in their armchairs. Plato and Aristotle taught in the Greek academies but were also deeply involved in politics. Socrates, the classic symbol of the activist political teacher, died for his heretical views. But his teaching method was critical: It examined the mistakes made by rulers and sought to reduce the ignorance of the ruled.

Although such critical teaching is essentially an intellectual activity it may lead to practical results. It seeks to show what is wrong with the ways in which power is used. This is why the intellectual tradition can easily become subversive of authority, leading to the disrespect of rulers and in every way contributing to political contentiousness. The teaching of politics is thus political, and political teachers are frequently "activists," independent and critical thinkers involved in public life. Similarly with political philosophers like Hobbes, Locke, John Stuart Mill, and Bryce. They all mixed political thinking with political action. So did Hamilton, Jay, Madison, and Wilson as well as Marx, Lenin, and Mao.

An intellectual perspective about politics is one which uses the self as a point of departure. If a person is troubled, angry, or wants to participate to improve a political condition, then that person's perspective is egocentric: "The way *I* see things . . ." It builds upon what an individual regards as wrong and the individual's thoughts about the action necessary to put it right. Some intellectuals concerned with reform seek to mobilize support for political actions they consider appropriate. Others prefer root and branch solutions, that is, to change the "system."

Any intellectual critique, whether reformist or radical, uses principles to define and project an appropriate *civic polity*. A political intellect cannot function without some sense of what is and what ought to be. That is why political intellectuals, more than others, debate the values people live by as well as the actions they take to pursue such values. Such debates improve understanding of the uses and abuses of power and form an integral part of political knowledge.

Many political theorists have started life as reformers, and by participating in political life directly or indirectly have tried to amend existing practice. Locke was concerned with increasing parliamentary power at the expense of the monarchy. His theories were designed to provide better arguments to supporters of this view, explaining why this was desirable.

Revolutionary tradition is represented best by Marx who, while not a professional philosopher or economist or sociologist or political scientist, was a sort of omnibus intellectual. He had something to say on all such matters in a critical but creative way. For him the life of the pen was also the life of revolutionary political action. By showing why a total transformation of social life was necessary to improve a political condition, he tried to convert enough people to his view to make revolution inevitable.

But whatever view is subscribed to, the intellectual side of politics begins with the individual who wants to know what politics is, what it can mean, and how the individual can change things.

The political perspective: The intellectual's view of politics is not so very different from that of the politician. The difference is that the politician is concerned with immediate things, the here and now, rather than with theoretical things (of which politicians are profoundly suspicious). The intellectual can become a politician by putting political concerns in the service of an interest or cause. He or she may play a key role in shaping or forming new political institutions. A case of mass conversion of intellectuals concerned with politics to politicians is that of the thirty-nine men who, in Philadelphia, signed the Constitution of the

United States on September 17, 1787. Nearly half were college graduates. Sixty percent were lawyers. Many had previously written important political pamphlets. Most were young (75 percent were under fifty and 40 percent were under forty years of age). But in the four months of discussion and argument required to prepare the Constitution, questions of theory were translated into a framework for practice.[4] The framers of the Constitution became politicians overnight.

The intellectual as politician is best at connecting constructive principles to practice. The politician will tend to remain critical and to be skeptical of theories. The intellectual side of the politician will thus often resemble the heretic.

The trouble is that someone needs to cope with the immediate problems of daily life that threaten to inundate modern society. In the ebb and flow of dispute, dissension, bargaining, and competing demands, the broad issues of principle are engulfed by the mundane. The politician needs to respond to these on the spot. Something happens on the way to the forum. Ideal solutions are quickly compromised by negotiations between contending parties. The working politician is thus concerned above all with the practicalities of power. The politician *needs* power and wants to use it. It represents means and ends.

The professional politician sees the political world the way a general does. If one side wins the other loses. The politician's model is therefore a strategy that defines what course of action is most likely to succeed. Politicians are the entrepreneurs of the political marketplace. They are lightning calculators of gains and losses, public pleasures and pains. They evaluate their strategies in support, votes, and offices. To win power and use it, a successful politician needs to be able to handle complex problems and difficult situations with determined common sense. For such politicians the quickest answer is usually the best.

In short, the politician's world is today's world, and the immediate tomorrow. The intellectual is concerned about yesterday and tomorrow as well as today. The decisions of the politician are tested in the harsh reality of public response. Votes come first and all too often principles come later.

If the politician's first rule is to gain power, his second is to keep it. It is not surprising that some politicians (including the best and the brightest) do terrible things. Intellectuals in politics lose their

---

4. See Robert Dahl, *Pluralist Democracy in the United States* (Chicago: Rand McNally, 1967), pp. 1–90.

intellectual perspective. But while dismay is the daily fare of the political intellectual, the politician is the eternal optimist, perpetually intrigued by the possibilities of power.

The political science perspective: The third standpoint from which to regard politics is as a science. Politics as a science is different from an intellectual's discipline or the politician's view of politics. It shares with the intellectual side a tendency toward critical judgment, but it involves more systematic criteria for the evaluation of politics. It is more concerned with the need to look ahead, to predict the consequences of both the political acts or policies of politicians and the principles and preferences of the intellectuals. If the intellectual views politics as an extension of the moral center of self, and the politician views it as the center of public power, politics as a science or professional discipline seeks to replace the self with a *corpus* or body of proven knowledge. Politics as a science then is concerned with propositions, validity, experimentation, laws, uniformities, the establishment of universal principles.

The professional political scientist considers politics as system, as organized, mutually interactive variables. The political system is considered to be analogous to information systems, feedback systems, made up of governments, parties, interest groups, policies. It may also focus on individuals, however. It is concerned with regularities in behavior, patterns, syndromes, and so forth. The professional's world is never idiosyncratic in the way the intellectual's or the politician's may be.

Both the intellectual and the politician may remain skeptical about whether politics is a science. Most would assume that politics is an art. Indeed, as practiced by the politicians, it is. The term "science" implies something dubious when applied to politics. It sounds glib, shady (like politics itself). We can recognize a "politician" when we see one. A politician is a fat man with a cigar buying votes in the Sixth Ward. It is an African leader with anger swelling inside, looking for a way to lead the African people to the political kingdom. Politics, we know, resembles religion in some of its aspirations, and crime in some of its activities. Politics can bring out the best (occasionally) or the worst in people. We also know that it will always continue to be a fact of life. Good, bad, or indifferent, there is no future without political life.

Well and good. But can the political facts of life be made scientific? If so, political science must be a dwarf among sciences. Its science is at best a diverse, problemmatical game of chance. Political events, from revolution to coups to winning elections, are products of chance. Trip an accidental chain of circumstances and it leads to a desire to transform the world. The search for peace with honor or glory without peace, the state of bureaucracy, the power of organizations and groups, all these are potentially political situations. No "science" can circumscribe the passions they evoke. The scientists' is a manageable universe: science may design a fine bomb. But political science must solve the problems of uses of atomic energy. There is no social physics.

The problem is not that the "science" of politics is so much dependent on chance that makes it dubious. The problem is rather with our conception of science. We think of science in terms of the physical world, as a cumulative body of laws explaining natural orders. But despite a few who hanker after finality, people do not believe that in politics explanations are an end in themselves. Political science is interpretive; it repeatedly reiterates first principles. It is cumulative in that it is based on the slow growth of a body of data, on probability analysis and the correlative connections between variables. But if its goal on one hand is to replace opinions with facts, its purpose on the other is to specify both necessary and sufficient conditions in a projective analysis of political theories.

The attributes of political science are openness, tentativeness, and the reduction of ambiguity. Precision in the use of concepts, yes; a better understanding of the relationship between hypothesis and validation, certainly; above all, an improvement in the ability to make valid generalizations—these are valued goals. How well science can be hitched to politics depends on the general questions asked as well as particular answers offered. But how "scientific" politics should properly be is an empty question.[5]

Political scientists are themselves unsure about the scientific status of their discipline. A few worry about it. Almost all are anxious to improve it rather than indulge in polemics. In a study of the profession made several years ago, roughly 66 percent of political scientists agreed that "much that passes for scholarship in political science is superficial or trivial"; 55 percent agreed that "political scientists in the United States are unhappy about the current state of their discipline"; and 66 percent believed that "political science cannot be said to have any generally agreed upon body of methods and techniques."[6]

5. See Maurice Duverger, *The Study of Politics* (New York: Thomas Y. Crowell, 1969), pp. 3–11.
6. See Albert Somit and Joseph Tanenhaus, *American Political Science* (New York: Atherton Press, 1964), table one, p. 14.

The situation has improved considerably since then. The development of a science of politics, whether "hard" (quantitative and positivistic) or "soft" (interpretative and qualitative), has opened up new and valid forms of political knowledge. Somewhere between "hard" science and "soft," the vast majority of political scientists do what suits them best.

Connecting the Three Perspectives

The three worlds—the worlds of the intellectual, the politician, and the professional political scientist—overlap a good deal. Emphases shift. The radical criticism and action of one period gives way to a reforming or improving emphasis in another. The evaluation of policy according to principles provides an intellectual background for those who actively enter politics, especially by way of law. As I have said, a surprising number of politicians are intellectuals voicing important criticisms and offering ideas for improvement.

The focus of professional political science is on research. Many of the topics so investigated are of importance to the politician who uses the results of political science research more and more. As the level of professionalism improves, political science becomes more important to the politician. In every field, from atomic energy to environmental problems, from election reform to methods of popular participation, politicians seek expert advice. Insofar as the professionals are good at their job and provide knowledge that can be relied on, the politician will make use of it. Thus the state of the "science" of politics is politically important. Its teachings rest on the clarity of its intellectual perspectives and on the understanding of its practitioners. Each of the three worlds have important consequences for the others.

As the social world becomes more complex, all kinds of knowledge become critical. To be a political intellectual without a practical outlook is to be ineffective. An effective revolutionary figure, like Lenin or Mao, combines all political perspectives. Continuously moving back and forth between an intellectual's critique, to more professional thinking about politics, to a politician's sense of practicability, such a political practitioner must be able to size up a situation at a glance, determine the strategy to be employed to gain certain ends, and specify appropriate tactics. Principles that are deeply philosophical in nature must be used to inform practice.

Today, more than ever before, there is an increase in the interaction between these three worlds. The professional aspect of politics is, by itself, sterile and abstract. The intellectual is egocentric and unrealistic. Where these conditions prevail, the practice of politics will be limited and uninformed.

The clarification of issues and formulation of alternative strategies in politics have become important to policy decision making in virtually all areas. In many developing societies, the civil servants are the intellectuals or theoreticians, the politicians are the practical men and women, while the universities provide the professional research facilities. There has been a great proliferation of political science institutes and research bodies in Asia, Africa, and Latin America.

All this raises important ethical questions. To what extent should the research emphasis of the professional political scientist be put in the policy-making service of the working politician? Should the political scientist, like the natural scientist, remain above politics in order to preserve objectivity and not become a servant of the state? What is the appropriate balance between relevance in the application of knowledge to the human condition, and objectivity, which requires a certain aloofness, independence of judgment, and loyalty to the status of knowledge itself rather than the demands of the politician? These questions will be debated again and again. There are no easy answers. Research in politics is bound to be sensitive. If it is to be acceptable it must adhere to standards of responsibility defined by the field of study itself and the canons of science and not yield easily to some external demand for relevance. Otherwise, research in political science can become a form of spying on individuals, whether at home or abroad. On the other hand, adhering too rigidly to principles of science might lead people to wonder what it is all for. Like the debate between "value free" and "value laden" science, relevance and objectivity do not have fixed boundaries. It is the debate itself that is important.

chapter two
Politics as a Science

Introduction

We now want to explore some characteristics of the professional side of politics. Let us begin by defining the minimum political system. For analytical purposes, politics begins with three persons in interaction. The reason for three rather than two is that in any two-person relationship interaction can only be direct and reciprocal; an "ego" interacts with an "alter." Not that such interaction is unimportant. It has infinite possibilities. Person A may dominate, while Person B tries to deduce the intent and purposes of the other's action. Person A scrutinizes the overt gestures of Person B—a smile, perhaps, or a frown—and decides whether or not the "tone" of the relationship will be pleasant. There is a limitless range of possibilities in the simplest of such relationships, and endless ways of evaluating them.

A three-person relationship, on the other hand, is all of the things that a dyadic relationship is, but the addition of a third "actor" means a quantum jump in the nuances of expression and meaning possible in the relationship. Even more important for our purpose, however, is the possibility that two actors will conspire against a third. Politics evolves when one actor is given an opportunity to arbitrate between two or more others, a situation in which two or more can check the power of one. This establishes a relationship involving a "ruler" and a "ruled," even if the level of interaction is very informal. A "public" element enters when a third person—able to judge, pick up the pieces after a fight, define a mutual interest, or otherwise assert leadership—becomes established. Such a relationship is different from that between parent and child, master and slave, friend and enemy, or rich and poor in that it lacks reciprocity or symmetry. *Power stems from an asymmetrical but reciprocal relationship among three or more persons.*

The more actors, the more complex the interaction and the greater the need to abstract the terms of the relationship. Abstraction takes place when we step back from the interaction at hand in order to select those aspects we consider strategic or critical. A good theory, then, depends on a few important variables with which one tries to explain much of what takes place. Today the professional side of politics is devoted to just such a search for theories that aim to abstract from real life certain critical and informative variables.

Different theories emphasize different variables. A "Marxist" will consider certain variables more significant than a "behavioralist." Which theory better serves what purpose will depend on the character of the questions being asked. In turn, this problem suggests another dimension of professionalization, namely, the appropriate criteria by which to judge different theories. If each concentrates on a selection of actions from real life, how do we know which method of selection to prefer?

Much current discussion deals with the problem of establishing valid and significant judgmental criteria. For the most part, of course, political scientists rely on good common sense. We can see important differences when we make case-study comparisons or consider how events fit together historically. But beyond common sense we use other tests—statistical validity, for instance—which may help predict the extent of error in a theory. We are also interested in the logic of our theories. Science implies consistency and empiricism, bringing the professional side of political science into contact with mathematics, computers, and more generally, the philosophy of science.[1]

Political Science Methodology

Abstraction or theory construction, the *criteria* for the selection of preferred theories, and the *evaluation* of the quality of the theories applied, are the major components of professional analysis. Without abstraction we are prisoners of events or, like journalists, we pursue the moment. Without criteria, we cling to whatever theories seem simplest or fit our personal preference. Without rules for evaluating the logic and technical power of theories, we may inadequately apply ideas to the

1. See David Easton, "The New Revolution in Political Science," *American Political Science Review* (December 1969), pp. 1051–61.

interactive world. For these reasons a great deal of the contemporary study of politics is concerned with **methodology**—the study of methods—and with "new techniques for acquiring knowledge, new criteria for judging the validity of claims to the possession of knowledge, and new analytical tools for refining the meaning of terms and raising the level of precision of logical inference, [all of which] were introduced more or less concurrently."[2] In sum, "professionality" in political science refers to the abstraction of rules for the selection, evaluation, and use of theories in practice.

The simplest form of abstraction is **selective description**, practiced by historians who mine certain facts from the field of historical events. The next higher level is **typology**, a process of abstraction that ascertains whether certain characteristics combine to form a composite concept such as "feudalism" or "capitalism" or "democracy." A third level of generalization occurs when relationships are seen to stand behind the types—distributions of power, for example, which form consistent patterns or **structures.** This is where abstraction really begins to be meaningful for political analysis. Structures in turn can be treated as **systems.** So-called "**systems**" analysis can be separated from data and treated as a set of rules in and of itself, as a set of techniques or operations, like statistical or computer techniques. These are important to an understanding of what happens as political scientists wrestle with the problem of complex interactive universes in which power is composed of an infinite array of economic, social, and cultural forces and a multiplicity of individual actors.

Fragmentation and integration: All systematic approaches to political science are concerned with abstractions, the criteria, and the modes of their evaluation. This is equally true of institutionalism, behavioralism, pluralism, and so on. But other aspects of the discipline also contribute toward making political science a profession in itself. We have already mentioned that there has been a quantum jump in the sheer accumulation of information in recent years. This is likely to continue as new methods and techniques become available. Although most new material comes from research done by political scientists, politicians too are important in this process. They employ pollsters to gather more and more precise information about issues and responses, and—in order to plan

2. See Eugene J. Meehan, *The Theory and Method of Political Analysis* (Homewood, Illinois: The Homewood Press, 1965), p. 10.

campaign strategies more effectively—about political behavior. For as
costs rise, efficiency becomes a matter of fundamental importance.

In addition, government increasingly commissions research studies
dealing with all sorts of practical political questions: energy policy, position papers on the Middle East, the trade-off between nuclear collaboration and controls, and so on. The total audience for political science
research thus grows by leaps and bounds and patrons who sponsor research become more diverse. One by-product of the search for efficiency
and predictability is specialization: efficiency improves with specialization. The problem of specialization is that we are collectively less able
to understand and use the knowledge that becomes available. It takes
an expert to understand an expert.

What happened to the physical sciences is happening to political
studies. That is, there is a fragmentation of the field as the body of
relevant knowledge grows. To compensate for the way in which precise
knowledge results in excessive specialization, it is important to find new
integrative ways of putting the pieces together. Otherwise the sublevels
of research become alien. Queries and hypotheses become increasingly
narrow.

The science of politics, then, works in both fragmented and integrative ways. There is a tendency towards increasing specialization of
knowledge, which in turn engenders an opposite tendency to link the
substructures of research back together again in new and different ways.

Max Born, the Nobel Prize-winning physicist, put the matter very
well in describing the explosion of knowledge in his discipline—physics.

*Physics has expanded in such a way that nobody is able to survey
the whole. The following data give some idea of it:* The Encyclopedia
of Physics *. . . is planned to have 54 volumes, each of them between
300 and 1,000 pages. Nobody knows more than a small fraction of this
enormous amount of material. Yet it goes on increasing from day to
day, and many a volume may be already outdated on publication.
Still more terrifying is the accomplished fact, that the* Transactions
of the International Congress on the Peaceful Uses of Nuclear Energy,
*held in Geneva in 1958, are now published in 27 volumes, many of 500,
some of 800 pages. Each volume addresses specialists of a narrow section
of this special branch: nuclear physics. This boundless increase of materials is common to all sciences. It is caused not only by the continuous
expansion of research inside the older group of civilized nations, but
through participation of newly developing nations all over the world.*

Thus the very meaning of the concept "knowledge" has under- gone a fundamental change. It does not refer any more to a single person but to the community of all men. While the total of what has been found and deposited in print grows in an unlimited manner, that part of it which an individual can possibly know and handle becomes relatively smaller and smaller. Thus, the gigantic increase of knowledge of the human race as a whole may mean that individuals become more stupid and superficial. There are, unfortunately, many indications that this is actually happening.[3]

The magnitude and scope of the political science discipline, the range of the literature, the complexity and the possible ramifications of political ideas have exaggerated differences between methodologies. There is a shift toward professionality in the field as a whole, to be sure, a bias toward a more scientific treatment of politics. But this is a recent, and perhaps peculiarly American, development.

Areas of specialization: We have suggested that in the United States the object of the discipline was, in early years, two-fold: to incul- cate civic responsibility through teaching and to improve government, at all levels, as a result of scientific investigations. So the management of government business led political scientists to emphasize pragmatic common sense and search out alternatives that would "work." In this respect the early Anglo-American tradition diverged from the Euro- pean tradition, the concerns of which were political philosophy, prin- ciples of jurisprudence, and the search for fundamental legal rules to be employed in the battles among absolutism, monarchy, and constitu- tional democracy.

Americans, more than any others, made political science into a practical discipline and the preferred style was always empirical. What has changed is the search for predictability, which emphasizes the quan- titative aspect of political phenomena. The research focus has shifted toward more individual interactive behavior, and away from institu- tions. After World War II, for example, political science professionals embraced the behavioral approach to the discipline. A huge increase in the number of journals handling political science materials of a behav- ioral nature became evident in both the discipline of political science, and in other fields of social science to which political scientists contribute.

Despite the proliferation of journals and articles dealing with be-

3. Max Born, *Physics and Politics* (New York: Basic Books, 1962), p. 5.

havioral aspects of political science, the profession has not lost its connection to political philosophy and its institutional focus. If the behavioral emphasis has been on methods, empiricism, and operationalism
in research, it still retains a concern for abstract moral principles:
authority, community, responsibility, liberty, the public interest, justice, rational decision, revolution, equality, and representation.[4] The
once conventional political science curriculum—political theory, comparative government, public administration, constitutional law, international politics, state and local government—has been drastically altered. New titles: legislative behavior, political modernization, political
socialization, political psychology have moved to center stage. Such
changes make the study of political science more confusing, but also
more exciting. Integrative efforts are now manifested in cross-discipli-
nary programs and area studies. The day of the standard program is
gone.

Despite the dangers of specialization, then, important unities remain in the study of political science. The point of departure is a belief
that people can change their social relationships by altering methods of
governing, and that they can alter methods of governing by design—that
is, by postulating philosophical alternatives.

The belief that, as life becomes physically easier, people prosper
morally, intellectually, and creatively, is auxiliary to this underlying
principle. Today we know that such progress is not self-evident. Private
purpose may be diminished by growth; individuals may become more
vulnerable rather than less so; society may batter as well as uplift the
individual. Catering to the social costs of progress is an increasingly
urgent task of government. How to deal with the task is what stimulates
the many different themes, theories, and fields of political science, which
all share a common concern with man's fate.

The language of political science: You will notice as you read this chapter that the discussion becomes highly abstract and generalized. We do
not describe political science in terms of specific events—wars, strikes,
elections. Nor do we deal specifically with various political demands,
needs, or interests. One of the problems of the discipline is that the
language, or jargon, is abstract. However, some abstractions, like power,
democracy, and freedom, are more familiar than others. Terms like *vari-*

---

4. These are the topics dealt with in the first ten volumes of *Yearbooks of the
American Society for Political and Legal Philosophy,* edited by J. Roland Pennock
and John W. Chapman.

ables, systems, structure, are really not so complicated either, if they are properly defined. As we move up the ladder of abstraction, at the end we must find something concrete: After all, ladders do not lean against air.

To facilitate dealing with some of the more important abstractions it will be helpful for us to define some of the words common to political analysis, whether of the empirical sort or the practical. Here are several:

1. *Paradigm.* A **paradigm** is a framework of ideas that establishes the general context of analysis. Fundamentally paradigms combine a mixture of philosophical assumptions and criteria of valid knowledge. The resulting combinations are sharply distinguished from each other. For example, an important paradigmatic change in people's social and political lives was from an essentially cosmic or religious view of universal order to a scientific and empirical one.

2. *Theories.* **Theories** are generalized statements summarizing the actions—real or supposed—of one set of variables. Any theory can be broken into (1) **dependent variables,** those whose action the theory seeks to explain, (2) **independent variables,** the causal or operating variables which effect changes in others, and (3) **intervening variables** which link the independent to the dependent. **Parameters** represent the conditions within which the independent variables operate. Theories may deal with large or small groups or units. Abstract theories are formal, or notational. Concrete theories are descriptive.

3. *Methods.* **Methods** are ways of organizing theories for application to data. They are sometimes called conceptual schemes. Some types of methods are comparative (using more than one case), configurational (using a single case study), historical (using time and sequence), and simulatic (using simulation). All sorts of mixtures of methods are possible. However, a distinction can be made between experimental methods, which allow precise observation and controlled procedure, and nonexperimental methods, which deal with on-going real-life situations.

4. *Techniques.* **Techniques** link methods to the relevant data. They represent various modes of observation and ways of recording empirical information. Techniques vary in appropriateness. Sampling, public opinion testing, interviewing, regression analysis, factoring, and the use of scales and tests, are some research techniques. In political science today there is a growing use of quantitative techniques, mathematical modeling, and statistical analysis.

5. *Models.* **Models** are simplified ways of describing relationships.

Models can be constructed from a paradigm, a theory, a method, or a technique. They are "inferential pictures" of these.[5] Models may be typological, descriptive, methodological, formal, and so forth. Some models are mechanistic, others are organismic or "biologistic." Cybernetic or input-output models are of the first variety, functionalist models are of the second.

6. *Strategies.* A **strategy** is a particular way to apply one or any combination of the above to a research problem. Professionality consists largely in the integrity and quality of a strategy; those that are simply stuck together, jerrybuilt, are eclectic. A good strategy fits together problem, theory, methods, and techniques in a systematic and coherent way.

7. *Research Design.* A **research design** converts strategy into an operational plan for fieldwork or an experiment. It is a prospectus or outline from which research is carried forward. A research design is the final stage in professional research preparation.

How well we put together paradigms, hypotheses, theories, techniques, strategies, and so forth to create a good research design is what professionality is about. But even the highest standard of professionality requires something more: a sense of purposes—ethical and material—for which professionality is a means, not an end. Knowledge of political things is itself political. We arrive at the threshold of political understanding when we become aware of what questions to ask.

A Face-off: Scientism versus Humanism?

Political science was originally a practitioner's field. How the institutions of government worked (and how they should work) was a matter of struggle and conflict in the political arena. Lawyers and jurists, politicians, leaders of factions, and parties, the citizenry, all, in one way or another, engaged in the battles. The great democratic accomplishment was the conversion of conflict from the battlefield itself to the field of freely competitive politics, the essence of constitutionalism.

Constitutionalism implies a way of defining the relationship between liberty and power. Jefferson's original purpose was to inform

5. R. B. Braithwaite, *Scientific Explanation* (Cambridge: Cambridge University Press, 1955) , pp. 88–96.

citizens about the Constitution itself, about the history and evolution of liberty as well as governing institutions. To know the principles subscribed to by society was to know its intent. Thus early political science became important as a form of civic learning, enabling citizens to act responsibly, and helping them pursue the interests of society in a rational and intelligent way. By being taught how to exercise their rights citizens could be taught to fulfill their obligations. To learn one was to pledge the other. These were the original purposes of political science.

But, as we have seen, the more political science becomes a technical discipline, like psychology or economics, the less it is a citizen's concern. The age of specialization has had its negative consequences at a time when issues which citizens and politicians are supposed to decide are too complex for a purely amateur understanding. Hence the paradox. As the research side of political science becomes more significant, and as knowledge becomes more technical, politics becomes more inaccessible to the public. Therefore, how good is political science from a technical standpoint? And who can make use of it as knowledge?

The first answer must be a bit equivocal (for the time being at any rate). Good for certain kinds of things and not others, political science has an uneven practical track record. Polling and sampling techniques have developed so that public opinion and voting behavior are fairly predictable. We know enough about political psychology, the learning process, political socialization, attitude formation, and so forth, to understand how ideologies and preferences form. Political scientists can and do provide strategic intelligence to politicians. There has also been a great increase in knowledge of organizational techniques, from techniques of mobilization to winning public support. And political scientists gather information about group, mass, and collective behavior.

Political science can also provide information about projected policies such as taxation or revenue sharing, or about the consequences of institutional changes such as an expanded Supreme Court system or the reform of Congressional committees. Political studies of a policy nature are increasingly useful. Budgeting, military decision making, party platforms, interest groups, ethnic factors, the bureaucracy, election systems, trade unionism in politics, business in politics, the role of professional organizations, the problems of the small community—all such topics represent opportunities for specialized policy study. The materials gathered represent a fund of useful knowledge, a form of intellectual capital.

Yet even particular or specialized studies can have larger implications. Aaron Wildavsky begins his study of the American budgetary process by commenting that a budget "is concerned with the translation of financial resources into human purposes."[6] Nothing would seem more down to earth and dry than a budget. But nothing says more about fundamental priorities. The best research studies always contain this sense of the general issue in the particular. At another level, we can just as easily see how the broadest constitutional issues may arise out of the most ordinary complaint by a citizen whose rights have been violated.

"Big" questions—those concerning the rights and values which specify our most fundamental priorities and which individuals seek to maximize—are always in a sense ambiguous. Indeed, it is hard to precisely pinpoint the meaning of terms like justice, equity, freedom, liberty, or democracy. The logic of any single principle, if pushed too far, and with enough singleminded attention, becomes contradictory. More practical concerns, when linked up with broad issues, clarify principle. In such give and take, political science as a research discipline helps to define and redefine fundamental beliefs.

As we define a particular system of representation, such as a single-member plurality constituency system (and we can define that better than, say, the principle of democracy), the principle becomes visible in the practice. Practice in turn raises questions of principle. In this respect political science, as it becomes more theoretically powerful, is also capable of providing valid knowledge on more and more concrete subjects. As a scientific field, it connects effectively with economic issues such as the politics of inflation and fiscal policy, or with sociological concerns like penal reform or urban development. Political scientists become more relevant in shaping policy as they make their knowledge useful. But as the discipline becomes more scientific, its theories go beyond the comprehension of ordinary citizens. As it becomes more "relevant," political science invades politics indirectly, in the form of expert advice, which reduces further the role of the citizen and the citizen's effectiveness in politics.

As knowledge becomes more technical it eludes the citizen. As this takes place, the influential elite, the social engineer, takes over. The problem of informed public opinion becomes more acute. When they don't understand, people lose interest in politics; moreover, when they

6. See Aaron Wildavsky, *The Politics of the Budgetary Process* (Boston: Little, Brown & Co., 1964).

do not understand the issues, they come to believe that they never will. They may come to feel stupid or inadequate, or to regard knowledge itself with contempt. Paradoxically, then, expertism endangers society by making citizens increasingly belittled and confused and by placing unchecked powers in the hands of government.

If the discipline is to use its resources to improve the general understanding, it cannot remain esoteric. No matter how specialized a study may become, as soon as an idea is proposed it should enter the mainstream of discussion. One does not need to be a nuclear scientist to discuss the issues of nuclear policy. One can make use of experts to describe impacts, contribute technical information about waste and disposal problems, evaluate cost systems and delivery networks, and so forth. But broad matters of priority easily translate to bread-and-butter concerns: How much will it cost? What effects will it have on my life? What will it do for my children?

Generative ideas: If technicism represents one side of the coin, the other side is creativity. A great many—perhaps most—of the new ideas about politics are not the result of scientific inquiry at all. One of the remarkable things about human beings is that they get their notions, theories, views, from quite unexpected sources. There is something about the human mind which, when confronted by a problem, enables it to ruminate onward without being particularly conscious of the problem. While we can study, scientifically, the way in which beliefs are formed, it is much more difficult to account for how a belief "forms itself."

Generative ideas, those which stimulate new ways of thinking and which are so important to modern life, are of this nature. They defy easy explanation. Generative ideas, whether from a politician's mouth or a militant revolutionary's, are articulated unexpectedly. They represent the single most important quality of political life, namely the capacity to see events in a fresh way. They are essential to our rational, intelligent ability to understand what goes on around us. They represent our efforts to transcend the limits of conventional thought. And they transcend science. Perhaps the best description of generative ideas was given by the philosopher, Susanne Langer.

The limits of thought are not so much set from outside, by the fullness or poverty of experiences that meet the mind, as from within, by the power of conception, the wealth of formulative actions with which the mind meets experiences. Most new discoveries are suddenly seen—things that were always there. A new idea is a light that fell on them. We turn the light here, there, and everywhere, and the limits of thought recede before it. A new science, a new art, or a young and vigorous system of philosophy is generated by such a basic innovation. Such ideas as identity of matter and change of form, or as value, validity, virtue, or as outer world and inner consciousness, are not theories; they are the terms in which theories are conceived; they give rise to specific questions, and are articulated only in the form of these questions. Therefore one may call them generative ideas *in the history of thought.*[7]

Generative ideas are not neatly contained in the scientific enterprise, but spring out of logical contradictions and arguments over principle as well as from data analyses. A discipline like political science is just a brokerage house for such ideas. If science stimulates them, then we want science. If it stifles or cripples them, then science is inadequate. What the generative idea requires is the free play of inquiry with imagination, which is the corrective to professionality. A generative force is an intellectual force. Generative ideas lend themselves to ethical debate, providing the intellectual focus or purpose. So generative ideas in political science analysis represent, above all, the humanistic state of mind within the professional shell. Factual research always poses the question: What is the relationship of the actual to the ideal? Furthermore, how does one implement changes to reduce the dissonance between these two states? To discuss these matters will require us to restrict Langer's concept somewhat to show the relation between generative ideas, theories, and specific questions.

The "Big" Questions

Generative ideas address problems that may be addressed by practitioners or intellectuals but which often must be scientifically understood. Some political scientists try to identify fundamental, long-term problems of the sort that interest intellectuals but which politicians, on the whole, cannot bother themselves with. For example, in a democratic society, all of the following questions are fundamental to

7. Susanne K. Langer, *Philosophy in a New Key* (New York: Mentor Press, 1948), p. 5.

one basic issue, democracy, but each approaches that issue from a different fundamental point of view. Is effective citizen participation possible? What are new and alternative methods of representation? What reforms can be effected? If better representation occurs, how will the society handle distribution of information? Will participation require new organizational facilities in government? If improved representation results in an information explosion, a technology of information processing, and information "delivery services," will this pose an "overload" problem? Will it result in new layers of bureaucracy? Will the old political system break down under its new burden of information processing?

The distortion and falsification of information can engender new forms of corruption. Information use requires checking, not to mention facilities for storage and retrieval mechanisms. All this increased bureaucracy affords new opportunities for power. In turn this implies new responsibilities for politicians who will need to organize and aggregate public information much more efficiently than in the past, transforming it into messages, or "inputs," more quickly. The pace of "inputting" will increase. Similarly, at the receiving end of such information, handling messages requires new bureaucracies, with new hierarchies of technicians and intepreters. Checks and balances? To check on the misuse of authority is a danger in itself. In a society in which everyone checks on everyone else, the politics of surveillance will prevail. How will this affect peoples' liberties?

There are other big questions. Will government follow the trend set by industry, where innovative activity depends on able "entrepreneurs" who use systems analyses to size up a situation, test a market, develop a product, implement a research design, and introduce an organizational change? Today industry involves research planning as well as more collective (and bureaucratic) forms of business leadership. The latest entrepreneurs are those politicians who operate in the political or economic marketplace identifying issues, packaging them, and selling them as programs on which voters pass judgment. But in politics individual leadership is gradually declining. Strategy in a campaign is a function of organization by professionals. Which candidates to select, where to spend limited campaign funds, issue saliency, candidate attractiveness, and a host of other issues are products of research and evaluation, a team delivery service.

The political systems of democratic societies in the West have effected considerable reallocation or redistribution of wealth. The poor have become wealthier, and more wealth inheres in the middle classes. But because of industrial growth the rich, for the most part, have not lost much either. One of the problems of democracy has been how to achieve greater redistribution of wealth—not just more collective wealth for each sector of society. Studies show that, despite overall improvement, the relative discrepancy between rich and poor has remained remarkably stable. Hence a problem for political scientists is how to stimulate more effective organization of the poor so that they can use the political system on their own behalf.[8]

These questions are difficult. They cannot be resolved by easy solutions, or by "wiping the slate clean" as if one could start fresh in politics, ignoring people's attitudes, vested interests, and cultural traditions. Politicians may search for villains and scapegoats when problems arise. "Capitalists," "communists," a particular ethnic or religious group may become the object of grievances. But, scapegoating is both simplistic and dangerous.

The issues of political science may be global problems or local ones. Urban redevelopment in Oakland, California, black paralysis in Watts, new forms of participation in Yugoslavia, the decline of democracy in India, revenue sharing and the decentralization of bureaucracy, and misuse of housing funds in St. Louis, all stimulate new questions. Attempts to answer them stimulates new generative ideas. They are debated. They change the meanings of old concepts such as equality, liberty, and the pursuit of political ends. They may be translated into scientific questions. Then criteria are defined, methods developed, comparisons organized, and techniques designated to answer them. The answers conjure up frightening political eventualities.

Nothing is more removed from public concern than the issue of penal reform. But let a prison be taken over by its inmates and issues of principle explode along with the violence of the events. Indeed, the uprising at Attica state prison in New York in 1973 was important precisely because it became, for a time, a moral decision point for the entire country. In the shadow of such energy the political scientist is a little like a priest who, officiating at the most boring day-to-day functions of the church—a wedding, a baptism, a funeral, a routine Sunday service— nevertheless can hear in such mundane activities the whisper of God (even in the tinkle of coins in the collection plate).

8. See Giovanni Sartori, *Democratic Theory* (New York: Praeger, 1965), pp. 72–92, and Robert A. Dahl and Charles E. Lindblom, *Politics, Economics, and Welfare* (New York: Harper & Row, 1953), pp. 472–526.

Generative ideas are connected to concrete research. Big issues are broken up into manageable smaller ones. Expert decisions help us give priority to certain policy questions. Criteria for evaluation and consequences make the field into a policy science. Politics is thus pitched between moral philosophy and empirical science. It draws its generative ideas (ideals) from moral philosophy, while more and more its policy depends on connections to the science of behavior. Between the two we can derive the following guidelines for political analysis:

1. Every research question should spring from a generative idea.
2. Every generative idea should be prescriptive as well as descriptive.
3. Every generative idea should be capable of being translated into explicit hypotheses.
4. Every hypothesis should cite criteria appropriate to furthering ideas. That is, what is it necessary to "know" in order to know more?
5. Every analyst should anticipate new generative ideas likely to emerge from a given analysis.

Indeed most political scientists would agree, with Engels, that "The philosophers have only interpreted the world in various ways; the point however is to change it."[9] Unlike Engels, however, most political scientists are less concerned with revolutionary solutions than with remedial ones. The discipline is, in the main, one of improvement measured by incremental change.[10]

The Application of Principle to Research

Hypothesis formation: The connection between moral philosophy and empirical science is secured when generative ideas become hypotheses. Hypothesis formation is thus the critical activity in professional political analysis. It can be defined as follows:

A **hypothesis** is a statement of the relationships between two or more variables when at least one is independent and one is dependent.

9. See "Marx's Theses on Feuerbach," No. XI, in Friedrich Engels, *Ludwig Feuerbach* (New York: International Publishers, 1935), p. 75.
10. See an extremely useful discussion of such matters by Alice M. Rivlin, *Systematic Thinking for Social Action* (Washington, D.C.: The Brookings Institution, 1971).

Any research starts with hypotheses. Sometimes, however, they are difficult to formulate precisely.

Before a hypothesis can be formulated, a preliminary stage may be required in which all sorts of open-ended questions are asked. Background work on available information is essential to help determine what hypothesis is likely to be useful. Once the question and criteria have been established, it is necessary to connect these to the problem that instigated the generative idea (otherwise a hypothesis is likely to be trivial).

The germinating or discursive stage is usually the most difficult because at this stage the analyst does not usually have a sense of clear purpose. The first mariners observed the stars. Gradually they discovered patterns; then they learned how to use them. This is essentially the procedure followed at a prehypothesis stage. Few astronomers simply observe the stars today. They extrapolate from the given knowledge new areas of concern.

Not all hypotheses are precise. It is common for an analyst to formulate preliminary hypotheses in order to better pinpoint the precise area of interest. Take, for example, an issue of social welfare. A common hypothesis is that if a welfare program is to be successful it requires participation by the people concerned. The theory is that participation increases interest and interest steps up motivation which, in turn, increases the efficacy of the program. An alternative hypothesis is that if a welfare program is to be successful, then participation must be limited and directed especially by experts who have a clear idea of what to do. These are "loose" hypotheses. They represent problems that should be subjected to all sorts of research programs to clarify and reformulate. Plenty of programs directed by experts have resulted in failures in part because public participation was lacking.

No matter how loose or tight, however, hypotheses should be phrased in a way as to extract specific answers about specific areas of research. Then knowledge of a practical nature will become increasingly available.

Limits to scientific research and analysis: Assume we have a policy question which not only is the product of an interesting generative idea, but also is phrased as a hypothesis. What then? The scientific experimental model relies exclusively on the *quantitative* rigor of the experiment. Hypotheses are confirmed according to statistical or other "hard" criteria. The danger of confusing the scientific method with "scientific" political analysis is that it drives out generative ideas. In the political arena, mere fact finding may so simplify the results as to make them spurious. A correlation may be statistically valid but theoretically misleading or unimportant.

Thus we have the danger of what we might call *false science,* the results of which, though exact, are yet not really true. A good example is the way intelligence tests work. The scores of blacks may consistently be lower than the scores of whites. But to infer from a correlation that blacks are intellectually inferior to whites is false. Too many other variables may account for the discrepancy, such as the effects of discrimination, poverty, broken families, and so forth. Moreover, the political implications of such false conclusions—including the idea that blacks should have different kinds of education than whites—should be immediately apparent.[11]

What then does constitute a valid political science methodology? Like all predominantly inferential and inductive or logical and deductive disciplines, political science uses common, garden variety ways of translating research findings into theory. These are mainly inductive. Starting with particulars, theories are built up into generalizations: When a variable X is repeatedly found in conjunction with certain types of events Y, then we say that X is likely to have a bearing—causally or associatively—on phenomenon Y. On the other hand (and this is what complicates the process), X may be a function of A and B, in which case it may be possible to transform the inductive generalization into a deductive one. Y may be a function of A and B. If A and B, then X. If X, then Y. This then is a deductive theory. The procedure is to build up general statements from many cases, either in terms of probabilities or in terms of a logical explanation of why the generalization holds true. If we can make the conversion to a deductive model, the deductive proposition (if X, then Y) can be separated from its inductive base to serve as a free-floating theory or "law." The explanatory "why" is the basis of theory.

The problem is that in political science analyses only a few valid deductive propositions can ever be made, although many inductive and inferential ones are possible. The reason for this is the sheer complexity of human beings. No science can stuff human behavior neatly into valid deductive propositions. This is why political science, as an empirical

11. For a discussion of such matters see Liam Hudson, *The Cult of the Fact* (New York: Harper & Row, 1972).

discipline, relies on correlations and regressions which identify *structural connections* between descriptive variables. While the "if X, then Y" equation is difficult to establish, it is not so risky to postulate that X and Y exist in *some sort* of relationship.

One problem is how to modify and organize techniques, many of which have been developed for quite other purposes than for use in political inquiry. Considerable research now goes to expanding the stock of techniques available. When political science knowledge becomes more systematic, experimental, and formalized, so more "laws" will be found.[12] Quantitative research of an empirical nature also requires "indicator data." Indicators are critical or important variables that measure something, like a thermometer measures temperature. How can we measure "political temperature"? We turn now to some of the kinds of indicators used by political scientists for empirical research.

Indicators: Using theory to predict behavior: In the social sciences, economists pioneered in the formulation of indicator methods. Using interest rates, "freight-car loadings," inventories, and other variables, they sought to identify certain trends that would allow them to better evaluate the overall performance of the economy. Such indicators are interpreted in terms of particular economic theories. For example, a *monetarist,* an economist specializing in interest theory, might interpret certain indicators differently than a Keynesian. The criteria for indicators are general: inflation, recession, depression. Indicators show the direction in which the economy can be expected to move, with respect to these general conditions.

Political scientists also develop useful indicators. The effort has been spurred by the use of new technologies. It is now possible to accumulate and store vast bodies of quantitative data in data banks. The problem is to locate the data under sufficiently useful categories, so that the material can be retrieved. There is also the problem of the growing expense of maintaining such archives.

12. Stages in the process include a variety of techniques including typologizing (or the organization of related characteristics) ; sampling, including biased, random, stratified, representative, and other samples; content analysis; survey methods; interviewing techniques; frequency distributions; indices; factor analysis; regression analysis; etc. These are only a few of the techniques which can be employed in combination. See Johan Galtung, *Theory and Methods of Social Research* (New York: Columbia University Press, 1967) . This is one of the best general reviews of methodological and technical combinations generally available. See also, Donald T. Campbell and Julian C. Stanley, *Experimental and Quasi-Experimental Designs for Research* (Chicago: Rand McNally and Co., 1963) .

An important test for indicators is that they be amenable to quantitative analysis. Perhaps the most systematic data collection pertains to voting behavior—in terms of both voting patterns in society, and specifically in the voting of members of legislatures. However, data are collected to aid research in the area of transactional analysis as well, particularly the measurement of flows—informational, economic, and social. The field of developmental indicators—economic, demographic, ethnic, and so on—also lends itself to quantitative analysis, as do general inquiries into political instability and, more recently, violence.[13]

Advances in computer analysis have also made possible rankings which employ qualitative mathematics.[14] Certain descriptive words can be used to "quantify" behavior in terms of broad "plus" or "minus" categories. Such "bits" of information can be fed into computers for analysis, allowing analysts to combine various kinds of indicator data with qualitative measures. The technique also enables an observer to combine very different kinds of information in a comparative way. Multiple regression analysis enables an observer to indicate the degree of variance in a variable according to the significance of two or more different independent variables. Much work has been done along these lines.[15]

Class analysis is slowly becoming amenable to indicator analysis. Take, for example, a hypothesis about ways to achieve a peaceful transition to socialism: *If a society has a large middle class, then a nonviolent transition to socialism will depend on the radicalization of the middle class.* (Assume that we can operationally define *middle class, radicalization,* and *violence.*)

A research design capable of evaluating the amount of "prosperity" devolving from a transition to a socialist system would depend on *operationalizing* the degree of radicalization of the middle class. It would have to enable one to compare middle-class radicalization in a variety of countries, say, France, Italy, England, and Germany, by using indicators that distinguish between trends toward conservatism and radicalization and show their respective political effects. The same is true of studies of working-class radicalism (Goldthorpe et al. have con-

13. See T. R. Gurr, *Why Men Rebel* (Princeton: Princeton University Press, 1970).
14. See Raymond A. Bauer, ed., *Social Indicators* (Cambridge: MIT Press, 1966).
15. See Hayward R. Alker, Jr., "Regionalism Versus Universalism in Comparing Nations," in Bruce M. Russett, Hayward R. Alker, Jr., Karl W. Deutsch, and Harold D. Lasswell, *World Handbook of Political and Social Indicators* (New Haven: Yale University Press, 1964), and Richard L. Merritt, *Systematic Approaches to Comparative Politics* (Chicago: Rand McNally and Co., 1970).

ducted such studies to help account for the conservatism of labor[16]) . If the hypotheses prove incorrect, then modification of much radical theory might be in order.

Questions dealing with class and political ideology are **macro**-level questions dealing with large political units. However, they may be stated in terms of **micro** context—that is, as pertaining to private political action. For example, if we are interested in the radicalization of behavior in a particular village or factory, we might ask individuals who live or work in that village or factory questions about leadership, their degree of militancy, and the way in which their militancy manifests itself in demands. We could establish appropriate indicators for all these political concepts and, in turn, we might raise questions about factory efficiency or industry productivity. In other words, by initially asking questions about a *micro*political situation, the radicalization of certain individuals, we confront the issue of the radicalization of a *collectivity* of individuals, thereby introducing *macro*political concerns into our analysis. We will deal more specifically with this distinction in the next section.

Coming to Terms with Abstractions

A political indicator exists in relation to some system, which may be one of two types: analytical or concrete. An **analytical system** is made up of a generalized set of relationships, that is, a theory. A **concrete system,** which is a membership group, consists of real people. An analytical system can be applied to the workings of a concrete system in order to make its operations understandable. For example, the term "democracy" does not represent a concrete system, but an analytical system. However, the government of the United States, a so-called democracy, is concrete because it is an actual operational system consisting of real citizens.

On the concrete side the central problem is size of the unit, whether it is broadly inclusive or small. The smallest political unit is the individual; the largest unit is a society. Small units are micropolitical units; large ones are macropolitical units. Whether a unit is macro or micro depends on how it is used in a particular analysis. For example, in examining microorganisms in the human body, the individual human

16. See J. H. Goldthorpe, D. Lockwood, F. Beckhofer, and J. Platt, "The Affluent Worker and the Thesis of Embourgeoisement" in J. A. Kahl, ed., *Comparative Perspectives on Stratification* (Boston: Little, Brown, 1968) .

is a macro unit. In contrast, in a system of international relations a nation as a single actor in a system of interaction is a micro unit.

In the Introduction to this chapter we showed how abstraction begins with description—with singling out from an infinity of objects or concepts those one wants to describe. A second level of abstraction is the search for characteristics which the objects of interest have in common. Identifying such characteristics enables us to define types or classifications of objects which, when seen in relation to one another imply a **system,** a network of interacting variables. When the variables are principles rather than objects or things, we reach a further level of abstraction. The most abstract theories are formal statements of principle as theorems.

Highly generalized analytical systems are those formalized in a quantitative or logical language. Few such systems are applicable to political science analysis, as we have said. Mostly political scientists still work at the typological level of analysis. Thus we speak of a democratic system with the central principle that a high degree of control over executive authority will be exercised by an elective legislative body, itself reflecting a diversity of views within a free population. As a model it does not *require,* for example, political parties or a particular form of electoral system, legislature, or bureaucracy. These are concrete characteristics and instruments, which may or may not operate democratically.

The model is made concrete when, in examining, for example, voting, ways of participating in decision making, or the struggle of legislators to check the decision-making power of the executive, we find that the actual process approximates the model. We can say that a concrete system (country X or Y) is more or less democratic according to how well the circular flow in the real world described in the abstract model of democracy is maintained. We use indicators to "measure" this degree of maintenance.

Different levels of research are a function of how abstract the categories of interest are, how macro or micro the units, and which concrete systems are used to test the resultant theories or hypotheses. Experimental methods lead to highly generalized and abstract analytical systems of human behavior, just as the structure of an atomic particle is relevant to all matter.

Years ago Harold Lasswell studied the behavior of inmates of institutions for the insane in order to form general theories about political behavior. Admittedly he shocked many people. Study the politics of the sane by extrapolating from the insane? Impossible. But Lasswell wanted to determine the extent to which the circumstances attending a person's early life affect public behavior. He came to the conclusion that private motives, when displaced onto a public object, become rationalized as public interest, thus resulting in politicization. Lasswell asserts that this model is as true in an insane asylum as in the Congress. Rationalization and displacement (categories derived from Freud) can occur in any setting.[16]

Certain kinds of macroanalysis (particularly that which has been developed for comparative analysis in developing countries) employ descriptive information. For example, Almond and Coleman list certain types of input and output functions characteristic of *all* political systems. These are: political socialization and recruitment; interest articulation, interest aggregation, and political communications on the input side; and rule making, rule application, and rule adjudication on the output side. Capable of being performed in a variety of concrete systems, these functions are general without being abstract ("courts not only *adjudicate* but also *legislate* . . . , the *bureaucracy* is one of the most important sources of *legislation*," and so on).[17] They illustrate a point that is critical to understanding the many forms of political science.

How to combine large questions of principle with concrete research is what the science side of politics is about. We have tried to provide a brief version of the problems of method and strategy which modern and empirical political studies involve. Unfortunately this has required the definition of technical terms. But most of the approaches to the subject only use these in research itself. For our treatment of the approaches themselves, more ordinary language will do.

We turn now to the generative ideas provided by political philosophy. The discussion is divided into three chapters, each representing a different tradition: classical, enlightenment, and radical traditions.

16. Harold D. Lasswell, *"The Political Writings of Harold D. Lasswell,"* *Psychopathology and Politics,* Book I, Chapter V (Glencoe, Ill.: The Free Press, 1951) .
17. Gabriel L. Almond and James S. Coleman, *The Politics of the Developing Areas* (Princeton: Princeton University Press, 1960), p. 17. Emphasis not in original. For a good review of the relations between macro and microanalysis, and the relation between theory and research, see Oliver Garceau, ed., *Political Research and Political Theory* (Cambridge: Harvard University Press, 1968) .

Political Philosophy

chapter three
The Classical Tradition

What we shall call the *classical tradition* took shape in ancient Greece with the emergence of the idea of science. Science meant explanation—the capacity to reason. Its object was to find reasons for the phenomena of the material world. Science meant taking things apart and reducing them to their constituent elements in order to understand the whole. Applied to human affairs, science took shape as what we would call history. The time and sequence of human events were a form of explanation, a way to order, or rationalize, societal development. This rationalistic paradigm displaced the more whimsical and mythic world view that had heretofore existed, a view in which gods like Hermes the trickster or Zeus the passionate progenitor could do violence as well as play favorites. Anyone who has read Greek mythology or Homer will recognize the role of chance in such a world.

Science, then, replaced chance with order. Order was no longer derived from the mythic paradigm, but from the scientific one. The Greeks replaced deities with a world of familiar objects. And, as such a view gained currency and drove out more mythical ones, nature itself became "reasonable." A crude physics replaced nature's folklore.

The notion that physical realities—the atom—were the irreducible bases of the world not only endured, it extended to social life. People came to view themselves as part of nature and subject to its rules. These rules, which the new, scientific frame of reference held to be immutable, determined order in all things; they were the psychological and social order to which people were subject as well as to natural forces. It was thought that perhaps individuals were human particles held together by society as by a field of force. (A derivative of this view prevails today. When the atom was smashed people began to appreciate what the Greeks had perceived—that at the center of the smallest unit of the universe is the largest kind of power. To structure and organize such force requires the *collective power of individuals* acting toward the common good.)

The trouble with Greek science—and history, too, for that matter—was that it was concerned with description rather than abstraction. It lacked a theory-making dimension, a way to separate those underlying principles that reason could discern and people could apply. To formulate theory it is necessary to conceptualize certain drives, to formalize their components, and to reduce the findings into either functional or predictive formulas. This the early Greeks were not capable of doing. Hence the intellectual (political) tradition we associate with the Greeks rejected science in favor of the analysis of morals.

Socrates was among the first who realized that the science of nature did not provide sufficient explanation for reason in the conduct of human affairs.

Socrates begins by saying that in his youth he had been eager to learn how philosophers had accounted for the origin of the world and of living creatures. He soon gave up this science of Nature, because he could not be satisfied with the sort of explanation or reasons offered. Some, for instance, had found the origin of life in a process of fermentation set up by the action of heat and cold. Socrates felt that such explanations left him none the wiser, and he concluded that he had no natural talent for inquiries of this sort.[1]

So political philosophy does not truly begin with science, but rather with the application of reason to human ends. But in political science, rationality, instead of being deductive, assumes a moral quality. If the smallest unit of power—in physics the atomic particle, in politics the individual—is smashed what will happen? Are the consequences like stepping on an ant? In terms of science, yes. In moral terms, no. Reason is the concern for justice and virtue that balances the rights of the individual and the collective.

Early science was not capable of formulating theories. It asked cosmic questions, but got no real answers. It needed to be shaped for moral ends: According to Socrates, to know one's self is to know ends, purposes and how these define what use is to be made of science.[2] Thus

1. F. M. Cornford, *Before and After Socrates* (Cambridge: Cambridge University Press, 1972), p. 2.
2. Ibid., pp. 29–53.

political philosophy was defined by ethics, which perhaps constitutes the highest "science." After Socrates (and indeed, until modern times) science was a peripheral subject and political philosophy a more central one in the hierarchies of political thought.

The question people have always asked is: What is political thinking? How does one derive criteria for moral principles? Well, the first step is to create a system, a political model sufficiently abstract so that different theorists or philosophers can supply their own ingredients while the model remains the same. The model specifies conditions of perfection, how such conditions might be obtained, and whether or not one can produce harmony by political means. For Socrates the purpose of such a model was to make one's soul as good as possible. The polity that could accomplish this end was the best polity.

But how does one go about making one's soul "good"? Plato followed the question to one conclusion. Aristotle took it in another direction. Plato believed that knowledge and virtue can go together. Aristotle asked what happens when knowledge tells us that perfection is unattainable. Should we strive toward a goal we know cannot be achieved? What consequence does knowledge have for deciding which is the best polity?

Balancing Order and Anarchy

Politics is a function of the relationship between rulers and ruled. Rule may be carried on by one (monarch, dictator, autocrat, tyrant), a few (oligarchy, junta, elite), or many people (the electorate). Rule by one person might be good or bad, depending on the ruler. Sometimes the rule of a few is wiser than the rule of one—but nothing prevents these few from governing on their own behalf. Moreover, an oligarchical or aristocratic method of governing is inclined to divisiveness. The few quarrel, plot, and intrigue among themselves. Even a government made up of a wise elite (like the Old Bolsheviks of the Russian Revolution) can destroy itself and play into the hands of a tyrant (like Stalin).

On the other hand, rule by the multitude—directly or by means of representatives—is always open to factionalism and favoritism. It is rule by the mediocre at best, or by the downright dishonest at worst. A system is needed that checks the power of autocrats and oligarchs who would prevent the selection of good rulers, but that does not prevent chosen leaders from ruling effectively. The problem is to make power rational and rationality equitable.

Each government is a kind of experiment in trying to find out what makes for "virtue." If the experiment goes sour, people pay the price in corruption, revolution, violence, and disillusionment. So politics begins where commandments leave off. It requires justiciable rules for the exercise of principled discretion. Such rules are expressed in commandments—whether fashioned by people or God—for the appropriate conduct of individuals and institutions. The political system becomes self-sustaining when it accepts the rights of all the "body politics," not just those of a favored few.

Plato said that those who possess exceptional ability to reason rightly (ethically) were those to whom it was given to rule. Reason, he deduced, was the first condition of politics and justice—including the principles of balance between equality and inequality, human versus property rights, and freedom versus order. Aristotle maintained, on the other hand, that since discrepancies between principles of equity and their practice generate conflict, conflict is thus endemic in politics.[3] Intellectuals' efforts to resolve this apparent split in the classical doctrine have generated repeated political predicaments throughout human history.

After the Greeks and Romans, reason was the special interest of religion. While virtuous conduct expressed God's revealed truth, reason served as a form of admonition, a guide to appropriate conduct. So a second continuous theme of the classical tradition is the idea of the immortality of the soul versus the immortality of the state. If political community represents justice as a morality higher than that of the state, then rulers must be subservient to God and man. Therefore a concerned morality is the basis of authority.

The alternative view—the origin of which can be traced to Aristotle —is more utilitarian. It is that virtue, in its political sense (that is, all the worthier feelings one manifests in public conduct), derives from each individual's pursuit of happiness, which is tempered by the fear of incurring penalties for excesses. A society in which public virtue and private happiness can be sustained is one based on policies of good judgment.

Abstract principles of goodness, duty, obligation, and commitment are continuously redefined in the context of debating the exigencies of harmony and conflict, the soul versus the society, and pleasure versus pain. These are the oldest and most enduring paradoxes underlying

3. *The Nichomachean Ethics of Aristotle,* D. P. Chase, trans. (New York: E. P. Dutton, 1911), p. 127.

politics. The utilitarian principle was one outcome of such debate, together with a number of other assumptions: that the individual, not the state, is primary and that human beings are perceptive entities who respond to external stimuli as a result not of isolation but of interaction. When pursuing individual goals becomes selfish, then politics has to deal with the question of how to regulate, and satisfy individuals' desires for property, power, and esteem by promoting cooperation without conflict.

(Political philosophy in this sense is a branch of moral philosophy. Later, in the seventeenth century, Hobbes saw the threat of chaos and anarchy in the utilitarian point of view. Hobbes believed that the prudential restraint postulated by Aristotle could not apply to the real world. Others, like Locke, hoped to avoid the Hobbesian solution by reexamining the place of reason and rationality in human affairs and redefining the kind of government that would enable both individualism and rationality to prevail. These matters are the subject of the next chapter.)

What was clear to the Greeks was that people fluctuate between two poles: their commitments to higher virtues and ideals of moral improvement, and the decay of such ideals. But if people innately have the capacity to recognize enduring and fundamental principles of virtue, justice, and obligation—how can they realize them? (Later the question would be whether an individual rationality is helped or hindered by a collective rationality.) That individuals can be helped by a collective rationality is the argument set forth in Plato's *Republic*. The concept is reiterated in the ideals of Augustine's City of God, the medieval religious utopians, and radical innovators including the early socialists—Saint Simon, Proudhon, and Robert Owen, not to mention Marx.

The Classical Model

Human beings have power to shape their lives and institutions as no other creatures do. Such power may or may not be used wisely and well. As human conduct was freed from the limitations and orthodoxies of a world view in which the gods prevailed over reason and priests were political interpreters, there arose the question of how to define reasonable priorities and put them into practice.

A "reasonable" paradigm assumes that people are reasonable, or that they can become that way given the appropriate political institutions. Political knowledge is represented by moral abstractions deriving from the search for purpose in the lives of individuals and societies. Such abstractions represent the goals of a community when the rulers (the micro unit) and the ruled (the macro unit) share in common beliefs about the purposes or ends of society and agree on means of governing that do not contradict those ends.

The classical political model, then, consists of rulers and ruled, means and ends. The model basically contains *all* the abstract ingredients of power. We can diagram the basic classical model of the political system as shown in Figure 3-1. Later philosophers merely fit various specific concepts into these broad categories.

Classical political philosophers sought to establish a balance between the rulers and the ruled so that each would serve the other's purposes as well as the common purpose (each would provide a means for the other). Rulers were the means by which stable and good government could produce a contented population. A contented population would work to produce the resources whereby government could carry forward its designs for the common good. Thus, through reason, the polity would achieve order, stability, and harmoniousness. The search for such balance continues to this day. The task of a democratic society is to enable the ruled to judge between rulers according to the ends to which they give priority.

But whatever particular theory one subscribes to about how to achieve harmony or balance, the Greeks created the framework of it. All subsequent political theory can be fitted into it. Working out the terms of the balance is the responsibility of all those who participate in politics—no matter what strategies are adhered to or what conditions

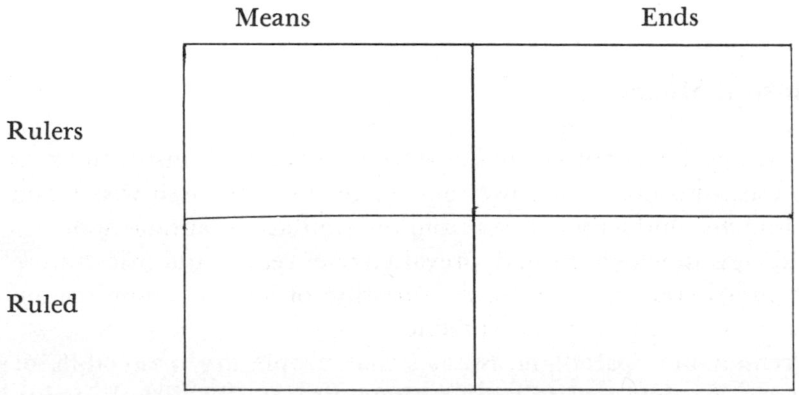

	Means	Ends
Rulers		
Ruled		

Figure 3-1. The Classical Model of the Political System

prevail between rulers and ruled. Despite the vast differences between Plato and Aristotle, or Hobbes and Rousseau, or Bentham and Marx, all doctrines can, without too much difficulty, be fitted into this general model of the political system. And in that respect, Plato is the ancestral figure of all political science.

In the next sections we examine some of Plato's ideas as well as the ideas of those who preceded and followed him. Due to the scope of this text, the purpose is not to give a detailed discussion of the work of the Greek philosophers, but to show some of the generative ideas they identified which remain part of today's understanding of political life. We shall also try to show how politics was plunged into the theocratic discourse which governed political philosophy during the medieval period, and which sought its ends in religious doctrine. In turn, this will help us to understand why the emergence of modern political philosophy—the enlightenment—from Machiavelli onward, is so essentially secular and in a sense so "Greek." It will also explain, to some degree, why the authors of the United States Constitution turned to the Greeks for inspiration and instruction as well as to Locke and Montesquieu.

Political Concepts Prior to Plato

The founding fathers did not emulate the classical model out of affection for Plato or Aristotle. Their motives were purely historical. They viewed in concrete terms the paradox we have described between the virtue of, say, a militant Sparta, whose spare strength was so enduring, and the civilization of a democratic Athens, whose brilliance and letters represented civility itself. The goal was to establish conditions that would allow both ideals to prosper.

Plato had been interested in the examples set by both Sparta and Athens, but in a more despairing way. Unlike the later utopians—from Sir Thomas More to Rousseau—who sought to describe an ideal state in order to instruct the improvement of people's ambitions, Plato tried to inculcate all the ways of governing with the pure truth that would create a better community. There is a vast difference between the Greek philosophers who sought a reasonable and truer basis for human life and the enlightened political philosophers who tried to discover workable conditions for human improvement. (In relatively modern times we have witnessed a similar difference between Marx, who sought ways to establish both the truth and the improving solution, and the social-contract theorists and utilitarians.)

And between Greek science and Greek moral philosophy there was a similar gap. It was bridged by several groups: The Pythagoreans saw a harmonious ordering of nature in numbers and music; the Sophists were concerned with the practicalities of politics. Pythagoras revered abstraction. The Sophists looked down to life itself, separating religion from culture, faith from indoctrination, and political education from philosophy.

Before the Sophists, there was none of the modern distinction between culture and religion in ancient Greek education: it was deeply rooted in religious faith. The rift between the two first opened in the age of the Sophists, which was also the period in which the ideal of culture was first consciously formulated. Protagoras' assertion that the traditional values of life were all relative, and his resigned acceptance of the insolubility of all the enigmas of religion were without doubt immediately connected with his high ideal of culture. Probably the conscious ideal of humanism could not have been produced by the great Greek educational tradition except at a moment when the old standards which had once meant so much to education began to be questioned.[4]

The political philosopher's quest was first to know the purposes of society by understanding its natural laws, and second to develop an appropriate method of knowledge. On these two principles, the study of politics began. By applying them in different ways, political philosophers produced the generative ideas most fundamental to politics as an intellectual's discourse and a practitioner's art.

The Greeks were not pious purists. They by no means limited knowledge to the high virtues. Knowledge was a practical business, the power of which produced visible results. General knowledge applied to specific things had consequence. Knowledge was power.[5]

4. Werner Jaeger, *Paideia: The Ideals of Greek Culture* (New York: Oxford University Press, 1945) , pp. 301–302. See also W. T. Stace, *A Critical History of Greek Philosophy* (London: Macmillan, 1950) , pp. 106–26.
5. Thales, of the Ionian city of Miletus, decided to demonstrate this precept. Using his general knowledge of the climate of Asia Minor, he prophesied a good harvest of olives, the main crop of the Milesian countryside. Then he cornered the market for olive presses. When harvest time came he hired the presses out for large sums of money, proving that philosophers can get rich too if they want to. He also used his superior knowledge in a more oracular capacity: to stop a battle. He wanted to show the superiority of knowledge as an intellectual skill over brute force. See Kathleen Freeman, *God, Man and State: Greek Concepts* (Boston: Beacon Press, 1952) , p. 14.

The same applied to government. Intelligence was the basis of a knowledge of natural law. The application of reason, or intelligence, was to be used to establish the conditions of the just society. Ergo the just society. Its government could be harmonious, as Plato showed. Taking Pythagoras' idea that the universe was composed of ordered and numbered relationships for which geometry was the language of form, Plato stipulated that, just as geometric designs fitted to concepts could establish the fundamentally orderly relationships of nature, so philosophical discourse could produce a geometrical, logical balance between rulers and ruled. For Plato, virtue was the "geometric" element of unity, with Socrates the symbol of rationality in human affairs. He represented both the promise that reason always wins out in the end, and the tragedies that occur when people are insufficiently schooled in reason. The vine of knowledge may be replaced by the poison of hemlock—the same cup will hold both.

Plato

Who was Plato? First he was the inheritor of what went before him in Greek thought. The Sophists had raised the question of ethics: Does the essence of things remain the same and survive all changes, or do all things change and pass away? What endures and what changes in nature and in human institutions? The answer to these questions is that interests determine changes in human nature. The problem is to make the overriding interest that of the community, rather than that of any one individual.

Socrates taught Plato that virtue consists of knowledge of the good, hence the problem was to fashion a state in which all were interested in virtue. Pythagoras taught Plato that virtue was abstract and that knowledge of the abstract was more real than knowledge of things manifested in the empirical or sensuous world. These concepts gave him an understanding of the metaphysics of ideal forms. The dialectical method—questioning by means of paradox—revealed that human beings could be made conscious of their abstract understanding.[6]

Plato also came to believe that abstract forms were at the basis of human immortality. An Athenian, he was born in 428 B.C. into a grim

6. See the discussion on dialectics in W. Windelband, *A History of Philosophy* (New York: Macmillan, 1896), pp. 130–31.

world. When he was young Athens was defeated in a war by Sparta. A wealthy aristocrat, Plato never married, but saw the influence of his position and his wealth erode with the rise of Athenian democracy, which to him simply meant the rule of demagogues. When Plato was thirty-one years old the Athenian state had Socrates put to death. Shattered, Plato became a wanderer, travelling to Egypt, Sicily, and elsewhere. Returning to Athens he founded an academy of learning which Aristotle is supposed to have attended for the last twenty years of Plato's life.

The death of Socrates showed Plato not only the importance of unfettered knowledge, but the need for public education as well. Education he saw to be the teaching of truths that make people wiser in the conduct of their affairs. The way to enlightenment is discourse, or the testing of the truth of one proposition against another. Plato called this method *dialectical*. Using the dialectic, with Socrates as his mouthpiece, Plato provides us with dialogues on truth, law, and justice and the derivation of the generative ideas of political and social life. By these dialogues Plato hoped to replicate the reason of nature—which was geometry—in society. The geometry of ideas is in the logical formulation of words and concepts. Just as the relationships of the natural world consist of proportions or balances mathematically stated, so relationships of the social world consist of a balance logically stated. Concepts replace numbers, but the intellectual structure is the same.

First Plato established a philosophical hierarchy of ideas. Then, assuming the role of the politician, he showed how his system of dialectical logic led to justice. The just society is harmonious and good. In the *Republic* he postulated the first utopia, in which those with the greatest power to reason were given the greatest power to rule. Such authority would lead to the virtuous and harmonious society.

Plato's greatness for us lies not in the freshness of his vision, nor in his theory of the "meritocracy" (although these are significant even today), nor in his theory of ideas, but rather in that his was the first theory of the ideal state. The model is so remarkable that it can be separated from Platonic theory and applied to *any* theory political philosophers have constructed to this day.

The Platonic model: A geometry of proportionality and balance in human affairs was the object of Plato's model. He had seen how societies could decay and how difficult it was to establish good ones not based on greed, deceit, and arrogance. He was much influenced by the Spartan form of society. Sparta was austere and simple. Education and training were strictly regulated. All aspects of life, from having children to the games children played, were the subject of conscious political design, and this went for women as well as men. Sparta's was a stable society. But its main business was war. Could a city equivalent to Sparta—but devoted to peace and justice (a permanent Athens) —be created?

Athens, a more intellectual society, was more concerned with commerce, the arts, and poetry than with war. Almost in spite of itself the Athenian empire was rich. The period of Pericles was its Golden Age; Solon was its great lawgiver. But in the Peloponnesian War (431–404 B.C.) it was rude Sparta that won, not Athens.

How could so great an empire with such cultivation and intelligence fail? For Plato the answer was that the critical knowledge and the wisdom necessary to sustain society is not equally distributed among all the people. The problem is to construct a society in which the multitude contributes to the prosperity of the community—all individuals realizing their fullest potentiality—without having the collective power to destroy. Then one could achieve the greatness of Athens using the method of the Spartans. Decay would be arrested. The just society would reflect the enduring harmony of the spheres.

The notion was that the perfect concrete system would reflect the perfect ideal or analytically abstract one. The perfect ideal one would be a system of mutually reinforcing parts. (A modern counterpart would be a physicist's invention of a frictionless machine, or an economist's model of perfect competition.) In the model distribution of power between rulers and ruled, rulers derive the right to use power to achieve public good from their exceptional intelligence. Public good in turn is the fulfillment of every individual's potentiality. The model therefore represents a flow of power according to what is right. Authority exercised by the ruling "philosopher-kings" establishes justice. Justice distributed among the ruled works toward the fulfillment of potentiality, which is achieved through work. Work, in turn, produces the necessary resources for authority. The model, which is diagrammed in Figure 3-2, is perfectly self-sustaining.

Plato represented what might be called the first "immersed" political theorist. He was immersed in politics and meant his model to serve as a form of propaganda for his theories. He proposed a way to discover political truth: "Truth—being the "real" reality—"ought" to follow "reality."

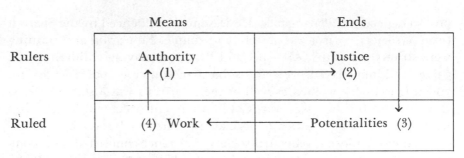

Figure 3-2. Plato's Political System

***The* Republic:** The good society then is the state of justice. Justice can be understood by philosopher-kings. In the just society all will be able to realize their potentialities. But how can such a society come into being? How does one know his or her potentialities? One must first perceive the model itself, the underlying "reality." The next step is to establish a system of competitive education. As in Sparta, all boys and girls alike must be exposed to the same educational system. As education becomes more complex, inferior people will fall out according to the level of their intellectual abilities. They cluster naturally into three main classes. The best, who are few, become philosopher-kings and thus the rulers. The next best become soldiers, who maintain and defend the society. The rest—artisans, farmers, merchants, and so forth—make up the ruled. Education and ability are the principles by which society is ranked, but education not only selects the classes, it indoctrinates the ruled.

Once the educational system is established a new problem must be faced. How does one ensure that the philosopher-kings will be single-minded in their pursuit of justice and not become corrupt? The state is not only a system of classes but a coalition of ethics, and the two cannot be separated. The responsibility for cohesion lies with the rulers. They must be noble, gracious, temperate, courageous, truthful and, above all, uncorrupted by "all the ordinary goods of life—beauty, wealth, strength, rank and great connection in the State. . . ."[7] For this reason they must be denied property and family. Property, and women and children are to be held in common. The purity of the philosopher-kings is ensured by their communism. They share common houses and means. All are fathers and mothers; all are their children.

No such condition applies to the commoners, the ruled, however.

7. *The Republic of Plato,* Benjamin Jowett, trans. (New York: The Colonial Press, 1901), p. 184.

The educational system will teach them temperance and music, as well as appropriate crafts so that they will learn to realize their potentialities. A worker will be most fulfilled knowing what he or she does best and having only one occupation. The basis of fulfillment is in the division of labor within the class. The ruled are carpenters, smiths, shepherds, farmers, traders. Work is their fulfillment.

Plato's system of rewards is based on the principle from each according to work, to each according to capacity. So, for Plato, justice is not the same for all, but varies between classes. The principle is that different people have different needs. Justice therefore does not depend on some mechanical condition of equality, but on a distributive justice. The philosopher-kings make possible the realization of the ends for each class, and so each individual is fulfilled. The business of the state is furthered by all individuals doing their work. The means so created by the ruled are then employed by the philosopher-kings to realize the just society. So self-reinforcing a utopian model is abstract in character. The model proposes an ideal city-state of about fifty thousand inhabitants.

To accept this model one needs to accept the premise that the basic qualities of individuals are naturally different. Some are "gold" (philosopher-kings) ; some are "brass" (soldiers) ; the rest are "iron" (the ruled). Because the structure of work and the structure of classes is based on a natural division of ability, justice differs from equality; therefore the just society is unequal. Indeed, according to Plato, it would be unjust to try to make all people equal for then the best could not rule. The good society would decay under the press of inferiors. The philosopher-kings would, like Socrates, take the hemlock or, like Pericles, fall from power, the prey of lesser and envious people.

The question Plato tried to resolve was how to prevent the mighty and good from being brought low—that is, how to prevent the decay of the good society. He asked how it happens that good governments can be allowed to decline, and mighty empires to fall apart, and good constitutions to be debased. Is it inevitable that standards of worthiness, austerity, commitment to ideals, and all the cooperative enterprise that a common raionality can produce, must in the end become empty, their meaning shallow, narrow, and dogmatic? (One can ask the question about our own society. The "revolution of the saints," the Puritans with their devotion to the ideal Christian commonwealth, prudence, and rational endeavor, has given way to a society hungering for material satisfaction and the pursuit of leisure. Happiness is the goal rather than virtue. Will our society decay as a result?)

Plato also raises questions about the character of education and its connection to civility and efficacy. If all people are not equal in their endowments, can they be equal in their rights? Should discipline and force be applied to keep harmony? Censorship will help ensure that ambitions will be limited, the realities of performance will serve as the basis of contentment, and public manipulation can substitute for force. Plato's treatment of property is particularly important. He wanted to prevent oligarchy so that the class of rulers would not become self-serving. Therefore power and property must be inversely related. For the multitude, properties are the necessities of work. For philosopher-kings, the sole property is the mind.

These perplexing, stubborn, and stimulating issues still are political-social concerns that turn up when we least expect them. How much is a meritocratic system of education the basis for our present ideas of political democracy? To what extent do we believe that a rough ordering of intelligence and occupation is a legitimate condition of rank or class? Arguments about quality versus quantity in education include the belief that excellence is an important attribute for an elite which, if it cannot rule, should at least influence policy more than its numbers might attest. Plato poses virtue against pleasure and finds the former "higher" in worthiness. On this principle rest a good many subsequent political beliefs.

We find in Plato's writings ideals of perfection, but also the ingredients of fascism and communism. Plato himself was no fanatic. In the *Laws* he climbs down from his lofty heights to take a clear look at likely and possible improvements that can be made in society, rather than dealing exclusively with the pure case. In the *Laws* he is much more realistic. However, he died before he could finish this work and whatever his later views, in the *Republic* not only did he open up a neverending debate about the relationship of knowledge and justice to power and equality, he provided the first systematic model of the political system.

Aristotle

Aristotle was very different from Plato. He was curious—his search for knowledge was insatiable. He was not concerned with gloomy prophecy or the making of poetical myths. He brought scientific inquiry into the realm of politics without sacrificing its ethics. Aristotle remained devoted to his master, Plato, but he was fundamentally different in personality and spirit. Born in Stagira in 384 B.C., his father died when he was a child and he was sent to Athens, where he entered Plato's academy, as a young man. He later founded his own school, called the Lyceum.

Aristotle accepted Plato's model but changed its emphasis. Instead of imagining a geometrical structure of concepts to be realized in social affairs, he tried to balance the logical need for ethics with a more practical view of the real world. Aristotle was doubtful about the virtues of wise men, preferring a government of laws.[8] He had good reasons for these views. After examining 158 constitutions (a number slightly less than the number of independent countries in the world today) to see how they came into being and how various distributions of power worked for the common good, he had few illusions about politics. The best one could hope for was *prudential happiness*. This "prudentialism" he extended into the dimensions of the Platonic model: the relations between rulers and ruled are determined by constitutional forms; authority can best be exercised by collective purpose when individual purposes are safeguarded against arbitrary power; the political emphasis is on law.

As for hierarchy, Aristotle believed that most people fall somewhere in the middle between high intelligence and low, just as most peoples' work puts them in the middle between wealth and poverty. His ideal was a society of the middle class, a class which knew its own self-interest. If Aristotle was not exactly a democrat, the spirit of his thought is democratic.

He was also an empiricist. Reality he believed to be that which is visible and tangible.[9] He began his analysis of politics with empirical investigation rather than deductive logic. But he did not reject the original rationalistic vision. Rather, he used it to establish a more realistic ethical foundation for the state. For Aristotle ethical goodness and practical wisdom must go together. What starts people along the line of goodness is not some abstract standard to be realized in a contemplative vision, but rather the concrete choices they make every day. Rulers make good choices and bad ones. "Good" and "bad" choices may be one of two kinds: moral or practical. A good practical choice may be a bad moral choice. A good moral choice may be a bad practical one. But to prefer the moral to the practical is foolish just as to prefer the practical to the moral is corrupt. Wisdom consists of striking a good balance and so becoming both practical and virtuous. For Aristotle,

8. See Alexander Passerin d'Entreves, *The Notion of the State* (Oxford: The Clarendon Press, 1967), pp. 69–81.
9. F. M. Cornford, op. cit., p. 88.

Pericles provided the model. He says, "We think of Pericles and men of that stamp to be practically wise, because they can see what is good for themselves and for men in general, and we also think those to be such who are skilled in domestic management or civil government."[10] The good society then is one in which men can be "practically wise." The problem is how to establish such a society.

The Aristotelian model: To answer this problem Aristotle turns his attention to the relationship between the ends of the community and the ends of individuals, both rulers and ruled. For Aristotle the ends of the community must evolve in such a way as to maximize the ends of the ruled. The state, as in the Platonic model, must realize individual potentiality: People are happy when they are both ethical and practical. So maximized, the ends of the ruled become the potentiality of the state.

Aristotle is concerned with describing the best state that will bring about fulfillment. He adapts Plato's model like this (see Figure 3-3).

For Aristotle practical wisdom leads to happiness. But happiness cannot derive from excess. Rather it is a form of virtue that stands between extremes. It is the supreme object of the state. Where happiness prevails, prudentially wise ends are maximized and reflected in good choices, which produce a middle class and a mixed constitution, which in turn ensures happiness. So the virtues of moderation and balance arise out of intelligent actions. (In this respect Aristotle remains close to Plato.) People making choices act politically, which is why "man is a political animal." The good society is the community that makes it possible for the best ethical and political choices to be made.

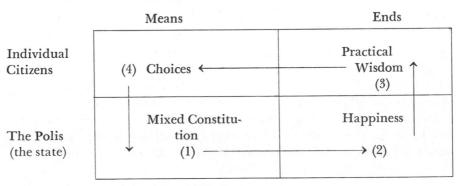

Figure 3-3. Aristotle's Prudential Polity

10. Aristotle, op. cit., p. 135.

Aristotle modifies the pure rationalism of Plato. He considers the relationship between the ideal and the actual, the theoretical and the practical, in terms of balances.

The Aristotelian method: Aristotle's method, like Plato's, is first of all logical. But unlike Plato's, it is not a logic of forms but one of *causality*. If one knows what causes something, one can control it.

Causality is inherent in nature. But nature, for Aristotle, is not a geometry—not a mechanistic balance. Rather it is organic growth unfolding in natural forms. For Plato, reality consisted of a system of ideal forms ordered from lower to higher, from multiplicity to unity. In society this unity was justice. For Aristotle there are lower and higher forms, but like the mighty oaks out of which little acorns grow, such forms are the result of natural processes. Hence he applies empirical science and naturalism to forms as causes. What causes growth? Aristotle identifies four kinds of causality: material, efficient, formal, and final. The **material** cause is the matter of which something is composed (for example, in a bronze statue the bronze is the material cause). The **efficient** cause is the method by which the material is produced, the requisite energy or motion (for example, casting the statue). The **formal** cause is what something looks like, how it graces the house, how it is suitable for worship, and so on. The **final** cause is the creative image that was in the mind of the sculptor.

These causes basically reduce to two: form and matter, or *potentiality* and *actuality*. How matter is converted into form—or potentiality realized in actuality—is as much a problem of politics as it is for the sculptor. The job of the political philosopher, like that of the sculptor, is to identify the final form of the state which best realizes the good life.

The final form for the individual lies in the individual's potentiality for practical virtue, the happiness of the soul. The formal cause of the individual is the mixed constitution, the charter of the state. The formal cause for individuals collectively is represented by the choices they make in occupational, familial, and other aspects of life. The efficient cause of the "polis" (state) may be a revolution, a war, civil strife, a wise leader or king, the murder of a leader, or some other political situation or event. The efficient causes for individuals depend on their personal situations, work, natural catastrophes, and so on. The material cause of the polis is human membership in families or clans. But since the polis exists by nature (and prior to the individual although composed of individuals), it helps to shape the individual. So if the individual contributes to the material cause of the polis, the polis contributes to the final cause of the individual.

We thus see that the polis exists by nature and that it is prior to the individual. Not being self-sufficient when they are isolated, all individuals are so many parts, all equally depending on the whole. The man who is isolated—who is unable to share in the benefits of political association, or has no need to share because he is already self-sufficient—is not part of the polis, and must therefore be either a beast or a god.[11]

Either beast or god, but not man—that is the essential point of Aristotle's causalities. The polis makes man and perfects him. For this he has an "imminent impulse" toward association. So, Aristotle goes on to say, when perfected man is the best of animals, but isolated from law and justice, "he is the worst of all."[12]

For Aristotle, the notion of causality and the transformation from potentiality to actuality is what unites nature and politics. People and polis are parts of nature and they cause each other to exist in whatever state they do exist. But the state exists prior to the people of which it is comprised.

The Polis: Given the foregoing critique of Aristotle's method, what is the best polis? To answer we must go back to the Platonic utopia.

The ordinary view is that Plato was describing a State which was the invention of his own fancy, and is therefore regarded as entirely unreal. This is completely to misunderstand Plato. So far was he from thinking the ideal State unreal, that he regarded it, on the contrary, as the only real State. All existent States, such as the Athenian or the Spartan, are unreal insofar as they differ from the ideal State. And moreover, this one reality, the ideal State, is the ground of the existence of all actual States. They owe their existence to its reality. Their existence can only be explained by it. Now since the ideal State is not yet reached in fact, but is the perfect State towards which all actual States tend, it is clear that we have here a teleological principle. The real explanation of the State is not to be found in its beginnings in history, in an original contract, or in biological necessities, but in its end, the final or perfect State.[13]

11. See *The Politics of Aristotle,* Ernest Barker, trans. (Oxford: The Clarendon Press, 1946), p. 6. Emphasis not in original.
12. Ibid., p. 7.
13. W. T. Stace, op. cit., p. 202.

Aristotle's formal cause corresponds to Plato's ideal (which is itself "real"). But for Aristotle the perfect state provides a basis for empirical evaluation. So he turned his attention to constitutions, or formal causes.

A constitution as a formal cause requires a final cause which, in the Aristotelian sense, is not at all similar to Plato's ideal state. Plato's ideal was deductive, based on a dialectic of established principles which could be applied to cases. Aristotle's final cause is inductively derived from the basis of evidence as well as the prudential ideal. Ethical considerations and practical experience embodied in a mixed constitution derive from a knowledge of the real world.

Aristotle begins the *Ethics* with a discussion of ends:

Every art, and every science reduced to a teachable form and in a like manner every action and moral choice, aims, it is thought, at some good: for which reason a common and by no means bad description of the Chief Good is, "that which all things aim at."[14]

He begins *The Politics* with a description of science:

Observation shows us first, that every polis (or state) is a species of association, and secondly, that all associations are instituted for the purpose of attaining some good—for all men do all their acts with a view to achieving something which is, in their view, a good. We may therefore hold, on the basis of what we actually observe, that all associations aim at some good; and we may also hold that the particular association which is the most sovereign and inclusive association is the polis, as it is called, or the political association.[15]

In both works, there is a concern with purpose, object, observation, species, and definitions. Here Aristotle is both didactic and empirical. The care he takes in formulating issues is impressive. His meanings are precise—unlike Plato's whose art is constructed on the grand design. By an argumentative sleight of hand Plato created a structure—the model for which is utopian—out of poetry.

Perfection in Plato's ideal is clear, explicit, modeled, and universal. "You are a sculptor, Socrates, and have made statues of our governors faultless in beauty. Yes I said, Glaucon, and of our governesses too; for

14. Chase, op. cit., p. 1.
15. Barker, op. cit., p. 1.

you must not suppose that what I have been saying applies to men only and not to women as far as their natures can go."[16]

Aristotle's emphasis is always on politics within the city-state. In the *Republic* Plato sought the static order. Aristotle is interested in political change. Plato hoped to reveal a fixed concept of justice. Aristotle considered the changing terms of equity. Plato regarded the appropriateness of rule in relation to the perfection of the governors. Aristotle saw it in terms of the perfection of the laws.

To understand what was potentiality before it became actuality requires historical knowledge. For example, in *The Constitution of Athens*,[17] Aristotle recapitulates the tumultuous historical events that propelled the Athenian city-state, from before the Golden Age through the establishment of the oligarchic Rule of the Thirty. History as it unfolds thus reveals empirical things—how councils work, how constitutions come and go, the role of magistrates and priests, and methods of impeachment and election. Theory emerges out of such a wealth of historical information, carefully sifted.

Here, then, according to historical analysis, is Aristotle's reasonable polity. The polis must be small. Size is to be determined by the following criteria: All citizens need to be able to know each other; all should be able to fit within a central square or plaza and be addressed by a single leader; the community must be economically self-sufficient. The state is necessary because of an imminent desire for perfection in all humans, but it cannot be attained by individuals. Individuals can try to realize their natural appetites, but moderation is required. The first job of the state is to educate its members. Since people are naturally unequal a "state of equality" is fairer for some than for others. The best state is that in which happiness is a reward in proportion to the individual's contribution. The best government is that in which the most virtuous rule.

But in real life, virtuous rulers do not necessarily stay virtuous; that is, the state of the virtuous magistrate or king is impermanent. Stability occurs when all the different classes of people are able to participate in politics; however, absolute democracy results in anarchy. The best compromise is for the state to reflect the power of the middle class.[18]

---

16. Ibid., p. 239.
17. *Aristotles' Constitution of Athens,* Kurt von Fritz and Ernest Kapp, trans., (New York: Hafner Publishing Co., 1950).
18. Aristotle quotes with approval the following couplet: "Many things are best for the middling:/Fain would I be of the state's middle class." Ernest Barker, op. cit., p. 182.

It is clear from our argument, first, that the best form of political society is one where power is vested in the middle class, and, secondly, that good government is attainable in those states where there is a large middle class—large enough, if possible, to be stronger than both of the other classes, but at any rate large enough to be stronger than either of them singly; for in that case its addition to either will suffice to turn the scale and will prevent either of the opposing extremes from becoming dominant. It is therefore the greatest of blessings for a state that its members should possess a moderate and adequate property.[19]

Aristotle goes on to comment about how tyranny can arise when there are extremes of wealth and poverty, and concludes that "it is clear that the middle type of constitution is best."[20]

Aristotle follows the Platonic classification of political systems according to rule by the one, the few, or the many. He analyzes the purposes of the good society and its relationship to individual happiness. He considers alternative forms of government in the context of the ends of both the polity and the individual. He shows the consequences of different kinds of connections between these in a comparative way. He considers the institutions of government and how they work, examines efficient causes in terms of revolutions and the rise and fall of regimes, but never loses sight of the connection between individual and social ends and means. (Unlike Plato, he takes a dim view of the Spartans.)

Plato and Aristotle represent the beginning of the classical tradition. Their two models—the original Platonic model and the Aristotelian amendment—have been tinkered with ever since. With them the paradigm of rational power was established.

They remain "model figures" for political inquiry of the sort which considers the ethical and purposeful basis of society as the rationale for politics. Rationalism and logic are critical to the enterprise. Argument over purposes and ideals is not simply a competition of one idea with another, juxtaposed, as it were, by main force (although sometimes that is what happens), but a competitive discourse aimed at establishing rational truths rooted in human nature. In the classical paradigm wisdom is a method.

Plato and Aristotle then, as the first two powerful figures in political philosophy, represent a "rationalistic paradigm." They show the intimate connection between what one wishes to know and the method

19. Ibid.
20. Ibid.

one applies to knowing it. Most of what was relevant to them is relevant to us. Any ordinary dinner-table conversation that rises above political gossip contains some element that would be recognizable in their terms. Stability and change, virtue and achievement, reform and revolution, tradition and innovation—all these are specifically dealt with and turned into particulars of rule based on the experiences of ruling. This is no mean achievement.

The Theocratic Paradigm:
From Reason to Law to Religion

Plato and Aristotle left an inheritance we still live off. Their stamp upon their successors was overwhelming. Just as they represented a paradigmatic shift away from magic and religion to rationalism, those who came after combined the earlier theocratic paradigm they displaced with the rationalistic paradigm itself.

The Romans extended the idea of natural law to human laws. In the Roman world magistrates replaced philosopher-kings. But the Christian world represents a return to a religious world view. Magistrates could be either sacred or secular—priests or kings. The problem was to combine a fundamental belief in the divine with natural law, expressing them both in the actual laws made for governing in a manner that would inspire cooperation between ecclesiastical authorities and secular ones. The question was how to render Caesar only that which belonged to him.

From God came revelation; from revelation reason; from reason natural law. From natural laws came practical ones governing property, inheritance, military service, and all other obligations. Such practical injunctions and regulations were made by people. Called *positive law,* these indicated what had to be done and how. So the theocratic paradigm consisted of a mixture of *natural law* derived from the Greeks and Romans, *revelation* derived from the Christian belief system, *positive law* which governed practical consequences, and *grace* which represents the attainable purpose. The mixture is diagrammed in Figure 3-4.

The above paradigm emerged with the triumph of Christianity. Grace is what all people must achieve. To live in a state of grace, the ruled must be governed by positive laws that ensure proper conduct, devoutness, devotion, piety, and work. Rulers establish positive law on the

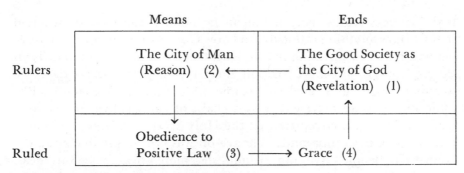

	Means	Ends
Rulers	The City of Man (Reason) (2) ←	──── The Good Society as the City of God (Revelation) (1) ↑
Ruled	↓ Obedience to Positive Law (3) ─┼──→	Grace (4)

Figure 3-4. The Theocratic Paradigm

basis of reason and natural law, which they comprehend through inspiration: God is in man, the city—which itself is ideal—is of God.

One can see how much such a vision owes to Plato. But now the ideal is a form of knowledge which takes revelation, or the knowledge of God's design, as its authority. The theocratic paradigm is not antirationalistic. The Platonic influence remained in the form of authoritative utopia. So did Aristotelian influences, and concern with a government of laws, not of men. The job of the Church and of medieval divines was to translate into rule what revelation outlined. So the Good Society became the City of God, and the city of man became the city of laws.

How the change occurred: What brings about such a change in the paradigm? A world of events lies behind the answer. The fall of Greece, the rise of Rome. In the transition, the world of human experience was transformed. The problems people confronted in their actual lives were perceived differently. Old ideas became detached from the common currency of daily transactions. New ideas arose. Fresh meaning was attached to old principles.

What was permanent was the idea of rationality. Once it was let loose on the world it could not be caged. But it is impossible to live in too rationalistic a world. People need religion, mystery, and divine guidance in their lives. Without these it is too difficult for most to think through all the issues of their lives. Socrates could believe in nonbelief, but most of us cannot.

The problem of rationality is whether or not intelligence in nature is divine. Is this ultimate intelligence, unity, orderliness—which the Greeks called *Logos*—God? Is God separate from life? Aristotle said yes —his god was purely intellectual. But if the universe originates with God, then the beginning can be known by knowing God. Unable to explain the mysterious roots of human rationality, the Divines assumed that to know anything rational is to know God. So a rationality of nature became mystical, blending nature with God, symbolized specifically in the incarnation of Christ. Platonic imagery was particularly adaptable to this thesis. Logical analysis became allegorical. (For example, Platonic images were represented by a chain of rings held together by a magnet. The magnet represented the Holy Spirit.) Allegory became a form of religious propaganda. The reason was not simply to elevate the aesthetic in people's lives but to establish a monopoly of religious ideas. The City of God was the new truth. If it was dogmatic, this was in keeping with Plato's tradition of political philosophy rather than Aristotle's. But in the long run, since revelation and dogma have to be supported by reason, the Platonic influence gave way to Aristotelianism.

The City of God and the city of man: The original purpose of theocratism was to ensure the uniformity of Christian life. In the hands of the popes, the unity of grace became a unity of politics. The church made salvation possible by envisioning the community of life transcended by a community of souls in immortality. The rationalistic universe of the Greeks was too mortal for medieval mortals to stand.

St. Augustine was the first great figure to state the issue of theocratic politicism. He had personally struggled with earthly desire. He saw heaven and hell and God and the devil as the personification of individual struggle between good and evil. For him politics had to resolve that struggle and with it the dualistic doctrine posed by the Manichaeans.[21]

In Augustine's hands, Plato's ideal city becomes the heavenly city, an intelligible archetype. Built on love of God and contempt of self, the heavenly city stands in contrast to the real or earthly city, which is built on self-love and contempt of God. The latter is material and narrow. Its inhabitants prefer possessions to virtue. The former is peaceful, universal, and harmonious. Life is a pilgrimage from the one to the other.[22]

---

21. Manichaeism was of Babylonian origin. *Mani,* or the apostle of God, was born in 216 A.D. He wrote a book called *The Living Gospel.* He preached a doctrine of the dualism of good and evil, light and darkness, truth and error, God and matter. The problem is to understand how the good side of such dualisms can be made to triumph. St. Augustine was, for a time, a Manichaean.
22. See the discussion of Augustine in A. H. Armstrong, ed., *The Cambridge History of Later Greek and Early Medieval Philosophy* (Cambridge: Cambridge University Press, 1967), pp. 354–419.

So the Platonists' stress on virtue and happiness is translated into religious purpose.

If, then, we be asked what the city of God has to say upon these points, and in the first place, what its opinion regarding the supreme good and evil is it will reply that life eternal is the supreme good, death eternal the supreme evil, and that to obtain the one and escape the other we must live rightly.[23]

How removed from the skeptical and relatively dry secularism of the Greeks is this mystic, demonological, Manichaean view!

Rationality Again

In the medieval period, Aristotle's ideas were connected to religious doctrine. For St. Thomas Aquinas, God was the equivalent of Aristotle's efficient cause, "For He is the universal efficient cause of all being."[24]

But what was God the efficient cause of? The answer is breathtaking: all the attributes of human society in which the ethical can prevail. Knowing the City of God is not enough. People remain preoccupied with their place in the city of man, earthly things, and material possessions. St. Thomas tried to resolve the paradox by going back to the problem of justice (Plato's original concern) and its relation to law. Justice consists of two forms: that which arises out of transactions, such as buying and selling according to market principles of distribution. A second is by rank: Proper justice occurs when a ruler or steward gives to each what he or she, by rank, deserves. The heavenly universe is ranked and ordered by Seraphim, Cherubim, and Thrones; Dominations, Virtues, Powers, Principalities, Angels, and Archangels. People are ranked as kings, nobles, clergy, masters, and slaves.[25] St. Thomas' doctrine was that rightness was achieved by each having his or her place. This structure provided the earthly reflection of heaven. Revelation taught the rules of the heavenly universe, and reason the rules of the earthly one.

23. St. Augustine, *The City of God,* Vol. 2, ed. Marcus Dods (New York: Hafner Publishing Co., 1948), p. 301.
24. Anton C. Pegis, *Basic Writings of Saint Thomas Aquinas,* Vol. II (New York: Random House, 1945), p. 3.
25. Ibid., Vol. I, pp. 995–1012.

The doctrine separated the two forms of authority: the ecclesiastical authority of the Church and the secular powers of kings.

Both St. Augustine and St. Thomas sought grace and salvation, but St. Thomas was much the greater thinker, while Augustine was a kind of architect of the divine. St. Thomas was a legalist, a logic chopper. His arguments became more unified as tension between representatives of the Pope and the Emperor of the Holy Roman Empire (ecclesiastical versus secular authority) hardened into competing claims of infallibility. Slowly, as the great Thomistic synthesis fell apart, so the ideal of the heavenly city disappeared. Grace was increasingly left to the individual. From that time on the arguments of political philosophers contend with human beings rather than God. People are the center of belief in the enlightenment tradition.

chapter four
The Enlightenment Tradition

The theocratic paradigm that largely replaced the Greek classical tradition nicely defines the boundaries of the classical period. The paradigm of rationality was sandwiched between a primitive theocratic world and a more sophisticated one.

The *enlightenment tradition,* beginning in the sixteenth century, was similarly bounded. On the one side was the deep religiosity of the medieval world. On the other, a new form of belief projected a radical vision of the world whose object is to transform the universe. This radical tradition—which we shall discuss in the next chapter—is essentially a product of the nineteenth century.

Late in the medieval period two important principles emerged which helped to make the transition to the enlightenment. One was that the ruler or monarch was a representative of the people with a constitutionally defined or limited sphere of power. The other was that the political community consisted not of the private rights of all individuals but of the rights of a representative assembly. People were represented not in their private capacities, but in a public one—that is, as citizens.[1] A representative assembly exercised control over rulers. These were the foundations of individual rights and representation. The problem was how to keep these from being made ecclesiastical.

Notions of the rights of citizens and constitutional limits on the power of rulers became secularized when they developed into a theory of *social contract,* in which the rulers and the ruled established their legal or constitutional relationship by agreement. The original idea of compact was between God and humans. This became a contract between

---

1. See F. W. Maitland, *Political Theories of the Middle Age* (Cambridge: Cambridge University Press, 1927) , pp. 62–63.

rulers and ruled. During the enlightenment, society, which had been re-garded during the medieval period as a sort of corporation—a legal entity—became based on a constitutional foundation. In the modern state the social "corporation" was no longer a fixed, religiously en-shrined set of social relationships, but a more mechanistic one based on the consent of the government. Newtonian physics replaced God as the center. The secular universe was composed of self-cancelling or mechanistic vectors. Politics, like physics, operated according to rules which were built upon the idea of the pre-eminence of the smallest unit —in physics the atom, in politics the individual.

But humans are not atoms. They can reason. Reasoning requires freedom. However, the free actions of individuals may be random, de-structive, and anarchic. Or they may be constructive. What political processes will ensure that freedom results in order? That was the funda-mental political question. But no matter how this question is answered, to the enlightenment it was certain that the social contract was a device that defined the sphere of freedom according to a division of powers between rulers and ruled. The problem is at the heart of modern con-stitutionalism.

Related questions were: Should there be freedom of religion (re-ligious toleration)? How much diversity of opinion should be allowed? How are rights to be secured? Answers were hard to come by because the questions were raised during a period of continuous rebellion, conflict, and war, when the danger of anarchy seemed to threaten all.

The wars were significant in and of themselves. They wrested power from popes and gave it to kings. The theory of constitutionalism in its medieval and modern forms was punctuated by a period of autocracy. For kings to be elevated over popes, the secular over the sacred, the nation state over the Christian empire was no easy transition. The Hundred Years' War, which was fought in the fifteenth century, resulted from continuous conflict over such matters. In the seventeenth century the same issues provoked the Thirty Years' War. With the emergence of the modern, secular state, came two principles: the idea of sovereignty, and the doctrine of the divine right of kings. The problem was how to keep the former and eliminate the latter. It became the job of a whole new school of writers, thinkers, and publicists to determine how to create a more durable political order.

Newton was not the only god of the enlightenment; Voltaire was his prophet. Both were the progenitors of a new "science of man." The British philosophers, John Locke, and David Hume, all contributed to this new concern, which was the antithesis to both the medieval spirit and autocracy.[2]

First, the imperial triumphed over the ecclesiastical in the great struggles between kings and pope. Then as the great synthesizing vision of medieval Christianity declined, rulers became increasingly preoccupied with maintaining power, which became an end in itself rather than a means to a higher or better end. Some political philosophers, dutiful apologists for kings and the doctrine of divine right, made up elaborate genealogies showing how kingly houses descended from Adam and Eve. But such doctrines were not very convincing. Then came rebellions—the English revolution. But not until the ideal of natural law in a Christian commonwealth was supplanted by the ideal of natural rights in a secular commonwealth was the medieval theocratic paradigm finally replaced by the enlightenment. From then on the people's rights, and how to secure them—not the powers of rulers—became the central consideration of politics. The universal solution was to be representative government, what is known as *political democracy*.

Machiavelli and the Resurgence of Secularism

A key figure in the transition was Niccolò Machiavelli. Weary of doctrinal disputes, Machiavelli led the way to the secular consideration of power. He differed from his predecessors, especially in his "entire discarding of any attempt to found a philosophy of right." Machiavelli never asked "What is the true science of politics?" but rather "What rules of prudence may be garnered from history or contemporary experience to guide us here and now?"[3]

Political theory thus became practical. It sought to answer the question of what needs to be done to remain in power. The answer—less a matter of principle than practical observations—was explosive. It was unrealistic to assume that "princes" needed to be good. On occasion they *had* to be bad. The necessities of political life often required the breaking of moral law. Plato's philosopher-kings ruled because they could create perfect justice in human affairs. Machiavelli's princes ruled

2. For a discussion of the "science of man" and the "pagan" spirit of the enlightenment see Peter Gay, *The Enlightenment: An Interpretation*, Vol. II (New York: Alfred Knopf, 1969), pp. 130–73.
3. J. N. Figgis, *From Gerson to Grotius* (Cambridge: Cambridge University Press, 1923), p. 74.

because they were shrewd in manipulating power. So power became separated from virtue.

There now began that dualism under which modern man has to suffer: that opposition between supra-empirical and empirical, between absolute and relative standards of value. It was now possible for the modern State, following its own most vital impulse, to free itself from the spiritual fetters that had constrained it; it was possible for it, as an independent power acknowledging no authority outside this world, to effect the admirable accomplishments of rational organization, which would have been unthinkable in the Middle Ages, but were now due to increase from century to century. But, it already contained the poison of an inner contradiction, from the very moment it began its ascent. On the one hand religion, morality and law were all absolutely indispensable to it as a foundation for its existence; on the other hand, it started off with the definite intention of injuring these whenever the needs of national self-preservation would require it.[4]

For Machiavelli, politics was the art of the possible. His life spanned the years from 1469 to 1527. His world was one in which politics was as erratic as any universe composed of crazy Greek gods. Magistrates survived on guile. Manipulation, skill, and shrewdness in the uses of power were the requisites of power. For Machiavelli and his princes the world consisted of human beings, not gods whose appetites were insatiable and whose capacity for mischief infinite. Machiavelli accepted that good and evil were traits possessed by all people. A successful ruler had to be "part lion and part fox."[5]

The Italy of Machiavelli's day gave obeisance to the ecclesiastical, but it was secular and modern. Florence, for example, was a thriving, vital, corrupt, commercial center of the Western world. The following describes how it appeared to Charles VIII of France when he and his nobles entered Italy in 1494.

They saw pride of life, sumptuousness and luxury, they saw symmetry and movement, new artistic effects produced by a technique that to them was new; and they saw, perhaps, little more. Behind all that was a mental

4. Friedrich Meinecke, *Machiavellism* (New Haven: Yale University Press, 1962), pp. 39–40.
5. See the discussion of Machiavelli in Sheldon S. Wolin, *Politics and Vision* (Boston: Little, Brown and Co., 1960), pp. 203–24.

world unknown to them or but barely suspected; a world of neopaganism and of Neoplatonism, a world of skepticism and materialism, of mockeries more audacious than those they knew of and of enthusiasms to them still stranger. They had stepped into the flood-tide of the Renaissance and did not know where they were. All about them in that Italy of Laurentius Valla and Leonardo, of Luigi Pulci and Aretino, of Michelangelo and Marsilio Ficino, of the Sforza and the Malatesta, the traditional and conventional Christianity they knew of lay in a ruin almost as complete as that of the monuments of old Rome. Theology had vanished from Italian universities; law, medicine, the classics, and a philosophy that owed nothing to the schoolmen reigned in its stead. They had come into a world which put images of pagan poets and demigods in its churches and prized the bones of Livy above all the bones of the saints. It was a world of which the hero was the successful adventurer in art or in arms, in study or in politics.[6]

Such a world was intolerable. It was dangerous. It was violent. It lacked basic civility.

The Social Contract

This then is the predicament. How can one transcend manipulative power without returning to the idea of natural laws as either a privilege of rulers or as the sacred inspiration of ecclesiastical dogma? People in the aggregate produce power and give it to rulers. But if this is true, then can they also take power back? The question is shocking. What defines the sovereign's power? If the answers are not based on opportunism, they require principle. But where are the principles to come from? The principles of the enlightenment paradigm begin with individuals, a mechanistic psychology, and a desire for order (see Figure 4-1).

The Newtonian polity: When rights are preserved, the ruled offer support to the rulers. When support is offered, power is generated. Power in the hands of rulers will produce the stability and order that are necessary for rights to be protected. No rights exist in a state of nature.

The first problem is to evolve from a state of nature to the civil polity, without which no rights can be secure. To evolve, one needs to improve on the state of nature by design. The concepts of the design

6. J. W. Allen, *A History of Political Thought in the Sixteenth Century* (London: Methuen & Co., 1928), pp. 445–46.

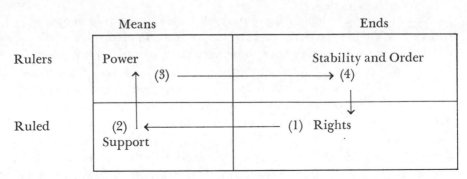

Figure 4-1. The Enlightenment Model

comprehend citizenship, public support, and obligations. The instrument for specifying rights and benefits is a *social contract*. The contract is the critical generative idea of modern constitutionalism.

If Machiavelli marked the turn away from religious philosophy as a political dogma, he opened the way for two brilliant successors. One was Thomas Hobbes, whose philosophy of materialism was the bridge from science to mechanics and whose logic was as elegant and brittle as any to be found in political thinking. The other was Jean Jacques Rousseau, who sought to redefine the moral personality in the moral community.

The Leviathan: Hobbes represents a complete break from the philosophical doctrines of Aristotle, medieval scholasticism, and humanism. Hobbes was interested in natural science. He rejected Aristotle's physics and metaphysics.

He certainly knew and valued the joys of knowledge no less than any other philosopher; but these joys are for him not the justification of philosophy; he finds its justification only in benefit to man, i.e., the safeguarding of man's life and the increase of human power.[7]

Like Machiavelli, Hobbes was concerned with practice. But he believed Aristotle to be the worst "teacher" he ever had. He rejected the primacy of epistemology or theoretical science and substituted for it a materialist metaphysics. He is philosophically the opposite of Plato, nevertheless he employs vigorous deductive logic. He roots his theory of nature in the idea of motions. In human beings these motions take the

7. Leo Strauss, *The Political Philosophy of Hobbes* (Chicago: University of Chicago Press, 1952), p. 34.

form of passions, which produce collisions. His method derived from Galileo.[8]

Hobbes' book, *Leviathan,* begins by developing a very different notion of the state from that employed by the medievalists. They were preoccupied with the organic community. The wise were the heads of state, the ecclesiastics the hearts, while the other various useful organs clustered to form families or households in the all-embracing fellowship of the community.[9] For Hobbes there was no natural community acting as some imminent force of life, but an artificial creation. The community is created because people—creatures of passion—have imagination, the ability to speak, and above all the ability to reason. But reason can be wrong, so society cannot depend on it in the abstract. "As in Arithmetique, unpractised men must, and Professors themselves may often erre. . . ."[10] Because people also have all sorts of less than charming attributes like rage, melancholy, and madness, the result is a natural propensity for conflict, which results in chaos. To prevent chaos (anarchy), private judgments must give way to authority.

But if truth is several, and no single rationality can prevail, how then can people be induced to pool their powers and convey power to a ruler? They will do so only when they achieve some benefit from it. What is the benefit? A state of order. For Hobbes, order is the supreme object, a self-evident benefit which people understand because of their own rational self-interest. Hobbes was the first to define the problem of how to convert private gain into public good. He determined that the value one sets on oneself varies from individual to individual. True, people cannot set their own "price" on themselves, but one's true value will be measured by the esteem in which one is held by others. Therefore compensations will be variable. However, since there is no single principle of compensation on which people can agree, distributions and compensations will result in conflict. Strong passions will be engaged. Vainglorious, fearful, ambitious, and ignorant people will plunge into conflict in which no one gains.

Will the strong triumph? No, says Hobbes, because in the end, despite their differences, people are really not so unequal in their powers. The "weakest has strength enough to kill the strongest." From this equality of ability "arises the equality of hope in the attaining of

8. Ibid., pp. 150–51.
9. See Otto Gierke, *Natural Law and the Theory of Society, 1500–1800* (Cambridge: Cambridge University Press, 1950).
10. See Thomas Hobbes, *Leviathan* (Oxford: The Clarendon Press, 1909), p. 33.

our ends."[11] And from this equality of hope arises the hope of equality. Each wants to be valued highly in the eyes of others. Equality in such a marketplace of self-esteem requires the demonstration of abilities. But without regulation the search for esteem again leads to conflict. Hence people need a common power above them to keep the peace. The pre-eminent virtue is to surrender authority to that power. The alternative is chaos.

Whatsoever therefore is consequent to a time of Warre, where every man is Enemy to every man; the same is consequent to the time, wherein men live without other security, than what their own strength, and their own invention shall furnish them with all. In such a condition, there is no place for Industry; because the fruit thereof is uncertain; and consequently no Culture of the Earth; no Navigation, nor use of the commodities that may be imported by Sea; no commodious Building; no Instruments of moving and removing such things as require much force; no Knowledge of the face of the earth; no account of Time; no Art, no Letters; no Society; and which is worst of all, continual feare, and danger of violent death; And the life of man, solitary, poore, nasty, brutish, and short.[12]

To prosper in all these things the commonwealth needs a magistrate —a magistrate required to be above all law. But sovereignty originally lies with individuals although they convey their individual sovereignty by means of a collective act—their ratification (tacit or otherwise) of a charter or social contract. This charter has the force of law. (A parallel is God's covenant to Abraham.) Under such circumstances, liberty does not inhere any longer in individuals. It is not the birthright of everyone, but the "right of the Publique only."[13]

Hobbes' *Commonwealth* sets up conditions of law. It specifies the place of knowledge, deals with the issue of dissent, and defines the character of duty. It outlines the powers of temporal rulers. At the core is pride and the other passions that "have compelled him [man] to submit himself to Government" and give great power to a governor.[14]

However one feels about the Hobbesian solution, what is important is that Hobbes defined the problem—that is, how to create order when

11. Ibid., p. 95.
12. Ibid., p. 97.
13. Ibid., p. 165.
14. Ibid., p. 246.

people's wants differ—in universal terms. His answer is that there must always be a supreme authority, and that such authority cannot be divided. (This is also the answer propounded by modern authoritarian rulers.) Too much diversity damages the community. For the benefit of all, a ruler—whether a military leader or a revolutionary—will prevent disorder and promote the harmonious efforts of all. Then the public will benefit.

We have said that the other brilliant figure of the enlightenment is Rousseau, who represents the alternative point of view and gives great power to the community as a whole. But between Hobbes and Rousseau is a figure who, if a lesser intellect than these two, had perhaps more direct influence on the English-speaking world. This was John Locke.

Locke and representative government: The international order is to this day Hobbesian. We do not need to accept his psychology. Even evil people are rational. They simply pursue their self-interest with greater ruthlessness than most. With strong authority they can be rendered useful citizens. Hobbes' emphasis on individuals is an important step *toward* a liberal model of the polity, but Hobbes was no liberal.

Nor was Rousseau. He offered a solution to the problem of variable rationality almost as absolute and overriding as that of Hobbes. Where power in Hobbes derives from order and resides in a single ruler, the sovereign monarch, Rousseau saw order produced as a consequence of equal rights. Rulers and ruled become the same when collective benefit is equal to the general will.

The *liberal* polity seeks to combine popular sovereignty with minimal government. The private sphere is large, the government small. As a result the popular power, although large, cannot dominate—there is no general will. The world is composed of private individuals going about their own business, tending to it in a rational, sober, and industrious manner. What John Locke (1632–1704) was to the liberal idea of politics, Adam Smith was, somewhat later, to economics.

The differences between Locke and Hobbes are profound. Locke saw the state of nature not as a condition of war but as a benign condition. But Locke, like Hobbes, is secular in outlook—he makes the church no more than a voluntary association. He also believes in the good effects of private property, the ownership of which is a form of insurance that people will be reasonable and cooperate with each other. Locke's secularism led him to attack both the doctrine of divine right of kings and the ecclesiastical arguments absolute monarchs used to authorize their exercise of unlimited power. His idea of property was directed against the Hobbesian principle that people were essentially conflictual. People, who are protective of and responsible for their property are willing to cooperate in the public interest. Therefore, private gain equals public good.

As Sheldon Wolin puts it, "Locke launched his attack against the traditional model of society, wherein ordered social relationships and institutions were sustained by the direction imparted from a political center, by substituting a conception of society as a self-activating unity capable of generating common will."[15] The political problem is to ensure that *all* the parts become self-reinforcing.

The exercise of labor and the pursuit of property were the crucial factors. Labor converts the products of nature into something of value. A person who labors endows those products, and property itself, with a proprietary feeling. It is the transition that is significant. In the state of nature, land and property are held in common. In civil society property is held privately and individually; therefore a state of capitalism exists. Locke says of the state of nature

The measure of property nature was well set by the extent of men's labor and the convenience of life. No man's labor could subdue or appropriate all; nor could his enjoyment consume more than a small part; so that it was impossible for any man, this way, to intrench upon the right of another, or acquire to himself a property to the prejudice of his neighbor, who would still have room for as good and as large a possession (after the other had taken out his) as before it was appropriated. This measure did confine every man's possession to a very moderate proportion, and such as he might appropriate to himself without injury to anybody. . . .[16]

On the other hand, because labor makes the land fruitful, labor becomes more important than the land itself. Therefore the more industrious become richer because they are willing to work harder and use more property; they are justified in their holdings because they add more value than they take out; and the critical difference between individuals is the productive capacity of their labor.[17]

15. Sheldon S. Wolin, op. cit., p. 308.
16. John Locke, *The Second Treatise on Civil Government* (Oxford: Basil Blackwell, 1948), pp. 18–19.
17. Ibid., p. 26.

It is labor which, applied to property, creates value, and value which becomes the patrimony of the individual.

The critical point of Locke's theory is thus the relation of property to consent. But we need to know what Locke meant by "property." His conception was different from our own. He says,

Though the earth and all inferior creatures be common to all men, yet every man has a property in his own person; this nobody had any right to but himself. The labor of his body and the work of his hands we may say properly are his. Whatsoever, then, he removes out of the state that nature hath provided and left it in, he hath mixed his labor with, and joined to it something that is his own, and thereby makes it his property. It being removed from the common state nature placed it in, it hath by this labor something annexed to it that excludes the common right of other men. For this labor being the unquestionable property of the laborer, no man but he can have a right to what that is once joined to, at least where there is enough and as good left in common for others.[18]

Locke's concept of property is extremely important, although it is a limited concept. It does not cover huge amalgamations of property very much beyond what a person can labor upon. The heart of his exposition is that labor is a value created out of a state of nature by human activity —the sweat of one's brow. On the other hand, the amassing of property is a right acquired by work. The ideal in Locke is a citizenry composed of small growers, farmers, yeomen of all kinds, and artisans. His vision was of people working like bees—sober, thrifty, and sovereign. Then the obvious question is: What sort of government will help facilitate such a society? Obviously, it is the one which will free people from restrictions and allow full expression of their energies as they cultivate the land or work a craft. This government must be limited. According to Locke, people form the commonwealth to preserve (not to create) "their lives, liberties, and fortunes; and by stated rules of right and property to secure their peace and quiet."[19]

Power is delegated by the people to a legislature. The method of governing must be according to established laws—not one law for the rich and another for the poor, but laws set down for the *common* good.

18. Ibid., p. 15.
19. Ibid., p. 69.

Political equality is essential under liberty. The medieval formula for liberty was *Salus populi supreme lex* (the "health" or "welfare" of the people is the supreme "law" or "virtue"). Locke reaffirms this idea of the public interest.

For Locke, then, political responsibility begins with property relationships. But society is not duly constituted until there is both freedom and government. The act of contracting with the monarch is the constituting of society.

That which makes the community, and brings men out of the loose state of nature into one polite society, is the agreement which everyone has with the rest to incorporate and act as one body, and so be one distinct commonwealth.[20]

The character of civil government is all-important. For Locke people are born "naturally free from subjection to any government" and will not put themselves politically in chains. The prince or magistrate has no right to restrict rights or to act despotically. The people have no need to accept despotism.

The reason why men enter into society is the preservation of their property; and the end why they choose and authorize a legislative is that there may be laws made, and rules set, as guards and fences to the properties of all the members of the society, to limit the power and moderate the dominion of every part and member of the society. For since it can never be supposed to be the will of the society that the legislative should have a power to destroy that which everyone designs secure by entering into society, and for which the people submitted themselves to legislators of their own making, whenever the legislators endeavor to take away and destroy the property of the people, or to reduce them to slavery under arbitrary power, they put themselves into a state of war with the people, who are thereupon absolved from any further obedience. . . .[21]

Locke not only stated a position in which the safeguarding of property is the basis of the community, but one in which limited property goes together with limited government. The Lockean world is one of small holdings and minimal supervision—the preconditions for individualism. The public interest is what furthers the private interest, but since private interests are more or less the same, the identity is secured.

20. Ibid., p. 103.
21. Ibid., pp. 107–108.

Montesquieu: This liberal ideal was by no means limited to Locke or the English political philosophers who developed both the labor theory of value and the idea of limited government. Adam Smith, whose economic writings were published in 1776—a prophetic year—turned the relations of property and its value into the theory of free enterprise, which liberal politics fitted together with entrepreneurial capitalism. So too in France. In 1758, François Quesnay published similar views in his *Tableau Oeconomique.*

The purpose of government was to prevent tyranny and to use political power in a way that did not interfere with the free workings of the market. It is not a big jump from man as citizen to the market as the foundation of society. Each individual makes a contribution to the functioning of the society by producing some kind of value. Together the laws of the social universe generate capitalism and representative government. Competition is the regulative principle in both economic and political life.

So conceived, political democracy is the polity that goes hand in hand with Newtonian science. Commerce, competition, and representative government go together. Montesquieu, in his book *Spirit of the Laws,* shows how the evolution of different forms of commerce in the ancient world affected political systems.[22] Moral commitment combined with material conditions and resources to organize society. Different conditions and resources produced different forms of government. Such interaction between commerce and the character of moral principles produced typical political solutions or ideal types.

Montesquieu was anxious to show—using the evidence of history—how such types evolved. Historical induction—from cases to observations, and from observations to systems—offered a method in accord with science. So in the liberal tradition, science—as it was applied to politics—was represented as the evolution of liberty (or individual rights) secured by checks and balances, the rule of law, and a mixed constitutional system of representation. Since this was to be the final political solution to all problems, from here on political life became an on-going process of compromises realized through mediating mechanisms. Societies that were prone to change needed governments that were stable because change had to be mediated. Montesquieu rejected the psychological theories of writers such as Machiavelli and Hobbes. Where Machiavelli believed that man is basically "rascally, mean, greedy, sensual . . . more ready to for-

22. C. L. Montesquieu, *Spirit of the Laws* (New York: Hafner Publishing Co., 1949), pp. 316–402.

give the murder of his father than the seizure of his property," his appetites "insatiable," his satisfactions few,[23] Montesquieu believed that people were not so consistently bad as that. Nor were they as good as Rousseau or Locke made them out to be, however. Whatever human nature, individual liberty was the basis of well-being.[24]

A stability-prone constitution, for Montesquieu as for Adam Smith, required the state to intervene in the affairs of citizens only when necessary. The marketplace was seen to regulate economic, social, and political activity as well. The biggest danger was conflict between nations.

As soon as mankind enter into a state of society they lose the sense of their weakness; equality ceases, and then commences the state of war.

"Each particular society begins to feel its strength, whence arises a state of war betwixt different nations. The individual likewise of each society becomes sensible of their force; hence, the principal advantages of this society they endeavor to convert to their own emolument, which constitutes a state of war betwixt individuals.[25]

It is to compensate for this condition of war that law is required. The law of nations governs relations between independent countries, civil law governs relationships between individuals, and political law determines the relations between rulers and ruled. A despotic polity is based on fear and coercion. A democratic polity must be based on virtue or it will destroy itself. Too much equality destroys respect between persons, too little equality produces despotism. The polity appropriate to maximize liberty and balance equality is the one in which the legislative, executive, and judiciary powers of government are separated so that civil law can be made according to the needs of all segments of the society. Such a polity produces that "tranquility of mind"—the ease a person might feel for the safety of his or her own person—which is the essential ingredient of political liberty.

The liberal solution: Montesquieu and Locke combined the view of a changing society with a stable government by means of a **liberal solution:** a constitutional government composed of free citizens, checks on the power of the executive by the legislature, and a political marketplace

23. S. W. Allen, op. cit., p. 450; See also Wolin, op. cit., p. 221.
24. See J. W. Allen, op. cit., p. 454.
25. Montesquieu, op. cit., p. 5.

of free ideas manifested in civil laws paralleling the economic market-place and laws of supply and demand. Their attention was on mechanisms of participation and representation, qualifications for voting, and the forms and types of electoral methods.

Both Locke and Montesquieu emphasized law and culture as the most important political considerations. (The word *spirit* in the title of Montesquieu's book is not implicitly religious, but refers to the concept of "ethos"—the cultural quality of norms and beliefs.) But preoccupations with such matters led toward rather than away from empiricism, in keeping with the spirit of science and historical investigation. Both Locke and Montesquieu represent the liberal solution. Between the imposed contractual order of the authoritarian sovereign and the imposed liberty of the general will, they posit a political marketplace in which rulers are connected to rule by a system of mutual obligations and loyalties. The purpose of the state is to ensure liberty.

Within this larger condition, individuals have ends that vary. How such ends are realized by rulers forms the basis of support, but two conditions are required to ensure that the rulers maintain liberty. First, the rulers can be peacefully removed if they do not do their job. Second, the people share in ruling by means of representation. Therefore majority rule replaces the general will and popular sovereignty is mediated by representative government. Representative government ensures the existence of a political marketplace which mediates gross inequalities, prevents threats to liberty, and promotes justice. The political marketplace adjusts any inequalities arising in the economic marketplace, and competition in politics combines with competition in economic life to constitute the vital force, the electricity, which makes it all work.

The liberal polity thus replaces Hobbes' order with that of a self-regulating mechanism. Wants are converted into motives for change, which, held in check by government, are not thwarted by excessive authority. The new problem was inequality. Too much inequality meant that exceptional power in the hands of some produced governments that favored the rich at the expense of the poor. This gave rise to the subordination of individuals to classes. Individual farmers, laborers, and merchants could only survive collectively as they sought to maximize their interests. Two alternative solutions were generated: the theory of utility versus the theory of equality. Rousseau represents the latter.

The opening lines of Rousseau's *Social Contract*—"Man is born free, and everywhere he is in chains. Many a one believes himself the master of others, and yet he is a greater slave than they"—had an impact which still reverberates around the world.

Rousseau and the Problem of Equality

Rousseau's words are beguiling. Their power draws on poetry and on metaphor. Rousseau returns to rationality to ask how rationality can be more appropriately used for the benefit of the individual in society. The sovereignty of the people must be actively exercised in the general will of *all*, not the will of a simple majority. The general will is total.

In part Rousseau believed that the general will should act as a supreme coercive authority because it equalled the general good. In this respect he had a good deal in common with Plato. Both admired the Spartan ideal in which the unity and simplicity of life enabled people to transcend their weaknesses. The alternative to Spartan communism is the supremacy of the individual household where intimacy, affection, and nurture prevail. The one is a harsh solution; the other is not. But both alternatives are utopian ideals.[26]

Like Plato, Rousseau took utopia as a model. But Rousseau was far more pessimistic. He did not believe that utopia would help society. He saw reform as relatively useless. "His sense of disaster was correspondingly total. Degeneration was the law of life. Utopia was an imaginative interruption of that process and a painful awareness of it. That was all."[27]

Rousseau uses utopia as a projective vision to sketch out solutions to the common predicament. The purpose is to define the moral issues of politics not as abstract principle but in the form of logical possibilities: What happens when magistrates become corrupt? How can corruption be prevented? How can freedom exist without equality? But how much inequality can be tolerated? This mode of questioning brings back some of the moral projectivism of the theocratic tradition, but stripped of its ecclesiastical implications. Indeed, the need for a renewed moral vision in the context of a political solution is Rousseau's contribution to the radical tradition which emerged in the nineteenth century.

Rousseau agreed with Locke that property must be protected, maintained, and guaranteed by the laws of the state. Property depends on the state for its existence. People can own property but for all to be equal in politics, all should enjoy its uses. It should not be a cause of inequality. In the city-state people can exercise their judgment about it uses. And the Rousseauan city-state (like Aristotle's) is to be a community of limited size, like a Swiss canton or commune.

26. See Judith Shklar, *Men and Citizens: Rousseau's Social Theory* (Cambridge: Cambridge University Press, 1969), pp. 3–8.
27. Ibid., p. 9.

Sovereignty is shared among all the members of a society, but the community is not like a family. The community lacks the love a father has for the family; rulers like power. Thus any rule is tantamount to rule by force. To merely acquiesce to an authority is to relinquish the rights of individuals because to alienate one's liberty is an unnatural act.

To renounce one's liberty is to renounce one's quality as a man, the rights and also the duties of humanity. For him who renounces everything there is no possible compensation. Such a renunciation is incompatible with man's nature, for to take away all freedom from his will is to take away all morality from his actions. In short, a convention which stipulates absolute authority on the one side and unlimited obedience on the other is vain and contradictory.[28]

Rousseau had a radical side, but he was no socialist. He believed that liberty and equality were the most important ends of society, although he doubted that perfect equality was possible. He considered ownership of property "unnatural"—an act of expropriation which makes some powerful and others weak, thus reducing the independence of each individual. But so is the political community "unnatural," for property creates civil society. Like Locke, Rousseau saw the connection very clearly.[29] Rousseau recognized as well how important equality was to human beings, and stressed the consequences of what Locke ignored: Inequality produced injustice and the foundations of disharmony.

What then was the solution? We have said that Rousseau was no socialist. His answer was that the general will rectifies economic inequities. Thus the object of a social pact is as follows: "To find a form of association which may defend and protect with the whole force of the community the person and property of every associate, and by means of which each, coalescing with all, may nevertheless obey only himself, and remain as free as before." This, Rousseau goes on to say "is the fundamental problem of which the social contract furnishes the solution."[30]

How does the contract work? The precondition is a "total alienation to the whole community of each associate with all his rights; for in the first place, since each gives himself up entirely, the conditions are

---

28. Jean Jacques Rousseau, *The Social Contract* (London: George Allen and Unwin, 1948), p. 105.
29. See Roger D. Masters, *The Political Philosophy of Rousseau* (Princeton: Princeton University Press, 1968), pp. 179–81. See also Shklar, op. cit., p. 49.
30. Rousseau, op. cit., p. 109.

equal for all; and the conditions being equal for all, no one has any interest in making them burdensome to others."[31] This may seem drastic for it
involves a total alienation of *private* power but,

> *. . . the alienation being made without reserve, the union is as perfect
> as it can be, and an individual associate can no longer claim anything;
> for, if any rights were left to individuals, since there would be no com-
> mon superior who could judge between them and the public, each, being
> on some point his own judge, would soon claim to be so on all; the state
> of nature would still subsist, and the association would necessarily
> become tyrannical or useless.*
>
> *In short, each giving himself to all, gives himself to nobody; and
> as there is not one associate over whom we do no acquire the same rights
> which we conceded to him over ourselves, we obtain the equivalent of all
> that we lose, and more power to preserve what we have.*
>
> *If, then, we set aside what is not of the essence of the social contract,
> we shall find that it is reducible to the following terms: "Each of us puts
> in common his person and his whole power under the supreme direction
> of the general will; and in return we receive every member as an in-
> divisible part of the whole."*
>
> *Forthwith, instead of the individual personalities of all the con-
> tracting parties, this act of association produces a moral and collective
> body which is composed of as many members as the assembly has voices,
> and which receives from this same act its unity, its common self, its life,
> and its will. This public person, which is thus formed by the union of all
> the individual members, formerly took the name of* city, *and now takes
> that of* republic, *or* body politic, *which is called by its members* State
> *when it is passive,* sovereign *when it is active,* power *when it is compared
> to similar bodies. With regard to the associates, they take collectively the
> name of* people, *and are called individually* citizens, *as participating in
> the sovereign power and* subjects, *as subjected to the laws of the*
> State.[32]

Rousseau then points out that such a contractual act involves a
"reciprocal engagement" between the public and individuals. Every individual is both a member of the sovereign toward other individuals and
a member of the state as a sovereign. The result is as follows: "So soon

31. Ibid., p. 110.
32. Ibid., pp. 110–11.

as the multitude is thus united in one body, it is impossible to injure one of the members without attacking the body, still less to injure the body without the members feeling the effects."[33] All for one and one for all. The sovereign, which consists of the individuals of the state, has no interest except that of the state. Individuals may, however, have interests which diverge from those of the community. By pursuing individual self-interests one runs into trouble, however, because

. . . whoever refuses to obey the general will shall be constrained to do so by the whole body; which means nothing else than that he shall be forced to be free; for such is the condition which, uniting every citizen to his native land, guarantees him from all personal dependence, a condition that ensures the control and working of the political machine, and alone renders legitimate civil engagement, which, without it, would be absurd and tyrannical, and subject to the most enormous abuses.[34]

"Forced to be free"—it is an ominous phrase, for it allows easy misrepresentation. What Rousseau intended to emphasize was that sovereignty derived from the people, not, as hitherto believed, the monarch. The "sovereignty" of the monarch represented his power over the people. Rousseau believed that the opposite was true. In his view, the old connection between rulers and ruled had to be destroyed. Sovereignty exists but no monarchy has a monopoly of power.

What is left of the conventional state is the legislator, the extraordinary person who is significant according to genius rather than office.

This office, which constitutes the republic, does not enter into its constitution: it is a special and superior office, having nothing in common with human government; for, if he who rules men ought not to control legislation, he who controls legislation ought not to rule men, otherwise his laws, being ministers of his passions, would often serve only to perpetuate his acts of injustice; he would never be able to prevent private interests from corrupting the sacredness of his work.[35]

The legislator deals therefore with the facilitation of government business, more or less on a day-to-day basis. The sovereign people, periodically, are the authors of the laws.

33. Ibid., p. 112.
34. Ibid., p. 113.
35. Ibid., p. 135.

The question of whether or not the general will is for Rousseau tyrannical and coercive is irrelevant. Here is what Rousseau has to say on the subject. "But, it will be asked how a man can be free and yet forced to conform to wills which are not his own. How are opponents free and yet subject to laws which they have not consented to?"[36] Rousseau goes on:

I reply that the question is wrongly put. The citizen consents to all the laws, even to those which are passed in spite of him, and even to those which punish him when he dares to violate any of them. The unvarying will of all the members of the State is the general will; it is through that that they are citizens and free. When a law is proposed in the assembly of the people, what is asked of them is not exactly whether they approve the proposition or reject it, but whether it is conformable or not to the general will, which is their own; each one in giving his vote expresses his opinion thereupon; and from the counting of the votes is obtained the declaration of the general will. When, therefore, the opinion opposed to my own prevails, that simply shows that I was mistaken, and that what I considered to be the general will was not so. Had my private opinion prevailed, I should have done something other than I wished; and in that case I should not have been free.[37]

This is a remarkable statement. The general will is seen to represent a priority of rightness. The individual will, inasmuch as it departs from the general, is imperfect or wrong. Freedom consists then in conformity. (We will see such principles iterated in Lenin's concept of "democratic centralism." For Lenin a decision—once taken—remains entirely binding as a moral obligation and discipline for all members.) On this basis societies can prescribe what citizens are required to obey. The general will has a higher morality than the individual. A general law of reason is the essence of such freedom, but it is also a tool of leverage which totalitarians can employ to subvert the common good.

Rousseau stands Plato on his head. Instead of placing the moral authority of reason in the hands of philosopher-kings, Rousseau gives moral authority to each of us—albeit in a conditional way. The right rule equals freedom plus the discipline of the general will. None of us is a philosopher-king, but collectively we achieve that condition.

36. Ibid., p. 105.
37. Ibid., pp. 200–201.

For Rousseau, together with other contract theorists, the problem is to keep societies from being plagued by continuous conflict over the diversity of wants such as those described by Hobbes. For Rousseau the solution is found when wants are shared to satisfy common needs. (Common needs are more common when there is equality in society.) Diversity is tolerable, if there is not too much of it. The Rousseauan system can be summarized as follows:

1. Individual wants are diverse.
2. Diversity leads to conflict, the prevention of which results in the coercive state.
3. Diversity is limited by equality.
4. Equality is based on a commonality of needs.
5. Satisfying the commonality of needs is the sole purpose of the community.
6. The community exists for its members, hence the legitimacy of the general will and the illegitimacy of a restrictive state.
7. The demands and needs of individuals, fulfilled through the application of the general will, creates a stable political system, that is, an equilibrium of forces.
8. Freedom and authority are reconciled.

Rousseau, like Hobbes, wants to rid society of the disruptive implication of passion and its subversive effects. He too seeks an orderly equilibrium, which requires that power be checked by individuals acting together. Behind the general will (as in Plato) stands education. However, Rousseau, like Plato, is forced to rely on censorship to maintain equilibrium. Homer is forbidden reading in Plato's Republic. Theater is a forbidden pleasure in Rousseau's. Censorship is their common weapon against public passion and irrationality. For all his protests, Rousseau is not without his chains.

Rousseau laid the foundation for a radical, transformational vision of the world, one which contrasts to the view of the political economy in which utility is the law of life. From Locke's social contract to political economy to utilitarianism to a modern form of behavioral science—a science of politics—is one series of distinct steps. From social contract à la Rousseau to equality to socialism to radical political theory is another. The connections between freedom and equality are critical ingredients of both syntheses. The radical tradition tempers freedom with the urge for equality. The utilitarian tradition tempers equality with the urge for freedom. The paradoxes of both represent a contemporary inheritance.

The Utilitarians

Bentham: The utilitarian answer to both Hobbes and Rousseau is to do away with social contracts. Instead of abstract formulation, what is needed is legislation, reform, education, poor laws, workmen's compensation, and so forth. To Bentham's secular thinking, happiness was a good enough universal purpose. To maximize happiness for the greatest number was the goal of the state. Jeremy Bentham, who lived from 1748 to 1832, was not much for principles and was no radical. "Bentham among the 'Jacobins' is like an engineer in a community smitten by an epidemic, who, while one agitator recommends the overthrow of the government and another advocates a reform of the religion, quietly suggests a repair of the drains."[38]

Bentham and the Benthamites involved themselves in reform—reform of prisons, reform of poor laws, reform of the legislature. They urged people to vote and advocated extension of the franchise downward through society. The resultant prosperity, knowledge, and education of the people to whom the franchise was to be extended would produce the greatest good for the greatest number. The primary emphasis was on educational reform. Voters had to be responsible and wise. Civic awareness was a necessity. The Benthamites believed firmly in the formula of civic benefits, hard work, individualism, and self-reliance. In their day the reforms proposed were a mixture of Radical and Whig politics. Bentham, especially in economic terms, was a classic liberal, a free-trader possessed of a very simple view of human nature.

It is impossible to understand Bentham without recognizing what it was he fought against. Bentham, like the Burkean conservatives, saw the events of the French Revolutions of 1789 and 1793 as basically destructive. To him these upheavals unleashed—in the name of fundamental human rights—both terror and the new Napoleonic autocracy. Bentham favored neither the American nor the French revolutions. But unlike Burke, he was no sentimentalist. He did not have much nostalgia for tradition as the social cement which would hold society together. He

---

38. D. C. Somervelle, *English Thought in the Nineteenth Century* (New York: Longmans Green, 1929), p. 43.

knew that this would only be as strong as public satisfaction in society. He believed that the theorists of the Rights of Man in France were victimized by the idea of society as a collectivity.

For Bentham the place to begin is with individuals. Individuals have interests: Satisfy those interests and you have the basis of the good society. Of course, there are limits to the satisfaction of interests. Such limits are reached when the satisfaction of one individual's interests takes place at the expense of others. There needs to be some formula for reconciling individual interests. This, Bentham proposed, was to find the greatest good for the greatest number. The formula is translated into practical politics by means of popular legislation.

In France in 1789 the Declaration of the Rights of Man specified four natural rights: liberty, property, security, and resistance to oppression. In refutation, Bentham pointed out that every law is a restriction on liberty. Government may be designed to maintain security, but how should individuals protect themselves against government? Property is in turn not at all sacred. Government can decide to build a road or a waterway or take over some land for public purposes. Finally, if the only way in which people resist oppression is to take arms that itself is a contradiction. So liberty, property, security, resistance to oppression, all have limits imposed by people's interests—private versus public.

That there are limits to human rights is demonstrated by any group in which majority or minority factions form coalitions. Coalitions continuously change according to priorities and issues. The basis of utilitarianism then is to translate the principle of the greatest good for the greatest number into the framework of shifting political coalitions, using factions and parties within a set of rules for appropriate governance. In contrast to the American and French revolutions, which were fought in the name of the social contract and inalienable natural rights, the utilitarian universe is made up of the common sense of individuals operating within a framework of rules in which parliamentary government and legislation reflect the changing needs and wants of the public. This, Bentham believed, represented the proper extension of Newtonianism into politics.[39]

At the center of Bentham's theory is the "pleasure principle," which essentially motivates whatever a person wants or wills to do. Since a "hedonistic" calculus of pleasures and pains results from legislation, to

---

39. He was delighted when, in 1790, he was referred to as the "Newton of legislation." Elie Halévy, *The Growth of Philosophical Radicalism* (Boston: Beacon Press, 1955), p. 178.

measure how much pain or how much pleasure something represents, one follows the rule of thumb of utility in economics. Just as the economic marketplace measures the individual utilities of goods and services, the political marketplace measures individual utilities in pleasures and pains. The law of diminishing returns prevails. The result is an empirical ethic in which natural law is replaced by prudence: Do unto others as they would do unto you—or else. . . .

Such a practical emphasis opened the gates for democracy by means of legislation. Practical thinkers like James Mill, who was concerned with how to rule ruder countries such as India, pressed hard for civil service and law reform. The Benthamites wanted to shift the emphasis away from the notion prevailing in England that the aristocracy was responsible for the welfare of the community and the embodiment of the country's best instincts. So, for example, the elder Mill wanted to institute civil-service examinations. Merit would substitute for class. Education would be preferred to "breeding." Such principles were all a result of the belief that people's wants are best known to themselves.

Mill: The emphasis on legislation and participation enunciated by Bentham and the elder Mill did not go far enough for John Stuart Mill. The younger Mill was disturbed by some of the implications of utilitarianism. He was not so convinced of the value of one's judgment of one's self-interests and he was more worried about the tyranny of the majority than the tyranny of a despot. Democracy depended too much on popular opinion (of which Mill took a dim view) . He stated his views in unmistakable terms in the beginning of the essay *On Liberty.*

When we consider either the history of opinion, or the ordinary conduct of human life, to what is it to be ascribed that the one and the other are no worse than they are? Not certainly to the inherent force of the human understanding; for, on any matter not self-evident, there are ninety-nine persons totally incapable of judging of it for one who is capable; and the capacity of the hundredth person is only comparative; for the majority of the eminent men of the past generation held many opinions now known to be erroneous, and did approve numerous things which no one will now justify. Why is it, then, that there is on the whole a preponderance among mankind of rational opinions and rational conduct? If there really is this preponderance—which must be unless human affairs are, and have always been, in an almost desperate state, it is owing to a quality of the human mind, the source of everything respectable in man either as an intellectual or as a moral being, namely, that his errors are corrigible. He is capable of rectifying his mistakes, by discussion and experience. Not by experience alone. There must be discussion, to show how experience is to be interpreted. Wrong opinions and practices gradually yield to fact and argument; but facts and arguments to produce any effect on the mind, must be brought before it. Very few facts are able to tell their own story, without comments to bring out their meaning. The whole strength and value, then, of human judgement, depending on the one property, that it can be set right when it is wrong, reliance can be placed on it only when the means of setting it right are kept constantly at hand.[40]

Mill formulates *the* political question as amendment—the self-correction of mistakes. "What, then," he asks, "is the rightful limit to the sovereignty of the individual over himself? Where does the authority of society belong? How much of human life should be assigned to individuality, and how much to society?" Mill's answer is to limit politics to what affects society and let individuals alone otherwise. "To individuality should belong the part of life in which it is chiefly the individual that is interested; to society, the part which chiefly interests society."[41] If a person's actions are of no account to anyone's interest but his or her own, then society had better keep out of it. If an individual wishes to commit suicide, take drugs, or drink, the individual should be able to do these things—as long as they cause no harm to others. On the other hand, social exchanges, selling, and commercial activities that necessarily affect the interests of others—these need regulation.

By rendering the private private and the public public, Mill wants to ensure that the self-correctives which individuals have at their disposal can be manipulated by individuals. This ensures self-reliance and independence of spirit, something too much government regulation reduces. On the other hand, by insisting on government regulation when public benefits are concerned, Mill wants government to be able to apply the correctives necessary to right wrongs and balance imbalances.

Mill extends the principle of the private sphere to education, arguing that, while every child has a need and a right to be educated, if education is undertaken by the state, it will become a "mere contrivance for the moulding of people to be exactly like one another" and lead to a

40. John Stuart Mill, *On Liberty and Considerations on Representative Government,* R. B. McCallum, ed. (Oxford: Basil Blackwell, 1948), p. 17.
41. Ibid., p. 66.

"despotism over the mind."[42] Mill's solution is typical for his thinking—that is, to provide public support for education for those who need it while enabling parents who can afford to pay to send their children to schools of their choice. The whole point to his essay *On Liberty* is thus to establish clearly the separate spheres of private and public purpose: to render unto the private the things that are of no injurious consequence and to make the public responsible for things that are or might be of consequence.

Just as Bentham, after establishing certain general principles, turned to practical reform, so Mill tried to establish the appropriate form of government which would realize the advantages of each sphere. Progress he saw as increase in the amount of good things. Order he saw as preservation of good things. So political ends, he thought, are determined by their effects on public affairs and the efficacy and abilities of the citizens. For Mill the ends of rulers and ruled are the same.

What connects the public and private spheres is representative government, that form of government in which

the sovereignty, or supreme controlling power in the last resort, is vested in the entire aggregate of the community; every citizen not only has a voice in the exercise of that ultimate sovereignty, but being, at least occasionally, called on to take an actual part in the government, by the personal discharge of some public function, local or general.[43]

Either the whole people rule or deputies rule who are periodically elected. Those who exercise power, who actually do society's business, require the consent of the governed (as through parliamentary control over the executive). A legislative body is unfit to actually govern. Its job is to review and control the executive. But an active executive is required to acquit the needs of the public sphere.

The balance between executive and legislative authority depends on the will of the people. That is the meaning of democratic or popular sovereignty: The greater the extent of the suffrage the more meaningful the democracy. However, there is a problem even with universal suffrage. Parliaments register the will of *majorities*. But more than majority rule is needed to safeguard the rights of *minorities*. Mill's solution is to advocate the Hare system of proportional representation, which has two objects. It gives voice to the needs of minorities whose views might other-

42. Ibid., p. 95.
43. Ibid., p. 141.

wise be ignored. But more important, *it enables the more intelligent minorities* to be heard, thus offsetting the "natural tendency of representative government, as of modern civilization . . . towards collective mediocrity."[44]

Mill is thus preoccupied with the double problem of how an elite minority can be combined with popular sovereignty, or how democracy can be enhanced without enthroning mediocrity. He was the first "pluralist." He also was very much an institutionalist. Concerned with electoral methods, plural voting, types of constituencies, suffrage, methods of voting, types of legislatures, upper chambers, and so forth, he did not much care for doctrines of class war. He paid little attention to Marx. But he was concerned with oppressed minorities, women's rights, and the protection of children. He favored workers' organizations. He came to believe in a vague form of *utopian socialism,* an intellectual socialism which would enable society to realize superior moral qualities. He was active in promoting land tenure reform, proposals favoring the aged, public health care, and accident insurance. He wanted greater democracy without too much levelling. He posed the problem of minority rights and liberty, eccentricity and moral improvement.[45]

Bentham was the practical optimist. Mill was more gloomy. Between them they established a tradition of moral improvement through social reform and legislative representation. They took the presuppositions of the traditional liberals like Locke and Montesquieu and transformed them into specific ways of organizing political life. In their hands moral ends or principles of political life became matters less of abstract theory and more of institutions of government. This also led to a concern with local government, rates and taxes, and health. They agreed that government should govern just up to the extent that it might sap the abilities and initiative of individuals and local communities to help themselves. That was the limit. Mill was very much in accord with Alexis de Tocqueville, whose delight at the American democracy was based precisely on its highly developed system of local government. The utilitarians remained ambiguous about certain problems, however. They favored the extention of the voting franchise, but they were afraid of uninformed popular opinion. They wanted to prevent excess of any kind. They regarded the intense religiosity of early Victorian England as a form of prejudice. Their problem was how to remove the social ce-

44. Ibid., p. 198.
45. See Crane Brinton, *English Political Thought in the Nineteenth Century* (Cambridge, Mass.: Harvard University Press, 1949), pp. 90–101.

ment of religious conviction and replace it with political conviction. Both were affected by the anticlericalism and scientific ethics associated with Saint-Simon, Fourier, Comte, and others in France. Hence the utilitarians were also concerned with such issues as determinism versus free will, and scientism versus metaphysics. They sought alternative ways to create out of the science of man, a new religion within the spiritual tradition of English nonconformism.[46]

Social Democracy

The utilitarian impulses were also expressed in idealism. In Germany, post-Kantian and post-Hegelian ideals revived the antique concern with ethical imperatives in relation to the state. How could the collective body express the highest moral qualities of the people? New theories of national economies, the legal structure of the state, and Christianity as the highest form emerged. In philosophy and *Staatslehre,* "the theory of the state," Plato and Aristotle were revived. The German liberal tradition embodied them in the conception of the *Rechtstaat,* "the state according to rights, i.e., constitutionalism." Roman law was exhumed, along with medieval jurists like Bodin. A state came to be thought of as a civil juridical association bounded by the limits of law. The functions of the state can only be discharged through intermediate institutions, particularly political parties. The private sphere is separate from the public. Individualism must be limited. Constitutional instruments of representation and social legislation to protect workers are necessary to bridge the gap. Liberty in excess is degenerate.[47]

The strong emphasis on the state as a corporate body which was embodied in German liberalism and bound up with Christianity as a political doctrine, had little counterpart among the English utilitarians. Moreover, the German fear of the French "radical disease," which had produced so much turmoil in France and which was squelched in 1848 in Germany, stimulated the growth of a limited constitutional monarchy as a substitute for more libertarian or revolutionary forms. Germany had no Babeuf, Fourier, or Jules Guedes to promote utopian socialism. Nor did it have a Wycliffe, a rebelling Methodism, or a dissenting chapel movement.

46. See D. H. Charlton, *Positivist Thought in France* (Oxford: The Clarendon Press, 1959) p. 106–107.
47. See Guido de Ruggiero, *The History of European Liberalism* (Boston: Beacon Press, 1959) , pp. 231–74.

It had instead Hegel, for whom the constitution must be sanctioned by the "law of reason." According to Hegel, political evolution is a function of transcendent human reason, which is a progressive historical force. Hence the improvement of human reason produces improvement in human society by means of improved political institutions. The executive or magistrate must subsume the particular problems of life under the universals of reason in a hierarchy reminiscent of Plato —with ordinary civil servants at the bottom, higher advisory officials above them, and supreme heads of departments in contact with the monarch above them. At the top, the cabinet consists of those who can handle the affairs of state and its policies in a manner maximizing human reason and the power to control man's destiny.[48]

Reduced to its simplest terms, Hegel's political thought consists of four fundamental propositions: (1) the modern state is a constitutional monarchy with a strong, bureaucratic executive balanced by popular participation in government and areas of individual, social, and local autonomy; (2) the legal and institutional structure of this state is in process of transformation by the thoughtful application of theoretical principles to the traditional framework. These are the ideas which chiefly permeate the nonphilosophical writings. The philosophical ones add two more: (3) political life in any epoch is shaped and determined by the dominant spiritual and material forces of that epoch, its total culture and civilization; and (4) the ultimate explanation of the character of each epoch and the transition from one to another is to be sought in the nature of a metaphysical entity called Spirit, Mind, or Reason.[49]

The emphasis was on culture, tradition, meaning, mind, and spirit, as these applied to the modern state.[50] Of those who followed in the neo-Hegelian tradition—historians and legalists primarily—a few British political philosophers like T. H. Green tried to find an alternative to radicalism and Marxism on the one hand and utilitarianism on the other. They wanted to combine the "radical" critique with a moral view of society.

It must be remembered that England had an authentic radical tradition. It included Diggers, Levellers, Chartists, and Methodist and

---

48. See T. M. Knox and Z. A. Pelczynski, *Hegel's Political Writings* (Oxford: The Clarendon Press, 1964), pp. 121–27.
49. Ibid., p. 137.
50. See Judith H. Shklar, *Freedom and Independence* (Cambridge: Cambridge University Press, 1976), pp. 163–79.

workingmen's associations. It evolved out of economic radicalism, religious evangelicism, chapel movements, and a popular fundamentalism associated with John Wesley. Radical demands had authenticity and dignity. They deeply affected those political philosophers in England who represented an educated rather than an aristocratic elite. Many among the intellectual upper-middle class joined forces with the dissenters. Some became the leaders of socialist movements. But Marxism never took hold. This "responsible elite" became the embodiment of change. How to provide an alternative to both utilitarianism and the evangelicals and attack the elitism of the alliance? This was the problem for the new democratic Hegelianism. Hegelians were out of sorts with the reforming utilitarian empiricists and disliked their arrogant style. Thinking in terms of whole systems—thinking deductively rather than inductively—and stripping out religion, they wanted reform to be replaced by social responsibility. Representing an "Oxford movement," they claimed among their ranks such great figures as Benjamin Jowett, the translator of Plato. Perhaps the central figure was Thomas Hill Green, whose *Lectures on the Principles of Political Obligation* emphasized the collective responsibilities of people to the community.

Melvin Richter put the matter very well when he said that Green "converted philosophical idealism, which in Germany had so often served as a rationale of conservatism, into something close to a practical program for the left wing of the Liberal Party."[51]

Green had a passionate belief in people—that is, the common people. He accepted radical views. He translated English nonconformist evangelicism into politics, but not the utilitarian kind. He rejected the notion of the greatest good for the greatest number as essentially shallow. Philosophical idealism as a method would replace Christianity as revelation, while retaining belief. The method is first to know the good and to try to perfect one's life accordingly. From good flows good, from evil, evil. The greater evil was not in the individual but in that aspect of society which punished some for the benefit of the rest.

In contrast to Marx and the philosophical radicals, Green began his agitation for change, not by denouncing asceticism and the official Christian values of charity and justice as sham, but by reaffirming their validity. And, this once done, he found no difficulty whatever in de-

51. See the excellent study by Melvin Richter, *The Politics of Conscience* (Cambridge: Harvard University Press, 1964), p. 13.

nouncing such abuses as the London slums as intolerable evils in a society which professed to believe in the moral dignity of the individual.

Green and his fellow idealists represent the renewed liberalism of the last quarter of the nineteenth century. They are all of them, for all their Platonism and Hegelianism, in the succession of the Utilitarians. They were all fundamentally individualists and democrats. But, they were convinced that Utilitarianism had become barren as a political creed because of the inadequate philosophy upon which it was based, and that no further progress could be made in an understanding of politics till a new philosophic basis was found for liberalism.[52]

Green's *Lectures on the Principles of Political Obligation* begin with the problem raised by Rousseau. But Green turns it around. "Since in all willing a man is his own object, the will is always free."[53] On the other hand, since there are various kinds of freedom in the concrete, what makes people free is how they fulfill their purposes and seek satisfaction in the process. Freedom is thus both a metaphor and a condition. It is a metaphor because the forms of *un*freedom can be overcome and are always particular conditions, like with slavery or dependency. One may be a slave but not feel like one. One may be dependent but act independently. People are as free as they have the power to make themselves free. The question is what conditions will help this purpose. The answer is an appropriate objective—known through reason—which inheres in all of us, plus will or the ability to act. Both will and reason constitute the moral life. What then are the conditions which contribute to it?

Political life begins with the doctrine that each individual has a capacity to conceive of good as the same for all, and of being "determined to action" by that conception. This is the foundation of rights. Conversely, every power should be a right. "Society should secure to the individual every power that is necessary for realizing this capacity."[54] Rousseau points the way in his notion of the general will. But the general will, if exercised in a manner reducing rights, becomes coercive. Then, either people are no longer interested in the maintenance of equal rights, or the sovereign has lost interest in sustaining rights. It is better to say that "law, as the system of rules by which rights are main-

52. See Thomas Hill Green, *Lectures on the Principles of Political Obligation* (London: Longmans, Green and Co., 1941), Introduction by A. D. Lindsay, p. vii.
53. Ibid.
54. Ibid., p. 47.

tained, is the expression of a general will than [that] the general will is the sovereign."[55]

This means that insofar as abstract principles maintaining rights are part of a general will, they are represented in laws rather than by magistrates. This shifts the concern to the type of obligations the state has to its citizens and the citizens have to the state. The state is not simply an aggregation of individuals under a sovereign but an aggregation of communities—family, tribe, whatever. Out of these obligations to the aggregate society comes understanding of duties and rights which the state must maximize. Such understanding begins in common humanity. Green then goes on to describe the various private rights, like life and liberty, and the limits of state rights, for example, during a war, the right to punish, the right to promote morality, and rights of property. These last are extremely important because they combine the a priori consideration of the good with the principles or collective purposes of the community. The state can intervene in morality. It can enhance consciousness and direct will towards morality in the same way that parents act to develop the independence of the child. Similarly, property rights need to be restricted according to the public interest. Private property does not need to be abolished, but harmful private usages must. The entire viewpoint was perhaps best put by Bernard Bosanquet. "The State is in its right when it forcibly hinders a hindrance to the best life or common good. In hindering such hindrances it will indeed do positive acts."[56]

The emphasis of Green and the neo-Hegelians is to establish norms of conduct for the state and to establish the meaning of collective purpose. Like that of the utilitarians, the result is an emphasis on practical reform—but reform of a principled kind. It was not the practical reform of the German state which simply bought off workers' demands with social welfare. It was not the reform of the French, who proposed changes in the total organization of life so sweeping that radicalism became acceptable only in theory, while French society became more and more bourgeois in practice. It was a mixture of a method which can only be called Platonic—stating the ideal as it seemed imminent in us all—and a political system which can only be called Aristotelian—in which prudential government could help realize the ideals, government being the final cause.

55. Ibid., p. 104.
56. Bernard Bosanquet, *The Philosophical Theory of the State* (London: Macmillan, 1951), p. 178.

It was left to another generation to translate all these prescriptive ideals into instrumentalities, to combine the utilitarianism of Mill with the philosophical convictions of Green. When this occurred political science as we know it began to take shape. On the Continent, theorists retained philosophy but expanded the analysis of law. In England, the law was extended as jurisprudence—a discipline following a tradition of political analysis which dates back to Bracton and includes the works of Blackstone, Stubbs, Dicey, Maine, Vinogradoff, Maitland, and Austen. The lawyers' interests intersected political science as institutional analysis, particularly influencing the work of Bryce, Barker, Laski, and others in England, and Lowell, Wilson, Finer, and Friedrich in the United States. With institutionalism we have the beginnings of modern political science. But before examining institutionalist solutions, we want to discuss a third perspective for which institutionalism purported to be an answer. This is the radical tradition in politics, which is above all associated with the French Revolution. If it can properly be said to have begun with Rousseau, it reached its peak in the theories of Marx. Fundamentally, the assumptions of the nineteenth century arose out of the terrible contradictions of industrial capitalism, which none of the earlier contract theorists had sufficiently understood and which produced results that neither the theory of natural rights, nor the simple reassertion of public morality could handle.

chapter five
The Radical Tradition

The radical tradition is very different in character from that of the enlightenment although it retains a belief in rationality and indeed elevates it to an even more central role. It has a different objective. Radicalism wants to break, not reconcile, the prevailing relationships of class, principles of rule, and behavior of individuals. The more radical a theory, the more it advocates the liberation of human beings from their limitations and predicaments, not only to change the circumstances of their lives, but to promote a better understanding of their situation. The most militant radicals believe such a transition is difficult to achieve, but that revolutionary action is furthered by "forcing people to be free," mentally as well as physically.

One can be a radical without being a revolutionary and a revolutionary without being a radical. Essentially, the English and American revolutions were of the latter sort. They sought to amend the relations of ruler and ruled in the name of representative or limited government in order to secure the rights of the ruled. They did not seek either to alter the social organization of society in some fundamental manner or to reform individual behavior; they took people pretty much as they were. The French Revolution of 1789 was similarly a revolution against despotism. It sought constitutional monarchy as a political solution.[1]

The goal of the French Revolution of 1793, however, was different. The radical wing, the Jacobins, consisted of activists who favored a social as well as a political revolution. They were radical revolutionaries in the true sense, but not socialists. Two-thirds of the membership were bourgeoisie. The Jacobins favored ownership of private property. They

1. See Georges Lefebvre, *The Coming of the French Revolution* (Princeton: Princeton University Press, 1947).

were secular libertarians.[2] But they were prepared to use radical methods to attain their ends. The term *Jacobin* has even come to imply extreme radicalism.

The radical tradition is an offshoot of Enlightenment political thought, but it contrasts particularly with the social contract and utilitarian theorists. First, it represents a return to the vision of a more balanced and harmonious society, as powerful in a secular sense as the earlier medieval paradigm was in a religious sense. It has more in common with the City of God than with the practical utilitarian view of interests. Indeed it seeks to transcend interests and regards these as subversive of rational action because "interests" reduce people to their most primitive appetites, making them slaves of passion, greed, and the desire for material objects. This ethical aspect of the radical paradigm makes it, like the religious ones that preceded it, militant.

Secondly, while the Enlightenment was concerned with political liberty and equality, its radical synthesis particularly espoused the problem of social equality. Radicalism sought to redress the human grievances incurred by inequality in political life. In this sense, insofar as the French Revolution attacked the instruments of feudalism and proprietary kingship, it was truly revolutionary. It swept away the class and social structure of an obsolete system. But because it did not pursue social equality with the same vigor with which it pursued political equality or the rights of citizens, it was an unfinished or incomplete radical revolution. This incompleteness became one of the foundations for the radical movement in France, and partially explains the reason for the persistence of communist and socialist movements there.

A third connection between the radical tradition and the Enlightenment is a preoccupation with the organization of work as the essential human activity. Radicals seek to replace labor-management relations with a new social connection, worker participation and control; they seek an end to the adversary relationship incumbent in class struggle; they want to build a state structure different from conventional forms of representative democracy. Hence the radical tradition is fundamentally antiutilitarian. It requires a more Rousseauan system, built on the general will, to operate at all levels of society. How to make that connection was the concern of the early utopian socialists in England as well as the early socialists, syndicalists, and anarchists in Europe. Marx sought to make radicalism into less of a vision and more of a

2. See Crane Brinton, *The Jacobins* (New York: Russell and Russell, 1961), pp. 50–51.

science of socialism by applying a specific interpretation of history. To-day, both the pre-Marxist and the Marxist emphases all form part of an elaborate discussion or debate about how to promote new forms of politics. Present-day proposals include the search for new generative ideas, which have emerged not only from the rejection of more utili-tarian theories, but also from experiences with autocratic socialism and the excesses of Stalinism.

Weaknesses in the Enlightenment Paradigm

Locke and Rousseau, Bentham and Mill were all primarily inter-ested in finding political solutions to social problems, and with the in-dividual in society. Public interest, they agreed, arose when politics con-sisted of appropriate mechanisms to aggregate individual interests. For Locke this required representative institutions of government. For Rousseau the collective public interest was what enhanced the freedom and well-being of the individual. For Bentham the rule was to find the greatest good for the greatest number by establishing priorities of de-mand in a political marketplace of ideas. For Mill, who saw liberty as threatened by the tyranny of the majority, the practical problem in democracies was to organize effectively those minority or disadvantaged groups (immigrants, the aged) who are inadequately represented.

But if we put the principle of equality as raised by Rousseau along-side the problem of inadequate minority representation, one sees weak-nesses of formidable proportions in conventional democratic theory. Minorities and majorities are not all that flexible. The Benthamite as-sumption that a minority on one issue may become a majority on an-other does not always hold. Instead of the continuous formation and reformation of impassioned interest groups, there are classes and perma-nent interests based on economic circumstances.

Hence the liberal solution, which relied on the political market-place as a more or less self-regulating device, catering to the diverse needs of a changing population by means of legislation, had serious de-fects. The reformers might try to organize minorities, widen the fran-chise, and make government more responsive to public needs, but to radical theorists these attempts were in principle bound to fail. Democ-racy, reason, and individualism were necessary—but not sufficient—in-gredients for a successful solution to political problems. The solution required an economic transformation. Among the poor and the growing working class, the liberal concern for greater political representation was inadequate. Radicals concerned with the plight of these groups looked at the liberal assumption that capitalism and democracy were adequately complementary (through the actions of the economic and the political marketplaces) and saw it as fundamentally an ideology favoring the rich or the successful. Instead of trying to solve the problem of capitalism, the radical tradition attempted to show why capitalism was the enemy of democracy. For the radicals, the relationship between capitalism and democracy, with their twin emphases on competition and individualism as self-regulating methods for establishing utilities, not only *did* not work, as Rousseau indicated, but *could* not work. The radical attack, while it began by favoring an inclusive democracy, became explicitly opposed to capitalism as a *system*. In Marxist ideology this belief extended to the theory of democratic government itself.

Utopia and Anti-utopia

The radical tradition is part of an earlier utopian tradition, which has its roots less in Plato than in the ecclesiastical vision of the City of God. But it is also a new form of rationalistic and scientific enterprise which, attacking the assumptions of liberalism, sought to "stand it on its head." Radicals hoped to establish that "liberalism" no longer represented liberty and individualism, but merely the political doctrine of capitalism, which they characterized as a kind of negative development in which ruthless competition, the survival of the fittest, and the exchange of commodities was the basis of human existence.

Many thinkers had tried previously (that is, even before the Enlightenment) to correct the negative impact of commercial economic activity. They saw the need for visionary goals not set by ecclesiastics.[3] One of the earliest was Sir Thomas More (1478–1535), who preached a return to innocence. He wanted to abolish private property, which he believed to be the root of all evil, and to promote humility as the way to redeem the world's plight. He sought to have all people participate in a self-governing community. And More, as Lord Chancellor of England, was no obscure figure.

Another figure, less mystical and perhaps the first to connect the

3. For a review of early utopias see Glenn Negley and J. Max Patrick, eds., *The Quest for Utopia* (New York: Doubleday Anchor Books, 1962).

theme of self-improvement to the application of modern scientific knowledge, was Francis Bacon. He too was to become Lord Chancellor of England. (He was subsequently fired for taking bribes and sentenced to life imprisonment.) For Bacon, new utopian opportunities were linked to the growth of science and invention. His was an age of exploration and the first beginnings of industry.

The notion of a utopia of reason was followed in different ways by a wide variety of thinkers who shared the method of science and the notion that our capacity to control nature included controlling the nature of human beings. The method of utopia was thus an early form of the method of scientific reason, observation, empiricism, experiment, and proof, but it added to it a moral goal. The advocacy of science plus morality runs through political analysis from the writings of Rousseau to Babeuf, Cabet, Saint-Simon, Fourier, Blanc, Proudhon, Bakunin, and others.

Some figures influential in their day, like the Abbé Morelly, believed that the one institution that caused misery and perverted human nature more than any other was private property. Others, like Francis Noel Babeuf (1764–1797) came to believe that absolute equality was the only solution. He founded the first communist newspaper, *The Tribune of the People,* attacked virtually all the institutions of society, and, during the French Revolution, favored continuing the Reign of Terror. He formed the first secret communist organizations designed to nationalize all institutions beginning with the corporations. He believed that, on the death of certain capitalist individuals, inheritance would cease. Production would be carried on by popularly elected officials who would rotate the responsibilities of management and be paid the same as ordinary workers.

Thus, in the seventeenth and eighteenth centuries, there were utopian movements galore which visualized communities in which land could not be bought and sold, and where the common stock of commodities would be made available to all.[4] In the eighteenth century another detrimental element, the destructive impact of the machine, became a factor. Precisely what the liberal economists like Adam Smith and the Benthamites saw as the force for progress, the radicals saw as the instrument of oppression. The Scottish philosopher Adam Ferguson (1723–1816) tried to show that, since institutions were interdependent, social

4. Indeed, Peter Chamberlen believed that the wealth and strength of nations was solely the product of propertyless working people who did all the necessary work of society.

appetite became the collective motive of social life—not individual insatiability or comparative utility. Competitive individualism and the desire for individual gain only intensified the division of labor, resulting in specialization and growing ignorance rather than greater civility and knowledge. Thinking was reduced to the level of a craft, valued only insofar as it was useful.[5]

Similarly in Germany Schiller believed the modern utilitarian state to be abhorrent.

Utility is the great idol of the age, which all powers must serve and to which all talents must kneel. In its crude scale the spiritual worth of art has no weight, and, robbed of all encouragement, art vanishes from the howling marketplace of the century. Even the spirit of philosophical enquiry seizes one province after the other from imagination, and the wider science spreads its bounds, the narrower shrink the frontiers of art.[6]

Schiller, Herder, Goethe, and Hegel all preferred an "organic" view of society. So did Wordsworth, who was much influenced by Rousseau. Colridge and Carlyle were influenced by the Germans. The interest in community and how to preserve it was not simply a matter of ideas held by a few sentimentalists capable of idealizing Greek history. The visible evidences of human suffering were everywhere. If one was on the one hand liberated from the fear of death and superstition associated with the medieval period, one was on the other hand confronted by the growing impoverishment of rural life and the brutalization of urban life (with child labor and other harsh conditions of the factory system simultaneously destroying human beings, the landscape, and the countryside).

All these ideas sprang from certain historical events. In a sense the liberal solutions—whether of the social contract variety embodied in the American Revolution or the utilitarian, which was the outcome of the "Glorious Revolution of 1688" in England—assumed that individual competition, innovative enterprise, and an expanding market, would gradually work such changes in material social conditions that morals would be benefited as well. Those who took a dim view of this position argued just the opposite. Competition, they said, was the very thing that

5. See Raymond Plant, *Hegel* (Bloomington: Indiana University Press, 1973), p. 21.
6. Quoted in Alasdair Clayre, *Work and Play* (New York: Harper and Row, 1974), p. 16.

would produce the alienation of individuals from themselves and their fellows. Thus the radical tradition, in one fashion or another, represented an urge to community, fellowship, and other characteristics of mutual help and intimacy similar to that which characterized the medieval society. Only the radicals wanted to translate this vision into the modern vernacular.[7]

The French Revolution was the watershed for such ideas. In 1789 the revolutionaries would have settled for an English-style constitutional monarchy and freedom from restrictions on trade; that is, a liberal revolution. By 1793, they would not. Although they were not socialists, as the revolution ran its course and the plight of the population in both rural and urban areas became more desperate, so the movement was radicalized. Paris became the center of radical revolutionary thought.

Indeed, it was not until the French Revolution that the term *revolution* was applied to social life. It came to mean upheaval, violence, bloodshed, and the barricades. As Hannah Arendt puts it,

Suddenly an entirely new imagery begins to cluster around the old metaphor and an entirely new vocabulary is introduced into political language. When we think of revolution, we almost automatically still think in terms of this imagery, born in these years—in terms of Desmoulin's torrent révolutionnaire *on whose rushing waves the actors of the revolution were borne and carried away until its undertow sucked them from the surface and they perished together with their foes, the agents of the counter-revolution. For the mighty current of the revolution, in the words of Robespierre, was constantly accelerated by the "crimes of tyranny," on one side, by the "progress of liberty," on the other, which inevitably provoked each other, so that movement and counter-movement neither balanced nor checked nor arrested each other, but in a mysterious way seemed to add up to one stream of "progressive violence," flowing in the same direction with an ever-increasing rapidity.*[8]

How to deal with the questions raised by the French Revolution was directly connected to the theme of suffering produced by industrial-

7. See E. J. Hobsbawm, *Primitive Rebels* (Manchester: Manchester University Press, 1959).
8. Hannah Arendt, *On Revolution* (New York: Viking Press, 1963), p. 42.

ization. These became the twin concerns of the radical tradition of the nineteenth century. Let us consider some of the proposals put forth by non-Marxist radicals and revolutionary thinkers before going on to a consideration of Marx.

The Radical Paradigm Before Marx

Precursors and enemies: Marx has been a successful monopolist in the realm of socialist ideas. He and his followers preempted "true" socialism and distinguished it from "false" or utopian socialism. Indeed, if one wants a match for Marx, the place to look is not among the socialists, but rather in that monumental apologist for a ruthless liberalism, Charles Darwin. Marx and Darwin both drew their inspiration from the natural sciences, as applied to history. Both believed they had discovered the secret of the universe. But while one offered the principle of natural selection as a means to justify the power of the rich over the poor, the other offered equality as the outcome of historical development. One justified the balance that existed in the world. The other offered a moral outcome to human activity.

The utopians had a vision similar to that of Marx but lacked the scientific awareness to apply it. Some—Saint-Simon, for example—sought a secular equivalent to the Catholic ideal. Born in 1760, at the age of nineteen Saint-Simon went to America, where he fought in the Battle of Yorktown. The American Revolution fascinated him, as it did other French politicists (most notably De Tocqueville). Saint-Simon went home to participate in the French Revolution and to devote himself to social reform. His vision is contained in three main works, *The Industrial System, The Catechism of Industry,* and *New Christianity.* According to these works, science, knowledge, and industry must replace faith, hope, and charity as the holy trinity, but for this transformation, the precondition is peace. (Saint-Simon called for a European parliament to mediate among the powers.) And along with peace, everyone must be able to labor. Universal associations are required to guarantee these conditions and ensure just rewards. Therefore the rulers of states, who must be those versed in science, must—like the people—conform to the Christian principle that all are created equal. This belief would improve the condition of the poor and, as a result, a cooperative commonwealth in which merit, work, and reward, graded hierarchically, would emerge under the benign rule of an aristocracy of science. The theory is reminiscent of Plato.

The Saint-Simonians believed in the natural inequality of people, but tried to turn this belief into the basis of cooperative mutual benefit. They established a Sacred College of Apostles, formed missions, dressed in costumes similar to clerical robes which indicated rank or degree, and sought in this way to manifest visionary goals in practical life.

Whatever one may think of the Saint-Simonians, one of their most important attributes was the desire to transform the symbols of ecclesiastical and Catholic order into symbols of a similar but secular order in which rank was a function of ability, instead of inherited position. The ideas of another radical reformer, Charles Fourier, provide a contrast to this desire. Born in 1772, Fourier (unlike Saint-Simon) was a commoner, the son of a cloth merchant. With a modesty characteristic of the period he believed that humankind was just reaching a stage of maturity whereupon it only needed to adopt his proposals in order for the new utopian age to appear. His point of departure from other philosophers involved a primitive psychology. Far from being repelled by or even competitive with each other, Fourier felt that human beings are naturally attracted to each other. People are essentially cooperative beings. To realize this condition a social organization must combine the human passions in a harmonious way. The passions are the five senses, plus friendship, love, family, ambition, and the passions for planning, change, and unity. All twelve passions, properly combined, form a single overriding passion—love for others within the society.

All this would be rather absurd except for one interesting point. Fourier envisioned the reconciliation of the passions through small communal societies, which he called *phalanxes*. The effective human group, he said, should be no smaller than four hundred members and no larger than two thousand. All would be required to live together in a common dwelling called a *phalanstery*. Here again the model is ecclesiastical. The phalanstery would be the secular equivalent of a monastery and, as for monks, the mixture of love and work creates a harmonious community. Each group would do work (mainly work of an agricultural nature) suited to the talents and interests of its members. The work would give people pleasure, and as people competed in friendly ways, efficiency would result and income increase. Those who performed necessary labor would receive the highest reward, useful labor the next highest, and agreeable labor the least. Hence, income would be inversely proportional to the unpleasantness of work. Fourier called the head of each phalanx a *unarch,* and the chief of the phalanxes (the equivalent of a pope) , the *omniarch.* There would not be much for such rulers to do. Even the family and the institution of marriage would disappear.

We mention the proposals of Saint-Simon and Fourier in part because they suggest how difficult it is to think up practical solutions to politics. Compared to their work the writings of the social contract and utilitarian theorists are the soul of sophistication. But absurd as they were, the ideas of both were influential. Each gave rise to sects trying to realize the teachings of the master. Each saw himself as a sort of latter-day Christ, possessed by the possibility of converting little bands of followers who would then give birth—as had the Disciples—to an ineluctable moral force. Such notions did not at the time seem far-fetched. Saint-Simon was the teacher of Auguste Comte. Fourier influenced such thinkers as Albert Brisbane, Horace Greeley, and Charles A. Dana, who established several Fourierist communities, of which Brook Farm in Massachusetts (1841–1847) was the most well known. It was in New England that the transcendentalists tried to combine social living with ideals of individualism, nonconformity, and spontaneous living in much the same fashion as do modern separatist communal experiments today.[9]

The socialist theorists: More significant in terms of modern radicalism were three quite different but more explicitly socialist theorists. One was Robert Owen, who also came to America to try to carry out on a political level the experiments he had started in his factory in Scotland. Owen represented a tradition of socialist *reform.* The second was Pierre Joseph Proudhon, who is remembered for radical *syndicalism.* The third is Mikhail Bakunin, who became the age's exponent of *anarchism* and the chief antagonist of Marx in the First International.

The first two, Owen and Proudhon, Marx called "bourgeois socialists." The third, Bakunin (who admired Marx) , Marx considered "a man devoid of all theoretical knowledge," whose program

was a hash superficially scraped together from the Right and from the Left—equality of classes (*!*), abolition of the right of inheritance *as the* starting point of the social movement (*Saint-Simonist nonsense*) , athe-

9. See Charles R. Crowe, "This Unnatural Union of Phalansteries and Transcendentalists," *Journal of the History of Ideas,* Vol. XX, No. 4 (October–December 1959) , pp. 495–502.

ism *as a* dogma *dictated to the members, etc., and as the main dogma*
(Proudhonist) : abstention from the political movement.

This children's primer found favor (and still has a certain hold)
in Italy and Spain, where the real conditions for the workers' movement
are as yet little developed, and among a few vain, ambitious, and empty
doctrinaires in Latin America, Switzerland and in Belgium.

To Mr. Bakunin doctrine (the mess he has brewed from bits of
Proudhon, Saint-Simon, and others) was and is a secondary matter—
merely a means to his personal self-assertion. Though a nonentity as a
theoretician he is in his element as an intriguer.[10]

The quote gives something of the flavor of Marx on the attack. It
must not be forgotten that Marx confronted Proudhon and Bakunin in
the various workers' movements of the day—most particularly during
the First International Workingmen's Association (1864) for which
Marx wrote the rules and the inaugural address.[11]

Despite Marx's deprecation of Bakunin, however, the latter was a
serious thinker. So were many others who wrestled with the problems
of their day. Indeed, despite the unworldly quality of their schemes,
most of the utopians and anti-utopians shared a tinkering rather
than a totalistic view of the universe. They were concerned with how to
put modern science to work for the benefit of all. They wanted to square
the need for equality with natural differences among human beings.
They wanted to generate participation around institutions of work
without alienating individuals from work itself. They sought some
means of breaking up the state rather than enlarging its powers. Indeed,
although none can compare in the power of their thinking with Marx,
who was a total social and political theorist, neither did they presume to
unlock the key to history with his dogged certainty.

Owenites, Proudhonists, Bakuninists, and many others were involved in the First International. That body was a testimonial to the
varieties of socialism which flourished by the mid-nineteenth century.
But the most important thing about Owen, Proudhon, and Bakunin is
that all were antistatists. The workplace was their key to peoples' social
existence. Otherwise, they were far apart in their thinking. Owen was
essentially a reformist whose principles were incorporated in the co-

10. Karl Marx, Letter to F. Bolte, November 23, 1871, in Karl Marx and Friedrich
Engels, *Selected Correspondence* (Moscow: Foreign Languages Publishing House),
p. 327.
11. See Julius Braunthal, *History of the International, 1864–1941*, Vol. I (New
York: Praeger, 1967), pp. 95–105.

operative movement. Bakunin believed in the liberating effects of violent revolutionary action.

The socialism of the workplace: The founder of "workplace socialism" was Louis Blanc (1813–1882). He believed that socialism would have to be created by, as well as for, the working class. Blanc himself came from a middle-class family. He was born in Madrid where his father was Inspector General of Finance under Louis Bonaparte. By the time he was twenty-six he had started a radical journal, *Revue du Progrès*. In the 1848 revolution in France he was a member of the Provisional Government and in 1871 he became a leftist member of the National Assembly. Blanc wanted to develop the human personality through the humanizing effects of work. He was opposed to competition. In place of the phalansteries of Fourier he proposed social *workshops*. Such workshops would be under the supervision of the state, which would subsidize them without interest and ensure that they worked for the common good. Workers would select the administrators of the workshops, however, and the entire system would be based on workers' control. The workshops would be united in a federation that would cover the losses of any individual workshop. Private capitalists could invest in them.

Like Saint-Simon, Blanc believed in a hierarchy of talent, but unlike him, he also believed that people had different needs. Hence his slogan, "from each according to his abilities and to each according to his needs." He believed in a doctrine of just proportions in which variable ability and variable need were mutually adjusted. Equality in the strict sense of the word, as favored by the extreme radical Babeuf, was an inadequate formula because it did not take into account human diversities on both counts.

Not content with putting his ideas forward in print, Blanc decided to put them into practice in 1848. His fellow members of the provisional government took a dim view of his proposals, however, and while pretending to support them appointed Blanc's worst enemy as Minister of Public Works, hoping that the results would be so disastrous that Blanc would be discredited. In this they were quite effective and the workshops came to a sticky end.

Blanc's fate was not so different from the experience of Robert Owen, who lived a generation earlier and who may have been the central figure in British socialism in the first half of the nineteenth century. Owen, who lived from 1771 to 1858, was the son of a Welsh saddler and ironmonger. He had a scanty education at the village school, but by the time he was twenty became manager of one of the largest factories in

Manchester. Later he went on to become a factory owner, and then a partner in one of the great manufacturing establishments of Scotland.

As superintendent of his mill in New Lanark, Scotland, Owen found himself in charge of a community of some fourteen hundred families. Theft, pauperism, and drunkenness, were common. The mill families lived under fearful conditions. Children worked; there was no schooling. Owen devised a scheme to make the mill more productive and at the same time improve the condition of the workers. He put in new, technologically advanced equipment. He established strict rules for sanitation. At company stores, workers could get their supplies at cost. Housing was provided. So was schooling for children. Drinking was severely restricted. Soon the New Lanark community became famous as a model of temperance, good workmanship, and cleanliness. The mills prospered. By 1816, Owen left business convinced that he had found the solution to the problem of rational human happiness. Combining in his person the spirit of philanthropy, commerce, and reform which for a long time exemplified English socialism and made it respectable, Owen took Bentham's objective—human pleasure or happiness—and tried to make it into a reality. He believed the key to rational happiness was through character formation: Good character breeds happiness; good working conditions breed good character. On the political level he favored factory reform. But all around him he saw the effects of over-production, depression, and unemployment, and realized that no factory legislation could eliminate these evils. His proposal was similar to Fourier's: establish unified and cooperative villages of five to fifteen hundred persons on a thousand to fifteen hundred acres of land for agriculture and manufacturing use. He believed these cooperative ventures, rather than reform of the House of Commons, were what was required to deal with the problem of human misery.

Unfortunately his scheme got nowhere. His outlines of the division of land were referred to as "Owen's parallelograms" and neither the rich nor the poor paid much attention. Everyone was preoccupied with parliamentary reform. Caught up in the reformist spirit Owen ran for office in Scotland and was defeated.[12]

Increasingly Owen's philosophy moved to the left. In 1821 he wrote a tract which expressed the need for pure communism. Individualism, accumulation of wealth, and competition, he believed, led to the degradation of labor. Property, like light or air, should be indivisible.

12. For an account of Owen's life see M. Beer, *A History of British Socialism* (London: George Allen and Unwin, 1958), pp. 160–88.

He left Britain and came to the United States where, in 1824, he purchased the Rappist community of Harmony. The Rappists were deeply religious German peasants who had converted about thirty thousand acres of land into a flourishing communist community. Owen collected about six hundred people—craftsmen and adventurers, idealists and intellectuals—to people the community, but his experiment failed. Endless bickering ran down the community and Owen lost all his money. Nevertheless he returned to England where he continued to work for the working-class movement, speaking in favor of labor exchanges and seeking to combine trade unions and cooperative associations. He wanted a general congress to replace parliament as a method of government. A good many of Owen's ideas were picked up by other militants, especially those who founded and participated in the Chartist Movement, the foundation of contemporary British radicalism.

Owen began as a Benthamite and ended his days as a communist. He, Fourier, and others centered their ideas about building different forms of community. None were powerful theorists although all propounded solutions they believed to be practical alternatives to the status quo. Proudhon, however, did not follow in their tradition, but decided to make a fresh start. For him, the reconstruction of society began with the radical alteration of the relationship between the social and the political order.

It can no longer be a matter of substituting one political regime for another, but of the emergence, in place of a political regime grafted upon society, of a regime expressive of society itself. "The prime cause of all the disorders that visit society," says Proudhon, "of the oppression of the citizens and the decay of the nations, lies in the single and hierarchical centralization of authority. . . . we need to make an end of this monstrous parasitism as soon as possible."[13]

With Proudhon began the tradition of anarcho-syndicalism.

Syndicalism and Anarchism

Syndicalism is a revolutionary theory based on the organization of workers, the unions or "syndicates" combining in appropriate units, economic, social, and political functions. Anarchism, a more inclusive term

13. Martin Buber, *Paths in Utopia* (Boston: Beacon Press, 1958), p. 27.

is a word with a strange sound to modern ears. One conjures up wild-eyed bomb throwers, terrorists, and those who believe in violence as a form of liberation. Anarchists are supposed to idealize the smashing of all those forms of social and political structure that represent the state's repression of the individual. But for the most part anarchists, like William Godwin, for example, were of very different stuff. They simply did not believe in the beneficial effects of political power in *any* form. Godwin, who wrote the *Enquiry Concerning Political Justice* in 1793, was the soul of reason. He wanted a simplified society in which decentralized authority and the voluntary sharing of material goods would make human life independent of government. He was extremely influential in his time, particularly with the romantic poets from Coleridge to Shelley, and with Ruskin, who looked on him as the source of the radical tradition.[14]

Work and political organization: In France, Proudhon was the central figure of the radical school, as we have said. Born in 1809, he died in 1865 a true syndicalist. He was poor but won scholarships which enabled him to become a printer. Profoundly suspicious of all forms of organization, he favored political policies based on mutualism, cooperation, and self-help. Regarding himself as the true expression of the revolution, he was perhaps the greatest single influence on the founders of the First International and the most militant leaders of the French Commune of 1871. Proudhon, like Godwin, emphasized the importance of the individual in society. In this respect the theories of both resemble liberalism. Reason in individuals requires human justice; justice, a collective condition, is only possible where life is natural and free. Proudhon became an atheist, and a militant member of the working class. Some of his views were translated into radical slogans: "Property is theft." "The control of man by man is oppression." He was sufficiently firm about these principles so that when the Revolution of 1848 broke out he took no part in it because he believed that *all* forms of government were bad. The only property a person could own, he argued, was that gained by labor, and not as a result of profit, interest, or rent.

Proudhon's opposition to government institutions was not limited to capitalism, but extended also to communism, which he felt denied independence just as surely as property destroyed equality. The ideal he proposed was an essentially rustic society of peasants and small craftsmen.

14. See George Woodcock, *Anarchism* (Cleveland: The World Publishing Company, 1962), pp. 61–93.

Proudhon rejected any reorganization of society that merely tried to rearrange its existing components. There was no point in simply shifting power from one group to another or in taking the ownership of capital from the existing proprietors only to replace them by a new set of monopolistic exploiters of the poor.[15]

For Proudhon, work was at the center of the social system. The closer people came to relating their work to their needs and abolishing the superstructure of banking, finance, and government, the closer they would be to seeing their needs fulfilled. Work was the dignifying human activity and the working class, removed from the imposition of machines and capitalism, would be the basis of a renovated society. Whatever the weaknesses of his ideas, they were nevertheless influential. Anticapitalist and antistatist, they posed the problems of modern life, rather than solving them. Among the important figures who were influenced by Proudhon's doctrines was his Russian friend, Mikhail Bakunin, born in 1814 not far from Moscow, in the town of Tver. It was Bakunin who became the prototypical anarchist—strong on deeds and daring, a true rebel. Although an aristocrat by birth he was a bohemian, a great talker, drinker, and a bear of a man. His life was dramatic enough to make others take notice, but he was no fool. He was aware of the authoritarian implications of Marxism, and during the First International, when the great struggle between libertarian and authoritarian conceptions of socialism began, it was Bakunin and Marx who led the factions.

Another influence on Bakunin was the German communist Wilhelm Weitling, a follower of Louis-August Blanqui and organizer of secret conspiratorial movements. Bakunin was thus a combination of Proudhon's mutualism—which he eventually came to reject—and Weitling's terrorism. Drawn into such movements himself, Bakunin became the object of police attention in a number of countries. He was kept on the move and he spent his life organizing followings and trying to avoid the clutches of the police. He became friendly with Guiseppe Garibaldi, the Italian nationalist leader, and settled in Italy where he founded his first secret Brotherhood, the prototype of underground anarchistic organizations.[16]

Bakunin rejected as insufficient Proudhon's belief that the essential basis of social life was mutual self-help. In 1866 he expounded his political and social program in the *Revolutionary Catechism*. The base of

15. James Joll, *The Anarchists* (London: Eyre and Spottiswoode, 1964), p. 63.
16. See Woodcock, op. cit., p. 160.

all political organization within a country, he said, should be the autonomous commune. The administrators of the commune are to be elected. Each commune would create its own constitution. Provinces were federations of free and autonomous communes, as was the state itself. Bakunin opposed Blanqui and the "neo-Jacobins" who elevated the role of the state. He believed that there must be spontaneity in organization, which resulted from direct revolutionary action.[17]

The seeds of Marxist thought: If the solutions offered by Proudhon and Bakunin seemed sentimental and nostalgic for the small-scale society based on mutual relationships and work, the problem of the tyranny of the state as an instrument of both capitalism and socialism was posed by them very clearly. Certainly Stalinism, when it came in Russia, was a realization of their worst fears. Marx, who fought against all these doctrines, was honest enough to recognize the dangers of the powerful state under socialism. His answer was a theory more general than theirs, which gave a definite, but constricted role to the state under socialism. The existence of this generalized state was limited to one specific stage, the transition to communism. After that the state would "wither away." Marx foresaw, then, that what the anarchists proposed for the beginning of the revolution would occur at the end. In between there would be a severe class struggle as the bourgeoisie fought the growing power of the working class with all the forces of repression at their disposal. The working class would then create a "dictatorship of the proletariat" which would give over the means of production to social ownership, abolish the property relations of capitalism, and liberate workers from oppression and exploitation. The Marxian vision both rejected and transcended the theories and goals of the contemporary anarchists. To do this properly required an entire system of thought. The one Marx constructed stands as a monument to creative social science.

Marx

Marx's ideas are so well established today that we forget that he was born as long ago as 1818. His grandfather was a rabbi, his father a jurist who turned Lutheran when Marx was six. On his mother's side, Marx

17. See Arthur Lehning, "Michel Bakounine, Théorie et practique du fedéralism anti-étatique"in Jacques Rougérie, *Jalons pour une histoire de la commune de Paris, 1871, International Review of Social History,* Vol. XVII (1972) , pp. 455–73.

was descended from a Dutch rabbi's family. He was a superb scholar, with a knowledge of classical literature, Greek and Latin. In his university days at Bonn, he came under the influence of Hegel, and studied philosophy rather than law, as his father would have preferred. His doctoral dissertation was on the *Natural Philosophies of Democritus and Epicurus.* Early a nonconformist in his views, his application for a lecturership at the university was rejected. (One can only speculate what might have happened if Marx had become a professor in the Prussian universities of his day. It is not very likely that he would have become such a passionate and original thinker.) He became a radical journalist. Attacking first religion, he quickly became interested in economic questions after being appointed editor of the *Rheinische Zeitung.* His studies convinced him of the thinness of socialist solutions and the need for their improvement. In 1844 he was impressed by an article written by a young German businessman working in Manchester, Friedrich Engels, and established a friendship and collaboration which was to last until Marx's death in 1883.

One of the reasons Marx is such an important figure is that he represents a successful mixture of the *intellectual* in politics, seeing the world with a sense of outrage and looking toward a more moral and free future for man; the *practical politician* who engages in conflicts with his political enemies, right and left; and the *professional* who develops a scientific theory of change as dialectical materialism.

It is of course impossible to do justice to the ideas of Marx in a short summary. No single thinker was so complex or had such a command over the issues and problems of his day, as well as such a sweep of historical knowledge. He was both a scholar's scholar and a politician's politician. Marx was not simply annoyed with the inadequacies of the early communists and anarchists. He actively fought them in the working-class movements of his time. A pamphleteer as well as a writer of scholarly tomes on capitalism, he recognized that his most serious contenders were not other radicals but the liberal economists and political theorists whose ideas had been put into practice very successfully in England and the United States, and who claimed equally universal solutions to the problems of an industrial age. His main attack, then, was focused on capitalism and political liberalism, especially because, in the early nineteenth century, it had became apparent that the liberal system might work. America was the place to see Montesquieu's theories of checks and balances vindicated. If in England and France liberalism was in trouble, it was also extremely powerful; for capitalism was innovative and productive in a way the world had never seen before. The protests of socialism were little more than ideologies for the protection of the working class, and as such either stimulated reform or were met with repressive measures. They were not to be taken seriously as political truths.

The Marxist method: If the socialist paradigm was to successfully oppose the liberal one it had to be as powerful intellectually. Indeed, it had to handle in a theoretical way what the liberal paradigm could not, that is, the problems of class conflict and polarization. It had to attack the Newtonianism of the self-regulating, competitive, market principles and show not only why these were faulty but why they broke down altogether. The required theory had not only to comprehend historical but developmental aspects of society as well. It had to show how industrialization effected changes in all social life and where its promise would lie. Libertarianism was to be the end-product. To achieve it required a transforming agent, exercising executive power for the proletariat. The proletariat, in turn, was the universalizing class. (Under capitalism the bourgeoisie was the universalizing class and the state was the executive committee for the bourgeoisie.) To win against the bourgeoisie required not only the historical destruction of capitalism but the enshrinement of the force of a higher logic of revolutionary strategy.

Marx recognized that evolution follows a prescribed arc, but not in some easy or immediate way. People need to work to bring about the revolutionary outcome by becoming conscious of their role in history as a class. So nature, liberty, government, science, and dynamic laws of industrial development are brought together by Marx in a revolutionary synthesis.

The main alternative to Marx—the equivalent historical figure—was Darwin. In the liberal view, the political marketplace would correct imbalances produced by the economic one, but in fact, it was slow to do so. As social Darwinism gained currency, liberals who ought to have been in the forefront of reform were divided. Some became reformers. Others became conservatives. But they mainly opposed reformers and were hostile to anyone who sought to arouse the multitude. Redressing economic grievances by political action was viewed as the devil's work, providing opportunities to troublemakers, misfits, adventurers, radicals of all sorts. Liberal democracy, which may have represented the triumph of capitalism over aristocratic rule, elevated the bourgeoisie, the commercial and entrepreneurial middle class, to power. But this was pre-

cisely the group that had economic power over the unrepresented workers and the poor in general. Thus it became obvious that political and
economic power did not check and balance each other, and that liberal
democracy was the instrument which supported by law the exploitation
of the workers. Marx believed that it would not help to reform government under such circumstances. To seek to correct the inequalities produced in the economic marketplace through compensatory political action would have provided a band-aid solution where an operation was
necessary. What was required was not reform but revolution—and with
it a social democracy which realized equality. For Marx, this premise
constituted a general historical law of motion in social affairs.

Dialectical materialism: Marx combined the empirical and the deductive in a formula for history called **dialectical materialism.** *Materialism*
in human affairs refers to the economic process and its modes of production. Marx's hypothesis was that inequality would grow with productivity until a quantum jump in the character of technology would enable
for the first time in human history a condition of abundance rather than
scarcity. But prior to such a condition, conflict between those with property and those without would grow at an unprecedented rate. This was
not a moral issue. The very nature of the capitalist productive process,
with its ruthless pursuit of efficiency and competition, would create
along with wealth and innovation social contradiction and crisis. Out
of such social crises would come a new solution—socialism.[18]

The misery produced by capitalism was the stimulus for revolution,
the potential source of mobilization against capitalist society. Such a
mobilization could be successful only when society was highly industrialized and distribution distorted. Then the imbalance between public
want and private gain would become so great that an inevitable struggle
for power would occur. The battle could only go one way—victory would
be to the producers of value, those who toiled and labored in the vine-
yards and the factories and who, by mixing their labor power with
materials, produced objects of value.

Of the harshness of capitalism and its social conditions there was
little doubt. What Engels described was accurate.

*The way in which the vast mass of the poor are treated by modern so-
ciety is truly scandalous. They are herded into great cities where they*

18. The best discussion of Marxism as science is in Maurice Cornforth, *The Open
Philosophy and the Open Society* (London: Lawrence and Wishart, 1968) .

*breathe a fouler air than in the countryside which they have left. They
are housed in the worst ventilated districts of the towns; they are deprived of all means of keeping clean. They are deprived of water because
this is only brought to their houses if someone is prepared to defray the
cost of laying pipes. River water is so dirty as to be useless of cleansing
purposes. The poor are forced to throw into the streets all their seep-
ings, garbage, dirty water, and frequently even disgusting filth and excre-
ment. The poor are deprived of all proper means of refuse disposal and
so they are forced to pollute the very districts they inhabit. And, this is
by no means all. There is no end to the sufferings which are heaped on
the heads of the poor. It is notorious that general overcrowding is a
characteristic feature of the great towns, but in the working class quar-
ters people are packed together in an exceptionally small area. Not satisfied with permitting the pollution of the air in the streets, society crams
as many as a dozen workers into a single room, so that at night the air
becomes so foul that they are nearly suffocated. The workers have to
live in damp dwellings. When they live in cellars the water seeps through
the floor and when they live in attics the rain comes through the roof.
The workers' houses are so badly built that the foul air cannot escape
from them. The workers have to wear poor and ragged garments and
they have to eat food which is bad, indigestible and adulterated. Their
mental state is threatened by being subjected alternately to extremes of
hope and fear. They are goaded like wild beasts and never have a chance
of enjoying a quiet life. They are deprived of all pleasures except sexual
indulgence and intoxicating liquors. Every day they have to work until
they are physically and mentally exhausted. This forces them to excessive indulgence in the only two pleasures remaining to them. If the
workers manage to survive this sort of treatment it is only to fall victims to starvation when a slump occurs and they are deprived of the
little that they once had.*[19]

But what Marx emphasized, above all, was not the *moral* aspect of
such conditions. Rather he tried to show how the *dialectic,* applied to the
mode of production, revealed the way in which the dynamics of exchange, which under capitalism produced *surplus value* or profit,
worked to undermine capitalism itself. It would do no good to *reform*
the conditions Engels described. The capitalist system itself would provide the means for the transformation of the proletariat from its present

19. Friedrich Engels, *The Condition of the Working Class in England* (New York:
The Macmillan Company, 1958), pp. 110–11.

condition to that of a universal class. Once that had occurred (and for the most part it would take revolution to accomplish it), the state as we know it would no longer be necessary. The liberation of man from the state, from his exploiters, and from his own alienation from himself would all be accomplished in a communist society.

The watershed of radicalism: Marx and Engels brought together a number of different intellectual strands. Their dialectical method they took from Hegel, bringing it down from its idealistic heights. Hegel's emphasis on the growth of ideas and the spread of these ideas as an evolving culture or ethos was given an economic emphasis. They discarded the antireligious emphasis of philosophical materialism as represented in the work of the German philosopher Ludwig Feuerbach and instead put it in the context of the political economy of David Ricardo and Thomas Malthus. The combination they called *dialectical materialism.* They applied it to relationships of capital, rent, and wages to show how contradictions necessarily arose out of the capitalist productive process. Historical evolution was integrated with scientific methods. Hence, the particular theories of Marx were a key to history, deductive in logic but empirical and pragmatic in relation to events. But they also incorporated Rousseau's original concerns with equality and freedom. The concern with freedom among human beings became for Marx a question of how people become socially *unalienated.* It was a process which required a particular economic form—socialism; a particular condition of development—abundance in material goods; and a particular state of consciousness—an understanding that the chains that bind people are political and that they are produced by class domination.

Marx provides (1) a method for the interpretation of history, and (2) an application of that method to a specific end. He seeks to show how the relationships of human beings evolve towards this end. But he believes that this comes about by intelligence and will. People are not instruments of blind history. Rather the key is human consciousness and the discovery of will.

Marxist ideology: Marx thus becomes for the modern era what Socrates was to the antique: the symbol of people's power over their destiny.

For Marx was before all else a revolutionist. His real mission in life was to contribute, in one way or another, to the overthrow of capitalist society and of the state institutions which it has brought into being, to contribute to the liberation of the modern proletariat, which he was the first to make conscious of its own position and its needs, conscious of the conditions of its emancipation.[20]

This is not a bad evaluation. Marx used a powerful deductive system for a prescriptive end. He sought to apply knowable truths as scientific laws, in order to define both potentiality and actuality. He believed that once the problem of material scarcity was solved, it would become possible to solve the philosophical problems posed by Plato and Rousseau, exorcise the ghost of Hobbes, and expose the liberal solution. Conventional politics would become unnecessary and disappear because public and private purpose would be the same. There would be neither rulers nor ruled. Marx, in short, proposed to abolish a political model that had prevailed from the time of Plato. In essence his argument was as follows.

Exchanges in work relationships result in class interactions, or concrete activities between people. These interactions stimulate people to think about the meaning of their exchanges, that is, what it all represents ideologically. Understanding these results from a consciousness expressed as opposing ideologies: liberalism versus conservatism, capitalism versus socialism, or Catholicism versus Protestantism. With Marx both forms of exchange—that of work and that of ideology—are sources of conflict. He looked toward the individual's liberation from alienation in a classless society, a society which is both egalitarian and noncoercive, having achieved that equilibrium that occurs in a stateless community.[21]

The Exchange Process. Marx begins his discussion with an analysis of the exchange process. The mode of production determines exchanges

20. Friedrich Engels, "Speech at the Graveside of Karl Marx," in Marx and Engels, op. cit., pp. 167–68.
21. See the discussion of Marx's view in Henri Lefebvre, *The Sociology of Marx* (London: Allen Lane, The Penguin Press, 1968), p. 184.

The proletarian revolution implies the end of the state. The internal relation between the two concepts is dialectical-contradiction and unity, a higher synthesis achieved via negation, the transitional period. In this period the objective is not simply to destroy the state (that is the anarchist position), but to take over the functions previously performed by the state. The incomplete rationality inherent in existing society, presently held back because of internal contradictions in the latter, has been taken in charge or, rather, captured by the state. Society must recapture and carry this rationality farther forward, toward its full realization.

of value and the social relations that result in a division of labor. The division of labor produces class interactions, which determine behavior. Marx distinguishes exchange relations and different forms of production by dividing history into precapitalist and capitalist periods. With capitalism, he posited, something major happens. A quantum jump occurs in human affairs which is brought about by the unique power of the capitalist productive process to produce commodities and money. In precapitalist forms, the social relations of exchange and the meaning of exchange are relatively simple: In feudal societies exchange was based on payments in kind. Marx says,

Instead of the independent man, we find everyone dependent, serfs and lords, vassals and suzerains, laymen and clergy. Personal dependence here characterizes the social relations of production just as much as it does the other spheres of life organized on the basis of that production. But for the very reason that personal dependence forms the groundwork of society, there is no necessity for labor and its products to assume a fantastic form, different from their reality. They take the shape, in the transactions of society, of services in kind and payments in kind. Here the particular and natural form of labor, and not, as in a society based on production of commodities, its general abstract form is the immediately social form of labor. Compulsory labor is just as properly measured by time, as commodity-producing labor, but every serf knows that what he expends in the service of his lord, is a definite quantity of his own personal labor-power. The tithe to be rendered to the priest is more matter of fact than his blessing. No matter, then, what we may think of the parts played by the different classes of people themselves in this society, the social relations between individuals in the performance of their labor, appear at all events as their own mutual personal relations, and are not disguised under the shape of social relations between the products of labor.[22]

In capitalism, then, social interactions take on a fantastic form, which is capital, money, congealed labor, and the embodiment of power. Capital begets capital, and capitalists compete for it, introducing efficiencies in labor to reduce costs and maximize profit or "surplus value." In so doing, however, they also produce contradictions. Competition in the interactions of exchange drives out weak capitalists and landowners.

22. Karl Marx, *Capital*, Vol. 1 (Moscow: Foreign Languages Publishing House, 1961), p. 77.

By the same token, the attempt to produce more and squeeze out more surplus value leads to increased efficiency through improved technology, and the employment of fewer and fewer workers. Marginal producers are squeezed out of the ranks of the capitalists. Those who are unemployed, or living at the subsistence level necessary to produce or work, have so little income that they cannot buy the burgeoning range of commodities. Hence, while there is dynamism, growth, and efficiency, there is also poverty, exploitation, and crises of depression and inflation.

This is the great structural paradox in Marx, which can be examined in many contexts as highly industrial societies confront increasingly serious economic crises. These crises are the cause of wars between industrial powers and the need for colonial possessions.[23]

The Value of Labor. For Marx the commodity of value was labor. Precapitalist relations had been in the form of exchanges measured in kind or in money. They were exchanges of "use values"; that is, people found that what they needed and wanted could be exchanged for what they produced. In capitalism, the exchange was no longer in kind. Rather, the entrepreneur was enabled—even encouraged—to extract more use value from a worker's production than was returned to the worker in the form of exchange value or wages. Thus, the capitalist system generated surplus value in the production of each worker. The worker received none of this value. In fact, while laborers got less than their proportionate share of the total output, those who contributed land got more, and those who contributed capital to the productive process got the most. Inevitably, a polarization developed, with capitalists dominating the society and the state coercing and exploiting the workers. The situation, Marx prophesied, would lead to a revolutionary break and a new form of exchange, without surplus value, in which work value reaped equal wage value. He wrote:

The life-process of society, which is based on the process of material production, does not strip off its mystical veil until it is treated as production by freely associated men, and is consciously regulated by them in accordance with a settled plan.[24]

The way it works is this. Labor creates value but labor does not receive the full return in the form of wages for the work that it does. Rather workers receive *exchange value*. This is a result of the competi-

23. See Shlomo Avineri, *Karl Marx on Colonialism and Modernization* (New York: Doubleday Anchor Books, 1969).
24. See Marx, op. cit., p. 80.

tion between workers. Exchange value tends to *subsistence:* that is, what it costs to keep workers alive and working. The buyer of labor is the capitalist. What he gets from labor is *use value:* that is, the labor time of the worker beyond subsistence or exchange value. The difference between the use value produced by the worker and the exchange value paid by the capitalist minus the cost of rent and capital equipment leaves the capitalist with a *surplus value* or profit. Some of this he pockets and some he reinvests. If surplus value is high, other capitalists will see profitable opportunities and enter the market. This means that competition intensifies where surplus value is high.

To increase his competitive position, the capitalist tries to decrease his labor costs. Labor is called *variable* capital. His object is to reduce his variable capital in proportion to fixed capital, or equipment. The capital equipment owned by the capitalist is *constant capital.* Reducing the ratio of variable to constant capital increases efficiency and productivity. This enables the capitalist to resist competition from others, and retain profits as competition intensifies.

The process produces capitalist crisis. Laborers squeezed out of the productive process or receiving only exchange value can not purchase what is produced. The result is *overproduction* which results in depression. As competition increases and new capital equipment and new technology is generated in order to increase surplus value, profits in fact go down. This is the "law of falling profit." Weaker capitalists are pushed out of the market. There is a *concentration* of economic power within an ever-narrowing circle of capitalists, and a *polarization* between the capitalists and a growing proportion of proletarians. The capitalists, or the *bourgeoisie,* use the organs of state power to oppress and control the proletariat. The result is a class struggle. The bourgeoisie, as a class, is overthrown by means of revolution. Revolution will be followed by a period in which the *dictatorship of the proletariat* replaces the old *dictatorship of the bourgeoisie.* After rooting out the remnants of the bourgeoisie, the state shall wither away.

The dynamic part of Marx's theory is the dialectic applied to the modes of production. How it works under capitalism—that is, the relation of use value to exchange value, variable capital and constant capital, surplus value and the law of falling profits, business cycle and polarization—is what Marx called the *organic composition of capital;* the variables are *systematically* related to each other in the way he describes. They underlie the capitalist mode of production wherever it may be. This is what Marxists call the "base."

The different groups of men and women who represent the social side of this, the social classes consisting of proletarians and bourgeoisie, or other classes, the ideologies they subscribe to, the political parties and interest groups which represent them, and the government which supports the dominant class, Marx called *superstructure*. The two interact. The long term changes, the intensification of crisis at the base, will be reflected in changes in the superstructure. But the latter is not a simple reflex of the former. Indeed, those who make the base the sole determinant of the superstructure are called "vulgar Marxists."

The Marxist Synthesis. So the precapitalist world, the world of feudalism, and the capitalist world of surplus value would eventually give way to modern socialism and communism. The world of socialist ideas flows logically out of the real world. The exchange system of capitalism makes possible not only predictable class relationships and their outcomes, but generates the evolution of a polar opposite form of consciousness. Exchanges then work to produce cooperation among classes. Classes become solidaristic. Class interest is perceived. The victory of the proletariat produces the individualization of man. Marx believed that capitalism produces individuals who find themselves in an extreme form of alienation, alienated both from their work and themselves.[25] He wrote that

> . . . *in money relationships, in the developed exchange system (and it is this semblance that is so seductive in the eyes of democrats), the ties of personal dependence are in fact broken, torn asunder, as also differences of blood, educational differences, etc. (the personal ties all appear at least to be* personal *relationships). Thus the individuals appear to be independent (although this independence is merely a complete illusion and should rather be termed indifference); independent, that is, to collide with one another freely and to barter within the limits of this freedom.*[26]

The jump to socialism eliminates inequality in exchange interactions and ends people's alienation in communism.

Marx transcended the ideas of the utopians. In doing so, however, he ignored what they thought most significant, the workplace itself.

25. See David McLellan, ed., *The Grundrisse* (New York: Harper and Row, 1971), pp. 66–67.
26. Ibid., p. 72.

He assumed that socialism would occur in the most highly industrialized countries. He believed that the state would become obsolete. It did not occur to him that Marxism would become the ideology of developing countries, and that a communist party would become, in addition to a vanguard, an instrument of the state which would itself become oppressive.

The Radical Legacy

After Marx, the radical inheritance became divided. In general, while the picture is extremely complex, we shall limit our discussion to stating two main traditions. One is the tradition of Lenin, who saw the need for a militant transformation of capitalism where capitalism was weakest, that is, its "imperial periphery." Lenin showed why the revolution had not yet occurred in the advanced industrialized capitalist societies: this was precisely because they were able to *export* their crises through colonialism and imperialism. Lenin believed that once the revolution occurred, it would spread from the periphery to the center.

Having to make a revolution in Russia under the circumstances prevailing in 1917, Lenin also improvised a good deal. He used "instruments of terror" similar to those of Robespierre in the French Revolution. These were elevated by Stalin into an instrument of intensification of the class struggle. Government became the instrument of economic transformation that was to bring about the conditions necessary to support communism without going through the creative and dynamic capitalist phase.

The second inheritance of Marxist thought was more democratic, taking off from a notion of Engels that a revolutionary transition could take place by parliamentary means, through *revisionism*. Eduard Bernstein, who was born in Berlin in 1850, the son of a locomotive engineer, became a friend of Engels. He believed that capitalism was not about to collapse, that polarization between workers and capitalists was not occurring, and that parliamentary institutions would provide a means to improve the conditions of the working class and bring them to power.

Bernstein represents a tradition that ties Marx to modern social democratic ideas. Other theorists of social democracy, like Karl Kautsky in Germany, the Fabians in England, and Jean Jaures and the reformist socialists in France wanted to use the institutions of liberal parliamentary government to shape the new socialist regime.

These two lines of thinking represented the revolutionary and re-visionist legacies of Marx. But the ideas of the utopians and anarchists also survived. Owenites were the forerunners of the *cooperative move-ment*. Proudhon and Bakunin were important in the evolution of mod-ern *syndicalist* movements, which take trade unionism as the basis for new forms of political organization. In the United States, Eugene Debs and Daniel DeLeon were instrumental in both.

In turn, the revolutionary Marxists have divided into other sub-groups—the followers of Leon Trotsky, for example, and those influ-enced by Antonio Gramsci, the founder of the Italian Communist Party. The most stunning impact was made by Mao Tse-tung. The Chinese Revolution is as powerful in its way as the Russian Revolution was under Lenin.

The radical tradition, then, is perhaps more diverse, alive, and realistic today than ever before. Although part of the Enlightenment paradigm, it stands against two of its offshoots—institutionalism, which translates the principles of the liberal model into practices and instru-ments of democratic rule, and behavioralism, which translates the prin-ciples of rational behavior into more general questions of what deter-mines human action itself.

Institutionalism

chapter six
Elements of Institutional Analysis

In the unit on Political Philosophy we discussed the more important generative ideas associated with political philosophy. The starting point for early political philosophers was the assumption of rationality, which is critical to any politics. Then came the idea of change and how to control it. Issues of rationality and control were used to define the relationship between freedom and obligation, or rights and responsibilities. And in the tradition of the Enlightenment, theorists tried to solve the political problems inherent in this interface by means of representative government. However, in a continuing debate, radicals consider the liberal solution to be inadequate, because it fails to resolve the problem of equality. Institutionalism favors the Enlightenment side of the debate. The institutional orientation seeks to effect universal solutions by translating libertarian ideals into representative government.

For institutionalists, libertarian political theories have emerged from history as moral objectives to be established in practice. Since these moral ideals have the capacity repeatedly to evolve new problems, various institutional strategies are required to implement solutions. No one theory or concept is fixed or permanent, nor is any solution final. As our needs change and our obligations and rights alter, the responsibilities of the state to its citizens change. Ideas about political solutions are refurbished and institutions modified.

We have seen how some political theorists would like to stop the process of change by resolving political problems once and for all. This was the tradition established by Plato, and also represented by Marx. Most institutionalists, following in the Enlightenment tradition, reject such final solutions. For them politics is "open." Conflict is converted to competition, which is made peaceful by means of the instruments of representative government.[1] The problem is to find out what *instrumentalities* work best to realize the ideals of political philosophy. It must be kept in mind that instruments can fail, leading to consequences different from those intended. (After all, some totalitarian countries provide mechanisms for representation and voting, for example. They may also have trade unions and at least one political party. Moreover, a given dictatorship may be popular with the public.) Therefore a proper concern with representative government and democracy cannot be limited to mechanisms of rule. It is necessary to determine whether or not these mechanisms embody principles of liberty and rights *in and of themselves.*

A special meaning attaches to valuable instrumentalities. In the United States, for example, the Supreme Court, or the office of the President or that of a Congressman or Senator, is an institution that represents certain principles. So institutionalism is a concern with how political ideals that evolved in the history of Western politics are embodied in particular connections between rulers and ruled. The best known political institutions are the *branches* of government. The executive branch has direct responsibility for policy making. The legislative branch reviews policy, and amends, innovates, and checks the power of the executive. The judiciary ensures that the constitution, which specifies the mutual obligations of the citizen to the state and the state to the citizen, is not violated. In free societies, the main principles on which these institutional branches of government are based are judicial review, executive responsibility, and the legislative exercise of sovereign power on behalf of the people.

Connecting links between people and governments are political parties, interest, pressure groups, and administration. The political parties enable the sovereign people to exercise their will by means of competitive elections, thus making legislators responsible to the people. The executive is responsible to the legislature, and through it to the people. In turn, policy is made by the joint collaboration of the people's representatives and the executive in the form of laws administered by the civil services and local authorities. There are two main forms of representative government: presidential and parliamentary.

The system summarized here is an *open system.* It seeks piecemeal solutions based on the consent of the governed. It works slowly; it is unwieldy; and it may be subject to malign influences. But it is capable

1. See Karl Popper, *The Open Society and Its Enemies* (London: Routledge and Kegan Paul, 1945).

of reform. Institutionalists believe that no matter how badly the system might work, it is still better than any other alternative system.

Institutional Generative Ideas

The main generative ideas followed by institutionalists can be summarized as in Figure 6-1. Power is a usable and controllable force. The great problem of history has been to turn absolute power to democratic uses.

Power is the basis of politics. In a democracy, its exercise must accord to standards of equity or justice. This in turn is manifested in law. Law generates authority and makes possible representation by means of which laws are made. In turn when representation is based on equality this is conducive to liberty and democracy itself. Democracy is a system that safeguards liberties. These are enshrined in rights, which are manifested politically in representation. In a democracy it is rights that, through the sovereignty of the people, give rise to authority—the same authority sanctioned by law. The result is a system of order on the basis of which the exercise of power is possible and which establishes principles of equity or justice.

The mutually enforcing basis of the institutionalist notion of democracy needs to be emphasized. *Equality and democracy secure liberty. Order and power secure justice. Justice and liberty are the critical or independent variables. Equality and order are the dependent variables.*

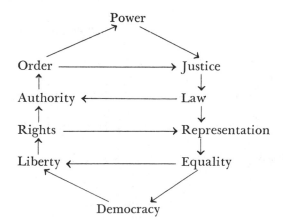

Figure 6-1. Basic Principles of Democracy

This outline leads to a second set of generative ideas about democratic government, as shown in Figure 6-2.

Popular sovereignty is required for democracy to work. But popular sovereignty requires the consent of the governed. And, without some reserved sphere of private life, popular sovereignty produces a tyranny of the majority. So government must be limited. How limited is a constitutional matter. But limited government nevertheless means that, in its sphere, government must be able to act in order to be efficient. However, the power to act also needs to be checked by the power of the legislature. Responsibility for the regulation of power is thus accorded to both the legislative branch and to the public. To effect public responsibility requires suffrage, which to be effective must be organized by parties that promote peaceful competition. Parties cannot peacefully compete without a prescribed electoral system. The electoral system assumes that people have reasons to vote on issues about which they are informed. An informed public needs the guarantee of a free press and the right to assemble to communicate opposing views. These ingredients check and balance power.

The democratic system operates in accord with the institutional structure outlined in Figure 6-3.

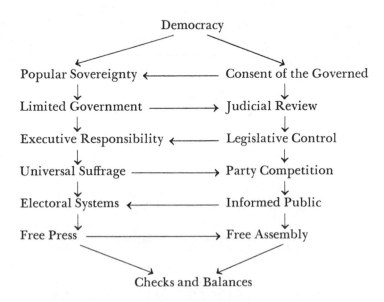

Figure 6-2. Institutions of Democracy

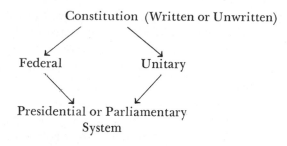

Figure 6-3. Types of Democratic Government

The main ingredients of institutionalist political analysis, properly put together, maximize the concept of freedom with order. For institutionalists the dilemma posed by political theorists from Plato to Hobbes is solved.

Freedom and order: How to achieve freedom with order is the primary institutionalist problem. There are two ways to establish the proper institutions: one is evolution, the other revolution. Edmund Burke represents the evolutionist view. He believed that each nation develops its own historical consciousness and works out its own national institutions. These, to be meaningful to the people, are rooted in the language, classes, manners, style, and commercial and economic activities of the national group. Public respect for authority requires a sense of national continuity and pride that is furthered by the institutions of government. Evolution, according to Burke, is to be preferred over revolution. A break or rupture with the past, such as that which resulted from the French Revolution, not only imposes terrible hardships, deprivations, and cruelties, but jeopardizes a nation's self-respect. It leaves a legacy of hatred, diminishes authority, and deprives a people of pride in their past.[2] Was America the exception?

America lacked a historical continuity. But uniquely, its self-respect depended on its rejection of the past and most of the traditions that went with it. The new institutions contained great promise. Rationality was applied to politics as a new measure of authority rather than continuity and reverence for time honored practices. The American

2. See Ruth A. Bevan, *Marx and Burke: A Revisionist View* (LaSalle, Ill.: Open Court Publishing Company, 1973).

concern with rational institutions, tested in the Revolution, required a confluence of libertarian ideals, in a constitutional document that would realize liberty and order under conditions of political freedom that did not prevail anywhere else in the world. This was the revolutionary tradition in America.

Americans were fairly quick to give the Constitution sanctity and to provide the Founding Fathers with a special authority to "institutionalize" the new form of government. The contributors to *The Federalist Papers,* for example, provided crucial interpretative materials on the meaning and scope of the proposed constitution. The American concern was to establish the principles of democratic government and to make these effective by means of a division of powers between people and government. So organized, government would promote distributive justice, once the prerequisite of order has been attained. The spirit of the United States Constitution, although it represented an ideal republic, was Aristotelian rather than Platonic. It was practical. It was prudential.

What made the early American democracy so impressive to contemporary political analysts like Alexis de Tocqueville was that it took full cognizance of all the passions and inconsistencies of which human beings are capable and rendered these into public policy.

In America the people appoint the legislative and the executive power and furnish the jurors who punish all infractions of the laws. The institutions are democratic, not only in their principle, but in all their consequences; and the people elect their representatives directly, and for the most part annually, *in order to ensure their dependence. The people are therefore the real directing power; and although the form of government is representative, it is evident that the opinions, the prejudices, the interests, and even the passions of the people are hindered by no permanent obstacles from exercising a perpetual influence on the daily conduct of affairs. . . .*

To a stranger all the domestic controversies of the Americans at first appear to be incomprehensible or puerile, and he is at a loss whether to pity a people who take such arrant trifles in good earnest or to envy that happiness which enables a community to discuss them. But when he comes to study the secret propensities that govern the factions of America, he easily perceives that the greater part of them are more or less connected with one or the other of those two great divisions which have always existed in free communities. The deeper we penetrate into

*the inmost thought of these parties, the more we perceive that the object
of the one is to limit and that of the other to extend the authority of
the people.*[3]

What are the critical institutions that exemplify the object of both
limiting and extending the power of the people? They are embodied in
the federal conception of checks and balances, limited government,
popular sovereignty, flourishing local government, and loose coalitional
parties—some favoring more, some less limited government; all converting into public policies the diversity of free opinions freely arrived at.

Americans have always admired de Tocqueville for the brilliance
of his analysis. He understood American institutions and, more important, the spirit in which they came into being. Moreover, he was a
foreigner, not one who had fought in the Revolution or participated in
the constitutional debates themselves. So admiring a commentator reinforced the already self-congratulatory tone of the American commentary
on itself. But, it also lifted it from its provincialism and helped make the
American solution into a universal one. The Preamble of the Constitution reads,

*We the People of the United States, in Order to form a more perfect
Union, establish Justice, insure domestic Tranquility, provide for the
common defence, promote the General Welfare, and secure the Blessings of Liberty to ourselves and our Posterity, do ordain and establish
this Constitution for the United States of America.*

As the objects of institutionalism became transformed into an influential political science, these purposes gained relevance for the whole
world.

Constitutions and sovereignty: Institutions require a framework of
principles from which they take credence. The framework is a constitution. The object of a constitution is "to provide a basic law for a governmental regime."[4] This basic law establishes the philosophical and organizational framework, divides responsibilities among public instru-

---

3. See Alexis de Tocqueville, *Democracy in America* (New York: Alfred A. Knopf,
1945), Vol. I, pp. 173 and 178.
4. See C. Herman Pritchett, "Constitutional Law," *The Encyclopedia of the Social
Sciences,* ed. D. L. Sills, Vol. 3 (New York: Macmillan and Free Press, 1968), p. 295.

mentalities, indicates how revisions of the basic charter should be made, and dictates the flow of government business, from decision making to policy implementation.

How basic is a basic document? In the United States, the Constitution is absolutely the last word, the embodiment of legitimacy. To violate the Constitution in practice or in spirit is to surpass the limits of political mandate. In countries such as the Soviet Union, the constitution is at best a blueprint for a framework of government observed in name rather than in reality, according to how and when it suits the purposes of the rulers of the state. Hence, violations of the constitutional rights of Soviet artists, or the political rights of dissenters, frequently occur even though such violations are constitutionally proscribed.

The most important feature of a constitution is how it distributes powers. In the American and French constitutions, these are spelled out in detail. In Britain, there is no single charter, but several constitutional instruments, such as the Magna Carta, that establish rights and principles. More broadly speaking,

Constitutional law . . . appears to include all rules which directly or indirectly affect the distribution or the exercise of the sovereign power in the state. Hence, it includes (among other things) all rules which define the members of the sovereign power, all rules which regulate the relation of such members to each other, or which determine the mode in which the sovereign power, or the members thereof, exercise their authority. Its rules prescribe the order of succession . . . , regulate the prerogatives of the chief magistrate, determine the form of the legislature and its mode of election.[5]

Whether dealing with a written or an unwritten constitution, however, the observance of its principles and practices as binding is a prerequisite to the "rule of law." Constitutions are *legal* instruments. But they are different from all others. They establish the conditions of power—both the power to make laws and to execute them. The functions and the organization of government provide the law-making mechanisms.

But a constitution does more than specify a division of authority between branches of government. It indicates a relationship between a

5. See A. V. Dicey, *Introduction to the Study of the Law of the Constitution* (London: Macmillan, 1959) , p. 23.

people and their sovereign, between their freedom, or autonomy, and the conditions of government on their behalf.

The Western constitutional tradition (especially in Europe) draws inspiration from Roman law and the contract theorists—especially Locke, Montesquieu, and Rousseau—and the utilitarians, Bentham and Mill. The legal tradition is an amalgam of natural law, or reason, operating in concert with positive or common law. The blend of natural and positive law in a constitution establishes the conditions of the just state, which provides a suitable framework for viable government—that is, a condition of political equilibrium as in Figure 6-1. Such a state preserves and protects justice, enlarges the public freedom, ensures the selection of capable office-holders, makes legislatures responsible, and prevents the capricious use of executive power, as indicated in Figure 6-2.

As we have said, there are two kinds of constitutional sovereignty. In Britain, the constitution rests on a lengthy constitutional history, a cultural tradition of common law, and a remarkable continuity of government, all of which have reinforced public support for and attachment to the parliamentary system. Although the real constitutional center is the force of public sentiment and its beliefs, if one were to ask, "Who or what in Britain is sovereign?" the answer would be clear. Sovereignty lies not in the people but in Parliament. Parliament can make any laws it wants. It checks the power of the crown. When sovereignty shifted from the monarchy to Parliament, and aristocratic government gave way to representative government, British sentiment became more democratic, but British sovereignty did not.

In the United States the people are sovereign.[6] Government exercises sovereignty on their behalf. This requires specific accords between the people and the government, a social contract in which the rights, duties, and obligations of both the government and the people are carefully spelled out.

The Institutions of Government

Early institutionalists were primarily concerned with the problem posed by John Stuart Mill—how to generate great power from the sovereign people and combine it with limited government. The institutional theorists assumed that (1) power is mainly private, to be used cooper-

6. Also in France, ever since the French Declaration of Rights in 1789.

atively, and is therefore mutually advantageous to both rulers and ruled
and (2) government is purposeful, helpful, mediating, and moderating.
The combination of right institutions with these principles would produce an Aristotelian prudentialism with the maximization of liberty.

But, if the sovereign power is great, how can it be kept in the
private sphere? Two great principles were brought together by the institutionalists within the framework of constitutionalism. Since a constitution provided the one principle of politics that was absolute, it came
to represent, in the institutionalist view, a social contract establishing
the conditions under which the sovereignty of the people extended to
their representatives. The constitution was supposed to result in a government that produced laws to carry out the wishes of a majority.

The first operating principle that makes this framework work, gives
it life, and produces results in the form of decision and laws, is competition. The problem is to prevent competition from leading to a Hobbesian condition by establishing an economic and political environment in
which private interests serve the public interest. The way to do this is
by means of elections. Through the elective process individual competition is made to produce collective benefits.

The second operating principle is Montesquieu's notion of checks
and balances. These work in several ways. They may be a product of
separation of powers between the legislative, executive, and judicial
branches of government. Or they may be the result of *parliamentary
control over the executive.* Separation of powers is what we have in the
United States. The three branches of government represent autonomous
spheres which must cooperate if laws and policies are to be made. Competition between the three branches helps keep them separate, as each
is jealous of any invasion of its powers by the others. As they are separate, each checks the power of the others. But the government must
produce policy or become impotent in the eyes of the electorate; therefore the separate branches must also agree on some common denomina-
tors of policy. So competition, combined with separation of powers
among the three branches of government and a voting system in which
candidates for office must compete on the basis of their performances
and their promises, keeps the power of government limited. But, because it must select priorities and agree to deal with matters that affect
the public, limited government can act powerfully.

In England the system does not operate on the basis of separation
of powers, but rather on the parliamentary control over executive
power. Whereas in the United States, the President is elected separately

from the Congress and is not a member of it, in England no one votes for the prime minister. The person designated as prime minister is elected by the constituency of a single district, just like every other member of Parliament. The party that emerges from each election as the majority in Parliament forms the government; that is, it selects a prime minister and cabinet from among its members in Parliament. The person selected to be prime minister, and that person's colleagues in the cabinet collectively make policy. Rather than upholding a separation of powers, the British Parliament is supreme, its authority based on a *unitary* constitutional legitimacy. Parliamentary control is exercised over the cabinet, which rules as long as it maintains parliamentary support. If a cabinet loses support, it must resign and a new election will be held.

So the doctrine of competition translates in politics into elections, competition between parties, and checks and balances organized either through separation of powers among the branches of government, or through parliamentary control over executive power. Constitutional frameworks outline the various powers and responsibilities of the branches of government. In the British case, certain landmark events, embodied in law, represent benchmarks of constitutional evolution. Of these, the Magna Carta, or Great Charter of 1215, which established the basis of personal liberties in England, is perhaps the most important.[7] Fundamental to the English tradition of constitutionalism is that the entire corpus represents the rule of law of which Parliament is the supreme lawmaker. Hence there is no provision for amendment; any law amends previous practice. If a law violates the spirit of the constitution as a corpus, a constitutional crisis is provoked.

When all the powers of the people remain with the people except as delegated to the government, and the powers of government are expressly divided between central and provincial government (as in Canada) or national and state governments (as in the United States) a *federal* constitution exists. Not only do the people have inalienable rights, but the states (or other administrative divisions) have rights as well. The federal government is thus not only checked by parties, but by the states. In turn, the states have governments which, with minor differences, are analogous to the federal government.

The power of the people is symbolically located in a single figure,

7. See William Stubbs, *Select Charters* (Oxford: The Clarendon Press, 1957), pp. 291–303.

a president, or monarch. But, whereas such figures of authority once exercised supreme power over the nation (as dictator or autocrat), in a parliamentary system such executive power does not actually reside in the head of state. In England the monarch reigns but does not rule. Power comes from the will of the people which is concentrated in parliamentary supremacy.

Federal and unitary systems operate on somewhat different mixtures of the two principles of competition and checks and balances. Checks and balances under a parliamentary government are imposed by parliamentary control over the executive. The executive can dissolve the parliament and call for new general elections. In a federal system with separation of powers, cooperation for policy making must be obtained among the branches of government.

The Branches of Government

A **federal state** is one in which authority and power are shared with the several states. A **unitary state** is one in which authority and power are centralized. Both systems are constructed with the same branches of government, but how they work is very different in each case. The problem of a federal constitution is that agreement for purposes of policy making is hard to get. Bargaining, dealings, and compromise on legislative items is needed to satisfy various and diverse groups.

Under a unitary or parliamentary system, if a prime minister has a powerful majority in Parliament and is able to maintain discipline over the party, the cabinet can garner great power, simply by its ability to win every parliamentary vote. However, there is always the danger of cabinet dictatorship. If a prime minister does *not* have a disciplined parliamentary party, and must rely for effectiveness on coalitions between several factions (as is often the case in France or Italy where there are many relatively active parties), then there is a danger of stalemate and instability. The government can easily lose the confidence of the Parliament and be forced to resign. Hence, in France during the Third and Fourth Republics, and in Italy today, governments endured only for very short periods, unable to make effective policy, and causing great public frustration.

We shall examine in some detail how the various branches and interest groups actually operate under these two types of constitutional systems. How the authority of these institutions is delineated is the institutionalist's main concern.

The legislative branch: In all democratic countries the most important check on power, real or potential, is the legislature. The legislature consists of the representatives of the people. All enactments of law must be approved by the legislature, but very little policy can be directly initiated by it. Factions, interest groups, and party coalitions interfere with the enactment of well thought out policies. Even when there is a crisis of major proportions, legislatures rarely initiate a specific bill. Instead they review, criticize, amend, ameliorate, and often refuse to pass critical legislation. Running the legislative gauntlet is a slow and complex process. A bill introduced in a legislature normally is read to the legislature as a whole several times, while going through a period of committee review and revision, each time being returned for further modification, and finally passed or refused by a plurality vote.

Federal constitutions have two houses, such as the United States Senate and House of Representatives. One is designed to represent states or other subdivisions of the federal authority, and the other to represent the people. The two houses do not have exactly the same powers, but they both must pass the same legislation. A bill introduced into both houses must be ironed out in committees of the two houses. Where a divided legislature exists—for example, in Germany as well as in the United States—the chairpersons of committees play an important part in steering bills through the various stages of consideration. In turn, continuous consultation is required between special committees to which bills are referred in the first place, and legislative floor managers. In addition, there must be close consultation between representatives of the legislative and the executive branches. The entire democratic law-making process requires continuous negotiation, between the legislative houses and among the legislative, executive, and judicial branches.[8]

In order to make intelligent decisions, committees may hold hearings on particular proposals. They also establish procedures for reportage from the executive to the legislature. For all these reasons—diverse responsibilities, the need to consult and bargain, and the need for information gathering—it is very difficult for a legislature to initiate policy, as we have said. If the legislators are critical of a government policy, they usually amend or overturn it, rather than offering a new solution. And, unfortunately, legislative initiative becomes less possible as political problems become more complex.

In unitary systems, the dominant power is always in the lower

---

8. See John C. Wahlke and Heinz Eulau, eds., *Legislative Behavior* (New York: The Free Press of Glencoe, 1959).

house, that is, the house that represents the people. The upper house is usually a vestigial organ of aristocracy, which has delaying powers and the right of review. It might also have special legal powers, such as obtains among the "Law Lords" of the House of Lords in England. The tradition, however, is that an upper house represents an elite, while the lower represents the mass. The great struggles over democracy in the nineteenth century were over first the people's right to establish parliamentary control over the executive (that is, constitutional monarchy or a constitutional presidency), and second, the need to increase the power of the lower house over the upper. (France, for example, suffered for years from the actions of a conservative and aristocratic Senate which effectively blocked reformist legislature passed in the lower house, the Chamber of Deputies—especially during the "popular front" days of the 1930s.[9])

In a federal system, because of the diversity of both state and private interests, the legislative parties tend to form coalitions consisting of sectional and special interests. These may coincide. Other interests may be less regional, and may be organized more on national lines. Trade unionism tends to coincide with high concentrations of population. States with big worker populations can deliver a labor vote which needs to be represented. Or coalitions can form around an issue. Hence, in a federal legislature, overlapping and shifting coalitions form the basis of legislative activity. Legislators who are good at putting such coalitions together are extremely valuable.

In unitary and parliamentary systems, which involve several parties, the same process goes on. Most European political parties are more ideologically distinctive than the two great omnibus political parties in the United States. Arrangements and deals need to be worked out in more formal ways, such as by electoral coalitions or agreements to form a cabinet composed of several parties. But such arrangements are often not effective. Legislators may not choose to follow party discipline, causing the coalition to fall apart, thus seriously limiting possible action. Indeed, a badly divided legislature in a parliamentary system makes government virtually impossible. Where strong party discipline exists, or where there is a two-party system or stable coalitions among parties, then it is possible for strong government to occur. Scandinavian countries are good examples of stable multiparty coalitions.

9. For a detailed discussion see Daniel Ligou, *Histoire du Socialisme en France* (Paris: Presses Universitaires de France, 1962), pp. 396–440. See also Nathanael Greene, *Crisis and Decline: The French Socialist Party in the Popular Front Era* (Ithaca, N.Y.: Cornell University Press, 1969)

The executive branch: The executive branch of government is responsible for just what the name implies: executing the wishes of the people.
In a democratic system the executive acts on behalf of the people. The
more support the executive has from the people, the more effective such
actions are. But a democratic executive differs from a general of an
army or a president of a business firm. The executive must lead, but be
responsive to the people as well. The public contradictorally expects an
executive to (1) take initiative and (2) not to do anything without
consulting them. A strong executive is always accused of dictatorial
tendencies. A weak executive is forever being castigated for not taking
initiative. That is the executive predicament.

The term *executive* is singular, but executive action is always a
plural affair. The term is used to refer to both the head of state and the
entire administrative organization of government. As a head of state,
the executive is singular, but conditionally so. The British monarch is
the head of state, but actually the executive branch of British government comprises the monarch in council, the members of the cabinet
(whom the monarch technically appoints on the recommendation of the
newly elected parliamentary leadership). In the United States, the executive is the president. But the president is, in practice, only the holder of
the office of the presidency. The president *presides* over cabinet and special advisors, senior officials, and the Diplomatic Corps as well as the
Civil Service Administration.

Most parliamentary systems have an executive who serves solely as
the symbol of government. Whether president, prime minister, or monarch, the executive undertakes the business of state, opening legislative
sessions, making speeches, accepting ambassadors, validating appointments, signing legislation, and generally representing authority in the
abstract. The real power of executing law is exercised by a prime minister and the cabinet, who make up an "executive committee."

In the United States, the president is both the symbol of government and the *actual* head of government. The buck, to paraphrase
Harry Truman, stops there. The president is expected to enforce the
laws, whether liking them or not, and to ensure that subordinates in the
executive branch do likewise.[10]

In addition to executing, or implementing, the administration of
law, the executive is also expected to *make* law. A president or prime

10. See John T. Elliff, "Aspects of Federal Civil Rights Enforcement: The Justice
Department and the F.B.I., 1939–1964," *Law in American History*, ed., Donald
Fleming and Bernard Bailyn (Boston: Little, Brown and Co., 1971), pp. 605–74.

minister keeps an ear to the ground, to the electorate. Issues raised in the press, or by representatives or interest groups, about the problems and needs of the people (funds, protection, special consideration, and so on) help the executive formulate policy. So the executive is in part a listening device which converts public information into policies, into initiatives taken in consultation with legislative leaders, into law. The executive initiates policy on the basis of information, consultation, and of course, judgments about priorities.

The third duty of the executive is to act as a party manager. The executive power comes from the party and through votes. In other words, the executive represents the party and its public supporters. The role is partisan, in the sense that it represents the party. Where the executive is a president, as in the United States, it is a difficult task to rise above party to represent the whole people. It is the job of the president to strike the right balance between bipartisanship and party loyalty. In parliamentary systems, a prime minister and cabinet can be much more openly partisan. The prime minister represents the party or party coalition, while the monarch or president represents disinterested public authority.

In all cases, the executive branch has the primary responsibility to enforce the law, make law, manage the party, and administer the constitution of the state.

The judicial branch: Federal systems are extremely complex. With constitutionally defined jurisdictions of power necessarily interconnected in the actual business of making policy, there are always possibilities that constitutional violations will occur. Also, because there is rarely some hard-and-fast rule pertaining to even the most precisely defined constitutional description of powers, the meanings change over time and as conditions change. This being the case, it is necessary to have a high court that serves as the ultimate arbiter in matters of constitutional interpretation. Such a high court represents the highest principle of an independent judiciary—the pinnacle of a system of courts and a legal structure that is above or aloof from politics. (One sees the effect of having a judicial structure tied to the vagaries of politics in constitutional crises such as that which occurred in India in 1975, when the prime minister, in effect, forced the Indian high court to suspend the civil liberties of the opposition.)

The point is that representative government and the defense of liberties against unwarranted governmental action is, in the last analysis, guaranteed by the courts. The constitution, whether written or unwritten, is a legal document or a series of legal interpretations of charters and ordinances. Together these comprise a tradition made up of law, precedent and custom. The resultant body of doctrine represents the meaning of the constitution, its principles and practices. In England, there is embodied in the Common Law the entire corpus of legal traditions and practices built up over the generations. In Europe, a similar tradition is associated with Roman Law which, modified by the scholastic and ecclesiastical authorities of the Middle Ages and incorporated in the law of the Holy Roman Empire, formed a common basis for relationships of rights, duties, property, descent, and constitutional powers. The American juridical tradition is based on English Common Law, but is embodied in a written constitution.

The interpretation of the constitution, the fundamental law, is always broad. In a sense there can be no narrow interpretation; or as some would describe it, "strict" versus "broad" construction. How flexible and complex the interpretation is depends on the intellectual bent and political outlook of a high-court justice. The interpretive construction of constitutional articles by a Supreme Court justice in the United States, for example, is a combination of politics translated into education, and education translated into legal interpretation.

The patterns of thinking associated with various forms of interpretation, tend to be conservative. There is always the problem of how to keep a court from representing the dominant money or property interests of the past. In a federal system, for example, if problems require strong executive actions that lead to an accumulation of power in the executive branch at the expense of the legislative (as has slowly occurred in the United States, particularly since the days of President Roosevelt), the need for strong executive action may be checked by the Court in favor of restoring balance to the legislature. This is one of the great problems of a system of checks and balances. At the same time, when there is erosion in the power of the Congress and power accumulates in the executive, then it may take more than the Supreme Court to correct the matter. For this reason checks on the power of the executive branch in the United States go beyond the Supreme Court to the representatives of the sovereign people through impeachment. (The House of Representatives decides whether or not to impeach and the Senate decides whether or not to convict. The Chief Justice presides over the Senate proceedings.)

Not all countries have a Supreme Court. The practice in Europe is to rely on *constitutional tribunals.* The French Constitutional Council only decides cases on request from the President of the Republic or the Prime Minister. In Italy and Germany there are constitutional courts similar to the American Supreme Court but more ambiguous in stature. Whatever the practice, it is clear that a high court provides the clearest indication of how democratic a regime really is in its respect for law. It is the repository of safeguards for liberties. It has no power other than the respect and authority it is granted by the people. Thus a supreme court represents, from an institutionalist point of view, the rule of law itself.[11]

A high court stands outside politics in order to interpret the constitutional conflicts generated by politics, when these affect the rights, liberties, and constitutional arrangements of government. It is, in this sense, aloof from the politics of the day although, of course, its interpretations have fundamental political implications. During the tenure of Chief Justice Warren, the Supreme Court of the United States was a "liberal" court, particularly in the area of civil rights. It effected a social revolution which has not only affected black–white relationships but the fundamental definitions of equality, compensation to the disadvantaged, the rights of cultural pluralistic groups, property rights, education, and so on. The implications of the decisions of that court, in such matters as school busing, educational tracking, neighborhood schools, metropolitan-suburban districting, and a host of other areas of life, will continue to be apparent for many years.

Constitutional or high courts represent what might be called the "myth of impartiality." Like the statue of justice represented by a blindfolded woman holding the scale before her, justice is blind. But the mind's eye represents wisdom, and the combination keeps the scales in balance. So a high court represents Plato's vision—the jurists and justices are to democratic societies what philosophers-kings were to the Republic, the rationality of the society—and Aristotle's distributive justice as well: the scales must balance.[12]

11. See the discussion in Carl J. Friedrich, *Constitutional Government and Democracy* (Waltham, Mass.: Blaisdell Publishing Company, 1968), pp. 249–65. See also Joseph La Palombara, *Politics Within Nations* (Englewood Cliffs, N.J.: Prentice-Hall, 1974), and S. E. Finer, *Comparative Government* (London: Allen Lane, The Penguin Press, 1970).
12. See Harold J. Laski, *The American Democracy* (New York: Viking Press, 1948), pp. 110–16.

The Roots of Government

Political parties: The judiciary and the administration are supposed to stand aloof from the politics of the day although they have profound political consequences. Parties, on the other hand, do precisely the opposite: they represent the connecting link between the public and the government. Parties build coalitions of interests and persuasions which most people support. They engage in open competition. They make the system work.

Political parties are the most important single instrumentality of politics, its competitiveness, its bargaining, its negotiations. They enable politicians to remain close to the public on the one hand and be a lot of different things to a lot of different people. On the other hand, when they achieve public office, politicians are supposed to be able to rise above the immediate morass of interests and represent a more general public interest. Some do and some do not, obviously, but that is all part of the party game.

While justice is blind, political parties have eyes in the back of their heads. They are on the lookout all the time for trends, problems, issues, and analyses of how these affect the basis of their support. Party politicians are like salespeople and entrepreneurs. They are the equivalent in the political sphere to the fellow who sells snake oil and horse liniment for sore throats. So politicians are supposed to be the very opposite of the civil servant or the robed justice. No robes for them, and no patrician tradition. If the idea of disinterestedness is the key to an efficient judiciary, the favors to be gained from interested service represent the patronage of the politician.

Political parties have various functions. The primary function of an organized party is to win elections. The better the organization, the more likely the party is to win, other things being equal. Good organization requires funding, talent, and a permanent staff. In pursuit of winning, political parties also seek out issues that concern the voters. They help to define policy needs, they shape legislation, and they facilitate government business.

Political party organization can be discussed in terms of elements of coalition, the extent to which the party is diverse or homogeneous in membership, the extent to which it is organized on a constituency basis, the extent of party control over the selection and elevation of candidates to public office, and the degree of discipline the party exercises over its members in the legislature. Some parties are ideological. Some are more pragmatic in conception. Others are bureaucratic.[13]

Some parties represent broad coalitions in order to appeal to the widest possible number of potential voters. Such *coalition parties* tend to be less ideological than pragmatic.

In countries in which parties are highly organized and reflect a relatively divided population, cleavage politics are practiced rather than coalitional politics. *Cleavage parties* are those that serve a particular clientele with a specific ideology. Cleavage parties reject the ideologies of other parties in specific respects, say, nationalization of industry. Cleavage politics tends to produce intense party loyalties. If there are many parties, legislative bargaining occurs to form coalitions to lead the government. (Italian politics are of this nature, two major cleavage parties being until recently at any rate the Communists and the Christian Democrats.) Where cleavage parties are large, the cleavages tend to be papered over by moderate appeals.

Cell parties, as Duverger calls them, are those composed of ideological purists and militants who require devotion to the party ends as a fundamental commitment. Such parties are like religious parties once were. Loyalty to party is the same as loyalty to country in the sense that, if the party captures power, then the ideals of the party will become the ideals of the country. Most communist, fascist, and other extremist parties are of this nature. They differ from the others, coalitional or cleavage, in the sense that they are monopolistic, using the rules of the electoral game in order to win power but then changing the rules so that other parties cannot oust them.[14]

Perhaps the most basic distinction is between democratic and totalitarian parties. Democratic parties are pluralistic. Totalitarian parties accept the idea of rectitude of only one party. They are monopolistic. The contrast can be set out as in Table 6-1.[15]

Democratic parties are really very different in their goals and objectives from totalitarian parties. They are the instruments of the people, using their many differences as a mosaic out of which to build programs to satisfy a broad spectrum or appeal to a particular clientele. But cell parties are willing to appeal to a mass only in order to gain power. We can sum up the difference in main functions between democratic and totalitarian politics in Table 6-2.

13. See Robert Michels, *Political Parties* (Glencoe, Ill.: The Free Press, 1949) .
14. See Maurice Duverger, *Political Parties* (New York: Wiley, 1954) .
15. See Harry Eckstein and D. E. Apter, eds., *Comparative Politics* (New York: Free Press of Glencoe, 1963) , pp. 327–32.

Table 6-1. Party Relationships and Characteristics

Unit	Democratic Parties	Totalitarian Parties
	Pluralistic: competitive with other parties	Monopolistic: seeks to eliminate other parties
Community	Representative: seeks to incorporate divergent views in order to win the widest following	Directive: seeks to amalagamate grievances in order to overthrow the existing order; or, if in power, to bend the community towards goals laid down by the party
Government	Constitutional: party action is limited by constitutional, conventional, and electoral rules	Extraconstitutional: accepts legal order only insofar as it is forced to. When in control of government, the party bends the government and constitution to serve party ends. The party makes the state subservient to itself.

Some countries try to avoid making these distinctions. A good many developing countries have experimented with single noncompetitive party systems using a cross between a cleavage party and a totalitarian one. For example, in Tanzania, the Tanzania African National Union (TANU) is a broad coalitional party based originally on cleavage parties. All other parties having been banned, electoral competition and factional dispute form the basis of the single-party politics.

What is most important about political parties today is that, while they were once based on class cleavages in both intent and purpose (the Conservative Party represented mainly the landed aristocracy, the Whig

Table 6-2. Party Functions

Democratic Parties	Totalitarian Parties
1. Control over the executive	1. Inducing solidarity
2. Representation of interests	2. Coercion
3. Competitive recruitment to office	3. Direction of government

Party represented mercantile interests, the Labor Party represented the working class) , cleavage parties have gradually given way to coalitional parties. This, in turn, reflects changes in social classes; the boundaries between them become more blurred as their social characteristics are altered with greater mobility.

Whatever their constitutional status, parties transmit public attitudes. They stand between the people and government. They thus convert public opinion into elective power by mobilizing support. Power, in turn, is converted into policy by government. The organization of governmental bodies, their duration, size, procedures, how (and why) they are dissolved, the character and powers of upper and lower chambers, the committees that compose them, their responsiveness to lobbies, how they establish priorities, their methods for ending debate, their methods in proposing financial legislation, the extent to which they defer to lesser jurisdictions like provinces or states or other units of local government—all this and more forms the descriptive substance of the institutional approach to politics (see Figure 6-4) .

A constitution puts a frame around the electoral system, legislatures, the executive, and executive administration. The people put life into these mechanisms by means of party. Where party politics are actively pursued and the connections between these bodies are well made and functioning, then the result is an appropriate flow of legislation and amendment.

In totalitarian countries, however, the courts are an instrument of the government. The government is the instrument of a single agency—Nazi or Communist party, for example, or perhaps the army. The legis-

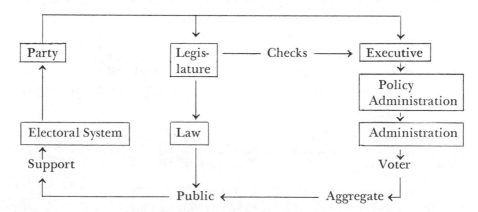

Figure 6-4. The Institutional Approach to Politics

lature responds to the executive. This totalitarian alternative can be diagrammed as follows:

The precondition of democracy is informed public opinion. Freedom of discussion, the press, and assembly are essential for making and acting out public demands. Public opinion, channeled by party leaders and activists, generates support. In turn, support, channeled through political parties and interest groups, generates power. Competition between parties and candidates for public support in the electoral system ranks public preferences and priorities; the conversion of preferences into support by electoral victory determines a mandate for public policy.

Parties are the source of some of the worst abuses in political life—corruption, manipulation by special interests, broken campaign promises. But parties are also transmission belts that transform the welter of conflicting and private opinions, factions, and demands into something approximating the public interest. A party, no matter what else it does, is always something more than a collection of parochial interests, if only because it must always convert special demands into a larger public platform in order to maximize support. If the result is that government is carried out by compromise, it is also to be hoped that the compromise carries with it some sort of consensus.[16]

Interest and pressure groups: Parties exist to win power. This is true of coalitional, cleavage, or cell, democratic or totalitarian parties. *Interest groups,* to the contrary, seek to influence policy without actually taking on the responsibilities of power. To this extent they are not responsible and do not want to be responsible for political action.

Some interest groups, like trade unions, represent particular segments of the population that have protective functions quite apart from their influence in politics. Influence is a by-product of other activities such as collective bargaining and direct dealing with management.

16. Parties are also "brokers" of ideas, and the connecting link between government and public opinion. See Sigmund Neuman, "Toward a Comparative Study of Political Parties," in S. Neuman, ed., *Modern Political Parties* (Chicago: University of Chicago Press, 1956), pp. 400–401. See also Giovanni Sartori, *Parties and Party Systems* (Cambridge: Cambridge University Press, 1976), and Kay Lawson, *The Comparative Study of Political Parties* (New York: St. Martin's Press, 1976).

Other interest groups consist of specialized interests or broad coalitions favoring business, or professional associations concerned both with the conditions of the profession and with lobbying for benefits.

Interest groups influence the selection of political party candidates, contribute to party campaign chests, and are close to, if not actually involved in, manipulating power for favors, which is what corruption is all about. At the same time, because of the diversity of interests prevailing in modern society and the fact that coalitional or even cleavage parties cannot cater to the diversity of prevailing interests, interest groups are a necessary and essential part of democratic politics.

Pressure groups are more limited in function. They form expressly for the purpose of influencing politicians and their policies. Pressure groups use lobbyists, peddle influence, and resort to a variety of practices mostly under the guise of "educating" legislators about their particular interest.[17]

Since interest and pressure groups can form around any issue, why is there such doubt about their propriety? Many doubt the methods by which they work. Acting behind the scene, they are not subject to public review and scrutiny. Their influence is recognizable less in terms of deliverable votes, than as possible secret kickbacks or payoffs to officials, party organizers, and so forth. Hence, they wield influence that not only is not above board, but that is considered to be an unfair form of access to power.

The most regular connection between interest groups and government is in the form of a lobby. A **lobby** is a registered and explicitly organized body devoted to the interests of a particular group in society. It may represent workers, blacks, school teachers, an association of railways, or some other interest group. Lobbyists try to make sure that the views of their supporting bodies are heard, particularly when hearings are held on legislation affecting them. Since every major piece of legislation affects all sorts of groups, lobbying becomes more rather than less important as time goes on.

In the United States, one of the problems with interest groups in the past was that they tended to favor the rich and the powerful, who had the resources to affect party politics. Slowly, however, the picture has changed somewhat. First trade unions became more effective in pursuing interest-group politics. Then representatives of minority groups followed suit. Finally, there is today a new kind of interest group, some-

17. See Richard Rose, *Politics in England* (Boston: Little, Brown and Co., 1964), pp. 124–39.

times called a *citizens lobby,* which attempts to pursue goals of a public interest rather than a private one. Such important figures as Ralph Nader and John Gardner have organized such lobbying in the interests of citizens and consumers without regard for political parties. These groups serve as watchdogs of the public interest in matters such as environmental protection.

The effects of interest groups can be conceived as sinister because their activities are kept relatively secret. But interest groups also help fill the gap between party representation and public policy making that affects particular groups in society.[18] They are the agents of powerful nonpolitical interests, but they may also give voice to smaller groups whose ability to voice grievances or affect the policy-making process would otherwise be totally ineffectual.

The influence of such groups and their extraparliamentary significance has been well recognized by institutionalists.[19] The problem is that, while the value of such influence may have beneficial effects, the chances are more likely that it will be deleterious and that the public interest will be undercut. The issue is how public interest can be reconciled with private interests outside of the usual and proper channels of representative government.

The civil service:[20] There is another part of government which, like the judiciary, is also supposed to be outside of politics in a democratic society. This is the civil service. The purpose of a disinterested civil service is two-fold: (1) disinterestedness prevents the administration from being corrupt; (2) civil service professionals should be able to serve, with equal conviction and faithfulness, whatever administration is elected by the people. The job of a civil service, then, is to help the executive execute the laws, but not become part of the law-making process.

Of course, like a supreme court, a civil service incurs politics at every turn. Just as judicial review produces decisions that are of great political consequence, so too does the administration of the law. Indeed, as the civil service systems of various countries have become elaborated and complex, some have established special courts to protect individuals from their arbitrary exercise of power. France, for example, has admin-

---

18. See S. E. Finer, *Anonymous Empire* (London: The Pall Mall Press, 1958).
19. See M. Ostrogorski, *Democracy and the Organization of Political Parties,* 2 vols. (New York: Doubleday Anchor Books, 1964).
20. The best description of a modern bureaucracy is still that of Max Weber. See H. H. Gerth and C. Wright Mills, eds., *From Max Weber* (New York: Oxford University Press, 1948), pp. 196–244.

istrative courts in which citizens who believe themselves to have been treated unfairly or summarily by a civil servant, can seek redress. In Sweden, where this idea was first introduced, a parliamentary commissioner, or ombudsman, is designated to investigate complaints about the behavior of officials. The system has spread through Scandinavia, Britain, and many Commonwealth countries. The ombudsman is usually a representative of the legislature endowed with investigative powers.[21]

Most people tend to think of an encounter with the civil service bureaucracy as, at worst, an infringement on their rights, and at best a necessary evil. But contrary to this attitude is the fact that the more participation there is by the public in political life and the more complex are the decisions made, the greater necessity there is for an active bureaucracy. The wish to do away with it is simply a nostalgia for a simpler time that will never return. A fundamental change in perspectives about the civil service is what is really needed. In Europe, it tends to be considered as a rational and hierarchical organization. Entry is by competitive examination, and individuals are promoted on the basis of their efficient performance of duties and intelligent and resourceful dealings with the public. Civil servants are protected from public scrutiny or pressure by appropriate ministers in charge of their departments. If something should go wrong, one minister must answer for it, not an individual civil servant.

Such a bureaucracy represents a cadre of specialists different from those of lawyers or politicians. Traditionally in Europe, members of the civil service were recruited from the educated classes and the best universities. Government administration had a noble tradition, representing an extension of the king's household, broadened to include the administration of the state. Its growth therefore has been coterminous with the growth of modern government. Hence, in most European countries the administration has come to represent—even more than the politician—government itself. Civil servants tend to have a sense of discipline. Exemplary behavior is expected of them and, in many societies, they constitute a kind of class. The organization of the educational system in France, for example, is based on a selective screening process to train future civil servants.[22]

21. See Joseph LaPalombara, *Politics Within Nations* (Englewood Cliffs, N.J.: Prentice-Hall, 1974) , pp. 165–66.
22. See Michel Crozier, *The Bureaucratic Phenomenon* (Chicago: University of Chicago Press, 1963) , pp. 237–58. See also Terry Nichols Clarke, *Prophets and Patrons* (Cambridge: Harvard University Press, 1973) .

Particularly where there is political instability, a government comes to be a creature of its civil servants. During the Third and Fourth Republics in France, cabinet instability was compensated for only by the continuity and power of the senior French civil servants who, as their ministers came and went, ignored the politicians as much as possible.

How to keep the bureaucratic class responsible to politicians and the public, and how to prevent it from becoming isolated and autocratic has always been a problem. How to have "representative bureaucracy" is one way to put the question.

Certain institutionalists, such as Woodrow Wilson, regarded the theory of administration that developed in France and Germany at the end of the nineteenth century as a science. Wilson also believed in a radical separation between the political arena—which was sensitive to issues, ideologies, and demands, and the politicians who served these— and administration, which had continuity, and whose members accepted the ideal of "disinterested" service to the state.[23]

A civil service is always in a delicate position. Standing apart from the politics and politicians of the day it nevertheless is the instrument for executing the laws. Without a civil service a chief executive is powerless.[24] Ideally, the administrator should balance the politician. The administrator can afford a longer view. The politician cannot. The one is a permanent member of a service, a career administrator. Politicians come and go, subject to the fickleness of the electorate. The civil servant relies more and more on finding effective principles of management, efficient processes, clientele, organizational relationships, and patterns of hierarchy.[25] Today's concern is on analyzing bureaucratic behavior, the psychology of bureaucratic agencies, and how bureaucracies act as information systems.[26]

Electoral systems: The connecting link between community and government is the political party. The legislature is the sovereign power of the

23. See the useful discussion of Wilson's point of view in Vincent Ostrom, *The Intellectual Crisis in American Public Administration* (Alabama: University of Alabama Press, 1973), pp. 24–29.
24. See W. W. Willoughby, *The Ethical Basis of Political Authority* (New York: Macmillan, 1930), pp. 385–409. See also Richard H. S. Crossman, *The Myths of Cabinet Government* (Cambridge: Harvard University Press, 1972).
25. See Luther Gulick and L. Urwick, eds., *Papers on the Science of Administration* (New York: Columbia University Press, 1937).
26. See Anthony Downs, *Inside Bureaucracy* (Boston: Little, Brown and Co., 1967). See also F. T. Haner, *Business Policy, Planning, and Strategy* (Cambridge: Winthrop Publishers, 1976), pp. 329–44.

citizen exercised by the representatives. Checks and balances, separation of powers, parliamentary control, all are contingent on the way the public selects candidates and elects some of them to office. How candidates are selected, the system of party caucuses, primary campaigns, and the methods of party organization are part of the institutionalist's proper concern with how the political system can be made to work. For present purposes the most important dynamic feature of democratic politics is the vote, and the mechanisms through which voting occurs, that is, the electoral system.

The problem of any electoral system is first of all to qualify the voters. Should suffrage extend to all citizens or only to those with appropriate education, say, or property? Do voters need something more at stake in society than citizenship in order to qualify? All democratic societies began with a limited franchise and in all, mostly gradually, by means of electoral reform, this franchise has been widened. The usual and original qualification was the ownership of property, then some minimum standard of education. Then came universal manhood suffrage, and finally universal suffrage. Women have been the last group to receive the vote.

Of course, as the franchise was extended two problems became apparent. One was that previously powerful and significant groups could maintain their power despite a widened franchise. The other was how the various diverse interests could be properly aggregated and focused for appropriate representation. In the first instance, an upper house—made up of a "responsible" elite—served the purpose of delaying the decline of previously important groups. Different systems of election, the size of the electoral constituency, the method of election, and the number of representatives from a constituency all affect the overall representativeness of the political system. It is to this aspect of electoral systems that we shall now turn.

Elections are institutionalized procedures for choosing representatives for political office. The simplest method is for each citizen to represent one vote, and for each constituency to elect one representative by means of a simple plurality, that is, the largest number of votes. This system is sometimes called the *first-past-the-post* system. The tendency is for parties to winnow out all appeals to the electorate, except those that are the most attractive to the largest number of voters. Then they find the next most attractive group of issues with which to appeal to the next larger group, and so on, until identifying the party with a particular issue is likely to cost more than can be gained (or be of too little general interest). The result is a tendency toward broad coalitional parties. Elections under such circumstances are what Lakeman and Lambert call a "plebiscite between two potential governments."[27]

This kind of electoral system tends to ride roughshod over differences. Where there are no fundamental cleavages in the society it works reasonably well, and tends towards stable government. But where cleavages exist in society, and are cross-cutting (class cleavage, for example, being somewhat different than ethnic or religious cleavage), then many groups are not effectively represented as such in an election.

To compensate for this a number of different solutions have been proposed, including systems of *weighted voting*—in which some votes count more than others, *gerrymandering*—manipulating particular constituency boundaries to favor the representation of some specific group, and others. The most common alternative to the first-past-the-post electoral system is *proportional representation*. The two most common forms of proportional representation are the Hare system and the list system. Both are designed to offset the problem that arises when, by a bare majority, one party wins everything.

Without going into technical details, the *Hare system* involves multiple-member constituencies in which some minimum proportion is necessary for an individual candidate to be elected. Candidates are ranked according to preference and the one who receives the minimum proportion is elected. Then votes no longer needed by that candidate are transferred to the next preferred candidate on the ballot and the weakest candidate with the poorest showing withdraws. This then provides the basis for preferential balloting and a second round of voting.

The other frequently used method of proportional representation is the *list system*. The list system works best where there are multiple cleavages in society represented by cleavage parties such as religious parties, or business parties, and so forth. Belgium, Holland, Denmark, Sweden, Finland, and several other countries all use list systems. In a list system, a voter votes not for a candidate but a party list. Constituencies are multimembered, but the voter casts one vote for the party list. The idea is that the number of seats are divided among parties according to their proportion of votes. Various methods have been devised for reapportioning votes according to the weight of party support after the first party reaches a certain quota and is elected. One method is the

27. See Enid Lakeman and James D. Lambert, *Voting in Democracies* (London: Faber and Faber, 1959), p. 39.

principle of the *highest average*. Seats are allocated one by one, and each goes to the list that would have the highest average number of votes per seat, *if* it received the seat in question (this method is called the *d'Hondt rule*). The other method is the *greatest remainder system,* which is a method of dividing total votes cast by the number of seats to be awarded, then reallocating remaining seats according to votes cast by competing lists.[28]

There are other methods of cleavage voting. In some countries communal rolls have been prepared that allow different racial groups to participate in a common election by means of votes weighted within the group. Few of these devices work very satisfactorily, but they may help to prepare the way for full elections by slowly lessening the power of a privileged election minority. That is what occurred in countries such as Tanzania and Kenya, in which small but superordinate, racially dominant groups slowly gave way before large, subordinated nonvoting majorities.

Proportional representation, then, favors cleavage politics and, depending on how deep the cleavages are, may be more representative. The proportional system may also be more unstable than single-member plurality systems of voting. Nevertheless, broad stable coalitional politics have resulted from cleavage politics plus proportional representation in Scandinavia. Where this occurs, the list system works to promote coalition out of cleavage, and has the combined effect of both generating more representative parties and the stabilizing of equivalent two-party systems.

Institutional Models

All the institutions discussed in the previous section combine to form representative government. The prerequisite is a population that knows its interests and is willing to convert competition into a peaceful selection of authorized representatives by means of elections. Power is fractionalized but cooperation renders it into policy. The bases are an informed electorate, individual liberty, the secret ballot, and a free press. The judiciary guarantees all of these. At the same time, how policy is carried out is up to the administration.

A flow of appropriate legislation maintains equilibrium. If at some

28. The best short treatment of the system of proportional representation and its variants is W. J. Mackenzie, *Free Elections* (London: George Allen and Unwin, 1958), pp. 75–84.

point this equilibrium begins to break down, reform is required. Reforms in the modes of participation, the methods of election, the flow of government business in the committee system, the reform of campaign financing, or any other aspect of the mechanism are the objects of institutionalist political science.

If too much checking without balancing is carried on, then a division of powers, basic disagreement over the terms of rule, and a lack of fundamental acceptance of the legitimacy of government can result. There will be no authority and no equilibrium. The English and American systems represent successfully equilibrated societies because the demands and needs of individuals versus groups are balanced by appropriate decisions of government and the successful enactment of these into legislation, followed up by effective administration. This flow of authority requires at least a minimum consensus by all parties about what constitutes the public good. Legislation, both by catering to the needs of people and by fulfilling the principles they regard to be appropriate to society, is, then, the active fulfillment of the mandate to rule. Only through legislating can an equilibrium society remain relatively efficient. The stalemated society lacks this minimum consensus. Accordingly, one of the key institutionalist problems is how to ensure that the equilibrium society will not turn into a stalemate society or, more positively, how a stalemate society can be converted into an equilibrium society.

If the institutionalist model of politics is based on a relationship of institutions with principles of rule, these will have different consequences depending on how much participation there is by the members of the society. Such representation needs to be balanced and distributed in multiple units of government. In principle, the greater the degree of participation, the more decentralized the units of governing and the greater the degree of democracy. This we can graph as shown in Figure 6-5.

At each point *a, b, c* in the diagram, there is an increased degree of sharing of the power among more and more instrumentalities of government. At point *a,* a political system is relatively *monistic,* with power concentrated in a few units of government, or even a single figure. At point *c,* the system is *pluralistic,* with power shared broadly in the community and distributed among many jurisdictions. One institutionalist question is: When does power become so participant and so broadly distributed as to make government impossible? A second is how to organize participation and distribute power among units so as to

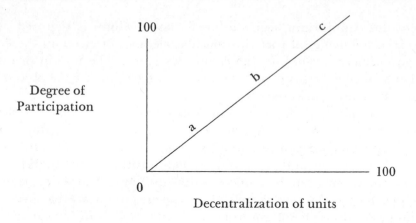

Figure 6-5. Power and Democracy

prevent a stalemate society and promote an equilibrium society. What is the optimal point? What is the model at the optimal point?

The model of democratic government at point *c* in Figure 6-5 looks like the diagram in Figure 6-6.

The promotion of ends and interests takes the form of legislation, which accords with principles of justice, liberty, and equality and satisfies both the public's needs and its sense of appropriateness about how things are done. Legislation provides the societal basis or consensus for stability, order, and control. At the same time, within that large consensus, government can act to control the political conflicts arising from factional conflict or party competition by means of improved electoral methods, changes in party financing, or other means.

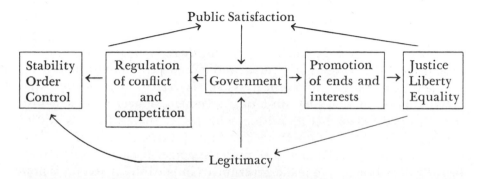

Figure 6-6. The Model of Democratic Politics

The institutionalist typology: Institutionalists have developed an elaborate typology of regimes, or governmental systems. These form, between two poles, the monistic versus the pluralistic versions of society, constituting ideal and opposite ends on a continuum along which various political systems—totalitarian, authoritarian, or democratic—can be pinpointed. Democratic systems are subdivided into two main types: presidential and parliamentary, with many mixed variations also occurring; that is, strong president combined with weak prime minister and parliament as in France, weak president combined with strong prime minister and parliament as in Italy, and so on.

These characteristics of institutionalist theory provide us with the basis of a standard typology of political systems useful for comparing concrete cases.

It is useful in limiting our discussion to a comparison of the two democratic types, presidential and parliamentary, to establish a set of questions for purposes of discussion. Each type concentrates power in a different way. Each shares a network of similar instrumentalities, electoral systems, political parties, legislatures, executives, and bureaucracies. The criteria used by institutionalists for their comparison are basically the following questions: How is power divided between executive, judicial, and legislative branches? Is the executive an elected president separate from the legislature or is it drawn from the majority party of the legislature or some plurality? Are elections held on the basis of universal suffrage, or are there discriminating qualifications? Does the judiciary have the function of judicial review? How critical is its role in protecting individual rights? How difficult is amendment to the constitution? How informed is the electorate? How free is the free press? How secure are rights to free expression? Is power centralized at the top of a national jurisdiction? If at the top, are these powers concentrated in the legislature with the executive being a special committee of parliament called a cabinet? Must members be elected to parliament? Is parliament supreme and how effectively does it exercise control over

	Totalitarian	Authoritarian	Democratic
Federal	USSR	Yugoslavia	USA
Unitary	Fascist Italy	Spain	Great Britain

Figure 6-7. The Institutionalists' Typology of Political Systems

the executive? Does the government fail if it loses the confidence of the parliament? Is power distributed between national and local jurisdictions in which residual rights belong first to the several jurisdictions and to individuals? Is residual power at the top further fractionalized by a system of checks and balances? Answers to such questions are essentially descriptive. But from them one can build up a textured, powerful, and informative picture of political processes.

The ingredients of a democratic government require analysts to examine institutions other than purely political ones, especially economic and social ones. Social institutions include the educational system. Economic considerations include the degree of industrial development and employment the society exhibits. In a good system, social legislation and laws affecting the protection of the individual are a result of needs of the electorate, expressed by political parties that dedicate their legislative programs to the task of satisfying those needs, relayed through the process of executive decision making, compromised so as not to offend other interests, and implemented in reaching policies designed to improve conditions overall.

The institutional dilemma: The two-fold predicament of democracy as defined by institutionalists is to prevent the stalemate society and to promote the equilibrium society. The problem of excessive decentralization and participation is that no decisions can be made. Too much democracy can result in stalemate. But, too much concentration of power to a few all-powerful individuals or jurisdictions will impair democracy. Finding the appropriate balance between these is to the institutionalist the main object of political science.

Where there are too many units and too much participation, agreement becomes difficult. At the same time, as societies become more complex, people agree less and less and their concern with principles gets pushed into the background. The political crises most people relate to in their daily lives are those of making ends meet, providing education for their children, establishing safety in the streets, solving problems of the environment, and so on. When these go unresolved or are continuously exacerbated, often by the very solutions that are proposed to alleviate them, then concern with principles is resurrected in the form of powerful ideological conflicts and totalistic solutions. The democratic tendency is to concentrate regulatory powers in the effort to solve problems; violence, for example, results in stronger and more centralized law-enforcement agencies. However, this solution may fail to handle the problem of violence because it represents an effort at controlling effects rather than removing the cause. Eventually ineffective controls increase public suspicion of the efficacy of government solutions, and of government itself.

The alternative is politically to induce promotion of more opportunities at a level so great as to effect a net increase in the satisfaction of people. This is more and more difficult to do as society becomes complex. An important inadequacy in institutionalist theory is its handling of this developmental problem.

Is it possible to decentralize power in society, adding many more units of participation—including worker participation in the decisions of management—while retaining the structure of private capitalism? Does more democracy require socialism? But does socialism produce such bureaucratic hierarchy as to deny pluralism? This extension of the institutionalist predicament into a more systematic and abstract form becomes "the pluralist dilemma." As we will see, it is much more universal than might appear and it stirs issues that will be preoccupying future political analysts for some time to come. We shall return to this theme later on, in the unit on pluralism, after first analyzing the bases of various specific institutions—how they came to be preferred, how they interact, what their variants are.

chapter seven
Institutionalism and Democratic Government

The Democratic Tradition

Until relatively recently, to survey political history was to observe a wavering but seemingly unbroken line of liberty winning out over autocracy as governments became more and more democratic. The ideal of a community of nations in which the rule of law, representation, and secure freedoms for all has prevailed. With such democracy all can realize their own potentialities. Each reinforces the other, society nurtures the citizen, the citizens contribute their measure to the community. Improvement in the prosperity of mind of the one betters the material condition of the other. The philosopher's model of the good society —rulers and ruled, means and ends—is thus realized in the institutionalist's model. The latter accounts for the sovereignty of the people, electoral competition, and political parties. These convey power to government, which, checked and balanced through the legislative system, is responsive to the citizens who, as voters, approve or disavow their representatives in periodic regularized elections. So the philosopher's models become reality, not merely in theory, but through a system of open government. History shows its progress throughout the world.

Modern models of representative government are England and the United States. The two share certain traditions: common law, freedom, dignity. The French state is more ambiguous. The French introduced the idea of equality as a social rather than a purely political condition. This radical vein in French politics is one of the causes of its instability. For a long time France was thus a puzzling case to institutionalists because it could not compose its social problems by democratic means.

Lord Bryce, a British journalist and member of Parliament, in the preface to his study of modern democracy, hit just the right self-congratulatory note in writing in 1920:

With 1789 the world passed into a new phase, but the ten years that followed were for France years of revolution, in which democracy had no chance of improving its quality. It was only in the United States that popular governments could be profitably studied, and when Tocqueville studied them in 1827 they had scarcely begun to show some of their characteristic features.

Within the hundred years that now lie behind us what changes have passed upon the world! Nearly all the monarchies of the Old World have turned into democracies. The States of the American Union have grown from thirteen to forty-eight. While twenty new republics have sprung up in the Western hemisphere, five new democracies have been developed out of colonies within the British dominions. There are now more than one hundred representative assemblies at work all over the earth legislating for self-governing communities; and the proceedings of nearly all of these are recorded in the press. Thus, the materials for a study of free governments have been and are accumulating so fast that the most diligent student cannot keep pace with the course of political evolution in more than a few out of these many countries.

. . . It is not the nature of democracy, nor even the variety of the shapes it wears, that are today in debate, but rather the purpose to which it may be turned, the social and economic changes it may be used to effect; yet its universal acceptance is not a tribute to the smoothness of its working, for discontent is everywhere rife. . . .

The time seems to have arrived when the actualities of democratic government, in its diverse forms, should be investigated, and when the conditions most favorable to its success should receive more attention. . . .

The new functions that are being thrust upon governments in every civilized country, should make it more than ever necessary that their machinery should be so constructed as to discharge these functions efficiently and in full accord with the popular wish.[1]

Bryce wrote these brave words at the end of World War I, defining the central task for political scientists for an entire generation. His emphasis was to show how representation worked in various parts of the globe to fit community and government together, and what diversity of instruments could achieve those ends. What we have come to call the

1. James Bryce, *Modern Democracies* (New York: Macmillan, 1921), p. 4.

machinery of government became the practical concern for a principled civility.

As Bryce and his liberal contemporaries saw the problem, democracy was not a fit subject either for Machiavellians or totalitarians. Parliamentary and representative institutions embodied in them universal principles of freedom, obligation, and responsibility. Those who did not subscribe to such views were disqualified from thinking about them. "Machiavelli's teaching would hardly have stood the test of parliamentary government," said Lord Acton, "for public discussion demands at least the profession of good faith."[2]

In the first part of this century, political observers saw democracy not as just one among many political forms. It was the universally *preferred* form. Today, while we are more cautious about ascribing to all societies the judgmental values incumbent in a society that learns to prefer competitive democratic systems, we still cannot deny, however, that democracy bestows special meanings on its instrumentalities. While it is possible to discuss the activities of political parties in totalitarian countries—for example, the Communist Party in the USSR—the meaning, purpose, and functions of those parties differ so fundamentally from the functions of parties in a democracy or representative system that using the same term for both is a misnomer. Democracy, or to put it less ideally, representative government, requires that the parties function in terms of purposes. Goals are self-evident: Liberty and order, which make up the good society, are molded under some constitutional form into an ideal of perfection that political scientists try to realize in practice.

Improvement, in the democratic tradition, means continuous reform; in representation, quality of legislation, organization, and so forth. Improvement requires at least two parties; one to press for more and quicker reform, one to hold back, helping to preserve the status quo and the continuity of the system. The confidence of the electorate is sustained between these poles. Since democracy requires a consensus between rulers and ruled, if the ruled lose confidence, the rulers sense this withdrawal of faith and act, hopefully, to dispel it. Confidence depends partly on getting good governors, on reverence for august institutions, and on the maintenance of dignity at the center.[3]

These issues, and the instrumentalities and processes through which

2. Lord Acton, *Essays on Freedom and Power* (Boston: Beacon Press, 1949), p. 68.
3. See Harold J. Laski, *A Grammar of Politics* (London: George Allen and Unwin, 1938).

they are made practicable, represent the raw materials of the institutionalist. We want to show how these are used by analyzing them in terms of their political function in England and the United States and, more briefly, France. In addition to relating more specifically the roles of those institutions discussed in Chapter Six, we shall examine their bases in national consciousness.

Constitutional Principles and Political Practice

In British practice, the "Crown-in-Council" represents the nation. In American practice, the nation is the people. The distinction may appear to be a minor one, but it illustrates why the rights and privileges of the American people must be so clearly outlined, and why limited powers and limited government are so important. To Americans, the growth of government infringes on private rights. The American legal conception is that any powers given to the government are powers taken away from the people. In contrast, in British theory there are no private rights, except those authorized, endowed, and secured by Parliament. In practice, rights may have time-honored and conventional effect, but they are not inalienable or specifically guaranteed as they are in the American Bill of Rights.

The spirit of the two constitutions, the unwritten and the written, differs. Conservative and proprietary, the British constitution represents those social attitudes towards government that have been built up out of a web of legal precedent and fought for over the years. The United States Constitution, although more populist and individualistic, does not easily accept government as the agent of primary responsibility for the well-being of the citizens. Each individual looks after himself or herself. What needs safeguarding is the individual's liberty, and that primarily against governmental encroachment. Hence, to most Americans, as to Ralph Waldo Emerson, that government is best which governs least. The two systems coincide in the common acceptance of the idea that personal freedom is inseparable from the rule of law. Both depend on law to safeguard the public against despotism.

The American Constitution is a brilliant and adaptive document. However, very much a product of the eighteenth century, its individualistic preconceptions and libertarian ideals do not square very well with the more modern concern with equality, or the effect of economic discrimination on liberty and individual rights. It balks at the principle, so accepted now in Europe, that an appropriate use of governmental powers is to promote the general welfare in social and economic terms.[4] Government intervention on the side of the poor and the weak is suspect. There is good reason for the Constitution's reliance on purely political notions of liberty and equality. Should political life become a jurisprudence of interests rather than of principle—social not individual—then who would interpret the various interests? If the state were to establish priorities, the danger would be that the principles of the Constitution would be vitiated by big government, the growth of which would gain momentum from the need to intervene in the public interest. Such a development would destroy the concept of limited government and pave the way for social democracy.[5]

The idea of social democracy puts a strain on the American constitution. It is far more easily absorbed in the British system, where there is no constitutional problem. There it is a matter of ordinary politics. To what extent can the Labour Party organize an attractive social welfare program, establish medical health schemes, revise taxation schedules, and intervene in any number of aspects of life? As far as Parliament wants to go. The programmatic test is in the political marketplace, a matter of majorities and pluralities.

Whatever the differences between British and American practice, and there are many, the constitutions of both comprise more than the letters of the laws. There is the matter of custom and principle as well as the distinction between the federal and the unitary systems. To examine the effects of the differences requires an evaluation of the political system in practice, but institutionalists do not restrict their analyses to the exercise of power, its legal limits, and its practices. They concern themselves with the scope and range of political action, that is, the give and take of the political process itself. Even the most elaborated constitution under the best circumstances remains only an *enabling* document that establishes boundaries around the exercise of power and organizes the flow of power. A constitution is silent as to the *content* of political interest, and also on a good many of the "transmission belts" of public power, most particularly political parties and interest groups. The nonspecific institutions, however, are what keep constitutional

4. For example, in Sweden, France, and elsewhere, there are much more extensive schemes for health, unemployment, modernity, and other benefits than in the United States.
5. For the best discussion of this point of view see Friedrich A. Hayek, *The Constitution of Liberty* (Chicago: University of Chicago Press, 1960) pp. 234–49.

principles attuned to everyday matters, allowing for development and change along the continuum of improvement. As such, these mundane manifestations of political activity in society are the stuff of institutional analysis.

The parliamentary model: The English parliamentary system is a model for institutionalists. Where else are stability, prosperity, and intelligence so effectively combined with representative government? The English form of representative government provides balance between the growing political education of the public and its opportunity to participate on the one hand, and the public's deferential willingness to let the elite rule on the other. This is a holdover from the tradition of postfeudal obligations. Deference was dressed up in the theater, drama, and mysticism of a nobility, not to speak of a monarchy, that still represented continuity while losing power. Libertarian views combined with a general attitude that the lower orders should be heard as much and seen as little as possible by those in the high places of rule.[6]

Reform created popular support. This was one visible aspect of English politics. The other, more radical—although not Marxist—inheritance in England is represented by the Levellers, the Diggers, Puritanism, Methodism, working men's chapel movements, Chartism, and the rest.[7] The course of English history has never been smooth. There were savage conflicts throughout the seventeenth and eighteenth centuries. Strikes and economic conflicts began early in the nineteenth century with the activities of the chartists. Perhaps it was because of such conflict that democracy in England survived and prospered. Indeed, without English radicalism the prevailing principles of participation were so limited and so tempered to a slow pace of change that they would have allowed few basic alterations in the political life of the people. Radicalism then was the driving force behind the expansion of the franchise, and after 1906, behind the establishment of a Labour Party and the move towards socialism. Still the balance was never lost. The key was gradualism. The party of the left was always practical and reforming (like the Fabian socialists). The party of the right, although imperial and ceremonial (the Tories), had a caretaker view of society. (Hence the term "Tory radical-

---

6. For an interesting discussion of the theatrical aspects of rulership, both in a conventional and radical form, see Ferdinand Mount, *The Theatre of Politics* (London: Weidenfeld and Nicolson, 1972).
7. See E. P. Thompson, *The Making of the English Working Class* (London: Victor Gollancz, 1965).

ism.") In contrast to Germany and its Prussianism, France and its instability, and Russia with its despotism, the English system balanced a
reforming left with a traditional but responsible right, a combination
that favored and preserved ceremonial monarchy.

How did it work? What made this slow evolution possible? It was
not economic well-being. Bagehot put the matter well.

*It cannot be said that the mass of the English people are well off. There
are those classes who have not a conception of what the higher orders
call comfort; who have not the prerequisites of moral existence; who
cannot lead the life that becomes a man. But, the most miserable of these
classes do not impute their misery to politics. If a political agitator were
to lecture to the peasants of Dorsetshire, and try to excite political dissatisfaction, it is much more likely that he would be pelted than that he
would succeed. Of Parliament these miserable creatures know scarcely
anything; of the Cabinet they have never heard, the Queen is very good;
and rebelling against the structure of society is to their minds rebelling
against the Queen, who rules that society, in whom all its most impressive part—the part they know—culminates. The mass of the English people are politically contented as well as politically deferential.*[8]

The picture is vastly changed today. Still there remains by American standards an amazing degree of deference. Despite depression, war,
loss of empire, and inflation the institutions of representative government remain highly valued for themselves. Are they understood? Bagehot believed not. It is the ceremonial part, the conservative aspect of
the monarchy that helps to preserve the English constitution, while the
efficient or legislative part does its work. (Today, unfortunately, the
efficient part creaks badly; one wonders how much longer the ceremonial part can carry the load.)

Bagehot's judgments, however, lucid as they are, lack the precision
and clarity of analysis modern-day institutionalism requires. But research tends to bear out at least some of his ideas. Certainly, the role
of the monarch as a ceremonial and symbolic figurehead, able to provide people with a sense of well-being and wise forebearance, and separating the onus of the politician from the status of the government it-

8. Norman St. John-Stevas, *Walter Bagehot* (London: Eyre & Spottiswoode, 1959),
pp. 386–87. See also the discussion of working class radicalism in E. P. Thompson,
op. cit., pp. 189–212.

self, survives. This separation is shown by the affection with which the institutions of the monarchy are held to this day.[9]

The presidential model: Such considerations could hardly apply to the United States. True, a ruling elite consisting of perhaps the most educated group of founders in the history of the world established the constitution. But, after Jackson at any rate, a rude populism took over in America and has never lost control. Deference is not an American trait. Populist coalitions may include a disproportionately powerful wealthy elite. But aristocrats? Rarely.

American political life is fundamentally egalitarian and individualistic. It is more "Lockean" than is the case with the English. Each unit of the polity—each person—has as much right as anyone else. Not deference, but a general hostility to being governed is perhaps the most fundamentally American characteristic. "Don't tread on me" is an old theme. However, because it is expensive to win public office (rigidly enforced laws restrict campaign financing in England), a power elite does exist. It is not hereditarily self-perpetuating. It is opportunist and often corrupt. The resulting privileged "establishment" includes those with money to "buy" the services of the less well endowed. The American (and it is peculiarly American) power elite relies hardly at all on class privileges and more on the competitiveness of the economic marketplace. The American political game reflects the rough and tumble of the business world. In fact, the principle of checks and balances is essential to prevent an all-powerful, oligarchic clique from perpetuating itself through monopolistic practices in government. The "imperial presidency" (which really began with Roosevelt and took a great leap forward under Nixon) has a good bit of tinsel about it. The ceremonial side of a working presidency is shabby. But it disguises huge accretions of power exercised on behalf of the powerful.[10] Fortunately, in America

9. See Edward Shils and Michael Young, "The Meaning of the Coronation," *The Sociological Review,* Vol. I (1953), pp. 63–81. See also Fred I. Greenstein, "The Child's Conception of the Queen and Prime Minister," *British Journal of Political Science,* Vol. 4, Part 3 (July 1974).

10. Corwin puts it this way: "Kept within bounds the power and prestige of the presidency comprise the most valuable political asset of the American people; they are, moreover, in a very true sense the creation of the American people. But centering as they do in a single individual who is free to advise, or to refrain from advising, with whomsoever he chooses, this power and this prestige are apt to become unduly *personalized,* thus inviting two dangers: the slowing down of the legislative process to an extent that unfits it for a crisis-ridden world in which time is often the essence

elites are competitive as well as powerful. Fortunately too, there is considerable reverence for the law.

The ceremonial part of the American system is the Constitution itself, not the presidency. The document is regarded reverentially. It is to Americans what the monarch is to the English, at least in terms of holding a part of government sacred as the embodiment of public good. It raises the collective circumstance of authority above the discretionary give and take of daily political life. As a consequence, the Founding Fathers have become larger than life. Americans have elevated these political forebears above politics as only "founders" can be. Their principles represent the ideal of democracy. They, like Aristotle's "unmoved mover," represent the legitimate basis of government.

The presidential system contrasts strongly with the parliamentary system. In the English system the spirit of government is centralized under the leadership of a prime minister. The symbolic or ceremonial part of the executive is a monarch who reigns, but does not rule. In the United States, the framers envisaged an institutional system of checks and balances on power by means of branches of government separated by function. Competition at all levels, from individuals and groups, right up to the legislative and judicial branches of government, prevents domination by any single party, faction, or social class. The problem was how to integrate this system to prevent fragmentation between the parts and a stalemate over policy. The system needs presidential initiatives and leadership to work.

The American system, which is so complex that it requires continuous mediation, also requires a very special form of presidential leadership. Personal intervention, indeed personality, counts for a lot. In England, personalities count for less than does a strong party system. In contrast, to implement policy a president depends on his ability to make coalitions across party lines and in the Congress. In the absence of strong party discipline, he must engage in continuous bargaining, cajoling, promises, payoffs, and deals.

Until recently the trend was toward a concentration of power in the presidential office and a simultaneous erosion of congressional power. The reason for this is that the responsibilities of office have escalated. Either the office of the presidency needs to be more powerful,

and—in consequence—autocracy," Edward S. Corwin, *The President, Office and Powers 1787–1957* (New York: New York University Press, 1957), p. 289. See also Arthur M. Schlesinger, Jr., *The Imperial Presidency* (Boston: Houghton Mifflin, 1973).

or parties need to be more disciplined.[11] The trend was checked but not reversed by the resignation of President Nixon in 1974. On the other hand, however, the congressional committee system has also produced strong leaders who can so counteract the exercise of presidential power as to make presidential government ineffective. Under the administration of Woodrow Wilson such an impasse was reached. Wilson came to believe that the opposition of the leaders of congressional committees was the worst defect presidential government had produced. He believed that only the British system produced responsible government, and that somehow this crucial element of responsibility was lacking in the American democracy.

If you would have the present error of our system in a word, it is this, that Congress is the motive power in the government and yet has in it nowhere any representative of the nation as a whole. Our Executive, on the other hand, is national: at any rate may be made so, and yet has no longer any place of guidance in our system. It represents no constituency, but the whole people; and yet, though it alone is national, it has no originative voice in domestic national policy.[12]

How then is the presidential system to work, when the combination of political relationships is so complex as to be unwieldy? The answer has been to centralize power in the president, who requires greater autonomy, freedom, and discretion for the efficient handling of affairs. But how will that discretion be used? If it avoids negotiating with specific interests—regional, occupational, religious—or the other special groupings of which modern society is composed, then the legislature must become more of an instrument of pressure groups in its effort to check presidential misuse of power.

Institutionalists have no real answer to this problem. Like the issue of centralization or decentralization, each is the answer to the other. If there is too much centralization, decentralize. If there is too much decentralization, centralize. No formula can be found. There is no legislative arrangement that can permanently hold back a dynamic president. There is no formula by which legislative power, even if broadly

11. See David K. Mayhew, *Party Loyalty Among Congressmen* (Cambridge: Harvard University Press, 1966).
12. Quoted in A. J. Wann, "The Development of Woodrow Wilson's Theory of the Presidency: Continuity and Change," *The Philosophy and Policies of Woodrow Wilson,* ed. Earl Latham (Chicago: University of Chicago Press, 1958), p. 58.

responsive to the electorate, can truly limit the scope of presidential power. There remains then a permanent tug of war which, if it threatens to get out of hand, is checked by the Supreme Court, or by impeachment. In turn, patronage, favoritism, the veto, and above all budgetary discretion—these are the tools of power in the office of the President.

Maintaining Balance

Control over the executive:[13] The principle of control over the executive is fundamental to any democracy. As we have seen, the two principal methods of control both involve the legislature. One is through a system of checks and balances, or the separation of powers between branches. The other is through parliamentary control. In the British system, two related mechanisms are built into the parliamentary system. The first is that a vote of confidence may be called for by parliamentary procedure. If the government is challenged by the opposition, and a motion to the effect is made in the House of Commons and accepted by the majority, then a *question of confidence* exists. The government must resign on the principle that a government that has lost the confidence of Parliament cannot govern. The prime minister and the cabinet tender their resignations to the monarch, who then may either choose replacements or call for a general election.[14]

For a government in England to lose a vote of confidence is rare. A government usually becomes aware of the fact that it is becoming unpopular when members of its own party ("backbenchers") become disaffected. Losing off-year elections for vacant seats to Parliament indicates loss of public support. Governments must in any case stand for a general election every five years.

Parliamentary control over the executive is exercised not under the principle of separation of powers, but under collective responsibility. The cabinet as a whole acts as an executive committee of parliament. A cabinet minister is responsible for the workings of a particular ministry or department. An attack on the minister's performance in Parliament is an attack on the cabinet. A minister comes under strong pres-

13. See A. V. Dicey, *Introduction to the Study of the Law of the Constitution* (London: Macmillan, 1959), p. 23, for the classic statement on British parliamentary responsibilities and obligations.
14. For example, from 1846–1860, Commons administered eight defeats out of which six cabinets resigned and two general elections were held.

sure to resign if there is evidence of wrongdoing or a misdemeanor by a senior official in the ministry. The prime minister—who is "first among equals—"[15] is responsible to the Parliament for the exercise of executive power and for running the business of government.

The second parliamentary method for controlling and reviewing government is by means of the parliamentary *question*. Members of Parliament prepare questions and present them to the government minister during a period reserved for that. Parliamentary questions may delve into all kinds of issues: from why an old lady in someone's constituency was not allowed her pension; to tracking down rumors of misdeeds in some government bureaucracy; to large questions of governmental intent. Parliamentary questions, if suitably embarrassing, may lead to governmental crises. However, since the entire system separates the formal head of government, the monarch, from direct rule, the government is not suddenly headless when a prime minister is removed. Residual functions exercised by the monarch, such as securing a transitional regime or asking a prime minister to stay on until a new general election is called, provide for orderly transitions.

Parliament consists of the House of Commons, the main lawmaking body, and the House of Lords, which now has mostly residual functions. The evolution of democratic government in England has been the slow transition from the power of Lords to the rule of the elective majority. In Commons this was accompanied by the expansion of the franchise through a series of reform acts beginning in 1832. As democracy increased, so the balance of powers between Commons and Lords shifted in favor of the former. Almost all cabinet ministers and all prime ministers are drawn from the House of Commons, although in years past both were drawn in good measure from among the Lords.[16]

In American as in English practice the active side of government is the executive. It would be difficult for the Congress actually to make major policy. The two houses operate to check presidential legislation more than to initiate independent policy. The original purpose in the two houses was to balance states' rights against general public needs and interests. The Senate has always been the more prestigious because of the six-year term of office and the responsibility that goes with it; plus,

15. See Sir W. Ivor Jennings, *Cabinet Government* (Cambridge: Cambridge University Press, 1947), pp. 219–27.
16. No peer since the Marquis of Salisbury has been prime minister. When Sir Alec Douglas-Home became prime minister, he resigned his peerage. Sir Winston Churchill refused to become a peer, preferring to remain in Commons.

its smaller size represents states' rights. The two-year term of office in the House of Representatives, the much larger size of that body, and its smaller constituencies make it responsive to special or local interests.

In order to effect policy a president must win over the leadership of both houses and their appropriate and joint committees. If a president represents one party and the Congress another, the chances of the president being able to accomplish much legislatively are restricted. Even under the best of circumstances it takes an artful politician to cope.[17] The effect is not to make the government responsible to the Congress, but in some ways the reverse, to stimulate the president to manipulate factions of all parties in the Congress by means of inducements and bargains. Cabinet government in Britain puts responsibility for governmental performance directly on parliamentary parties and their discipline. In the United States, legislative parties break up into sectional, ideological, and interest groups and other factions that can be wooed or propitiated, as necessary. The result is a more diverse set of pressures on the president and more need for manipulation.

An important contrast between American and British practice is apparent in the amending process. In the American system, amendment is difficult. The reason is that many fear that should the process be simplified, the executive could amend the constitution to increase its power practically at will. In England, amendment requires only parliamentary action. Parliamentary government is thus directly responsive to the changing needs and problems of political life.

Similarly with impeachment. In England the principle is followed of an "immovable but powerless Crown and a powerful but removable ministry." A minister, to be impeached, must be tried before the House of Lords.[18] In the United States on the other hand, impeachment requires a majority vote in the House of Representatives followed by a trial and conviction in the Senate. The process is intended to be difficult because stability is a key element in presidential government. For example, if a president believed that many important but unpopular measures were necessary, and was able to win the support of enough factions in Congress to gain a working majority, those who opposed him might be tempted to use the impeachment weapon and thus reduce his role to impotence. The proper restriction upon presidential action

17. See Richard Hofstadter, *The Idea of a Party System* (Berkeley: The University of California Press, 1969), pp. 212–71.
18. See Herman Finer, *The Theory and Practice of Modern Government* (New York: Henry Holt and Co., 1949), p. 601.

is thus not impeachment but *judicial review,* that is, the Supreme Court's determination of the constitutionality of presidential actions. The president is not simply the head of a party, but also the only representative of the national constituency as a whole, and therefore not only responsible to the legislature, but to the people. The people review executive acts through their legislature, protected by the Supreme Court which checks on the constitutionality of both.

The role of the cabinet: In the American system the cabinet is outside the Congress. Actually, it is not a cabinet at all in the parliamentary sense; that is, cabinet ministers are not elected to their posts. It is a group selected by the president to help administer the executive department for which the president is responsible. Heads of departments— State, Treasury, Interior, Agriculture, and so on—are secretaries to the president. Often they are personal friends or associates of the president. In England ministers are selected among members of Parliament who have worked their way up to positions of leadership in their party, and are important in the parliamentary party. A British cabinet minister must win election to Parliament, while no American cabinet secretary is allowed to be a member of the legislature, as this would violate separation of powers. A minister in England is never without a constituency. In the United States no cabinet secretary has a constituency.

The British cabinet is not precisely defined in number either. How it works varies at the discretion of the prime minister. At times a small inner group is designated the effective cabinet, while a large number of departmental heads who have ministerial rank are not included. The two key figures in the cabinet are the prime minister and the minister of finance. One figure, the Lord Chancellor, who is the senior judicial officer, is always a member of the House of Lords, which in certain ways acts as a supreme court. Not all ministers are attached to certain departments—these are "ministers without portfolio." If a minister resigns, he retains his seat in Parliament.

In the American system, the powers of the cabinet have been eroded in recent years by the expansion of the White House staff, the Office of Management and Budget, the National Security Council, and numerous personal presidential aides. This has tended to diminish access by cabinet secretaries—except, perhaps, for the Secretaries of State and Defense —to the president. The White House staff is essential if the president is to handle a large flow of government business, but its position can be abused (as during the Nixon administration when the staff virtually sealed off access to the president from all other governmental agencies and officials) .[19]

In Britain, while the cabinet collectively is responsible for policy, the emphasis is on partisanship. Every Parliament has in addition to the "front bench" of cabinet ministers of the government, an opposition bench consisting of a *shadow cabinet*—that which the opposition party organizes as a potential alternative government.

In Britain the government, practically speaking, is the cabinet, even though no constitutional provision is made for a cabinet. It is a matter of convention. Technically, the government is headed by the Queen-in-Council (or King-in-Council) —the Privy Council. Its functions are (1) the final determination of the policy to be submitted to the parliament, (2) the supreme control of the national executive in accordance with the policy prescribed by parliament, and (3) the coordination and delimitation of the authorities of the various departments of state.[20] In the United States, if one were to ask "What is the government?" the answer would be much less precise. The government is primarily, of course, the president and cabinet. But the power of certain congressional committees or individual members may be so great that for all practical purposes these people become part of the effective government. More and more institutionalists tend to reserve the term *government* to mean the executive "team," and save the term *political system* to include the other branches of government.[21]

Functions of the Representative Legislature

In all democratic systems the functions of the legislature are first, to represent the people and second, to make laws on their behalf. There are both historical and procedural differences in ways these things are done. A presidential-federal legislature is quite different from a parliamentary-unitary one. British democracy is a history of conventions and practices, which recognize the primacy of the Commons. The expansion of the franchise in England by means of reform acts was an explicit recognition that as wealth, education, and public civic practice improved, the public gained the right to share more in electing public officials. In the United States, sovereignty inheres solely in the people,

19. See Schlesinger, op. cit., pp. 208–77.
20. See Jennings, op. cit., p. 177.
21. Woodrow Wilson preferred to use the term *congressional government*.

whether they are ready or not to rule, and representation is a fundamental right. Historically, in British practice there was suspicion of the citizenry by aristocratic elements and both deference and hostility to the aristocrats by the citizens. In the American experience the citizenry feared aristocratic government. This fear was especially manifested against the Federalists, even though they did not represent much of an aristocracy.

Between these positions there is a world of difference. In England the tendency is to assume that responsible government knows best. In the United States the individual, one presumes, knows what is best, at least for himself or herself. As a result, in the United States that government is best which governs least. In England, government is best which governs most, that is, assumes responsibility and does the best job it can. Legislators in the United States are much more closely attuned to their constituencies than in England, where legislators are expected to vote by conscience instead of constituency. Legislators in the United States are much less party oriented than in England, although they rely on party machinery to be elected.

The House of Commons has come to mean *Parliament* in England, just as the cabinet has come to mean *government*. The Commons is represented on the basis of single-member constituencies. Its business is the debate, review, and passage of bills. Private members have little room to act. There are few strong antagonists of government, except in the opposition, whose function is to oppose the party in power and whose leader is paid for that purpose.

The atmosphere in Parliament is that of a club. To preserve intimacy, not enough seats are provided in the House of Commons for all members to sit down. One does not get the feeling of an empty chamber even when only a few members show up to debate. The house is divided in two, with the government front bench sitting across the aisle from the opposition front bench. To "cross the aisle," that is, to change party affiliation, is a solemn act, rarely undertaken.

In Congress, as we have said, the lower house, the House of Representatives (435 members) has less prestige than the Senate (100 members). But, although it is the "popular" house it does not compare in power with the English House of Commons. The Senate, on the other hand, has been steadily increasing its significance, as the upper house in England has been losing significance. Here something of the same intimacy and club-like atmosphere of the English Commons prevails. There rules of debate include the option to use the "guillotine," a procedure worked out in advance to enable the Speaker of the House of Commons to terminate debate. In the Senate "cloture" requires a two-thirds vote. There is great emphasis on senatorial courtesy and privilege.

In both Parliament and Congress, most of the legislative business is accomplished in committees. The most important committees in the Congress are standing committees, the chairmen of which reach their positions and hold on to them by virtue of tenure, making them into preserves of power, legislative fiefdoms. Until recently the House of Representatives had twenty standing committees and the Senate had sixteen covering the major policy and departmental areas of the federal government, banking and finance, defense, foreign policy, and so on. Today, due to congressional reform, there are fewer committees, but they still retain their power. Bills are reviewed by the appropriate committee before they are recommended to the White House. (Most of them die in committee.) At times a bill falls under several committee jurisdictions.[22]

The situation is the reverse in England. Amendment to legislation takes place on the floor of the House of Commons—one of the reasons why there is so much emphasis on its character as a debating institution and why the chamber housing is smaller than its membership. There are standing committees but these are appointed for each session; therefore there is no seniority principle. Committees reflect the composition of the entire house. Committees facilitate. They modify proposed legislation between "readings." But they lack the power of their counterparts in the United States.

Special committees can be established for particular purposes, such as select committees composed of experts to deal with particularly pressing problems in a manner leading to reform. *Select commissions,* as they are called, or Royal Commissions, have dealt with subjects such as homosexuality or the condition of the poor, and their recommendations usually lead to major legislation. Such special functions are ordinarily performed by ad hoc or special committees of the Senate in the United States, but the parallel is remote.[23]

In the House of Lords, the principal legislative options are to delay

22. See Kenneth Wheare, *Government by Committee* (Oxford: The Clarendon Press, 1965). Wheare speaks of committees to advise, inquire, negotiate, legislate, administer, scrutinize, and control.
23. See Roland Young, *The American Congress* (New York: Harper and Bros., 1958), p. 115. See also, Richard Fenno, *The Power of the Purse* (Boston: Little, Brown and Co., 1966).

and to reconsider. In the United States, not only is the executive power checked by the Congress but the houses of Congress check each other's power. This condition could paralyze government, making the president a prisoner of the Congress, but this has never been the case because the president has so much patronage and power. Nevertheless a small group of Senators can filibuster against legislation and prevent it from being properly considered. And special interests can manipulate the House. An effective president exerts leverage on the key members of committees to prevent their stalling important bills. Moreover, the president can veto bills passed by both houses. In Britain the right of veto resides in the Crown, but is never used. No bill can pass that a prime minister does not want to pass. The constitutional rights to veto, and disallowance by the monarch, have not been used in England since the days of Queen Anne.

The Apparatus of Popular Sovereignty

Political parties: In Chapter Six we discussed several aspects of party function and control. But it is useful to compare the party as it works in the legislature with how it works in the country at large. Party organization in Britain has traditionally been more class-based than has been the case in the United States. American parties are more or less dormant between elections. When the need arises they expand, like a balloon filling up with air, to organize rallies, raise money, and put on the usual funfairs that attend both local and national party caucuses. The parties ready themselves for general elections every four years. Local elections at one-year or two-year intervals do not generate the same furor. There is a sporadic urge to organize at the grass-roots level, however, to solidify support in election off-years and to heal party wounds. In Britain party organizers are more likely to be paid and hold permanent offices. They must always be ready for a general election due to the possible consequence of a vote of confidence.

In both the United States and Great Britain, political parties are mass coalitional organizations, appealing to voters by means of regionally defined, demographically drawn constituencies. In both countries they are responsive to special interests. While in theory representing individual voters, in practice parties represent organizations. Organizations—business, interest coalitions, voter groups—intervene at every stage, helping to structure the nominating processes, offering support to party candidates, and influencing party politicians. Nevertheless all parties are pluralistic within, and competitive without. They are broadly representative and constitutional. Parties remain organizations of individuals, despite the manipulation of special interests and organizations, and their support can be won by good staff work (as when Senator George McGovern captured the Democratic Party presidential nomination in 1972). That is the real significance of the principle of "one man—one vote."

Party politics in both countries develop out of factions, on a "clientelistic" basis.[24] In the United States, party politics stem from conflicts between people representing different principles—like Thomas Jefferson with his notions of limited government and Alexander Hamilton with his desire for stronger executive authority.[25] Jackson was perhaps the great turning point in American party politics; it was the supporters of Jackson who established its populist base. The English system, developing under such prime ministers as Walpole and Fox, Peel and Canning, Disraeli and Gladstone, turned the same corner during the administration of Peel.[26]

In both countries, the practice of democracy has become almost synonymous with the idea of a responsible two-party system. Efforts to build a third party have been made, of course. But by and large the systems settle down to two main contending parties: Whigs versus Tories, Liberals versus Conservatives, Democrats versus Republicans. In England after a so-called Lib-Lab (Liberal-Labour) coalition in 1906, the Labour Party developed rapidly. It came to power in a coalition government in the period between the two world wars, and as it did the Liberal Party declined.[27]

In Britain, as we have said, a party must be prepared for a general election at almost any time because a prime minister may resign, or dissolve Parliament and call a general election in order to increase his support in Parliament. This stimulates interest in the party as a vehicle of influence. Constituency organizations, the trade union movement or other clienteles are represented at yearly party conferences to remain

24. See the discussion by D. E. Apter, "Political Parties," *Comparative Politics*, ed. H. Eckstein and D. E. Apter (New York: Free Press of Glencoe, 1963), pp. 327–332.
25. See Hofstadter, op. cit., pp. 74–121.
26. See Norman Gash, *Politics in the Age of Peel* (London: Longmans Green and Co., 1953), p. x.
27. See R. T. McKenzie, ed., *British Political Parties* (London: William Heinemann, 1955).

close to party leadership. The leadership is, in turn, mindful of its constituencies, trade unions, the cooperative movement, and so forth. In both England and the United States (although mostly in the latter), a good many party politicians are lawyers who know how to make legislation and who have gained experience working for special and powerful party interests that then support them as candidates. The leadership of British parties, however, is more directly responsible to the members than in the United States.[28]

In the American system the substitute for regular organization is the party caucus which, at all levels, operates to bring coalitions and policies together. Party caucuses vary a great deal. Where one party is dominant, as has been true in the South, senior party politicians, whether Senators or old line leaders, indicate who they want selected as candidates. (At the 1972 Democratic National Convention, for example, a key argument in favor of minority quota representation was the need to break the power of old-line forces of the party and reduce the longevity of city bosses like Mayor Richard F. Daley of Chicago. The attempt was only partly successful.)

On the other hand, precisely because there has never been any kind of quota system in the past, parties have tended to favor two types of oligarchies in the United States: business, which is rich, and labor, which has numbers. The Republican Party has tended to favor the former and the Democratic Party the latter.

Tendencies toward a class clientele must be tempered by what they cost in votes. If too much attention is paid to labor at the expense of business, there will not be enough money for winning elections, nor enough support from those who admire or uphold the rights of business. Too much influence from business or populist anticorporate traditional American radicals can cause a party to lose elections as well. Both these factors act as constraints. Policies tend to be broad rather than narrow, class-based coalitions. However, groups without influence or money lose out. Other factors count in constructing party platforms too, including religion, ethnicity, language group, race, and so on.

Perhaps the sharpest differences between American and British parties are seen at the level of parliamentary organization. British parliamentary parties are disciplined. If the party whip makes clear that at the end of debate on a certain issue the party is required to vote as

28. See Samuel H. Beer, "The Representation of Interests in the British Government" in *American Political Science Review,* Vol. LI (Sept. 1957), pp. 613–60.

the Chief Whip lays down (a "three-line whip"), then to vote otherwise is to risk expulsion from the party. Individuals have to work their way up through the party and, since there is not much lateral entry, no one wants to throw a good position away. Those who rise to become party leaders are noted by the party when young. After they have done a good deal of party dirty work they are graduated to higher and better posts. It is a process that demands performance at every stage. Characteristically, as is also the case in the social democratic parties in Europe, the British Labour Party is composed of older representatives or those of longer standing, and is more bureaucratic than the Conservative Party.

The American system is much looser. Legislative parties tend to be coalitions that split from the official party line on many issues. For example, on many issues Southern Democrats have much more in common with Republican middle westerners than with the northern liberals in their own party. Therefore, legislative coalitions are loose, and interests play a large part in their formation. This is due in part to the fact that the population is much less homogeneous than in Britain. The party programs are therefore blander and less ideological. The appeal is always to the mythical middle—"Middle America," middle class. The most coalitional—that is to say, the most pragmatic—political parties in the world are the Republicans and Democrats, who appeal to the same broad mass of voters although the Republicans have traditionally sought business representation, while the Democrats have been more responsive to labor and ethnic and religious minorities. Although the Democratic Party is traditionally more liberal and the Republican Party traditionally more conservative, it is hard to say which party will support what policies when in office. (No one would have believed, for example, that a Republican administration under Richard Nixon would have opened the door to rapprochement with Communist China and détente with the Soviet Union.)

In Britain the term *middle* has, until recently, meant *upper-middle*. Today, however, the political center of gravity is changing rapidly, residing more in the lower-middle and working classes.[29]

Robert Dahl summarizes the characteristics of the American party system as follows. It is a two-party system. Party competition varies but in general declines with the size of the unit, particularly in towns and cities. There is diffusion and decentralization of control. Ideologies

---

29. As England declines economically relative to other countries, the working class forms a proportionally larger part of the electorate than in other industrial countries. "Working-class Britain" may thus be a consequence of economic decline just as, say, middle-class France may be a function of economic growth.

tend to be similar between parties, but there is conflict on issues. There are differences in party followings; for example, Catholics and blacks are more consistently Democrats than Republicans. The parties are durable. The history of the Democratic Party goes back to the time of President Jackson in 1830, and the Republicans to 1856. Party support is variable, so that the electorate appears fickle. Parties are not cohesive.[30]

In both countries, the principle of representation is motivated by the desire to win elections. In democratic theory, what links society to government is representation, with representation being a function of the voting system. The business of winning the election is the main preoccupation of politicians, who represent people because they have to. Nevertheless the high principle of democracy coincides with the baser goal of maximizing votes.

Interest and pressure groups: In both Britain and the United States, institutionalists have paid a good deal of attention to pressure and interest groups such as unions, trade associations, and ethnic associations organized to protect and advance the welfare of their specific membership as distinct from the welfare of the society as a whole. Just as political parties technically operate outside the specific confines of constitutional arrangements of power, so do interest and pressure groups. If party politics and politicians are sometimes regarded as unsavoury, interest and pressure groups are regarded with even more suspicion.

Interest groups differ from pressure groups. The former are organized in pursuit of corporate purposes beyond politics itself. They may establish rules for professionality and ethics, as the American Medical Association does. They may try to work out common needs and targets regarding matters affecting their group. Pressure groups are more specific. The National Association of Manufacturers or the Federation of British Industries have well-defined positions on such matters as nationalization, interest rates, and tariffs.

Much of the corruption in American politics has been put down to the influence of such bodies as the milk lobby, multinational corporations, and so on. In Britain, however, where elections require far less money and the level of ethics required of a member of the government or Parliament is correspondingly much higher than in the United States, interest and pressure groups are nevertheless also strong.

Influence peddling is one way to describe the problem—the public

30. See Robert A. Dahl, *Pluralist Democracy in the United States* (Chicago: Rand McNally, 1967), pp. 213–38.

senses that government cannot work democratically. But there is, of course, another way to analyze such groups. Interest groups can be legitimate representative bodies, despite their using informal consultation to conduct their affairs. Their formation can bring response to the needs of groups that may be important but unable to muster votes. We shall also note that lobbying in the committees of Congress, behind-the-scenes consultation between government and various interests, occurs all the time.

In the United States interest groups affect the political process in two principal ways. One is through influencing legislation. The other way, which is more crucial in the United States than in Britain, is in the nomination of candidates favorable to their cause. Precisely because the party system is less well organized in the United States, it is more susceptible to more organized bodies. This *nomination vulnerability,* when combined with campaign financing, means that in this country groups mesh with party politics at the two crucial points of politics: (1) in selecting candidates favorable to specific interests and getting them elected, and (2) in using elected officials to exercise their legislative votes as bargaining leverage with the executive.[31]

The civil service: As the functions of the executive increase and the need to establish regulatory agencies, administer social welfare, organize and promote reform, and otherwise ensure that legislative policy is efficiently carried out, so a civil service expands its scope, size, and the number of its activities. The growth of bureaucracy is a function of the expansion of governmental responsibility. The origin of the idea of a civil service in England began with the servants of the king's household. These servants, drawn mainly from the nobility, administered the king's domains, his private lands, his finances, and so forth. In the nineteenth century, and particularly after the establishment of a disinterested civil service administration in India, the notion of a career civil service developed in Britain. The ideal was the notion of a senior class of civil servants—not members of the aristocracy but people exceptionally qualified by education and moral stature—to be recruited by means of a competitive examination that had to be passed with a high standard. One could look forward to a good pension on retirement and the possible distinction of a knighthood or title as an additional reward for

31. See David B. Truman, *The Government Process, Political Interests and Public Opinion* (New York: Alfred Knopf, 1951), pp. 262–320.

meritorious service.[32] No one could be recruited from private life or other occupations and advanced over the head of a senior official. A career official would be promoted in due time and course. The individual administrator would be protected from politicians by the minister of the department and, in turn, owed to the minister responsible advice and service.

In Britain the career service is not aristocratic, but educated people most likely to pass the examinations are those who attend Oxford or Cambridge. The career senior civil service, or those in the Administrative Class, as it is called, are drawn mainly from the upper-middle class, from which the universities principally recuit their students. The transition to a "democratic" civil service meant a corresponding change in the availability of education.

Such a civil service produces a class or "old-boy" network in which a great deal, in terms of standards of appropriate conduct, can be taken for granted. There is a high level of propriety and corruption is rare, and at the same time, the civil service is able to carry on despite changes in governments. It closely approximates the ideal of the disinterested civil service which can serve any party in power, is discreet, stays out of politics, and indeed, is not allowed to engage in party activity. Much of this ideal remains intact in Britain although gradually the British are becoming aware that the ideal civil servant, rather than being a highly educated "generalist," is more likely to be a technically trained specialist.[33]

The American system has never been like the British system. As suggested in Chapter Six, the civil service was, for a long time, based on a "spoils" system. An incoming administration turned over government posts to cronies in whom the president and the party had confidence, or to whom was owed some political debt. Bureaucratic patronage was an important source of presidential power. But although such a civil service tends to recruit mediocre people—party hacks paid off with civil service sinecures—and in general leads to corruption and inefficiency, it also had an advantage. It prevented the formation of an administrative class of like-minded, educated, possibly arrogant elites.

Only gradually, as the need for expertise grew, was a career service

32. The ideal "breathed" reform and efficiency. See Sir Edward Blunt, *The I.C.S.* (London: Faber and Faber, 1937). See also Eric Stokes, *The English Utilitarians and India* (Oxford: The Clarendon Press, 1959).
33. The tradition has favored "educated generalists" and opposed "narrow" technicians. See Crossman, *The Myths of Cabinet Government* (Cambridge, Mass.: Harvard University Press).

movement organized. And, as various civil service reform acts were passed, a career service did somewhat grudgingly become established, first in the Foreign Service and then elsewhere. But it was never extended unambiguously to the top levels of the government. Lateral entry into the civil service from business or other fields is still common and acceptable. Finally, eligibility examinations ensure a broad recruitment from diverse universities and from nonuniversity candidates who possess compensatory experience. There is no such thing as an "administrative class," as in England.

Electoral systems: In both the United States and Britain the assumptions prevail that political stability depends on having a two-party system, that more than two parties would produce instability, and that the two-party system results from plurality or majority voting. There is strong evidence for these assumptions, but none which is conclusive. Parties can form stable coalitions based on proportional representation, as European experience shows.[34]

Moreover, many coalitional tendencies are directly related to the electoral system as a whole. The British divide the entire country into electoral constituencies based on population. The idea is that constituencies should be large enough and sufficiently diverse to reflect more than narrow pressures or demands, but small enough to distinguish differences from region to region—rural versus industrial, and so forth. Such differences are reflected in the composition of the House of Commons. On the whole, with modifications appropriate to a federal system and state representation as such, the same principles apply in the United States.

In turn, the mechanism of election includes the simple plurality system, that is, the winning candidate is the one who gets the largest number of votes, rather than a required majority (this is the first-past-the-post principle discussed in Chapter Six). In England the constituencies are single-membered, that is, there is one representative in Commons for each constituency. In the United States there are two Senators and there is a Representative for each congressional district. In both systems, differences of opinion, attitudes, and needs become part of a common pool of opinions and interests. The primacy of certain regions with more influence and money, also fluctuates. The Boston–

34. See Enid Lakeman and James D. Lambert, *Voting in Democracies* (London: Faber and Faber, 1959).

New York establishment dominated the American electoral scene for generations, but is now losing out to other parts of the country. Southern influence, once strong, declined (except in the form of legislative committee chairmanships) and once again is growing. First southern influence was wielded by third-party movements (like those of Alabama Governor George Wallace). Now as the electorate "changes its color" and its ethnic proportions, so new groups attain electoral significance. The changing composition of the electorate, as a result of various demographic shifts, is the ultimate factor determining party composition.

At the same time, minority interests can easily be excluded or given perfunctory treatment, unless they are exceptionally well financed or organized. The plurality electoral system systematically works against the unorganized or small group. To compensate, unorganized or small groups must coalesce with other sympathetic groups. The great advantage of proportional representation is that it emphasizes more differentiated groupings.[35] Hence, the combination of a single-member or dual-member constituency system plus plurality voting requires that, to be effectively represented, groups must be organized, and small groups must join together into significant coalitions. In the formation of the British Labour Party, for example, it was precisely the effort to organize labor into trade unions that first produced the coalition between labor and the Liberal Party that allowed the first labor representation in Parliament. Similarly, in the United States trade union and civil rights organizations have brought about more effective party representation for Puerto Ricans and blacks in the Democratic Party. Since now minority groups appreciably affect swing votes, no candidate can continue to ignore them. Once a group reaches this effective point, the electoral system that may previously have worked against it, then works for it.

Thus there is a threshold of voting power and salience which, once crossed, increases minority significance. In both Britain and the United States, it is widely believed that changing the electoral system into one favoring minorities and more specialized group interest—as by proportional representation—would maximize the number of parties, help keep marginal interests alive, and foster ideological sectarianism. But although this solution to some electoral problems might be more democratic, it would also tend to produce instability (as we shall see in our later discussion of the French Third and Fourth Republics).

35. In Britain, as Asian, Caribbean, and foreign immigration increases, and as Scottish and Welsh nationalism rises, there is renewed interest in proportional representation.

Strengths and Weaknesses of the Institutional Paradigm

The institutionalist tradition, as we have emphasized previously, is one of continuous reform. Institutionalists take the long view, favoring slow change that works its way to the surface of legislative and parliamentary institutions and is modified by debate. In this tedious change-making process, since any important legislation is bound to affect the interests of many, only the most important issues, the most enduring problems require major attention. By the same token, these need to be resolved piecemeal. Institutionalism is decidedly not crisis politics, although parliamentary "minicrises," hurried consultations in back rooms, and a concern with particular and momentary issues—as opposed to comprehensive schemes—is the usual rather than the exceptional way of doing business.

Institutionalists take for granted that the slow conduct of governmental affairs is, in the end, the best way of taking into account the widest range of views. It is on this basis that they justify the slow and frustrating democratic decision-making process. The problem is that the unorganized, or poor, or otherwise relatively voiceless elements of the electorate always find their interests to be the lowest priority. Institutionalists also tend to take it for granted that the area of private discretion, which includes a good deal of economic life, should not become too much of a governmental affair.

Nevertheless, since the New Deal in the United States and the first Labour government after World War II in Britain, there have been changes. Indeed, in Britain there has been something of a social revolution. The deference Bagehot spoke of was based on a class system that depended not only on inequalities of money, property and privilege, but even more on a highly segregated educational system. This educational system began to be modified by the Educational Act of 1944, which provided for examinations, to be taken by all students, that would enable the gifted from *any* class to go on to university with financial scholarships from local or other authorities. This bill was more helpful to the lower-middle class than to the working class, but more recently there has been a move towards comprehensive schools, similar to those in the United States, in which, for the most part, rich and poor (black and white) are schooled together.

The United States, as an immigrant society, relied heavily on the school system to integrate diverse groupings into a common political culture. On the whole the British system (which had much more ethnic and religious homogeneity in the first instance) used the school system to perpetuate class differences.[36] Under the circumstances, while neither country has been much influenced by Marxist ideology, in both there has been an authentic radical tradition. In the English case, as we have seen, it goes back to the Puritan reformers, the Levellers and the Diggers, the Chapel movements, and so forth. The concern with reform came from the upper classes of society as well as the lower. The Fabian Society, for example, which comprised mainly middle class and highly educated people, conducted detailed research on everything from alcohol use to insurance, the poor laws, and the organization of industry. Its proposals became very much the basis of both liberal and labor reform.[37] But the Fabians represented an elite. A more communalist tradition of socialism, identified with the nineteenth century revival of medievalism in England, was represented by William Morris and John Ruskin. Reacting to industrialism, statism, and the "administrative socialism" desired by the Fabians, they wanted to decentralize all political institutions. One proposal was that Parliament should become a bicameral body, one house to be made up of representatives of constituencies and the other based on representations of interests, particularly labor and industry. The voter would be the "consumer," who would determine what should be produced. A council of guild representatives—producers— would be responsible for the management of industry, with each guild being self-governing. National planning systems and guild self-government would then work together. This system of "guild socialism" was particularly the work of G. D. H. Cole, who was a professor at All Soul's College, Oxford, and a Fabian.

None of these schemes came to much. But neither does the present political system of England seem adequate. Britain today is in deep crisis due to a marked decline in the quality of industrial management and efficiency. England's empire melted during the post–World War II years. The economy suffers increasing hardships. Labour Party strength has grown, and with it the power of the trade unions. A situation now exists in Britain in which industrial enterprise steadily deteriorates, while industrial labor is unwilling to compensate for technological

36. See Fred I. Greenstein and Sidney Tarrow, *Political Orientations of Children: The Use of a Semi-Projective Technique in Three Countries* (Beverly Hills, California: Sage Publications, 1970) . See also Paul R. Abramson, *Generational Change in American Politics* (Lexington, Mass.: Lexington Books, 1975) .
37. See George Bernard Shaw, ed., *Fabian Essays in Socialism* (New York: Doubleday, no date) .

obsolescence by increased labor productivity. Industry and labor mutually blame one another, and to an extent both are right. Meanwhile, the England that was a beacon of liberal modern politics is in difficulty, and the crisis challenges all the institutions of parliamentary government.

The American case has been different. While in England there has been a relative decline in economic conditions, there have nevertheless been great gains toward equality. In the United States, while there have been steps made toward integration of black and white, little change has been made in the economic disparity between rich and poor.[38] By and large, over the past twenty-five years in the United States, 5 percent of the population commands approximately 16 percent of the income, while the bottom 20 percent receives roughly 5 percent.[39] In both Britain and the United States, welfare costs have increased, the burdens falling mainly on the middle class. In the United States very little ideological radicalism has been manifested. Both black radicalism and student radicalism in the sixties and seventies proved to be limited and episodic. In contrast British labor is increasingly militant, without being particularly radical.

The questions of institutional reform, radicalism, and threats to the stability of democratic institutions have not been seriously raised in either country. But no one knows for how long the institutions that have served adequately up to the present will be equal to the tasks that lie ahead.[40]

The French Connection

Until recently France had been an example of a government made ineffective by weak and fragmented institutions. Excessive centralization of the monarchical government and administration was violently ruptured by the French Revolution, but the revolution decided little. France remained a country divided against itself. The legal and constitutional instruments were periodically violated by revolutions and coups.

38. See the *President's Annual Economic Report* (Washington: D.C.: Government Printing Office, 1974).
39. Ibid.
40. See Warren E. Miller and Teresa E. Levitin, *Leadership and Change* (Cambridge: Winthrop Publishers, 1976). Considerable change can be expected in Britain as a result of the 1975 referendum supporting membership in the European Economic Community.

The spirit of French democracy was punctuated by heroic monarchs like Napoleon who, combining modernity with autocracy, made France the most powerful country in the world. "Men on horseback" acted as instruments of an unreconstructed bourgeoisie. Rural and Catholic France stood apart from urban and bourgeois France. Bourgeois France stood aloof from the radical working class, the populist France symbolized by the Paris Commune. To chronicle the diversity of post–Revolutionary France requires the talents of a Balzac or Flaubert. Clericalism, radicalism, conservatism, radical-conservatism, royalism, Bourbonism, and Orleanism all flourished simultaneously among a deeply divided population. Cleavage parties, a weak cabinet government, and a strongly centralized administration combined with regional provincialism. Highly organized trade unions—Christian, communist, and socialist—manipulated the most powerful parties. Such were characteristics of France up until the time of Charles DeGaulle, when democracy was saved again by a "man on horseback."

Stanley Hoffmann has picturesquely represented the conditions that existed before DeGaulle as a period of "immobilisme." He called France a "stalemate society" (a term that applies to Italy today), centralized but limited in power.

In a way, then, the centralized but limited state was a faithful translation of the two key features of the stalemate society. But establishing a political system remained a very complicated task; for, between a society and a political system, there is a crucial problem of transmission belts and institutional arrangements.

It is true that there are authority patterns in all groups, from the family to the state. But, precisely because the state is the "group of groups," the way in which authority relations prevalent in society will or will not operate in the political system depends to a large extent on what may be called the political formula, or political legitimacy: the way in which political leaders are selected and power distributed among them. There will usually be strong connections, of course, between the style of authority and the political formula; however, a given style of authority in society is compatible with a variety of political formulas.

It is also true that in studying the question of political legitimacy one must take into account the presence or absence of a social consensus. But its mere existence is not a guarantee of political stability, because a consensus on the nature of society does not determine the regime which will be based on it. Thus, in France, the previously described social con-

sensus was not enough—a political consensus was missing; there was no agreement either on the objectives for which political power is to be used, or on the procedures through which disputes over such objectives can be resolved. Whoever undertakes to arrange the political institutions and transmission belts to society ought to consider not only the main features of society but also the main political opinions—and to remember that his work is at the mercy of the most unmanageable of all variables: events.

France, ever since the Revolution, had been split into rival schools of thought, differing not only in the judgment of the merits of the stalemate society but also in their views about how society should be governed.[41]

What were the institutions? Those pertaining to cabinet government and parliament. What were the transmission belts? Party and interest competition, proportional representation, and parliamentary maneuvering. What was the result of centralized administrative regulation? Cabinet instability. Under the Third and Fourth French Republics, the average life of a cabinet was seven to nine months. A legislature consisting of temporary coalitions made legislative leadership impossible. What was lacking was a system of administration that would outlast individual governments and changes in the constitution, and carry out the actualities of rule.

France was the original example of the unstable parliamentary democracy. In this respect it represented one end of the spectrum that includes other multiparty parliamentary systems like those of Belgium, the Netherlands, and the Scandinavian countries. But despite their similarities to the French political system, these latter have been closer to England in terms of stability. What makes for the stability of some and the instability of others?

One answer is popular consensus, which was conspicuous by its absence in France (and is still absent today in Italy). Certainly in Holland, Scandinavia, and Belgium there are profound political differences —ethnic, religious, and so forth—dividing the electorate. But in these countries, as in England, conflict occurs within the political system, not over its appropriate form, whereas republicanism in France began with a radical repudiation of centralized and monarchical govern-

41. Stanley Hoffmann et al., *In Search of France* (New York: Harper & Row, 1963), pp. 12–13. See also Isser Woloch, *Jacobin Legacy* (Princeton: Princeton University Press, 1970).

ment. The tradition is much more radical than that found in England. In England constitutional reform took a big jump in the Glorious Revolution of 1688, and in so doing the country avoided the carnage of the French Revolution.[42] Continuity and tradition were modified but sustained. Then electoral reform from 1832 on slowly inducted more and more sectors of the population into the mysteries of representative government. After the Revolution, France (like the United States) began with perfection and then tried to improve it. But, with its more open social condition, the United States was blessed with a self-congratulatory sense of superiority, optimism, and hope as a legacy of revolution. There was little internal bitterness.[43] Not so in France. As Wahl describes the French political tradition,

France has long been known as the nation of the Great Revolution, the cradle of democracy and reason, the mother of innovations in style and ideas. But, it is often forgotten—and particularly by Americans— that France was also the nation that perfected political absolutism and that this epitomized reverence for the traditional above all in economic and social customs. In political ideas, therefore, France has developed a split personality that has been perpetuated by the historical experience of the nineteenth-century revolutions and by the peculiar resistance of French society to social and economic change.[44]

France, then, was no model of democracy. It has had a long history of self-defeating results, although today this is no longer an appropriate view. For the time being at any rate, Italy has become the appropriate substitute. Indeed, France has changed all the old traditions; from family farm and family firm to innovative rural and industrial corporatism, from antitechnology to advanced technology and from rural-urban cleavage to suburbanization. All this and more has been accomplished, with startling results, so that France of the 1940s was wholly different from France of the 1970s.

What is not clear is the extent to which changes in the French political system will prove to be permanent. The catalog of French politi-

42. See Alfred Cobban, *The Social Interpretation of the French Revolution* (Cambridge: Cambridge University Press, 1968), pp. 145–61.

43. See, for example, J. Hector St. John Crevecoeur, *Letters From an American Farmer* (New York: Doubleday Books, no date).

44. See N. Wahl, "The French Political System" in *Patterns of Government*, ed. Samuel H. Beer et al. (New York: Random House, 1958), p. 217. See also Henry W. Ehrmann, *Politics in France* (Boston: Little, Brown, 1971).

cal vices was a long one and a good many of them remain. The old dualism between popular republicanism and reactionary aristocracy has disappeared; DeGaulle provided the executive with a more effective scope for action, although at the expense of legislative stalemate; and economic development has suddenly "taken off." But, potentialities for conflict—between president and prime minister, legislative and executive branches—remain.

The stagnant society transformed: So fearful were the shapers of the constitution of the Third Republic that a strong centralized executive would result in either restoration of the monarchy or Bonapartism, that they created a parliamentary system in which the legislature was extremely powerful. The Senate was indirectly elected with nine-year terms of office, with electoral methods favoring rural over urban areas. The Senate was consistently conservative, and re-election was common. Something like the seniority system found in the American Senate worked in France as well, but on an overwhelming scale. The Senate could stop bills emanating from the Chamber of Deputies (the equivalent of the House of Commons or the House of Representatives) by using its important financial powers.

As in Britain, there was a parliamentary question (interpellation) period that gave legislators the right to interrogate the administrative branch on matters of policy. Party coalitions in the Chamber of Deputies were very fragile. Governments were at the mercy of coalitions that fell apart with appalling regularity. Whereas in England, because of parliamentary discipline, there was control of government business to the extent that one could speak of "cabinet dictatorship," in Third-Republic France party fractionalization was so complete that cabinet instability was the most regular feature of government. Between 1879 and 1940 France had ninety-five governments.

As in England, the executive was separated by symbolic and working functions. There was a president, who was indirectly elected by both houses, and a premier. The cabinet had no rule of collective responsibility—ministers could, and did, publicly disagree—and could not dissolve the parliament. The president could dissolve parliament with the agreement of the Senate. Parties were ideologically oriented and divided among left, right, and center coalitions.[45]

Under the circumstances, it was the civil service that effectively ran

45. See Maurice Duverger, *The French Political System* (Chicago: University of Chicago Press, 1958). See also Roy Pierce, *French Politics and Political Institutions* (New York: Harper & Row, 1968).

the country, departments being insulated against normal political turn-overs.[46] Interest groups operated freely—the more conservative ones exerting influence over the Senate, the more radical ones over the Chamber of Deputies. Such a mixture of power plus factions plus weak coalitions plus a weak executive plus a divided legislature created in-stability, intensified conflict, and increased public suspicion of govern-ment. In society generally, the rule was "every man for himself." In the rural areas the family and Catholicism, the ideological mainstay of the family, reigned supreme. In business, family firms defined the heart of the bourgeoisie. Aligned against the provincial and bourgeois powers were the trade unions—communist for the main body of industrial workers, socialist for the more skilled, and Christian for those who op-posed the others. France was highly organized and divided against itself. Each group favored parties more or less class-based. Minor differences inspired minor parties; twelve, fifteen, or more parties were not un-usual. Unfortunately the Fourth Republic, which tried to eliminate some of these problems by eliminating the Senate, for example, only exacerbated party competition by providing for proportional representa-tion, thus enlarging the electoral base for the proliferation of minor parties.[47]

Our purpose here is not to discuss the French system in any detail, but rather to indicate the kind of contrasts that can be drawn using the British model of parliamentary government. Each of the points of com-parison—control of the executive, role of the cabinet, functions of the legislature, political parties and electoral systems, the working of interest groups, and the significance of the civil service—all contrast in striking ways. In this regard, just as it could be shown that the British par-liamentary system works as a system because these elements are comple-mentary in theory or practice, likewise the reasons the Third and Fourth French Republics failed to work, or worked badly, were because each was at cross purposes with the others. The civil service was aloof from the cabinet because the latter was constantly being changed. The cabinet changed because party coalitions disintegrated. Party coalitions disintegrated because the legislature was powerless to make effective legislation. Legislatures could not legislate because parliamentary par-

46. See Michel Crozier, *The Bureaucratic Phenomenon* (Chicago: University of Chicago Press, 1963).
47. See Richard F. Hamilton, *Affluence and the French Worker in the Fourth Re-public* (Princeton: Princeton University Press, 1967). See also Roy C. Macridis and Bernard E. Brown, *The DeGaulle Republic* (Homewood, Ill.: The Dorsey Press, 1960), pp. 119–59.

ties were too divided and the Senate was too conservative. Lacking the discipline of parliamentary dissolution, cabinets could be removed without it being necessary for legislators to stand again in a general election. Because of such instability, which was made even worse by proportional representation, the divided electorate clung to outmoded or irrelevant social groupings and political and religious ideologies that kept alive the old conflicts germane to political disgruntlement and revolution. The legacy of revolution was a self-perpetuating division of the nation into urban–rural, Paris–province, Catholic–left, bourgeois–worker factions. Compromise, inaction, cynicism, political distrust, and the unwillingness to concede to government the idea of a public interest stalemated impulses toward the just society.[48]

However, these conditions were reversed after the mid-twentieth century. After the prolonged agony of the Algerian war, the emancipation of the French Community of Nations, the association with Europe in the Common Market, friendship with West Germany, the promotion of trained technocrats to critical civil service positions in the ministries, the renovation of agriculture, the emergence of new kinds of industrial enterprise, and a host of associated changes, these characteristics no longer apply. There is no longer a split between the Catholics and the left; there is today also a Catholic left. The distinction between urban and rural no longer disguises completely different life styles; there is mobility between the two. The old working class is still, by and large, antibourgeois, but it enjoys a measure of security and opportunity that makes it more and more resemble the bourgeoisie. (The organized left, for example, showed its contempt for radical students in the 1968 Paris uprising.) In short, the old self-perpetuating cleavages in the social body are slowly melting as new, more complex forms replace them. These changes, developmental in character, may have more to do with the new French stability than the present constitution. Today it is the President who exercises real power. The President, who is not responsible to the parliament, the French National Assembly, designates a Prime Minister who is. The President can also dissolve the Assembly without being directly accountable to it. In this hybrid parliamentary system, there is no doctrine of either separation of powers or checks and balances, and the parliament is neither impotent nor very powerful. The President is elected by an electoral college, and thus not a directly

48. See Nathanael Greene, *Crisis and Decline: The French Socialist Party in the Popular Front Era* (Ithaca: Cornell University Press, 1969). One could change the terms slightly and apply more or less the same description to the present condition of Italy.

elected representative of the whole people. But neither is the President a creature of parliament. The President can bypass approval of the National Assembly and seek direct mandates through referenda. The National Assembly is restricted in its ability to alter or review the budget. A Constitutional Council supervises presidential elections and reviews constitutional matters, but it lacks the final power the U.S. Supreme Court has.

Has the stalemate model in France finally given way to an equilibrium model? When a high concentration of executive power exists, the system works well. But who can say what will happen under a bad executive. When a bad president is elected, we shall then see how much equilibrium will prevail.[49]

Totalitarian versus Democratic Institutions

Representative government must be libertarian. However, if it produces gross inequities, then the extension of political liberty is not followed by a similar extension of economic and social liberty. Rather the reverse occurs. The rich and powerful are free to act against the poor and defenseless. The problem is how to extend economic and social rights without restricting liberty. Political liberty that leads to inequality in economic and social terms means a divided nation, a political system riddled with conflict, a polarized rather than cooperative society, and political instability.[50]

How to deal with such a situation is a central concern of institutionalists. In a nation too badly divided the democratic polity does not work. History is strewn with democratic failures like the Weimar Republic, not to speak of virtually all the nations of Europe created by the downfall of the Austro-Hungarian Empire after World War I.[51]

Contrary to Bryce's optimism, only a few successful democratic governments survived after World War I, notably Czechoslovakia and

49. See Phillip M. Williams and Martin Harrison, *DeGaulle's Republic* (London: Longmans, 1965), p. 123. Williams and Harrison describe the situation as follows: "The result is a Hanoverian monarch masquerading as a Republic President, who is also head of state, guardian of the ark of the covenant, one head of a two-headed executive, mediator within his cabinet and between the government and Parliament, and in a great crisis constitutional dictator."
50. See Sir Ernest Barker, *Principles of Social and Political Theory* (London: The Clarendon Press, 1951), pp. 236–68.
51. See Agnes Headlam-Moreley, *The New Democratic Constitutions of Europe* (Oxford: Oxford University Press, 1929).

Finland. Just after Bryce wrote that the future belonged to democracy, the situation changed. If democracy remained the natural system, it was so only under special circumstances—circumstances that did not apply where the tradition of liberty was missing, or where economic and social freedom did not or could not obtain.

A collectivist solution has become the alternative to the individualistic ideal. But does this compromise necessarily take place at the expense of freedom? Certainly in the two main forms of collectivism—communism and fascism—the answer is yes. The single-party state replaces the multi- or two-party system: totalitarianism replaces pluralism. Diversity disappears in an enforced unity of goals under the guise of "will" and discipline. The meaning and certainly the functions of the term *party* change. The legislature no longer acts as a check on the executive. The military or the police become the basis of authority of the state.

Single-party systems use the party to "block up" all the channels between the state and society, except one. The single channel thus left, just because it is single, becomes something more than a channel of information and approval. It becomes the fountainhead—the original and the only moving power. Instead of responding to social movement and receiving social impulses, it works back on society as a controlling force that determines what society will be and what it says and does.[52] Thus the meaning of institutions like parties or parliaments or the executive are irretrievably altered in a collective society, but with variations. The main difference between Soviet collectivism and fascist collectivism is that the first obliterates private ownership of the means of production, and the state intervenes directly in economic development. Social relations and benefits are directly regulated, as are conditions of employment. In the fascist case, enterprise is privately controlled although trade unions, businesses, and other economically based groups are organized and regulated by the state. Fascism organizes interests into corporations; the result is greater economic inequality than exists under communism. A fascistic government also has, as a long-term object, the goal of replacing legislative government with functional representation.[53]

52. See Ernest Barker, *Reflections on Government* (London: Oxford University Press, 1942), pp. 300–11.
53. See A. James Gregor, "Fascism: the Classic Interpretations of the Interwar Period," University Programs Modular Series (Morristown, N.J.: General Learning Press, 1973). See also Ernst Nolte, *Three Faces of Fascism* (New York: Holt, Rinehart & Winston, 1966).

Communism claims to exemplify political universality, while fascism makes the national state into a doctrine of "sacred egotism" or racial superiority. In Hitler's Germany, this combined a folk nationalism with a nonproletarian mixture of socialism and capitalism. The leadership embodied the Protean spirit—Germany rising out of the depth of defeat in World War I to transcend a decadent Weimarism. (Both Italian and German totalitarianism were populist in their appeal to nationalist sentiments.) The Soviet appeal espouses a future in which *all* are brothers and sisters. But the Communist Party is more elitist, acting as a vanguard for the future, than are the party organs in fascist regimes (although under fascism the party, military, and police elites and the bureaucracy have a privileged life style).

What is the solution? What happens if, in modern society, more democracy—that is, more participation, more equality, more community involvement, and more effective and better executive efficiency—all prove contradictory to the institutions of rule as we know them? What if government cannot intervene more effectively in the social and economic life to promote greater equality? "Equality in liberty of thought, if it is to have substance and content, must mean a large measure of equality in the education of mental capacity."[54] What is needed, as in Aristotle's day, is a common material and mental "equipment" so that, out of the fraternity produced by reason and equality, a more resolute and purposeful democracy will become possible.

Are there institutionalist solutions to the dilemma? There are some. Social democracy is more important than ever before. During the Fourth Republic in France, the demand for greater governmental efficiency (voiced by scholars such as Duverger) took the form of constitutional reform, which changed the shape of the French parliamentary system and provided for executive efficiency.[55] Others have sought to adapt Marxist thought and socialist doctrine to the political system, especially favoring greater degrees of nationalization, the abolition of private property, and the expansion of worker's influence and control. Such a tradition of social democracy, powerful in France and Germany,[56] has antique elements; Blanquism, Proudhonism, Jacobinism, and so on. But these are shadowy figures in the dialogue of today. (So are Bernstein, Kautsky, and others who tried to blend Marxism with democracy in Germany.) In England, the social democrats included Fabians, guild

54. Barker, op. cit., p. 418.
55. See Maurice Duverger, op. cit., p. 185.
56. See George Lichtheim, *Marxism in Modern France* (New York: Columbia University Press, 1966).

socialists, and others whose object was to use the prevailing political system, but to permeate it with programs and pressures for reform, and in other ways bring about more social and economic democracy.[57] These included institutionalists like Laski, whose concern with the failure of democracy to promote equality moved him further and further toward the left. It also included Leonard Woolf, G. D. H. Cole, and many others whose belief in the institutions of democracy made them insist that social democracy was the precondition of political democracy, and not the other way around.

It should be clear, however, that institutionalists are concerned with reform as a means to improve democracy by (1) expanding the power of libertarian government to balance public preference with effective policies; (2) evolving appropriate electoral, party, and legislative systems in order to create a bond between the community and the state; (3) facilitating representation that contributes to the efficacy of the individual and the public interest; and (4) buttressing popular sovereignty to ensure the loyalty and cooperation of the citizenry. How these powers can be made more effective has been the subject of institutional political science.[58] It is becoming more and more the subject of modern pluralism. It is also the concern of those interested in the activities that people perform in political life, their ideas, beliefs, and actions. Before discussing pluralism, it is necessary to examine the "behavioral persuasion" in politics.

57. See M. Beer, *A History of British Socialism* (London: George Allen and Unwin, 1940).
58. See Carl J. Friedrich, *Constitutional Government and Politics* (New York: Harper & Row, 1937).

Behavioralism

chapter eight
Public Opinion and Political Behavior

Institutionalists discovered that, despite the importance of electoral systems, parliamentary and presidential forms of representation, and constitutional principles such as parliamentary control over the executive, checks and balances, or separation of powers, institutions, in themselves, did not determine how or even whether a political system would work. The French case was distracting because it showed that some of the very instruments that produced stable government in England could do the reverse elsewhere. A constitutional form could not unify a deeply divided electorate in which continuing instability had left a heritage of political failure and cynicism. The same problems are occurring in Italy and most developing countries today, where one not only needs to believe that representative democracy *can* work, but needs to see evidence that it *does* work. More than faith is required of an electorate. Commitment to a democratic political culture requires effective mediating of interests and good policies. Where these have been lacking, democratic experiments have failed—in highly developed countries like post–World War I Germany and Italy and today in less-developed regions of Africa, Latin America, and Asia. The surprising thing is that, for the most part, people still desire political democracy—"when conditions are right." Belief in democratic systems and institutions may come and go but, on the whole, when they are absent, they are missed. When is representative government preferred? When are people apathetic to it? These are some of the questions that behavioralism deals with.

Behavioralists turn their attention away from political systems (especially legal and constitutional arrangements) to observe individual political action.[1] The change in perspective is important. The main

1. For a discussion of behavioralism, see D. E. Apter and Charles F. Andrain, eds., *Contemporary Analytical Theory* (Englewood Cliffs, N.J.: Prentice-Hall, 1972), pp.

emphasis of behavioralism is on the *relationship between* political knowledge and political action, including how political opinion is formed, how political acumen is acquired, and the ways people learn about political events. Such categories of thought are commonly referred to as ideologies, or **belief systems,** which create meaningful patterns of behavior.

Let us take busing as a form of desegregation as an example of how belief systems are formed and applied—decided less on its technical merits—that is, on its consequences for education and changing neighborhood and racial patterns—than by generalized ideological predispositions, the "conservative" or "liberal" interpretations of those affected by it. After exhibiting their initial stance on busing, people then develop technical arguments that support their views. Busing, or any other political matter, from the behavioralists' point of view, is a question of how groups come to share opinions, preferences, and beliefs. The behavioral approach takes into account factors of socialization, how we "internalize" values and prevailing beliefs, and how changes in outlook occur.

Intellectual Origins of Behavioralism

The intellectual origins of behavioralism are complex. Its spiritual ancestor was the skeptical philosophy of David Hume. Its American forerunner was the pragmatic philosophy of William James (1842–1910), which emphasized empiricism, voluntarism, the actions of individuals, and the connection between consciousness and purpose. Such concerns were congenial to Lockean principles of individualism, adding to them psychological variables that can be used to explain individual behavior.

Another forerunner of the behavioral school, who was similar in outlook to James, was the philosopher Charles S. Pierce (1839–1914), who invented the term *pragmatism*. And perhaps even more important was John Dewey (1859–1952), who sought to construct a practical philosophy of truth based not on ideal principles, but on the observation of experience. Experience in an open political system could be used to help people shape the instruments of life to solve social problems. Dewey's "instrumentalism," in particular, saw truth as conceived and tested in experience.

14–28, 459–84. See also Heinz Eulau, *The Behavioral Persuasion in Politics* (New York: Random House, 1963), pp. 13–55.

This general predisposition toward learning in action linked philosophy to the emerging discipline of psychology, and with this emphasis philosophy became a "scientific" or observational pursuit: One observed human behavior. The term *behavioralism* was coined by John B. Watson (1878–1958), a psychologist who considered learning to occur as a result of observations of the connections between stimuli and responses. Such "behavioral instrumentalism" inspired a new outlook on political life as a mode of social learning accomplished by trial-and-error experience. What went by the board was the speculative mode, the rationalistic or logical deductive analysis of the political philosophers.

Philosophy and history seemed fundamentally at odds with behavioral experimental methods. If they were interested in philosophical questions at all, behavioralists inclined toward the philosophy of science exemplified in the work of figures like Alfred North Whitehead, Rudolf Carnap, Carl Hempel, or Karl Popper. The object was to supplant metaphysical perspectives, replacing certainty with probability, rationalism with measures of central tendency, and description with distributions and measures of dispersion. Disparaging generalized and intuitive hypotheses in favor of more rigorously empirical ones based on observation, the behavioral point of view was ahistorical and nonevolutionary.[2]

The institutionalists were partly to blame. So concerned were they with mechanisms of rule, that they had left a philosophical vacuum. As institutional political analysis focused on means rather than ends, it lost its normative connections, which had apparently become self-evident. Appropriate legislation, reform, and a rich and voluminous body of law was the institutional "how" of governing, but it diluted understanding of "why." Behavioralism, while it did not fill the philosophical vacuum left by institutionalism, sought to examine the "why" of politics by examining individual action. Favoring a natural science paradigm, the behavioral movement was linked to Saint-Simon's doctrine of *positivism*, which emphasized scientific methods. Indeed, some political science behavioralists have become particularly interested in the link between experimentalism and scientific philosophy, a tradition represented by Mach, Poincaré, Frege, Wittgenstein, and those of the "Vienna Circle" who sought to locate principles of a unified science of human behavior and to link politics to "system theory." The *Encylo-*

2. For a discussion of the basic philosophical tendencies of behavioralism, see Abraham Kaplan, *The Conduct of Inquiry* (San Francisco: Chandler, 1964); and A. J. Ayer, ed., *Logical Positivism* (Glencoe, Ill.: The Free Press, 1959).

pedia of Unified Science,[3] for example, which encapsulated most of the great theories of logic, language, and biology, offered a new scientific orientation called *general systems analysis,* whose foremost exponent in political science was David Easton of the University of Chicago. But this gets us ahead of our story. Here we want to explore some of the characteristics of the scientific paradigm as applied to politics.

Behavior as action versus metaphysics

The political behavior of the individual person is the central and crucial empirical datum of the behavioral approaches to politics. This does not mean that research is restricted to the individual person as the theoretical focus of investigation. Indeed, most behavioral researchers are not concerned with the individual political actor as such. A small group, an organization, a community, an elite, a mass movement, or a national society may be the focus of behavioral inquiry and events; structures, functions, processes, or relations may serve as categories of behavioral analysis.[4]

Ideally, behavioral inferences are the result of careful generalizations based on observation conducted by means of explicit, empirical, and predominantly inductive methods, and mathematical and statistical techniques applied through interviewing and sampling. Behavioral study includes the use of indicators that identify regularities in conduct. The emphasis is on distributions rather than dichotomies, continuous variables rather than ideal types. Moreover, behavioralists insist on knowing what is "true" of public activity, and therefore turn their attention to variables: relationships, strategies of action, and the effects of size, number, and saliency variables. Behavioralists avoid large omnibus categories like "power" or "authority" because such terms, although seemingly providing explanations for behavior, are really only substitutes for them. If one explains the difference between the behavior of the French from that of the English by saying that the "cultures" are

3. See Otto Neurath, Charles Morris, and Rudolf Carnap, eds., *The International Encyclopedia of Unified Science* (Chicago: University of Chicago Free Press, 1955). Topics include theory of signs, logic and mathematics, linguistic aspects of science, procedures of empirical science, principles of the theory of probability, foundations of physics, cosmology, foundations of biology, and the conceptual framework of psychology. See also, Richard von Mises, *Positivism* (Cambridge, Mass.: Harvard University Press, 1951).
4. Heinz Eulau, op. cit., pp. 13–14.

different, one is merely saying that the French behave the way they do because they are French, or the English because they are English.[5]

To explain political events as a distribution of "power"—who has it and who does not—puts the cart before the horse. Power, as an omnibus term, or even the effects of power, do not "exist," nor can they be measured. Political events identify who has power and who does not. Power is behavior. As Brian Barry puts it,

[I]f we had an analysis of the state of society (etc.) that was sufficient to enable us to talk confidently about the distribution of power and the lines, and amounts of conflict, we would already be in a position to be able to explain political events. In other words, as a means to being able to describe the situation in terms of power and conflict, we would have to build up information and ways of analyzing that information, so good, that we would indeed be able to explain political events. But the logical relationship among the elements would be not that because we could talk about power and conflict we could explain political events but rather that because we could explain political events, we could talk about power and conflict.[6]

Behavioralists, then, work from the "bottom up." Their techniques for establishing important independent variables include regression analysis, factor analysis, Guttman scaling, indicator analysis, and other statistical measures. They use aggregate data that lead to determinations of saliency, or "vectors" that show the direction of change. Their theories derive from learning theory. Childhood experiences, the impact of education on attitudes, and the formation of public opinion all represent behavioral focuses.

The connection to politics was first made by Graham Wallas (1858–1932), a member of the executive committee of the Fabian Society and contributor to the *Fabian Essays in Socialism*.[7] Wallas, annoyed with the Fabian stress on economic explanations for human affairs, wanted students of politics to look at other facts of human nature—the effects of modern society on personality, the tensions produced by urban concentration, and so forth—to gain insights into the social psychology of

5. See David Easton, *The Political System* (New York: Knopf, 1953), pp. 115–24.
6. Brian Barry, "The Economic Approach to the Analysis of Power and Conflict," *Government and Opposition,* Vol. 9, No. 2 (Spring 1974), p. 189.
7. See George Bernard Shaw, ed., *Fabian Essays in Socialism* (New York: Doubleday). (First published in 1889.)

modern life. His book *Human Nature in Politics* was the first to deliberately shift from an economic model of politics to a psychological
one.[8] He was interested in how attitudes and opinions form and the
effects of the division of labor on the individual personality.

The "Chicago School": Similar questions arose in the United States
from the work of a scholar whose perspectives were very different from
those of Wallas, A. Lawrence Lowell. Lowell was an institutionalist, but
he emphasized government as the art of action and practice. The dynamic part of government he saw less as a matter of instrumentalities
of rule, than as the activities of politicians and particularly as the outcome of their conduct in political parties. The influence of these two
thinkers was so profound that the new issues of social psychology in
politics as well as the group activity model were given a special place in
the political science curriculum at the University of Chicago. There
under the influence of Harold Gosnell, who saw the possibilities of
statistical and behavioral analysis in the use of voting data, and Charles
Merriam, who made the break with institutionalism by concentrating
on group interaction, behavioralism properly got started. Harold D.
Lasswell, perhaps its most influential spokesman, was Merriam's student, adding a specifically Freudian dimension to psychological theories
going well beyond the applications attempted by Walter Lippmann
in his book *Preface to Politics*.[9] (The pursuit of behavioral concepts at
Chicago became contagious and eventually went far beyond the political
science arena to permeate the fields of educational testing, urban sociology, and statistical measurement.)

We can summarize some of the formative influences of the
"Chicago school" of behavioralism as follows:

1. It shifted the emphasis away from political ideals and institutions to the examination of individual and group conduct.

2. It favored a natural science paradigm over a normative one (how
people act, as opposed to how they should act).

3. It preferred explanations of behavior derived from theories of
learning and motivation rather than from models of institutional power.

4. It subdivided behavioral political science into two new lines of

8. See Graham Wallas, *Human Nature in Politics* (London: Constable, 1908).
9. Discussed in Bernard Crick, *The American Science of Politics* (London: Routledge and Kegan Paul, 1959), p. 109. It was Harold Lasswell who helped inject
frustration-aggression theory directly into political analysis with his book *Psychopathology and Politics* (Chicago, Ill.: University of Chicago Press, 1930), p. 261.

inquiry: the distribution of individual attitudes, beliefs, opinions, and preferences; and models of social learning.

The Democratic Aggregate and Public Opinion

Let us define the ruled as a *public*. Each unit of the public has preferences, wants, desires, and motivations. The political community is an aggregate, a political marketplace of preferences. So conceived, the public can be *operationalized* (systematically analyzed in terms of specific functions) as a set of relevant sample categories; that is, as a population to be surveyed. The object is to explain the variable support relationship between rulers and ruled. In a democratic system, since voters make periodic collective judgments through elections, elections and voting data are particularly good subjects for behavioral research.

Behavioralists share with institutionalists the belief that the people ultimately are the judges of rule. This idea is, in democratic political theory, analogous to the idea of consumer sovereignty in the economic marketplace—an expression of the sovereignty of the people. While politicians may ignore public opinion for a while, they cannot ignore it completely. Otherwise they would be in a position equivalent to that of a firm that ignores public taste in designing its product: If left with a large inventory, it faces a marketing crisis. Politicians who ignore public opinion are likely to find themselves without support.

Public support of policy is fundamental to democratic or liberal politics. But what if the people cannot judge? Walter Lippmann, whose view of the world was as gloomy as it was Platonic, saw public opinion as forming a triangular relationship "between the scene of action, the human picture of that scene, and the human response to that picture working itself out upon the scene of action."[10]

The pessimist's view: Since what people believe in, they believe to be real, the job of the politician is to create political reality by molding public opinion. The "picture" is not likely to trace reality, but to represent in some fashion—not necessarily "true" fashion—the exigencies of rule. The picture is often deliberately exaggerated, for the simple reason that politicians posture and clown for public viewing because doing so helps them manipulate voter responses. Yet what is really needed in a democracy is an educated understanding, greater clarity of

10. Walter Lippmann, *Public Opinion* (New York: Macmillan, 1932), p. 17.

vision, and shrewder judgments on the part of the public. The behavioral question therefore is two-fold: How can public opinion be manipulated? And how can a public learn to penetrate such falseness and achieve a more fundamental understanding of the processes of rule?

Informed judgment is hard to come by. It is not a matter simply of civic education, but of a host of assumptions that order the individual voter's world. Most of us rely on snap judgments to place complex issues in simple categories of rights and wrongs, moral justifications, and shallow beliefs. Thus humans, although moral beings, are easily mistaken in their political judgments. But given the range of stimuli received by individuals, the impinging events, activities, conflicts, and incidents to which they are subject, how else can they react?

At the core of every moral code there is a picture of human nature, a map of the universe, and a version of history. To human nature (of the sort conceived), in a universe (of the kind imagined), after a history (so understood), the rules of the code apply. So far as the facts of personality, of the environment and of memory are different, by so far the rules of the code are difficult to apply with success. Now every moral code has to conceive human psychology, the material world, and tradition some way or other. But in the codes that are under the influence of science, the conception is known to be an hypothesis, whereas in the codes that come unexamined from the past or bubble up from the caverns of the mind, the conception is not taken as an hypothesis demanding proof or contradiction, but as a fiction accepted without question. In the one case, man is humble about his beliefs, because he knows they are tentative and incomplete; in the other he is dogmatic, because his belief is a completed myth. The moralist who submits to the scientific discipline knows that though he does not know everything, he is in the way of knowing something; the dogmatist, using a myth, believes himself to share part of the insight of omniscience, though he lacks the criteria by which to tell truth from error. For the distinguishing mark of a myth is that truth and error, fact and fable, report and fantasy, are all on the same plane of credibility.[11]

Behavioralism addresses itself to the question of whether or not the circumstances of democratic life are self-defeating. Are citizens, as a mass

11. Ibid., p. 123.

or aggregate, capable of making rational and effective decisions? Or, in the name of democracy and rationality—the core of the Enlightenment ideal—does the individual become the dupe of the politician? And if so, is democracy a flawed doctrine, no matter how good its ideals, because an "intelligent public opinion" is not possible? If capable only of ideological understanding, a public cannot be expected to make informed judgments. And, this being the case, the idea of the sovereignty of the people—and indeed virtually all the assumptions of both the liberal and radical theorists as well as those of institutionalists—need revision. Lippmann's views challenged the liberal tradition of democracy as participant government.

The self-rectifying society: The notion that democracy is too good for the common people goes back to Plato. Modern political scientists with a more positive view of the force of public opinion recognize not only that the questions are extremely complex, but seek to redefine the issues along a fact-oriented model. Were Lippmann's assumptions psychologically correct? Does long-term public opinion in a democracy differ from short-run public opinion? Or, granted ill-informed judgments, manipulative political leaders, and a fatuous citizenry, is there also in a democracy a self-correcting process? Most behavioral political scientists conclude that democracy, as a system, is able to rectify its worst errors. As Merriam put it, the system is not "static."

The normal American system has evolved, and by evolving it has survived. It has evolved and survived from aristocracy to mass democracy, through slavery, civil war, the tentative reconciliation of North and South, the repression of Negroes and their halting liberation; through two great wars of worldwide scope, mobilization, far flung military enterprise, and return to hazardous peace; through numerous periods of economic instability and one prolonged depression with mass unemployment, farm "holidays," veteran's marches, tear gas, and even bullets; through two periods of post-war cynicism, demagogic excesses, invasions of traditional liberties, and the groping, awkward, often savage, attempt to cope with problems of subversion, fear, and civil tension.

 Probably this strange hybrid, the normal American political system, is not for export to others. But so long as the social prerequisites of democracy are substantially intact in this country, it appears to be a relatively efficient system for reinforcing agreement, encouraging, and main-

taining social peace in a restless and immoderate people operating a gigantic, powerful, diversified, and incredibly complex society.[12]

The answer to the problem raised by Lippmann is not, simply, how to evaluate the quality of public judgment at any moment, but how people learn by experience; how they see their needs as individuals and members of society. The emphasis on individual learning as a cumulative process is not the same as the idea of the individual in the eighteenth century, which held that aggregate interests produced the societal or the public interest. Nor was it similar to the nineteenth-century, evolutionary, individual-in-society view, which was preoccupied with how changing societies affected individuals. The questions one needs to answer to deal with modern behavioralism concentrate on the circumstances of adaptive behavior: When are individuals willing to take risks, to involve themselves in politics, to reconsider long-standing views?

To understand these things it is necessary to consider society from an individual standpoint, to learn how and why broad group affiliations —of class, region, occupation, income, religion, ethnicity, and so on— shape beliefs, attitudes, and ideas. While psychology investigates the properties of the individual *qua* individual, behavioral political science studies both aggregate, or mass, behavior and individual motivations. The connecting links are social groups, whether faction, trade union, political party, or interest cluster. It is the organizational capacity of individuals, the way people form and shape their lives by acting in concert with others, that links the individual to society. It is group activity that helps create individual and aggregate norms, not in some abstract way, but in relation to the needs and concerns of individuals. Therefore, although a collective public opinion might be faulty, especially when confronted with a difficult or perplexing problem, public opinion can be disaggregated. In a variety of more particular concerns, the picture becomes very different: People know a great deal.

The behavioral task is to redefine the relation of the individual to the group in general, and to different kinds of groups in particular. Which groups are strategic ones that affect individual learning? When does the school or work group limit or transcend parochial and narrow views? When do ideas that might not be encountered in the home, church, or other domestic relationships broaden rather than restrict the

---

12. Charles E. Merriam, *Systematic Politics* (Chicago: University of Chicago Press, 1945), p. 220–21.

individual's sensibility and efficiency? Under what circumstances does group interaction lead to greater personal security? Under what circumstances does the reverse occur? Where prejudice exists between different communities living side by side, proximity sometimes reduces hostility and sometimes increases it. Given the selective way we perceive each other, when do negative or hurtful examples reinforce stereotypes, while positive and friendly examples go unnoticed? When is the opposite true?

The liberal and radical ideals minimize differences between individuals. But in reality, differences between groups based on cultural traditions, race, religion, language, and nationality are persistent and self-perpetuating. Particularly in primarily immigrant societies (like the United States or Argentina), how should these be regarded? Should they form the basis of group competition? Or do such groups prevent adherence to common values, a public interest, and a national culture? If public opinion is a consequence of values that emphasize differences in traditions that stimulate grievances (such as exist among the Basques in Spain, Biafrans in Nigeria, French in Canada, and Catholics in Northern Ireland), then public behavior is likely to be touchy, hostile, negatively informed, uncompromising, and prone to conflict.

Behavioral analysis also considers questions of fundamental groups, and the importance of class, occupation, and other factors Marx saw as deriving from the people's relation to the means of production. But it considers other issues from a more individualistic perspective. The idea of public opinion replaces the idea of "class consciousness." The concern is how individuals perceive their situations. For example, how do working-class attitudes cluster? Are they primarily the result of exploitation, fear of unemployment, and individual vulnerability? How does membership in trade unions affect them? Do such organizations and the labor discipline that enables them to accomplish their purposes necessarily make working-class individuals "conservative" or "liberal"? What is the effect on workers' attitudes of trade union research and the identification of pertinent issues? How do these promote more effective collective bargaining with employers? What effects do trade unions' concerns with legislation have on how workers perceive their interests, scrutinize the voting records of politicians, and vote? When do such groups become more or less ideologically active, screening ideas through the filter of preconceived notions—liberal, communist, socialist, or pragmatic—focusing on specific issues?

A great many questions of behavioral politics stand between the

Lippmann and the Merriam assumptions. Empirical evidence used to facilitate answers is derived from measures of the movements of populations, social mobility, changing class relationships, social opportunities, educational improvements, and the effect of all these on new modes of participation, ideological commitments, and affiliations.

Motivating Self-Interests

We have suggested that the original behavioral concern was fear, or mistrust of public opinion. An ill-formed or uninformed electorate was seen as a threat to democracy. Research has shown that public misinformation, and the extremism that it invites, can result in the election of demagogues or those unconcerned with the public interest, not to speak of lowering the level of public trust. Lowell once called public opinion the "motive force of democracy," the foundation and precondition of democratic participation. The research that has stemmed from this view has been remarkable in both its diversity and extent.[13]

Key's "political game" analogy: Perhaps the most important early study was V. O. Key's *Public Opinion and American Democracy.*[14] Key, a utilitarian theorist, considered self-interest an essential motivating element in politics.

Politics is not, like marbles, a game played for sport. It is a game played for keeps, a game in which the stakes are high. The way the game is played and who wins effect every citizen and perhaps even his children and grandchildren.[15]

A game is, first of all, played by players. Then the play itself is competitive; some win and some lose. What is lost is of value to both losers and winners; that is, they agree on a prize that is of value. However, winning is more than just victory, although that implies an excit-

---

13. See A. Lawrence Lowell, "The Nature of Public Opinion," *Reader in Public Opinion and Communication,* ed. Bernard Berelson and Morris Janowitz (Glencoe, Ill.: The Free Press, 1950), p. 27.

14. See V. O. Key, Jr., *Public Opinion and American Democracy* (New York: Alfred A. Knopf, 1963). See also Robert A. Dahl, *Who Governs?* (New Haven, Conn.: Yale University Press, 1961).

15. See V. O. Key, Jr., *Politics, Parties and Pressure Groups* (New York: T. Y. Crowell, 1948), p. 1.

ing struggle in which triumph is attended by some public token of recognition. It means winning individual or team (group) benefits and opportunities. In a game the strategy of the players is a means of outwitting opponents. But since wits, knowledge, and skill are all essential elements for taking part in the game, strategies also stimulate learning. One needs not only to know one's opponents but to know the network of rules and processes (institutions) by which the game is played. In the political game, one's occupational and educational opportunities, living conditions, social affiliation, religion, and other factors are the stakes. The "teams" are various cultural, social, or political groups with different bundles of utilities, diverse interests, and various perceptions of scarcity.

Winning translates composite demands into policy. Political parties package social utilities in the form of legislation. Part of the game is to gain a privileged place among governmental priorities for a certain interest, by whatever means possible according to the rules of the game. The strategy may be for one group to mix its priorities with those of another, forming a package representing a larger public interest. Then the ensemble of such packages is used to define the public interest, according to the judgments of those in office. According to these judgments, potential losses and gains to be incurred at the polls, and actual policies validated or invalidated by the electorate, the compromise distribution of interests occurs. The behavioral model is outlined in Figure 8-1. (Notice that the structure of the model is the same as that of Plato's model.)

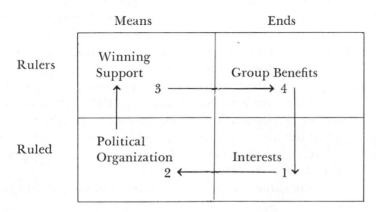

Figure 8-1. Key's Behavioral Model

In Key's model of behavioral political functions, group benefits define individual interests, which in turn are promoted by political organizations. Candidates for political office woo organizations by promising to pay off in terms of group benefits.

Key elaborated the model by showing that when each cluster of players pursues privileged priorities, opinion is converted to interests—agrarian, labor, business, and so forth. As such groups proliferate, specialized knowledge replaces generalized knowledge. Add sectional and urban "players" and we find more, not less knowledge generated, but of a different sort than that envisaged by the liberal theorists. Interests and sectionalism intersect class; therefore class becomes the omnibus group, with parties mediating between classes. Differences between, say, Northern industry (to use the United States as an example)—manufacturers and workers—and landowning Southern agrarians and sharecroppers are great, but coalitions form between Northern industrialists and Southern landowners in the Democratic party. Intersectional conflict can be mediated despite vast differences in loyalty, dialect, ethnicity, religion, occupation, and class. This multiplicity of possibilities lends itself to more precise study, and to comparisons over time. Some variables are more salient than others. Changes in political "ecology" occur, as those induced by the large-scale black immigration to northern U.S. cities that began during World War II. Public opinion, then, is abstract until it is applied to specific issues, and manifested in the platforms of organization and electoral coalitions.

In *Public Opinion and American Democracy*, Key argued against Lippmann's attack on the ability of people to generate an informed public opinion. People, reckoned Key, have all sorts of opinions. On some issues they have very strong or intense views. On some they may be very well informed. But their judgments will not be uniformly motivated or reasoned, because opinions are distributed along occupational, sectional, geographical, and other structurally differentiated lines. Some attitudes are latent, representing potential opinion. Most immediate, or manifest, beliefs are determined by one's social situation, family, education, or the impact of the media. But these beliefs are *measurable*. And the relationship of such variables can be described on various indices and factored for significance.[16]

In turn, motivating variables such as education and so forth can be

16. See Key, *Public Opinion and American Democracy*.

linked to one's affiliation with certain institutions. These may be interest groups, or political parties. What is unique about the behavioral concept of institutional relationships is that the institution represents a body composed of many interests, which it tries to mold into aggregate opinion. Politicians need to transcend provincial views and approximate this wider public interest perspective if they are to win institutional endorsement. To study how this works goes beyond studying the methods of party organization, to extracting its ways and purposes of extending patronage, favors, contracts, and other political "goodies" to recruit support.

A successful political party makes payoffs to various interested groups. But unless these transcend the interests of a favored few, the voters, who are more numerous than members of specific interest groups, will come to regard the party as a tool of the special interests. Hence political behavior among leaders forms a mixed strategy in which personal pressures and the politics of the parish pump stimulate the political processes.

Key's emphasis was on the game itself. He was less concerned with institutions, the role of the president, the functions of the executive branch, or the efficiency of public service than with the players and what they represent. Key defined a broadly based empirical field of study that points in two directions. Using Key's model one can examine how attitudes, opinions, and ideologies form, concentrating on social learning. Or one might focus on how group interaction works, at any level of politics (especially in terms of party and voting behavior), to form specific ideologies.

Learning models: The question "How can we account for beliefs deeply held or attitudes firmly formed?" was asked by the psychologist H. J. Eysenck, who attempted to formulate some relatively simple answers. He tried to find correlations between social status and political class, education and political attitude, religious affiliation and political attitude, and sex and voting preferences. Intercorrelations between these indicate ideological preferences. He showed how public opinion polls could be used to locate essential data, and how to evaluate opinions according to "scalograms" and other types of measurement. He put together findings in terms of dichotomous personality types. For example, given a sample of attitude testing on issues like capital punishment, birth control, war, and communism, Eysenck found that two attitudinal typologies emerged among the sample population: a radical/

conservative dichotomy and a tenderminded/toughminded one. Depending on the temperament of people judged according to these categories, conclusions could be drawn about people's personality structures, degree of intellectual rigidity, their need to dominate, and so on.[17]

Other studies dealing with the effect of personality on public opinion are more sophisticated than Eysenck's early work. Some use personality types to describe pathologies like the "authoritarian personality." Others delineate cultural styles or "national character," showing how these determine patterns of socialization.[18] After Key, the psychological dimensions of public opinion study rapidly became more elaborate and experimental, and today it is an enterprise in which social psychologists, sociologists, and statisticians, in addition to political scientists, engage. Various refinements of the original ideas have developed. Cultural groups have become known as *reference groups,* and much research posits how salient attitudes of group members tend to reinforce each other and create sustained beliefs, as well as exerting group pressure against backsliding. Yet there is a threshold beyond which group analysis does not sufficiently explain processes of political attitude formation. People do change. If most of us inculcate and reiterate the views of our parents and social and institutional affiliates, there are times when we do not. Moreover, what is true for the aggregate may be untrue for the individual.[19]

Learning models stress precisely the persistence and change of political attitudes. But what are the circumstances under which one belief is transformed into another? Why do some beliefs inculcated as values stick, while others change? The largest proportion of children of conservative parents wind up as conservatives too. Why? Does the answer lie in the pattern of childhood socialization? Are the needs of the human organism so strong that the hunger for affection, security, and nurture builds up attitudes of trust, affection, and attachment so deep that loyalty to a political ideal is basically no more than a function of the transfer of parental attitudes to the child? Does the degree of internalization of such attitudes during primary, face-to-face socialization form so

17. See H. J. Eysenck, *The Psychology of Politics* (New York: Praeger, 1954) .
18. See M. Brewster Smith, Robert W. White, and Jerome S. Bruner, *Opinions and Personality* (New York: Wiley, 1956) ; Fred Greenstein, *Children and Politics* (New Haven: Yale University Press, 1965) ; and H. McClosky and H. E. Dahlgren, "Primary Group Influence on Party Loyalty" in *American Political Science Review,* Vol. 53, (1959) , pp. 757–76.
19. Perhaps the best discussion of the formation of public opinion is Robert Lane and David Sears, *Public Opinion* (Englewood Cliffs, N.J.: Prentice-Hall, 1964) .

necessary a shield of protective psychological armament that the child will in later life select peer groups that replace family with a network of supplementary supporting links and associations, reference groups, and friends? Or, if one repudiates family belief systems, does this produce guilt and conflict? Do divergent views occur most noticeably during periods of rapid economic change?

These and other behavioral questions require analysts to find ways to link up empirical observations of individuals, politicians, voters, and groups influential in the competitive politics of democratic society to models of learning and group life. The "game" of which Key spoke is not simply played by a commonwealth of voters, each member being a competitor capable of joining "play" or withdrawing from it at will. The formation of the capabilities and sensitivities of the players themselves is part of the action. To measure the players' abilities requires statistical evidence—on voting, attitudes, social background, and other indicators—all of which provide a data base representing a realistic construction of the world as people live in and perceive it.

Behavioral considerations also take us beyond the rational dimension of political behavior, to the realm of deeper sentiments and feelings, particularly those which—although they may take the form of logical arguments—are disguises for unsound arguments for pseudological thinking.[20] After all, we all know that words stir emotions and symbols affect thought.[21] Rationalistic beliefs are not the whole story.

Indeed, today we know that all beliefs represent bundles of notions that organize and systematize the wealth of stimuli that assaults our senses at every moment. To phrase this psychological concept in terms of its importance to politics, one might say that we attach meanings to words beyond what the speaker or writer says. We *interpret* what others say and attribute motives to them which add context to content. A politician making a speech is not simply an individual voicing private opinions, but the representative of a party as well as various social, economic, and other institutional reference groups. A position on issues makes us feel sympathetic or antagonistic and these "gut" feelings connect to our experiences, resonating with previous connections to friends or enemies, family, and significant events. Political ideas connect to our own per-

20. See Harry Stack Sullivan, "Tensions Interpersonal and International," *Tensions that Cause War,* ed. Hadley Cantril (Urbana, Ill.: University of Illinois Press, 1950), pp. 21–124
21. See S. E. Finer's discussion in the introduction to Vilfredo Pareto, *Sociological Writings* (London: Pall Mall Press, 1966), p. 41.

sonal histories and, by making us feel part of an on-going process, link us to history itself.

The range of formative influences and personal experience, screened through the ideas commonly held by both individuals and organizations, needs to be analyzed in component parts. It is most important to remember that, as politics becomes increasingly specialized, the general public's political opinions are increasingly less well defined, and judgments rely more and more on pre-existing patterns of belief. The political process connects decision-making processes to these broad belief systems. It is through such systems, and what they imply for our behavior as participants in representative government, that we are conscious of politics. Schools, the media, political events, campaigns, and the degree of relevance of these to our private lives, all influence our belief structures and our behavior.

Ideological belief structures: Key's second emphasis was on the study of *ideology*, which can be approached in any one of four ways. One may see it as a popular manifestation of a particular political philosophy or tradition, a more or less coherent body of views, ideas, or dogma subscribed to by a group. Liberalism, Marxism, fascism, nationalism, socialism, "Americanism," all are examples of ideologies. Such ideologies are described by particular terms which emphasize significant values. The ideologies with the best-defined terminology are *doctrines*, bodies of principles having some degree of internal logic and prescribing "dos" and "don'ts."

A second way to examine an ideology is to ask, "What are its determining factors?"—class, social position, or ethnic or religious affiliation. To examine an ideology in this way is to relate it to social learning theories. One might study to what extent a person's social position determines ideology, or how a person's role or position in society decides that person's values and beliefs. This approach leads us to attribute doctrinal preferences to social determinants.[22]

For example, Marxists who treat ideology as "superstructure" consider it a manifestation of the class affiliation of an individual. Since classes form out of the organization of factors of production, people who make their living under common conditions share common views. The views of each class are limited and the perspective false or partial, unless

22. See Karl Mannheim, *Ideology and Utopia* (New York: Harcourt Brace Jovanovich, 1946), p. 46.

the class is one capable of transcending its position. Marx hoped that by a more scientific examination of society partial views could be transformed into whole truths to foment a class struggle that would end with society so transformed that individuals would understand their free relationships with one another. Then false consciousness and partial understanding not only would disappear, but the relationship of ideology to truth would be "unmasked."

Behavioral interpretations reject this view and treat the Marxist ideology like any other.[23] But both behavioralists and Marxists agree on the significance of ideology as a possible determinant of behavior. From this standpoint, ideology can be treated empirically; that is, the way specific political beliefs arc distributed in a population can be measured.

In addition to the analysis of the nature of belief systems and the distribution of them according to social class or interests, a third way to examine an ideology is to look at the needs it fulfills for both individuals and societies. For individuals, ideologies help make coherent one's sense of self. To accept a particular philosophy or set of beliefs allows one to reject others and identify with people who see things similarly. This affects what some psychologists have called a "need for affiliation," a need satisfied by joining an association that stands for certain principles that represent what might be called an *ego ideal*. A child models his or her ideals on the example set by parents, but seeks the public validation of these in terms of belief systems as well. So ideology is a way of relating the self to society and the ego to the environment. As *ego identity,* or the consciousness of self, develops, one's self-image becomes the picture one has of the self in the community. It may be active or passive, accepting or rejecting, radical or conservative. One might say that the third dimension of ideology, then, relates to personal identity.[24]

The implications of this identity element are varied. Identity can include one's feeling of pride in the history of one's national achievements in contrast to other nations' "failures." When the failures of others are regarded as coming from a particular defect of that people or society—a lack of character, perhaps—then "identity" can lead to prejudice and discrimination. One's own society is seen as "good"—committed to moral ends, freedom, accomplishments in science and art, and the

23. See Charles E. Osgood, "Behavior Theory and the Social Sciences," *Behavioral Science,* Vol. 1 (July, 1956), pp. 167–185.
24. See Erik H. Erikson, *Identity, Youth and Crisis* (New York: Norton, 1967), pp. 225–231.

attainment of ideals—while the "other's" values are seen as opposite in every way. This polarized perception allows one to view one's own political system as superior to all others.

Following this line of argument, it is easy to see how people become troubled when they no longer take pride in their political identity. For example, precisely because it has supposedly been principled, the American identity has suffered severely in recent years. Today the American identity includes being violence-prone, philistine, and imperialistic. (Since Vietnam and Watergate, Americans are not sure of the purity of their national identity.) For some, personal identities have become separated from the national one, producing individual crises and the search for new solutions, new ideologies, and new principles.

If the connection between ideology and identity has weakened in the United States, most Americans still believe in their capacity to reform themselves. They have faith in both their intelligence and the democratic political process. So the identities of most Americans remain connected to liberal ideologies, democratic institutions, and constitutional boundaries. Only a relatively few Americans prefer to change their personal political identities to subscribe to ideologies that may threaten or, at least, challenge the conventional positive image we have of ourselves. Indeed, challenges to the notion of our utilitarian, greatest-good-for-the-greatest-number society, upsets those with high positive identities, perpetrating witch hunts, persecutions, spying, and other actions that violate the very principles embodied in the Constitution. A threat to our identities can make us act in ways that can violate fundamentally self-defining ideals.[25]

The fourth aspect of ideology is related to the third. Ideology not only links the individual to society in a principled way, but also links the rulers to the ruled. Ideology represents the basis of legitimacy, the justified use of power. It establishes moral principles on the basis of which power can be exercised. If some individuals come to believe that their government either does not live up to such principles, or if they want to change the principles, then the legitimacy of the government is threatened. When legitimacy is in doubt, one can expect deep, polar divisions within the population. Each cleavage becomes symbolically loaded with moral significance.

25. See Kurt Lewin, "Field Theory and Learning," *Field Theory and Social Science* (New York: Harper & Row, 1951), pp. 60–84. See also Martin Seliger, *Ideology and Politics* (New York: The Free Press, 1976), pp. 233–55.

There are, of course, many forms taken by such ideological conflicts. But it was the French Revolution that connected ideology to legitimacy. Subsequent revolutions were no longer fought for "freedom" (as were the English or American or French), but rather for the "happiness of man." It became permissible to think about "forcing men to be free." Struggles over moral priorities or ethical imperatives are not easily compromised. Identities forged in battle develop intense convictions, and a propensity for extremism surfaces—all, usually, in the name of morality. Legitimacy, and the struggle for it, may be protracted, only to be put down by authoritarian means. Order often becomes the supreme commandment, by virtue of which can be justified the violence of the state against the citizen.[26]

Thus the four different ways we can break down the study of ideology enable us to obtain several perspectives on the effects of ideology on behavior. Ideologies can be compared as relatively coherent systems of meaning including moral and philosophical preferences. How they are distributed can be analyzed in terms of the connection between social position and the expression of ideology as class interest or preference. The intensity, or the significance, of an ideology to various persons, can be analyzed according to the need people have to clarify who they are in relation to others (particularly regarding religion and nationalism). Finally, the relation between ideology and legitimacy implicates the other three issues as well, particularly with respect to conflict behavior which, in its most extreme form, can challenge the basic consensus about principles of government themselves.

All four systems of study affect how people perceive themselves and others, what they consider to be important, who or what they will or will not support, when they will join parties or movements, when they can be relied on to sacrifice, support, and give loyalty to a cause (and the limits on all these), the character and intensity of their prejudices, and so on. In these terms we cannot divide public opinion into the ideas of true believers and nonbelievers. All people—in one or more senses of the term *ideology* as used above—have an ideological construction by which they mold their beliefs, whether they are active or passive or apathetic. The question is: What enables one of these four modes to become significant?[27]

26. See Hannah Arendt, *On Revolution* (New York: The Viking Press, 1963), pp. 13–52.
27. See Hans Toch, *The Social Psychology of Social Movements* (Indianapolis, Ind.: Bobbs-Merrill, 1965).

Public opinion versus ideology: Ideology differs in a number of ways from public opinion in general, even though public opinion helps us to see how ideologies are distributed, and ideologies help us understand some of the determinants of public opinion. The two can be distinguished on the basis of support, that is, whether the belief is broadly based or limited to an elite. A specific ideology (like that of the communist parties in Italy or France) may belong to a particular political elite. The problem is how to convert it into a mass ideology. Using propaganda, persuasion, argument, and confrontation will, if the effort is successful, cause adherence to the ideology to become widespread. It will govern public opinion and affect voting and the like. The object is to universalize the ideology in the mass so that it becomes internalized and involuntarily governs public opinion.

In democracies the reverse is true. Elites hold competing ideologies with which they hope to appeal to the mass, but public opinion is only loosely connected to these. The situation in turn helps reduce the ideological convictions of the elite.

It is when we go from public opinion to ideology that differences between ideas held by an elite and opinions distributed throughout a population become striking. The difference between Lippmann's distrust of mass beliefs and Merriam's restoration of faith in popular judgment is partly due to a difference between how opinions in general and beliefs as ideologies interact in competitive politics. Competitive political elites have to connect a following with some kind of political action. They seek middle ground between simplistic or populist opinions— some of which are no more than prejudices, most of which are ill-thought out if not ill-conceived—and more ideologically defined notions. It is in this middle ground between popular public opinion and elite idea systems that the behavioral side of ideology connects to institutionalism.

As we have indicated, ideology refers to broad patterns of beliefs which attain some degree of coherence as ideas and establish certain moral priorities, rights and wrongs, and principles of rule and equity. Ideological labels, imprecise though they may be, indicate some broad distinctions along the lines suggested and are perhaps best understood in terms of alternative or antagonistic views: During the seventeenth century in Europe, Catholicism and Protestantism shaped opinions in the context of contending religious ideologies; in eighteenth-century England, conservatism and liberalism were their secular equivalents; in modern times, liberalism (much modified from its original designs) stands in contrast to various radical doctrines. The principles each favors—political freedom versus economic equality, for example—go deep enough to establish different political priorities. And each defines public opinion. But out of the varieties of opinions held by a mass public, new elites may arise to voice new ideologies. Social democracy and Christian democracy, for example, represented mixtures of the liberal concern with political freedom and socialist reforms for economic and social equality.

Ideologies may be independent of political parties, but all parties can be distinguished by the degree to which their ideology varies with the flow of mass opinions and preferences. Indeed, as instruments they link the broad or populist views of mass publics to the more specific interests of various elites. Ideologies add elements of principle to interests. So, whether one is in favor of more social welfare, public higher education, greater social services, compensatory programs for the poor, socialized medicine, publicly supported legal defenders, or whatever, does not depend merely on simple self-interests, but on other ideologically defined principles of fairness or equity as well. Those who, in principle, regard it as the fault of society that some are poor and in greater need of public assistance than others who are rich, are more prone to support parties and leaders willing to redistribute wealth on behalf of the poor. Those who, as a matter of principle, regard poverty as the fault primarily of the individual support those who regard it as unfair to penalize the rich to pay for the poor.[28]

To one extent or another, doctrines and ideas characteristic of modern ideologies do not differ much from earlier religious beliefs. Conflicts over principles of justice and equity were as much a part of the Reformation as were arguments over the nature of salvation. The churches saw themselves as a link between poor and rich, and undertook seriously to ameliorate the suffering of the poor. Similarly, modern political parties are not only defenders of a particular clientele, they offer their version of an appropriate political society.

Belief Systems

Constraints on belief: As research on belief systems progresses, the purpose is more and more to predict, rather than to explain, when ideas will determine action. Philip Converse uses the term *belief system* to denote

28. See Robert E. Lane, *Political Ideology* (New York: The Free Press of Glencoe, 1962), pp. 432–35.

"a configuration of ideas and attitudes in which the elements are bound together by some form of constraint or functional interdependence."[29] By "constraint" Converse means the extent to which it is possible to predict—from a list of critical indicators like welfare, nationalization, aid to education, and so forth—the position a person might take because he or she already holds a specific set of attitudes or beliefs. When such ideas are interdependent, changing one idea will require also changing others.

To determine what constraints imposed by interdependent factors can be used to increase predictability, it is useful to suppose that, in forming beliefs, individuals are placed in a choice situation. How, given a problem, does a belief system preselect a person's reactions? No one encounters a problem in political life without some prejudices, if only as part and parcel of one's personal attitudes about human nature. After all, in our hearts many of us take a basically Hobbesian view of "human nature." We regard fellow human beings with suspicion. If they are not downright evil, they are out to "rob you blind."

But the same notions may, without too much alteration, be interpreted in a Lockean way. One might regard most people as reasonably good, or suppose that they prefer to be that way, given half an opportunity. Then, to maximize the potential for good, what is required is the prosperity and freedom of the individual. Since poverty and restriction may apparently make people perverse, this position can lead to a preference for moderate reform. One who prefers a more extreme view (such as that freedom does not produce the general good if tainted by inequality) may desire radical change. On extreme grounds militant elites may favor transforming ideologies that propose to forcefully reshape public opinion for its own good.

Belief preferences remain at the core of most modern ideologies. By combining them in diverse ways, analysts can measure peer group and other reinforcements of belief according to political commitment. Most belief systems, even quite opposite ones, can be mutually accommodating, except when they collide in confrontational situations. (When one gets hit over the head by a police officer wielding a club one's belief system tends to be strengthened. The police become an enemy rather than a symbol of authority.) However, some ideologies embrace "contestation" (as it is called in France) as a principle, pre-

29. Philip E. Converse, "The Nature of Belief Systems in Mass Publics," *Ideology and Discontent,* ed. D. E. Apter (New York: The Free Press of Glencoe, 1964), p. 207.

ferring conflict to compromise because it forces a public to take sides. Not only is this a way of establishing ideological commitment and loyalty, but conflict makes the ideology more defined. For example, in war, the most accommodating and mildly held belief systems turn into powerful and mandatory dogmas.

Value orientations: Thus, while belief systems are closely affiliated with interests, as Key indicated, there is more to it than that. Interests are negotiable. And, in a democratic system, continuous bargaining is a way of adjusting differences. But when the differences are deeply held values, it is not so easy. People dig in their heels on matters of deep concern. If their degree of adherence to certain beliefs could be scaled, we would see that the more a belief system is value laden, the more it constrains behavior (see Figure 8-2).[30]

Figure 8-2 suggests that the greater the degree to which ideological *values* are formed and subscribed to, the greater the likelihood of conflict *(c)*. The lower we move down the ideological scale, to *interests* and *preferences,* the greater the likelihood of successful mediation of conflicting ideals through political parties, trade unions, and other organizations that bargain and convert conflict into competition *(b)*.

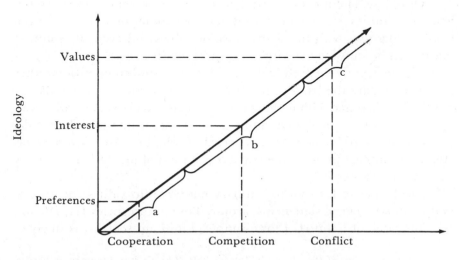

Figure 8-2. Belief System and Behavior

30. See Arnold M. Rose, ed., *Human Behavior and Social Processes* (Boston: Houghton Mifflin, 1962), pp. 3–19.

Finally, when ideological factors represent simply *preferences,* it becomes possible for people to cooperate in order for all parties to gain (*a*).

Democratic societies give a special twist to this hierarchy of beliefs. Because they place high value on holding preferences (for example, those preferences according to which one votes), values and preferences conjoin. Negotiation and bargaining become a matter of principle. For those who subscribe to democracy, then, it appears that a high degree of commitment to the principle of bargaining is itself the end of ideology. "Ideologues" are those who subscribe to all values save that of allowing the free expression of preferences over all values.[31]

In short, in democratic systems there is a tendency toward ideological agreement. Intransigence in practical politics declines in favor of preference bargaining and the accommodation of interests. Ideological dogma declines.[32] Even in France and Italy, where politics have been based on long-standing value-laden cleavages, and political associations work to convert preferences into interests and interests into values with high potentiality for conflict, ideological dogmas have declined. Even communist parties in both countries are slowly becoming parties of interests, rather than values, and are striving more and more to cooperate with others. Cleavages such as those based on class, race, ethnicity, age, and so on become more latent.

Of course, latent conflict can become manifest again, transforming issues into values that elicit extraordinary confrontation or contestation. Conflict increases with the significance of values and even the simplest matter can become loaded with ideological significance.

Where negotiable preferences and interests, and competition rather than conflict, are the bases of political life, the portion of a population explicitly concerned with ideological matters is usually very small. Measuring this portion involves dividing a society according to different degrees, or levels, of ideological conceptualization. The American electorate, for example, can be divided on a continuum of ideological intensity as shown in Table 8-1.[33]

Ideologues seek to make ordinary matters into values which, embodied in ideological statements, arouse those in categories III, IV, and V to the pitch of I and II. (For example, a militant socialist is likely to

---

31. See the discussion of this theme in Daniel Bell, *The End of Ideology* (Glencoe, Ill.: The Free Press, 1960), pp. 269–70.
32. See Erik Allardt, "Finland: Institutionalized Radicalism," *Decline of Ideology?* ed. M. Rejai (Chicago: Aldine: Atherton, 1971), pp. 117.
33. See Converse, op. cit., p. 218.

Table 8-1.

	Proportion of total sample (*percent*)	Proportion of voters (*percent*)
I. Ideologues	2.5	3.5
II. Near-ideologues	9	12
III. Group interest	42	45
IV. Nature of the times	24	22
V. No issue content	22.5	17.5
	100%	100%

perceive a collective bargaining arrangement between trade unionists and management as an opportunity to instigate a confrontation that would radicalize workers and stimulate a more revolutionary consciousness.)

Near-ideologues are less dogmatically involved in ideologies than real ideologues, but they are likely to maintain identifiable positions—socialist, conservative, liberal, or whatever. A public conscious of such affiliations rallies appropriate ideological persuasions; then, within each group, pressures are generated to reinforce and support such views. A dissident becomes an object of suspicion, and changing one's mind is considered backsliding or even betrayal. In contrast, ordinary interest groups in which ideological forces are weak express their opportunism in negotiation. For example, in the United States many business organizations contribute to both Republican and Democratic parties. Indeed, interest groups are usually willing to affiliate with or support any or all parties catering to their specific concerns, regardless of where they stand on other issues.

For some who do not differentiate among ideological preferences, politics, especially corrupt politics, is simply part of the "nature of things." People are the victims of chance, fortune, and uncontrollable events. For them there is no general rationale. On the other hand, ideologues will always see in an event something they "knew" all along. For example, if there is a depression in a capitalistic society, a militant Marxist ideologue will interpret it as an inevitable effect of contradictory forces at work in the capitalist system. A near-ideologue socialist might argue that, because capitalism engenders contradictions that can have harmful consequences, something should be done to mitigate the ill effects, for example, nationalizing industry or increasing social welfare. Those with a strong group interest in the matter, like trade union-ists, will argue the need for more secure welfare payments, a broader jobs program, better social security coverage, and other reforms en-abling the unemployed to go back to work or offering more of a cushion against depression. When an event is viewed as part of the nature of the times, chances are people will act primarily on their own behalf, "weath-ering the storm" if they can. They are less likely to seek solutions in organized action. It is not that apolitical people are necessarily apa-thetic, but rather that they lack a belief system that converts issues into more generalized but cognitive patterns.[34]

Many people perceive no issue controversy at all, even in events affecting their well-being or happiness. In this condition people attach no significance to an action, beyond the action itself. Whereas, to an ideologue, a beggar in the street represents defects in society as a whole, to one who apprehends no issue content, a beggar in the street is just a beggar in the street.

Ideology as Political Behavior

We have suggested how ideology is connected to public opinion, and that it stands at the intersection between philosophical principles or ends, individual preferences and beliefs, and general and particular values. These intercepts are outlined in Figure 8-3.

Values, interests, and preferences obviously overlap. Ideologies are combinations of these attributes—sometimes coherent and sometimes not. Preferences can be converted to interests and interests to values, or they may be elevated to the status of values in order to achieve interests.

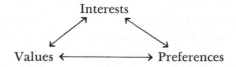

Figure 8-3. Components of Ideology

34. Sartori has distinguished ideology in knowledge from ideology in politics; we regard this as an interesting, but false distinction. See Giovanni Sartori, "Politics, Ideology, and Belief Systems," *American Political Science Review,* 63 (1969) : 400–404.

Some political parties transform ideology into dogma, which follow- ers are obliged to accept in most particulars. Most American political parties represent vague and general ideologies that do not demand un- questioning support, yet there are differences between them, as reflected in the views and policies they represent. The Democratic Party is more reformist and welfare-minded than the Republican. Likewise in Eng- land, the Conservative Party is reformist, but less socialist than the Labour Party.

Does it matter how ideology affects public opinion as long as we know what opinions really are? If ideology, like culture, cannot be shown to have a determined or causal relationship to action, then why is it significant as a practical political weapon?

Theoretical versus common sense ideologies: Despite ambiguities, ideologies help people judge political happenings. They are capable of being studied by content analysis, or can be viewed as a symbolic lan- guage that encodes clues as to how we think, and cues to which we re- spond. Even flags, patriotic songs, and other sentimental attachments are ideological signs subject to interpretation.

Such a combination of objective and subjective analysis was used by Robert Putnam to compare the beliefs of politicians in Britain and Italy. First Putnam established certain categories of characteristic styles of thought: generalized-particularized, inductive-deductive, explicit or vague, and so forth. Then he ranked the political "styles" of various countries according to questionnaire responses obtained from a sample of those active in politics. He was able to link stylistic factors to personal- ity characteristics such as degree of authoritarianism, willingness to compromise, and so on, all the way up to determining subjects' views about conflict, decision making, and democracy.[35]

Putnam's behavioral analysis reveals some of the difficulties politi- cal analysts encounter in using ideology as an explanatory variable. Some ideological elements correlate with behavior, certainly. But commonly accepted simplistic notions that make belief a consequence of class or status affiliation are suspect.

At the urging of sociologists and under the aegis of Marxist and neo- Marxist social theories, countless scholars have counted the social back-

35. See Robert D. Putnam, *The Beliefs of Politicians* (New Haven, Conn.: Yale University Press, 1973).

ground characteristics of political leaders. But there have been persistent complaints that these studies assume the unproved: that social back-ground conditions behavior. Recently, these murmurs of discontent have been amplified by evidence that many aspects of the belief systems of political leaders are virtually unrelated to their social origins. The present study [sic] adds another refinement to the argument. If one wants to predict a politician's position on economic planning or Euro-pean integration, his social background may well be irrelevant. But if, on the other hand, one wants to predict his orientation toward social conflict or his commitment to political equality, his social background may be considerably more important.[36]

Whatever factors condition ideology, or behavior, both describe a set of properties, a political culture, as described in Chapter One, as the fundamental basis of political life. The properties can be dichotomized or treated as continuous variables depending on whether one wants to isolate specific functions or generalize norms of political behavior.

Of course, it makes a difference whether an ideology is (like Marxism) doctrinally explicit about what values, ends, and preferences it advocates, or whether these are more loosely outlined by the nature of shared preferences, values, and philosophical predispositions. In the first instance, ideology, in its most behaviorally significant state, is a form of motivation. To motivate action ideologically it is necessary to stimulate a common consciousness. (For example, in the People's Re-public of China exemplary behavior is still that which personifies Mao's precepts, whereas general principles of Marxism-Leninism lead to the end of establishing the all powerful communist society.) There is a strong element of utopianism in the defined ends of an ideology. These determine the values and dictate the preferences of individuals. In this form, "ideology," said Daniel Bell, "is the conversion of ideals into social levers."

What gives ideology its force is its passion. Abstract philosophical in-quiry has always sought to eliminate passion, and the person, to rational-ize all ideas. For the ideologue, truth arises in action, and meaning is given to experience by the "transforming moment." He comes alive not in contemplation but in "the deed." One might say, in fact, that the most important latent function of ideology is to tap emotion. Other than re-

36. Ibid., p. 238.

ligion (and war and nationalism), there have been few forms of channel-
izing emotional energy. Religion symbolized, drained away dispersed
emotional energy from the world onto the litany, the liturgy, the sacra-
ments, the edifices, the arts. Ideology fuses these energies and channels
them into politics.[37]

Bell's comment describes an extreme ideologue, the revolutionary.
Revolutionary political beliefs he likens to religious beliefs because
religion, in its day, was perfectly capable of channeling energy for political purposes. In the sixteenth and seventeenth centuries, religious motivations were manipulated by secular as well as Church rulers for the
purposes of sustaining authority and maintaining hegemony over the
ruled.

Where ideology is loosely knit, it is based generally upon ordinary
common sense. It involves not so much the conscious manipulation of
ideas as loyalty to a set of predisposed values, such as the independence
of the individual, the value of the idiosyncratic, and so forth. Common
sense ideologies may be contradictory—that is, individualism may be an
ideological value in the United States for certain purposes—but it may
not be one of the motivating preferences that individuals rank high. So,
for example, in the United States, individualism is a common value to
which the ends of democratic society are devoted. But while most Americans believe passionately in individualism as a fundamental part of a
liberal ideology, in practice, many are influenced by what neighbors,
peers, and associates think. People are often afraid to assert their individuality for fear of being regarded as peculiar (or even anti-Ameri-
can). Hence the most individualistic of societies, in terms of ideology,
is behaviorally among the most conformist. This fact is very well described by Robert Lane in a study of "common man" ideologies.

. . . *[T]he common man asserts his independence, asserts that he would*
not, even to relieve his ignorance, consult anyone in particular about the
issues and candidates in an election—but would rather make up his own
mind (or possibly go to anonymous man-in-the-streets sources—as
Tocqueville said he would) . Independence is prized; men say they
would rather be known for their independence than for their capacity
to get along in a discussion; they value leaders who give the impression
of independence. . . .

37. Bell, *The End of Ideology* . p. 371.

But the fact is that [the common man] is one of the most conven-
tional of all men. . . . [T]hey rarely made it appear that their inter-
pretation of the concept of freedom includes casting off the bonds of
public opinion or the pressure to conform that their friends and neigh-
bors impose on them. Rather, I believe, these pressures are interpreted
in an unconscious way as supports, like buttresses on a wall that cannot
bear the stress without them. They do not want to be "told"—that pro-
duces a strong negative reaction—but they want to be clued, they want
to be "filled in," they want to receive the right sign at the right time, so
they won't look foolish. And this, as they see it, is no more a restriction
on their freedom than is a libretto a restriction on the freedom of the
opera star.[38]

Bell's idea is related to Marx: Powerful ideological "superstructures" (whether religion or politics) have motivating effects on human
activity. Lane's view is closer to Freud: Ideologies are rationalizations,
ways of coping with the pressures, threats, tensions, and conflicts to which
the human organism is subject.

Marx's belief in a strong, working-class, revolutionary or proto-
revolutionary ideology presumed a powerful, solidaristic subculture.
Lane's vision is the opposite.

Marxism implies a strong social identity rooted in a working class group.
It anticipates, and helps to form, a proletarian sub-culture with values,
morals, codes of behavior that a person acquires by virtue of his social
identification. The strong personal identity combined with the diffuse
social identity of the . . . common man is exactly the reverse of this.
[He] gets almost no guidance from his class membership, no sense of
brotherhood, no common goals or shared purposes. Marxist appeals
to him as a member of a working class fall on deaf ears.

The inevitability of social conflict is central to Marxism. At the
very core of the ideology is the notion of class conflict; indeed this is
the mechanism through which the promised perfect society is to be
gained. But [the common man] believes there is a general public interest
that, once understood, will be grasped and agreed to by everyone. So-
cial conflict, then is a product of misunderstanding. Moreover, as a
personal style as well as a social goal, compromise, adjustment, obscur-
ing of differences are much preferred to open conflict. . . .

38. Lane, op. cit., pp. 19–20.

The "selection" of an ideology, or of bits and pieces of an ideology, or of an opinion, is, of course, dependent upon how useful it is to a man or group. But, as we have tried to show, this selection is a matter of matching and fitting and searching for congruences with the experience and premises and personal qualities and ongoing social conflicts of a society.[39]

Lane's discovery of the "common man's" blandness and urge toward adjustment describes the mixture of ideology and behavior that characterizes much of American life. It might be argued that such low-keyed ideological persuasions are necessary to the give and take of democratic society, as more intensely held and narrowly defined ideologies would be divisive. But at the same time, it is quite possible for the blandness to disappear, without the ideology changing very much, and for a quite different behavior to emerge. For example, many working-class Americans have been attracted to populist political efforts with strongly demagogic appeals (such as the presidential campaigns of Alabama Governor Wallace). It is altogether possible for a group in any society—democratic or otherwise—to ascertain grievances, seek scapegoats, and find "ideological" solutions. In England, the followers of Enoch Powell find his racial attacks expressive, in an ideological way, of fundamental traditions and values of the English "race."

Lane's psychological emphasis on political behavior helps to explain how schismatic groups intensify ideologies, while undergoing little change in their beliefs. In an analysis of the John Birch Society, an example of a radical right, ideologically oriented organization sprung from the most basic American principles, Lipset shows how the "common man" can be radicalized.

Many of the analysts of the extremist right have suggested that the assorted movements draw from those groups in the population which are most subject to status frustrations. These may include both groups which feel themselves to be "dispossessed," to be declining in status as a result of the rise of other types of communities, occupations, or ethnic groups, and groups which have recently risen, but find themselves barred from being able to claim the concomitants of success. The term "status discrepancy," as used here refers to possession of status attributes which may lead a man to feel that he is granted less prestige, income, or power

39. Ibid., pp. 431–32.

*than he feels he deserves. Status discrepancy often has meant in the so-
ciological literature discrepant status attributes, as in the case of the
college-graduate factory worker, the grammar-school-educated business
executive, the wealthy Negro, and the like. However, it may also refer
to the president of the family-owned corporation who finds his power
in his factory to be less than he believes should be associated with ownership. In general, it refers to the conditions which result in violations of
expectations about the varying positions which should be concomitant
of a given status.*[40]

Ideology, then, expresses a more or less well-defined admixture of
enduring values, the pursuit of which produces fluctuating outcomes.
These values are related above all to roles and organizations more than to
class and status. The diversity of role demands affects human personalities and, indirectly, affects public opinion.[41] All people have, besides
the opinions they hold on particular issues, fundamental commitments
by means of which their views on any particular issue are likely to be
slanted. No one participates in supporting or opposing the issue of socialized medicine, or a more expanded range of welfare benefits, or taxation to pay for these things, without fitting these beliefs into some previously defined system of notions or prerequisite preferences (like the
value of the individual over the state, self-reliance over socialism, freedom over bureaucracy, or some other advocacy). Ideologies may not always be consistent, but they are interrelated. Political parties sometimes
clearly and strongly, sometimes more vaguely, stand for the primacy of
some of these sets of interests over others.

The dimensions of political culture: Belief systems and ideologies represent, as Converse put it, a "configuration of ideas and attitudes in
which the elements are bound together by some form of constraint or
functional interdependence."[42] Converse was particularly concerned
with the stability of beliefs and what mixtures are more or less likely
to change, as well as the problem of knowing what meaning can be attached to the influences that work to shape opinion.

40. S. M. Lipset and Earl Raab, *The Politics of Unreason* (New York: Harper &
Row, 1970), pp. 306–307.
41. See Theodore M. Newcomb, Ralph H. Turner, and Philip E. Converse, *Social
Psychology* (New York: Holt, Rinehart and Winston, 1965), Chapter 13.
42. Converse, op. cit., p. 207. For an amplification of Converse's original findings see
also Herbert McClosky, "Consensus and Ideology in American Politics," *American
Political Science Review*, LVIII (June 1964); Gabriel Almond and Sidney Verba,
The Civic Culture (Boston: Little, Brown, 1963), pp. 11–39.

Almond and Verba treat ideology as an aspect of political culture; that is, as an "object of orientation" consisting of three dimensions: (1) the *cognitive* dimension—one's knowledge of and beliefs about the political system; (2) the *affective* dimension—feelings people have about political matters; and (3) the *judgment* dimension, which uses performance as an indicator of the political system.

The cognitive aspect of ideology connects fundamental beliefs to "deep structures" (to borrow a linguistics term), or the internalized values that make up a person's mental process. These are formed early in life and are inured to change. When political cultures take an explicit ideological form as an established set of ideas they become dogmatic. People holding dogmatic opinions are not likely to change their views. They only interpret events to confirm what they already believe. Ideology, then, gives meaning to "ends" or values. Meanings that are closest to deep structures often contrast to those that represent "surface structures." While a deep structure provides deep emotional satisfactions or arouses strong positive or negative affect, a surface structure ideology is like an ordinary benefit or interest, the political resonance of which we discussed previously. An ideology relevant to one's deep-structure beliefs provides a powerful form of gratification to the subscriber.[43]

"Americanism" was a deep-structure ideology in the early days of the American republic. It is less so today, when the term *Americanism* is associated by many with imperialistic economic and political practices. "Our system is the richest in the world and if you don't like it here go someplace else." That is the common ideology which prevails. In Communist China the picture would be very different. The concepts of Chairman Mao, and the analects of Marxism establish a meaning of political life by means of continuous discussion and indoctrination.[44]

Of course, ideas change, and opinions vary even among the most orthodox. What remains? Consider what would happen if everyone held drastically different opinions about everything. Suppose that blacks and Jews and Italians, racial, religious, and ethnic communities all believed exclusively in the values of their particular subgroups of the society, while regarding the values subscribed to by others with an implacable hostility. No political society built upon such animosities could remain viable. Ideological values must be converted into interests, with groups

43. See Milton Rokeach, *The Open and Closed Mind* (New York: Basic Books, 1960).
44. See Franz Schurmann, *Ideology and Organization in Communist China* (Berkeley, Calif.: University of California Press, 1966), pp. 102–103.

competing, though not engaging in conflict. Then very different clusters in a population will add diversity to the political culture without destroying the society as a whole.

Sometimes deep conflict can be released in an explosive outburst which has a cathartic effect. Then conflict over values may recede. This is what occurred in Nigeria after the struggle over Biafra. It has not happened in Northern Ireland. Some conflicts simply persist, waxing and waning (as did the linguistic conflicts in Ceylon or Canada). Yet if all people spoke the same language, or had the same religion, or belonged to the same race, all the diversity and cultural richness that these differences represent would be lost.

One problem is to find that minimum of ideological agreement on which diversity can flourish, or that degree of commitment to an evolving ideal which makes it possible to phase out old loyalties with the promise of new opportunities.

Finding the right mixture is a subject for political experimentation. But no society is likely to experiment too much. Each society teaches its citizens a kind of ideological conviction that represents the civic culture. In our model this culture is the admixture of ends embodying the good society and the benefits that flow from it.

It is precisely the congruence of such convictions, and their effect on the relationships between rulers and ruled, which make the work of Almond and Verba so significant. For them, the successful civic culture "maintains the balance between power and responsibility."[45] High congruity in the political culture equals great stability in the political system. The ingredients, and the style, of various political cultures are thus of critical importance. Comparative analyses of different systems can be useful in analyzing the validity, or the durability, of various political cultures.

One common criticism of political parties in the United States is that they stand for basically the same values. But the advantage of this sameness is that it renders diversity and potential cleavage into competition. The question is, "What is left of ideology?" Both Republicans and Democrats share the same ideologies so completely that voting seems to be merely a ritual, or epiphenomenon, that is, without substance. It seemingly serves only to rearrange political offices among like-minded politicians and wins only marginal changes in policy. (This has been a

45. Almond and Verba, op. cit., p. 249.

critique particularly of those who favor the view that parties represent interests derived from classes. The dominant classes, whose interests are well represented, put their leaders in power to prevent basic and much-needed changes.)

Whatever the merits of this view, one way to examine the extent to which there are ideological differences between Republicans and Democrats, or between members of any parties, is to survey samples of them on key issues. In one classic study, Herbert McClosky and associates took samples of delegates to the national conventions of both major parties and asked them to respond to questions regarding issues carefully selected for their significance: public ownership, government regulation of the economy, egalitarianism and human welfare, tax policy, and foreign policy. The results were striking. On twenty-three of the twenty-four issues, significant differences were obtained between parties. McClosky concluded that

. . . differences which typically separate Democratic from Republican leaders seem also to reflect a deep-seated ideological cleavage often found among Western parties. One side of this cleavage is marked by a strong belief in the power of collective action to promote social justice, equality, humanitarianism, and economic planning, while preserving freedom; the other is distinguished by faith in the wisdom of the nature of the competitive process and in the supreme virtue of individuals, "character," self-reliance, frugality, and independence from government. To this cleavage is added another frequent source of political division, namely, a difference in attitude toward change between "radicals" and "moderates," i.e., between those who prefer to move quickly or slowly to reform or to conserve.[46]

McClosky also points out that to hold attitudes is not necessarily to act on them. Hence the determinants of action, the type of action, and the possibilities for action remain open questions. Ideology is thus a predisposition, a long-term orientation of thought. How precisely it determines a course of action depends on many factors influencing the political system in which it operates. If, as in China, an ideology is a way of organizing opinion according to doctrine, then discrepancies between behavior and ideology can be cause for coercion.

46. Herbert McClosky, Paul J. Hoffman, and Rosemary O'Hara, "Issue Conflict and Consensus Among Party Leaders and Followers," *American Political Science Review,* Vol. 54 (June 1960), pp. 406–27.

Cleavages, then, do exist in the United States. They form the basis for how people perceive events and issues. The point is that ideologies represent a conscious conceptualization of political life. They are the structure by which people interpret significant events. Included in that interpretation is a person's preferred concept of the world, whether it consists of hostile forces, or merely competitive ones, or positively cooperative ones. Which view becomes dominant depends in part on which interpretation people are taught in their first encounter, and the particular situation in the second. McClosky's work is important because it shows that the American political system works as a network of competitive elites operating within a democratic legislative framework that converts values into interests, interests into competition, and competition into cooperation. All factions, groups, or parties, no matter what their attachments, need to give priority to a system of values that makes all other values into interests and preferences. In so doing, it enables decision making on a cooperative basis. If this basic commitment does not prevail, then democracy can be bargained away. There will be no rules to limit the game, no central value around which all others can be negotiated. This is the classic problem of belief systems in democracies: What should be of central significance? (For generations the central problem for France was the lack of a core value that addressed the democratic system itself. And this is the central problem for government in Italy today.)

If ideology is so important to democracies, then we need to look more in depth at how ideological "deep structures" form, how people embrace the values they hold, and when they become deeply committed. We need to understand the way in which belief systems are "internalized" as part of the superego, or the conscience of individuals. We need to study the effects of peer groups, schools, and the workplace on the reinforcement of political attitudes and the shaping of beliefs in the context of identifiable interests.[47] We need also to examine the circumstances under which, for whatever reasons, beliefs can be so deeply offended by the failures of government, or by policies badly wrought, or by situations too complex to be treated effectively by the decision-making process, that people prefer totalitarianism to representative democracy.

47. See Daniel J. Levinson, "Role, Personality, and Social Structure in the Organized Setting," *Journal of Abnormal and Social Psychology,* Vol. 58 (March 1957), pp. 170–80.

chapter nine
Behavioral Models and Political Actions

In the previous chapter we described how behavioralism evolved out of institutionalism. As democracy became more representative, interest grew in the character of the electorate. Institutions of government, bureaucracies, constitutions, civil liberties, political parties, and international relations became less of a focus for political science. With new theories of individual and aggregate behavior new questions arose: How do citizens perceive politics? How do political values become socialized? To what extent do voters follow their own self-interests?

The behavioralists did not reject the concepts of institutionalism outright. But by and large, they sought primarily to call attention to empirical methods and data-gathering techniques that could be used to define political activity. While the models used by institutionalists classified the state according to rule by the one, the few, or the many (monarchic, oligarchic, or democratic), behavioral models, similar to those employed by psychologists and economists, reflect how people determine their needs and priorities—or in a more straightforward sense, how they aim to maximize pleasure and minimize pain. With such a perspective the purpose of political science itself changes. Suddenly the traditional preoccupation with moral ends (which since the Greeks had defined the purpose of politics) and the idealism of ecclesiastical or reformist political thinkers abruptly changed. (One can imagine the dismay among many political scientists of the old schools. Suddenly, too, the study of politics itself became political; conflict arose over curriculum, the substance of courses, and definitions of purpose.)

Behaviorists responded to denunciations by philosophical and institutional political analysts with a positivistic argument. For example, one of the more tough-minded positivistic thinkers has this to say in answer to a question about the higher moral ends of politics: "Do political appraisals express moral attitudes?" Weldon argues that this basically institutional concern is badly put, suggesting the false belief that "morals" and "politics" represent two distinguishable spheres and implying also, that actions described as "moral" are invariably more important than those described as "political." All this is very misleading and is liable to cause unnecessary confusion. Certainly the rules made up by politicians are not the only rules we recognize; among the non-political rules is an important group usually called "moral" which comprises (1) formalized rules laid down by religious authorities, and (2) conventions recognized by groups of people who may be, but are not necessarily organized in definite associations.

In the second and more important sense of "moral," moral conduct is not a matter of obeying rules, and therefore it is useless to say that political rules depend on moral rules. But it is true that people who tend to act in an unselfish or impartial way are likely to support humanitarian or inoffensive measures both in political legislation and in conventional codes of behavior. In other words morality in this sense has a definite though seldom a decisive influence both on morality in the other sense and on the explicit rules of association of all kinds.[1]

In so far as groups are politically influential, it is to be expected that they will attempt (and to a greater or lesser extent will be successful) to get their codes written into the laws of the State. In this sense it is correct to say that political rules are derived from moral rules, though it would be more accurate to say that the codes of behavior of influential minorities tend to be enforced by law on majorities for whose use they may or may not be suitable. In states that adopt representative institutions, the reverse process can also be observed, that is to say, the conventions the majority find convenient may be enforced by law on influential minorities.

If morality is not decisive, then neither are rules. Hence the discrepancy between what ought to be and what are political truths. Hence too, the empirical concern with political behavior. If not morality and rules, what then are the determinants of conduct, or how do the two intersect?

Behavioral political theory has increasingly been promoted be-

1. T. D. Weldon, *The Vocabulary of Politics* (London: Penguin Books, 1955), pp. 188–89.

cause institutional reforms have failed to resolve certain problems of government. Legislation designed to protect various interests reduces individual freedom and enlarges bureaucracy so that the need for more government is offset by growing antagonism to it. The greater the participation, the more bewildering the issues. As political decision making becomes more sensitive to public opinion it becomes less judicious and less well balanced. If voters cannot discriminate the "right" answers on key issues, this failure induces manipulation, opportunism, and demagoguery. To the behavioralist such a scenario foretells a return to fundamentals, but fundamentals of a new order.

General Systems Theory

A utility model in politics consists of a relation between inputs, demands, and outputs as governmental policies. The original stimulus to political action is the desire to maximize benefits. In economics such a system is measured in money; in politics the equivalent of money is power. To explain the outcome of a vote, or the salience of an issue, one needs to investigate a voter's "price,"—the priorities of his or her belief constructs—as a function of several variables (for example, income in relation to inflation). Utility theories represent political behavior as a political economy of choices and opportunities. The variables are good predictive indicators of how individuals interact, form coalitions and alliances, and maximize self-interests through group cooperation. One can expect a sudden rise in the cost of living to be reflected in shifting party or governmental support. The primary influences on behavior are changes in the economy. If these can be used to accurately predict ensuing political behavior, then these can be called indicator variables similar to economic indicators used by economists. The better the indicator, the better the prediction of public support and opinion.

The **psychological model,** which is not so different from the utility model, speaks of stimuli and response, instead of inputs and outputs. However, the significant variables are different—psychic rather than economic, having to do with identity, self-esteem, personal well-being, personal efficacy, and how these affect a person's ability to adapt his or her response to uncertainty, capacity to learn, capacity to take risks, and so on.

The notion of *equilibrium* is common to both utility and psychological models. An appropriate response relieves a disturbing stimulus. In the utility model, the input of, say, high inflation and its impact on voters will trigger a policy which, if successful in coping with inflation, will remove the source of the problem. In turn, this is likely to increase support for those in power responsible for the policy. A political equilibrium exists when the political system is thus able to feed back appropriate responses.

Both utility and psychological models are also similar in their reliance on the notions of stimulus and response or inputs and outputs, concepts which relate to feedback and equilibrium. A political system, then, is the continuous relationship between rulers and ruled according to certain criteria. The best statement of what might be called a *general systems approach* to political science is that of David Easton:

All scientific research, it is maintained—and with considerable justification—ultimately deals with determinate systems of behavior. From this premise, the further conclusion is developed that since all systems are determinate, they must show the property of striving to achieve equilibrium, variously called steady state, homeostasis, adjustment, balance and the like. For this reason it seems logical to the advocates of this position to propose first, that scientists interested in developing the most general model or theory for understanding all kinds of human behavior ought to devote themselves to the study of the properties common to all systems—general system theory as it has been called; and second, that this inquiry into system theory must be couched in the form of equilibrium analysis.[2]

A "general system" is more than a way of organizing variables. It emphasizes the connection between abstract models and both empirical and experimental research in a variety of fields. If we consider information as input and government's actions as mechanisms for the conversion of information into decisional outputs, then politics is a feedback system, a cybernetical model similar to engineering models of servomechanisms.

The general systems paradigm: All political problems can be studied from a single general system point of view. The following excerpt from one of the original group of systems theorists sums up the idea:

2. David Easton, "Limits of the Equilibrium Model in Social Research," *Symposium: Profits and Problems of Homeostatic Models in the Behavioral Sciences* (Chicago: Behavioral Sciences Publications, No. 1, 1953), p. 27.

Our definition of "system" is very general and at first sight might appear to apply to almost everything in the world. And, of course, the function of general theory is to be inclusive. However, it may be helpful to indicate what is not a system. The dark-colored half of the Pied Piper was not a system. The opposing lines of two football teams in scrimmage, independent of their backs, would not ordinarily be considered together as a system. If the Headless Horseman of Washington Irving had not been fictional, he could not have held his head in his arm and yet behave like an intact system. All the blonds in the United States are themselves not a system unless they are organized by some sort of communication, like the Red-headed League of A. Conan Doyle. In simple, naive, commonsense terms, then, a real system is all of a thing. Even though it is possible to construct a conceptual system which includes grandpa's mustache, Chinese hokku [sic] poetry, and the Brooklyn Bridge, this would not correspond to a real system of general systems theory, because these things are not surrounded by a single boundary, are not continuous in space-time, and do not have recognizable functional inter-relationships.

Some may wonder whether "system" is not identical with "Gestalt." Are there laws of the whole which do not apply to specific parts? We hold that both the parts, or subsystems, and the whole behave according to similar laws. However, the fact that subsystems are equilibrated together by system-wide organizing processes (even though these mechanisms can be explained by the behavior of component parts) means that there are characteristics of the whole which do not apply to any part. This is true of systems at every level.[3]

We may, then, restate the characteristics of systems as follows:

(1) Systems have boundaries within which there are functional interrelationships mainly based on some form of communications;

(2) Systems are divided into subsystems, with exchanges existing between the subsystems (as, for example, between a city and a state, or a state and the national government) ; and

(3) Systems have a capacity for coding—that is, they take informational inputs, are able to learn from inputs, and translate inputs into some kind of output.

In short, in a system there is a relationship between information and the use of energy. The relationship between coding and the use of

3. James G. Miller, "Toward a General Theory for the Behavioral Sciences," *The State of the Social Sciences,* ed. Leonard D. White (Chicago: The University of Chicago Press, 1956) , pp. 33–34.

energy—outputs—is transformational. The result is a general systems paradigm which can be applied to different system levels, each with its own boundaries: cells, organs, individuals, groups, societies, or whatever. The *general system model*, then, uses energy and information inputs, control mechanisms, memory banks, checking instruments, calculating instruments, and outputs which generate new energy and information.

The Utility Model as a Political System

A general utility model can be stated in the form of a political system. It draws on principles derived from general systems theory, such as information distortion, tendencies to reduce internal strain, lags and overcompensations. It uses the notion that the more energy in a system that is devoted to processing information, the more likely the system is to survive. David Easton has constructed a utility model of politics.[4] The model describes certain relationships between the subsystems and systems of a "unit" (which may be a society, a trade union, an administrative organization, or a new nation). Easton's model of politics, somewhat simplified, is shown in Figure 9-1.

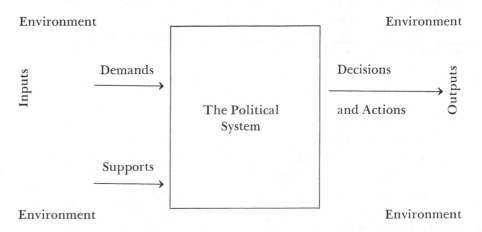

Figure 9-1. The Political System

4. See David Easton, "An Approach to Political Systems," in *World Politics*, Vol. 9 (1957), pp. 383–400.

Inputs in the system are demands made on government, and its supports, as from political parties, citizens, and the like. The political system as a governmental subsystem responds to inputs by making decisions and taking actions. These outputs "feed back" in the form of inputs, that is, demands and supports. The entire political system can be *operationalized* by using income, voting, class, and other precise or measureable data.

Connecting this general model of the political system to the utility model enables us to understand or predict a relatively high proportion of the immediate responses or actions of a public and its government. The central focus of utility models is on rational choice, rationality being a function of information. Information is reflected in a schedule of political demands, with support representing degrees of preference for parties and politicians. The political marketplace is much more complicated than the economic. Wants are more diverse. Policies that satisfy some offend others. Finding the right balance is a central problem.[5]

Many explanations of behavior fit within the contours of a political economy of behavior, one development of which is **polimetrics,** the study of voting.

Utility and public policy: Polimetrics shows, in the political marketplace, how, by voting, public and private utilities are connected. Individual private utilities cannot be realized if they maximize benefits without minimizing social costs. These imply *potential* benefits only, when established without providing for social public utilities; each increase in social public utilities increases opportunities for individual private utilities, but at a cost. Equilibrium occurs when the cost of increased social public utilities balances that of individual private utilities at the point of effective political demand. Beyond this point, social utilities become more expensive than individual ones and individual benefits are less than social (see Figure 9-2).

In Figure 9-2, unless there is an expansion of social public utilities (SU–E), individual utilities cannot be satisfied. Social utilities are those public policies aimed at expanding the cost of benefits exacted from individuals; they are like a tax which must be paid before individual utilities become possible. Policies that increase individual private utilities will win support for politicians; but those increasing public

5. See Anthony Downs, *An Economic Theory of Democracy* (New York: Harper and Brothers, 1957).

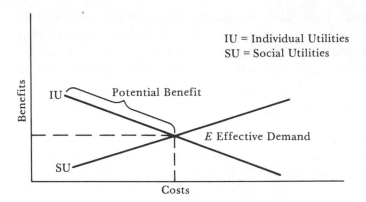

Figure 9-2. A Utility Model

social utilities at the expense of individual private ones will lose them support.

The model assumes beneficial consequences for public policy, and is thus not quite parallel to the economist's model of the pure theory of economic competition. However, it adumbrates a theory of relationships that specifies when coalitions form and power is concentrated. Each relationship is drawn as a ratio of benefits to costs. The organization of political power is to the "polimetrician" what growth is to the economist.

In these terms democracy is seen as a method for reconciling private wants and public goals in terms of the relative costs of each. Policy is the search for strategies that minimize costs and maximize gain.[6]

Finding the right strategies and minimizing costs motivates voters to maximize interests with their votes and politicians to maximize access to power through payoffs. Rationality and a high level of available information about interests and policies are assumed. Maximized interests and support manifested by votes represent a complete motivational system. The theory produces as well behavioral predictions about party activity, the formation of coalitions, and so forth.

Refinements in efforts to calculate utilities on the basis of economic considerations have led to the isolation of strategic economic variables such as the cost of living index, inflation rates, and unemployment figures. These variables can be used to account for changes in

6. See Robert A. Dahl and Charles E. Lindblom, *Politics, Economics and Welfare* (New York: Harper and Row, 1953).

voting support, or the effect of percentage changes on numbers of seats won or lost in a legislature, thereby enabling analysts to correlate economic conditions with voting behavior.

Much quantitative data are needed to activate models, especially data which can be stored, retrieved, and correlated over time.[7] More and more regional centers or consortia (such as the University of Michigan Survey Research Center) store figures on voting at both national and state levels in data banks. As material is gathered from more parts of the world, it becomes possible to correlate shifts in attitudes, ideologies, voting, and other behavior not only with changes in economic conditions, but with variables like education, sex, income, occupation, religious preference, race, age, and so on, all of which affect public responses. Hence economic variables are not the exclusive basis for the explanation of utility models even though they possess salience. Nevertheless, economic variables are good predictors of political behavior. Voting preferences are likely to shift during times of economic crisis; changes in party or candidate support can be predicted as unemployment grows. Economic conditions and party loyalty do, after all, have something to do with one another.

But all this is, in a sense, too easy. Let us use an example to qualify our model building: Does militancy in trade unions fluctuate according to economic advantages? Yes and no. In the first stages of their organization, when unions were illegal, the workers' militancy was directly related to their vulnerability. An outright war against the government-business coalition versus trade unions was what was required of them to effectively organize. Police, in league with employers, fought against the unions and their organizers. Militancy had more to do with struggle than with fluctuations in the business cycle (although those were of course a significant cause of organization in the first place). Later, the coalition between business and government weakened, with government at times allying itself with unions. For example, under the National Labor Relations Act in the United States (1935), government protected the right to organize, which it had before prevented. Elections enabled unions to be certified as bargaining agents and required business to recognize unions and bargain with them.

Worker militancy today takes other forms; in some countries work-

7. See Heinz Eulau, "Policy Making in American Cities: Comparisons in Quasi-Longitudinal, Quasi-Experimental Design," *Experimentation and Simulation in Political Science,* J. P. Laponce and Paul Smoner (Toronto: University of Toronto Press, 1973), p. 93.

ers want to share directly in management. How these new demands will affect parties, the economy, and government decision making is not at all clear. The relevant variables are being explored by means of what is called *polyvalent modeling*. Information about why issues or demands become salient and what new coalitions are likely to form are required. Accurate prediction of such matters, however, is also a function of other variables like how workers' self-management might affect the personal security of the participants. These and a host of other factors associated with the psychology of learning—how people respond to danger, when they minimize risks, when they are prone to act individually rather than collectively—go even beyond utility modeling to include models of psychology. Personality formation, national style, culture, authoritarianism, civic mindedness, all represent different clusters of significant behavioral variables.[8]

Psychological Models

Psychological models are variants of general systems theory models which, although not antithetical to utility theories, employ different variables and emphasize different kinds of explanations. While the latter assume motivation, the former try to explain behavior. Hence the emphasis on social learning. A utility calculus puts motives in a measurable relationship of wants, goods and services, jobs and money, or other rational needs. The psychological models, where the motivating effects of personality are concerned, replaced power in the utility calculus with the idea of energy transformation. Learning and learning reinforcement are directly linked to this because energy tension creates need, and learning to satisfy need is the primary human activity, the aim of interaction between and among persons. When personal need is transformed into public interaction, individual behavior becomes political.

8. The connection between benefits and support can be evaluated in terms of the costs and benefits of either articulating the issues or exiting the political arena, by leaving the community, becoming a revolutionary, or otherwise withdrawing support for the ruled. This choice is seen as one of the special circumstances of pluralism, or *polyarchy,* which we shall discuss further in Chapter 10. A recent and more sophisticated expression of the behavioral relationships we have been discussing is the formulation by Albert O. Hirschman, *Exit, Voice, and Loyalty* (Cambridge, Mass.: Harvard University Press, 1972) , and "Exit, Voice and Loyalty: Further Reflections and a Survey of Recent Contributions," *Social Science Information* Vol. 13 (1) 1974, pp. 7–26.

Most psychological theories employ some of the following independent variables: (1) a stimulus situation which generates action within the environment (This stimulus may be the result of some immediate action like failing an examination or getting into a fight, or a more general one like trying to gain access to power by joining a political party); (2) response situations which satisfy the arousal of drives such as anxiety (In political life the rewards of party loyalty, the satisfaction obtained from holding public office, and the sense of esteem or accomplishment derived from the power to make policy are all ways of satisfying drive arousal); and (3) individual variables like heredity, age, sex, and physiological condition, all of which determine the way people perceive their opportunities and the alternatives available to them (The dependent variable, when applied to politics, is political action of some sort—voting, joining a party, or affiliating with an active interest or pressure group).

There are many ways to research such variables. One strategy is to determine from the observation of many cases, samples of political action, and population clusters, typical reasons why some people participate more than others, what factors generate leadership, who acts, and who is acted on. Such questions are ignored by utility models, which assume leadership—that some people will control others. While utility models are more concerned with distributions of disposable surpluses and economic resources, the condition of the economic market (depression, recession, inflation), or how the capacities of individuals are distributed in a population (degree of literacy, extent of communications, rate of exchange of goods and services), converting these tendencies into a causative basis for voting strategies and power, the psychological model accounts also for individual efficacy, people's abilities to innovate, their psychic strength or vulnerability, and risk taking *Together the two models represent objective versus subjective factors in behavioral politics.* For example, objective factors are depression, inflation, and the inability of government to control the situation. Subjective factors serve to establish how tension rises during crises and how this, in turn, affects the actions of individuals to seek solutions.

Intervening variables used by both models are also interesting. Utility models of politics include actual political institutions or procedures like roll-call voting or coalitions between political groups among possible intervening variables. Psychological theories are built upon interactions among *qualitative* variables: neurophysiological variables, such as brain fields and genetic imprinting: holistic variables, such as

Freud's notion of the id, ego, superego, and libido; and social or relational systems, such as Lewin's topological, or vector, psychology.

The latter also can lead to inquiry into biological aspects of personality, carried out through the study of gene structure, to discover the extent to which such tendencies as hostility and aggressiveness, or cooperation and adaptiveness are biologically determined. Much experimental knowledge of human behavior has been accomplished by laboratory study of animal behavior (of rats, for example), but recently techniques have made possible the observation of the collective behavior of primates in their natural settings. This, plus the experimental isolation of actual genetic strains, represents two areas of inquiry of growing importance to political scientists.

The study of animal colonies has, in behavioral analysis, replaced the kind of inquiry once represented by the study of so-called primitive societies by anthropologists, who studied the politics of such communities to locate "basic" characteristics common to all: What are the differences and similarities of behavior in communities simpler than our own? *Ethologists,* and others, study colonies of baboons in natural settings, for example, for much the same scientific purpose. To do so helps us to understand instincts of territoriality, aggression, affection, cooperation, and "unlearned" or genetically based behavioral patterns, some of which may be applied to human political conduct. **Ethology,** or the study of genetic imprinting on hierarchies of organization and power, represents a fertile field for political examination.[9]

But ethology is a very specialized field. Most psychological behavior treats political phenomena as the results of purposeful individual behaviors that emphasize relationships between perception and motivation, defining, for example, how a stimulus, arising in a given situa-

9. See Lionel Tiger and Robin Fox, *The Imperial Animal* (New York: Holt, Rinehart & Winston, 1971). Tiger and Fox argue that it is:

natural to man to create hierarchies, to attach himself to symbolic causes, to attempt to dominate and coerce others, to resort to violence either systematic or lunatic, to assert, to connive, to seduce, to exploit. The only possible Utopia, in our perspective, would lie in a return to a simple hunting existence. But this is impossible. We have crossed the divide in terms of population alone. Our societies of the future will be places that will have to deal with the continuing tension between the needs of a hunting primate on the one hand, and the conditions it has created for itself on the other—conditions that often work to negate the very needs that move it in the first place. Neither the state nor bureaucracy will wither away, and we are not evolved to cope with either (pp. 238–39).

See also Derek Freeman, "Human Nature and Culture," *Man and the New Biology* (Canberra, Australia: Australian National University Press, 1970), pp. 50–75.

tion, triggers action by the individual within a complex network of response judgments and leads to certain actions (the expenditure of energy), aimed at satisfying the need triggered by the stimulus. How do these form into both actions and ideas? They lead to learning, cognition, symbolization, and understanding.

Some theories also emphasize genetic factors, kinetic and sexual tension, theories of repression, and positive or negative valences (such as affection and approval, esteem or the lack of it). Some translate individual into group motivations—especially studies of informal organizations. Others describe the human capacity to transform situations into abstract or cultural absolutes or symbolic or ideological projections.

The psychological model makes certain cost-benefit assumptions similar to those made by utility theories, but the key variables in these are stimuli and responses. The famous stimulus–response (S–R) model represents the degree to which a stimulus, say, food given to Pavlov's dog, will cause a response, salivation. If the experiment were repeated a sufficient number of times while the bells of St. Basil's Cathedral in Moscow were rung, St. Basil's bells would eventually produce salivation in the absence of the food. How long this condition would prevail without food depends on the capacity of the dog to live without food and the extent to which the salivation reflex has been conditioned (and the durability of St. Basil's bells).[10] Whatever form they take, both utility and psychological theories follow what we might call a *natural science model.* They are experimental, inductive, and concerned with the replication of experimental outcomes under controlled settings.

The most common form of the basic psychological model relates frustration as a form of tension to the question of when the individual responds to stimuli by coping or becoming aggressive. Can we predict when one response or the other is more likely? Since coping is a "peaceful" response, while aggression is not, the matter is of fundamental concern to the study of war, peace, and cooperative behavior as

---

10. Soviet authorities have been very impressed with Pavlov's dog. They have based a good deal of their educational and propaganda efforts on the assumption that individuals can be taught to respond in similar ways. Moreover, in Soviet prisons, the method has been applied with great specificity. In order to receive more food, it has been necessary for prisoners to overfulfill the work norm, the principle being "he who works harder eats better." However, the work has, at times, been so hard that people literally worked themselves to death. Trained to overfulfill, and otherwise kept on the verge of starvation, inmates were placed in the awful predicament of Pavlov's dog multiplied to the *nth* degree. They salivated, worked harder, and died. See Aleksandr I. Solzhenitsyn, *The Gulag Archipelago,* 1918–1956 (New York: Harper & Row, 1973–4).

a potential political alternative to a politics of conflict. The basic model appears in Figure 9-3:[11]

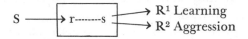

Figure 9-3. A Learning Aggression Model[12]

These two main lines of behavioral inquiry—utility versus psychological —lie behind the analyses of public opinion, ideology, and socialization we described in Chapter Eight.

The Models Compared

The two models can be used separately or in tandem, since they approach questions from different angles. For example, some people, when confronted with a period of rising inflation and unemployment, tighten their belts, work harder, become more active in their unions, and step up their political party activities, engaging in greater problem-solving efforts on their own behalf and in concert with others. Others become demoralized; lassitude sets in along with an apathy of personal decay. Available solutions elude such people. A utility model, which helps to correlate material costs with aggregate responses, might be most appropriate in the first instance. The psychological model uses personality factors to discriminate among the aggregate, to *disaggregate* collective behavior, and should be used in the second.

Another example: People see their savings disappearing from rising inflation, their pensions being made inadequate, and the cost of medical care rising to astronomical proportions. One can measure the response in shifting political support by opinion polling and other means. But this would not answer the question of why some see the situation as hopeless, while others are spurred to seek out strategies of survival, and still others perceive the situation in terms of new oppor-

11. See Ernest R. Hilgard, *Theories of Learning* (New York: Appleton-Century-Crofts, 1956) ; and B. F. Skinner, *Science and Human Behavior* (New York: Macmillan, 1956) .
12. Adapted from Charles Osgood, "Behavior Theory and the Social Sciences," *Approaches to the Study of Politics,* ed. Roland Young (Evanston, Ill.: Northwestern University Press, 1958) , pp. 313–44.

tuniti̇es which can be exploited. How can these individual responses be determined, even predicted, and possibly compensated for?

It is very hard to know what complex of factors leads to depression, passivity, and apathy and what leads to greater activity, or a desire to control the situation, or to dominate others, or to institute an authoritarian solution. Why does one individual learn (or want) to manipulate others? When does the promise of greater security become translated into a commitment to higher moral purposes? Such questions are fundamental to the understanding of political action. It is interesting to note that it is precisely in societies efficiently organized for utility maximization—that is, in industrial societies—that the psychological problems have been the greatest. In modern society people look forward to the future, to innovation and change. But many also are backward looking and nostalgic, yearning for some bygone golden age or just a simpler time. Sometimes the national state becomes like a political cult. The individual is expected to derive satisfaction through a wholehearted commitment to the state; then private frustrations are displaced onto public objects, and politics becomes a form of mass therapy.[13]

This leads us to an interesting contradiction between the two models. According to a utility model, increasing the stream of economic benefits and enlarging the stock of available utilities should increase satisfaction, enabling a political system to achieve a stable equilibrium as long as continuous growth is converted by an appropriate political mechanism into equitable distribution. Thus a stable polity becomes possible. This is the behavioral core of the liberal political model. People, so satisfied, will show their better natures to the world and to each other, acting as increasingly moral personalities as their satisfaction is prolonged. Then the rules governing the polity, the relationships of property, and power and wealth will be sustained. People will support the rules.

Today, from the standpoint of the psychological model, these assumptions are open to question. It is not so clear that increasing utilities can lead to greater psychic satisfaction, even under conditions of equitable distribution. It is commonly observed that anxiety increases (as well as tension, conflict, and dissatisfaction) during periods of rising rather than falling economic prosperity. During prosperity, expectations begin to rise rapidly, making what might have previously been regarded as a satisfying condition of equity—a good job, a home, reason-

13. See Harold D. Lasswell, *Psychopathology and Politics* (Chicago: University of Chicago Press, 1930). It is with this book that the frustration-aggression hypothesis entered the field of political studies.

able educational opportunities, for example—suddenly change. The job seems boring. The home is suddenly too small or shabby, in the wrong neighborhood. The school is no longer the instrument of improvement but a center of conflict, competition, and favoritism. As such social problems accumulate, tension levels aggregate. Individuals become petty, aggressive, and narrow. As their intolerance grows, previous solutions to the main problems of ordinary social life come full circle, turning back on themselves as the seeming sources of the problems they were once thought to avert.

How to find solutions to such problems is perhaps the most pressing behavioral concern of all. Some of the solutions necessarily lie at the level of individual behavior; that is, we may say that by improving the mental and psychic health of individuals, we may hope to overcome some of our less desirable social instincts. But this method is extremely expensive and slow as well as risky. Permanent individual improvement does not come easily and cannot be forced. The need is for large public solutions, but certainly not mechanical ones.

Between the extremes pressing questions require us to find answers to how people learn in politics and why they do what they do. We now turn to the ways behavioral scientists have dealt with some of them.

Socialization

One of the most important behavioral questions is socialization, or social learning. How does it happen? We know a good bit about it. For example, children are largely socialized through imitation. They want to fulfill the expectations of loving parents by emulating their ideals, and very early they become aware of the ideals or preferences (including political ones) of their elders. Psychocultural explanations of early childhood socialization by parental preferences show how initial socialization becomes reinforced by peers, in school, and by other reference groups. Political participation affects socialization too. The experience of doing political things, from voting to running for office, builds on the original socialization patterns and provides opportunities for new social learning. The total pattern of *interpersonal transference* establishes and fixes certain networks of belief, defining social conformity and deviance. For the most part, later relations reinforce earlier instances of social learning. The study of socialization turns behaviorists away from studies of ideology to how orientations are instilled by society in the individual. These fundamental orientations help determine his or her political personality.[14]

Primary, secondary, and tertiary stages: A lot of information has been developed concerning the formation of political attitudes. One special area of inquiry is how children learn about politics. Children personalize politics. For example, they are not interested in the office of the presidency as much as in the personality, smile, and good feeling the President as a symbol can generate. Children gain a sense of identification with the person who is the living representative of authority. Greenstein and others have found that authority so personalized tends to be benign, providing a sense of order.[15]

Fundamental values, especially those associated with fairness or equity, begin to be internalized at a very early stage in the maturation of the individual. Largely a function of primary socialization, the first phase is learning within the family, which is political in the sense that adults are citizens who express attitudes about society or their like or dislike of political leaders and party chiefs, and react to issues that affect them. Such matters are sensed by children long before they are understood. A parent's social satisfaction or job security, his or her attitude toward prices or taxes, and his or her orientation to other ordinary issues penetrate the psychic makeup even of the child who appears to be oblivious to them. Moreover, the saliency of certain political problems are revealed within the family before the child becomes consciously aware of them.

14. See Robert D. Hess and Judith V. Torney, *The Development of Political Attitudes in Children* (Chicago: Aldine, 1967); Herbert Hyman, *Political Socialization* (Glencoe, Ill.: The Free Press, 1959); Robert E. Lane, *Political Life* (Glencoe, Ill.: The Free Press, 1959); Wilbur Schramm, *The Process and Effects of Mass Communication* (Urbana, Ill.: University of Illinois Press, 1961); Fred I. Greenstein, *Children and Politics* (New Haven: Yale University Press, 1965); Robert Hess and David Easton, "The Child's Changing Image of the President," *Public Opinion Quarterly,* 24 (1960): 632–44; David Easton and Robert Hess, "The Child's Political World," *Midwest Journal of Political Science,* 6 (1962): 229–46; David Easton and Jack Dennis, "The Child's Acquisition of Regime Norms," *American Political Science Review,* 60 (March 1967): 25–38; David Easton and Jack Dennis, *Children in the Political System* (New York: McGraw-Hill, 1969); and Kenneth P. Langton, *Political Socialization* (New York: Oxford University Press, 1969).
15. See Fred I. Greenstein, "A Note on the Ambiguity of 'Political Socialization': Definitions, Criticisms, and Strategies of Inquiry," in *The Journal of Politics,* Vol. 32, 1970, pp. 969–78. See also Robert D. Hess and Judith V. Torney, *The Development of Political Attitudes in Children* (Chicago: Aldine, 1967), pp. 46–47.

A second line of inquiry is into how political orientations are generalized by the child as he or she matures and encounters group situations outside the family. As the child comes into contact with values that clash with his or her own, this is the beginning of secondary socialization, which occurs in school and among school-related peer groups. Here inquiry centers about questions of self-esteem, personal anxiety, how leaders are chosen, and how groups form. The rules of political life are grasped in play interaction as well as through formal instruction.

A third line of inquiry deals with problems of "adultness." How do reference group affiliations—occupation, church, party, clubs, and other associations—affect socialization through participation? Participation requires an investment of psychic energy because a person's social personality is defined in relation to significant others. One's own self-image and self-esteem depends to a high degree on the discriminations of positively valued persons.

These three main lines of behavioral inquiry correspond to three stages of socialization: primary, secondary, and tertiary. In each stage, different processes are at work within the confines of the same psychological model. The primary period establishes fundamental predispositions which, once ingrained in the personality, are very difficult to change. They "program" the individual, predisposing him or her toward those secondary and tertiary groups most congenial to values previously taught. At the same time, the secondary stage, which introduces a much broader range of contacts, can be shocking to the individual (as, for example, when a young adult leaves home for the first time and goes to college). Some individuals try to protect themselves from secondary-stage shock by creating a closed universe. They associate only with those who hold beliefs similar to their own, thus reinforcing primary dispositions. Such individuals are likely to learn only what reinforces what they already know and reject what they find strange. Values embodied in the family are then again reinforced by affiliations in church, political party, and other groups. Yet others react differently. Some even consciously shed in adult life the religion or basic political ideology or even the national or ethnic identity with which they were raised.[16] Research on these matters continues. To what extent does education produce rigidity or flexibility? When do political values become fixed and hardened?

16. See Richard E. Dawson and Kenneth Prewitt, *Political Socialization* (Boston: Little, Brown, 1969). See also Edward Shils and Michael Young, "The Meaning of the Coronation," *Sociological Review,* Vol. 1, 1953, pp. 63–81.

Consistency: The validity of the democratic assumption that rational individuals are in a continuous state of learning based on information gathering is important to such queries. The old liberal ideal presumes that citizens try to become better informed and better able to make decisions based on reason and common sense. This is a democratic article of faith. But some experiences of socialization reduce that capacity, and lead us to ask, how does one differentiate between political learning and indoctrination?

Political learning is a consequence of the organization of motivation around perceptions of appropriate values of affiliation and participation. It works by bringing children into a political culture and converting them into responsible adults capable of exercising the judgments and rights pertinent to that culture. The two go together in an open society, but this, in turn, requires an active politics. Participation is itself a socializing influence.

Each citizen, each participating individual, has a profile of political characteristics. These include his or her view of human nature and determination of acceptable or appropriate forms of action. Insofar as each person's profile tends to be consistent, they form into recognizable types.

Out of the variety of research into the stages of socialization, certain results are notable: There seems to be a need by individuals to make their various perceptions consistent and coherent, and there are definite limits on the degree to which one can tolerate inconsistency. (It is rare that a person will hold wildly different perceptions about the same experiences.) If a person cannot put two and two together in the realities of the political world, the degree of inconsistency will be troubling. So, for example, a person who is "liberal" can be expected to make the same or similar responses to items on a scale of conservative-liberal preferences as others who are "liberal." One can expect a certain congruence of opinion among those who cluster around each significant point in relation to social as well as political attitudes.

Of course, no one ever achieves perfect consistency. Some people actually increase amounts of inconsistency in their political views by formulating theories that explain or account for inconsistencies, making them consistent within a closed framework. So the more independent a voter is, the more likely he or she is to be "intellectually sophisticated." In this way intelligence is intimately related to the ability to absorb knowledge and make it logical and consistent within a given framework. The more strongly entrenched an unquestioned item of social learning is, the harder a person will strive to make it consistent with similar, and even intrusive, issues. We all try to rationalize our prejudices.[17]

We know also that personality predispositions extend to group affiliations. While there is never a complete fit between personality and affiliation, it is possible to measure the degree of fit according to such variables as social class, occupation, regional location, religion, education, place of residence, language group (or ethnicity), and so forth.[18]

Childhood socialization: But let us see in greater detail how socialization in the form of political learning occurs. Robert D. Hess and Judith V. Torney, in *The Development of Attitudes in Children,* have been particularly concerned with the way in which the individual child is prepared for membership in the adult political community.[19] Using a sample of public school children, Hess and Torney attempted to correlate political awareness with social maturation. Their hypothesis was that, with social maturation (that is, going from lower to higher grades) comes maturation of judgment, and particularly an increased shrewdness about the real world of politics. They tried to show that such maturation is not just a matter of knowing more, but a consequence of changes that take place in the *way* we learn. Hess and Torney describe four main models which identify significant ways children learn to make political judgments. They find that the main variables determining the degree of social maturation are stimuli received from family and school that reinforce certain characteristics at certain ages. Religious affiliation, peer group participation, social class, intelligence, and sex-role orientations are *mediating,* or *contingent,* variables which affect but do not determine political attitudes to the same degree as do family, school, and the grade level achieved.

It is impossible even to summarize briefly Hess and Torney's diversity of findings. However, one that is particularly interesting is that children from high-status families consider their fathers to be more powerful than children from low-status families. Because they respect the father's position in society, such children also become aware of distinctions of prestige and power which they in turn project onto the sphere of government and politics (usually under the same set of con-

17. See Charles E. Osgood, "Cognitive Dynamics in the Conduct of Human Affairs," *The Public Opinion Quarterly,* XXIV (Summer 1960), 341–65.
18. See Fred I. Greenstein, *Personality and Politics* (Chicago: Markham Publishing Co., 1969), *passim.*
19. See Hess and Torney, op. cit.

structs they associate with their father's views). In lower-status families, children rely less on their fathers as sources of information about such matters. In both cases, however, those who have "strong" fathers more easily attach themselves to figures or institutions in the political system (particularly the President and the police) than those whose fathers are perceived to be relatively "weak."[20]

Concerning political learning and school level, the assumption is that as a pupil progresses through school political interests grow and attitudes toward political things and toward oneself as a citizen become more and more clearly formulated and defined. For example, Hess and Torney found that among younger children, the image of the President was more positive: "Of 51 second-graders, 60 percent saw him as 'the best person in the world,' and 75 percent said they thought 'the President likes almost everybody.' "[21] With greater social maturation the picture becomes more complex and differentiated. The presidency, for example, becomes less personalized and is perceived more as "a group of attributes having to do with the office or the role demands of the presidency."[22] So the hypothesis seems to work.

The capacity to differentiate personal qualities from the standards and requirements of role and office should enlarge as a child progresses through the educational system. But instead, it was found that, while children do learn to discriminate between the ideal and the real, this process does not continue automatically. According to the hypothesis, a child in junior high school should have a better political understanding than one in elementary school, and political learning should be maximized at the high school level. In fact, it was found that most political learning occurs at the pre–high school level. A pilot study showed that

an unexpected degree of political learning and experience had occurred at the pre-high school level. Compared with seniors, the freshman classes were relatively advanced in their attitudes and they displayed opinions about a wide range of political matters. It was the extent to which attitudes had been acquired before the freshman level and their stability during the high school period that directed our research efforts towards the study of political socialization during the elementary years.[23]

20. Ibid., p. 101.
21. Ibid., p. 11. See also David Easton and Robert Hess, "The Child's Political World," *Midwest Journal of Political Science,* 6 (1962) : 229–46.
22. Hess and Torney, p. 11.
23. Ibid., p. 9.

On most issues tested—mainly attachment to the "system" and regard for law—pupils were found to be most sensitive to and aware of issues between the sixth and eighth grades. After that, attitudes and knowledge hardened. The ability to change, to comprehend the flexibility of law, the place of leadership, and other basic attitudes towards citizenship and politics, crystallized during this period.

Socialization models: To say that the greatest changes in political understanding occur between the grade- and middle-school years does not mean that everyone learns the same way. Hess and Torney distinguish different ways of learning. Between the fourth and fifth grades, for example, the rate of learning is fastest, but the way learning takes place is not very sophisticated. So then there are two problems, not only how fast learning occurs, but the way children learn: The person who learns most but matures less may be well informed but unable to use knowledge intelligently. The problem led Hess and Torney to postulate four models of socialization:

1. *The accumulation model.* The acquisition of political role expectations is furthered by the addition of *units* of knowledge. This is the most straightforward learning model; it states that the more information fed to a child, the more knowldege the child acquires. It depends on the acquisition of specific items of information—What are the Articles of Confederation? What was the Dred Scott decision? Such a model involves little conceptualization.

2. *The interpersonal transfer model.* The child, by virtue of familial and other associations, develops diverse relationships to figures of authority. The child extends these relationships, based on experience, to all subsequent relationships. The power of the President, for example, can be understood as a projection of similar powers represented in the figure of a father. The formation of political attitudes this way depends very little on specific information.

3. *The identification model.* Children take their attitudes from significant older persons, usually a parent or teacher. The child, identifying with such figures, uses them to establish a self-image which, once fixed, offers the basis for affiliation and group attachments. Hence, children take on the political party preferences of their parents, and a high proportion stick to such affiliations for the rest of their lives even though they had little understanding of what these affiliations represented when they were first indoctrinated.

4. *The cognitive-development model.* The child's thought processes are based on a conceptual understanding of an order which will allow him or her to translate an understanding of the individual figure into an understanding of similar individuals and to their roles in a whole political system. To ensure growth in conceptual understanding is a problem for civic education, which should not simply seek to indoctrinate pupils with the "right" attitudes towards political leaders, or citizenship, or society but, particularly in a democratic society, to enlarge the cognitive capacity to understand issues and politics in a network sense. This model hinges on the development of a capacity for abstraction.[24]

One might take exception to some of the outcomes of the Hess and Torney study; however, it raises certain key behavioral questions. If most political attitudes are shaped at the fifth- or sixth-grade level, before the cognitive-developmental form of learning has progressed very far, how good is that knowledge? Indeed, will it not necessarily represent indoctrination? Hess and Torney point out that, while the interpersonal transfer model represents the way in which the child is most likely to learn from a first contact with the political system, it is possible to build on such knowledge. Although one cannot fathom conceptual knowledge prior to having discrete knowledge about the system, and despite the fact that many affiliations are formed not on a cognitive basis but according to the principle of identification, we may nevertheless suggest that political attitudes are formed without political understanding. These quickly harden into ideologies that predetermine the way a person will perceive and define political issues in the future. However, the picture is certainly more complex than that. For one thing, learning can take place outside of school and without pressures. Abstraction results from language learning processes, imitation, and forming symbolic attachments. Children learn easily to dissociate themselves from their universe and see the universe as larger than themselves. Intellectual development is thus, in many ways, a continuous process. It continues thoughout adult life as a result of participation in work, in politics, in political campaigns, in trade union organization, and in a myriad of other activities and relationships. In short, political learning is a function of political experience.[25]

24. Ibid., p. 21.
25. See Jean Piaget, "Developmental Psychology: A Theory," *International Encyclopedia of the Social Sciences*, Vol. 4, ed. David L. Sills (New York: Macmillan Free Press, 1968), pp. 140–47.

But what about participation? Why does it occur, and under what circumstances and in what ways are children or adults induced to participate? We must also raise the issue of what kinds of participation enlarge the cognitive capacities of individuals. Is learning a function of high-level participation? Does low-level participation have the same effect, or is it the case that at lower levels what is required is a form of organization in which participants are not encouraged or expected to think for themselves but to do as they are told? Indeed, there is some evidence that participation must be egalitarian in small groups, and carried out through continuous discourse, if it is to be cognitively meaningful.

Even aside from these concerns, other criteria need to be taken into account to explain the socialization phenomenon. Work has been done, for example, to determine how individuals evolve a moral personality. Despite the fact that children appear to be amoral, to be totally preoccupied with themselves and their own wants unless explicitly taught otherwise, there is more to it than that. Following Piaget's work on cognitive development, Lawrence Kohlberg and his associates found not only that children do learn from instruction, and that their ways of learning mature, but also that they develop *levels* of moral thinking. Not all judgmental capacities are internalized from parents or teachers or even friends, but some are internal to the individual himself or herself.

Kohlberg recognizes a definite pattern of three levels of moral awareness: "preconventional," "conventional," and "postconventional," or autonomous. Preconventional children interpret behavior in terms of physical consequences rather than moral principles, that is, as rewards and punishments. This occurs between the ages of four and ten. Then comes a period of reliance on conventional attitudes, basically conformist, during which children try to fulfill expectations in order to win and maintain familial or group esteem. At the postconventional level there is a shift to more independent judgment about rights and wrongs. This last level can also be divided into two stages. The first is a "social contract" orientation with legalistic and utilitarian overtones.

Right action tends to be defined in general rights and in terms of standards which have been critically examined and agreed upon by the whole society. There is a clear awareness of the relativism of per-

sonal values and opinions and a corresponding emphasis upon procedural rules for reaching consensus.[26]

The second stage is more abstract. Here the emphasis is not only on moral principles, but on their logical comprehensibility (like that of the Golden Rule or the Ten Commandments). This brings us back to the need for consistency in the form of universal principles: a recognition of the need for justice, reciprocity, and equality of human rights, and the dignity of human beings.[27]

Such principles can be stated in many ways. They constitute the basis for both a philosopher's political theory and that of the "common man," in whom these beliefs activate a desire for reform, improvement, and fairness, the pursuit of which may occur within or without the regularly organized channels of politics. Kohlberg suggests that this progression is common among all people. It extends beyond schooling and is not limited to a single class or elite. It extends beyond any single political culture.

This is because the ideal principles of any social structure are basically alike, if only because there simply aren't that many principles which are articulate, comprehensive and integrated enough to be satisfying to the human intellect. And most of these principles have gone by the name of justice.[28]

Saliency

The idea of socialization centers about how the individual is introduced into and made part of an ongoing society, and how he or she learns how to function within it. This is partly a matter of organizing the individual's system of needs and gratifications so that in learning how to perform, a person also learns how to *learn,* or to perceive opportunities and make use of them. The assumption is that a society offers a wide range of opportunities for individuals; and becoming socialized into

26. Lawrence Kohlberg, "The Child as a Moral Philosopher," *Psychology Today,* (September, 1968) : 25–30.
27. Ibid.
28. For further discussion about such matters see D. E. Apter and Charles Andrain, eds., *Contemporary Analytical Theory* (Englewood Cliffs, N.J.: Prentice-Hall, 1973), pp. 459–682. See also, Charles F. Andrain, *Children and Civic Awareness* (Columbus, Ohio: Charles E. Merrill Company, 1971).

various roles integrates the individual into society and enables him or
her to utilize the benefits of society. But there are circumstances under
which this does not happen. There are those who, for a variety of
reasons, can be socialized into a counter culture but are unable to become part of the existing network of opportunities.

If many people refuse to become socialized according to prevailing
convention, and decide that they want to change the society, government is confronted with the problem of how much control or how much
adaptability is needed to keep the society functioning smoothly. This
degree of proneness to change on the part of individuals and governments is marked by tension on both sides. Issues become charged with
meaning, as any ordinary demand can be regarded as threatening. The
interface between individual (or subgroup) and government demands
determines what is called *issue saliency.*

Defining salient issues: Saliency is associated with extremism and radicalization (that is, the rejection of prevailing roles and refusal to be
socialized to participate). The most salient political issues are those
most fraught with tension. But radicalization tends to be an episodic
phenomenon. It becomes politically important only when significant
numbers of individuals fail to define their position in terms of values
both sides share.[29]

Radical movements, apathy, or unsocialized social anger such as
random violence, street violence, rape, and other forms of antisocial
behavior, affect the daily lives of the public as well as the policies of
governments. They do not occur as isolated incidents, but are related
to overall needs for remedial policy. Will increasing social welfare programs at the disposal of the poor substantially improve the socialization
of the least socialized, or the most penalized? There is a good deal of
evidence to suggest that this would not provide the whole solution. Expanding welfare programs might resolve the problem of alienation or it
might increase economic overhead costs to such an extent that the upper
strata of society—its most effectively functioning parts—might suffer reactive alienation. The tendency of authoritarian, corporatist, and fascist
regimes to put things right by overcorrecting against imbalances is associated with such shifts in alienation.

Which issues become salient and how they affect politics is closely
connected to problems of inadequate socialization and also to the ways

29. Warren E. Miller and Teresa E. Levitin, *Leadership and Change: The New
Politics and the American Electorate* (Cambridge: Winthrop Publishers, Inc., 1976).

individuals develop moral personalities. Hence self-interest is not the only basis for saliency; the implications of both the Piaget and Kohlberg studies is that saliency is above all a function of moral significance. For example, one might perceive a potent contrary ideology as an evil and wicked force, and such a perception, false or not, would inspire many to sacrifice self-interest in favor of the worthy cause of opposing such an enemy. But if the moral purpose of resistance becomes doubtful and the issues obscured, self-interest may be reasserted.

Self-interest and morality are both ingredients of saliency, that much is clear. But what issues are salient and under what conditions is not clear. Several conditions must be met before a particular issue emerges as an overwhelmingly—both in the moral and practical sense—salient social concern. The most obvious forms of self-interest saliency are economic. Here's a simple example. Suppose that large sections of the community watch their economic capacities decrease, their old-age security devaluate, or their income erode. They experience anxiety. A failure of policy to correct the backsliding will lead to hopelessness, despair, and aggression—fertile ingredients for the growth of ideologies offering quick solutions and panaceas. (The rise of Nazism in Germany is a classic case.)

The most common issues of moral saliency are war, revolution, and basic reform. These often combine (for example, as when moral corruption in war and protective self-interest became two sides of the same coin during the United States involvement in the Viet Nam war, eventually leading to America's defeat and withdrawal). By combining the models developed by Hess and Torney and Kohlberg, however, we can hypothesize about issue saliency and the interpretation of behavioral tendencies according to one position or another. It depends on what learning model one subscribes to.

If the predominant mode of learning and socialization is by the accumulation model, the more information the public is given about an issue, the more that issue will become salient. Degrees of salience will be defined by the most significant source of information to which the public has access. Those who depend on newspapers for information will gain a sense of saliency from headlines or articles prominent in the media. Those who derive information from professional or trade journals, trade union pamphlets, and similar organs will consider information gleaned from these sources as most salient. Issue saliency, then, is determined by interests.

If the predominant mode of learning is by means of the inter-

personal transfer model, saliency will be defined by important and respected public figures. Stands made by preferred political leaders will
identify the key issues for those who rely on authority for judgment.
Under this model saliency is very much a matter of who says what.

If learning takes place under the identification model, most of the
issues considered to be salient will be those advocated by one's political
party and the interests whose ideology it represents, and the policy
statements of other affiliations to which the individual subscribes. The
predominant emphasis will be on interpretation, supplied by those
whose job it is to make such interpretations—party officials or the leaders of churches, trade unions, or other groups. The identification model
is one that seeks to promote a coherent ideology. It is also the mode of
learning which, in Kohlberg's terms, would represent a *conventional*
level of behavior because membership in groups reinforces conformity
by promoting the desire for esteem from other members; in other
words, through peer-group pressure.

If we take the cognitive developmental model as the basis of learning, saliency will depend on the general knowledge and capacity for abstract thinking which an individual has achieved. What is salient is
not necessarily what hits the front pages of the newspapers, but rather
one's interpretation of long-term trends, the patterns of change in the
political system, organizational and group activity, and so forth. This
model most closely approximates a professional understanding of political problems and, indeed, the "scientific" understanding of the
problems. It also conforms to Kohlberg's pattern of moral development,
in which saliency is determined by one's sense of fairness or unfairness.
In short, the most salient issues are those which affect principles of
justice in terms of abstract imperatives of "right" and "wrong." The
most salient issue is one which either most offends or most inspires
morality.

Issue saliency and modes of learning are not separated. All people
learn according to some combination of these; moreover, although from
the standpoint of political behavior, the movement from type one to
type four represents an improvement in the level of political understanding, or the capacity to understand and make judgments, the internalization of certain values and beliefs does not follow such a neat
progression.

If basic attitudes are determined to a large extent by early childhood socialization, then saliency will vary to the extent that the public
has evolved from preconventional to conventional behavior. Conventional behavior manifests itself in a respect for authority and standard-

ized moral values. But since intellectual activity during the period in which this evolution occurs coincides with that which takes place in the accumulation and transfer models of political learning as well, it can be said that most learning occurs *prior* to the evolution of moral and cognitive understanding. Hence a good deal of "learning" merely consists of finalizing one's reasons for holding to values and beliefs formed earlier.

We may say that (1) primary socialization, by means of accumulation and interpersonal transfer modes of political learning, correlates with the maximum period of political personality formation—that is, the period of time during which one most internalizes political values. (2) Such values represent persistent "deep structures" which are difficult to change. (3) They help to determine which ideologies we prefer and in what order of preference. Ranking systems help to elaborate both the moral personality of the child and the cognitive ability of the adult. (4) Finally, once moral development, cognitive ability, and group reinforcement according to secondary and tertiary affiliations evolve to a certain point, issues, although decided on the basis of values, ideologies, and preferences, are interpreted by individuals according to more sophisticated modes of learning. We diagram the process in Figure 9-4.

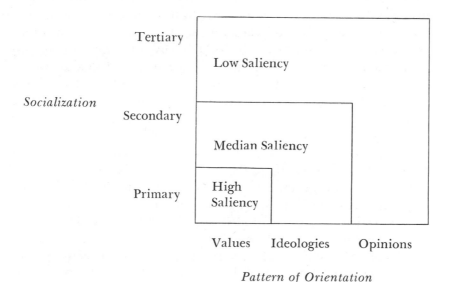

Pattern of Orientation

Figure 9-4. The Relationship between Socialization and Political Orientations

Figure 9-4 suggests that the human personality has a need for consistency. Political values help select which ideologies will be preferred. Ideologies shape political opinions and establish saliency preferences. If incongruities arise between values and ideologies the conflict will be manifested in various forms of anxiety and alienation. For example, children who become "radicalized" in school to accept ideologies representing values at variance with those prescribed by their families are likely to exhibit erratic love-hate, guilt-accusation behaviors and to make extreme judgments of "moral" criteria.

Adaptive behaviors: Although these hypotheses incorporate the idea that primary socialization is more powerful and fundamental than secondary, and secondary than tertiary, it is clear that values once learned can be unlearned or relearned. Mostly the values inculcated early remain permanent endowments of an individual's personality. But during periods of great personal stress or political upheaval, values and ideologies can be altered. Indeed, at the peak of upheaval, it may appear that all pre-existing values have been swept away, but quite often people also reconcile what they were taught during the period of primary socialization even against contradictory evidence. (We discussed this urge for self-justification previously). This is one reason the government of the People's Republic of China continues to attack Confucianism, for example. Not only does primary socialization indelibly imprint on the psychic makeup of the individual values that are not easy to alter permanently, but it also helps to explain why ideology is so important where radical change is sought. Socialization is used to organize moral ideas to change values. It requires leadership with a shared ideology and both the willingness and the means to control political learning, combining it with moral "regeneration." So, for example, the definition of freedom in Communist China is "freedom with leadership," and democracy is "democracy under centralized guidance, not anarchy. Anarchy does not conform to the interests or wishes of the people."[30] A great deal of revolutionary method is simply the inculcation of new values fostered by identifying moral contradictions within old belief systems which violate the individual need for consistency, and the subsequent resolution of these inconsistencies.

Ideologies help to square discriminations between values and preferences which might be at odds. The more logically structured an individual's ideology, the more consistent the political behavior of the

30. Mao Tse-tung, *On the Correct Handling of Contradictions Among the People* (Peking: Foreign Languages Press, 1969), p. 12.

individual. But the more open and reflective the ideology, the more the burden for consistency, or conformity, is placed on the individual rather than on the society as a whole.

Predisposition: One of the more careful attempts to establish how socialization and saliency variables are perceptualized was undertaken by Fred Greenstein. Challenging predictive theories, Greenstein uses probability not to necessarily predict behavior, but to describe the link between individual and aggregate behavior. Greenstein does this by an equation:

Personality structures + Political belief + Individual political action + Aggregate political structures and processes = Behavior

Greenstein sees personality structure, for example, as the result of many variables: from the degree of family authoritarianism to the ways in which psychic needs are expressed. All he can say about certain types of personality structures is that they *predispose* people toward particular political beliefs. Those who feel the need for stability and security, and who identify with a figure of authority, *may* also favor tough "law and order" ideologies, or more dogmatic ideologies, and they *may* prefer simple solutions to more complex ones.[31] But such tendencies do not enable us to absolutely predict what will be an individual's preferences, political or otherwise. Personality structures and political beliefs strongly affect political behavior by establishing predispositions which form a kind of "code," an imprinting on the mind of tendencies observable through people's selection of parties, their reactions to issues, and how they wish to be perceived. Such coding affects how we perceive each other. (In white-supremacist South Africa, a white person looking at a black person may see not another individual but an *object,* possibly of fear or contempt. The black has become a symbol to the white perceiver of the oppressed, of potential aggression, or of some other stereotyped response. The white person in such an instance has reacted to both external and visible "cues" which triggered a chain of precoded meanings.[32] In Northern Ireland, Catholics and Protestants so coded might perceive each other in terms of reactive cues triggering

31. Greenstein, op. cit., pp. 123–27.
32. A. Kornberg, J. Smith, and David Bromley, "Some Differences in the Political Socialization Patterns of Canadian and American Party Officials: A Preliminary Report," *A Comparative Study of Party Organization,* ed. William E. Wright (Columbus, Ohio: Charles E. Merrill, 1971), pp. 135–69.

violence.) The key term is *predisposition*. We cannot predict when predisposed responses will occur.

It was once accepted that those most receptive to the Nazi ideology in Germany were those with authoritarian personalities. Now it is clear that these persons actually were more likely passive personalities who sought to scapegoat Jews (as symbols of corruption and subversion) for their own failings. Individual weaknesses were converted into a group response, one so powerful that it could transform individual passivity into collective power. Coding, then, is also related to needs, dependency, and vulnerability, and to the conditions evident in any given situation. To generalize on the basis of personality formation alone is wrong.

The empirical examination of these matters represents a large part of behavioral analysis in politics. Behavioral theories seek to explain how innovating, changing, adapting, and learning new attitudes relates to political action.[33] While it is not difficult to link social attitudes to social class and to assess the impact of distributions of attitudes on, say, voting and public policy, it is more difficult to explain why some people act one way and others act differently given the same external circumstances.[34] This continues to be a dilemma to behavioral analysts.

Political Culture and Modal Personality

Let us look briefly at the problem of authoritarianism itself, and the question of how different political cultures act to form different modal personality types.

One old query is: Why do some people want to inflict terror and violence on others? What causes such tendencies in some personalities and not others? Well, every society has people who enjoy the exercise of power over others, but it is usually likely to be exercised responsibly, democratically, and on behalf of the plurality of citizens. So when is power exercised on behalf of a favored few; unfairly, or vindictively;

33. See Dawson and Prewitt, op. cit., pp. 81–97.
34. See Bernard Berelson, "The Study of Public Opinion," *The State of the Social Sciences,* ed. Leonard D. White (Chicago: University of Chicago Press, 1956), pp. 299–319. See also Herbert H. Hyman, "The Value Systems of Different Classes: A Social Psychological Contribution of the Analysis of Stratification," *Class, Status and Power,* ed. Reinhard Bendix and Seymour Martin Lipset (Glencoe, Ill.: The Free Press, 1953), pp. 426–42.

punitively and violently? One might also ask: Why do prisons and concentration camps attract abusive guards or persons prone to personal violence, some of whom delight in sadistic exercises of power? And, to what extent are persons whose behavior is pathological distributed among all societies? That is, if such tendencies persist in every society, when and why are sadistic minorities able to seize power, as they did in Nazi Germany or Stalin's Russia, and monopolize the organs of state terror and control?

To answer such questions requires a great deal of behavioral research. A variety of tests based on the isolation of authoritarian characteristics have already been developed.

As we have mentioned previously, some tests seek to measure universalized, or *culture free,* clusters of characteristics capable of indicating an individual's authoritarian predispositions. One such measurement is the **F-scale,** which can be used as a measure of predisposition to authoritarianism both universally and comparatively. The *F*-scale can be used to help pinpoint what type of individual subscribes to certain political views and holds what ideological preferences. Janowitz and Marvick found, for example, that in the United States, the more authoritarian personalities tended to be more isolationist in foreign affairs.[35]

Theories of national character have also been used to explain authoritarian responses to violence. In societies in which civic culture is democratic, conflict is more likely to be mediated. The prevailing style of behavior prevents ideological conflict and polarization. Manifestations of national conflict are avoided. This tendency in turn, can be correlated with other variables: the extent of individualization, privatization, atomization.[36]

Some theories seek to discover "tolerance thresholds." When and under what circumstances will people no longer be able to accept the burdens of modern life? What forms of irrationality are directly traceable from the pressures we confront in our work? When will people tend to withdraw from active social and political life, or become apathetic? When can the apathetic be aroused and/or manipulated by political leaders?[37] By what *kind* of political leaders?

35. See Morris Janowitz and Dwaine Marvick, "Authoritarianism and Political Behavior," *Public Opinion Quarterly,* No. 17 (1953) : 185–201.
36. See Masao Maruyama, "Patterns of Individuation and the Case of Japan: A Conceptual Scheme," *Changing Japanese Attitudes Toward Modernization,* ed. Marius B. Jansen (Princeton, N.J.: Princeton University Press, 1965) , pp. 489–531.
37. See Erich Fromm, *Escape from Freedom* (New York: Rinehardt, 1941) .

Evidence in all such studies shows that ideological preference, issue saliency, and type of participation are all affected by personality factors. However, we must be careful in generalizing to what extent. Alex Inkeles makes the point very well:

There is a substantial and rather compelling evidence of a regular and intimate connection between personality and the mode of political participation by individuals and groups within any one political system. In many different institutional settings and in many parts of the world, those who adhere to the more extreme political positions have distinctive personality traits separating them from those taking more moderate positions in the same setting. The formal or explicit "content" of one's political orientation—left or right, conservative or radical, pro- or antilabor—may be determined mainly by more "extrinsic" characteristics such as education and social class; but the form or style of political expression—favoring force or persuasion, compromise or arbitrary dictation, being tolerant or narrowly prejudiced, flexible in policy or rigidly dogmatic—is apparently largely determined by personality. At least this seems clear with regard to the political extremes. It is not yet certain whether the same characteristics make for extremism in all national groups and institutional settings, but that also seems highly likely.

Prominent among the traits which make for extremism appear to be the following: exaggerated faith in powerful leaders and insistence on absolute obedience to them; hatred of outsiders and deviates; excessive projection of guilt and hostility; extreme cynicism; a sense of powerlessness and ineffectiveness (alienation and anomie); suspicion and distrust of others; and dogmatism and rigidity. Some of these terms have been or will be shown to be merely alternative designations of the same phenomenon, but some such general syndrome of authoritarianism, dogmatism, and alienation undoubtedly is the psychological root of that political extremism which makes this type actively or potentially disruptive to democratic systems.

If political extremism is indeed an accompaniment—and even more a product—of a certain personality syndrome, and if this syndrome produces the equivalent extremism in all national populations and subgroups, that fact poses a considerable challenge to the student of national character in its relation to political systems. At once we face this question: Are the societies which have a long history of democracy peopled by a majority of individuals who possess a personality conducive to democracy? Alternatively, are societies which have experi-

enced recurrent or prolonged authoritarian, dictatorial, or totalitarian government inhabited by a proportionately large number of individuals with the personality traits we have seen to be associated with extremism? In other words, can we move from the individual and group level, to generalize about the relations of personality and political system at the societal level?[38]

The original landmark study of the authoritarian personality was by Adorno and his associates.[39] The emphasis was on how personalities form, especially those that are rigid, compliant, and disciplined, capable of only slight or conditional affection, and marked by a predisposition toward father-figure leadership and an acquiescence to prejudice. According to Adorno, such individuals search for scapegoats when confronted with problems; they desire the extension of military-like conformity to civilian activity; they willingly abdicate privacy and favor state intervention in all aspects of life. In terms of ideology and opinion, they show a willingness to believe in what they are told by those who wield power. Their opinions are easily molded by sentiment. Such traits can be manipulated by ideologues and techniques to alter prevailing public opinion. It is also true that salient values which can be altered by propaganda may induce compliance to authoritarian leaders by means other than coercion. Individuals can be made into willing co-conspirators by effective propaganda. Certainly, where essential utilities are not provided, the disintegration of democratic systems is fertile ground for authoritarian alternatives. But a need for authority can also be manifested during times of *psychic* rather than material distress or confusion, even when utilities are adequately provided.[40]

Studies of the emotional roots of political behavior point out important relationships between self-esteem and self-hatred, aggression and frustration, and violence, as well as such phenomena as the internalization of social anger, and the need for order versus random behavior or anarchy.[41] Many theories dealing with such issues are Freud-

38. Alex Inkeles, "National Character and Modern Political Systems," *Psychological Anthropology,* ed. Francis L.K. Hsu (Cambridge, Mass.: Schenkman, 1972), pp. 226–27.
39. See T.W. Adorno et al., *The Authoritarian Personality* (New York: Harper, 1950).
40. See L. Festinger, H.W. Riecken, Jr., and S. Schachter, *When Prophecy Fails* (Minneapolis: University of Minnesota Press, 1958).
41. See Hans Toch, *The Social Psychology of Social Movements* (Indianapolis, Ind.: Bobbs-Merrill, 1965). Often the impact of these relationships is best revealed in a culture's drama or fiction. To understand the famous Moscow trials during the

ian, or were influenced by Freudian doctrines.[42] Their explicit focus is on personality and the pathology of repression; their solution to problematic behavior is through reducing anxieties.[43] The repressed individual, however, can also be seen as a product of a repressive society. The liberation of the individual may then require, as a cure, a new freedom, or a more appropriate new society.[44]

Aggregate Behavior and Violence

Attempts have also been made to use aggregate data to indicate how tensions engender conflict or general frustration sparks aggression. For example, if people are led to believe they will make rapid gains in social mobility due to increased education, welfare, and other benefits, and if these gains are too slow or are not forthcoming, grievances soon develop which may lead to aggressive acts. Large discrepancies between aspirations and their realization produce what is called *relative deprivation*. This is a condition in which anticipated benefits have been frustrated. Relative deprivation tends to increase exponentially as opportunities increase in more modest integrals. In developing countries this syndrome often gives rise to the "revolution of rising expectations." The literature of relative deprivation emphasizes the frustration of hopes.[45]

Conflict, then, is more likely to occur when conditions improve and social mobility increases, rather than the other way around. That is to say, the really poor are rarely revolutionaries. As conditions improve, expectations rise and incongruities appear among social status

height of Stalinist repression in the USSR, one can gain more insight from Arthur Koestler's *Darkness at Noon* than from many more "scientific" treatments. Similarly with Solzhenitsyn's *First Circle,* which gives substance and reality to such analytical treatments as Nathan Leites and Elsa Bernaut's study of why people confess, *Ritual of Liquidation* (Glencoe, Ill.: The Free Press, 1954) .
42. See Sigmund Freud, *Civilization and Its Discontents* (New York: W. W. Norton, 1962) .
43. See Irving Sarnoff, *Personality Dynamics and Development* (New York: Wiley, 1962) . See also Harold Lasswell, "Impact of Psychoanalytical Thinking on the Social Sciences," in Leonard D. White, op. cit., pp. 84–115.
44. See Herbert Marcuse, *Eros and Civilization* (New York: Random House, 1962) . See also Frantz Fanon, *The Wretched of the Earth* (New York: Grove Press, 1968) .
45. See Hadley Cantril, ed., *The Tensions that Cause Wars* (Urbana, Ill.: University of Illinois Press, 1950) . See also W. C. Runciman, *Relative Deprivation and Social Justice* (London: Routledge & Kegan Paul, 1966) .

hierarchies. *Status incongruity* refers to the condition in which status and rewards are out of balance. Status incongruity theory goes hand in hand with theories of relative deprivation, which state that as opportunity grows, so does the potentiality of conflict between those who gain in status versus those who decline.[46] A violence prone situation (as exists today in Northern Ireland) mainly pits higher-status groups against lower-status ones. This results in militant social movements when the higher-status group recruits to their side similarly interested lower-status groups which then combine against a third, most often a minority, segment. Most religious, ethnic, and racial movements are of this nature. The most extreme militancy leads to the formation of totalistic parties and private armies. The primordial radical-ideological movements of Nazi Germany and Fascist Italy, and the cadres of militant and disciplined communists in Latin America seeking to replace the prevailing social order are all examples.[47] Ideological fanaticism, with attendant simple authoritarian political solutions, is in many ways analogous to millennial religious movements.[48]

When does the aggregation of tendencies toward violence lead to revolution? While many measures have been suggested to deal with that question, one of the more interesting is the *J*-curve, which describes a revolutionary syndrome or pattern as follows:

Revolution is most likely to take place when a prolonged period of rising expectations and rising gratifications is followed by a short period of sharp reversal, during which the gap between expectations and gratifications quickly widens and becomes intolerable. The frustration that develops, when it is intense and widespread in the society, seeks outlets in violent action. When the frustration becomes focused on government, the violence becomes coherent and directional. If the frustration is sufficiently widespread, intense, and focused on government, the violence will become a revolution that displaces irrevocably the ruling government and changes markedly the power structure of the society.

46. Ibid.
47. See I.K. Feierabend et al., *Anger, Violence and Politics* (Englewood Cliffs, N.J.: Prentice-Hall, 1972).
48. See A.L. Nieburg, *Political Violence* (New York: St. Martins Press, 1969), pp. 99–133. See also Seymour Martin Lipset and Earl Raab, *The Politics of Unreason, Right-Wing Extremism in America, 1790–1970* (New York: Harper and Row, 1970), pp. 22–31; and Morris Janowitz, *Political Conflict* (Chicago: Quadrangle Books, 1970).

Or the violence will be contained within the system, which it modifies but does not displace. This latter case is rebellion.[49]

There are many examples of such development in history. The French Revolution was preceded by a period first of enormous growth and agricultural prosperity and then a drastic rural depression. Similarly, the period just before the American Revolution was one of great prosperity antecedent to acute commercial crisis. Since World War II, nationalistic revolutions in developing countries have most often occurred when colonial regimes loosened up their control, engendering expectations of democracy and freedom which have all too often been followed by a tightening of political control by a privileged sector of the colonial society. There are many other examples which seem to follow the hypothesis of the *J*-curve. Moreover, the notion can be applied generally to outbreaks of violence of any sort, not necessarily revolutionary.

Under certain conditions revolutionary ideologies stimulate the popular acceptance of extremist leaders who offer simplistic solutions.[50] Hostilities can be transformed into hate, the prejudiced into the "storm troopers" of the new society. A reconstitution of value oriented beliefs can occur which may be revolutionary or take the form of revivalist nostalgia.[51]

Clearly we need solutions. Most of us would like to find democratic ones, but if the old notions of democracy are no longer suitable, behavioral models work better for suggesting what is wrong than for stipulating what is right. They define the problems to which political solutions must be found; they describe why what goes wrong goes wrong. Obviously there can not be a one-to-one correspondence between behavioral predicaments and political solutions. However modern theories of pluralism, which direct themselves to the problem of mediating extremes, seek to find partial solutions to the tensions we have discussed rather than total answers.[52]

49. James C. Davies, "The J-Curve of Rising and Declining Satisfactions as a Cause of Some Great Revolutions and a Contained Rebellion," in Hugh Davis Graham and Ted Robert Gurr, *The History of Violence in America* (New York: Bantam Books, 1969) p. 547.
50. See Neil J. Smelser, *Theory of Collective Behavior* (New York: The Free Press of Glencoe, 1963) , p. 83.
51. For a discussion of "revivalist populism" see Richard Hofstadter, *The Age of Reform* (New York: Vintage Books, 1955) , pp. 23–59.
52. See Norman Frolich, Joe A. Oppenheimer, and Oran Young, *Political Leadership and Collective Goals* (Princeton: Princeton University Press, 1971) .

Pluralism

chapter ten
The Premises of Pluralism

Pluralism, the dominant approach to political science, builds on both institutionalism and behavioralism. Like the former it emphasizes party participation as the link between society and government, and thus postulates certain dynamic relations between them; for instance, as when an increase in the scope of political involvement in either numbers or effectiveness significantly alters the degree of centralization of decision making, accountability, and other aspects of governmental policy making. Like behavioralism pluralism emphasizes the active side of politics and adaptive learning by means of public participation at multiple levels of politics and in diverse social and political bodies.

Combining institutional concerns with behavioralism emphasizes *process* over structure. Less attention is given to how governmental agencies, legislatures, committees—the usual instruments of government—work than to how power is shared among a variety of groups, both public and private. These may be ethnic interest groups such as the South London Pakistani Association or the Italo-American Club of Hartford, or others like the Elmira P.T.A., petitioners before the Consumer Protection Agency, or the League of Women Voters.

Viewed in the light of pluralism, politics is seen to be an interactive process in which involved citizens affect the course of policy. This view brings up two fundamental questions with which pluralists have been concerned. The first is the problem of the nonparticipant, the inactive citizen who is excluded or who excludes himself or herself from the process. The second, which could be called the pluralist paradox, has to do with too much participation. A very high degree of participation by diverse groups may immobilize policy makers if and when a decision on any significant issue offends too many interests.[1]

1. See Robert A. Dahl, *After the Revolution?* (New Haven, Conn.: Yale University Press, 1970).

On the first point it may well be the case that in voting, at any rate, there are few significant differences between voters and non-voters with respect to attitudes, beliefs, and preferences. Regarding the second, it is certainly true that participation increases democracy. But it also increases the need for coordination and control. In short the problem escalates as graphed in Figure 10-1.

The more who participate in the political process, and the more diverse the modes of participation, the more competition there is between groups. Indeed, unless there is some way of coordinating and controlling, or directing, such competition the political system can become "overloaded" and break down. Examples abound: in Latin America, for example, many pluralist countries have experienced military takeovers in the name of control; Italy suffers severely from a lack of political organization and control. Conversely, in a political system which lacks coordination, participation becomes pointless. People become cynical or disillusioned. As they lapse into disinterest or apathy control is left unchecked.

How to find the right balance is partly a question of appropriate institutional mechanisms. But it is partly a question of appropriate political behavior too. Attempts to find the right pluralistic ingredients divide adherents into two main schools of thought. The dominant form, **liberal pluralism,** calls for the formation of competitive political

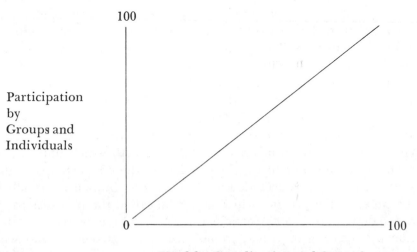

Figure 10-1. The Pluralist Paradox

elites drawn from diverse clienteles and accountable to both supporters and the political system. **Radical pluralists** oppose this solution, emphasizing instead the generation of new modes of participation which should reduce the need for coordination and control.

Class Differentiation and Pluralism

Pluralists utilize and expand on two key principles of institutionalist political thinking in their analyses: legislative control over the executive and popular sovereignty, or how the power of the state is checked by the people and how the people are represented as citizens. Pluralists assume from these principles that since citizens pay for the services and activities of government, their right to representation is a precondition of paying taxes.

The two principles are related. The historical significance of legislatures is their link with representation in terms of who pays the bill. For example, the French Revolution of 1789 was brought about partly over the issue of the right of the Third Estate to check the power of the monarchy because it represented the taxable public. In England as well, as power shifted from the House of Lords to the House of Commons, so the franchise extended downward and the taxable public expanded. And in part the American Revolution was about "no taxation without representation." It is also true that in today's world, there is no representation without taxation.

In pluralist theory these two principles have been extended beyond the formal limits of politics. A condition of pluralism is that the electorate includes all citizens: universal suffrage. From a pluralist's point of view, there can be no discriminatory restrictions on voting. In turn, the principle of legislative control over the executive extends not only to lower levels of government—regional, provincial, or state, county and municipal—but includes virtually all aspects of organized life. The key principle is *accountability*—of business managers to stockholders, civil servants to the public, party leaders to followers, university administrators to faculties and alumni (and sometimes students!), and so on. The hitherto private domain becomes quasi-public.

All institutions, then, are invested with new political significance. But for this to occur the social composition of society needs to be changed. Institutionalists differentiate society on the basis of classes. Particularly where classes are clearly and rigidly demarcated, the main job of parties is to mediate between them. But where class systems break down, parties change as well. They become broad coalitions composed of representatives of various strata of the community. When this happens thère is simultaneously *greater* emphasis on interest groups than on classes and *less* emphasis on the representation of the citizen as a private person with private rights and property. A pluralist society is established.

Not surprisingly, pluralism is a so-called "American," rather than a European, notion. In Europe, the idea of class based on feudalism was converted into that of class based on economic or productive relationships. In America, while classes certainly exist, the hard and fast distinctions characteristic of Europe never formed clear-cut social cleavages.[2] With parties here less ideologically oriented than those in Europe, politics are regarded as a science of compromise. France, in contrast a highly class-based society, had at one time the most ideological parties, the most profound cleavages, and the greatest instability of any country. Where parties are less ideological, factions and coalitions replace party cleavages.[3]

In Europe class differentiation was always greater than in the United States, but as the old feudal forms gave way during the earliest industrial transition period (an age demarcated by the English and French revolutions), a new basis for economic class differentiation emerged. Greater industrialization expanded the middle sectors and an erosion of the aristocracy occurred. Increases in the number of persons attaining higher education (not to speak of increased taxation of the upper middle class) was one of the factors reducing cleavages between classes and promoting greater social mobility. Changes in the class composition of society reflected themselves in the growth of interest groups and coalitional political parties (see Figure 10-2).[4]

There is an established body of class theory which considers democratic government in the United States to be restricted to a ruling elite to which government is accountable. This power elite is supposedly composed of those ordained by the hidden hand of capitalism. Just as Marx saw government as essentially the "executive committee of

2. See Louis Hartz, ed., "A Theory of the Development of the New Societies," *The Founding of New Societies* (New York: Harcourt, Brace and World, 1964), pp. 3–122.
3. See Robert A. Dahl, *Pluralist Democracy in the United States* (Chicago: Rand McNally, 1967), p. 58.
4. Mobility rates in France, England, and the United States during the late, or most recent, period of industrialization since World War II are as follows: United States 34%, Great Britain 31%, France 29%. See Gerhard Lenski, *Power and Privilege* (New York: McGraw Hill, 1966), p. 411.

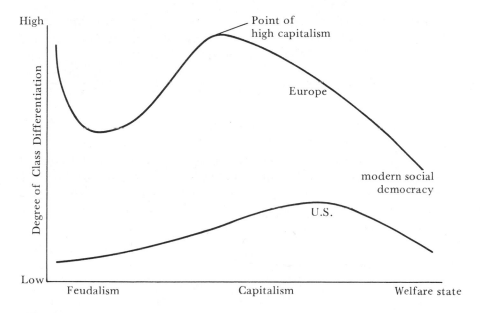

Figure 10-2. Class Differentiation in Europe and the United States

the bourgeoisie," so in contemporary society old families, the wealthy, and the most highly educated rule both in local and national politics. If true in practice, this means that there is a huge discrepancy between the theory of pluralism and actual pluralism.

In support of this view, a large number of studies conducted in the United States from the 1930s to the 1950s, showed that on all levels of government and in all cities and towns, there was a high behind-the-scenes concentration of hidden power. Studies done during the Great Depression reflected the sharp polarization between rich and poor which existed at that time. Why then did class conflict not occur? The same studies also showed that even when extreme class differences exist, in the United States they are not usually recognized as such. People translate democracy not in terms of their own share in the making of policy but by "getting ahead." Hence social and political institutions can remain stable even when they do not function properly; the blame for failure falls on the individual, not the "system."[5] The American belief in democracy persists even when the practice is faulty.

Proponents of the power elite theory agree that on a national scale

5. See for example Robert S. Lynd and Helen Merrell Lynd, *Middletown in Transition* (New York: Harcourt, Brace and Company, 1937), pp. 487–94.

the power elite operates by means of class and status dominance. As one astute commentator writes: "Although our democratic heritage makes us disapprove, our class order helps control a number of important functions. It unequally divides the highly and lowly valued things of our society among the several classes according to their rank."[6]

Max Weber: Even if there is one pluralism for the rich and one pluralism for the poor, what unites them is mobility. Max Weber distinguished between classes on lines primarily economic in origin—based on property ownership or control—and "status," a particular set of qualities or characteristics representing a position within a class.[7] Such position, Weber showed, when high enough in rank, garnered respect and prestige and could command authority for the status holder. Therefore class hierarchies result in the formation of power interests. Status, derived from honor, represents a style of life and its concomitant privileges.[8] Each can be acquired incrementally.

Class is combined with status to differentiate between social groups. It becomes possible to divide classes more precisely into upper-upper, middle-upper, lower-upper, upper-middle, middle-middle, lower-middle, and so on. Such differentiations emphasize status distinctions and social mobility as well as the ever greater differentiation within each class that is produced by modern industrial life.[9]

The idea is that power flows from the dominant sectors of the society downward. The rich and the prestigious continue, however, to exercise exceptional influence on decision-making processes, even as social mobility occurs from the lower to the higher status positions.

Pluralists take issue with Weber's model. They argue that a view of politics as a system through which benefits filter from the top down, is too simple. It undervalues the importance of the political process itself, particularly that of voting as a means of participation and the effect that organized groups have on decision making. For pluralists modern electoral and party systems do not result in a politics controlled simply by class and status elites but in a highly complex and differentiated

6. W. Lloyd Warner et al., *Social Class in America* (New York: Harper Torchbooks, 1960), p. 23.
7. See Max Weber, *The Theory of Social and Economic Organization* (London: William Hodge, 1947), p. 319.
8. See Max Weber, "Class, Status, and Party." *From Max Weber: Essays in Sociology,* ed. H.H. Gerth and C. Wright Mills (New York: Oxford University Press, 1946), pp. 180–94.
9. See Warner et al., op. cit.

process of participation by means of organized bodies at all levels of societies.

The political side of pluralism reflects this diversity. Accountability and consent are diffused throughout society. Whether the government is parliamentary or presidential, sovereignty is, in effect, shared by many. Such a polity is the opposite of a *monistic* structure where power is concentrated at the top of a political hierarchy and the ends and purposes of such power are defined by those who have it. Monism is associated with autocracy, totalitarianism, and authoritarianism; pluralism with democracy. An authoritarian regime may have a considerable degree of pluralism, as Linz and others have shown,[10] but the more pluralism, the more democracy. Today's concept of pluralism even includes tentative steps toward worker participation in management and the representation of consumers in government decisions.[11]

Instead of the class conflict and polarization between classes predicted by Marx, pluralists see the widening of the franchise and the more democratic application of institutions of representative government as expanding the middle, while eroding other class distinctions. Then, as the middle class is increasingly broken up into status groups, differentiation becomes more complex and prestige and power gain importance in the immediate community rather than just on a national scale.[12]

As additional criteria become relevant to power and prestige, behavior is no longer contingent on class and tradition. The attitudes of the "expanded middle" toward citizenship, property, manner, civility, responsibility, and commitment depend on the degree to which new political opportunities are opened up as new leaders are drawn from an ever-widening pool. The more participation there is in a common political culture, the faster rigid class distinctions disappear. The liberal pluralist ideal is a welfare state in which "leadership and power are exercised from many stations in life, by politicians, judges, ecclesiastics, businessmen, trade unionists, intellectuals and others."[13] Such finely

10. See Juan Linz, "An Authoritarian Regime: Spain," *Mass Politics: Studies in Political Sociology,* eds. Stein Rokkan and Erik Allardt (New York: The Free Press, 1970), pp. 251–75.
11. See Ralf Dahrendorf, *Class and Class Conflict in an Industrial Society* (London: Routledge and Kegan Paul, 1957), pp. 257–67.
12. See S. N. Eisenstadt, *Social Differentiation and Stratification* (Glenview, Ill.: Scott, Foresman, 1971), pp. 171–77. See also Albert J. Reiss, Jr. et al., *Occupations and Social Status* (New York: The Free Press, 1961).
13. T. H. Marshall, *Class, Citizenship and Social Development* (New York: Doubleday, 1964), p. 254.

tuned notions of differentiation in society reject more class-bound theories. The focus is on how politics works as a network intersecting at all levels—community and national.

Primordial Pluralism

Predating class is a range of ethnic and other attachments, the remnants of which hold over into the postclass period. These, to a pluralist, represent "premodern" affiliations and attachments which still continue to survive in modern societies. These can be called *primordial*. Primordial attachments are strong cultural and emotional loyalties to one's race, language group, religion, or ethnic affiliation.

Institutionalists regard primordial attachments as essentially vestigial remnants of earlier times. Parochial affiliations might survive in local areas or primitive parts of the world, but the spread of the Enlightenment, with its emphasis on science and technology, and the universalizing effects of modernization should have generally brought an end to them.

But if this is happening it is certainly not happening at as rapid a rate as it was once thought it should. Primordial affiliations can reassert themselves in the most highly industrial societies. They can intertwine with class; hence Scottish nationalism in Great Britain, or Breton nationalism in France, or black nationalism in the United States. Where such attachments occur in regional concentrations the significance of historic ethnic roots and languages grows, raising problems of minority representation and rights.

These problems in industrial societies are not of recent vintage. The principles of democratic representative government have always had to reckon with primordial attachments and affiliations. The problem was to prevent separatism by converting primordial values into interests in a working partnership. Unity within diversity was the goal.

Indeed, the term *pluralism* referred originally to the problem of plural societies, those whose populations were not homogeneous but divided by tribal, ethnic, racial, and religious cleavages and where, as quite often happened, several of these factors combined to increase the propensity for conflict rather than compromise. The problem was of particular significance in colonial territories. As these became independent, democratic constitutional formulas had to recognize the differences. A good example is Malaysia. A colony under Great Britain, it was divided between ethnic Malays, ethnic Chinese, and other groups with religious, linguistic, and cultural differences. There was a powerful communist movement among the Chinese, while the Malays were on the whole anticommunist. The problem was to find a democratic solution which would bring the two together and at the same time re duce the communist threat.[14]

What political cement could hold such social cleavages together? The assumption was that a unified people could develop itself more rapidly. Economic growth would erode differences, contributing to the mutual interdependence of all groups under a nationalistic ideology that could embrace all groups and mobilize them for independence, freedom, and development.

The primordial pluralist problem was how and where to draw the lines. How much power needed to be given to each group? The question of representation was thus related to whether people were prepared to make democratic institutions work in cooperation with other primordial groups. Pluralists began by confronting questions like whether large-scale primordial groupings should be divided between two or more countries (as British India had been divided between Pakistan and India) or contained in a single jurisdiction (as in Ceylon or Indonesia).[15] As Rupert Emerson put it,

The crux of the matter in a plural society is that it is not one people which is determining itself but two or more, and it should not be ignored that the United Nations Charter speaks in the same breath of self-determination and of equal rights of peoples. If they are actually to be equal then the subordination of one to another is evidently ruled out.[16]

Hence, pluralism consists of experiments with various forms of representation: communal voting rolls where different racial groups hold different proportions of the vote and vote for different lists of candidates. In some cases pluralist communalism has meant that various

14. One could cite many other examples of societal cleavages pertaining to Asians in East Africa, castes in India, and Arabs in Israel, for example, among others. For a good sourcebook see Donald Eugene Smith, ed., *Religion, Politics and Social Change in the Third World* (New York: The Free Press, 1971).
15. See J. S. Furnivall, *Netherlands India* (Cambridge: Cambridge University Press, 1939).
16. Rupert Emerson, *From Empire to Nation* (Cambridge, Mass.: Harvard University Press, 1960), p. 330.

communities establish their own separate legislative and representative bodies. Regionalism and federalism have also been tried. On the whole, however, such forms of political pluralism have not succeeded. Where such experiments were instituted, strong military governments have for the most part replaced democratic pluralist regimes as nationalism eroded and local primordial groups re-engaged in provincial conflicts.

The pluralist solution to primordial plural societies has not been a source of much inspiration to pluralists.[17] But the problems and the solutions have been very different in modern industrial societies.

Liberal Pluralism

We have suggested that liberal pluralism depends on fractionalization of class, the disappearance of primordial cleavages, and the differentiation of roles, so that no individual is wholly identified with a single class, occupational, ethnic, religious, or other affiliation. Then participation produces coalitional parties, mediation is not just a function of party, and accountability extends throughout all organized life.

Coordination and control of all this occurs primarily at two political levels. One is at the community level where a *pluralism of the base* exists. The other is at the national level where a *pluralism of the center* takes hold.

Pluralism of the base: The process of "pluralization" at the base has been described by three important theorists in somewhat different terms. First we will discuss the views of a "power elite" theorist, the sociologist Floyd Hunter. The contrasting interpretations are offered by two other political scientists, Robert Dahl and Nelson W. Polsby. All three use the notion of the community as a frame of reference for a network of power relationships. All three are concerned with the behavior of citizens as people who act in accordance with their values and beliefs but whose interpretation of these at any moment may not be expressed explicitly. It is from the countless ways people conduct their business vis-à-vis each other that we infer what they believe: Taking action is making choices. All agree too that power is a complex concept in which

17. See Lucian W. Pye, *Politics, Personality and Nation-Building* (New Haven, Conn.: Yale University Press, 1962), pp. 244–66. See also Clifford Geertz, ed., "The Integrative Revolution," *Old Societies and New States* (New York: The Free Press, 1963), pp. 105–57.

any and all the factors of income, prestige, knowledge, institutional affiliation, and "connections" may be involved. They agree that the purposeful actions of individuals in the community are only random or unconnected when seen as a whole. From the micro point of view on the contrary, each person devotedly pursuing his or her own ends is seen as working within or endorsing or changing given patterns of social life and organization.

While cities are an ancient phenomenon, the modern city is a dynamic network of functions: a hub of transport, industry, finance, employment and education, welfare and health facilities. It offers exceptional amenities: markets, theaters, newspapers and other media, and so on. It also has its special dangers. Despite all these, however, it is mainly in the city that one can observe groups: the rich, the middle class, the poor, the unemployed, marginals, teenagers, community college students. Each lives in a characteristic manner, in a characteristic neighborhood, but each sustains networks of affiliation with similar others as well. Within each network there are those who believe in "an honest day's pay for an honest day's work." There are others who are "angry at the system." Some are on welfare. Others work hard in white-collar occupations and put in over-time without recompense, trying to "get ahead." Some elites represent old wealth, others new. Clubs might be desegregated and school busing might be introduced. But any changes produce ripple effects throughout the social network, as a result of which traditional or status quo habits and feelings are uprooted, people affronted. All three of the analysts whose work is assessed here ask, How can a community, subject to the continuous pressure of change, uncertainties, and upward and downward mobilities which juxtapose antagonism and power with compromise and mediation, remain relatively stable?

Hunter: The Power Elite. For Hunter different socioeconomic institutions, government, religious and educational bodies all represent official inputs into the policy-making process, along with professional, civic, and cultural associations whose connection to policy making is direct. More informal constraints are exercised by a special elite which commands great influence and respect. Each of the institutional and associational bodies in turn subdivides into smaller groups with their own leaders and their more particular objects. Yet each subgroup contains a kernel of respect for the original power elite. Behind the formal and informal networks of power, then, there is another pattern of power based on deference. This is sustained by influence and informal surveillance such as by neighbors who know "appropriate" conduct, peers, and associates in work and recreation. This informed system is peculiar. Nothing goes unobserved and little goes unreported. Yet despite gossip and rumor and innuendo, everyone minds his or her own business, or so it seems.

These informal patterns of deference and influence become visible in a community when certain projects or issues attract attention because they are important in a great many people's lives. Community interest will always be greater than community participation. Participation is mainly by more affluent and organized groups. Those who are least able to participate are minorities—blacks, Hispanics, those on welfare, and others.

Structurally the Negro [for example] community is isolated from the power group through the individual Negro's inability to rise in the organizations which are community-wide in scope. The professional groups in the under-structure of power do not get into the policy-making meetings. Both of these groups represent relatively weakly organized bodies in Regional City. The Negro citizenry is becoming increasingly organized, however, and the politicians are paying more attention to the demands of this group. The key to participation in power decisions would appear in finding strength through perfecting social organizations along interest lines.[18]

Hunter shows that leadership and decision-making power in what he calls "Regional City" is formed, shaped, and distributed from the top down. He shows how access to power is related to organizational and suborganizational strength, and the connection of the latter to policy making by the leaders themselves. While Hunter recognizes the changing structure of power, he is less concerned with how new groups get power than with how those in office organize, lead, and affect policy.

Dahl: Reward Structures. Robert Dahl is more concerned with how power changes hands, with the dynamics of the process and how the distribution of power is itself altered. When communities seek to break

18. Floyd Hunter, *Community Power Structure* (New York: Doubleday Anchor Books, 1963), p. 250.

the monopoly of power or rule by the "patricians," control shifts to the entrepreneurs, the "ex-plebs" and the "new men." Dahl is less concerned with leaders as such than with the concept of leadership and its ambiguities. A leader requires a follower, therefore

> . . . [F]rom one position, leaders are enormously influential—so influential that if they are seen only in this perspective, they might well be considered a kind of ruling elite. Viewed from another position, however, many influential leaders seem to be captives of their constituents. Like the blind men with the elephant, different analysts have meticulously examined different aspects of the body politic and arrived at radically different conclusions. To some, a pluralistic democracy with dispersed inequalities is all head and no body; to others it is all body and no head.[19]

The problem is to distinguish among the rituals of power, the trappings of formal office, and the reality of power. Those close to decision making are able to exert more influence than those further away. But indirect influence is also great, and more difficult to measure or account for. Hence, according to Dahl, the relationship between leaders and citizens is more likely to be reciprocal than hierarchical. Power does not simply flow from the top down but, despite elite or political substrata more directly involved than ordinary citizens, generates a back-and-forth or reciprocal relation between leaders and their clientele.

The problem is to assess more precisely how such reciprocities work in the long term and the short term. What is the immediate political significance of the politicized substrata? To answer that one can call upon any of several political axioms. One is the utility notion that (1) there must be a "reward structure" before political coalitions will be effective, and (2) coalitions must be broadly based on a sufficiently diverse membership. This structure favors multiple-group support for leadership rather than a single-group, class, or interest monopoly of power. Any group can veto a coalitional objective if it feels strongly enough about it—this is a condition of participation, particularly by important ethnic groups. Coalitions generally follow the lines of economic and social needs and structures.

In a coalitional or utilitarian society, leaders dispense services as

19. Robert A. Dahl, *Who Governs?* (New Haven, Conn.: Yale University Press, 1961), p. 89.

rewards. These services must be substantial enough to initiate sublevels of reward dispensation by subleaders. Reward dispensation always fulfills both overt and covert commitments but, as Dahl points out, such characteristics

> *. . . are not necessarily dysfunctional to a pluralistic democracy in which there exists a considerable measure of popular control over the policies of leaders, for minority control by leaders within associations is not necessarily inconsistent with popular control over leaders through electoral processes.*
>
> *For example, suppose that (1) a leader of a political association feels a strong incentive for winning an election; (2) his constituents comprise most of the adult population of the community; (3) nearly all of his constituents are expected to vote; (4) voters give heavy weight to the overt policies of a candidate in making their decision as to how they will vote; (5) there are rival candidates offering alternative policies; and (6) voters have a good deal of information about the policies of the candidates. In these circumstances, it is almost certain that leaders of political associations would tend to choose overt policies they believe most likely to win the support of a majority of adults in the community. Even if the policies of political associations were usually controlled by a tiny minority of leaders in each association, the policies of the leaders who won elections to the chief offices in local government would tend to reflect the preferences of the populace. I do not mean to suggest that any political system actually fulfills all these conditions, but to the extent that it does, the leaders who directly control the decisions of political associations are themselves influenced in their own choices of policies by their assumptions as to what the voting populace wants.*[20]

Dahl discusses how the process of pluralistic policy making works with respect to those who participate—their income and wealth, affiliations, and so on—using certain key policy issues—urban renewal, education—as examples. To Dahl, while the rich are clearly more influential than the poor, they are a smaller number. The less affluent therefore are often able to have more of a long-range effect on policy *when they participate*. In other words, they can have a negative impact on the power of the rich. On the other hand, the very poor or the working class lack the resources to engage in politics, and this reduces their self-

20. Ibid., pp. 100–101.

confidence, their sense of political efficacy. Organizational participation will partly compensate for this lack because ordinarily those who participate in organizations are those who are likely to participate directly or indirectly in politics as well. Also, the better off a citizen is, the less likely he or she is to work for the city itself. Therefore patronage systems tend to favor the less well off, providing a direct route to influence within the governmental organization.

Dahl concludes that active participation in politics is for most people confined to the act of voting and one or two other occasional activities like donating to or electioneering for a particular candidate. (Of a sample taken in New Haven, Connecticut, 47 percent reported that they "get together to talk about local politics and affairs"; 27 percent had ever "contacted local public officials or politicians"—and only 16 percent had done so in the past year—while 13 percent had over the previous year participated in an activity connected with local issues or problems—"political or nonpolitical."[21])

So pluralistic local politics is reciprocal. Power is dispersed, participation is low and episodic, and political interest is very limited unless some issue happens to affect people's primary focus of attention regarding, for example, food, social mores, family, work, shelter, and the like.

Activities like these—not politics—are the primary concerns of most men and women. In response to the question, "What things are you most concerned with these days?" two out of every three registered voters in [a] sample cited personal matters, health, jobs, children, and the like; only about one out of five named local, state, national, or international affairs. It would clear the air of a good deal of cant if instead of assuming that politics is a normal and natural concern of human beings one were to make the contrary assumption that whatever lip service citizens may pay to conventional attitudes, politics is a remote, alien and unrewarding activity. Instead of seeking to explain why citizens are not interested, concerned, and active, the task is to explain why a few citizens are.[22]

Polsby: Choice Alternatives. Nelson W. Polsby analyzes such questions in a more comparative and theoretical way. His particular concern is to make precise the meaning of power as a decision-making force.

21. Ibid., p. 279. The sample numbered 525.
22. Ibid.

Where decisions are choices between alternative courses of action leading to outcomes A and B, an actor can be said to possess a certain amount of "power" if, by acting on others, he changes the comparative probability that these outcomes will take place. The amount of power the actor has in this situation is expressed by the magnitude of the changes he introduces.[23]

Among the questions to be answered are these: To what extent are certain common "power elite" assertions—for instance, that an upper class "rules" local community life—true? Are political and civic leaders subordinate to the upper class? Is there a single ruling power elite that performs in the interests of the upper class, causing conflict between the upper and the lower classes? In short, Polsby poses pluralist alternatives to the common view that in a democratic and capitalist society, the few rule the many, the few are the rich, and the ruled are their servants. Where Dahl's hypotheses are largely drawn from a case study of New Haven, Connecticut, Polsby uses findings from studies taken in diverse localities: Muncie, Indiana; Newburyport, Massachusetts; Morris, Illinois; Philadelphia, Pennsylvania; Atlanta, Georgia; Baton Rouge, Louisiana; Ypsilanti, Michigan; Seattle, Washington; *and* New Haven, Connecticut. By closely reading the comparative studies of each of these cities and towns, Polsby shows that many findings of the power-elite theorists are not warranted by the data overall, and that there is an insufficient fit between their findings and the validation of hypotheses. Above all, studies, which purport to confirm the power elite thesis, not only fail to do so but contain enough counterfactual observations that they contradict themselves.[24]

Polsby also challenges Hunter's assumption that there is a relatively closed circle of leaders consisting of members of the business elite in the community. Defining the economic elite in terms of the top economic stratum of the community, Polsby established a sample elite in New Haven based on the following criteria:

(1) the president and the chairman of the board of every company having a total assessed evaluation putting it among the city's top 50 taxpayers during any of the five years 1953–1958; (2) any individual whose total assessed evaluation during the years 1957 or 1958 was greater than

---

23. Nelson W. Polsby, *Community Power and Political Theory* (New Haven, Conn.: Yale University Press, 1963), p. 4.
24. Ibid., pp. 14–44.

$250,000; (3) the presidents and chairmen of the board of all banks
and utilities; (4) any individual who was a director of a New Haven
bank or of three or more local corporations having an assessment
of $250,000 or more or employing more than 50 if a manufacturer,
or employing more than 25 if a retailer.[25]

From this set of criteria it was possible for Polsby to obtain a list of
239 people in a study of the New Haven-area "power elite." He also
collected the names of a second elite, the "status elite," from the New
Haven *Blue Book,* an exclusive social register of two thousand families,
from which he extracted 231 names. Then, comparing the names on
both lists with the critical participants in key urban renewal issues on
which he expected power and influence to be directly involved, he
found that there was a minimal amount of overlap between the power
and status elites, and then only in ordinary activities like the P.T.A.
Thus, only a very small proportion of the two elites were involved in
any important decisions studied. Since many of the key issues involved
concrete matters of policy, Polsby inferred that conflicts or disagreements were between professionals—teachers and school administrators,
for example—and not between classes.[26]

In addition to the question of "Who governs?" much work has
been done on "How?" Detailed studies have been done on the links
between local, regional and state level politics by a number of political
scientists in the United States and abroad. Heinz Eulau in particular
has concentrated on the complex of factors relevant to the political
process at local levels of decision making in cities, and explored their
linkages to state governments and legislatures. Through his painstaking
and careful investigations he has provided elaborately detailed findings,
and more statistically refined data than anyone else, making possible
the thorough examination of specific questions affecting the relations of
local power. What emerges from such efforts is a picture of local and
regional politics today vastly different from that drawn by the older
"class-status-power elite" school.[27]

25. Ibid., p. 85.
26. Ibid., pp. 88–95.
27. See Heinz Eulau and Kenneth Prewitt, *Labyrinths of Democracy: Adaptations,*
Linkages, Representation, and Policies in Urban Politics (Indianapolis, Ind.: Bobbs-
Merrill, 1974.) See also Heinz Eulau, *Micro-Macro Political Analysis* (Chicago:
Aldine, 1969).

Dahl, Polsby, Eulau, and others have made a positive case for pluralism as a combination of diverse power networks, and a negative case against power elite theories with their view of politics as dependent on a ruling class holding the reins of an obedient or subservient ruling elite. Research on pluralism at the community level has revealed the complex forms of interaction that occur among highly organized groupings in society and interested individuals, describing the network of activities by means of which a community is governed.

Pluralism of the center: In pluralist theory the same principles at work at the local level are at work at the level of central government, but in a much more elaborate way. Several schools of pluralists can be named, all of which have proposed theories of central government, including those of David Truman, Robert A. Dahl, Charles E. Lindblom, Edward Banfield, Robert Lane, Sidney Verba and Norman H. Nie, Douglas Rae, Stein Rokkan, Brian Barry and others. Here we cannot discuss even the highlights of the work of all of these, but taken together, their studies represent an important segment of today's corpus.[28] The following speculations run through their work:

1. If greater differentiation in society produces greater differences among people, what does the term *equality* mean? How can equality be made *politically* meaningful? How does modern pluralism connect to ideas which were significant among Enlightenment and radical political theorists?

2. In liberal political theory the political marketplace balances inequities of wealth arising from the economic marketplace, and the private economic marketplace provides alternatives to public power in the political marketplace. Private wealth should balance public power, and public power reallocate private wealth, according to the preferences of (a) consumers and producers and (b) citizens and politicians. How can the political marketplace be used to induce greater equity in distribution without government accumulating centralized powers which can be used against private citizens?[29]

3. As political participation increases and rights are respected, conflicts among parties will increase. How can political stability be re-

28. For a short review, see Andrew S. McFarland, *Power and Leadership in Pluralist Systems* (Stanford: Stanford University Press, 1969).
29. See Anthony Downs, *An Economic Theory of Democracy* (New York: Harper and Bros., 1957), pp. 257–58.

tained and decisions reached which are mutually acceptable to all parties?[30]

4. Given political differentiation plus the desire for participation, representation needs to become more and more indirect, reducing the effectiveness of and the sense of sharing in the decision-making process which democracy requires. How can the need for more indirect representation in the interests of manageability and the need for more direct representation, or the representation of one's own interests, be resolved? Which is the preferred emphasis: the liberal pluralist concern with the accountability of elites or the radical pluralist concern with breaking up units into smaller and more participatory subgroups?[31]

To answer these questions different solutions have been offered. Our discussion of pluralism at the center will emphasize two liberal pluralist solutions: *consociational democracy* and *polyarchy*. Before discussing these theories specifically, however, it will be useful to develop the assumptions of pluralism a bit further.

Rights and equality in a pluralist system: The British sociologist T.H. Marshall described the rise of the modern social welfare state as the result of the organization of different sectors of society in defense of their rights. However, as people defend their rights, through trade union organization for example, they also need to live up to the obligations of citizenship. And this they are not always prone to do. Moreover, the effects of status differentiation—that is, the modern tendency to divide people up along relatively smaller and smaller degrees of differentiation until they become stratified by means of minute classifications —results in the higher grades acting more "responsibly." Such status

30. See Douglas Rae, "The Limits of Consensual Decision," *The American Political Science Review,* Vol. LIX, No. 4 (Dec. 1975) : 1270–94. Rae cites as an example the "famous Pigouvian chimney":
  (*1*) *A chimney emits smoke, reducing the welfare of the people living nearby.*
  (*2*) *The victims of this diseconomy would gain from its elimination, but the chimney owners would lose from its elimination.*
  (*3*) *It is proposed that government eliminate the smoke by simple prohibition. This is rejected.*
  It is proposed that government eliminate the smoke by the combination of a prohibition and a tax on former victims sufficient to make this a gain for the chimney owners (p. 1288) .
31. See Dahl, *After the Revolution?,* pp. 140–66. See also Steven Lukes, *Power: A Radical View* (London: Macmillan, 1974) , pp. 46–56.

inequality produces differing degrees of citizen responsibility.[32] Equality and responsibility, therefore, do not coincide. Conversely, to get more equality people need to exercise their rights, but some people will exercise them more than others. How can equity result?

The pluralist argument is that in addition to modern electoral systems, organizational openness in society is what provides the ingredients for the defense of rights and interests. But this requires organization at every level of society, not only to mobilize people and public opinion, but money and other resources as well. While once the working class was not only poor, but ineffective in competition with big business, today this is not the case. It is highly organized. (In Great Britain, for example, virtually no government policy affecting the economic life of the country can be made without the agreement of the trade unions. Much the same situation prevails in the United States, France, and other democratic societies.)

Pluralism starts with a predisposition toward the principle of organizational equality as distinct from individual equality. This makes for a system of countervailing powers. At the same time some method of control is necessary in order to prevent organizational anarchy. As Dahl and Lindblom put it,

Why, then, is political equality significant in governments—*that is, in organizations that have a sufficient monopoly of control to enforce an orderly settlement of disputes with other organizations in an area? Precisely because whoever controls government usually has the "last word" on a question; whoever controls government can enforce decisions on other organizations in the area. Thus so long as the condition of political equality is approximated, citizens can always decide in what situations and in what organizations they wish to tolerate hierarchy in order to achieve goals that cannot be satisfied by organization on an equalitarian basis. The condition of political equality assigns to the electorate the position of an ultimate court of appeal to decide where else in society the condition of equality may be enforced or foregone.*[33]

Organizational pluralism creates opportunities for equality by ensuring that each group is publicly accountable for its actions. But that requires a principle of equality based on equal rights in the first place.

32. See T.H. Marshall, *Class, Citizenship, and Social Development* (New York: Doubleday, 1964), pp. 112–13.
33. Robert A. Dahl and Charles E. Lindblom, *Politics, Economics, and Welfare* (New York: Harper Torchbooks, 1963), p. 42.

What follows after are majority rule, security, an emphasis on progress, rationality, the delegation of authority to experts, a willingness to make gains incrementally, effective controls by means of rewards and penalties and effective communications between parties. These are all characteristics of the pluralist society. The problem is to make these work without their confounding each other. Behind them a multitude of objective groupings—interest groups, bureaucracies, political parties —convert the public concern with principles into specific issues for policy making. All functions relate in one way or other to institutions— the legislative process, the committee system, the courts, and other bodies permitting access to power. The stress, however, is on the dispersion of political information by political elites, diverse methods of bargaining and negotiation within and among government agencies, and accountability.

Equality is a condition of absolute fairness or justice, and it is an elusive condition. Relative fairness or justice is more common. But equity is more likely to be realized as political leaders become more responsible to their followers. Responsibility generates cooperation.

One of the problems in promoting equity is to prevent elites from maintaining bureaucratic controls over their followers. The stockholders in most large private corporations, for example, do not really supervise or hold managers accountable, except when the company fails to show a profit. Few trade unions, similarly, even those whose leadership is elected, hold their leaders accountable. A high degree of apathy is characteristic of both stockholders and rank-and-file union members. Thus, for pluralism to succeed a society must disprove what Robert Michels called the "iron law of oligarchy."

Organization implies the tendency to oligarchy. In every organization, whether it be a political party, a professional union, or any other association of the kind, the aristocratic tendency manifests itself very clearly. The mechanism of the organization, while conferring a solidity of structure, induces serious changes in the organized mass, completely inverting the respective position of the leaders and the led. As a result of organization, every party or professional union becomes divided into a minority of directors and a majority of directed.[34]

How to reverse this condition and open up organizations to greater control by the membership is thus a critical concern for pluralists, par-

34. See Robert Michels, *Political Parties* (Glencoe, Ill.: The Free Press, 1958), pp. 37, 393–409.

ticularly for radical pluralists. It is possible to call a society where all the subunits are relatively closed pluralist and democratic in the sense that each organization competes in order to promote its own interest. But that means pluralism at the top, not at the base of society. Modern pluralists are concerned with pluralism at both the top and the base.[35]

In a pluralist democracy it is not enough that group membership in society becomes more differentiated. Nor is it sufficient that the elites become more accountable. True accountability means the reduction of inequality among the various segments within society. When people feel more equal to each other, they are less likely to accept absolute or bureaucratic rule. True equality, then, is the final form of equity. But true equality, as we have said, is an elusive condition which can never really exist because of natural differences among people. While equity is a condition that falls short of equality, people nevertheless regard it as fair and just. In pluralist terms *equality,* to be meaningful, requires a precondition of equal rights.

The active pursuit of rights requires participation, and in modern society participation on a mass basis requires organization. Various political organizations mobilize opinion, voters, and interests. In turn, they publicize a broad spectrum of local, national, and special interest concerns. Each organization has some hierarchy, but at the top one finds powerful *cadres* of leaders, elites. In pluralist theory these elites should be responsible to their followers; that is, they are expected to be accountable to their supporters. However, the concept of accountability implies also (1) the continuous threat of being thrown out of office and (2) that leaders can be held legally and morally responsible for their acts. Such accountability generates a complex interchange between leaders and led, elites and followers, of influence and information. By such exchanges responsibility for specific acts is focused on one political group or another. In pluralist theory, however, no organization can assume a monopoly role in society, nor for that matter can any group.

Facets of a pluralist model: Pluralism extends the liberal theory of the political marketplace. The notion of individual competition is replaced

35. One important study of pluralism at the base is Seymour Martin Lipset, Martin Trow, and James S. Coleman, *Union Democracy* (Glencoe, Ill.: The Free Press, 1956), particularly pp. 403–12. This book examines how the International Typographical Union avoided bureaucratization and oligarchy. The authors suggest a general proposition about equality and democratization, which reads that if a reduction of differences in status due to differences in skill is associated with more education, knowledge about politics, and egalitarian principles, then the more likely are people to participate in politics.

by a network of organizational competition, influence, accountability, and information in which groups can organize and, by exercising rights, realize interests to affect policy outcomes. The emphasis on transactions and exchanges of influence, information, and accountability has the further effect of converting passionately held political beliefs and values into interests. But even here such a conversion does not take place on a one-way street. Those with little power try to convert interests to values (such as the desire for rights) and those who have power try to reduce values to interests (the payment of benefits). The stability of a pluralist system, then, is based on (1) maintaining the rules of consensus, (2) converting values to interests by means of organizational competition, (3) gearing the society increasingly toward equality, and (4) anticipating the conversion of interests to values by the relatively powerless.

A good example of a pluralist process is the American black movement. Before the 1960s blacks were excluded from competitive politics. They were badly organized. They measured low on standard scales of equality—economic, social, and political. Then the welfare of blacks came to be perceived as a problem of fundamental values. The discrepancies between principles of equality and their practice challenged the professed aims of American society. Commitment to the actualization of such values among religious figures like Martin Luther King, Jr. and activist organizations like the Black Panthers, increased the organizational basis of black competition. Through such organization blacks converted their values to interests in jobs, busing, increased educational opportunities, and neighborhood desegregation. However, the rules of the game were participatory rather than revolutionary, and insofar as some success was obtained at both the legislative level and in shifting public attitudes in general, consensus about the rules was maintained as the benefits sought were, to some extent, rendered and inequities reduced.[36]

The capacity to absorb demands which begin as value-loaded threats is one of the most important aspects of pluralist societies. But it assumes that the commitment to consensus, and to the right of *all* parties to participate in negotiations and transactions, outweighs all other considerations. It also assumes that, despite the incidence of individual violence, collective violence will not be permitted.[37]

There are, of course, many problems. Some people can be or-

36. See Everett Carll Ladd, Jr., *Negro Political Leadership in the South* (New York: Atheneum, 1969).
37. See Morris Janowitz, *Political Conflict* (Chicago: Quadrangle Books, 1970), pp. 171–203.

ganized more readily than others, and quite often those who have the least advantage, the least wealth, and the least education—those who are likely to need the most benefit from society—are also those least likely to be able to organize or mobilize. Thus they obtain the least from society. While the positions of minorities of the rich and powerful in most modern societies have eroded as a result of such policies as transfers of welfare benefits, majority coalitions are still reluctant to pay the cost of providing exceptional opportunities for the most disadvantaged. Except in a few countries like Sweden and the Netherlands, compensatory inequality is still not possible. The middle class in most Western cultures grumbles about the high cost of welfare. It will not insist that unemployment be reduced, if this goal implies higher taxes. Popular sovereignty and taxes are not always harmonious principles.

On the other hand, if marginal members of society can organize, they may be able to make significant differences by voting, especially where parties are otherwise equally matched in coalitions. Raising the "values" question helps too. But if the situation is sufficiently desperate, acts of violence and terrorism can be expected, such as occurred during the 1960s race riots in American cities, in the Biafran war in Nigeria, or urban rioting in South Africa. If a government fails to heed the causes of extremist acts, it does so at its own peril.

What interests fuel the pluralistic system of political competition? Jobs and taxes; inflation and depression; poverty and disadvantage; rents and housing; the basic costs of food, clothing, and education; roads and railways; sewage and waste disposal; power and water supplies; recreation and environment; community services, health and medical facilities, care of the aged, family assistance, children, marriage and the rights of the sexes; law and order; busing and integration. These are the issues that dominate ordinary political life, interspersed with momentarily salient questions of ethnicity, race, and class. If group rights are exercised by means of organization, the political problem for government is how to reconcile conflicting interests and mediate between conflicting claims. Thus the emphasis in pluralism is on continuous negotiation so that rights and benefits, values and interests, remain in balance. Since these are always getting out of balance, the process is continuous.

Should the poor have equal organizational access with the rich if the latter are 1 percent of the population and the former 20 percent?[38] Is there a political difference between subjective and objective equality?

38. Dahl and Lindblom, op. cit., p. 505.

One may have equality before the law and feel discriminated against in a thousand ways. Indeed, in many countries where differences in religion, language group, or cultural traditions are strong—whether in Africa or Asia or Europe—the intensity of attachment to a particular grouping may inflame a sense of economic grievance and compound feelings of discrimination. How then can consensus be achieved? How do different kinds of problems cluster? For example, from the standpoints of rich and poor, the problems of recreation and environment are very different. For the rich "recreation" may mean visiting a foreign country or having a relaxing golf weekend. For the poor it involves confronting the danger of hanging out on the streets. The environmental concerns of the middle class are clean air and water. For the poor they are rats and decaying houses. For research purposes such "gut" issues must be treated as complex. They require detailed study using proper techniques to evaluate the significance of many variables.[39]

Data Gathering Techniques. Pluralists use "ecological analysis" to obtain data pertaining to (1) individuals and (2) territorial units. Both *primary data* and *derived data* are sought. Primary data for individuals include measures of personal attributes or qualities such as sex, age, church attendance, voting, and so forth. Primary data for territorial units include the global attributes of the whole society such as aggregate data on population size, national income, and other quantifiable matters. Derived data on individuals show the impact of global attributes on the individual. Aggregate derived data show the consequence of individual behavior as a distribution of global data. Using these four types of data assessment techniques allows one to examine all kinds of interactions leading to issue saliency and its effect on organization; for example, the global effects of a dominant language on those minorities in a given territorial unit who speak another language (for example, Finnish-speaking people living in Sweden). How does the use of a minority language (or even dialectical differences) affect neighborhoods, residence, income, and party affiliation of speakers, and thus issue salience and bargaining?[40]

39. An example is the so-called *F-scale* which was discussed in Chapter Nine. The *F-scale* shows the difference between the variance of each individual variable and the residual variance, thus demonstrating how each of these factors of class and issues interrelate.
40. The most elaborate and detailed single work using ecological analysis is by Mattei Dogan et al., *Quantitative Ecological Analysis in the Social Sciences* (Cambridge, Mass.: Massachusetts Institute of Technology Press, 1969).

The attempts of conventional pluralist analysts to answer these kinds of questions have not been satisfactory. There is a difference between societies which are *plural* in the sense described earlier in the chapter (that is, in terms of "primordial" differences of race, ethnicity, religion, and language), as opposed to those that are *plural* as relates to diverse interests and affiliations. Indeed, where societies are plural in the first sense, virtually any of the bread-and-butter issues of politics can be transformed from a matter of interests into a values-laden controversy over which people fight to preserve their rights and freedoms. Where they are plural in the second sense, rights may be infringed simply because some are unable to or will not participate. Solutions in each case are somewhat different, and in the following sections we shall discuss two possibilities.

Consociational Pluralism

The term *consociational pluralism* has come into common usage today, particularly with respect to societies in which deep primordial cleavages have successfully been converted into instruments of effective pluralist democracies. The term itself is an old one, reaching back to the sixteenth and seventeenth centuries (to the work of Johannes Althusius[41]). It means simply the *associating* of groups in a way that maintains the distinctive characteristics of each of the constituents without inhibiting the pursuit of collective aims.

In modern use the term was first applied to African societies with strong primordial, ethnic, and other cleavages.

For example, in an analysis of the problem of how to create a political framework for an about-to-become-independent Uganda, Apter contrasted the term *consociational* with two other forms of pluralism: that of a modernizing autocracy—an essentially innovative but traditional form of monarchy—and a mobilization system in the form of a mass radical, nationalist single-party state.[42] Uganda, like many African societies, was deeply divided along ethnic, religious,

41. J. Althusius (1557–1638), a professor of law who lived in Holland, believed that the state is *the* association of all other associations. He was a federalist whose themes were important to the idea of the state as a social contract. See Otto Gierke, *Natural Law and the Theory of Society* (Cambridge: Cambridge University Press, 1950), pp. 70–74.
42. See D. E. Apter, *The Political Kingdom in Uganda* (Princeton, N.J.: Princeton University Press, 1961).

regional, and racial lines. Some of these combined with class differences so that some groups were economically far better off and more educated than others.[43] *The problem was to find some common denominator for representative government, or a form of government which could join together the constituent units so that they maintained their identity while still merging in some form of union.*

Modern consociations may range from relatively loose confederations of groups and states to federal systems or parliamentary arrangements. Whatever the form, however, they must ensure consensus—a framework of shared interests within which groups will be willing to interrelate, compromise, and accommodate one another. The internal politics of such a system must be flexible and since consociational politics lacks, or does not require, a total commitment on the part of its members, common agreement is necessary before action is possible. In an unstable consociation, crisis, fission, and recombination limit possibilities of action to the wishes of recurrent pluralities which ebb and flow with continual arguments over values, interests, goals, and tactics.

The main characteristics of consociational polities are as follows:

1. *Pyramidal authority* based on power that is dispersed and shared among the constituent units and a central agency.

2. *Multiple loyalties* between units formed on different criteria (racial, religious, linguistic). The individual may belong to several units which all fall along a single line of cleavage or these affiliations may be blurred (religion cutting across language, race across religion, and so forth). Political parties and interest groups do not require the sole allegiance of individuals. Parties cannot discipline their memberships.

3. *Necessity for compromise* is built into such a system because of its voluntary character.

4. *Competition* between different groups for support outside their own interests is necessary in order to form coalitions and keep leaders accountable.

5. *Ideologies* can be inclusive rather than exclusive, and they may symbolize the larger purposes of the consociation (such as historical continuity).[44]

43. The problem was particularly interesting because powerful "kingdom states" were in conflict with organized ones: Bantu versus Nilotic; Catholics, Muslims, and Protestants against each other; and Africans, Asians, and Europeans in a three-tiered racial class conflict.
44. Ibid., pp. 24–25.

The consociational system has also been applied to those European countries where primordial conflicts (like those in the Netherlands between Protestants and Catholics and in Belgium between Flemish and Walloon populations) survive in society. This application has required changes in the consociational model. Perhaps the most important example of positive adaptation has taken place in the Netherlands, where different groups sharing conflicting values have learned to live together in a prosperous and advanced welfare society. Indeed, in the Netherlands cleavages have encouraged effective interaction among groups rather than producing conflict.

One theorist, Val R. Lorwin, has used the term *segmental pluralism* to suggest powerful and distinctive units which need to be composed into a single political system.[45] But perhaps the most elaborate application of the consociational model of pluralism is in Arend Lijphart's study of the Netherlands.[46] Taking off from Gabriel Almond's distinction between stable and "immobiliste" democracies[47] (Great Britain, the United States, and the Old Commonwealth democracies as well as the stable, multiparty democracies of Switzerland, the Low Countries, and Scandinavia), Lijphart suggests that a third type of consociational system exists which consists of fragmented but stable democracies, or "consociational democracies."

The leaders of the rival sub-cultures may engage in competitive behavior and thus further aggravate mutual tensions and political instability, but they may also make deliberate efforts to counteract the immobilizing and unstabilizing effects of cultural fragmentation.[48]

Examples of such consociations are democratic Austria after World War I, Belgium in the early nineteenth century, modern Canada, the Netherlands, and others.

The European cases emphasize the point that separatist or segmental subunits help stimulate political awareness and participation. While the identity of each group is preserved, the groups nevertheless

45. See Val R. Lorwin, "Segmental Pluralism," *Comparative Politics,* Vol. 3 (1971), pp. 141–75.
46. See Arend Lijphart, *The Politics of Accommodation: Pluralism and Democracy in the Netherlands,* 2nd ed. (Berkeley, Ca.: University of California Press, 1975).
47. See Gabriel Almond and Sidney Verba, *The Civic Culture* (Princeton: Princeton University Press, 1963), pp. 473–505.
48. See Arend Lijphart, "Consociational Democracy," in *Consociational Democracy, Political Accommodation in Segmented Societies,* ed. Kenneth McRae (Toronto: McClelland and Stewart, 1974), p. 75.

remain isolated from each other. However, the elites of all groups, while highly accountable to their own communities, need also to be devoted to mutuality and compromise. The Dutch case, where cleavages were religious and ideological resulted in a politics of compromise which accommodated everyone.

Conversely, as various separate communities lose some of their uniqueness and become less segmentalized, the politics of accommodation begins to erode. In the Netherlands the left has become both more powerful and less willing to negotiate along traditional lines, pushing for more participatory forms of democracy. The effects of the mass media, generational changes, and a variety of other factors have made the Dutch political culture less and less divided. Bloc cohesion breaks down. There is a decline of deference. Demands for democratization grow and polarization occurs between extremists and those who are increasingly passive or "depoliticized."[49] Thus the paradox of consociational democracy: The more homogeneous the segments, and the more each bloc breaks down into a common political culture, the more the commitment to compromise and negotiation declines and the more apathetic or withdrawn from politics is the bulk of the electorate.

Bargaining: The key to consociational accommodation is elite bargaining. The key to elite bargaining is a responsible leadership highly accountable to its community. But the existence of various communities must not be threatened by consociation. Identities must be preserved. If the cleavages become separatist, accountable leaders will have more severe limits imposed on their capacity to bargain with other leaders and thus compromise will be drastically curtailed. (This is the situation that is occurring in French Canada. It is also the reason for the stalemated consociation between Greek and Turkish Cypriots. Tendencies toward cleavage and fragmentation exist among the more militant Basques in Spain, the French in Quebec, and the Scots in Great Britain.) In contrast, one of the best examples of successful cohesion is Norway's "community system." Cohesion exists despite division and there is a high value placed on consensus as an end in itself even where people are divided. The elites cultivate

> . . . *a certain political considerateness of others: deference to their expertise or experience, sympathy with their special interests, or reluctance to raise issues that might exacerbate feelings of hostility of any*

49. Ibid., pp. 196–219.

kind and so prevent agreements even where they might be reached. But, of course, communal sentiments tend themselves to make for certain kinds of political agreement, most of all in areas that the communal values themselves involve.[50]

On the whole, given tendencies to fragmentation as well as cohesion, the theory of consociational pluralism raises questions about what conditions will prevent the former and sustain the latter. This places the emphasis on the regulation of conflict or ensuring that groups deeply concerned with the preservation of their own identities will not resort to violence. One of the more interesting theories about this has been advanced by Eric Nordlinger.

1. When intense conflicts are successfully regulated, one, or more, of six conflicting-regulating practices is always employed. The six practices are the stable coalition, the proportionality principle, depoliticization, the mutual veto, compromise and concessions.

2. An exclusive reliance upon majoritarian institutions and practices does not facilitate conflict regulation, and may even contribute to conflict exacerbation.

3. Efforts to regulate conflict by creating a national identity in a short period of time will not only be unsuccessful, they will more than likely lead to widespread violence and governmental repression.

4. Conflict group leaders play a critical role in the process of conflict regulation. They, and they alone can make a direct and positive contribution. As for conflict group members, their impact on regulatory outcomes can only be directly negative or indirectly positive or negative.

5. Conflict regulating motives are a necessary condition if elites are to engage in conflict regulating behavior. More specifically, one or more of four motivations must be present if elites are to make regulatory efforts: the strong desire to ward off pressure from external states, to maintain or increase the level of economic well being, to acquire or retain government offices and power, or to avoid bloodshed among the leaders' own segment.[51]

50. See Harry Eckstein, *Division and Cohesion in Democracy* (Princeton, N.J.: Princeton University Press, 1966), p. 194.
51. Eric A. Nordlinger, *Conflict Regulation in Divided Societies* (Cambridge, Mass.: Center for International Affairs, Harvard University, 1972), pp. 117–18. Nordlinger lists seven other interesting conditions as well, which should be examined for a more in-depth representation of theoretical consociation.

Consociational pluralism emphasizes the way elites bargain and compromise spurred on by nonseparatist cleavages. They use such instruments as proportional representation to ensure minority representation, but strong coalitions between parties prevent politics from being factionalized at the center and producing the kind of *immobilisme* which virtually paralyzed the Third and Fourth French Republics. It also helps to be prosperous and small. (But not too small; pluralists do not favor mini-states. Indeed, what would Switzerland become if it were divided into French, German, and Italian speaking mini-states?[52])

Polyarchy

Almond and Verba—Democratic culture: Consociational pluralism deals with the special case, but it suggests more general characteristics of pluralism. Perhaps the most important study dealing with the comparative character of democratic culture and the commitment to the values of democracy is by Gabriel A. Almond and Sidney Verba.[53] Using a sample of five countries—United States, Great Britain, Germany, Italy, and Mexico—Almond and Verba collected cross-national survey data which they then evaluated according to several variables of which pluralist political cultures are comprised.

The first variable is political cognition. How much importance do people attribute to national and local government? To what degree are people exposed to politics and public affairs? How much political information do they possess?

The second variable is partisanship, the degree of political feeling people have. If open and moderate partisanship is regarded as essential to stable democracy, what attitudes—positive or negative—do partisan groups have toward each other? Do they see each other as selfish? intelligent? Evaluations can be made of the psychological distance between parties and how multiple affiliations affect this.

A third variable deals with the extent to which citizens feel obligated to participate in politics, their idea of the "good citizen," the effects of local government, and differences in attitudes toward civic obligations. These concerns relate to the extent to which people feel

52. For an alternative view see Benjamin R. Barber, *The Death of Communal Liberty* (Princeton, N.J.: Princeton University Press, 1974).
53. See Gabriel A. Almond and Sidney Verba, *The Civic Culture* (Princeton, N.J.: Princeton University Press, 1963).

that they count in politics, and that their participation will actually affect an unjust or mismanaged condition. Included in the notion of competence are ideas about how people influence each other, the strategies they use, and the extent to which they cooperate.

The fourth variable tested whether competence, participation, and political allegiance were positively correlated. (The hypothesis held true in all except the Mexican case. "In Mexico the competent citizen is not more likely to evaluate actual government performance positively."[54]) Pride in the political system and political competence also went together in the United States, Britain, and Mexico, more so than in Germany and Italy. In the latter cases pride and competence are associated with specific outputs of government, but not with the political system as a whole.[55]

These cognitive and emotional qualities were not the only variables used by Almond and Verba in their analysis. They also measured patterns of social relationships, degrees of civic cooperation, the values associated with the community as a whole, and the extent to which the family and socialization are critical in connecting the local or segmentary group with the national polity. Particular attention was paid to political socialization—including reports of the age and character of entry into participation in school debates, discussions, disagreements with teachers, and other forms of "activism." Finally, the character of group life, social preferences based on education, the role of women, and the quality of family life were all evaluated.

From these different variables organized around specific hypotheses, a series of profiles of national political cultures was compiled. The study concluded by emphasizing the diverse ways in which a political culture evolves and the extent to which a pluralist or civic culture specifically depends on complex processes of training, the experiences of the individual in institutions, and the extent to which people learn to participate in politics or live in a vital political atmosphere. Almond and Verba suggest new channels of political participation and more effective means of establishing a powerful political identity.

It is impossible to describe the richness and imaginativeness of the Almond-Verba study briefly. It investigates the conditions of pluralism not only by means of a comparative behavioral method, but also mobilizes behavioral hypotheses relevant for survey research about attitudes and feelings. (It has been criticized for emphasizing the high civic sense

54. Ibid., p. 246.
55. Ibid., p. 247.

inherent in those of Anglo-American culture, but because the study was concerned with social and psychological factors rather than principles of government such criticism seems to miss the mark.) It is precisely issues of this character that have provided the basis for Robert Dahl's special theory of polyarchy.

Democratization: Democracy is a set of conditions which can only be approximated in real life. A key characteristic of democracy is the "continuing responsiveness of the government to the preferences of its citizens, considered as political equals."[56] This is a classical liberal definition in which the "utilities" of all participants in the political marketplace are equal although their wants and needs are different, requiring government to select the most satisfactory mediating responses it can.

For a government to be responsive its citizens need to have the ability to formulate their preferences, inform both their fellow citizens and the government of those preferences through some kind of individual or collective action, and have their preferences weighed equally without discrimination in terms of content or source. The institutions required to ensure these criteria include freedoms—to join and form organizations, to express oneself, to vote, to run for office, to have alternative sources of information.

Democracies have such characteristics to varying degrees. Not all citizens have the ability to formulate their preferences equally. Not all groups have equal access to alternative sources of information. Social inequalities inhibit the exercise of these rights and the use of their institutional opportunities in real life. But what most "democratic" societies represent in real life are different kinds of polyarchies. **Polyarchy,** which simply means rule by the many, is more effective the more closely it approximates the democratic ideal.

Just as Lipset and his associates concluded that in a trade union the more equality there was, the less bureaucratic, autonomous, and hegemonic the leadership was likely to be, likewise in societies as a whole the more egalitarian the polyarchy, the more democratic the society is likely to become. Moreover, the more developed a society is and the more differentiated, the more likely it is to be based on a competitive and democratic politics, while the less developed the more authoritarian its regime is likely to be.

56. Robert A. Dahl, *Polyarchy* (New Haven, Conn.: Yale University Press, 1971), p. 1.

Dahl concludes that

The higher the socioeconomic level of a country, the more likely
that its regime is an inclusive or near-polyarchy.
    If a regime is a polyarchy, it is more likely to exist in a country at
a relatively high level of socioeconomic development than at a lower
level.[57]

In Table 10-1, increase in socioeconomic level implies the proliferation of organizational subgroups. Also it implies that participation
will be high at both a national and subnational level, and that the
greater the degree of competition and contestation, the more effective
the right to participate in elections and policy making. At the higher
stages of development there is an increase too in liberalization, in-
clusiveness, and the polyarchy of the society.

We have suggested that a society can be a polyarchy at the top but
not at the base. For example, in the United States, hegemonic controls
over blacks in the South prevented their effective participation in politics. The dualism of the system implies a lack of democracy. We also
suggested earlier that one way to overcome this in pluralist systems is
for the weak to convert their interests into values and demonstrate to
the ruling majority how violations of those values challenge the dominant principles of the society. Figure 10-3 illustrates certain patterns by
means of which this translation of interest into values occurs.

At any point the connection may break down. Members of the disadvantaged group may not compare themselves to the most advantaged.
Or they may not consciously articulate a sense of "relative depriva-

Table 10-1. Economic Development and Political System[58]

| Political System | "Stage" of Development | | | | |
	I	II	III	IV	V
Competitive	13%	33%	12%	57%	100%
Semicompetitive	25	17	20	13	0
Authoritarian	63	50	68	30	0
	(8)	(12)	(25)	(30)	(14)

57. Ibid., p. 65.
58. Dahl derives his figures from Bruce Russett, *Trends in World Politics* (New
York: Macmillan, 1965). More up-to-date data would confirm the conclusions even
more sharply as the number of authoritarian regimes in Latin America and Africa
has increased substantially since the Russett data were gathered.

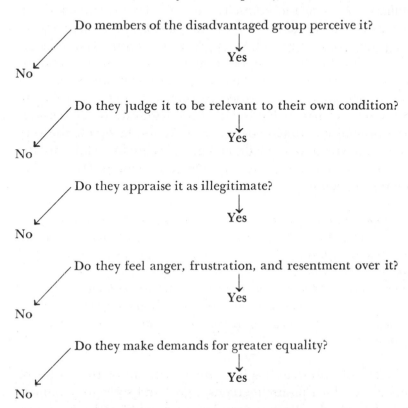

Objective Inequality Exists

Do members of the disadvantaged group perceive it?
Yes

No

Do they judge it to be relevant to their own condition?
Yes

No

Do they appraise it as illegitimate?
Yes

No

Do they feel anger, frustration, and resentment over it?
Yes

No

Do they make demands for greater equality?
Yes

No

Figure 10-3. The Transition from Objective Inequality to Demands for Greater Equality[59]

tion."[60] But if they do make such a comparison and do find extreme inequalities, this discovery is likely to produce extreme instability. Indeed, one could argue that in many Latin American countries as growth and development increased but inequality did not decline, the stage was set for the overthrow of semipolyarchies and their replacement by hegemonic military regimes.

Evidence shows that polyarchies are not *likely* to function where there are extreme inequalities; they are nevertheless plausible alternatives to totalitarian rule. They are not likely to succeed when cleavages

59. Ibid., p. 95.
60. For an illustration of the case of Britain see W.G. Runciman, *Relative Deprivation and Social Justice* (London: Routledge and Kegan Paul, 1966), pp. 120–35.

in a society are extreme, particularly cleavages of the primordial variety. (Both conflicts over caste and ethnicity in India, for example, and extreme inequality contributed to the erosion of polyarchy there and to the growing authoritarianism of Prime Minister Indira Gandhi's regime in the 1970s. Leaders of opposition parties, newspaper editors, and influential figures who criticized the government were jailed on the argument that they had "refused to cooperate in the public interest.) Deep-set and irremediable cleavages aggravate other tensions in a society, prejudice national goals, and make less favorable the very conditions for growth, development, and greater equality which appear to be necessary for a stable polyarchy. On such matters Dahl makes several interesting points.

Opponents in a conflict cannot be expected to tolerate one another if one of them believes that toleration of another will lead to his own destruction or severe suffering. Toleration is more likely to be extended and to endure only among groups which are not expected to damage one another severely. Thus the costs of toleration can be lowered by effective mutual guarantees against destruction, extreme coercion, or severe damage. Hence a strategy of liberalization requires a search for such guarantees.[61]

The theory of polyarchy begins with a critique of two forms of pluralism, one of which posits liberty as a goal and seeks to maximize it and the other of which posits popular sovereignty and equality as goals, and seeks to maximize them. Neither of these is sufficient as theory, however. Nor is it sufficient to merely establish some ideal descriptive characteristics of democracy based on subjective judgments of various rules. The question of what prerequisites are necessary to make democracy work in the "real world" is the question to which the special theory of polyarchy addresses itself.[62]

Maximizing majority rule: Polyarchy functions well to the degree that it realizes what Dahl calls "The Rule"; that is, the principle of majority rule which prescribes that

in choosing among alternatives, the alternative preferred by the greater number is selected. That is, given two or more alternatives, x, y, etc., in

61. Dahl, *Polyarchy*, p. 218.
62. See Robert A. Dahl, *A Preface to Democratic Theory* (Chicago: University of Chicago Press, 1956), pp. 63–64.

order for x *to be governmental policy, it is a necessary and sufficient condition that the number who prefer* x *to any alternative is greater than the number who prefer any single alternative to* x.[63]

A host of problems attends the realization of this rule, including the intensity of preferences, costs of compromises, fluctuations in commitment, and so forth. Polyarchy is a system which compensates for these difficulties in the degree to which the following conditions prevail:

During the voting period
1. Every member of the organization performs the acts we assume to constitute an expression of preference among the scheduled alternatives, e.g., voting.
2. In tabulating these expressions (votes), the weight assigned to the choice of each individual is identical.
3. The alternative with the greatest number of votes is declared the winning choice.
During the pre-voting period
4. Any member who perceives a set of alternatives, at least one of which he regards as preferable to any of the alternatives presently scheduled, can insert his preferred alternative (s) among those scheduled for voting.
5. All individuals possess identical information about the alternatives.
During the post-voting period
6. Alternatives (leaders or policies) with the greatest number of votes displace any alternatives (leaders or policies) with fewer votes.
7. The orders of elected officials are executed.
During the inter-election stage
8.1 Either all interelection decisions are subordinate or executory to those arrived at during the election stage, i.e. elections are in a sense controlling.
8.2 Or new decisions during the inter-election period are governed by the preceding seven conditions, operating, however, under rather different institutional circumstances.
8.3 Or both.[64]

Dahl himself points out that in no instance have all eight points been achieved at any single moment in any political system. Hence poly-

63. Ibid., p. 38.
64. Ibid., p. 84.

archy remains an ideal goal as much as democracy does. The value of
the theory is that it points out what conditions of the polity need to be
maximized. It also shows the kinds of information necessary for these
conditions to work. For example, bargaining depends on preferences
and has costs. To understand the relation between costs and benefits it
is necessary to utilize some political calculus like game theory to show
how maximization will operate under a given set of options. To understand the options it is necessary to ascertain the costs and benefits by
using certain variables to measure the strength, durability, and intensity of attitudes and opinions. In order to prevent groups from over-
powering the unorganized, special requirements are necessary. These
favor the representation of the weak, protecting minorities so that during interelection periods their options are preserved and acted on. In
short, the special theory of polyarchy draws attention to specific items
necessary to promote a more perfectly functioning democratic system.

All this implies the need to identify the ways and means of political
participation at all stages of the political process—the voting, prevoting,
postvoting, and interelection stages. In the prevoting period, individuals can substitute alternatives they prefer to those being offered. However, a corollary to this is that everyone has equal information about
alternatives. (This qualification approximates the ideal of the perfect
competition model in economics, where perfect information regarding
the conditions of the market is said to prevail.) At the voting stage,
everybody votes and all votes count the same. The winner in the election gets the most votes.

During the postvoting and interelection periods several other
factors become important. The alternatives that receive the greatest
number of votes take precedence over all others. Those officials who
have been elected have their wishes carried out. Meanwhile, between
elections the kinds of alternatives which arise as policy must in a sense
be subordinate to the bigger ones decided during the elections, unless
there are ways to create new opportunities for voting on the issues.[65]

The idea of polyarchy is designed to minimize some of the crucial
difficulties inherent in the relationships of democracy. Take the eight
characteristics of polyarchy, for example. The American system of government, with its checks and balances, its periodic elections, and its
ways of registering preferences, has certain obvious drawbacks. How
can an emphasis on polyarchy reduce them? Well, one needs first of all
to re-evaluate how well voting, constitutionalism, and other factors

65. Ibid.

characteristic of the American system work according to criteria implied by the conditions of polyarchy. We have regional representation in an upper house based on the several states. But does this house really improve representation? How does it add to our knowledge of alternatives? What other means are available or possible which might provide better access to the business of locating alternatives than those currently existing? Concrete questions like these are raised immediately when polyarchy is applied to the American presidential system.

We might also ask, does the usual parliamentary system found in Europe work better than the presidential system? Following the implications of polyarchy as laid down by Dahl, we note that European nations are subject to more frequent elections, as when a parliamentary majority fails on an important issue or loses a vote of confidence. A motion of confidence, when introduced by a member of parliament, is actually a request to parliament to show whether or not a government has exhausted its mandate. If it has, and no confidence is voted, a new election or a new government replaces the old one. In this sense no government is guaranteed that its office will be completed between scheduled general elections.

The polyarchic model answers five questions: (1) How can preferences best be expressed? (Through group representation.) (2) How do increased alternatives affect the methods of expressing alternatives? (Through group power and group competition.) (3) How do increased alternatives and means of expressing them affect the appropriate exercise of political power? (Through countervailing pressures of equality and inequality.) (4) To what extent is political power increased, and with it arbitrariness, when more and more preferences become available and voters have more and more difficulty expressing alternatives? (The tendency toward group competition stimulates political monopoly.) (5) To what extent is the increase in political power reflected in the growth of executive power, monopoly at the center (as in a "cabinet dictatorship"), or the "concentration of presidential powers" an irreversible process (unless the unit changes or there is an opportunity for more effective political competition).

Pluralism and Information Availability

By putting the theory of polyarchy into a developmental form, Dahl links dynamic processes of change with those of political structure. Other theorists have tried to link developmental change with pluralism as well and we shall discuss one such formulation in Chapter Fifteen on developmentalism. However, it might be useful to indicate some variants on the theory of polyarchy, especially in regard to competition and information.

Some of the general conclusions were achieved using a differing set of variables in Apter's theory of modernization, in which development is regarded as a set of stages based upon technological and other innovative changes. If contradictions, conflicts, and inequalities grow rather than decline the situation requires bureaucratic controls or the exercise of power by *vanguard elites* to mobilize society. The cost of both controls and mobilization, however, is increasing coercion, which brings about decreasing information availability. Since the more modernized and industrialized a society becomes, the greater is its need for information, high coercion will slow growth and innovation and prevent changes. Hence what we may call a *reconciliation system* is similar to Dahl's polyarchy. This system, however, is more appropriate to highly developed societies dependent on high inputs of information. Conversely, the more hierarchy in a system or hegemonic the bureaucracy, the greater the degree of coercion, and the lower the amount of information (see Figure 10-4).[66]

Under this system, while all regimes try to maintain equilibrium between coercion and information in order to best maximize their goals, the less organizational hierarchy that exists, the more the goals will be a result of the spread of information, the responsiveness of the government through parties, interest groups, and other bodies, and the more conciliatory and therefore pluralist the political form.

Perhaps the most elaborate attempts to translate pluralist theories into information feedback systems have been made by Karl W. Deutsch

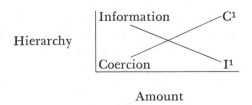

Figure 10-4. Information and Coercion

66. See D. E. Apter, *Choice and the Politics of Allocation* (New Haven, Conn.: Yale University Press, 1971), pp. 143–44.

and David Easton. Deutsch, much influenced by engineering and mechanics models, has dealt extensively with information flows, feedback systems, and the conditions that produce equilibrium.[67] Easton uses a similar general systems approach but is more intent on specifying the variable factors to show how wants in society are transformed into political demands and supports, and how different societies respond to both.[68] A more philosophical interpretation which deals with rights, equity, choice, and the public interest is Brian Barry's *Political Argument*. Barry tries to clarify such terms as equity, interest, welfare, and public interest to show how a clearly delineated hierarchy can in many ways effectively further the goals of a given culture.[69]

While pluralism is not a single theory or idea it defines relationships of democracy with reference to equality, participation, responsiveness, cleavage and consensus, stability, and growth. All these factors can combine and recombine in many forms. They represent the basic ingredients in which modern theories of democracy are composed. In Chapter Eleven we shall examine some of the processes by means of which pluralist democracies work.

67. See Karl W. Deutsch, *The Nerves of Government* (New York: The Free Press, 1963).
68. See David Easton, *A Systems Analysis of Political Life* (New York: Wiley, 1965).
69. See Brian Barry, *Political Argument* (London: Routledge and Kegan Paul, 1965).

chapter eleven
The Process of Pluralism

In Chapter Ten we showed how societal pluralism, the result of differentiation in society, produces political pluralism. Many opportunities for and diverse modes of participation result in continuous mediation among groups. Influence is spread by means of a growing network of interacting groups, voluntary associations, and parties. The distinction between the private and the public spheres breaks down. As politics becomes more complex, questions about propriety—proper conduct —arise. Influence penetrates the corridors of power, and quite often lobbyists are those able to draft the legislation that will most affect their clients' enterprises or activities. In a system in which information equals power, organization mobilizes information. Access to information gives those who obtain it privileged power.

As class distinctions—once the critical factor in assessing an individual's worth—decline, other factors become important in the hierarchy of judgments people use as criteria for assigning power and prestige. For example, in the United States, women (and men) fight for an Equal Rights Amendment to the Constitution to guarantee an end to discrimination based on sex. Today age discrimination is a subject of concern as well. Differentiation between blacks and whites, Protestants, Roman Catholics, and Jews remains important, but education and professional experience have emerged as more potent selective forces than one's cultural associations and connections. Income groups too are increasingly intersected by consumer groups. Class groupings break down into small divisions: unskilled working, skilled working, lower-middle, commercial middle, professional middle, and so on. Urban, suburban, and rural residence distinctions are being altered and these are reflected in changing percentages and distributions. Changes are occurring in the pattern of trade union organization; and in the composition of membership of business, trade, and professional associations.[1]

Important new nonclass distinctions are those based on one's drive, and to a lesser degree one's life style. The new organizational breakdown of the monied and powerful represents an elaborate "multi-factored" hierarchy which ranks income, occupation, religion, education, and other affiliations conglomerately. There is today a need for what Stein Rokkan calls a "stock taking" on a multisectorial as well as a cross-national basis.[2] We need to find how variables combine to affect the character of society. Which are the most important variables in a society composed of so many overlapping memberships?

No longer is one label seen to be a sufficient definition of anyone's personality—social or political. Single-interest groups remain, but they are no longer politically cohesive. For example, abortion is an issue which may mobilize a militant Catholic group, but the significance of the "right to life" pales for many alongside the "facts of life"; the rising cost of bringing up children and the need to educate them properly in an increasingly complex world. The difference in degree to which Roman Catholics, compared to other religious groups, abjure contraceptive devices is declining all the time.

There is also a growing rate of intermarriage between Jews and non-Jews (which some members of the Jewish community still condemn). The point is that factors other than, say, Jewishness are today used to define both the group basis of life and the personality of the individual. (In the long run this may have important effects on Jews not only as an interest group, but as a pro-Israel constituency, for example.)

In turn what may disappear from one context may reappear in another. One of the interesting problems in this regard is the revival of primordial affiliations in, for example, Northern Ireland. There "particularism" has again become politically a vital force in society. Alternatively, to mobilize as large a proportion of the population as possible, in many countries new public interest groups have sprung up,

1. For a discussion of these distinctions see W. Lloyd Warner and Paul S. Lunt, *The Social Life of a Modern Community*, the Yankee City Series, Vols. 1 and 2 (New Haven, Conn.: Yale University Press, 1941, 1942). For a different view in a British context, see Barry Hindress, *The Decline of Working Class Politics* (London: MacGibbon and Kee, 1971). See also David Butler and Donald Stokes, *Political Change in Britain* (New York: St. Martin's Press, 1969), pp. 101–15.
2. Stein Rokkan, *Citizens, Elections, Parties* (Oslo: Universitetsforlaget, 1970), pp. 169–80.

such as those advocating environmental protection and other contemporary causes.[3] The consumer movement is another which affords
a basis for the mobilization of public-interest groups.

The Cybernetic Model of Pluralism

Pluralism thus emphasizes individual *and* group wants and preferences,
and is concerned with how these are converted into policy outcomes.
Although building on institutionalism as well as behavioralism, its
larger perspective remains closest to the philosophical tradition of
utilitarianism. The behavior theory of utility is concerned with how
coalitions form, voting behavior, and preferences. The basic model
is in many respects similar to that of classical economics, and like economics lends itself to greater and greater quantification. Utilities and
maximization can be measured by indicators, such as how frequently a
legislative coalition wins debate, and how much its voter and party
support fluctuate. Political stability is a measure of the government's
implementation of the "greatest good for the greatest number" by
means of establishing and realizing beneficial agendas and programs.

Pluralists turn either the utility or psychological political models
to their purposes. The first helps them evaluate government policy-
making strategies by means of feedback. According to this model, group
stimuli and competition produce various forms of input, and government produces appropriate policies ("appropriateness" meaning maximized satisfaction for the largest plurality of citizens) . From a citizen's
point of view, the best government is that which best ameliorates conflict and increases benefits. The dynamic ingredient, however, is
competitive maximization.

In economic theory the economic marketplace is a device which
converts utilities into consumer preferences. Priorities are determined
according to price, quantity, supply, and demand. In pluralist theory the
voting place serves an analogous purpose. In what can be called a cybernetic adaptation of pluralism, participation is both a cause and a
consequence of "feedback" based on the free access of individuals and
groups to the vote. According to rules of fair competition, candidates for
office present programs aimed at identifying specific problems and offer-

3. The Social Democratic Party in Sweden lost the General Election of 1976 over the
issue of nuclear energy.

ing their preferred solutions. Finalists in the competition must eventually adhere to a party platform which not only defines a set of priorities, but is a contract and an agenda for action as well. The vote is the device which indicates to politicians the degree to which their programs fit the maximum need. To win, a candidate requires as much accurate information in advance about voters' needs and preferences as can be obtained. In turn, voters need knowledge to evaluate the candidates' programs and their respective abilities. Successful candidates not only form governments that reflect a plurality or majority distribution of public preferences and public wants but, by being responsive to the electorate through the formulation of suitable policies, try to ensure their reelection. The government's accountability to the public involves a continuous exchange of information, review, and adaptation according to certain standards of cost-benefit analysis.

The crucial element, as we have said, is feedback. In this sense the political model conforms to an engineering model for the self-corrective mechanisms of homeostatic systems. An initial failure to satisfy public utilities by means of good policies will be reflected in protests, crises, and public denials. Appeasement policies are then instituted in an attempt to rectify discontent and assure satisfaction.

How are discrete bits of information held by individuals and groups converted into authoritative public policies? How are minority concerns aggregated into issues of significance to a plurality or majority? How do monitoring devices work both to aggregate demands and to provide a continuous flow of information at all levels? These are the concerns of modern pluralists, whose pluralistic cybernetic model (Figure 11-1) seeks to account for such functions.

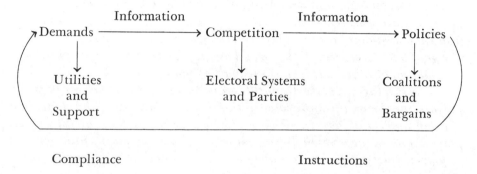

Figure 11-1. The Pluralist Cybernetic Model

One can see that the pluralist model puts a heavy emphasis on informational give and take. The better the information feedback, the more likely it is that policies will satisfy the electorate and the greater the likelihood of government's compliance with societal demands. "Information" is not just a matter of transmitting messages, however, but a critical activity in a pluralist system where the primary concern is with improving the flow of information for effective decision making. A high rate of informational access is a condition necessary for balance, or homeostasis. However, the polity, unlike mechanical engineering devices, comprises a multiplicity of subsystems, some of which work at the expense of overall balance. Wiener aptly describes the trade-off as follows:

In connection with the effective amount of communal information, one of the most surprising facts about the body politic is its extreme lack of efficient homeostatic processes. There is a belief, current in many countries, which has been elevated to the rank of an official article of faith in the United States, that free competition is itself a homeostatic process: that in a free market, the individual selfishness of the bargainers, each seeking to sell as high and buy as low as possible will result in the end in a stable dynamics of prices, and rebound to the greatest common good. This is associated with the very comforting view that the individual entrepreneur, in seeking to forward his own interest, is in some manner a public benefactor, and has thus earned the great rewards with which society has showered him. Unfortunately, the evidence, such as it is, is against this simple-minded theory. The market is a game, which has indeed received a simulacrum in the family game of Monopoly. It is thus strictly subject to the general theory of games, developed by von Neumann and Morganstern. This theory is based on the assumption that each player, at every stage, in view of the information then available to him, plays in accordance with a completely intelligent policy, which will in the end assure him of the greatest possible expectation of reward. It is thus the market game as played between perfectly intelligent, perfectly ruthless operators. Even in the case of two players, the theory is complicated, although it often leads to the choice of a definite line of play. In many cases, however, where there are three players, and in the overwhelming majority of cases, when the number of players is large, the result is one of extreme indeterminacy and instability.[4]

4. Norbert Wiener, *Cybernetics* (New York: Wiley, 1948), p. 185.

Wiener's exposition shows that, systematically, maximizations or optimizations—striking bargains—can lead in two opposing directions, one toward stability, the other toward instability. The lack of good homeostatic devices, then, generates the need for politics. The politician's job is to produce mediations which head off crises. The predicament in virtually all modern pluralist political systems today is accurately summed up in Wiener's invocation of "indeterminacy and instability."

How to improve the situation is, as we have said, the central pluralist problem. It may be phrased in terms of how to resolve tension, conflict, international crises, wars, industrial disputes, how to work out urban renewal plans, how to abate pollution, or as other kinds of formulations. But one should remember that what really is at stake is not how to make a more perfect democracy, but a better mouse trap.

The key to pluralist theory, then, is not only the determination of how power is shared and allocated, but how in the process politics acts to cultivate social choice. Pluralism basically defines a method by which all participants—individuals, groups, governmental bodies at all levels, private bodies—continuously canvass each other's relative gains and losses. By this activity and its outcomes, social choice invests the political system with critical significance.

But difficulties arise (just as they do in the pure competition model of economics) because conditions of rationality, party competition, and the self corrective and regulating consequences of public policy in reality do not always equilibrate between public wants and governmental policies. The problem of feedback is complicated by the size of the constituent group, unequal access to information, propaganda, and sometimes by the coercive power of larger coalitions. But although the classic model of pluralism (like its equivalent in economics) is faulty, it is nevertheless useful. Newer models of the cybernetic type emphasize how group coalitions form and break apart, and how in the process an accord between public need and the distribution of benefits can be struck. The comparison to economics is a good one even under modern conditions. Just as giant conglomerate enterprises compete through advertising, product differentiation, and profit maximization, so big political coalitions like major parties also seek to become monopolistic by driving out small competitors or internal dissidents if they can. Competitive bargaining occurs inside large, monopolistic political groupings—at federal, state, local, or central, provincial, and regional levels. Initiatives at all levels activate inter-sector bargaining.

Each party has its clientele of interested groups and organizations

—interest groups, institutional groups, and pressure groups—which enable parties to intersect with governmental units. As part of the process of exchange each tries to obtain commitments to uphold its expectations about possible direct policy benefits. Bargaining takes place in the environment of previous relationships, which shape and condition future decisions.[5]

The Significance of Parties

In Chapter Ten we stressed the breaking up of class and other group distinctions and the conversion of values into interests as crucial to the emergence of pluralist democracy. Political parties are essential to the process. Indeed, party politics represents the critical factor serving to aggregate interests in a pluralist society. Parties convey information from the public to the government, articulate interests, and recruit candidates to political office. In turn, on the feedback side, they help to ensure that legislative rules are properly made and fairly applied.[6]

Parties have always been significant in both institutionalist and behavioral analyses. The classic study of political parties by Robert Michels[7] emphasized relevant criteria for the differentiation of parties as loose associations of interests: mercantile, shipping, planting, speculating. He interpreted the United States Constitution as a sort of embryonic national party platform based on relevant interests. Out of those various interests the powerful coalitions we today call political parties formed. In the United States the Federalists came first. They possessed the bulk of the financial resources of the country. Then more popular and agrarian interests came to power during the Jacksonian period. Later the rural populism of the South was incorporated into the Democratic Party, which was the antagonist of the rich, mercantile Northern Republicans. Class interests were at the center of party conflict over who gets what, when, and how. "Whether Hamiltonian Federalists, Jeffersonian Republicans, Jacksonian Democrats, Clay Whigs, or Lincoln or McKinley Republicans are in power, the principle runs true

5. See Heinz Eulau and Kenneth Prewitt, *Labyrinths of Democracy: Adaptations, Linkages, Representations, and Policies in Urban Politics* (Indianapolis, Ind.: Bobbs-Merrill, 1973), p. 467.
6. See Gabriel Almond and James S. Coleman, *The Politics of the Developing Areas* (Princeton, N.J.: Princeton University Press, 1960), pp. 11–58.
7. Robert Michels, *Political Parties* (Glencoe, Ill.: The Free Press, 1958).

to form, no matter how it may be modified by high idealism or patriotic purpose."[8]

Today parties throughout the world are losing their specific class characteristics as they take on more complex mediational roles. Modern political parties can be divided into essentially two types: broad coalitional or caucus parties, and class interest parties. In Europe, where social differentiation by class was more important and clearly articulated than in the United States, parties were formerly regarded as mediators between classes. Fear of class struggle induced parties to act as go-betweens to promote social mobility through wider access to power.

Michels believed that because the working class cherishes the hope of rising to higher social status, members of the working class are inhibited from engaging in class politics. He argued against "cleavage" politics as the basis of class, asserting that workers are no more homogeneous than the bourgeoisie. Discrepancies between different kinds of workers prevent them from acting out of class interests.[9] It does hold true, however, that where class, religion, ethnicity, race, or other factions combine, highly ideological parties, which are those least likely to negotiate interests, form. (We have previously cited much evidence that documents this fact.) Therefore the intensity of conflict between opposing parties remains under such conditions as long as each issue, no matter how ordinary, is charged with saliency.

But the more characteristic situation is the advent of coalitional parties in which class, religion, ethnicity, and other such factors do not follow the same lines of cleavage—where there is not one primordial religious affiliation among members but a number of religions represented, not one ethnic sector but several, not one dominant racial group, but a confluence of two or more. Such multiple membership characteristics describe coalitional parties, what Duverger calls "indirect parties," or parties of the mass, not restricted to a particular elite in society.[10] They contrast with ideologically disciplined and organized parties which pursue monistic goals. The coalitional party, with its loose organization, diverse composition, and emphasis on the dynamics of bargaining both within the party and between parties, does not stand for anything in some fixed or permanent way.[11]

8. Wilfred E. Binkley, *American Political Parties* (New York: Knopf, 1947), p. 379.
9. Michels, op. cit., pp. 304–5.
10. See Maurice Duverger, *Political Parties* (London: Methuen, 1954), pp. 17–132.
11. See Sigmund Newmann, ed., *Modern Political Parties* (Chicago: University of Chicago Press). See also Kay Lawson, *The Comparative Study of Political Parties* (New York: St. Martin's Press, 1976), pp. 4–20.

Indeed, because of the emphasis of coalitional parties on assimilation, those who cannot see the difference between major parties often have a mistaken notion of what parties are supposed to do in pluralist systems. Coalitional parties affect the way people vote. They affect government policy. The connection between them is the network of influence which affects the *process* of politics. Let us briefly review the landmark study of party differentiation by Berelson, Lazersfeld, and McPhee.[12]

In a sample of residents of Elmira, New York, a supposedly typical, medium-size American town with industrial and labor diversity, religious differentiation, and high accessibility to the media, researchers asked: What are the differences in opinion between Republicans and Democrats? What makes the differences between the parties? What makes some voters more or less constant in their party affiliation and others independent? To what extent are social and political perceptions affected by group affiliation—socioeconomic occupational groups, ethnic groups—and how are groups perceived by their opposites? How do social perception factors affect how each group *anticipates* the other, and to what extent do such "anticipations" affect voting?

The study broke down the notion of interests along a complex of attitudinal factors revealed by respondents' stances on a number of issues like U.S. relations with Russia; labor-management relations; the cost of living; and attitudes toward Jews, Communists, Negroes, and others. These and other perceptions were correlated with party affiliation. Because a modern political campaign tries to make its appeal widespread, the popular multitude is affected by far more than individual observations or perceptions. The study concludes that what successful politics requires is a mixture of

. . . social *consensus and change—in effect pluralism—in politics. Such pluralism makes for enough consensus to hold the system together and enough cleavage to make it move. Too much consensus would be deadening and restrictive of liberty; too much cleavage would be destructive of the society as a whole.*[13]

Thus parties are great mediating devices. Where they are not, they represent sources of continuous trouble for pluralist governments.

12. See Bernard R. Berelson, Paul F. Lazersfeld, and William N. McPhee, *Voting* (Chicago: University of Chicago Press, 1955) .
13. Ibid., p. 318.

Reluctance to extend the definition of polyarchy to include militant communist parties, for example, weakens the degree of democracy in the system according to the standards laid down by Dahl, though it might strengthen the polyarchy by reducing the likelihood of its over-throw. In turn a restrictive, but "protective," strategy can result in the acceptance of the "rules" of democratic pluralism. This has happened with the French and Italian Communist Parties. As they become willing to compromise, they strengthen democracy. As they help to promote equality, they strengthen democracy. In turn, this compromise affects their own internal control. Will participation by communists in a poly-archic system make people less contentious, compliant and accepting of the hegemonic and bureaucratic control characteristic of communist parties? Or will the ideological devotion of those of the communist persuasion mitigate the apathy and/or alienation of those who reject the "sameness" of purpose of broader-based coalitions? No one knows.

Political parties are the chief proponents of the political culture. They socialize the different sectors of the population. Campaigns and electioneering affect the behavior of citizens, therefore parties in this sense represent a structure of opportunities, an "overall context of re-wards and deprivations, of pay-offs and sanctions. . . ."[14]

Cleavage and consensus: Cleavage and consensus, then, are the two poles which parties mediate by means of electoral coalitions in a plural-istic system.[15] Party competition is the balance wheel. But what about groups that cannot or will not compete in the system on their own behalf? How can they expect to benefit from politics? Study after study has shown that those with the greatest need are the least likely to participate. Not only are such people likely to be apathetic, but they are also likely to distrust efforts by party organizers to mobilize their support. The poor lack resources.

The poor man can contribute no significant sums of money, nor is
his individual social and occupational position likely to give him as an
individual, much influence over governmental actions. Poor people can
exert influence only by collective action; really only through organiza-
tions designed for this purpose. The more prosperous individual, how-

14. Giovanni Sartori, *Parties and Party Systems* (Cambridge: Cambridge University Press, 1976), p. 93.
15. For a different view, see Michael Mann, "The Social Cohesion of Liberal Democracy" in the *American Sociological Review,* Vol. 35, No. 3 (June 1970), pp. 423–39.

ever, can make larger financial contributions and can use his personal and professional influence to some effect. The working class person must speak through an agent; the business or professional person may delegate his politics in the same way, but he may also exercise personal influence.[16]

Thus the problem of pluralism is how to promote equity, particularly at the lower ends of the socioeconomic scale. Otherwise, as in the thirties in Europe, the appeals of militant communists, fascist, or other extremist parties for a "new order" will be strong.[17]

Verba and Nie: Methods of Participation. The most important single value in pluralist politics is participation, in voting and other forms. The best overall study of participation is by Sidney Verba and Norman H. Nie, *Participation in America.* Verba and Nie used multiple correlations to identify rates of participation, preferences, who votes, civic orientations, and many other factors.[18] Their study challenges many of the conventional pluralist assumptions about how socioeconomic variables affect voting and participation. They base conclusions on their evaluation of the social circumstances of individuals, the conditions of their cohorts in institutions, and what combinations determine what attitudes. They evaluate stimuli which affect whether individuals participate or do not participate in politics, correlating participation with alternative circumstances, consequences, or outcomes.

Questioning some of the earlier hypotheses of Key, Robert Lane, Robert Dahl, and others, Verba and Nie found that most Americans eschew participation in politics other than voting. A limited but active segment of the population performs a variety of other functions such as carrying on the work of voluntary associations, activating community organizations, attending political party meetings, and joining in other political activities. Participation, then, is limited to a relatively small percentage of the population, a highly salient and intensely active elite drawn from an overlapping network of roles. It is not a power elite in the old class sense of the word, but it has extraordinary influence.[19]

16. Robert E. Lane, *Political Life* (Glencoe, Ill.: The Free Press, 1959), p. 222.
17. See Giuseppe DiPalma, *Apathy and Participation* (New York: The Free Press, 1970), pp. 201–15.
18. See Sidney Verba and Norman H. Nie, *Participation in America* (New York: Harper & Row, 1972).
19. The Verba and Nie study evaluates political activity—electoral and nonelectoral, conflictual or not, outcomes and the initiative required to further goals, and how a participation-elite uses party organization. Pearson correlations were used to evaluate

In addition to the Verba and Nie concern with participation, other factors as well help explain the environment in which participation occurs, particularly those related to voting and party affiliation. Spatial relationships—clusters of locational groups in neighborhoods, towns, districts, provinces, regions, states, and national units—affect participation, political support, and authority and its exercise differently. Party identification can be crosstabulated with education, attitudes towards government policies—foreign and domestic—and the use of mass media. The danger is that crosstabulation of indicators that appear to be significantly different may simply represent different measures of the same phenomenon. Neighborhoods may consist of relatively homogeneous class, occupation, and religious groups simply because people sharing the same characteristics often like to live close to each other.[20]

Butler and Stokes: Patterns of Participation. Perhaps the most thorough analysis of the connection between participation and party is the study by David Butler and Donald Stokes, *Political Change in Britain*.[21] Butler and Stokes made the effort to go beyond correlation to put together a picture of what goes on in people's minds. (In this respect their study closely approximates the traditions of V.O. Key, whose knowledge of the intricate happenings of political life in America constituted the flow of his discussion, while the data were used illustratively at key points.) The emphasis is on party as comprising both individual electors and the aggregate electorate. The electorate has characteristics made known by aggregating the individual elector's characteristics. The leadership constitutes an elite similarly aggregated. The analyst's task is to disaggregate the various characteristics and reaggregate them for analytical purposes. The connection which Butler and Stokes make between individuals and their characteristics, and leaders and their characteristics posits a model relationship of party affiliation as follows:

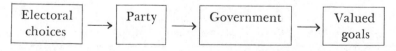

types of political activities, while the various modes of participation were ranked in clusters. Then profiles of participation by groups and types of activists were derived. These, in turn were related to cycles of participation, the organizational context of participation, leader responsiveness, and other factors.

20. See the discussion of the "ecological fallacy" by Kevin R. Cox, "Geography, Social Contexts, and Voting Behavior in Wales, 1861–1951," ed. Allardt and Rokkan, pp. 117–59.

21. See David Butler and Donald Stokes, *Political Change in Britain, Forces Shaping Electoral Choice* (London: Macmillan, 1969).

The arrows in the diagram represent aspects of the voter's consciousness; what the voter thinks will be the effect of his or her electoral choices on the party, and the effect of party on government. Butler and Stokes indicate that for the British voter, the party–government connection is "very real in the public's mind."[22] The full chain may be a little more dubious; nevertheless, party and partisanship represent to some degree "generalized dispositions," or ideological preferences which are more stable than actual voting preferences. These dispositions manifest themselves in several ways; for example, as a correlation of party self-image with class self-image. See Table 11-1.

Findings on the basis of occupational status and party affiliation follow the same lines; that is, the higher his or her occupational status, the more likely it is that a person will be conservative. As a result there are aspects of class conflict reflected in the British party system, and party conflict and class conflict correlate to a much larger extent than is the case in the United States.

The Butler and Stokes study tries to account for changes in patterns of voting mainly in terms of class formations, although the impact of mass media, qualities and characteristics of leaders, the effectiveness of party campaigns, and other influences are evaluated. They identify some of the reasons for the institutionalists' observation that in Britain people vote for parties rather than for candidates.

The study raises questions about what happens when a "working-class consciousness" changes and the class alignment aspect of party politics alters. The study shows how change depends on the extent to which economic interests are affected.[23] Many utility models of coali-

Table 11-1. Party Self-Image by Extended Class Self-Image in Britain, 1963

		Class Self-Image						
		Upper Class	Upper Middle	Middle Class	Lower Middle	Upper Work-ing	Work-ing Class	Lower Work-ing
Partisan	Conservative	100%	84%	79%	76%	48%	28%	23%
Self-Image	Labour	0	16	21	24	52	72	77
		100%	100%	100%	100%	100%	100%	100%

From Butler and Stokes, p. 77.

22. Ibid., p. 29.
23. For a more cyclical or "surge and decline" theory using psychological as well as interest variables see Angus Campbell, "Surge and Decline, a Study of Electoral

tion, showing methods of optimizing satisfactions, and the translation of wants into utilities according to costs and benefits are being elaborated in the context of electoral politics. As new methodological and mathematical techniques are developed, maximizing matrices can be used to predict political action. The logic behind minimizing losses and maximizing gains, using the cybernetical model, reveals what James M. Buchanan and Gordon Tullock call the "calculus of consent."[24] Highly specialized mathematical and statistical techniques, including regression analysis, time series, and other items are employed to test the validity of such hypotheses. Participation subsumes most of the "behavior" intrinsic to the processes of democracy.[25]

Information and party strategy: The power of political elites is their ability to process information into a set of predictions. Information derives from both the characteristics of the voters and the goals the elite wants to achieve. The strategy involves putting information into an appealing package for voting purposes without, by and large, altering the prevailing political culture. Since evaluation and prediction are the main ingredients of strategy, they are called *utility* and *probability components,* or U- and P- components. These represent a politician's basis for calculating. The more powerful the tools for U- and P-, the more effective the strategy. The U-/P- calculus depends on being able to serve up information regarding goals, objects of influence, means, and capability in attractive packages—party platforms, manifestos, and, in the end, legislative policies.[26]

The best single source of political information is data on the swing of party support in elections. In this respect parties are the geigercounters of public information. Using an implicit U-/P- calculus, issues are coded, weighted, ranked, and computed by politicians. Both the intuitions of politicians and the computations of social and political scientists help a party infer the pattern of information about the public on which it bases its strategy.

Information and messages are "heard" by politicians, coded

Change," *American Governmental Institutions,* ed. Aaron Wildavsky and Nelson W. Polsby (Chicago: Rand McNally, 1968), pp. 373–85.

24. See James M. Buchanan and Gordon Tullock, *The Calculus of Consent* (Ann Arbor, Mich.: University of Michigan Press, 1965).

25. See William H. Riker and Peter C. Ordeshook, "A Theory of the Calculus of Voting," *American Political Science Review,* Vol. 62 (March 1962): 25–42.

26. See Gunnar Sjöblom, *Party Strategies in a Multiparty System* (Lund, Sweden: Studentlitterature, 1970), pp. 36–38.

mediated, and transformed into strategies. These are used in a number of ways.[27] The most obvious way, of course, is by getting out the vote. But legislative action—from roll-call voting to committee bargaining—also involves strategies. Some are of a payoff or "back-scratching" variety. Also "listening" activities must be carried on by legislators. The information provided by representatives of interest groups or lobbyists, the protests or demands of a constituency, and reports on the flow level of campaign financing are all indicators in the calculus. We now turn to how the U-/P- calculus works with politicians and parties.

"Rulers": Legislators and Leadership Style

To really judge the methods and the motives of "shirtsleeve" bargaining, coalition formation, and the working out of compromises requires going beyond statistical analyses. The actual practices that prevail reflect the "real world" judgments of politicians, not professional expertise; politicians are the real brokers and bargainers. Legislative leadership is particularly important for the power elite. What Eulau calls "governing practices" take several different forms of leadership, five of which are worthy of note: limited exchange, bargaining, coalition formation, compromising, and general exchange. These are the styles and manners of relationships that occur in legislative behavior.[28]

Leadership style is a function of legislators as individuals communicating in a pattern of interaction with others. The context of their evaluations in formulating strategies may be (1) constituency oriented or (2) legislature oriented. Between these two orientations information is presumably objectively heard and evaluated, and a context established. How the process functions is a primary concern of political scientists and a focus for research designed to expand our knowledge of the legislator as decision maker. Variables include the social background of the legislators and their professional expertise.

For example, in the United States a very large proportion of politicians are lawyers. This helps create a special legalistic subculture which is pervasive in legislatures throughout the United States. The subculture favors certain modal personalities. A case in point: From a

27. See Karl Deutsch, *The Nerves of Government* (New York: The Free Press, 1963), pp. 75–110.
28. Eulau found these to be relevant to the analysis of city councils, but the principles are more generally applicable to legislative behavior. See Eulau and Prewitt, op. cit., Chapter V.

sample of state legislators in four different states Eulau suggests four modal personality types of politicians. These are *ritualist, tribunalist, inventor,* and *broker.*

The ritualist is concerned with propriety and protocol. He or she will try to fit all relevant messages into standardized and acceptable categories. Messages about a farm union strike in California, say, will come under the conventional heading of "farm programs," requiring consultation perhaps with an ensemble of Farm Bureau and other leaders, who may be entirely out of sympathy with the strikers and their aims. The ritualist is concerned above all with voting and how it is done.

The tribunalist considers himself or herself to be the representative of a "people's forum." The tribunalist's ideas usually approximate popular needs. He or she is a specialist in finding out what the grass-roots responses are. This is a populist's role.

The inventor sees himself or herself as an initiator of policy, a person of imagination, seeking new formulas and new strategies. The inventor is likely to be progressive, anticipating problems and recognizing incipient confrontations that have not yet reached full bloom. In modern legislatures the inventor's role is administratively difficult because legislatures are not much good as policy-making bodies.

Finally, the broker is the classic go-between who balances all points of view, makes deals, and all the while seems to be neutral. Former President Lyndon Johnson during his days in the U.S. Senate was the broker personified.[29]

The types are closely derived from data on the social backgrounds of politicians: their places of birth, residence, and upbringing; their educations and occupations; the occupations of their parents; age; political experience; legislative experience—duration in office, committee participation, position in the party; and effectiveness in manner and style or role.[30] Other variables include the politician's relation to his or her constituency, accessibility, responsiveness, and leadership ability. These affect the way the legislator or other politician interprets in-

29. See Heinz Eulau, "The Roles of Legislators in the Legislative Process," *The Legislative System,* John C. Wahlke et al. (New York: Wiley, 1962), pp. 237–66. Lasswell's original types were the agitator and the administrator. See Harold Lasswell, *Psychopathology and Politics* (Chicago: University of Chicago Press, 1930).
30. See Donald R. Mathews, *The Social Behavior of Political Decision-Making* (New York: Doubleday, 1954).

formation, from whom information is obtained, and to whom credence is given.[31]

Legislative behavior stands at that sensitive point in the political system which intersects the flow of information upward, from people, interest groups, and technical experts to governmental officials, and the downward flow of information to the public.[32] Within this information system the politician is encased in a complex network and can be observed in action as, for example, when a bill is formulated and presented, by examining roll-call votes, or in the way policy is heard in legislative committees.[33]

A recent study of U.S. Senate committees makes the point very well. How legislators translate public preferences into public policies at a legislative level is, in part, the work of key individuals in critical committees. For example, key Senate committees like Commerce, Finance, and Labor have their own representational clientele which consists of political elites and interest groups. The extent to which they restrict their policy activities to the clientele narrowly or broadly defined is a product of the following kinds of activities or functions:

(*1*) Instigation and publicizing—*the public or private advocacy of an issue as one worthy of attention and ameliorative action. Typical instigators include the staff man or lower-level bureaucrat who calls a problem to his superior's attention, the congressman who highlights an issue through investigative hearings, or the author who documents and dramatizes a social need.*

(*2*) Formulation—*devising and advocating a specific legislative remedy for a supposed need. The formulator draws boundaries around an issue and establishes a focal point for its further consideration.*

(*3*) Information-gathering—*collecting data on the nature of hazards and abuses; the alternative schemes for solving problems and their costs, benefits, and inherent difficulties; the likely political impact of each scheme; and the feasibility of various compromises. Information-*

---

31. Perhaps the best detailed study of legislators' behavior is Richard Fenno, *The Power of the Purse: Appropriations Politics in Congress* (Boston: Little, Brown, 1966). See also David R. Mayhew, *Congress, the Electoral Connection* (New Haven: Yale University Press, 1974).

32. See Deutsch, op. cit., p. 150. See also David Easton, *A Systems Analysis of Political Life* (New York: Wiley, 1965).

33. See Stephen K. Bailey, *Congress Makes a Law* (New York: Columbia University Press, 1950). See also Duncan McRae, *Dimensions of Congressional Voting* (Berkeley, Ca.: University of California Press, 1958).

gathering is crucial to each of the other functions—to devising a work-able proposal, as well as to plotting its political course and building a sense of need and legitimacy.

(4) Interest-aggregation—responding to the needs and wishes of individuals or groups affected by a given proposal. In one instance, it might mean the championing of one group over or against others, in another the assumption of a mediating, "balancing" role, in yet another the stimulating of latent group sentiments. Such activities may both re-solve and exacerbate conflict; they may, on the one hand, contribute to the instigation and mobilization effort, or on the other, give rise to attempts at modification or obstruction.

(5) Mobilization—the exertion of pressure, persuasion, or con-trol on behalf of a measure by one who is able, often by virtue of his institutional position, to take effective and relatively direct action to secure enactment. Whether an issue goes beyond the publicizing and formulating stages usually depends on the support it receives from in-dividuals, groups, or governmental units that possess authority and legitimacy in the policy area and on the extent of "intra-elite organiz-ing" by key leaders. Mobilizers may become involved in other func-tions as a part of these efforts, but they may benefit from—or be stimu-lated by—those who were active at the "earlier" stages as well.

(6) Modification—the marginal alteration of a proposal, some-times "strengthening" it, sometimes granting certain concessions to its opponents in order to facilitate final passage. Modification may or may not complement actions taken at earlier points, but in any case the mod-ifier shares responsibility for a bill's final form.[34]

We have seen how complex the representational base really is. The process of conversion indicates how much the power structure is a matter of individual discretion and compromise as well as overlapping group interest.

Coalitions and the Distribution of Benefits

The two behavioral models discussed in Chapter Nine can be incorpo-rated into the cybernetic model. The utility model suggests how

34. David Price, *Who Makes the Laws?* (Cambridge, Mass.: Schenkman, 1972), pp. 82–84.

maximizing private and group interests will produce the greatest support for the leaders and parties that offer the most benefits. Finding a good balance between demands and support will represent a cybernetic equilibrium or "steady state." The assumption is that the public will continue to observe the rules of the voting place. The model does allow for changing preferences. It represents a method of responding according to a maximizing principle within libertarian rules.

However, the psychological model implies that as social life becomes more complex and differentiated, the expression of concepts of socialization, saliency, and modal personality do too. Individuals may lose their sense of civic responsibility. Moral ends become perfunctory when values are converted to interests. The password of political life is "every man for himself." The greater the economic opportunity, the greater the competition; the weak will be driven out by the strong. As a political system seeks to satisfy individual and group utilities by means of political strategies, the more anxiety-ridden and uncertain the public becomes. This state can lead to an inverse correlation between increasing utilities and political commitment, which we diagram in Figure 11-2.

In Figure 11-2, positive feelings for the collectivity, or the public interest, decline as utilities are maximized. This means that the most successful utility system is, from the standpoint of the psychology model, an increasingly unsuccessful system. The paradox is visible in the form of growing alienation, anger, and political apathy prevalent in the most advanced democratic societies.

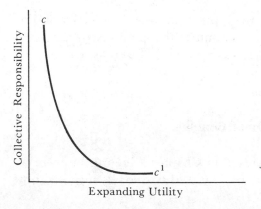

Figure 11-2. The Commitment Hypothesis

The solution to the problem, in terms of the utility model, is to increase utilities, thus offering the promise of greater growth and improved distribution, and if necessary the compensatory reallocation of benefits to the disadvantaged parts of the society. But increasing development and growth require more training and higher skills; differentiation in work; new technological innovations; and greater mobility, efficiency, and so forth. Such innovations are hard to cope with, and individuals may become more distrustful of society as conditions improve, withdrawing from collective responsibility. Efforts to control the process by means of political participation to a large degree frustrate themselves; hence to expand utility merely compounds the problem.

One solution is to teach individuals to adjust to such problems by enabling them to handle the psychological load. This is the perspective of therapy. However, this is not a feasible solution. Another is to initiate greater political control to reduce the uncertainties which accrue with increased utilities. This would involve authoritarian restrictions, controlled socialization, manipulated social learning, and value indoctrination. It would spell the end of polyarchy.

Is there any way out? To find an acceptable combination of institutional practices capable of increasing utilities and avoiding the problems which the psychological models have indicated is the objective of modern pluralism. Pluralism defines a set of political theories aimed at resolving the high utility–high anxiety paradox.

The built-in contradiction of modern pluralism, however, is that it cannot deal with big issues—only small ones. As society becomes more complex representative systems fail to develop sufficiently flexible and fast-adapting mechanisms to keep public utilities and public policies in proper balance. In prolonged periods of change people may "disaffiliate" from the system. They may become alienated and believe that the pluralist system not only will not but cannot respond to their needs. The idea of a public interest dissolves. Why then do polyarchies or democratic societies survive at all? It is clear that there is a compensatory mechanism built into the pluralist political model, despite its inadequacies. Power may concentrate, but it can also be fractionalized through competition among political parties, interest groups, regulatory agencies, and other bodies. There is a hierarchy, but there is no single hierarchy. Moreover, every hierarchy breeds a countervailing force. In the pluralist model human potentiality is seen to be exemplified by individual choice—not by homogeneity but by diversity, not through hierarchy but through fractionalization, not as a result of polarization of ideas but by their proliferation.[35] The pluralist model may creak, but the public interest does not disintegrate altogether. How, then, does a pluralist system work?

Countervailing power: Political parties in a pluralist system are loose coalitions which maximize membership around dominant issues and themes. They are creatures of coalitions in their internal make-up and in their relations with other parties. But each unit in the coalition is interested in realizing its own specialized demands. The party coalesces around common objectives even though the coalition fractionalizes as distribution occurs. Group competition thus results in an attempt to create political monopolies. As we stated previously, an election is a form of monopolistic competition. All resources are directed toward building one grand party and telescoping all utilities under one banner. Party leaders are natural monopolists. Any party leader who claims to want to keep the party small is suspect. However, political monopolies need members to be monopolistic, so the more monopolistic the party, the more representative it is likely to be, and the more hospitable to diverse interests.

If a coalition wins a given election or legislative battle, there is a division of the spoils. The desire to achieve gains causes groups to proliferate. To increase their membership is to gain a position advantageous in bargaining for marginal gains on the basis of strength. The bargaining process leads to the distribution of rewards such that those who have claims will be paid off. The grey area between the tendency toward coalition or fractionalization represents an arena for compromise among all groups represented in the process. A complex system of maneuvers results in games and strategies in which payoffs depend in part on how effectively subgroup fractionalization works to "bleed" the large coalition for the small gain.

The matter is complicated because each individual has more than one interest or utility demand and multiple group affiliations. Each wants to maximize the power of groups with which he or she is affiliated at the expense of others. If one contributes money or time to a coalition, one expects a payoff in due proportion. Hence, complementary forces are at work to maximize individual preferences and to monopolize

35. See the discussion of such matters in Robert A. Dahl and C.E. Lindblom, *Politics, Economics and Welfare* (New York: Harper & Row, 1953) . See also Anthony Downs, "Why the Government Budget in a Democracy is too Small," *World Politics,* XII, No. 4 (July, 1960) : 541–63, and Brian Barry, *Political Argument* (London: Routledge and Kegan Paul, 1965) , pp. 207–85.

power through group affiliation. These forces describe a *monopolizing tendency*.

On the other hand, the more interests there are, the more sub-groups are contained within the coalition, and the greater the competition for benefits. Where there are many organized monopolistic groups, there are many countervailing groups. These diverse organizations institute a *competitive tendency*.

The first results in greater inequality (group and individual). The second results in greater equality (group and individual). How the two tendencies operate can be graphed in terms of the diagram in Figure 11-3.

As individuals try to maximize their preferences, they form groups. Each group strives to become more powerful and monopolistic (just as firms try to become more powerful in economic life). However, the more monopolistic the tendency, the more likely other groups are to compete (although they may not all be of the same kind). Those left out of established groups form compensatory new ones. These may then draw off dissatisfied splinter groups from the monopoly.

To the extent to which monopoly prevails, it services the preferences of some individuals over others, producing a drive to inequality in the system. To the extent that group competition (and splintering) occurs, greater equality results. One process concentrates power, the other divides it. Political equilibrium exists at the intersection of these two opposing forces.

The model highlights the central ingredient of a stable pluralist

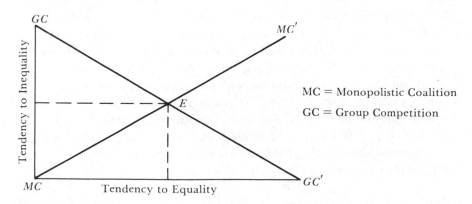

Figure 11-3. Degree of Fractionalization

democratic system—the theory of countervailing power. A tendency toward monopolistic coalitions will be counterbalanced by a tendency toward new competitive groupings. Stability is a point between equality and inequality. All strive for those forms of inequality most in their favor. Everyone strives for equality against subjectively unfavorable inequalities.

These characteristics of competition are fundamental to the representational system. From one point of view, the joining together of many interests into broad coalitions maximizes informational utility demands, from another it represents competition among groups and the need to effect utility demands in the form of policy payoffs. In turn, payoffs depend not on the size of a coalition but on the efficiency of groups engaged in the "bleeding" process. There is a proliferation of highly efficient small groupings which claim particular objectives. Some groups will be more skilled at bleeding than others.

The greater effectiveness of relatively small groups—the "privileged" and "intermediate" groups—is evident from observation and experience as well as from theory. Consider, for example, meetings that involve too many people, and accordingly cannot make decisions promptly or carefully. Everyone would like to have the meeting end quickly, but few if any will be willing to let their pet concern be dropped to make this possible. And, though all of those participating presumably have an interest in reaching sound decisions, this all too often fails to happen. When the number of participants is large, the typical participant will know his own efforts will probably not make much difference to the outcome and that he will be affected by the meeting's decision in much the same way no matter how much or how little effort he puts into studying the issues. Accordingly, the typical participant may not take the trouble to study the issues as carefully as he would have if he had been able to make the decisions by himself. The decisions of the meeting are thus public goods to the participants (and perhaps others), and the contribution that each participant will make toward achieving or improving these public goods will become smaller as the meeting becomes larger. It is for these reasons, among others, that organizations so often turn to the small group; committees, sub-committees, and small leadership groups are created, and once created they tend to play a crucial role.[36]

36. Mancur Olson, Jr., *The Logic of Collective Action* (Cambridge, Mass.: Harvard University Press, 1965), p. 53.

To win political power, then, requires large coalitional parties or interest groups, which in turn generate smaller organizational groups, which bleed off the gains of the larger ones. Bleeding is the result of small-group competition for the distribution of public, or collectively won, benefits. This is the basis for the theory of countervailing powers.

How well groups optimize is the key problem of democracy. But such group representation raises the question of the public interest as well. If groups compete, do they not plunder the society? How can the public interest be defined? If effective group representation requires organization, and organization requires power, especially financial power, then those with great need but small resources (such as the poor or the marginals in a society) lack precisely the most important ingredients of effective organization. The social cost of pluralist democracy can be measured by the extent to which those with the greatest need have the least representation. This concept is called the *marginal theory of democracy*. Under the circumstances how much public interest is possible?

Even liberal pluralists view the public interest as something more than a simple symposium of private interest. Moreover, Dahl notes:

> . . . *When one looks at American political institutions in their entirety and compares them with institutions in other democracies, what stands out as a salient feature is the extraordinary variety of opportunities these institutions provide for an organized minority to block, modify, or delay a policy which the minority opposes. Consequently, it is a rarity for any coalition to carry out its policies without having to bargain, negotiate, and compromise with its opponents; often indeed, it wins a victory in one institution only to suffer defeat in another.*
>
> *The multiplicity of checkpoints that American political institutions provide organized minorities results from three interrelated factors. First, there is a great diversity of political institutions. Second, among these institutions there is no clear-cut hierarchy of legal and constitutional authority. Third, there is no de facto hierarchy of power.*[37]

In a pluralist design it is crucial that power be multiple. Minorities on one issue may become majorities on another because pluralism at the social level is reflected in the political culture. Bargaining is endemic, and organization is the key to effective bargaining.[38]

37. Robert A. Dahl, *Pluralist Democracy in the United States*, op. cit., pp. 326–27.
38. See the discussion of these matters in Andrew S. McFarland, *Power and Leadership in Pluralist Systems* (Palo Alto, Ca.: Stanford University Press, 1969), pp. 32–49.

Coalitions and political power: In the pluralist world, political power is based on electoral support. Increasing electoral payoffs means building coalitions that unite groups and individuals with a variety of interests into a single voting bloc. The larger the coalition, the greater its electoral power. Coalition formation is thus a basic tendency in pluralist political life, but while coalitions attempt to maximize *electoral* payoffs, they receive corresponding *interest* payoffs as their political power grows. This is, after all, why they are in business. But coalitions are based upon bargains and bargains involve mutual sacrifice. Thus coalitions generally yield higher electoral payoffs than they do interest payoffs, as one can see from Figure 11-4.

Different kinds of coalitions yield different relationships between electoral and interest payoffs. The most common coalition in pluralist politics is naturally the party. Parties may be loosely organized from among a large body of disparate interests, in which case their electoral payoff is high because they are able to mobilize a large number of votes. But their interest payoff in such a case is low because the bargains made between disparate groups obligate them to share the spoils widely. Parties may also be tightly disciplined and organized around a small body of closely aligned interests. In this case, the electoral payoff is low as the number of groups is small, but interest payoff is high because there are only a few internal bargainers demanding mutual payment. See Figure 11-5.

It has often been observed that different types of electoral mechanisms tend to foster different kinds of parties. Single-member majority-rule mechanisms tend to favor large, loosely organized parties, while P-R (proportional representation) systems tend to favor small, dis-

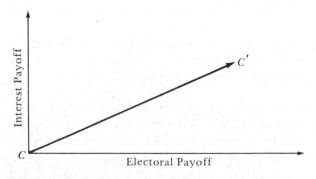

Figure 11-4.

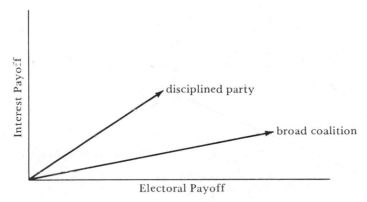

Figure 11-5.

ciplined, single-interest parties. But electoral mechanisms also have a direct impact on the relationship between electoral and interest payoffs. All electoral systems have a minimal threshold below which coalitions are considered too small to be represented. For example, under a majority-rule system, a coalition representing nearly half the voting population may be defeated and receive no interest payoff whatsoever. In a P-R system the threshold for interest payoff is much lower; almost all coalitions are viable and receive immediate interest benefits. It is this threshold property (see Figure 11-6) of electoral systems that partially accounts for the tendency of different types of electoral mechanisms to yield different types of coalitional parties.

We now are able to represent two properties of pluralist coalitions. The slope interest/electoral payoff represents the degree of solidarity of the coalition. The distance *d* represents the minimal vote criterion for representation under the electoral mechanism. Together the two determine the balance between interest and electoral payoffs for a given combination of electoral mechanism and coalitional solidarity.

Fractionalization and short-run benefit: Unfortunately the story of coalition formation in the pluralist world does not end here. Coalitions are based upon bargains, bargains are based upon trust, and trust can be violated. The broader the coalition, the less the interests of its members coincide, and the greater is the opportunity for betrayal. Betrayal may yield a great deal of short-run interest benefit because the betrayer gains the payoffs of coalitional bargains struck previous to betrayal, but

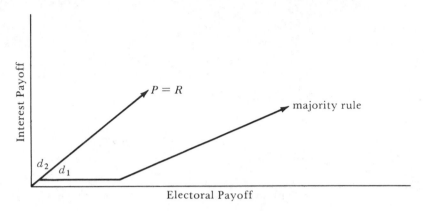

Figure 11-6.

does not forfeit their costs. But the result for the coalition is fractional-ization; interest groups break off and the coalition is destroyed.

The pull toward fractionalization grows increasingly stronger as coalition formation proceeds. The number of bargains which defines a coalition grows at a higher rate than the number of members, thus in-creasing the possibilities of betrayal. At the same time, as electoral payoffs grow, the potential rewards incumbent on betraying the coali-tion grow. It is important to point out that betrayal can only succeed once. Afterward the betrayer is an outcast; electoral payoff and subse-quent interest payoff slip to a very low level in the next round. But the short-run rewards of fractionalization can be immense. The decision to betray thus involves weighing gains against losses, but this involves a complicated decision as gains and losses are in this case difficult to com-pare. The gain of betrayal is immediate interest payoff. Its cost shows up in interest terms only in the long run; all that is lost immediately is electoral power.

This betrayal decision is easily treated in "gaming" terms. For ex-ample, in a coalition with two members, the game of coalition forma-tion and betrayal is very like the familiar "prisoners' dilemma" game where the parties, in order to cooperate, need to be not only trusting but trustworthy. Each party's decision is either to maintain or to betray the coalition. If one party betrays the other, that player receives addi-tional interest payoff, but if there is mutual betrayal the coalition is fractionalized. Consider the following situation.

Imagine two betrayal situations. In situation 1 the fractionaliza-tion curve is not far from the coalition curve. Short-term interest gain is probably not sufficient to motivate betrayal. But in situation 2 short-term interest gain is immense relative to that obtained by maintaining the coalition. Experimental studies using the prisoners' dilemma framework have shown that the relative magnitudes of the utilities involved in the various cells of the game matrix are the most important determinants of betrayal decisions. The dynamic is exactly the same here.

But we must remember that the payoff structure of any given betrayal decision is itself partly a product of the type of coalition involved. Earlier we stated that different types of coalitions could be described by different slopes of the interest/electoral payoff curve. The "profit" of any given betrayal is the difference between the interest payoff to be derived from the betrayal and that of the intact coalition. Two alternative situations are shown in Figure 11-7.

Case 1 shows a low-solidarity mass party, while case 2 shows a high-solidarity single-interest party. By comparing the gains of betrayal at the extremes, it is easy to see that the first is far more vulnerable to fractionalization than is the second. But the second is able to mobilize only a very limited electoral strength and is thus at the mercy of larger groups, or must depend on a P-R electoral mechanism for survival.[39]

The pluralist world of coalitions is also a world of instability. Examining the dynamics of coalition and fractionalization reveals that the prime source of instability is the contradiction between short- and long-run benefits. The game of politics is played continuously. Betrayal

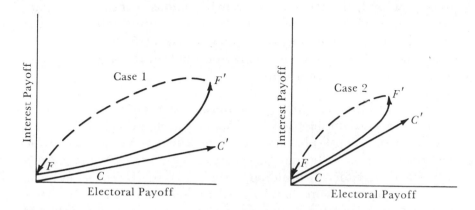

Figure 11-7.

39. See David R. Mayhew, op. cit., and *Party Loyalty Among Congressmen* (Cambridge, Mass: Harvard University Press, 1966). See also Steven J. Brams, *Game Theory and Politics* (New York: The Free Press, 1975), pp. 30–33.

requires the sacrifice of future benefits for those of the moment; coalition maintenance requires the opposite sacrifice. But this statement of the problem reveals that there is more at work than just a contradiction between the present and the future. The real contradiction is between private and public interests. The solution to the prisoners' dilemma involves the perception of a public interest summing up the utilities of both parties. In choosing not to betray, both parties sacrifice individual for collective gain. Therefore the decision to maintain a political coalition in spite of a pull toward fractionalization involves a commensurate sacrifice. Pluralism focuses on individual values and gains, but sanctifies the bargain. Yet we have seen that in many cases bargains may be broken for individual gain. In the last analysis pluralist theory, despite its preoccupations with institutions, rests upon the faith that such cases are not the rule but the exception.

We have tried to show how the basic constructs of pluralism relate the behavioral tendencies of political groups to the party system and the party system to equality and inequality. The tendencies just described are coalition formation and fractionalization. Structural consequences have been treated in terms of the amount of interparty competition in the political system. These range from a pure competition, multiparty system on the one hand to a monopolistic one-party system on the other. Two types of expansion phenomena have been treated: first, the tendency for alliances to break up through a "bleeding" process; second, the tendency for small factions to evolve into large parties. Each of these phenomena takes place within a different range of variation on the competition-monopoly axis, the first being associated primarily with the low-competition half of the scale, the second with the high-competition half.

1. The "bleeding" phenomenon begins at a middle range of structural competition in the party system, perhaps in a three- or four-party system where each party has a distinct constituency—but not too distinct. The basic movement begins when parties begin trying to encroach on each other's territory by building coalitions. Initially, coalition formation proceeds at a more rapid rate than fractionalization. Coalitions peak as party competition increases in response to the threat, following which further efforts at building coalitions only result in an increase in competitiveness among parties. But fractionalization continues to grow with the increasing coalitional emphasis. Splinter groups form as

ideological boundaries blur. Then fractionalization yields a rapid decline in monopolistic tendencies for the system as a whole.

2. Party building (a "clotting" phenomenon) also begins at a middle level. Suppose a party with clearly delineated ideological boundaries accepts the loss of less committed members of its constituency. Then if competition between parties decreases, battles are fought not in front of the electorate, but in the legislature. Tendencies toward coalition increase when there is a possibility for achieving ideological goals. But increasingly, small parties see their position in the legislature as nonviable, and seek to increase their legislative power by maximizing electoral support. Coalitional behavior first occurs *outside* the legislature, perhaps in the form of a "popular front" or other electoral coalition. The result is a rapid decline in competition in the party system as a whole.

How coalitions form and how they are bled will continue to be the topic of much research because the bargaining process represents "exchanges" among groups. Such exchanges may be primarily in terms of economic payoffs or they might involve other organizational factors. Whatever the form such analysis takes, however, it is clear that when coalitions form around consistent cleavages which serve as lightning rods for all other conflicts in society, then the danger is that coalitions will be replaced by a monopoly. To prevent that from happening is one political problem. Which brings up the matter of equality: The greater the degree of equality in a system, the less likelihood there is of such cleavages engulfing the more diverse pluralistic demands.[40] Another issue is that if a pluralist system fails to meet some minimum standard of benefits, then a monopolistic effort to change the rules of the game becomes more desirable. A good deal of the activity of modern autocratic societies is devoted to minimizing pluralistic tendencies.

The Radical Pluralist Critique

Critics of the liberal pluralist position have argued that it is elitist. They regard as too limited the liberal position that the characteris-

40. See Douglas Rae, *The Political Consequences of Electoral Laws* (New Haven, Conn.: Yale University Press, 1967). See also Douglas Rae and Michael Taylor, *The Analysis of Political Cleavages* (New Haven, Conn.: Yale University Press, 1970).

tically democratic element is the method of competition among leaders (elites) for the votes of the people in periodic, free elections.

Elections are crucial to the democratic method for it is primarily through elections that the majority can exercise control over their leaders. Responsiveness of leaders to non-elite demands, or "control" over leaders, is ensured primarily through the sanction of loss of office at elections; the decisions of leaders can also be influenced by active groups bringing pressure to bear during inter-election periods. "Political equality" in the theory refers to universal suffrage and to the existence of equality of opportunity to access to channels of influence over leaders. Finally "participation," so far as the majority is concerned is participation in the choice of decision-makers. Therefore, the function of participation in the theory is solely a protective one; the protection of the individual from arbitrary decisions by elected leaders and the protection of his private interests. It is in its achievement of this aim that the justification for the democratic method lies.[41]

There is a good deal to the criticism, but as Dahl has suggested democracy "is not, in a strict sense, a single form of authority."[42] Who are "the people" and how they are represented is very much a function of what they want and how they are organized. Hence participation and representation are more and more related to participating and representing functions which, in the ebb and flow of political groups, are increasingly flexible and malleable. It may be efficient to have highly organized political parties whose routine activities at election times are their main justification, but the trend is in the opposite direction. Parties are more and more creatures of social pluralism—not *representative* of the political life of citizens but *part* of that life. This makes them simultaneously more intertwined with the social experiences of people and less likely to be able to take strong stands on anything.

Thus the more representative a party is of a broad spectrum, the less decisive is that party's activity, but the more information it generates and circulates. What bodies, then, are able to best utilize the instrumentalities of political life? This is the large question which pluralism as a method raises, without offering a clear-cut solution. One possibility is that what were formerly influence groups—lobbies and interests ma-

41. See Carole Pateman, *Participation and Democratic Theory* (Cambridge: Cambridge University Press, 1970), p. 14.
42. See Robert A. Dahl, *After the Revolution?* (New Haven, Conn.: Yale University Press, 1970), p. 59.

nipulating parties by their financial support or some similar access to power—should bring their attention to bear more directly on government and regulatory commissions, thereby providing government with private expert advice and other services.

The most successful example of the pluralistic model is the United States. Here the attempt was made to establish an explicit set of mechanisms of rule which would render intentional the practices of political life described by the models. But while establishing a government of laws is no easy task, and intentionality and good practice, plus suitable amendment procedures, have given a moral strength to the American constitution bordering on the sacrosanct, there are nevertheless fundamental defects which require further comments.

Pluralism, as embodied in the ideas of the framers of the Constitution, had as a central concern the fair treatment of factions. There was fear that factions would destroy the union because they would divide it, but since division is also essential to a democracy, the right medium was thought to be one which would promote compromise between factions and convert that to the public interest.

Hence the liberal idea of pluralism is based on multiple and competitive centers of power.

Instead of a single center of sovereignty power there must be multiple centers of power, none of which is or can be wholly sovereign. Although the only legitimate sovereign is the people, in the perspective of American pluralism even the people ought never to be an absolute sovereign; consequently no part of the people, such as a majority, ought to be absolutely sovereign.[43]

It is precisely this axiom which was used to create a political marketplace of ideas. To find the circumstances under which the marketplace could flourish with due regard to the rights and obligations of all—individuals acting as individuals and groups acting as groups— became the basic political problem, raising among others the issues of minority rights, representation, and the effects of the exercise of power. Dahl, summarizing the more significant concerns of the Founding Fathers, puts the matter as follows:

Because one center of power is set against another, power itself will be tamed, civilized, controlled and limited to decent human pur-

43. Dahl, *Pluralist Democracy in the United States,* p. 24.

poses, while coercion, the most evil form of power, will be reduced to a minimum.

  Because even minorities are provided with opportunities to veto solutions they strongly object to, the consent of all will be won in the long run.

  Because constant negotiations among different centers of power are necessary in order to make decisions, citizens and leaders will perfect the precious art of dealing peacefully with their conflicts, and no more to the benefit of one partisan but to the mutual benefit of all parties to a conflict.[44]

  Mancur Olson has challenged these assumptions.

The view that groups act to serve their interests presumably is based upon the assumption that the individuals in groups act out of self-interest. If the individuals in a group altruistically disregarded their personal welfare, it would not be very likely that collectively they would seek some selfish common or group objective. Such altruism is, however, considered exceptional, and self-interested behavior is usually thought to be the rule, at least when economic issues are at stake; no one is surprised when individual businessmen seek higher profits, when individual workers seek higher wages, or when individual consumers seek lower prices. The idea that groups tend to act in support of their group interests is supposed to follow logically from this widely accepted premise of rational, self-interested behavior. In other words, if the members of some group have a common interest or objective, and if they would all be better off if that objective were achieved, it has been thought to follow logically that the individuals in that group would, if they were rational and self-interested, act to achieve that objective.

  But it is not *in fact true that the idea that groups will act in their self-interest follows logically from the premise of rational and self-interested behavior. It does* not *follow, [that] because all of the individuals in a group would gain if they achieved their group objective, that they would act to achieve that objective, even if they were all rational and self-interested. Indeed, unless the number of individuals in a group is quite small, or unless there is coercion or some other special device to make individuals act in their common interest,* rational, self-interested individuals will not act to achieve their common or group interests. . . . *The notion that groups of individuals will act to achieve*

44. Ibid.

their common or group interests, far from being a logical implication of the assumption that the individuals in a group will rationally further their individual interests, is in fact inconsistent with that assumption.[45]

Clearly, if Olson is right, the conventional notion of pluralism as acting for the conversion of pluralistic interests into a collective public interest, is flawed. Olson applies his idea to large groups rather than small ones because by and large pluralistic groupings are large coalitions maximizing support. The problem is this: Competition, the foundation of pluralism and the representation of interests, introduces contradictions between common and competitive interests. For example, the common interest of farmers is high prices for foodstuffs. But, in order to maximize their incomes, farmers try to produce more. Each farmer is a maximizer; therefore the collective effect of maximizing behavior is to drive prices down. It is easier to state the problem than to find a solution to it. In a world of social inequality, few are willing to give up comparative advantages to help the disadvantaged. Those economically or socially disadvantaged groups that can organize may be able to use the political arena to rectify social and economic inequality, but this effect, which is precisely that which mass voting in democracies is supposed to accomplish, may or may not be forthcoming. Real life is a bargaining process carried on among those who seek to gain advantages for themselves at the expense of the others.

Rousseau tried to deal with the problem by insisting on equality for political purposes along with limited social inequality. The general will and all individual welfares would coincide. The Industrial Revolution viewed the problem of economic injustice from a purely redistributive point of view and translated it into a question of growth. Robin Hood was replaced by the entrepreneur. Modern theorists have cast the problem in a developmental role. Let the rich perform a role in development and expand opportunities by investing their wealth. They can keep their riches as long as they perform their economic functions. Given the growth potential they provide, society can be "leveled *up*" (according to the concept of *collective mobility*) rather than "leveled down."

One of the differences between liberal and socialist pluralisms is in the definition of social justice. Social democratic ideas of pluralism retain the idea of the political marketplace but seek a leveling down in the economic sphere; social welfare benefits should be taken away from

45. Olson, op. cit., pp. 1–2.

the rich and given to the poor. Liberal pluralists assume that the right way to handle the problem is to level up; that is, to use the political marketplace to share the opportunities made available by the rich and the powerful.

A governmental system based on the principles of a political marketplace is the idea common to both forms of pluralism. A liberal pluralism is traditionally one which levels up the benefits of society in the hope that this will stimulate more rapid growth, greater collective benefits, and in the long run greater social justice. The preference for capitalist versus socialist forms of pluralism also disguises certain premises about behavior. In the old liberal paradigm capitalism is a system which uses pluralism to make greed virtuous. Socialism is a system which uses pluralism to make the desire for power virtuous. Socialists under pluralism try to use power to repress greed. Capitalists under pluralism use greed to check power.

The criticisms: The radical critique of pluralism rejects both points of view. It advocates instead participation at all levels as a way of ending passive alienation and the loss of efficacy experienced by those normally excluded from the political process. It attacks the notion that elite accountability really works. It assumes that the existence and influence of a power elite, even one perhaps composed of more than a simple dominant class, create conditions which exclude some people at least from exercising more than formal expressions of approval and disapproval in the electoral mechanism. Widespread apathy, absenteeism, and even violent disapproval are all indicators of pluralist failure.

Moreover, at any moment those with power can exercise it more or less unchecked by any form of countervailing power. For example, during the Cuban missile crisis in 1962 President John F. Kennedy did not ask the American people what they thought he ought to do. He acted alone. Similarly, instruments designed to restrict or regulate various powerful interests, such as regulatory commissions, all too often become in the normal course of affairs responsive to the very organizations they are supposed to monitor. Collusion can occur.

Liberal pluralism profoundly mistrusts the people themselves. It is a "revolt against the masses," or "from" the masses as Peter Bachrach puts it:

With the disenchantment with the common man, the classical view of the elite-mass relationship has become reversed: it is the common man, not the elite, who is chiefly suspected of endangering freedom, and it is the elite, not the common man, who is looked upon as the chief guardian of the system. The revolt from the masses has led to a second shift in theory: the emphasis is no longer upon extending or strengthening democracy, but upon stabilizing the established system. The focus, in short, is upon protecting liberalism from the excesses of democracy rather than upon utilizing liberal means to progress towards the realization of democratic goals.[46]

What in effect happens is that the issues which come forward are not actually the issues which concern people, but only a selection of those which the elites in their judgment-making capacity anticipate will be acted upon. Hence the effect of the complex process of liberal pluralism is to make ordinary people co-conspirators in elite manipulation. In their belief that they can act, they allow others to act against them.[47]

Still another fundamental criticism is that polyarchy, the various utility and psychological models, the cybernetic flow, and the notion of equilibrium operate on a too simple idea of one-dimensional power; that is, the reciprocal power of A and B. That A becomes accountable to B is a facile explanation of the interchange. Missing from the formulation is that those forces which operate to constrain the individual, forces which indeed constitute a "hidden agenda," may go entirely unnoticed. Thus liberal pluralism and its method structures the attitudes of people and builds into their way of thinking the illusion that they are independent decision makers, capable of really influencing and acting upon a ruling elite.[48] This is not only untrue, but those who are excluded from the political process under pluralism are likely to remain excluded, their only recourse being periodic threatened or actual violence.[49]

The main attack on pluralism, however, is that it does not go far enough to protect the weak, the poor, and the unorganized. The answer to this criticism is greater participation. Radical pluralists are interested in increasing direct participation by citizens in decisions that affect their lives. Unlike conventional pluralists, who are concerned mainly with competitive centers of power and group interaction, radical plural-

46. Peter Bachrach, *The Theory of Democratic Elitism* (Boston: Little, Brown, 1967), p. 32.
47. See Peter Bachrach and Morton S. Baratz, *Power and Poverty* (New York: Oxford University Press, 1970), pp. 104–6.
48. See Steven Lukes, *Power* (London: Macmillan, 1974).
49. See David Ricci, ed., *Community Power and Democratic Theory* (New York: Random House, 1971), pp. 193–201.

ists shift the focus back to the individual and seek to identify possible agencies of direct participation.

The solutions: One main line of thought pursued by those interested in participatory democracy is the analysis of greater worker self-management, a return to an old concern in political theory associated with Proudhon, the early French radicals and syndicalists, English guild socialists, and German Social Democrats. It is different from the liberal pluralist construct for labor-management relations, collective bargaining between unions and employers, or compromise as a set of wage and work agreements or contracts. It involves the sharing by workers in ownership and the decisions affecting all aspects of production and employment. Thus participatory democracy focuses on work and living groups. Radical pluralists want compromise and consensus, but they are less interested in solutions from "above" that is, from the standpoint of government—than from "below," through worker participation and representation.

They argue that of all activities of human beings the most important is one's work. Work will produce alienation or fulfillment. To be responsible and participate fully in society is therefore a result of participation in one's workplace experience. While pluralists rely on socialization instruments like schools to prepare people for their place in a democratic and pluralistic society, the efficacy of such an approach holds true only for the elite. Those less capable of resolving the problems that confront them in everyday life—those victims of big bureaucracies or "power centers" remote from their experience but having the ability to reach down and by impersonal means transform their terms of existence—need to be constantly monitored, controlled, manipulated, and policed. But they will only become bigger burdens all the time.

Evidence has now been presented to support the argument of the theory of participatory democracy that participation in non-government authority structures is necessary to foster and develop the psychological qualities (the sense of political efficacy) required for participation at the national level. Evidence has also been cited to support the argument that industry is the most important sphere for this participation to take place and this does give us the basis for a possible explanation of why it is that low levels of efficacy are more likely to be found among lower SES [socioeconomic status] groups.[50]

50. Pateman, op. cit., pp. 50–1.

Yugoslavia has gone further than any other country in developing a system of self-management at the factory level; workers decide on investment policy and output, whether or not to expand, or to use company income for health, housing, and other social benefits on a collective basis. Indeed, so well established is the system of self-management committees that they are the critical units of policy. The managers are actually employees of the factory workers. The system has been expanded over the years so that today self-management and workplace socialism are the central institutions of the society, with both reflected in political organization as well. For example, the constitution has been established around the institutions of worker participation.[51]

There are many other examples. Tanzania has experimented with *Ujamaa* villages in which communal ownership and community decision making have replaced individual tenure, especially in tobacco and coffee growing areas.[52] In Sweden some automobile companies are experimenting with worker participation (particularly the Volvo company). In West Germany the movement is particularly strong. In France there is an important journal, *L'Autogestion,* devoted to reporting on and analyzing self-management experiments.

Naturally enough a great deal of interest has been generated by the Yugoslavian experience as well as other experiments in worker self-management. The impetus for it is growing particularly where the efficiency of production-line techniques has fallen off sharply. There will no doubt need to be more and more experimentation with various self-management schemes especially as work loads of governments increase and overburdened executives try to operate within the framework of decentralized decision making. Every decentralization of power will also add another level of discussion, debate, and paperwork. Greater cooperation will be required to accomplish less. The solution is to get people to solve their own problems. The question is how.

Radical proponents of participatory democracy offer to eliminate the problem by dismantling the complex interactions of modern life and returning to the more directly democratic style of face-to-face representation in the workplace and in communes. The communal solution would eliminate hierarchy.

51. See Ichak Adizes, *Industrial Democracy: Yugoslav Style* (New York: The Free Press, 1971). See also the *Reports of the First International Conference on Participation and Self-Management,* Eugen Pusić and Rudi Supek, eds. (Zagreb: Institute for Social Research, University of Zagreb, 1972), 7 vols.
52. See Julius Nyerere, *Freedom and Unity* (London: Oxford University Press, 1967), pp. 162–71.

Examples of interest are the Israeli kibbutzim where communal forms have been practiced quite successfully. Other nations too are experimenting with communal and village forms of social-political units, for example, the Chinese communes and Tanzanian Ujamaa villages where collective farming on a self-help basis is the foundation of a social collective on which a political unit is built.

The desire for such communal forms of social life is of course an old one, harkening back to historical experiments in group living. In the 1820s in New Harmony, Indiana, for example, a group of New England transcendentalists, followers of Robert Owens pooled their resources and turned to the simple life. But their experience, unlike that of the Israelis, was unsuccessful. Communes need to be bound together by profound religious convictions (as were those of the Shakers) or passionate political commitments. Otherwise sectarian disputes and ideological bickering usually prove fatal. Recent experiences with communes have not been any different. Perhaps too much is required of individuals in the way of self-discipline. Often the freedom anticipated in communal life disguises a too great loss of privacy, or even worse, intolerance for idiosyncrasies.

In any case the actual practice of direct democracy has distinct limitations. Contemporary pluralists have alternatively become concerned with mechanical or absolute limits. Dahl states the problem thus:

Choose a polyarchy of modest size, so as not to bias the presentation. Sweden, say, or if you want a city (only a little smaller in population), New York. Imagine that the citizens of Sweden or New York amended their constitution in order to guarantee every citizen the right to participate in government decisions at any and every stage, through final enactment. Consider now the situation of the chief executive. Suppose that in order to fulfill his obligations under the new amendment the prime minister (or mayor, as the case may be) decides to set aside ten minutes for any citizen, or any group of citizens, who wish to see him about some matter. He details the task of working out a schedule to an assistant. Moments later, we may imagine, the assistant returns. (The arithmetic is simple, as you will see.) If the prime minister (or mayor) were to meet one person at a time, allow ten minutes for each meeting, and set aside one hour a day for meetings of this type every day of the year, in a year he could meet with about three-hundredths of one percent of the total population. Of course, by devoting ten hours

every day of the year, he could meet with three-tenths of one percent.
If instead of meeting only one person at a time he were to meet with
groups of 100 for ten minutes (participation, you notice, becomes pretty
symbolic at this point) , he could meet with 3 percent of the population
in a year if he set aside one hour and met six groups every day; and 30
percent if he set aside ten hours and met sixty groups every day.[53]

Despite both the sobering and humorous aspects of Dahl's scenario, it is easy to foresee that the need for participation is likely to grow rather than diminish. Participating in politics will become more difficult as the urge to democracy becomes more widespread. Moreover, as modern societies place greater emphasis on requirements for social welfare, reform, and the expansion of services, the greater the need for executive efficiency will become.

One danger of too much participation is a general impatience with the burdensome aspects of the process, leading to more desire for quick and decisive political action. Periodically the desire grows for drastic reduction in representation in order to free government from public control. This can lead to a change from a democratic to some other form of government.

But it may be that we will have to ask whether or not the political units which we are accustomed to think of as "given" will remain appropriate in the future. Are there boundaries of autonomous states within which authority is becoming obsolete? Extending the concepts of pluralism not to communes but to nation-states raises the possibility of using different systems of authority for different purposes. Many economic activities (the modern multinational corporation, banking systems, flows of goods and services) are impeded by national boundaries. While national boundaries at one time helped to stimulate growth and benefited citizens, this is not necessarily so today. Welfare needs are so diverse that the need to handle them on regional or other terms is increasingly urgent. National policies are more and more often turning out to be expensive failures. Pluralism also implies that we live in a world of overlapping jurisdictions. Regional jurisdictions are emerging in Western Europe, where different jurisdictions exist for defense as well as for industrial, commercial, monetary, and other purposes. Perhaps this broad focus will provide the basis for tomorrow's political orientation.

53. Dahl, *After the Revolution?*, pp. 144–45.

Conclusion

Pluralism, a method which converts private wants into public policies, is also an instrument for achieving social justice. The first emphasis, a liberal one, emphasizes individuals and their rights. The second emphasis, a radical one, emphasizes distributive allocations of social benefits. Pluralism, then, defines both the theory and practice of democracy. Pluralists have come to regard the theory and practice of pluralism as the essence of democracy. Distinguished from all other forms of political life, it arose when civil power replaced ecclesiastic, autocratic power was limited, and expedience was contained by adherence to principles of equality of justice. Pluralism draws directly on the inheritance of institutionalism. In philosophy, no matter how technical the form or abstract the formulation, it retains its roots in natural law, the belief in nature, and the principle that the governor must have due regard for the good of the governed; that is, it updates and extends the concepts of contract and constitutional as well as utilitarian theory.[54]

Modern pluralists use behavioral rather than legal analyses. While institutionalists are interested in civil law and legal status, pluralists are interested in the flow of power among diverse interest groups—ethnic communities and the like. They emphasize a behavioral concern with community action.

Pluralism, then, is also concerned with how aggregated political groups produce democratic solutions given the diversity of these groups, the multiple membership individuals have in them, and the extent to which representation and decision making, occurring on a piecemeal basis, make politics a continuous process of negotiation. Pluralists break down large units and societies into the individuals and interacting groups which compose them, with due regard for the influence and interaction patterns which occur between them. From the standpoint of social inquiry pluralism is a statement of condition about organizational competition; about how social organizations and leaders, in order to sustain loyalties, need skillful techniques in negotiation; about the way multiple affiliations and multiple attachments reinforce each other in the form of many coalitions.[55]

Modern pluralism is thus concerned with such matters as the effects

54. For a good statement of the original principles see J.N. Figgis, *From Gerson to Grotius* (Cambridge: Cambridge University Press, 1907) , pp. 7–30.
55. See Pateman, op. cit.

of size on representation, and better methods of participation, including workplace democracy.

Pluralism as elite theory seeks to study both how leaders determine politics and the means available to a public by which it is controlled. All pluralist solutions fall within a continuum. Between two contradictory political systems—democratic and totalitarian—the question is how the elements of hierarchy needed for increasing the marginal or incremental gains which leaders might be able to obtain by virtue of their authority and power, will be tempered by multiple and reciprocal obligations. The liberal solution is polyarchy, a form of democratic hierarchy: the Soviet Union is not a polyarchy; the United States, Great Britain, Canada, New Zealand, Australia, France, Norway, Sweden, Denmark, Mexico, and Israel among others are.[56]

But how can public policy be made when there are too many conflicting demands or when satisfying one group means offending another? Pluralism is not a maximizing system but one built on realizing partial incremental gains. Nor can pluralist systems be bound by long-term plans, which are likely to become unstuck because of contingent compromises which it is necessary and expedient to make along the way.

Political promises are vulnerable to betrayal not merely because politicians are cynical or corrupt manipulators, but rather because there is often no effective way to put them into practice without offending large numbers of followers. The course of pluralistic politics never can run smoothly and never will. The remarkable thing is that it runs at all.

56. Ibid., p. 277.

Structuralism

chapter twelve
The Foundations of Structural Analysis

While pluralism is in the mainstream of the contemporary study of politics, particularly in the United States, structuralism constitutes a less well-known subject. To make matters more confusing, there are different kinds of structuralism. The most interdisciplinary of the approaches we have introduced so far, it derives from linguistics, anthropology, philosophy, and sociology. Political scientists are becoming more interested in structural analysis because it deals with political questions in ways obscured by pluralism. The latter regards the world from the standpoint of action, while ignoring the limits within which action can occur. Structuralism tries to discover the hidden *agendas,* the rules of play that determine action. It "frames" human activities.[1]

Politics—national or local, in voluntary associations or bureaucracies—is structured. If one knows how it is structured, then it is possible to locate gaps in one's knowledge, missing pieces. Freud, for example, developed a set of rules describing the structure of personality. By doing so he located the boundaries of knowledge in such a way as to project new knowledge; something must be going on just beyond what we know. Structuralism frames this potentiality in terms of *functions.* Freud gave the names *ego, id,* and *superego* to psychological functions. Political functions have other names, like information, communication, and aggregation.

We shall concentrate on two among the many forms of structuralism: *the method of contradiction* and *the method of equilibrium.* The first emphasizes conflict, the second equilibrium. The one is dialectical. (Its ancestor was Marx although Marxists vigorously reject being called structuralists.) The second is functional, the descendant of the

1. See Erving Goffman, *Frame Analysis: An Essay on the Organization of Experience* (Cambridge, Ma.: Harvard University Press, 1974).

work of Emile Durkheim. A third structural form associated with linguistics was founded by Ferdinand de Saussure (1857–1913), a Swiss linguist interested in the way Indo-European language systems diverged. We shall not deal in depth with this form, but it is useful to know that de Saussure studied language as a system of signs (semiology). The rules governing the use of signs are like the rules of a chess game; grammar is structure.

All three approaches to structure emphasize different rules of order. All can be applied to beliefs and relationships, and how each affects the other. For example, the French anthropologist Claude Lévi-Strauss showed how the categories people use to define kinship, the terms whereby people "relate" to each other, follow certain general rules. After examining many different kinds of kinship systems Lévi-Strauss concludes that despite great diversity, kinship is one of the ways the human mind expresses reciprocity and obligation—through family structure. Such reciprocity involves obligations within a family-based system of exchange. Modern societies establish rules of reciprocity and obligation in more complex systems of exchange. But whether in kinship systems or in market systems different versions of the same structural processes will go on.

The structures of kinship, reciprocity, and exchange occur both as categories of the mind and in the environment in which human beings live. The way people cope with these structures (and hand them on to succeeding generations) generates functions that result in social order. Nevertheless such order is always being upset. In every society some people will ignore rules of exchange or leave their obligations unfulfilled, and just as such willfulness in human beings can be disruptive, so the social and physical environment can be risky, chancy, whimsical. Primitive societies deal with the element of willfulness and chance by myth. The myth represents a language of order.[2] Modern societies use ideologies to perform the same function. Both myths and ideologies deal with the unruly quality of life, which is itself both a cause and an effect of political action. In political science terms, the structuralist is interested in belief systems not simply as a distribution of public opinions, but as a way of ordering the world according to principles of equity, or moral right and wrong. One aspect of structuralism is that it restores the normative, or moral side of reciprocity and obligation. In this it resembles political philosophy.

2. See Claude Lévi-Strauss, *The Elementary Structures of Kinship* (London: Eyre & Spottiswoode, 1969), and *Structural Anthropology* (New York: Basic Books, 1963).

Structural psychologists have studied how human beings generate moral rules. The psychologist Jean Piaget (whose work was mentioned in Chapter Nine) developed a concept of the "structure of mind." Piaget shows that in the evolution of the human being from childhood to adulthood, change constitutes a development from egocentricity to a more generalized moral comprehension based on knowledge.[3]

Replace the idea of kinship with politics, the relations of kinship with political power, and myth with ideology and you have structural politics. Politics is the acting out of a drama of power, therefore the meaning people attribute to power relationships is as important as action. Each leader *means* something. So does each form of government. Structuralists are interested in the *symbolic* side, the intuitive meaning, of politics as well as its exchanges.

Structuralists also have much in common with Marxists. Marx wanted to know how a system of productive relationships affected class consciousness. He emphasized the rules of economy and developed a method which adapted the dialectic of Hegel's philosophical idealism. Marxists use Marx's method, applied to "historical materialism," to show the "hidden agenda" behind politics.[4]

Some schools of thought have tried to combine the psychoanalytical structuralism of Freud with Marx. Perhaps the most important of these is the school of "critical theory," the Frankfurt School. The philosophers and sociologists of the Frankfurt School were particularly interested in the relationship between ideology and social structure.[5]

Despite major differences between the schools of thought, they share common concerns. They interpret events, episodes, and the activities of social life—including politics—in terms of "contours." Seeking underlying principles, they represent paradigmatic thinking; that is, thinking in terms of wholes. They use deductive methods. Structuralism in politics has more in common with psychoanalytical and Gestalt psychology than with the experimental psychology of behavioralism and pluralism.

The method of contradiction began in social science with Marx, the

3. For a discussion of Piaget see Howard Gardiner, *The Quest for Mind* (New York: Vintage Books, 1974), pp. 51–110. See also Jacques Lacan, "Of Structure and Inmixing," *The Structuralist Controversy*, ed. Richard Macksey and Eugenio Donato (Baltimore, Md.: The Johns Hopkins Press, 1970), pp. 186–95.
4. See Louis Althusser and Étienne Balibar, *Reading Marx* (New York: Pantheon Books, 1970). See also Dan Sperber, *Rethinking Symbolism* (Cambridge: Cambridge University Press, 1975).
5. See Max Horkheimer, *Critical Theory* (New York: The Seabury Press, 1972). See also Martin Jay, *The Dialectical Imagination* (Boston: Little, Brown, 1973).

method of equilibrium with Emile Durkheim. We will call these thinkers *pre-structuralists*. Concerned with how societies evolved from preindustrial to industrial types, they were the precursors of today's
structuralism.

Basic Principles of Structuralism

Despite the varieties of structuralism and different disciplines in which
they have appeared, one common concern is to delineate the rules
whereby events are governed. Another is to show how rules derive from
the minds of human beings. In social and political life the rules apply
to reciprocities based on exchange, work, family obligations, and responsibility. The normative rules governing social relationships are
political ideas.

As the forms of exchange alter, beliefs alter (both are "systematically" related) . Structuralists are preoccupied with "system-transforma-
tions." Some regard transformations as evolutionary; from lower to
higher stages. Others regard change as advancing from type to type.
However, the nineteenth- and early twentieth-century theorists—Marx,
Darwin, Durkheim, Weber—believed in an evolution based on knowledge. They saw society as a social organism. While classical economics
resembles physics, structuralist theory is like biology.[6]

Just as the body has functional needs, so does society. These needs
must be met or the organism will not survive. Often needs are interrelated; for example, respiration is a structure which performs more
than one biological function in the body. In human society structures
are functionally related to the survival of society itself, to its subunits
and its individual members as well as to the whole.

A simple model of structuralism in the social sciences is presented
in Figure 12-1.

The model emphasizes the interaction between meaning and exchange, which different theories explain in different ways. According
to Marx, for example, exchange is not only based on the factors of production, land or rent, labor or work, and capital or money, but on the
dynamic relationships among these under, say, capitalism. This is the
base. The "organic" composition of capital generates an "organic"
composition of society in terms of reciprocities between classes. Therefore classes perform functions corresponding to the factors of produc-

6. The term used is *organismic.*

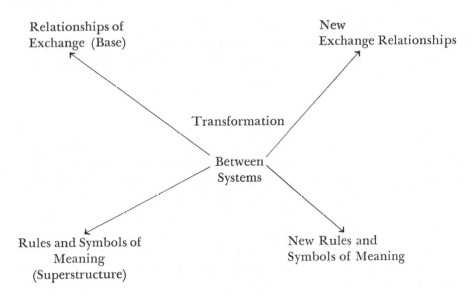

Figure 12-1. A Simple Structural Model

tion; some rent, some work, and some employ capital. Each class, with its own interests, suffers conflict with others. In turn, conflict creates meaning in people's lives, meaning in terms of class interest. This is the *superstructure*. Each class holds certain immutable beliefs about its relative position, both singly and in contrast with others.

The capitalist productive process is dynamic, continually inducing changes in technology, and producing and reprocessing wealth—some who were poor become rich; some who were rich become poor. As social conditions change, an evolution takes place. People exchange or modify their beliefs about each other, and their modes of expressing belief as well. In early forms of capitalist societies, religion is the main expression of meaning. In a more developed period, religion declines, to be replaced by secular ideologies of class interest—liberal versus socialist, for example. These *superstructural* changes were, for Marx, very important because changes in meaning can also alter concepts of exchange. Each system of exchange and meaning represents a higher stage in an evolution: feudalism gives way to capitalism, capitalism to socialism, socialism to communism. Each stage is punctuated by conflict; each new synthesis develops higher contradictions. The relationship between exchange in meaning and meaning in exchange is inherently unstable, therefore further contradictions succeed unity in all transitions to higher, more complex levels. It is this thrust which Marx called dialectical: the move-ment from lower to higher forms, with technology unfolding from the simple to the complex. It is the basis of the method of contradiction.

The Pre-Structuralists

The alternative to the method of contradiction is the method of equi-librium. The method of equilibrium emphasizes the mutual and com-plementary relationships of the parts, i.e., how the needs of the social body can be met. It is just the opposite of contradiction. We contrast the two in terms of meaning and exchange in Figure 12-2. In the chart we list the names of four important pre-structuralists. Marx is shown as a proponent of the method of contradiction to whom exchange repre-sents the basis of the structure, while meaning is superstructural. For Max Weber (1864–1920), the German historical sociologist, exchange is an independent variable, but the meaning of "normative systems" replaces it as the foundation of political structures. What, Weber asked, is the significance of religion in the emergence of modern capitalism?

Emile Durkheim (1858–1917) was a French historical sociologist. Like Weber, he was interested in religion as a form of "collective repre-sentations," or ideas about things and events or moral facts. He sought to balance changes in meaning with alterations in the division of labor in society. Finally, Bronislaw Malinowski (1884–1942), a Polish-born social anthropologist, was particularly interested in comparisons of so-cieties. He opposed undertaking cross-cultural analyses to determine the "evolutionist" and "diffusionist" tendencies (others believed that cul-tural traits diffused across cultures). Instead Malinowski saw culture as

	Exchange	Meaning
Method of Contradiction	Karl Marx	Max Weber
Method of Equilibrium	Bronislaw Malinowski	Emile Durkheim

Figure 12-2. Some Pre-Structural Theorists[7]

7. See Raymond Firth, *Marxist Analyses and Social Anthropology* (London: Melaby Press, 1972) (paper presented to the British Academy, May 3, 1972).

a response to functional needs, the satisfaction of which contributed to the on-going character of society. He used the method of equilibrium.

All the early structuralists lived through the period of transition from pre-industrial to industrial society in the nineteenth century.[8] Indeed, in his lifetime Marx observed first-hand the ravages wrought by industrialization, revolutions, coups, repression, machine-makers, and machine-smashers, and the rise of professional armies and bureaucracies. All this impressed him with the power of forces of production in exchange.

Marx applied his method to the evolution from primitive communalism to "slave" societies based on the exploitation of slave labor, to feudalism which exploited serfs, to capitalism which exploited workers. Exchange he saw as based purely on exploitation because reciprocity among classes was unequal—one class dominating, the other dominated. Capitalism he believed to be unique because it found a way to change over the more primitive forms of accumulation of wealth to a modern system which separated value from the laborer in the form of capital (disembodied labor). Capitalist production smashed all previous forms of social life and in the ensuing search for profits polarized reciprocal relations. Also the meaning of exchange differed between capitalist and worker. For the worker it meant the expropriation of labor. For the capitalist it meant higher profits. To "expropriate the expropriator" meant initiating a transformation which would eliminate capitalists. The meaning of exchange would be socialized, private property abolished, and equality promoted. The Marxian analysis concentrated on the dynamic study of capitalism as a system of exchange and meaning. Marx did not devote a great deal of attention to what society would look like under socialism.[9]

Durkheim—Organic society: Durkheim and Weber were also interested in the transformations occurring within modern industrial society. Durkheim believed that norms would be endangered by an excessive division of labor. He too sketched out a kind of socialist solution, dividing the functions of society into two types of equilibrium. Pre-

8. See Raymond Aron, *Main Currents in Sociological Thought* (New York: Basic Books, 1967), pp. 179–252.
9. For appropriate reading on socialism see Karl Marx, *The Critique of the Gotha Program* (Moscow: Cooperative Publishing Society, 1937). See also Karl Marx, "The Civil War in France," and Frederick Engels, "On Authority," in Marx and Engels, *Selected Works,* Vol. 1 (Moscow: Foreign Languages Publishing House, 1962), pp. 473–98, 636–39; and Karl Marx and Frederick Engels, *The Communist Manifesto* (Moscow: Foreign Languages Publishing House, 1962), pp. 25–65.

industrial society he called "mechanical." In mechanical societies individuals performed similar roles: fathers, husbandmen, hunters, priests,
and so on. All such roles, or functions, were handed down from generation to generation with as little change as possible. In contrast, modern
society was "organic," the product of a division of labor and the differentiation produced by industrial processes. Organic society is innovative
and complex. Religion pervaded all aspects of life in the first society, but
its place became more restricted in the second.

If there is one truth that history teaches us beyond doubt, it is that
religion tends to embrace a smaller and smaller portion of social life.
Originally, it pervades everything; everything social is religious; the two
words are synonymous. Then, little by little, political, economic, sci-
entific functions free themselves from the religious function, con-
stitute themselves apart and take on a more acknowledged temporal
character.[10]

Durkheim sees social life as organic, with all the parts interacting
as a compensatory system. In an organic system, as religion declines, for
example, other beliefs must replace it. Otherwise, instability would
arise as various functions were not performed. Thus, for example, if
the function of religion were not replaced by, say, ideology, then the
solidarity of the society which religion once promoted would decline.

Suicide. Durkheim began as a hard-nosed empirical sociologist. He arrived at his notions about the importance of religion in social life after
studying suicide. Why, he asked, do people destroy themselves? Why is it
that in some societies people are more prone to suicide than in others?
From a sample of eleven European countries, a rank ordering of suicide
rates consistently showed that certain populations tended to register
higher suicide rates than others. From such data Durkheim established
a typology of suicide. He related it to sex, insanity, religion, idiocy,
alcoholism, race, age, region, climate, and other factors. However, no
one correlation appeared to be particularly critical; some who commit
suicide are rich, others poor, some are this, some are that. Durkheim
concluded that suicide is a *social* phenomenon which must be explained
sociologically.[11] But what is a sociological explanation? A structural
ordering. According to Durkheim:

10. Emile Durkheim, *The Division of Labor* (Glencoe, Ill.: The Free Press, 1933),
p. 169. See also Steven Lukes, *Emile Durkheim, His Life and Work* (New York:
Harper & Row, 1972).
11. See Emile Durkheim, *Suicide* (Glencoe, Ill.: The Free Press, 1951), p. 299.

Each social group really has a collective inclination for the act, quite its own, and the source of all individual inclination, rather than their result. It is made up of the currents of egoism, altruism or anomie running through the society under consideration with the tendencies to languorous melancholy, active renunciation or exasperated weariness derivative from these currents. These tendencies of the whole social body, by affecting individuals, cause them to commit suicide.[12]

One might ask, what has Durkheim's preoccupation with suicide got to do with structuralism? The answer is this: Durkheim's first concern was to explain a puzzling bit of behavior, the willful self-destruction of individuals. Second, using a method that was empirical and behavioral (although statistics were primitive), he discovered that his correlations lacked depth, substance, and explanatory power. Third, he began to search for societal patterns that seemed to favor suicide (and of different types such as altruistic and egotistic) in belief systems or a society's collective morality—that is, its set of shared values. These moral and collective factors, Durkheim concluded, were the determinants of suicide.

The discovery persuaded Durkheim to concentrate an investigation on the relations between the social structure of group life and the moral or collective conscience among members. This collective conscience represents the *normative*. Durkheim studied primitive societies and contrasted them with modern society. He found that in ancient kingdoms, to transgress the law was to transgress the community. To be discovered in an adulterous relationship, for example, might be punished by being excluded from community life, or left to perish in some dangerous place, or stoned to death. The outrage of the entire community would be focused on the crime. In modern societies, in contrast, most crimes can be atoned for by completing a sentence in jail, or by compensating a victim for some ill. One kind of law was repressive, the other restitutive. Repressive law, the law of public vengeance against wrong-doers, does not fit with modern society.

In two important works, *The Division of Labor in Society* and *The Elementary Forms of Religious Life*,[13] Durkheim relates the characteristics of exchange to the characteristics of belief. In the first vol-

---

12. Ibid., pp. 299–300.
13. See Emile Durkheim, *The Division of Labor in Society* (Glencoe, Ill.: The Free Press, 1949); *The Elementary Forms of Religious Life* (London: Allen & Unwin Ltd., 1957).

ume he shows the effects of growth, differentiation, and complexity on human society. These transform preindustrial societies based on mechanical solidarity—imitation and similarity—to modern industrial societies with an organic solidarity and all the interconnections based on the differentiation of specialized functional activities. The political problem is that as the division of labor expands, the collective conscience becomes weaker and the moral side of life progressively indeterminate. What holds society together is the complexity of the division of labor itself.[14]

Anomie. This weakness of conscience produces the danger of "anomie," or loss of moral meanings. Therefore, although the division of labor in modern society goes hand in hand with individualization, freedom, and personal autonomy, such progress also separates and isolates people from each other.[15]

Government must check this dissolving character of the division of labor and assert the common sentiments of solidarity. The job of government is to maintain society as its parts become morally separated as a result of increasing specialization. As collective sentiments become more and more impotent, society is in danger of anarchy. One way out is through socialism. As the conditions of exchange are equalized, so there is less conflict and more mutual cooperation and benefit. And because everything that is a source of solidarity is moral (the greater the exchange, the more mutualism in it), the individual becomes "cognizant of his dependence upon society; from it come the forces which keep him in check and restrain him. In short, since the division of labor becomes the chief source of social solidarity, it becomes, at the same time, the foundation of the moral order."[16] The division of labor, then, leads to exchanges which in turn become the basis for the moral order itself.

For Durkheim the problem is stated as individualism versus socialism. Durkheim did not favor the socialism of Marx, but an organizational socialism or form of collective consciousness. He propounded a form of "normative socialism," under which equality, planning, and the organization of economic activities would offset the individualizing effects of the division of labor.

For Durkheim, "the generality of men" must be "content with

14. Durkheim, *The Division of Labor in Society,* p. 283.
15. Ibid., p. 356.
16. Ibid., p. 401.

their lot." It is not necessary that they have more or less, "but that they be convinced that they do not have the right to have more. And for this to be, it is absolutely necessary that there be an authority whose superiority they acknowledge, and which lays down the law. For never will the individual left to the pressure of his needs acknowledge that he has reached the extreme limit of his right."[17]

Durkheim sees the re-establishment of the moral order as a condition of social order. Socialism purports to be a way to accomplish that —to put sense at the center of things. The emphasis on change defines the theoretical task. Durkheim's work assesses the effects of development on the social organism, but Durkheim was not a simple evolutionist. The evolutionists, like Herbert Spencer, were very different from Durkheim. They saw social life as a series of stages in which history was *progress*. Spencer and others also saw that the division of labor produced specialization even among political functions.

The differentiation of the regulating part and the regulated part, is, in small primitive societies, not only imperfectly established, but vague. The chief does not at first become unlike his fellow savages in his functions, otherwise than by exercising greater sway. He hunts, makes his weapons, works, and manages his private affairs, in just the same ways as the rest; while in war he differs from other warriors only by his predominant influence, not by ceasing to be a private soldier. And along with this slight separation from the rest of the tribe in military functions and industrial functions, there is only a slight separation politically: judicial action is but very feebly represented by exercise of his personal authority in keeping order.

At a higher stage, the power of the chief being well established, he no longer supports himself.[18]

This evolutionist idea of progress in the form of stages from lower to higher is *unilinear*, as is the idea of the specialization of political functions. It was common in the nineteenth century. Spencer, for example, believed that society, although initially savage or primitive, surpassed that stage. Other evolutionists, like Henry Sumner Maine, contrasted "primitive" obligations based on status, the bonds and security of family obligation, and the extended family with its network of kinship to the impersonal contractual relations among individuals in

17. Quoted in Aron, op. cit., p. 81.
18. See Herbert Spencer, *The Study of Sociology* (Ann Arbor, Mich.: University of Michigan Press, 1961), p. 55.

modern society. He emphasized the change in focus from the family as the corporate unit of which societies are composed in a primitive state, to the individual, whom he saw as the essential political unit in the modern state. His concern was with both the anthropology of law and authority and the corporate, or structural basis of social life.[19]

Weber—Traditional versus modern societies: In contrast to such evolutionist theoreticians, pre-structuralists pointed out the distinction between the intimate, traditionalistic, change-resistant pattern of pre-industrial life and the more impersonal, innovative, change-prone character of modern life (as exemplified in such ideal type distinctions as the *Gemeinschaft,* or community form of life, and the *Gesellschaft,* or more impersonal and business-based, or corporate, form of life). But this contrast they did not define as "progress." The pre-structuralists also wanted to determine how change affected the way people invest social life with purpose. Durkheim had been afraid that too much differentiation, and its concomitant specialization, would lead to anomie, a loss of meaning or a falling off of moral principle, apathy, and moral disintegration. Max Weber had a more positive view. He wondered how it was that capitalism first arose in the nineteenth century when the requisite conditions for it seemed to have been available in many parts of the world and at different times in history. His answer was that the particular values and norms of Calvinism were realized extremely well in economically oriented action. The two ideas were mutually reinforcing. Through Calvinism and Puritanism the "moral conduct of the average man was thus deprived of its planless and unsystematic character and subjected to a consistent method for conduct as a whole."[20]

Weber tried to show how certain ideas manifested in Calvinism helped to produce that form of motivation which resulted in hard work, which in the form of economic activity produced capitalism.[21] He compared this quality of Protestantism with the mandates of Mandarinism in ancient China, Brahmanism in India, and the priesthood of ancient Israel, to show how each of these produced a different set of objectives and motivations. He also showed, following Marx, how the transforming manifold of capitalism produced new forms of

19. See Henry Sumner Maine, *Ancient Law* (Boston: Beacon Press, 1973).
20. Max Weber, *The Protestant Ethic and the Spirit of Capitalism* (New York: Scribner's, 1958), p. 117. See also his *Religion of China, Ancient Judaism* and *The Religion of India* (Glencoe, Ill.: The Free Press, 1951, 1952, and 1958).
21. See Max Weber, *The Theory of Social and Economic Organization* (London: William Hodge, 1947).

social organization, new ideal types of behavior, and particularly bureaucracy as the special form of modern capitalist activity. All affected the modes by which power was exercised. Weber distinguished three different forms of power: traditional and patrimonial, rational and legal, and charismatic. As contradictions occur between types of societies, charismatic or near charismatic leaders arise as prophets of populist mass movements, idealized by their following. Charisma serves as an engaging theoretical focus showing how a transitional form of authority interposes between traditional forms of the past and the new legal-rational system of modernity.[22]

Weber also connected ideal types and comparative methods and tried to define how social analysis differed from that of the natural sciences. Unlike Durkheim, who emphasized that social facts required social explanations of a functional nature (rather than, say, psychological ones), Weber reflected on the relationship between the conditions of existence and the types of experience by means of what has been called *Verstehen* (literally, "empathetic understanding"), an "interpretive method" or an "existential psychology." The concept of *Verstehen* proposes the capacity of the observer to penetrate the state of mind of those being observed and comprehend the logic of their thinking as well as their attitudes. The observer should examine social processes objectively, stripping out his or her own value preferences. Weber's science was as determinedly value free as it could be made. Objectivity was as important as in any scientific enterprise.[23]

The politics of change: Durkheim and Weber were among those scholars concerned with *change* rather than *progress* (as were Darwin, Spencer, and Maine). Changes were from the antique to the modern, the heavenly to the earthly, the sacred to the secular, social to individual obligation. The pre-structuralists were also aware of the psychic costs of such change. In the preindustrial community blood ties, neighborhood, and friendship count. There life is cooperative. But in modern society, the *Gesellschaft,* on the contrary, relationships are contractual. Business life is competitive. The two perspectives may endure if some people remain rooted in the folk basis of community, while others separate from it. Leaders who speak for the people, the *Volk,* regard themselves as representatives of the mystic racial bonds of the past, however, and can manipulate this nostalgia (as Italian Fascist and

22. Ibid.
23. Max Weber, *The Methodology of the Social Sciences* (Glencoe, Ill., The Free Press, 1949).

German Nazi leaders have done, for example) . The *Volk* tend to regard capitalists as entrepreneurs loyal only to their own self-advancement and alienated from their past. The pre-structuralists were aware of the negative quality of capitalistic middle-class society. Their theories touched the roots of fascism long before fascism became a doctrine.[24]

The *Gesellschaft* is the opposite of the tribal or medieval community. The modern corporation exemplifies its qualities and character. In such organizations individuals are independent, competitive, and engaged primarily in exchange.

In the conception of Gesellschaft, the original or natural relations of human beings to each other must be excluded. The possibility of a relation in the Gesellschaft assumes no more than a multitude of mere persons who are capable of delivering something, and consequently of promising something. Gesellschaft as a totality to which a system of conventional rules applies is limitless; it constantly breaks through its chance and real boundaries. In Gesellschaft every person strives for that which is to his own advantage and he affirms the actions of others only in so far as and as long as they can further his interest.[25]

Notice that what is threatened is the moral definition of the basis of obligation—to heaven, to the holy, to the community, to common sentiment. Weber showed how the *Gesellschaft* was basically organized around legal-rational authority, while the *Gemeinschaft* was organized around the principle of traditional authority—that is, authority memorialized in antique practice.

The typological interpretations of the pre-structuralists, then, were designed to explore what happened when modernity impinged on traditionality. Traditional systems organized around kinship, the *Gemeinschaft,* represented a mechanical solidarity. Modern societies organized around contract, voluntarism, and the division of labor produced an organic solidarity, the *Gesellschaft* (for which the prototype was the modern corporation with its rational emphasis). Such typological structuralism is particularly useful in historical study. For example, it provokes such questions as these: Why did capitalism arise? What form of mixture between one type of society and another is viable? What are the effects of the mixture in terms of peaceful change,

---

24. See Ferdinand Toennies, *Community and Society* (New York: Harper & Row, 1957) .
25. Ibid., p. 77.

class formations, ideologies, and the formation of modern parties, legislatures, parliaments, and so forth? When does "Caesarism" arise or the society fall under the influence of charismatic leadership? Does it make a difference whether a society is Catholic or Protestant? Typological distinctions help make history systematic, suggest comparisons— between past and present, preindustrial and industrial—and invite ethnographic and field studies of primitive societies as compared with contemporary ones.

Functionalism

With the exception of Marx, the pre-structuralists were concerned with change rather than transformation or progress. Some tried to examine the role of particular groups by explaining the rise of capitalism.[26] Others were particularly troubled by the prospects of socialism. Some tried to apply economic theory to societal structure.[27] Still others applied structural principles to political parties and bureaucracies.[28] Case studies were produced of countries which showed a mixture of preindustrial and industrial qualities within an autocratic political framework.[29] Typologies were used for making comparisons between one phase and another.

The step from structural type to function is not very great. Functions rather than types facilitate the comparison of diverse kinds of systems (a way of comparing apples and pears). A model adapted from the natural sciences, functionalism accepts the "organismic" analogy— that a social or political unit will have certain adaptive qualities—in contrast to a cybernetic or mechanistic analogy. (Since machines are inert, it takes an external intelligence and power to activate them.) Living organisms inherently possess organismic properties, including the capacity to reproduce themselves, the capacity to perceive and learn, and the capacity to adapt and adjust to new circumstances or

26. See Werner Sombart, *The Jews and Modern Capitalism* (Glencoe, Ill.: The Free Press, 1951).
27. See Vilfredo Pareto, *Manual of Political Economy* (New York: Augustus Kelley, 1971). See also Sammy Finer, *Vilfredo Pareto, Sociological Writings* (London: Pall Mall, 1966).
28. See Robert Michels, *Political Parties* (Glencoe, Ill.: The Free Press, 1958). See also Moisei Ostrogorski, *Democracy and the Organization of Political Parties* (New York: Doubleday, Anchor Books, 1964).
29. See Anatole Leroy-Beaulieu, *The Empire of the Tsars and the Russians,* 3 Vols. (New York: Putnam's, 1893).

changes in the environment.[30] The functional analysis of politics begins by assuming that these properties which inhere in human beings have their counterparts in communities. Societies reproduce themselves. They perceive and learn. They can, within limits, adapt to problems. Societies also adjust to change by means of collective problem solving. They have a built-in tendency toward integrating collective symbols, language, and beliefs into the system to assert coherence, just as individuals have a built-in tendency toward speech. So we may say that functionalism begins with *system*. It is not a method of classification, but a system of ingredients.

A.R. Radcliffe-Brown summarizes the difference between class types and system as follows:[31]

Class	*System*
Relations simple	Relations complex
Relations of similarity	Relations of interconnectedness
Mathematical relations	Spatio-temporal relations
Without form	Characteristic form
No quality of integration—coordinated by similarity	Integrated—coordinated by interdependence
Members may be separated without violation to them	Units violated in separation
Members may be moved about without violence to them or to their class	Units may not be moved about without violence to them or to the system
No cohesion between members of a class	Units cohere and thereby isolate the system from the rest of the universe
No functional relationship between members	Functional consistency
An aggregate	A genuine whole, having a structure
The sum of its parts (members)	Organic unity; not the sum of its constituent units

30. For a useful and easily comprehensible discussion see Roy E. Jones, *The Functional Analysis of Politics* (London: Routledge and Kegan Paul, 1967).
31. See A.R. Radcliffe-Brown, *A Natural Science of Society* (Glencoe, Ill.: The Free Press, 1957), p. 22.

The first category, *Class,* comprises aggregates identified on the basis of certain traits and characteristics, while the second category, *System,* constitutes relationships of properties. Functional analysis may begin with classification as a preliminary exercise, but the idea of system is necessary in order to locate and identify functions—a process of abstraction showing *necessary* relationships within systems.

The politics of process: The functionalists were less concerned with history than with the composition of different societies, their needs, and the structures that satisfied those needs. Functionalism begins with these questions: What are common needs in all societies? How are these needs satisfied in different societies? The emphasis is both *synchronic* and *comparative.*

Bronislaw Malinowski: Ethnography. Perhaps the simplest way to show how functionalism became a specific device for the analysis of systems (other than those of Western industrial society) is to trace the progress of an ethnographer at work. Bronislaw Malinowski was a Polish anthropologist who was well trained in mathematics and physics and skilled in languages. He was interested in psychology, linguistics, and anthropology. Studying Australian aborigines, he was particularly anxious to discover the "structure" which made comprehensible their patterns of marriage, descent, and organization.

This structure was the kinship system, which established the rules of descent, marriage, and inheritance that were followed by the people. From 1915 to 1918, while World War I raged in Europe, Malinowski was marooned in the Trobriand Islands. He thus had plenty of time to catalogue the behavior of the islanders, what they believed, and how their beliefs affected their work (which was primarily gardening). But such exotic people were about as different from a Polish intellectual as anyone could be. How indeed could Malinowski make sense of their world?

Malinowski, much influenced by Durkheim, sought to establish universal categories by which to identify the activities of the Trobriand Islanders. First he observed their actual behavior. Then he asked what the behavior revealed. Much was familiar—the gathering of foodstuffs, gardening, weeding, storage of crops, harvesting—after all, everyone must eat. But soon these ordinary activities began to yield symbolic meanings. Each person cultivated in much the same way, without variation. The rules governing when and how to cultivate were fixed, based

on the need to ensure a ready food supply for all during the unproduc-
tive seasons. Biological regularities also revealed much about the belief
systems of the Islanders. As some people died and others were born,
Malinowski observed the society's manner of conducting inheritance,
the assignment of tasks, the mode of educating (and socializing) the
children. A "structure" of land tenure represented the fundamental
character of exchange. This provided the basis of many of the systematic
rules whereby activities were performed.

But Malinowski discovered too that behavior was never completely
defined by tasks. One can weed a garden in several ways. Why do it one
way instead of another? Gradually Malinowski observed that the acts
themselves were complex. Their meanings implied more than just the
results of the activities performed. Magic and ritual attached to the
harvest, for example, and to marriage and other institutions. To understand these one had to discover their meaning from the standpoint of
the interconnectedness of social life and activities. Any concrete unit
performed many functions.

The family, however, is not merely a group where agricultural produce
is consumed. It is also a productive unit. And here again the law of mar-
riage affects land tenure profoundly. Land tenure vests the title to land
in the father of the family. He is the citizen of the local group, the mem-
ber of the sub-clan, and as such has the fundamental right to cultivate
soil. The law of marriage joins his wife to him. By marriage she ac-
quires the right to assist him in garden work—a right which is also a
duty; and she acquires a claim to part of the joint produce. In a way
the claims to land of a woman resident by marriage are as firm and un-
questionable as those of her husband. They are less fundamental be-
cause they depend on the contract of marriage which, in the Trobriands,
can be dissolved by divorce.[32]

Malinowski projected beyond the observation of familiar concrete
behavior to the connections among relevant membership groups on the
basis of functions. Once he was able to describe more fundamental
structures, he showed how families embodied much more than their
mere ostensible activities. From such observations Malinowski formed
abstract categories which, put together in a general scheme, became a
theory of culture change, a "functional theory of culture." He established a sequence for change from the original culture, or "zero point,"

32. See Bronislaw Malinowski, *Coral Gardens and Their Magic,* Vol. 1 (London:
Allen and Unwin, 1935), p. 354.

to the impact of innovation under colonialism. Innovative influences, interests, and intentions had their impact on the traditional culture. Under the resulting cross-cultural contact, surviving forms of tradition, the reconstructed past, and new forces of spontaneous reintegration all acceded to generalized patterns.[33]

Using Malinowski's structural categories, an observer can generate hypotheses about the rate, direction, and conditions of cultural change. He or she can collect data in each of the categories that will lead to the identification of concrete structures—those carrying European influences, perhaps. The categories form columns within which specific agencies or organized bodies can be placed (for example, administrative, missionary, entrepreneur, or settler). Criteria for evaluation include the degree of "autonomism" of each phase, the "relatedness" of each phase, "asymmetry," "multiplicity," and the presence or absence of "common factors" and "new Nationalisms."[34]

The way Malinowski worked is quite instructive for understanding modern structuralism. Beginning with detailed observation, Malinowski generalized observations into functional categories that linked concrete activities. Then he organized functions into structures. These structures inspired a method for creating a sequence of change. They represented boxes to be filled in with relevant data.

Malinowski's work has been roundly criticized as being too simple. Nevertheless, he tried to be scientific. He developed a specific research procedure based on a functional method. He also showed how structuralism helps one understand what goes on in unfamiliar or exotic societies. Functionalism offers important advantages as a research strategy, even despite failings it may have, especially where not much is known or understood about a society.

Class analysis and comparative history: Malinowski's work represents one example of how structuralism can be applied as a method to a field situation. His form of structuralism had a great many faults; for one thing, it assumed that every function fulfilled a need. Malinowski did not recognize that sometimes in the fulfillment of one need, another was offended—that is, that functions could be malintegrative as well as integrative. His was a form of *naive* functionalism; nevertheless, it shows some of the basic characteristics of modern structural methodology—the

---

33. See Bronislaw Malinowski, *The Dynamics of Culture Change* (New Haven, Conn.: Yale University Press, 1945), p. 73.
34. Ibid., pp. 74–75.

application of universal functional categories to intensive field studies of exotic societies. It represents a method of equilibrium.

We turn now to a case of conflict analysis based on the method of contradictions and using class as the unit for historical comparison. We will illustrate the contrast from the work of Barrington Moore.[35]

Barrington Moore: Conflict Analysis. Moore is interested in a question rather like the one which preoccupied Max Weber. (Remember that Weber tried to place the origin of modern capitalism in religious pietism and Calvinism.) Moore's is a political query: Why did England become a free society under the impact of industrialization while other countries did not? Using a sample of six societies, Moore was interested in finding how exchange, in the form of commercial activity and patterns of trade, creates functional classes. In each case he isolated a strategic reciprocal relationship prevailing between lord and peasant. The structural question was whether, and to what extent, both were absorbed into a growing middle class.

England was a case of early transformation. Commercial stimulation, the wool trade, and the growth of urban trading centers ripped apart the feudal system as early as the fifteenth century, long before the English civil war. Commercialism grew up in opposition to the crown. The Enclosure Acts stimulated urban crowding and created a labor force simultaneously with the growth of a commercial agriculture, giving rise to agrarian capitalism. English society broke apart from the top downward. When the English civil war, the Glorious Revolution, occurred it took the form of a political revolution. Parliamentary democracy went hand in hand with the growth of rural capitalism.

New technology and other innovations made it possible for the commercial and laboring classes in England to replace gentry and peasant. The gentry used the parliamentary system to retain power but accommodated to the need for reform. No matter how reluctantly, they became a responsible aristocracy, standing out of the way of the rising commercial and industrial bourgeoisie. Changes in exchange relations occurred in a context of expanding opportunity, not at the expense of any single class. The nobility came to represent an ideal of civic responsibility whose power was shared with less aristocratic classes.

In France, on the other hand, kingship and nobility reinforced each other by exploiting the peasantry. Any attack on exchange relations

35. See Barrington Moore, Jr., *Social Origins of Dictatorship and Democracy* (Boston: Beacon Press, 1966).

and the nobility as a class was equivalent to an attack on the king. The economic system of mercantilism meant economic control by a monarchy hostile to capitalism. Innovation arose not through an entrepreneurial class but as a function of state enterprise. The crown restricted what it could not control. Under these circumstances, to emerge in its own right as a class the bourgeoisie had to attack the crown, which they did. The large patrimonial estates were subdivided; then, to make smaller farms pay, the nobility squeezed the peasants mercilessly. Sharecropping increased, and tenant farming produced a "rural proletariat." Then when the bourgeoisie demanded free trade in response to this impetus, they were opposed by the large, relatively impoverished nobility. The bourgeoisie joined forces with the peasantry against the landed aristocrats. The French Revolution became the transforming event. It was more a peasant revolution than a bourgeois one. It resulted in the consolidation of a small, rural capitalist class which eliminated the feudal nobility. But it did not foster industrialization. The result was the formation of a society somewhere between rural capitalism and urban financial industrialism. The factions remained hostile and were unable to resolve their differences.

Moore compares these two European situations—England and France—with China, India, and Japan. The Chinese class relationships were based on a three-fold class structure made up of the landed aristocracy, the peasantry, and a bureaucratic class. All were intersected by the family system. Landlord and officials worked together, the former dependent on the bureaucracy to guarantee property rights and enforce the collection of rents from tenant families. In turn, the bureaucracy carried on imperial projects such as public works, irrigation, and so forth. As a consequence the bureaucrats became corrupt as landlords manipulated the monarchy (which represented the mandate of heaven on earth). The Confucian religious system taught deference to family, landlord, and bureaucrat, and therefore, while not a feudal system, the Chinese family subsistence economy offered few incentives to a commercial agriculture. Moreover, landlords were more difficult to eliminate than a feudal nobility and, in the late nineteenth century as the imperial system declined, landlords turned into warlords and bandits. The Kuomintang (founded in 1912) attempted to establish a commercial system, but failed. The society continued to rely on a centralized bureaucracy, hoping that infused Christian ideals would supplement Confucianism with the right innovative values. However, the result was not at all what was intended; eventually the peasantry became radicalized and overturned the entire structure.

In India, on the other hand, after the decline of the Mogul Empire around 1857, the pattern of revolt against British domination took the form of an alliance between a British-educated commercial and administrative elite and the local villages under a doctrine of "villagism" glorified by Gandhi.

The bourgeois revolution in England resulted in democracy. The rural conservative revolution led to fascism. Peasant revolutions led to communism in Russia and China. An independent nobility, which would have helped stimulate the growth of democracy was absent in India and Manchu China. So was a vigorous and independent class of town dwellers. Conversely, a fusing of labor-repressive agriculture with links to a central authority created, or rather reinforced, a military ethic among the nobility like that which distinguishes the Samurai class in Japan. We can see that no peasant revolution can occur without a peasantry being linked to other strata or classes.

We can not include all of Moore's cases. Those we have discussed show how he establishes structural variables derived from exchange interactions embodied in class relationships. Such variables lead some societies toward democracy and others toward totalitarianism. Moore singles out key aspects of exchange which determine certain fundamental structural characteristics of preindustrial societies. These, in turn, determine the resulting historical political evolution. Variables include the way in which the mobilization of capital occurs, the degree of political access of the mobilized class, the decline of the nobility, and the absorption of the peasantry. How these variables cluster determines which specific historical alternative options occur.

The study combines the traditions of Marx and Weber. Moore examines England, France, America, China, Japan, and India within a common structural framework. And Moore's findings were that the experiences of all six countries represent three broad, structural transformation patterns of politics: (1) the bourgeois revolution culminates in Western democracy; (2) the conservative revolution ends in fascism; (3) the peasant revolution leads to communism. A theoretical conclusion identifies four independent variables: the persistence of royal absolutism (or, "more generally, of a preindustrial bureaucratic rule into modern time"), the reduction of absolutism by a nobility independent of royal power, the necessity for a vigorous and independent class of town dwellers, and the emergence of commercial agriculture.[36]

36. Ibid., pp. 417, 418.

Moore's "promontories," or sets of revolutionary transformations, are affected by the character of society, the character of classes, and exchanges—from peasant to commercial and agricultural, from pre-capitalist to capitalist and socialist, from monarchical and feudal to democratic or totalitarian systems. Within these broad transforming types, Moore sketches out the way classes, commercialization, a bureaucracy, a system of land tenure, and other factors all fit together to produce both an evolutionary or historical picture and a comparative one. For Moore, history unfolds not as a series of events, but as a flux of growth and denial in various relationships. The exchange relationships are networks of classes.

Malinowski's description of the ethnography of the case builds an elaborate framework involving a functional theory of observed needs. Moore's emphasis is on the structure of historical process.

The works of Malinowski and Moore exemplify simple functional and structural forms of analysis, although, as we have said, Malinowski represents a "naive" functionalism, while from a structuralist point of view Moore suffers from two defects: his independent variables are not abstract (or "systematic"), but historical, and they neither link directly to exchange processes nor follow from a single or overriding principle such as a class struggle or the transformation of classes according to some *necessary and sufficient* set of causes. Nevertheless, Moore's work is full of fascinating insights even if it is not a purist's ideal of applied structuralism.

Structural Functionalism

Structuralism can consider politics from the standpoint of changes in the organization of *order*. This represents a concern with politics at its broadest. If the method of contradiction is concerned with polarities— conflict versus adaptation, revolution versus bureaucratization, and democracy versus alienation—the method of equilibrium implies that if needs are not met, a society will die. If certain fundamentals are disregarded or handled inappropriately, society will change.

Structural functionalism is different from the descriptive functionalism of Malinowski. Developed in the 1940s and 50s by Talcott Parsons and others influenced by Durkheim, Weber, and Pareto, structural functionalism sought to incorporate behavioralism within an *action scheme*. Action is motivated, and behavior is determined by combinations of structural relationships. But motivated behavior determines structure. The two are reciprocal.

Parsons identified three levels of analysis, each of which has "framing" or limiting characteristics for the others, and is a function of the others as well. One is *culture,* or learned symbols, beliefs, and value orientations. A second is *social system,* or the interrelationships of action based on networks of roles. The third is the structure of the *personality,* its needs and gratifications. Each of these structures is analytically abstracted from the world of the acting individual: personality represents perceptions and motivation; social systems represent the universe of relationships; culture represents the universe of public meanings and symbols.[37]

Pattern variables: Culture, personality, and social system are all expressed in terms of the same set of contrasting *modes.* The five commonly accepted modes, or paired variables, are as follows:

1. *Affectivity or affective neutrality.* This refers to whether or not an impulse should be gratified or disciplined.
2. *Self-orientation or collectivity orientation.* This refers to whether private or collective interests are dominant.
3. *Universalism or particularism.* This refers to the norm governing relationships—whether or not these transcend any particular relationships or characteristics. [I may give my brother a job because he is the best qualified for it (universalism), or because he stands in a blood relationship to me (particularism).]
4. *Ascription or achievement.* This refers to whether or not norms should prevail based upon specific qualities related to either the situation or ascription, a condition of status.
5. *Specificity or diffuseness.* This refers to the kind of relationships or obligations contained in a role, that is, whether it should be a narrowly prescribed one, such as might pertain to priests and their parishioners or fathers and their children, or a more broadly based one.

These five pattern variables constitute alternatives among systems. They "formulate five fundamental choices which must be made by a [political] actor when he is confronted with a situation."[38]

37. See Talcott Parsons, *The Social System* (Glencoe: The Free Press of Glencoe, 1951), pp. 4–23. See also Talcott Parsons and Edward Shils, eds., *Toward a General Theory of Action* (Cambridge: Harvard University Press, 1951), p. 81.
38. Parsons and Shils, ibid., pp. 76–91.

Movement from one side of the pair to the other constitutes a change in culture, social system, and personality—a transformation made through adaptive changes in other pattern variables operating within the personality system, the social system, or culture. The five fit together. If recruitment to roles in a social system is based on achievement, then the personality will be motivated toward gratifying needs by achieving the cultural norm through one's own accomplishments rather than connections. In turn, the social system will provide opportunities for competitive action via a reward system, like that based on one's grades in school and scores on achievement examinations. This system will provide for the recruitment of high achievers according to standardized and accepted measures. Achievement and competition also will be built into functionally significant public roles. The place of activities based on ascription will be very limited, mainly because families are organized not on the basis of achievement but ascription. The obligations of children to parents, and vice versa, and other familial bonds are defined in terms of kinship, obligational affection, and mutual support rather than competition.

If familial norms of ascription extend to achievement-based institutions and cultural values, then trouble ensues. (An example of such an extension is the system of political nepotism.) Mixing ascriptive criteria with achievement criteria in a culture may produce corruption. A society divided on all three levels—culture, personality, and social system—will experience disorder. Then if equilibrium is lost, government must step in to maintain the functioning of the system.

Every society has a set of *functional imperatives*—that is, minimal functions on which order rests. These include *adaptability,* with a degree of accommodation or ability to see the world "realistically"; *goal gratification,* or the ability to satisfy the needs of the members; *integrative* functions which mediate between the opposite tensions of the pattern variables; and, finally, what Parsons calls *latent pattern maintenance,* or the capacity of a society for self-renewal. These four functions are jeopardized when the equilibrium of the system is upset. The job of the polity or political subsystem is to guarantee that the system is in working (functional) order. For example, a breakdown in the economy due to inflation impairs the adaptive function of the system; if goal gratification is jeopardized, the polity directs its efforts to restoring the goals of society.[39]

39. See Talcott Parsons, Robert F. Bales, and Edward Shils, *Working Papers in the Theory of Action* (Glencoe, Ill.: The Free Press, 1953), pp. 179–264.

To use structural-functional analysis properly, one first needs to follow the rules. Beginning with the most generalized unit (a whole society), one must explain the determinants of action. Only when the limits of explanation have been exhausted at the general level does one proceed to subunits. Second, since the emphasis is on balance—the maintenance of equilibrium of the system and its parts according to the criteria of the functional imperatives—an examination can often best be achieved by detailing what is *out* of balance. Hence equilibrium theory is actually process related; it deals with the politics of change. Adaptations of the theory and applications to politics have been attempted, the most notable being those based on comparative cases evaluated according to the pattern variables and the functional imperatives.[40]

In theory, a condition of *congruence* exists in society if and when culture, personality, and social system are normatively and structurally "fitted" so that the pattern variables are congenial. For example, *affectivity,* or feelings of love, should be expressed to one's family but not to one's job. It does not take much imagination to figure out that if this link is reversed, so that affectivity is attached to the work group and not to the family, strain results. High affectivity in politics takes the form of absolute loyalty to party leaders, such as occurs with the rise of a charismatic leader. Followers suspend their ordinary judgment when the appeal of such a leader is perfectly congruent with other social, cultural, and political imperatives. (Such a congruence existed in China in 1934 when people were willing to take their families and follow Mao Tse-tung on the Long March to Yunan.) Then political loyalty becomes the emotional center of life. Society takes priority over private affairs, and the state over the family. One's self-orientation may be submerged in favor of a *collectivity orientation.* A militant communist elect, or a vanguard party, encourages precisely such boundless loyalty, an orientation which provokes some interesting questions. If collectivity orientation is associated primarily with primitive societies or feudal ones, can it be revised under and applied to modern socialism?

To summarize: Incongruous distribution of the pattern variables in society, the functional imperatives, and the three framing dimensions—culture, personality, and social system—has political implications. Inasmuch as such incongruities produce disequilibrium and disorder, government must step into the breach. Without such intervention the in-

40. See Robert I. Holt and John E. Turner, *The Political Basis of Economic Development* (Princeton, N.J.: Van Nostrand, 1966). See also William C. Mitchell, *The American Polity* (Glencoe, Ill.: The Free Press, 1962), and *Sociological Analysis and Politics* (Englewood Cliffs, N.J.: Prentice-Hall, 1967).

stitutionalization of the roles that compose the social system will be challenged, the values threatened, and behavioral motivations destroyed. In the extreme case, authority breaks down and society becomes fragmented and helpless.[41]

Efficiency: The *polity* is a functional subsystem of society that is equivalent to the economy. The polity is primarily concerned with the pursuit of collective goals. How well it achieves its goals is a measure of its efficiency. Efficiency is for the polity what utility is for the economy. Choice is the central problem because there is no single or completely universal goal. The polity selects a particular goal at the expense of alternatives.

Government is a concrete subsystem of society that is responsible for ensuring efficiency and making selections among goals. It has the legitimated right to make decisions binding on a collectivity. To carry out decisions it exercises power, which is to the polity what money is to the economy. Power, to be effective, requires that those in authority (in government) be able to mobilize the members of society to realize collective goals. How power is exercised determines the organization of the polity—its degree of bureaucracy, participation, and leadership. How well the goals of the society are implemented determines stability. In turn, the polity interacts with the economy (the adaptive subsystem) to maintain cultural and motivational commitments (pattern maintenance) and reinforce legitimacy through the law and other institutions of social control (the integrative subsystem).

Operationalization begins with asking the following kinds of questions. What happens when norms change? When structures are modified? When behavior does not follow the patterns of institutionalization?[42]

There are many operational problems involved in the use of structural functionalism. Few categories can be quantified and validated or tested. Few tests reveal or demonstrate when functional imperatives are met (except in obvious cases of failure). There is no standardization of

41. See Talcott Parsons, *Structure and Process in Modern Societies* (Glencoe, Ill.: The Free Press, 1960), pp. 195–225. See also "The Political Aspect of Social Structure and Process," *Varieties of Political Theory,* ed. David Easton (Englewood Cliffs, N.J.: Prentice-Hall, 1966), pp. 71–112.
42. It has been argued that this form of functionalism contains a political bias favoring the status quo. However, this fault is neither inevitable nor intrinsic to the approach. It is possible to use this same form of analysis "radically" or "conservatively." See Robert K. Merton, *Social Theory and Social Structure* (Glencoe, Ill.: The Free Press, 1949), pp. 40–47.

functions, nor are the meanings of functions precise. The main value of the approach is to point out contradictions and "dysfunctions" which societies are likely to experience when undergoing change. The concept of structural functionalism provides a framework for handling contrasts.[43]

Parson's theory is extremely complex and we have only just touched upon it here. However, it has inspired a number of important theorists interested in the political aspects of social change, some of whom have tried to make Parson's scheme more amenable to empirical research. Some have been interested in the way economic and political processes create "boundary exchanges." Here the political emphasis is *integrative,* and the economic *innovative.*[44] Others have been concerned with the problem of culture first raised by Max Weber: the extent to which a change in religious beliefs affects the way economic and political innovations occur—that is, the effect of religion on political life and social order, and the implications for change.[45]

Still others have been more interested in the class and role relationships of structure, particularly in what Parsons called the "social system." Differentiating the organization of classes and roles and their changes has been a common concern of social analysts Seymour Martin Lipset, Robert Merton, Paul Lazersfeld, Wilbert Moore, and Juan Linz. Their investigations have primarily enlightened those interested in what is properly called *political sociology.*

Equilibrium Versus Contradiction

Requisites: Tracing the evolution of structuralism is difficult. Many structuralists simply regard themselves as proponents of modern behavioral theory. Most Marxists would take exception to the term. However, structural functionalists consider their approaches to differ fundamentally from those of the Marxists.

The "requisite form" of equilibrium analysis can be used to make structural analyses more operational and more deductive. This method

43. See William Flanagan and Edwin Fogelman, "Functional Analysis," *Contemporary Political Analysis,* ed. James C. Charlesworth (New York: The Free Press, 1967), pp. 72–85.
44. See Talcott Parsons and Neil J. Smelser, *Economy and Society* (London: Routledge and Kegan Paul, 1956).
45. See Robert N. Bellah, *Tokugawa Religion* (Glencoe, Ill.: The Free Press, 1957). See also Clifford Geertz, *The Religion of Java* (Glencoe, Ill.: The Free Press, 1960).

assumes that since a functional system is concerned with societal needs and their satisfaction, the functions indicate what is necessary for a unit to survive in its setting. Structures will indicate how such needs can be handled. The survival of societies, or their disappearance or absorption, constitutes a test of the society's viability. A requisite is any function or structure necessary to enable a unit to persist in its setting. Marion J. Levy has developed a set of *functional requisites* for society.[46]

1. Provision for an adequate physiological relationship to the setting and for sexual recruitment.
2. Role differentiation and role assignment.
3. Communication.
4. Shared cognitive orientations.
5. Shared articulated goals.
6. The regulation of the choice of means.
7. The regulation of affective expression.
8. Adequate socialization.
9. Effective control of disruptive behavior.
10. Adequate institutionalization.

Abstracting from the functional set provides a minimal set of *structural requisites*—that is, the means of handling the functional requisites of a society. It is this structural set that is employed for empirical analysis:

1. The structure of role differentiation.
2. The structure of solidarity.
3. The structure of economic allocation.
4. The structure of political allocation.
5. The structure of integration and expression.

These functions and structures are *requisites*. Designed for comparing many societies, or the same society over time, analysis proceeds through the examination of combinations of structural relationships, their contradictions and resolutions in the real world. The object is the discovery of recurrent combinations leading to adaptive survival behaviors.

As with Parsons' approach, the political element is relevant at two levels: societal and governmental. The structural requisites of society

46. See Marion J. Levy, Jr., *The Structure of Society* (Princeton, N.J.: Princeton University Press, 1952).

are performed under different empirical conditions (for example, in a preindustrial or industrial society). Analyzing the transition from one stage to the other points out contradictions identified by the requisites, contradictions which need to be handled by government. Meanwhile, the structure of political allocation refers specifically to how government uses its power to mediate change.

Requisite analysis directs attention to the unevenness of change and the difficulties of maintaining some of the requisites. It focuses on government, a concrete structural requisite of society. All societies must have some subgroup responsible for making authoritative decisions.

Motivations: A good way to compare the method of contradiction with the method of equilibrium is to compare conflict theory with structural functional analysis as suggested by Dahrendorf, who says that structural functionalists make the following assumptions:

1. Every society is a relatively persistent, stable structure of elements.

2. Every society is a well-integrated structure of elements.

3. Every element in a society has a function, i.e., renders a contribution to its maintenance as a system.

4. Every functioning social structure is based on a consensus of values among its members.[47]

In contrast, conflict theory depends on quite different assumptions:

1. Every society is at every point subject to processes of change; social change is ubiquitous.

2. Every society displays at every point dissensus and conflict; social conflict is ubiquitous.

3. Every society is based on the coercion of some of its members by others.[48]

47. See Ralf Dahrendorf, *Class and Class Conflict in an Industrial Society* (London: Routledge and Kegan Paul, 1959), p. 161. It might be noted that these points are similar to the notion of rationality in economic theory: they constitute a standard for comparison with real life, not a statement of how life is in reality. For every one of the above statements the functionalist is interested in the exception, that is, the unstable elements of society, the poorly integrated, the "dysfunctional" elements which contribute to the breakdown of society, and the dissensus that can arise among members.
48. Ibid., p. 162.

Functional theories assume that conflict can be rendered harmonious through the interaction of and satisfaction of interests and claims by contending groups. Conflict theorists from Marx to Georg Simmel regard conflict as the motivational basis of political life. Compromise or conciliation, debate, and competition are foundation stones of social life.[49]

We said that Marx believed that each stage of social development generated a level of contradictions which "explode" to instigate a new stage. So the contradictions resolved in one stage generate new contradictions. Mao restated this theory in the context of Chinese development:

Marxist philosophy holds that the law of the unity of opposites is a fundamental law of the universe. This law operates everywhere, in the natural world, in human society, and in man's thinking. Opposites in contradiction unite as well as struggle with each other, and thus impel all things to move and change. Contradictions exist everywhere, but as things differ in nature, so do contradictions. In any given phenomenon or thing, the unity of opposites is conditional, temporary and transitory, and hence relative; whereas struggle between opposites is absolute. Lenin gave a very clear exposition of this law. In our country, a growing number of people have come to understand it. For many people, however, acceptance of this law is one thing, and its application in examining and dealing with problems is quite another. Many dare not acknowledge openly that there still exist contradictions among the people, which are the very forces that move our society forward. Many people refuse to admit that contradictions still exist in a socialist society, with the result that when confronted with social contradictions they become timid and helpless. They do not understand that socialist society grows more united and consolidated precisely through the ceaseless process of correctly dealing with and resolving contradictions.[50]

Whether basing one's analysis on pattern variables, stages of growth, or the analysis of contradiction, the central emphasis is two-fold, being based on exchange and meaning. *Exchange* represents the relationship of classes and roles. *Meaning* represents norms. The transformation may be from traditional to the modern or primitive, feudal,

49. See Georg Simmel, *Conflict* (Glencoe, Ill.: The Free Press, 1955).
50. Mao Tse-tung, *On the Correct Handling of Contradictions Among the People* (Peking: Foreign Language Press, 1960), pp. 21–22.

capitalist, socialist, or communist stage of development, emphasizing processes of primitive unification, industrialization, welfare, or abundance.[51] However, in all cases the role of government is prescribed in terms of the following:

1. Conflict between sets of norms (preindustrial—industrial, and so on) ;
2. Conflict between systems of exchange (roles appropriate for the family are not functionally appropriate for the business corporation) ;
3. Conflicts between both of the preceding.

Structuralism represents macro-analysis. It uses whole societies as its units. It is useful for combining historical change with comparison. Its central political concern is how one system changes into another and why, or how a system adapts to innovation and survives and persists. These points require further discussion.

51. See A.F.K. Organski, *The Stages of Political Development* (New York: Knopf, 1965).

chapter thirteen
Structural Crises and the Political System

In Chapter Twelve we discussed functionalism and requisite analysis as aspects of structural analysis. We describe contrasting forms of political structuralism—the method of contradiction and the method of equilibrium. We turn now to a structural model of politics, the variables of which can be used in both radical theories of conflict and liberal theories of congruence. How they are used depends on the user rather than on the theory itself.

When Marx criticized capitalism he wanted to show the causes of contradictions built into the very structure of capitalism itself, thus revealing its deficiencies as a system. This was something the classical economists, with their emphasis on equilibrium, supply, and demand, could not properly do. Structure in this sense resulted in a theory. Analyzing capitalism, Marx not only used concepts of logical analysis (derived from Hegel) which could be applied to all history, but compared different concrete forms of the same structural type in order to demonstrate the logic of the theory. The comparisons were necessary because in theory the basic logical structure of capitalism remained the same, while its application in different countries varied. As in a mathematical statement, the relationships and logic remain the same while the variables change. Likewise, the application of a model to actual conditions (as in engineering) requires new variables relating to the available materials. Hence, for Marxists, the logic of capitalism is the same for all capitalist societies even though in practice the materials—the specific qualities of each concrete form of capitalism—affect the speed, direction, and velocity of the evolution of the system. The way the infrastructure works, the "base" (the mode of production) varies with the resources, the raw materials supply, the comparative advantage of the nation, the degree of industrialization and innovation, the value of colonial or imperial possessions, and so on. The superstructure—the classes, historical factors, political regime, ideology—all mediate the process. One can *project* difficulties and contradictions in the system, but not *predict* if and when a revolutionary condition might arise in any particular country.

Despite this emphasis on application, the broad analysis of capitalism (and its preceding systems) does reveal a pattern of evolution.

The new facts made imperative a new examination of all past history. Then it was seen that all *past history, with the exception of its primitive stages, was the history of class struggles: that these warring classes of society are always the products of the mode of production and of exchange—in a word, of the* economic *conditions of their time; that the economic structure of society always furnishes the real basis, starting from which we can alone work out the ultimate explanation of the whole superstructure of juridical and political institutions as well as the religious, philosophical, and other ideas of a given historical period.*
. . . [The] mode of production peculiar to the bourgeoisie, known, since Marx, as the capitalist mode of production, was incompatible with the feudal system, with the privileges it conferred upon individuals, entire social ranks and local corporations, as well as with the hereditary ties of subordination which constituted the framework of its social organization. The bourgeoisie broke up the feudal system and built upon its ruins the capitalist order of society, the kingdom of free competition, of personal liberty, of the equality, before the law, of all commodity owners, of all the rest of the capitalist blessings.[1]

What is of interest here is not so much whether the Marxian interpretation is correct, but the emphasis on whole systems—epochs, historical periods, economic organization, and class—which delineate the contours of specific juridical or legal superstructures, beliefs, religions, and so on. These, in turn, act on the individual, *structuring* his or her world, way of thinking, motives, attitudes, and behavior. Capitalist society makes the modern French and English more alike than were feudal French and capitalist French. By the same token do Chinese communists have more in common with Yugoslavian, Russian, or East German communists than Chinese under the nationalist regime of Chiang Kai-shek

1. Frederick Engels, "Socialism: Utopian and Scientific," *Selected Works,* Karl Marx and Frederick Engels (Moscow: Foreign Languages Publishing House, 1962), pp. 37, 135.

or the last Manchu dynasty? If Mao and his successors have their way the answer would be yes.

The question can be turned around. To what extent do common characteristics of Chinese culture and tradition represent an unbroken line from the teachings of Confucius to Mao?[2] Reverse the question like that and one changes the basic descripton of the *system,* making it cultural. But either way one needs to know certain things about the system to talk of analysis. First it is essential to know what constitutes the system itself. Second, a clear, explicit method is required to enable an observer to discover which systematic characteristics apply in concrete situations. (Marx described his method as dialectical materialism. A modern structuralist might use functionalist methods.) Third, the application of method to units must cluster characteristics in some fashion.

Structural theory is *constructed* theory. In the same way an architect designs a building with the idea of controlling the flow of movement within it, so the structuralist oversees the *design* of whole societies, or subunits within societies, and their specific forms—the family, religious institutions, productive enterprises, schools and universities. The structuralist seeks to discover what provides the ability to control, direct, manage, shape, and constrain—"structure"—behavior. Each structural theory, like each architect's design, is different. But the purpose is to observe the *whole*—a whole epoch or period in history, a whole mode of production, a whole system of language—in order to understand the parts. The leg of a table, detached from the whole, means nothing. But connected to the table, one of four, it is understood. The relationship, then, is what counts. The contribution of one part to the whole can only be understood if one knows how the whole system works. Feudal, capitalist, socialist, and communist societies all have similar basic functions, but these are satisfied in quite different ways.

We can summarize as follows:

1. The observer uses classes and roles, organized in relationships of exchange and reciprocity, to determine constraints and opportunities.

2. Beliefs—moral values, ends, priorities, and goals phrased as myths, religions, and ideologies—affect constraints.

3. Connection between the two is the subject of detailed empirical examination.

4. Such relationships are best observed at certain high points in

2. See Joseph R. Levenson, *Confucian China and its Modern Fate* (Berkeley, Ca.: University of California Press, 1968) .

history; for instance, after a revolution, a war, or some other "promontory" establishing event.

    5. Both establish boundaries around behavior.

The Language of Structuralism

Structuralism is a concept used in literature, psychology, anthropology, art history, sociology—in short, wherever the relation of parts to wholes is the main burden of analysis. Although institutionalism, behavioralism, and pluralism all differ, these may be converted into a structural form. For example, a pluralist approach can become a structural approach if we consider, for example, the opposite political types we detailed in Chapter Twelve: totalitarianism and democracy. Each has certain typological characteristics. Power in the one is vertical, stemming from the top down. Power in the other is more horizontal. To the degree to which a society is more or less pluralistic, it moves along a continuum between totalitarianism and democracy. The key is the structure of power and how it is divided among subunits. Polyarchy, from a structural point of view, comes closer to democracy as its rules for the distribution of power are observed. For example, a concrete system like the United States can be evaluated as a polyarchy that is more or less closer to the democratic pole than, say, Sweden or the Netherlands. Similarly, some societies with totalitarian regimes are considered more pluralistic than others. For example, contemporary Yugoslavia is more pluralistic than the Soviet Union in that it is authoritarian in structure rather than totalitarian.[3] Thus we can construct a continuum using the comparative analysis of concrete political systems according to their degree of pluralist distribution.

    We summarize the methods and emphases of structuralism in terms of *sets,* or "languages."

Set one—transformational languages: Transformational language consists of terms used to refer to changes of systems. Engels spoke of capitalism being built on the ruins of feudalism. Marx spoke of socialism being built on the ruins of capitalism.[4] Durkheim considered the transforma-

3. See Andrew C. Janos, "Group Politics in Communist Society: A Second Look at the Pluralistic Model," *Authoritarian Politics in Modern Society: The Dynamics of Established One-Party Systems,* ed. Samuel P. Huntington and Clement H. Moore (New York: Basic Books, 1970) , p. 439.
4. See Marx and Engels, "The Manifesto of the Communist Party," op cit., p. 39.

tion from mechanical to organic solidarity essential. Others spoke of folk societies being transformed into urban ones, and so forth.[5]

Each transformation, to be seen as a system, requires some abstraction. Highly abstract language uses mathematical equations or logical symbols. Most structural analysis in political science is just one step above descriptive history—it is typological. Even so a few employ abstract forms of structure.[6] The more abstract the language, the more likely it is to produce theory in the form of laws governing transformations. The object of structural theory (derived from case studies of the evolution of a system or comparative study of similarities and differences) is to identify possible laws which govern change.[7]

Summarizing briefly, we can say that the language of structural analysis defines the following concepts: system, transformation, formalization, exchange, and boundary. *System* refers to the relation of parts to wholes. *Transformation* refers to changes from system to system. *Formalization* refers to laws of transformation.[8] *Exchange* is the process by which transformation occurs. *Boundaries* refer to the units within which the process occurs.

Set two—theoretical languages: We have already described the two dominant modes of structural theory. The method of contradiction emphasizes the projected and/or unresolvable problems each kind of system engenders, unavoidable predicaments it confronts along the paths of its evolution. Such a method led to the development of *conflict theory*. The method of equilibrium is concerned with how structural imbalances are rectified by the components of a system that mediate and make congruent what might otherwise threaten the survival of the unit (*congruity theory*). The first uses the language of *dialectical* analysis, while the second uses the language of *functional* analysis.

In a dialectical process, each changeover between systems is marked by crisis—revolution or some overt conflict. But over time crisis is evolutionary, particularly with respect to growth and development. Growth and development produce contradictions which are then resolved, im-

5. See Robert Redfield, *The Folk Culture of Yucatan* (Chicago: The University of Chicago Press, 1941).
6. See David E. Apter, *Choice and the Politics of Allocation* (New Haven, Conn.: Yale University Press, 1971). See also Karl Deutsch, *The Nerves of Government* (New York: The Free Press, 1963).
7. See Jean Piaget, *Structuralism* (New York: Harper Torchbooks, 1970).
8. "Nomothetic," or law-giving propositions.

plementing a higher stage of growth and development. This circular doctrine is shown schematically in Figure 13-1.

Take two variables, S and D, and follow them through time T. The dialectical process shows that the variables collide at point R. which is a revolution or other form of confrontation, after which they reverse the terms of thesis-antithesis. What had been the dominant variable in T_1 becomes subordinate in T_2, and so on.

Any analysis of such a dialectical process would, of course, require us to add content to the variables and provide a theory to fulfill the model. For example, the variables might be revolutionaries versus conservatives, labor versus management, socialists versus communists, centralizers against decentralizers. A theory that would explain these contradictions might follow a Hegelian "idealist" tradition or a Marxist "materialist" tradition. Mao's analysis of "correct contradictions" might be contrasted to those of Lenin or other Marxist thinkers.[9]

Equilibrium, or congruity, theorists deal with *reciprocals* in roles, not classes—that is, with functionally defined relations. These include doctor–patient, sales person–customer, politician–voter, teacher–student, parent–child. While each actor in a role has a function to perform that satisfies a social need, any one person occupies many roles. A father is also a businessman. A professor may be an economic advisor to a politician. The functions they perform satisfy the need of society for

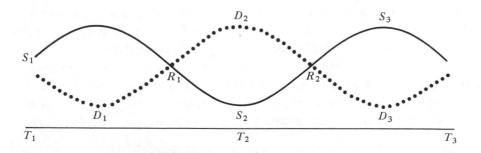

Figure 13-1. Dialectical Change

9. See Kenneth E. Boulding, *A Primer on Social Dynamics* (New York: The Free Press, 1970), pp. 38–40. The simple structural model used in the previous chapter (Figure 12-1) represents an example of a dialectical model using relationships of exchange and rules and symbols of meaning.

maintaining the health of the individual or the "health" of the economy. The analogy to living organisms is not accidental. Human societies are after all organized by human beings *for the satisfaction of human needs*. Beneath the wide variety of arrangements designed to satisfy such needs, lie certain basically similar processes. Hence, while it is true that each human group is unique, having its own special characteristics and its own intrinsic qualities, it is also true that there are common needs as well. The functional emphasis is on the extent to which all human groups share in the same sets of core problems. In other words, it is a method with an emphasis different from the dialectical method. It is concerned with how the fundamental social needs of people are met by their living together in groups.

Functionalism is the method which compares the different ways role systems operate to satisfy people's needs. Research expounds similarities, through which the more specialized and peculiar needs of each community can be identified. Function, then, defines what needs are satisfied. Structures organize how they are satisfied. A minimal, irreducible set of functions and structures is universalized in *all* units of the same kind, and is necessary for the survival of the system. This set is made up of *requisites* of the society. The special form of equilibrium analysis that links functions to structures in a minimal or irreducible set is *structural-functional requisite* analysis. This form of requisite analysis does not contain independent variables. It demonstrates *syndromes* or *uniformities*. It sensitizes the observer to anticipate problems. Projective rather than predictive, it is not a theory in the highly generalized sense of the word.[10] Rather, the general structural-functional model is a matrix (see Figure 13-2).

Note that the same function may be handled by many structures. For example, the functional need to control deviant behavior may be handled by political structures or economic ones.[11]

In conflict theory, reciprocals are polar and contradictory—antagonism leads to ruptures and explosions. In congruity theory, reciprocals are multiple; they change bit by bit. We can summarize this set of terms as *reciprocity of class* versus *reciprocity of role,* or *dialectical* versus *functional* change, or as change from *lower* to *higher* levels of system, from less complex (preindustrial) to more complex (industrial) societies.

10. See Michael Banton, *Roles* (London: Tavistock Publications, 1965). See also S.F. Nadel, *The Theory of Social Structure* (Glencoe, Ill.: The Free Press, 1957).
11. See Marion J. Levy, Jr., *The Structure of Society* (Princeton, N.J.: Princeton University Press, 1952), for a full treatment of these matters.

Structures

	y_1	y_2	y_3	y_4	y_5
x_1					
x_2					
x_3					
x_4					
x_5					
x_6					
x_7					
x_8					
x_9					
x_{10}					

Functions

Figure 13-2. Requisite Analysis Matrix

The political implications of the two types of structural methods are quite different. The first kind, which is concerned with contradictions and with finding new solutions to them, sees history as an unfolding process in which each stage represents a higher one than the last (and correspondingly has more powerful contradictions which need to be resolved) . It also produces new and better opportunities for improving the conditions and finding new solutions to the predicaments of human beings. If the most modern societies show the greatest and most striking contradictions, they also offer the greatest opportunities for benefits. Hence conflict theorists study contradictions in order to devise possible new solutions. Indeed, most are interested in radical solutions through new systems. Congruity theorists regard change as a method of increasing diversity and complexity. To them no single contradiction is critical, and no single new system is capable of resolving incongruities. Therefore, since change is bound to occur, attention must be turned to controlling functions toward moderate reform, adaptation, and adjustment. Disequilibrium can be rectified by policy; therefore there is a tendency in all systems toward equilibrium. Conflict theorists and congruity theorists, then, differ on how they deal with change. The former are interested in how conflict brings about innovation in systems. The latter are interested in how mediations produce an equilibrium flow so that a change in one set of roles will be absorbed by compensatory changes in others.

Set three—the language of comparison and case: Both kinds of structuralism can be applied over time or comparatively. A structuralist can follow the evolution of a single case, or compare cases at a single moment or period. The first is called *diachronic* analysis. The second is *synchronic*. We diagram these different tendencies as in Figures 13-3 and 13-4.

Assume a system *A*. (It might represent France, an African territory, a tribal society, or any other unit.) Consider three variables: *x*, which refers to patterns of exchange; *y*, which refers to reciprocities of class; and *z*, which refers to a belief system or ideology. Assume three time periods: an initial period (which for France might be feudal) ; a transitional period (which for France might be capitalist) ; and a resultant period (which for France might be, perhaps, described with a question, such as, will the country become socialist?) . The structuralist will ask, how do the different variables change between the first two systems and lead to projective hypotheses about the third? (See Figure 13-3.)

Assuming that *x*, *y*, and *z* will be partially transformed by each successive evolution, then their characteristics in time period one, the initial period, will be transformed in two and three. The question is how. A conflict theorist would speculate on clashes occurring at each stage, with the transitional stage being the focal point of contradiction. A congruity theorist would concentrate on how adaptations in variables *x*, *y*, and *z* materialize in increasingly complex ways.

With synchronic analysis time is a constant, and history is excluded from the study. (See Figure 13-4.)

Assume that *A*, *B*, and *C* are different forms of the same general type of political system. England, France, and the United States, for example, are all capitalist countries with common characteristics *x*, *y*, and *z*. However, these variables are exhibited in different forms. The patterns of exchange, reciprocities, and belief systems in all three countries differ. Compared to, say, Brazil or the USSR or China, the differences, however, are small.

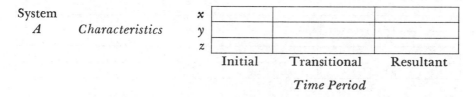

Figure 13-3. Diachronic Analysis

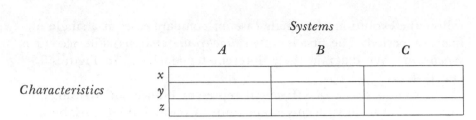

Figure 13-4. Synchronic Analysis

Contemporary structuralists combine diachronic and synchronic analysis, making a very complex synthesis. This is one of the reasons for the tendency towards formalization. If those variables which characterize different systems both comparatively and historically can be made precise and quantitative, they can be used for computer analysis. Then the models can easily be expanded to include more systems and variations (see Figure 13-5).

	Unit A	Unit B	Unit C
X			
X_1			
Y_2			
Y			
Y^1			
Y^2			

(Structural Variables; Units)

Structural Variables	Units A, B, C Time 1	Units A, B, C Time 2	Units A, B, C Time 3
X			
X_1			
Y_2			
Y			
Y^1			
Y^2			

(Unit in Time)

Figure 13-5. Expanded Synchronic and Diachronic Models

A Generalized Structural Model

So far this chapter has dealt mainly with the character of exchange in terms of functional role and class relationships, ideas, and beliefs. Structuralism contrasts sharply with behavioralism where the observation supports comparison.[12] We now want to bring together belief systems and exchange relations in structural terms.

Go back to the distinction between dialectical and functional congruencies. Reducing the differences between conflict or congruence, contradiction or equilibrium, let us consider all exchange relations and their reciprocities as referring to structure and ideas, and belief systems as norms. Assume further that structure and norm determine the limits of behavior by establishing boundaries around it.

The model in Figure 13-6 assumes that there is a connection between exchange and belief system. The validity of an explanation of some kind of behavior—perhaps the reason why a revolution occurred in X place at Y time, or the innovation that led to the employment of a bureaucracy, or the evolution of democracy rather than a totalitarian system—requires an evaluation "across some range of circumstances."[13]

Belief systems are *symbolic* systems. The problem is to reconstruct the depth and coherence of idea systems (or the "ideational") in the model without forfeiting any of their richness. It is possible to face this problem in many ways, through the study of language and the deep structures of the mind; the study of myth, ideology, and religion; or the study of the core, or central values, of a culture.

Exchange relations are based on *work,* defined as all those life giving activities on the basis of which reciprocity, social interactions, and social constraints occur.

The generalized structural model can be reduced to the terms shown in Figure 13-7. In this model, norms as belief systems and structures as exchange systems determine behavior.

In dealing with macrosystems—whole societies—government is a subsystem of society whose primary task is to deal with the changes that occur when incongruities between structure and norms affect behavior. We diagram the relationship of society to government in Figure 13-8.

12. See Claude Lévi-Strauss, *Structural Anthropology* (New York: Basic Books, 1963) , p. 21.
13. See Guy Swanson, "Frameworks for Comparative Research: Structural Anthropology and the Theory of Action," in *Comparative Methods in Sociology,* ed. Ivan Vallier (Berkeley, Ca.: University of California Press, 1971) , p. 142.

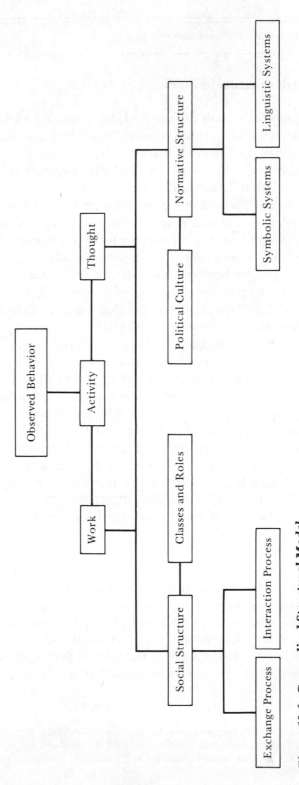

Figure 13-6. Generalized Structural Model

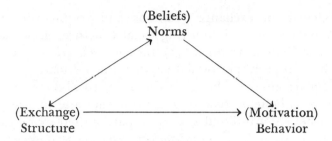

Figure 13-7. Simplified Structural Model

Government, pictured at the center, is responsible for maintaining structural and normative congruity in society, thereby ensuring appropriate behavior. This model emphasizes the *equilibrium aspect* of structuralism. We can apply an equilibrium or a Marxist or a conflict theory to the model and focus on modifications in exchange that affect reciprocal relations of classes and roles and the relationship of structures to norms. Conflict will arise in the relationship between norms and structures with consequences for government, as follows:

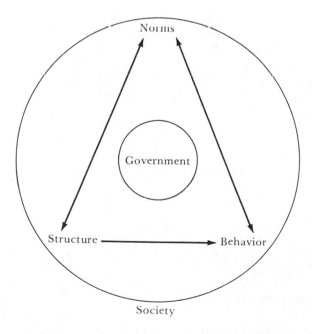

Figure 13-8. Society and Government

Any change in exchange relations and reciprocities produces changes in the network of interacting social structure, classes, and institutions. These conflicts result in (1) *institutional crises;* that is, functions are not properly performed so that the normative boundaries around them are altered. Change at the normative boundaries of roles effects change in belief systems or general norms, altering the way people perceive beliefs or internalize them as part of their moral identity as citizens. This leads to (2) *internalization crises* like that experienced by Marx's "alienated man" or expressed in Durkheim's concept of anomie; rebelliousness; anger, and so on. In turn, changes in structure result in the breaking up of reciprocal relationships so that processes of socialization no longer are effective. This leads to (3) *socialization crises.*[14]

We summarize these interrelationships in Figure 13-9.

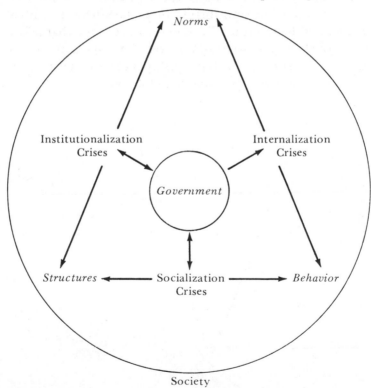

Figure 13-9. The Sociopolitical Model[15]

14. See D. Apter and Charles Andrain, *Contemporary Analytical Theory* (Englewood Cliffs, N.J.: Prentice-Hall, 1972) , p. 8.
15. Ibid., p. 8.

From this sociopolitical model we can restate the structural argument as follows:

1. Systemic contradictions at the level of society produce crises.
2. The critical societal crises are institutionalization, internalization, and socialization.
3. Governments attempt to solve these crises by policy making, using coercion or force, or mediating through adaptive political means and organizations.
4. If governments fail, and system-level contradictions continue, the system will be transformed from one type to another.

Crisis Variables

Crisis variables result from incongruities arising among norms, structure, and behavior. They have been the object of considerable research. In the field of social change and development, studies of "institution-building" have emphasized how new role networks carrying the needs of structural change need to be integrated with old ones. The concrete structures on which the job depends are educational, or administrative, or financial, or some others. Governments mediate directly in the process to increase institutionalization, to improve the fit, and to help lock roles and functions together.[16] But often these efforts fail.

Government requires political *sensors,* indicators of trouble occurring in terms of these crisis variables, to gauge when remedial action should be undertaken. Government depends on a flow of information about the concrete causes of such crises in order to discover how best to resolve them. Without the sensors, authority would be undermined because government might fail to respond appropriately.

Institutionalization crises: The work of the historical sociologists began with speculations on the organization of preindustrial society. It was basically organized around exchanges between kinship groups, each of which was highly integrated; norms and structures were congruent. Historical sociologists also considered industrial society as being relatively well integrated around functional exchange processes of economic

16. For an analysis of institutionalization see Samuel Huntington, *Political Order in Changing Societies* (New Haven, Conn.: Yale University Press, 1968). For a study of political institutional transfer see D. E. Apter, *Ghana in Transition,* 2nd rev. ed. (Princeton, N.J.: Princeton University Press, 1973).

activity. Societies which were mixtures of the traditional and the industrial suffered from a kind of institutional "indigestion." Kinship obligation in traditional societies was considered "dysfunctional" to modernization, for example.

Modernization is a form of system change, which results in institutional conflict. But roles and institutions that survive the transitions adapt in ways which dilute and restrict the growth of innovation functional to industrial activity. It is easy to see why. For example, many developmental projects designed to expand economic growth fail because there are not enough people to perform the new roles properly. Old roles may restrict the performance of new ones.

One indication of lack of fit, or failure to institutionalize effectively, is corruption.[17] Another is conflict. Attempts to increase institutionalization have seen the construction of single-party state regimes in which all roles and classes serve first the party, and its normative priorities. State enterprise and socialism also provide ways to produce a more coherent network of functional relationships. Hence, in many formerly colonial societies where a variety of role institutional conflicts prevail, ethnic or tribal affiliations based on rural traditional versus urban modern sectors, attempts have been made to transcend the old modes by effecting a grand mobilization. Then the conversion of old interests into new values becomes an integrative political strategy for the institutionalization of roles.

Institutional conflicts are perhaps better understood in modernizing societies than in industrial ones, but virtually all the pre-structural theorists we have discussed—from Marx to Maine, and Rousseau to Weber—were concerned about the strategic discontinuities arising out of the institutionalization crises of industrial societies.

Socialization crises: Socialization crises occur at the intersection between structure and behavior. Socialization deals with role performance. Behavior is fitted into relationships which govern and shape action. Individuals *learn* to perform in socialized ways. They perceive their identities in terms of social roles: male–female, parent–child, teacher–pupil, employer–employee. We might say therefore that if identity is shaped in the context of roles and behavior is conditioned by identity, then efficacy reinforces a person's willingness to accept both

17. See James C. Scott, *Comparative Political Corruption* (Englewood Cliffs, N.J.: Prentice-Hall, 1972) .

the obligations to perform and to attain a standard of performance. Each role embodies power, albeit in a structured and limited sense. (The teacher cannot apply the power of the parent. The parent cannot usurp the power of the employer.) Hence role relationships also imply sanctions that can be applied if any actor fails to comply with acceptable behavior.[18]

Socialization ensures the continuity of roles, and is in part a function of educational systems. As Durkheim puts it,

If, as we have tried to establish, education has a collective function above all, if its object is to adapt the child to the social milieu in which he is destined to live, it is impossible that society should be uninterested in such a procedure. How could society not have a part in it, since it is the reference point by which education must direct its action? It is, then, up to the State to remind the teacher constantly of the ideas, the sentiments that must be impressed upon the child to adjust him to the milieu in which he must live.[19]

The same idea is expressed by Rousseau when posing the difference between the individual and the citizen.

The natural man is all for himself; he is the numerical unity, the absolute whole, who only has relations with himself or his fellows. Civil man is only a fractional unity who depends on the denominator and whose values are in his relations with the whole, which is the social body. The good social institutions are those which know best how to denature man, to remove his absolute existence in order to give him a relative one, and to transport the man to a community unity; so that each private person no longer believes himself to be one, but is part of the unity, and is no longer sensitive except in the whole.[20]

Socialization, then, transforms the "natural man" into the citizen, the transformation being the essence of education.

Governments attempt to ensure a proper flow of new recruits to the existing ensemble of roles in society and to generate new and mu-

18. See Geoffrey Vickers, "Institutional and Personal Roles," *Human Relations,* Vol. XXIV, No. 5 (October, 1971) : 433–47.
19. Emile Durkheim, *Education and Sociology* (Glencoe, Ill.: The Free Press, 1956) , p. 79.
20. Jean Jacques Rousseau, quoted in Roger D. Masters, *The Political Philosophy of Rousseau* (Princeton, N.J.: Princeton University Press, 1968) , p. 11.

tually supportive roles for people to play. In a situation where a government is trying to promote change, socialization can become a form of radical indoctrination. For example, in recent decades the establishment of new networks of roles under socialism in Cuba or China has been a state responsibility. Government and party take a direct hand in the socialization process. They teach people how to perform appropriately in the new roles, and choose and select people to fill them. To the extent the roles themselves become institutionalized, the socialization process becomes more conservative.

Socialization, where institutionally established roles are locked into organizational settings, is one way to define the actions of incumbent role-fillers. Prescribing appropriate conduct is the first step toward socialization. The second is to teach an individual the limits of his or her role. Both actions presume appropriate motivation.[21]

If there is low institutional coherence in a society, and role sets are disjunctive or incongruent, a random quality enters the socialization picture. Loyalty to subgroups takes precedence over loyalty to the society as a whole. Government may take drastic steps to rectify this condition. Socialization becomes more uniform, and each socialization experience is undertaken at the expense of subgroup loyalties. In extreme cases, integrative socialization may take the form, for example, of genocide.

Where government establishes mandatory socialization patterns, relevant institutions are mobilized in the service of the state. For example, in China under communist leadership the family was downgraded as an outmoded Confucian ideal. Communist Chinese schools became instruments of indoctrination as much as education. Party units established in places of work and wherever people congregated were used to obliterate old patterns of behavior as well.

In a democratic society the problem of socialization is adaptive rather than transformational. Democratic sustaining values, such as tolerance and accommodation, may be taught by exemplary people— teachers, ministers, and high public officials. Political socialization represents principled conformity to democratic ideals. Deviant impulses are curtailed by laws and customs.

The most common socialization predicaments occur when individuals or groups refuse to accept the prevailing role ensemble or to be

21. For a criticism of this "unitary conception" of social role, see D. J. Levinson, "Role, Personality, and Social Structure in the Organizational Setting," in Apter and Andrain, op. cit., pp. 563–76.

socialized into a new set. In the first instance, we infer that significant sectors of the population are dissatisfied with the actions, and possibly the goals, of society. They find the roles which society makes available to them inadequate, immoral, or in other ways inappropriate to their set of beliefs. In the second instance, significant sectors of the population refuse to give up the prevailing ensemble for a *new* set. A revolutionary government faced with this predicament can make any of several characteristic responses. It can liquidate, severely chastise, or otherwise dragoon, or forceably persuade, the dissenting sectors of the population to change their position (as occurred in the USSR during the purges in 1936–1939).

Internalization crises: If institutionalization refers to the activities of a network, or set, of role reciprocities, and socialization refers to processes of learning and accommodation, internalization describes the incorporation of norms into the individual personality. Externalization is the reverse process, which details how an individual "expels," or rejects norms. The process of externalization often results in alienation.

Alienation is a state of mind as well as a social condition. It is found wherever individuals feel that their own efficacy is diminished rather than enlarged by the social roles available to them and where the values they believe in have soured. Barrington Moore offers an example.

In the advanced countries it is not only our obviously destructive use of technology but also its presumably constructive aspects, from flush toilets through refrigerators, that with large numbers impose a dangerous strain on the physical environment, dangerous in the sense of contributing to human misery. To make the point in as offensive a form as possible, there are grounds for holding that the attractive young upper middle-class mother, driving a station wagon (nowadays often decorated with a peace sticker) full of happy sunburned children, represents a major threat to the prospect of a humane civilization, even one defined according to the purely negative criterion of reducing misery.[22]

The very symbols of benign values thus become transposed.

Lack of effective internalization, or the lack of commitment to norms, opens up the way for new norms to take effect. One can argue

---

22. Barrington Moore, Jr., *Reflections on the Causes of Human Misery* (Boston: Beacon Press, 1970), pp. 42–43.

that alienated people, unlike anomic ones, are looking for a new normative synthesis. They are therefore susceptible to new ideological persuasions and, more particularly, to charismatic or populist leaders who inspire them beyond their usual rational cautions. One of the great consequences of alienation, then, is that it produces an innocence in the midst of high cynicism—a cynicism about what is possible under existing circumstances and an innocence about what is possible under future circumstances. In the right combination of new ideologies, new political systems, and new leaders, alienation prepares the way for political hope. In this respect alienation leads towards hope, but a hope that fastens certainty to what is certainly ambiguous; that is, the apparent solution, the "lead out of darkness" ideology, that people cling to when all partial solutions have failed and they believe that the existent system is destined only to failure. Simply put, political disillusionment, if sufficiently pervasive, leads the way to naive totalistic solutions. Old political norms atrophy, or ancient ones may be revived by new leaders. Both communism and fascism feed off this syndrome.

To summarize, institutionalization relates norms to structures. Socialization relates structures to behavior. Internalization relates behavior to norms.

Issues affecting institutionalization, socialization, and internalization are complex. Rather than dealing with them any further here, it will be useful to treat them as "loadings" for governments. How do governments handle specific situations to mend things that might otherwise break?

Indeed, let us consider the crises described above as forming the basic work load of government, the concrete manifestations of which take the form of specific problems. These are the public policy issues which stare at us every day from the newspapers and the nightly television news. The government's job is to render the incongruous congruent, the disorderly orderly.

Political Systems[23]

We shall now deal with the ways different governmental systems handle crises in institutionalization, socialization, and internalization. Our

23. See David E. Apter, "Government," *International Encyclopedia of the Social Sciences*, Vol. 6, ed. David L. Sills (New York: Macmillan, The Free Press, 1968), pp. 214–30.

concern is not with specific policies so much as different types of government. We want to show how political norms and political structures define different kinds of government as subunits of society. The new focus shifts from society and its crises and contradictions to governments. Particular types of governments each deal with the three crises quite differently.

Democratic governments: Democratic governments respond to the crisis variables by trying to mediate between contending groups in order to produce effective policies that can ameliorate the causes of tension. Their success depends in part on the effectiveness of the links between society and government. Government is the dependent variable; society is independent. The basic democratic model is shown in Figure 13-10.

The social system comprises a national society. Government responds to societally generated crises as inputs. Since the democratic government model is above all an instrument of tension reduction, it responds with instruments that act on society, government, political parties, electoral systems, and the like. The ability of governments to resolve crises depends on their relationship to the social system and the quality or appropriateness of policy decisions.

Government is cast in the role of mediator and judge. Its functions are to reduce tension and mediate. Its political norms are embodied in law, which serves as a framework for instruments of rule. And the legal framework is itself important to the tension-reducing and mediating activities of the government.

Totalitarian governments: In totalitarian governments the situation is reversed. The government tries to deal with institutionalization, socialization, and internalization by mobilizing the population. It transforms the entire society. It does not mediate within it. It mobilizes the population to this end. Participation which checks the power of elites, in which people establish priorities over their own circumstances, is restricted. The mobilization of all toward the achievement of certain goals is facilitated in the hope that this will coordinate all efforts, unify

Figure 13-10. Government as a Dependent Variable

all objectives, and provide collective power for transforming and transcending the restrictions of society (see Figure 13-11).

In this instance government is the instrument by means of which radical change is produced in the social system. Defining the purposes and objectives of such change (normative characteristics) establishes new structural characteristics of society.

Sacred and secular systems: In democratic society, where government is the dependent variable and society the independent variable, governments must solve crises by catering to the interests of society. This is not true in the model in Figure 13-11, where mobilization requires a centralized, hierarchical form of government. If the goals of government are to be achieved they must become sacrosanct or *sacred*. Ethical precepts become political symbols which provide legitimacy. Where democratic governments resembling the model in Figure 13-10 tend to be competitive and pluralistic, those resembling the totalitarian model tend to be monopolistic and monistic. Normatively, the first are more *secular* than the second. Structurally, they are less hierarchical. Behaviorally, they rely heavily on internalized norms and self-control, rather than on external authority. These two generalized types—sacred and secular—in their various concrete formulations, are perpetually vulnerable to attacks from the other. Indeed, one can see over time that they engage in a permanent dialogue of conflict. They represent two fundamentally different approaches to government.

We have narrowed the pertinence of the discussion to two concrete units. Rulers in the classical formulation now come under the collective title *government,* a unit with particular responsibilities for the maintenance and adaptation of society. The ruled, organized in classes and role networks functional to the exchange process, represent *social systems*. The largest social system is a *society*. Government is the one sub-unit among all others that has a unique responsibility to society. To fulfill this responsibility it exercises a virtual monopoly over the instruments of force, and is the sole legitimate agency for the exercise of

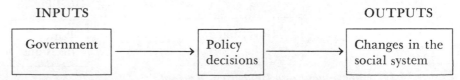

Figure 13-11. Government as an Independent Variable

public power on behalf of society. The societal-governmental relationship creates a *political system*.

Depending on whether government acts on behalf of society or to direct society, its actions imply two structural and two normative alternatives. Where government acts on behalf of society power tends to be more or less egalitarian and decentralized. Where the opposite is true, power is likely to be highly centralized. Where the latter condition prevails, leaders usually attempt to make the goals of society sacrosanct; that is, to elucidate moral principles by which all roles are institutionalized, serve as values to be internalized, and represent the basis for socialization. For example, in contemporary Communist Chinese society, the Maoist method of instruction is designed to ensure all three variables by means of continuous discussion in all work centers, communes, and other instruments of society.

This gives us a four-fold classification of types of political systems. (See Figure 13-12.)

The figure represents four distinctive types of political systems. Each will deal with crisis variables differently. Where there is centralized power or authority with sacred norms and belief systems, the political system is likely to be monistic and ideological, seeking to create a society for the future. Its emphasis is on the realization of moral purposes. Lenin's ideal of the communist party is an example. The party takes over the government. The government transforms the society and achieves the final goal. Why? Lenin's answer is that this process is necessary because the corrupting influence of society is what it is. According to Lenin, the bourgeoisie

. . . encircle the proletariat on every side with a petty-bourgeois atmosphere, which impregnates and corrupts the proletariat [externalization] and causes constant relapses among the proletariat into petty-bourgeois spinelessness, disintegration, individualism and alternative moods of exaltation and dejection [desocialization]. The strictest centralization

		Norms and Beliefs	
		Sacred	*Secular*
Structures of Power	*Centralized*	A	B
	Decentralized	C	D

Figure 13-12. A Structural Typology of Political Systems

and discipline is required in the political party of the proletariat in order to counteract this, in order that the organizational *role of the proletariat (and this is its* principal *role) may be fulfilled correctly, successfully, victoriously [institutionalization]. The dictatorship of the proletariat is a persistent struggle—sanguinary and bloodless, violent and peaceful, military and economic, educational and administrative— against the forces and tradition of the old society [enforced resolution of crises].*[24]

The direct opposite of Lenin's proposed solution is represented by set D in Figure 13-12. In this model society is decentralized as regards power and has secular norms whose principle is to convert internalization crises in terms of value conflicts into mediated interests. This combination pretty well describes pluralism. Highly centralized and secular systems represented by set B in the model are modern military bureaucratic regimes run by army officers. Decentralized sacred communities, like those in set C, are represented by theocratic communities like the Puritan colonies of America, where equality in the political "congregation" required absolute commitment to the theocratic ideology.

The four types never appear in a pure form. For example, Israel is a good example of a society that is predominantly of the D-type—a pluralist polyarchy with certain A-type characteristics regarding the historical destiny of the Jews in Israel and the significance of the army to protect it against invaders, yet it also has certain C-type characteristics insofar as only Jews can be fully equal citizens.

The typology outlined in the model in Figure 13-12 can be used to examine ancient societies and modern ones, highly industrial society or modernizing society.

The Significance of Different Polities

Political norms: We can now begin to explore some of the implications of the political system types.

Sacred Political Norms. Governments based on sacred norms cover a wide range of cases, ancient and modern. They include ancient China

24. See V.I. Lenin, *"Left-Wing" Communism: An Infantile Disorder* (New York: International Publishers, 1934) , pp. 28–29.

and early Semitic kingdoms. Consider the following description of ancient Egyptian civilization:

The Egyptian of historic times did not have our doubts and difficulties. To him the kingship was not merely part, but the kernel of the static order of the world, an order that was divine just as much as the kingship was divine. . . . From the earliest historic times, therefore, the dominant element in the Egyptian conception of kingship was that the king was a god—not merely godlike, but very god.[25]

Or take the case of ancient Greece. There the principles of patrilineal authority and ascribed status were linked to an ancestral and religious source, not only for kings but for every citizen.[26] Ascribed status applied particularly to priests and to the distinction between nobles and commoners. Hence political norms represented an explicit validation of the structure of authority.

Sacredness does not apply only to theocratic or primitive societies. It applies as well to many modern states. The sacred qualities of Marxism-Leninism in the Soviet Union are today enshrined in an elaborate philosophical system. Many of its sacred attributes were cruelly visible in the various purges and trials of the 1930s. They appear even today in the Soviet controversies over the political role of literature and the arts. Clearer still is the case of modern China. During his lifetime Mao's perceptive sayings assumed a sacred characteristic potent enough to define the basis of political legitimacy. Many new nations share this characteristic (although to a lesser degree), particularly those where attempts have been made to ritualize the authority of a charismatic or highly personalistic leader by endowing that person's words and teachings with special insight.

No government is entirely free from sacred qualities, whether these be elaborate ideological or token symbols (such as a flag or a constitutional document). These aspects of government may be merely ceremonial, taking what Bagehot called the "dignified part," or they may provoke high sentiments which express the solidarity and unity of a community.

---

25. See H.W. Fairman, "The Kingship Rituals of Egypt," *Myth, Ritual and Kingship: Essays on the Theory and Practice of Kingship in the Ancient Near East and in Israel,* ed. Samuel H. Hooke (Oxford: The Clarendon Press, 1958), p. 75.
26. See Charles Hignett, *A History of the Athenian Constitution to the End of the Fifth Century B.C.* (Oxford: Clarendon Press, 1962), p. 63.

It is possible to distinguish three main varieties of sacred attachments which, even if they overlap, are analytically separable. Ranking them in ascending order of sacredness, they are (1) primordial attachments to or beliefs about race, language, and nationality (a typical expression of primordial attachment in modern society is nationalism); (2) philosophical attachments (socialism is the most generalized moral and philosophical ideal in which a total synthesis is expressed relating mankind to the environment and specifying the way of the future); and (3) religious attachments (such as religious beliefs that propose the origin of the society, moral purpose, and a particular pattern of transcendental beliefs associated with a universal religious doctrine like Christianity).

In practice, all three levels of sacred attachments may be blended. Modern populist and totalitarian regimes (as in Nazi Germany) mixed primordial attachments of race with theological religious attachments. In the Soviet Union during World War II, the symbols of government became more and more primordial—that is, nationalist—and less and less philosophical or Marxist.

Secular Political Norms. Secular norms are built on a framework of rules rather than on some higher purposes of the state. The most common secular systems are those in which the sacred elements have declined through internalization. They do not disappear, but they become so completely a part of the accepted pattern of right and wrong that to more than refer to them on ritual occasions is unnecessary. Thus ceremony, rather than the substance of belief, is characteristic of secular systems.

By tacit agreement, secular systems reserve the "higher" goals for the individual sphere and these goals inhere in the individual's body of private beliefs. If governments should violate these norms, they run the risk of overstepping their limits of variation and of being terminated.

The structure of authority: Cutting across the sacred-secular normative distinction is the pattern of centralized or decentralized authority. A word of warning: It is always difficult to use dichotomous variables to divide concrete cases. What is in theory decentralized may be quite the opposite in practice. Or, highly centralized systems may show informal patterns of consultation and accountability to various groups in the community. Indeed, at any given time even the most highly centralized system may act on certain issues in a highly decentralized manner.

Moreover, centralized government includes monarchical and bureaucratic systems, represented by ancient empires, that combine monarchy with decentralized administration. This configuration includes different types of government: systems where the hierarchy, as in many tribal governments, is based on a king who is a "father" of his people, deriving authority from a totemic ancestor, or systems where authority lodges in a patrimonial figure and the relationship between ruler and ruled is that of patron and client.[27]

Centralized Authority. Let us ignore all these variations in form and say boldly that centralized power begins at the top and is applied downward through a specific delegation of authority. A military organization or a bureaucracy represents a clear-cut "command" case, with autocratic and totalitarian governments defined as those that employ this system of hierarchy. Government may then be represented by a single figure, a king or dictator, or by an oligarchy or junta.[28] Such highly centralized systems show the following characteristics: concentrated power subject to few checks; power inherent at the top; derivative subordinate authority; and strong reliance on the personality of a particular leader.

Decentralized Authority. Decentralized authority represents an opposite conception of power. Power is generated by the public through the aggregation of their political wants, expressed through various groups, and regulated by an abstract system of rules. (Its usual normative expressions include the acceptance of the principles of majority rule and the rights of all citizens.) This is what we mean by a democratic government. It is characterized by checks and balances, parliamentary control over the executive, and some form of electoral system as the method of political recruitment to sensitive positions. Of course, such practices do not exhaust the forms of decentralization. Decentralization may be functional, based on the allocation of the economic power in society among various groupings such as guilds, protective associations, professional associations, and other interest groups.

Sacred and centralized governments: The modern sacred-centralized type of system is likely to be associated with the establishment of a new

27. See Lloyd A. Fallers, *Bantu Bureaucracy* (Chicago: University of Chicago Press, 1956).
28. See Carl J. Friedrich and Zbigniew K. Brzezinski, *Totalitarian Dictatorship and Autocracy* (Cambridge, Mass.: Harvard University Press, 1956).

political system. Government is the independent variable associated with a new moral framework. Such conditions commonly apply after a major revolution or in territories that have recently gained independence.

Communist Governments. The distinguishing feature of the sacred-centralized communist government is the high degree of centralization encompassing the total community. The sacred object of government is to transform the material conditions of life and the consciousness of the people at the same time. The evolution of the community becomes a moral goal, to be sought under the leadership of a militant vanguard—like Communist Party membership—serving as the spearhead of government. In the classic Leninist form of the communist regime, no competitive sources of power can be tolerated. In recent times, however, a trend toward secularization and decentralization can be seen in the Soviet Union.[29]

Historically, the Soviet Union is an interesting case in that a set of external beliefs influenced internal social groups to revolt against a highly autocratic monarchy, a weak parliament (the Duma was only founded in 1905), and a centralized bureaucracy liberally sprinkled with foreign—particularly German—immigrants. Not only was the revolutionary instrument based on a small but dynamic working-class movement; Marxism itself was largely restricted to Russian middle-class intellectuals. It was essentially an alien doctrine (transformed by Lenin to meet Russian conditions) which led to a revolutionary organization that later became the centralizing mechanism of state power. When the religious beliefs of the Greek Orthodox church were replaced by the secular ideology of Marxism-Leninism, the goals of political development were "sacralized" to form the new basis for the legitimacy of government. Of course, a wide discrepancy existed between the theory and practice of government. Power was in fact centralized in the hands of the First Secretary of the Politburo of the Central Committee of the Communist Party, while constitutionally the Soviet Union was a federal system with an elected "supreme organ of state power," the Supreme Soviet, which in theory had the exclusive right of legislation.

Until relatively recently this system formed the model of state organization for all other communist systems as well as for the Soviet

29. See Richard Pipes, *The Formation of the Soviet Union* (Cambridge, Mass.: Harvard University Press, 1964). See also Chalmers Johnson, ed., *Change in Communist Systems* (Stanford, Ca.: Stanford University Press, 1970).

Union. Since the death of Stalin, however, two interesting features may be noted. The sacred quality of Marxist-Leninist ideology has declined, particularly as younger generations find it less significant as a doctrine than as a ritual, and a trend toward decentralization has begun. A struggle is on between the communist political leaders and the technical specialists—economists, scientists, and the like. Moreover, as *polycentrism* on an international level is more widely accepted, the necessity for a more liberal approach to Marxism-Leninism reduces its orthodoxy. Alternative structural experiments are increasingly common—such as those in Hungary, Yugoslavia, and Poland—where cultural decentralization (in the cases of Hungary and Poland) and economic decentralization (in the case of Yugoslavia) represent experiments in greater freedom.[30]

The communist examples are particularly relevant because these countries are attractive models to governments of developing areas bent on following the Soviet pattern of rapid industrialization.[31]

Fascist Governments. Fascist governments are more secular in orientation. The developmental, or evolutionary-sacred, ideology around which communist governments are organized embodies certain universalized moral aims. In contrast, the sacred attachments of fascist governments are more easily attributable to primordial sentiments, including race and nationality. Although there are structural similarities between communist and fascist governments, particularly with respect to the roles of a powerful totalitarian political leader and a weak set of parliamentary institutions, one important difference should be pointed out. In the communist case, government is monolithic, emphasizing the evolution of the entire community. Fascist governments, on the contrary, tolerate certain corporate groupings.

Three fascist governments are of interest here: Germany (1939–1945), Italy (1919–1943), and Spain (1939–1976). All were highly centralized, but they varied considerably with respect to the sacredness and secularity of political norms.

The strongest attachment to sacred primordial political norms was exhibited in Nazi Germany. The supremacy of one race and the liberating effects of war and conflict were embodied in the revived Nordic myths (as the doctrine of "Odinism") and blended into a set of na-

30. See Walter Laqueur and Leopold Lebedz, eds., *Polycentrism* (New York: Praeger, 1962).
31. See Adam B. Ulam, *The Unfinished Revolution* (New York: Random House, 1960).

tionalist political norms. Structurally, although the government was highly centralized under a personal dictatorship, four main groupings were given exceptional attention: the army and secret police; large-scale industrial enterprises; labor organized into fronts and battalions; and military scientists and technicians. The Nazi case also shows that even under a highly centralized form of government, economic control can be kept separate from ownership, with private industry continuing to operate under government regulations. Unlike the situation that exists in communist systems, in Nazi Germany a market system of economic allocation *coexisted* with government-organized fiscal and credit manipulations. Each corporate group obtained special conditions of privilege.

Italian fascism showed less commitment to primordial political norms than Nazism, as well as a somewhat less-centralized governmental structure. The norms themselves were composed of ambiguous combinations of primordial sentiments, appeals to historical precedent, and claims to philosophical universality. Primordial claims were mixed with the corporate organization of the state, under the inspiration of the Collegia of the Roman Empire. The "corporation" was thus associated with the great period of Italian imperial and cultural achievement and became the legitimizing basis of the regime.

A second claim to universality, which was of minor importance during the period of Italian fascism, may yet prove to be highly significant. This is the view that the proper way to organize the state is around corporate groupings functional to development and industrialization. In arguing the case of corporate government, it is sometimes pointed out that fascism as a form of government, although totalitarian, emphasizes the role of the corporation as both the point of reconciliation between state and individual and the instrument of individual expression.[32] This function remains an important structural device of governments midway between highly centralized and decentralized systems.

Both the German and Italian systems contained important normative ambiguities, which they attempted to resolve in the apotheosis of violence. This was most apparent in their total repudiation of democratic, decentralized forms of government (which were regarded as catering to human weakness). Both the Italian and German forms of fascism represented authentic *totalitarian populism* (a modern form of tribalism), in which medieval ideas of corporatism, organic concepts of

32. See Ernest Barker, *Reflections on Government* (New York: Oxford University Press, 1958), pp. 329–66.

the community, and primordial sentiments were intertwined with a highly centralized system of administrative government.[33]

In Spain the fascist regime of Francisco Franco was less ideological and less centralized. Despite the exceptional power of Generalissimo Franco and the concentration of authority in the national cabinet, the Falangist Party played a lesser role in government than did the National Socialist Party in Germany or the Fascist Party in Italy.[34] One reason is that, within six years of Franco's accession to power, Italy and Germany were defeated by the Allies in World War II. Their systems no longer served as models of successful dictatorship. Even more important was the Catholic tradition, to which the right wing of the Falange and significant proportions of the Spanish population generally subscribed.

More decentralized than the others, and therefore more autocratic than totalitarian, the Spanish system represented an extension of an old and established bureaucratic system which traced its roots to the imperial Spanish tradition, to the Inquisition, and to a centralized monarchy. Today the Spanish government has reasserted its commitment to monarchy as a traditional form of legitimacy, while continually feeling its way to a more liberal parliamentary regime. This commitment reduces the government's ability to revive memories of Spanish grandeur, and thereby to treat communism, secularism, and socialism as agencies of the devil (as Philip II and Archbishop Carranza of Toledo treated Protestantism, Islam, and Judaism in the fourteenth century).[35] The lack of fervor of this conviction indicates the decline of sacred political norms derived from Catholicism even though they are more or less indifferent to the structure of authority. (Many of the same norms served equally well in Juan Peron's Argentina (1946–1955), and can be embodied in modernizing and authoritarian governments; for example, in Chile.)

Secular and centralized governments: The most pronounced characteristics of a secular-centralized system of government are (1) autonomous power in the hands of a president or monarch (or perhaps a "presidential monarch") ; (2) a single political party, whether in the form of

33. See Hans Rogger and Eugen Weber, *The European Right* (Berkeley, Ca.: University of California Press, 1965) .
34. See Stanley Payne, *Falange: A History of Spanish Fascism* (Stanford, Ca.: Stanford University Press, 1961) .
35. See Reginald Trevor Davies, *The Golden Century of Spain* (London: Macmillan, 1937) .

an elite (a communist party) or a populist mass party with an elite center (most nationalist parties) ; (3) a truncated or largely ritualistic parliament, which has no real veto power over the executive; and (4) an elections system which does not allow effective competition among candidates for political office.

Such centralized systems generally exhibit several characteristic problems common to all forms of centralized government with the exception of institutionalized monarchies. The most important of these are that (1) succession to high public office is usually accompanied by a severe struggle for power, and (2) the outcomes of disagreements are institutionalized.

The normative content of both communist and fascist forms of government gives direction and shape to the entire society. Historically, however, there have been many cases where the normative content has been relatively low (or largely ceremonial and ritualized) , while power has remained centralized. These include most nineteenth-century monarchical forms of government. Indeed, precisely because their sacred characteristics were emptied of content (though retained in form) they were unable to survive as types and were either transformed or eventually removed from power. In France the monarchical form, revived periodically during the nineteenth century, was effectively destroyed by the French Revolution. Only Bonapartism had any genuine normative success.

In Britain the secularization process began with the transformation of the monarchy or, symbolically, with the beheading of Charles I in 1649. The Act of Settlement of 1701, whereby the sovereign occupies the throne under a parliamentary title, established parliamentary supremacy, although it took many generations before the full implications were realized.[36] Real structural changes in the form of decentralization were embodied in the widening of parliamentary control over the executive and in popular representation from 1832 onward.[37]

If the record of historical cases of secular-centralized government is any guide, then one useful proposition can be stated as follows: Because its legitimacy disappears, government must decentralize as sacred political norms become secularized or ritualized.

Examples of secular-centralized governments include czarist Russia (although there were important theocratic elements in the role of the

36. See A.V. Dicey, *Introduction of the Law of the Constitution* (London: Macmillan, 1961) .
37. See Norman Gash, *Politics in the Age of Peel* (London: Longmans, 1953) .

czar) and Bismarck's Germany. More recent cases have been colonial administrative governments in British and French Africa and South Asia, the Netherlands East Indies, and the Belgian Congo.

Many new nations have gone from one form of highly centralized system, under colonialism, to another in the form of one-party government, but with a change in the quality of political norms. These norms often become endowed with intense attachments to primordial loyalties and, to a lesser degree, with aspects of socialism and public ownership, all wrapped up in a particular, pointed ideological message (such as those bespoken by Nasserism in Egypt, Nkrumahism in Ghana, or "Communocracy" in Guinea).

Sacred and decentralized governments: Where new constitutional governments have been most successful, they have evolved a shared set of political norms deriving from a previous period when such norms were explicitly sacred, either in an ecclesiastical form (as was the case in the Puritan commonwealths) or in a more directly political form. Modern democratic governments emerge from historically sacred-centralized or sacred-decentralized forms where norms of self-control are behaviorally widespread. The decentralization of authority and the secularization of political norms proceeds more or less simultaneously with a corresponding increase in the standard of individual civic obligation.[38]

The origins of Western democratic governments derive from a synthesis of generally agreed religious values that are associated with a generalized Christian ethic. The theocratic origins of democratic government are not to be taken lightly. Even the forefathers of the American experience assumed a unified set of Christian (mainly variants of deistic and Protestant) theological precepts. Law was based on the prior conception of agreed-on principles of political propriety. The formulation of these principles was articulated in many theologically based experiences, including religious wars. The body of precepts within the Catholic Church was even more unified. Conflicts over conciliarism and the role of the Church councils, not to speak of the nationalization of the Church itself within various countries, were resolved explicitly by political means. These issues have been historically so important to politics that much of the process of secularization can itself be traced to the search for some mutually agreeable and satisfactory common denominator to render politics more secular and democratic.

38. See Gabriel Almond and Sidney Verba, *The Civic Culture* (Princeton, N.J.: Princeton University Press, 1963).

In the United States this process of secularization was most clearly recognized in the works of the brothers Brooks[39] and Henry Adams, both of whom saw the modern economic state, with its emphasis on instrumental values, economic exchange, and corporate finance, as destroying the implicit basis of original Christian values. Nowhere is this more explicit than in Henry Adams' essay on Mont-Saint-Michel.[40] Adams' views, which tend to idealize the classical and medieval civilizations, romantically express his religious ideal. But in addition politicists having a sacred bent also know the importance to the system of doctrine and creed. The church militant was not always composed of simple stuff. (Even in Catholic Spain during the "golden century," the political aim of the conquistadors, who combined their adoration of the Virgin with a voracious appetite for plunder in the New World, were vastly different from those of the various religious orders—Jesuit, Benedictine, and Dominican—which in turn had their constitutionalists, such as Juan de Mariana, Francisco Suarez, and Bellarmine.[41])

The secularization of political norms occurred in three historic steps. The first was nationalization of the Church. By this means the political universalism of the Church (symbolized by the name Holy Roman Empire) was restricted and various national churches arose.

The second step was the extension of that process of nationalization to government. This was symbolized in the expression "divine right of kings," whereby authority was actually traced to God through the principle of royal inheritance and kinship. The doctrine of divine right established the idea of a sovereign government as a legitimate unit having a right to protect itself against external sacerdotal influence.

The third step was the growth of Protestantism, associated first with the unfolding of Christian principles through equity and then with the radicalization of instrumental values. The transition was particularly significant because Protestantism emerged as a particular religious ideology based on a mutually reinforcing synthesis between sacred values and instrumental objects germane to industrialization. In this sense, Protestantism provided the mode of transition from the more explicitly religious forms of government to the more secular ones which merely reflected religious values. This is why the roots of modern Western constitutional ideas are so deeply embedded in the Protestant ideal of the community.

39. See Brooks Adams, *The Law of Civilization and Decay* (New York: The Macmillan Company, 1898).
40. See Henry Adams, *Mont Saint Michel and Chartres* (New York: Collier, 1904).
41. See Ewart Lewis, *Medieval Political Ideas*, 2 Vols. (New York: Knopf, 1954).

In some ways the secularization of religion was a result of the loneliness implicit in the Protestant vision of salvation, which in Calvin's doctrine excluded even the church from participation in individual salvation. Weber makes the point that this is the singular difference between Catholic and Protestant doctrine, the result being an emphasis on an individualism held in check by the idea of the priesthood as a "calling" embodying good works and sobriety. Rationality came to be reflected in a political community of individuals. Thus self-control became the founding ethic of representative government, in conjunction with the economic doctrine of capitalism. In sharp contrast, Catholic doctrine implied a system bent on "punishing the heretic but indulgent to the sinner."[42] The Catholic projection retained a conception of the organic community which, although not necessarily antagonistic to decentralized government, did not glorify its basis in individualism and the doctrine of individual representation.

The consequences of Protestantism along with Dutch, British, and American capitalism helped to create the conditions for political secularization with a greater degree of emphasis on legal and constitutional political devices. Weber quotes John Wesley: "I fear wherever riches have increased, the essence of religion has decreased in the same proportion."[43] This view was (and is) central to modern secular democratic government where law has replaced religion as the foundation of the community. Thus, in political terms, secularization is important in the Western world because it is a process containing a constitutional element, the object of which is to establish a framework of government responsive to change. Therefore secularization leads to an explicit acceptance of the idea of the *sovereignty of the people*. Secularized governments particularly encourage the accumulation of wealth as a citizen's *duty,* thereby favoring rapid economic growth. However, both the advantages and the failings of the process are circular. Secular and decentralized governments wrestle with the question of how to retain the idea of obligation and responsibility in the face of continuous radical secularization.

One should not assume that there is a linear progression from centralized to decentralized or from sacred to secular systems. The opposite was true (and took place in a peaceful manner) in Weimar Germany. In the popular elections in 1933 legitimacy was withdrawn from the con-

---

42. See Max Weber, *The Protestant Ethic and the Spirit of Capitalism* (New York: Scribners, 1958). See also John T. McNeil, *The History and Character of Calvinism* (New York: Oxford University Press, 1954).
43. Max Weber, ibid., p. 175.

stitutional government when the voters freely elected the Nazi party ticket instead. We can infer from this event that this is likely to result when the norms of a secular and decentralized and democratic system are relatively weak and insufficiently internalized. But it is more to the point to say that such a system can operate only when *self-control* and *nonpolitical restraints on behavior* predominate in terms of the internalization of democratic values, and the socialization of political action.

Secular and decentralized governments: As secularization occurred in Western societies, theological obligations were worked into codes of civic responsibility. Law replaced religion as the basis of political norms. With the rising prosperity of Europe, there developed a general belief that free, democratic governments providing maximum political participation for all would provide a beneficial political condition. Indeed, nineteenth-century political struggles were largely fought over debates about the appropriate speed and thoroughness with which constitutional democracy should incorporate the entire membership of a system, not over structural principles of government.

A model of government analogous to the classical economic model was widely accepted as the basis of the pluralist model. As we suggested in Chapters Ten and Eleven, the community is composed of voters who are like consumers. Their political choices are tantamount to consumer sovereignty. The election system represents the market and voters choose their representatives on the basis of stated preferences. Government, consisting of a legislature and cabinet as well as appropriate administrative cadres, is similar to the productive unit. It manufactures decisions, which the public evaluates through the electoral mechanism. The courts are present to ensure that the rules of the system are not violated.

The principles on which the system rests include a high level of information, rationality as an attribute of voting and decision making, and equal representation.[44] (Such principles underlie the American form of presidential government and the utilitarian systems advocated by John Stuart Mill and the Benthamites in England.) Advocates of this form emphasize the improvement of information processes, the im-

---

44. See Anthony Downs, *An Economic Theory of Democracy* (New York: Harper Bros., 1957). See also David Easton, *A Systems Analysis of Political Life* (New York: Wiley, 1965).

portance of education in achieving rationality (only the informed voter can be rational) , and especially the improvement of electoral systems in order to achieve maximum communication of public wants in a representative chamber. We suggested previously that important questions concern the role of political parties acting as agents by which public desires are transformed into government cognizance. In this respect political parties are designed to emphasize and make explicit certain publicly held priorities, so that as the problems confronting government compound and the voices of individual citizens are lost, politicians stand for some symposium of priorities and on this basis are accepted or rejected by the voters.

The principle of majority rule implies, in effect, that the rightness of a doctrine be measured by the degree of electoral support it obtains. That support creates power. Hence majority rule is a principle of power which credits the rationality of the majority and elevates reason (plus numbers) over abstract morality. It is because of this orientation that instrumentalities begin to take on their own moral properties.

Not all democratic polities tolerate this highly individualistic form of government. Two alternative forms—one older and one very modern —have stressed the idea of the organic community rather than the more mechanistic doctrine of individualism. The first of these forms, an extension of medieval doctrine, incorporates Catholic beliefs within the context of a decentralized state. Examples of this *social democracy* approach to democratic government include states where Christian socialism and Christian democratic parties exist. The second form is *democratic socialism,* or social democracy, which emphasizes the democratic state as a means of fulfilling conditions of equality and freedom in conjunction with the development of the moral and material bases of the community.

Both of these forms see inadequacy in political democracy as resulting from a contradiction between the principles of private ownership of the means of production and the maintenance of civic obligation. How can government be secular and decentralized yet retain authority? If the achievement of democratic government is that it is secular in practice and therefore free of formalized commitments to a higher set of priorities than those desired by a majority, then the problem is how to retain that self-control implicit in Calvin's formula. One way is through endorsing new roles in government, particularly those which provide a "calling" (such as the roles of civil servants, members of professions, and scientists) to those whose sense of responsibility and commitment to the exchange of free ideas remains one of the most important characteristics of democratic government in highly industrial societies.

Government in Developing Nations

Governments formed in "new" nations—those achieving independence since 1945—present some of the most interesting challenges confronting constitutional experts, political theorists, and politicians alike. New governments tend to include characteristics of *all* the forms we have discussed.[45] For example, in Africa and parts of Asia societies retain attachments to ethnic governments which compete with central government for the loyalties of the population. Regional clusters with religious or linguistic affiliations represent powerful primordial loyalties that deny legitimacy to a central government or counter it with local attachments. Thus unity and legitimacy within the context of the nation are urgent problems facing political leaders of modern emerging states. Inasmuch as certain aspects of traditional government represent a rightful heritage, it may be that traditional bastions of legitimacy should be incorporated into modern governmental forms, as has been attempted under such ideological labels as "African socialism" or "communocracy." Furthermore, new nations commonly emphasize the positive role of government as the great engine of social change actively intervening in all aspects of life, from family relationships to educational opportunities, from road building to the development of local airways. Government in this respect is seen as an independent variable; much as it is, for example, in the Soviet Union.

At the same time, many newly established constitutional patterns follow the outlines of Western parliamentary government. With sufficient control over parliament, applied through the instrumentality of party discipline, it is possible to retain popular government based on parliamentary practice and a cabinet system with few formal checks on executive authority.

In a very real sense, then, the governments of new nations tend to be amalgams of the other types we have discussed—theocratic, communist, fascist, and democratic. Their roots in ethnic or traditional forms

45. See David E. Apter, *The Politics of Modernization* (Chicago: The University of Chicago Press, 1965). See also Ronald Cohen, "Anthropology and Social Science: Courtship or Marriage" in *Politics and the Social Sciences,* Seymour Martin Lipset, ed. (New York: Oxford University Press, 1969), pp. 29–48.

of government are identified in normative terms, with a mythical past providing a national identity. In some countries, like Angola, Mozambique or Somalia, there is a search for some equivalent to the communist emphasis on puritanism, public ownership, and discipline as represented in the recruitment of a developmental elite and as a method of exercising power. The representation of corporate functional groups has much in common with fascist governments. And the desire for a populist democratic rule and the pattern of parliamentary government foster Western democratic ideals and some of its procedures.

All this is confusing because the various systems of government described appear at first to be so antithetical that it would seem impossible to make them into viable and effective systems. This is to a certain extent true; hence virtually all new governments face problems with stability. It is not surprising that quite often what holds such a government together is allegiance to a particular political leader who is associated with revolution or with the seeds of development of a mass nationalist movement. Indeed, the outstanding feature common among new governments is their dependence on a highly personalized leader supported by a dominant political party or the army. This tends to be the case whether or not the system is *formally* organized as a single-party state so long as one dominant party is capable of controlling large regional areas. In the special case of new governments, therefore, the crucial factors regarding functions and structures are the relationship between the leader of the government and the leader of the party, and the role of the party. (Ordinarily one person controls the reins of both party and government.)

In terms of the various models employed here, new governments incline in theory to the position that government is an independent variable. In practice, however, government is likely to be an expression of an elite which manipulates a mass party that is itself a reflection of a wide diversity of interests. In other words, government and the social system tend to be subsumed under the broad tenets of a single party. Party becomes the independent variable, with government an intervening variable, and social system the dependent variable. (Even where more than one party exists, the situation is not very different. There may be several dominant regional, tribal, or linguistic parties, rather than one party; however, usually none is deeply committed to a single ideology, and in this they differ sharply from communist or fascist parties.)

The situation illustrated in Figure 13-13 is realized in its clearest form under conditions of radical transformation from dependent to

INPUTS   OUTPUTS

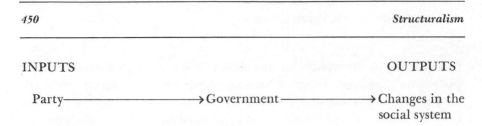

Figure 13-13. Government in the Single-party State

independent status, or directly after a revolution. Since the framework within which the parliamentary and cabinet systems operate is not entirely eliminated, it intervenes between government and the implementation of changes in the social system. In other words, the role of government derived through the formal decision-making process is the making of *technical* decisions, while the main lines of policy are generally laid down by governmental leaders who are also senior party leaders. Classic examples are Nyerere's Tanzania, Ghana under Nkrumah, Nasser's Egypt, and Algeria under Ben Bella.

How can we evaluate new governments? This will be the topic of Chapters Fourteen and Fifteen. Normative criteria involve those associated with democratic systems and include the adequacy of the protection of individual rights and the degree of pluralism tolerated in government and parliament. On this score governments in new nations show a mixed record. Some, such as Ghana under Nkrumah, possessed a declaration of fundamental principles to which the president swore adherence, but these declarations could not be enforced in the courts. Nigeria had a bill of rights. Burma emphasizes the social ownership of the means of production. Ghana and India have preventive-detention ordinances. It is safe to say that the protection of civil rights and liberties varies less with governmental form than with the general spirit in which government functions.

Since the legitimacy of new governments tends to be rather weak and is often associated with highly personalized leaders (a very vulnerable structural condition), another normative criterion is how successfully a government cultivates primordial loyalties. The quality of such attachments provides a basis for evaluation of new governments and describes the depth of the emerging political culture.

Primordial attachments tend to be linked to problems of economic growth. Planning, technical skills, manpower surveys, and the like, are important areas of governmental decision making. In addition, they provide moral or normative concepts associated with objectives that commonly take the form of socialism (since socialism explicitly validates a development ideal and is represented, through party and government, in evolutionary, ideal terms). Socialism also justifies political demands for personal sacrifice and loyalty. How well socialism (or its variants) can embody new economic rationality and enforce commitment to savings, work, education, and development is a fourth evaluative criterion.

Behavioral consequences of normative beliefs emerge as a combination of political norms, nationalist primordial sentiments, and the philosophical ideological expressions of socialism, which combine to form the motivational system of the society. Structurally these elements are organized less frequently in parliamentary or representative institutions than in functional or corporate bodies built within and around a political party. Party wings and various related interest groups are the devices that link individuals to the government.

Despite all integrative efforts, the most striking feature of new and emerging governments is the behavioral weakness in their population vis-à-vis government. Changing allegiances and the ritualization of authority, not to speak of the stresses and strains of rapid economic change and industralization, all require much study of motivation, of the sources of personal identity, and of learning. Indeed, what is now called the *identity problem*—the conditions under which individuals are able to establish a set of personality boundaries compatible with changing normative and structural conditions—is a growing concern. Only a few studies of the relationship between government and identity have been attempted, though many problems of governing derive from the search for identity.[46]

Conclusion

In Chapters Twelve and Thirteen we have traced the complex evolution of the structural study of politics. Two major points have been emphasized. First, structuralism is highly interdisciplinary. This is because the structural issues which arise at the level of history or comparative system change pertain to the politics of change in its broadest sense: transformation, the formation of new societies. Second, struc-

46. See Lucian Pye, *Politics, Personality, and Nation Building* (New Haven, Conn.: Yale University Press, 1962). See also Erik H. Erikson, *Young Man Luther* (New York: Norton, 1962).

turalism includes not only concepts of change in societal systems, but in governments. When we focus on government in structural terms we must ask, what types of systems are represented and what consequences for society do different political systems have?

Structuralism, then, deals with broad questions of change. It serves as an excellent introduction to the politics of development.

Developmentalism

chapter fourteen
The Analysis
of Development

We come now to the last of our six systematic approaches to the study of politics. **Developmentalism,** or the study of development, implies a progression toward a goal by means of economic growth. Just as institutionalists consider the evolution of democracy to be the embodiment of philosophical ideas of societal "good," so to developmentalists the conclusion to a period of change is part of an evolutionary, cyclical or repeating, history of industrial nations. In the West, those who see development as a recapitulation of historic stages of progress generally regard the goal not simply as economic growth, but also as the realization of political democracy. For a Marxist this idea is foolish: "Liberal" developmentalism results in intensified capitalist contradictions, resulting in imperialism.[1] But while for liberals the goal is democracy, for Marxists it is the stateless society. Both liberal and Marxist thinkers, however, consider development as a process which contains a *telos* (something like Aristotle's final cause), where the end is contained in the beginning in the form of potentiality, or goal. Experience has fallen far short of both ideals. The faith in development as mankind's hope is dimmed by practice. Nevertheless, while the search for a better system continues, politics takes command. Most developing countries build tough one-party states, military regimes, or corporatist governments as the practical political answer to the question of how to make societies modern. *Modernity* remains the critical issue even though the bloom is off the rose.

The change from a nondeveloped or underdeveloped to a devel-

---

1. See Shlomo Avineri, *Karl Marx on Colonialism and Modernization* (New York: Doubleday Anchor Books, 1969). See also V. I. Lenin, *Imperialism: The Highest Stage of Capitalism* (New York: International Publications, 1939).

oped society is an extremely complex transition. Growth—that is, increasing the net contributions to society that give people the ability to enjoy more choices and alternatives and so improve the conditions of their lives—is difficult to accomplish. This is because, as most people rightly assume, the industrial process is a universalizing force whose essential ingredients are based on scientific and technological innovation.

It will be useful to indicate at the start some of the terms used to describe "developing" countries, for there are many. Most of them are loaded words. Take the word *develop,* for example. All societies "develop" in some ways. But if the term *develop* has a favorable sound, *underdevelopment* implies a defect. Yet is large-scale industrial or economic development such a grand achievement? Many of the problems of postindustrial societies result from changes that have altered or modified virtually all the practices and institutions of political life. The problem for developing countries is this: How should emerging nations develop, expand their capacities and capabilities for a "modern" society, without being victimized by the problems that are known to beset highly industrial societies? Framing an answer to this question is not easy.

"Loaded" Words

Most terms used to describe countries aim to cluster them in a typological way. For example, before World War II, the term *have-not nations* applied to Germany, Italy, and Japan. This appellation referred to their lack of colonial empires, their late and uneven industrial growth, and in a sense "justified" their fascist or corporatist and militaristic inclinations. These nations were considered "up-and-coming"; they had "legitimate claims" to empire as the natural consequence of industrialization. The argument went thus: Because industrial metropolitan centers were the most powerful and civilized among nations, they had a right to colonies. "Have-nots," as they became "haves," staked out and pursued such claims. Conversely, since developing countries were "backward," it was their fate to become possessions and territories. So, as they developed technological superiority, Germany expanded in Europe, Japan invaded China, and Italy conquered Ethiopia. It was not until the end of World War II that the colonial claim itself was deemed illegitimate for all countries and the term *decolonization* was accepted by "metropolitan powers" like England, France, the Netherlands, and Belgium, as they slowly and reluctantly gave up imperial possessions. Today the claims are reversed; "poor" countries are demanding a fairer share of the wealth of the "rich."

Similarly, the term *socialist* (which applies to the USSR and the Peoples' Republic of China) emphasizes not the Marxian ideal of advanced capitalist countries undergoing a transition to communism, but rather the need to use political means *to intensify the pace of economic growth* and mobilize the resources of the nation, material and human. "Catch-up socialism" describes a way to set up and realize priority goals that will result in speeded-up growth rates. Less-developed countries using this political mechanism can hope to catch up with and surpass "advanced" Western nations. The Soviet Union, a recently developed giant, measures its development in "five-year plans" concentrating on heavy industrial production. Its scheduled targets are plotted by centralized planning. Quotas assigned to all productive units up and down the line must be fulfilled. It is assumed that the efficiency of planned growth demonstrates the moral and practical supremacy of the socialist ideal.

The expression used today to refer to developing countries allied with neither the Western democracies nor the socialist bloc is *Third World*. This political-economic designation distinguishes between the "first world" of political democracies operating under capitalism, and the "second world" of the newly risen USSR and associated socialist states. In some Third World nations, such as Guinea and Tanzania, vanguard parties organize state planning and socialism. Others are ideologically closer to the West, like Kenya. But the Third World is on the whole uncommitted; some countries lean toward socialist ideals and others toward Western democratic principles. (China is a Third World country that is close to the "second world" in method but that pursues an independent line. Cuba is overtly aligned with the USSR.)

The general terms *developing areas* or *underdeveloped countries* are primarily based on economic judgments of per capita income statistics. The areas included under this category are some countries within the Mediterranean basin (Southern Italy, Portugal, Turkey) as well as those in Asia, Africa, and Latin America. The breadth of land area and resources involved illustrate the need to correct imbalances between rich and poor countries. For example, the United States accounts for more than one-third of the Gross National Product (GNP) of the world as a whole and for more than one-half of that of the developed, non-communist countries. Per capita income in the United States is over $7,000 (as of 1970). In contrast, in at least ten African countries, yearly income per capita is below $100. Behind the statistics is not only the injustice of the unequal distribution of wealth, but also the idea of the obligation of advanced societies to help improve the lot of the less fortunate.[2]

The goal of Third World solidarity is to act in concert. Third World organization is today where trade unionism was a generation ago; that is, it represents a way to organize the collective power of the weak against the strong. The common predicaments of underdeveloped countries are not only that they are poor, but that they are subject to exploitation and manipulation by the major powers. Both governments and other instruments of power politics like multinational corporations perpetrate inequities (as well as providing certain benefits), but to a certain extent this cannot help but be so. The United States, for example, through international financial and trade policies, dominates a large part of international markets. Its domestic crises and the steps taken to resolve them have repercussions in the Third World. Also, the combined power of the United States and the other advanced Western powers is so great that it is not difficult to see why the domination of the Soviet Union and its allies is often regarded in emerging states as the lesser of two evils.

Much of the literature dealing with such problems points to a simple solution: Become rich. But this is like asserting simplistically that criminals should become good citizens, or the unscrupulous generous. What does getting rich mean? Indicators of growth like per capita or national income reveal much, but some forms of growth do not show up on such indicators. For example, a country may decide to concentrate its resources on building up its educational infrastructure or a suitable network of roads, ports, communications, or other facilities that will guarantee industrial opportunities in the future. Such forms of investment do not indicate "growth" over the short run, but a country that boasts such improvements is "getting richer."

The English specialist on development, Dudley Seers, describes the quandary in which inexact terminology places political analysts as follows:

2. See Robert E. Asher, *Development Assistance in the Seventies* (Washington, D.C.: The Brookings Institution, 1970), p. 9. See also Bert F. Hoselitz, "Theories of Stages of Economic Growth," *Theories of Economic Growth*, Bert F. Hoselitz et al. (Glencoe, Ill.: The Free Press, 1960), pp. 193–238

We must avoid the very tempting trap of saying that since poverty consists of low income per head, therefore development means economic growth. One could hardly talk of development having taken place in any true sense, i.e., in the sense of the nation having moved to a better situation, if average incomes had risen but at the same time inequalities had grown more severe, unemployment had increased, educational levels had fallen and political liberties had dwindled.[3]

Experience in most developing countries shows that this contradiction is *precisely* what happens under conditions of economic growth, whether or not average incomes rise.

Political goals such as greater liberty, greater equality, a more productive life with more opportunities, and a greater range of choices open to individuals within a context of peace and stability are not likely to be achieved. They are more often than not shunted in favor of immediate policies capable of enhancing economic development. Nationalism is the ideology favored to stimulate productivity and kindle public enthusiasm, often while applying harsh methods of rule. Ideologues of nationalism place the stress on creating a viable, independent, nation-state unencumbered by a colonial past and free of imperialism. But this requires giving priority to economic projects capable of sustaining growth. In many regimes, however, leaders are unable to realize *any* goals. And the results of failure are dwindling resources and growing political cynicism. No wonder, then, the increased frequency of military coups d'états. Where centralized government is backed up by army-imposed stability, freedom goes by the board.[4]

It is clear that latecomers to the company of modern, industrialized nations are penalized in many ways. They labor under terrible handicaps, and if it is, perhaps, true that all societies must traverse the same developmental road, progressing from poor to rich, underdeveloped to developed, then most are doomed to fall relatively farther behind as time goes on. Hence the urgent search for alternatives. However, if one replaces ideas about "early" or "late" development with terminology about predicaments and strategies, then the search for new solutions becomes geared to open up *new* political options. This is not,

3. Dudley Seers, "Other Ways in which Rich Countries Affect Development," *Journal of World Trade Law,* Vol. 4, No. 2 (March–April, 1970) : 377–82.
4. I use the term *pre-democratic* to refer to this type of situation. See D.E. Apter, *The Politics of Modernization* (Chicago: University of Chicago Press, 1965) .

however, to assume that because the first and second worlds represent relatively coherent *systems,* that *mixed* strategies will work in the Third. Indeed, such combinations are likely to produce the worst rather than the best of both. The search for alternative solutions requires, therefore, not some eclectic mix of liberal and socialist practice, but the formulation of totally new systems, however hard these are to come by.

Political thinking generally follows what might be called a *unilinear model* of development. In a liberal view, even though people disagree about the character of the process, they accept the idea that societies go through phases, which correspond roughly to stages of economic growth. Each stage places certain limits on political options. As Clark Kerr explains,

> *The world is currently undergoing a great economic and social transformation. In essence, this transformation is in the commitment of man to a new way of life. Throughout history most of mankind has been committed to a constant way of life, even though particular ways have varied from one place to another and, to a much lesser extent, from one time to another. Commitment to a constant way of life seems to be the natural state of man.*
>
> *The current period of history is distinguished from all others, however, by the immensity of the process of destroying old commitments, no matter how constant they may have been, and by the worldwide uniformity of the new commitment. Men everywhere are transferring themselves fully and finally into the industrial way of life. Great uniformity is developing out of great diversity.* Industrialization, itself, is the significant new form *of social affiliation.*[5]

Kerr's view emphasizes stages of development within a broad pattern leading to uniformity, sameness, and similarity. To promote unilinear growth is the objective of developmental assistance, an instrument of foreign policy. For Marxists the paradigm of developmentalism is seen as an evolution from primitive communalism to, sequentially, slave, feudal, capitalist, and socialist societies, effected by means of transformations. The key question is: Is it possible to go from feudalism

---

5. Clark Kerr, "Changing Social Structures," *Labor Commitment and Social Change in Developing Areas,* ed. Wilbert E. Moore and Arnold S. Feldman (New York: Social Science Research Council, 1960), p. 349.

to socialism bypassing capitalism? The long-run objective is a common and universalized condition of freedom from poverty and freedom from constraining institutions which alienate men and women from themselves.[6] The problem is that to skip the capitalist stage requires the application of state power to the base, the modes of production. And this opens the door to coercion, manipulation, state capitalism, or a host of other ills.

The Idea of Development

Developing countries, then, are damned if they do and damned if they don't. The liberal capitalist solution poses the problems of inequity. The Marxian socialist requires coercion. Nevertheless no country gives up the idea of development. Development embodies hope. Aristotle saw it long ago as the realization of potentiality. Each individual has within him or her qualities which can be realized in an appropriate political setting. The better the politics, the more likely is individual potentiality to be achieved. That Aristotelian idea, combined with the notion of distributive justice, remains the foundation of all development politics. The best polity maximizes growth with equity; it effects the proper balancing of individual wants and needs against the collective good. Growth plus equity therefore equals fulfillment. This was also the ideal of the Enlightenment. The Industrial Revolution opened up the vision of unlimited possibilities.

Today's basic goals are the same, but modern political practice involves more realistic trade-offs between growth and equity. Development foreshadows economic or political inequality. Some may prefer economic inequality; in other words, acquiescing to the right of the rich to enjoy a disproportionate share of wealth so long as they help further the growth of society as a whole. Inequalities can be worthwhile if the poor are in the long run able to benefit. Others prefer political inequality and more controls over economic growth. A communist state with a firm hand, represses political liberties in favor of creating more industrial capacity, justifying its methods with the argument that it promotes an infrastructure of growth; there is gain for all as well as

6. See Joseph Schumpeter, *Capitalism, Socialism and Democracy* (New York: Harper and Brothers, 1947), p. 364.

costs. On the other hand, capitalist modes of rapid growth produce severe economic *and* social inequality, while bureaucratic socialism implements great political inequality. Each system justifies itself on the grounds that it achieves modernization (a goal that has only recently been challenged). The Soviet Union offers the prospect of liberalization after the main force of development has been accomplished. The United States offers the hope that the poor and the marginal will find greater opportunities in social betterment.

Progress does occur by means of democratic politics, but it is slow and discouraging. European countries that have become less growthminded and more equity-minded, like Britain, also find themselves in trouble. To achieve a just distribution without growth is expensive. A society needs to continue to develop if it is to meet its human obligations for public health, education, old age and survivors insurance, and other such programs. Yet if it puts too much money into social welfare at the expense of development, it lives beyond its means.

How much development is needed? At what rate of growth? How much equity? Where does one strike the balance? These are crucial questions. What forms of government are necessary to promote growth? How? What are the costs in human freedom? These issues confront political leaders anxious to promote development and concerned about its social costs. How they have dealt with them is varied. In terms of the relationship between development and liberty the picture is not very satisfactory.

The question of freedom and development can be boiled down to three topics for analysis. The first is economic growth, particularly the impacts of technological change and scientific innovation. Next is social change and differentiation, which results from the first. (How have technology and economic organization affected public behavior?) Third is political development—that is, the growth of an articulated governmental structure differentiated from other social subsystems—and the degree of public participation.

An historical perspective: The idea of economic growth is associated with the initial wave of technological development that began around 1750 and transformed the world. It began in Britain and spread. In Britain, inventiveness, parsimony, and the tradition of saving for investment in commercial opportunities, combined with an available labor force willing or forced to work for virtual subsistence wages, stimulated

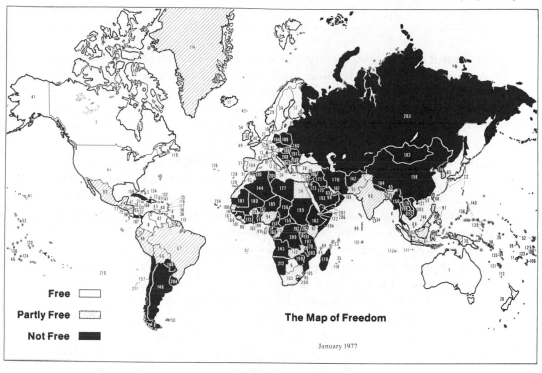

Free ☐

Partly Free ▨

Not Free ■

The Map of Freedom

January 1977

Free

Nations

1 Australia
2 Austria
3 Bahamas
4 Barbados
5 Belgium
6 Botswana
7 Canada
8 Colombia
9 Costa Rica
10 Denmark
11 Fiji
12 Finland
13 France
14 Gambia
15 Germany (W)
16 Greece
17 Iceland
18 Ireland
19 Israel
20 Italy
21 Jamaica
22 Japan
23 Luxembourg
24 Malta
25 Mauritius
26 Nauru
27 Netherlands
28 New Zealand
29 Norway
30 Papua-
    New Guinea
31 Portugal
32 San Marino
33 Seychelles
34 Sri Lanka
35 Surinam
36 Sweden
37 Switzerland
38 Trinidad
    & Tobago
39 Turkey
40 United Kingdom
41 United States
42 Venezuela

**Territories &
Dependencies**

Denmark:
43 Faroe Islands
France:
    (*Overseas Territory*)
44 Mayotte
Netherlands:
45 Antilles
New Zealand:
46 Niue
United Kingdom:
47 Belize
48 Bermuda
49 Channel Islands
50 Falkland Islands
51 Gibraltar
52 Gilbert Islands
53 Hong Kong
54 Isle of Man
55 Montserrat
56 St. Vincent
57 St. Helena
58 Solomons
59 Tuvalu
60 West Indies
    Ass. States
United States:
61 Puerto Rico

Partly Free

Nations

62 Andorra
63 Bahrain
64 Bangladesh
65 Bhutan
66 Bolivia
67 Brazil
68 China (Nat.)
69 Comoro Islands
70 Congo (Rep.)
71 Cyprus
72 Dominican
    Republic
73 Ecuador
74 Egypt
75 El Salvador
76 Grenada
77 Guatemala
78 Guyana
79 Honduras
80 India
81 Indonesia
82 Kenya
83 Korea (S)
84 Lebanon
85 Lesotho
86 Liberia
87 Liechtenstein
88 Malaysia
89 Maldives
90 Mexico
91 Monaco
92 Morocco
93 Nicaragua
94 Nigeria
95 Pakistan
96 Peru
97 Philippines
98 Qatar
99 Sao Tome
    & Principe
100 Senegal
101 Sierra Leone
102 Singapore
103 South Africa
104 Spain
105 Swaziland
106 Tonga
107 United Arab
    Emirates
108 Upper Volta
109 Western Samoa
110 Zambia

**Territories &
Dependencies**

Australia:
111 Christmas Island
112 Cocos (Keeling)
    Islands
113 Norfolk Island
Denmark:
114 Greenland
France:
    Overseas Depts.:
115 French Guiana
116 Guadeloupe
117 Martinique
118 Reunion
119 St. Pierre
    & Miquelon
    Overseas Territories:
120 French Polynesia
121 New Caledonia
122 Territory of
    Afars & Issas
123 Wallis & Futuna
New Zealand:
124 Cook Islands
125 Tokelau Islands

Portugal:
126 Azores
127 Macao
128 Madeira
Spain:
129 Canary Islands
130 Places of Sov.
    in No. Africa
United Kingdom:
131 British Indian
    Ocean Territory
132 British Virgin
    Islands
133 Cayman Islands
134 Turks & Caicos
135 New Hebrides
    (British-French Condo.)
United States:
136 American Samoa
137 Canal Zone
138 Guam
139 Micronesia
140 Northern Marianas
141 Virgin Islands

Not Free

Nations

142 Afghanistan
143 Albania
144 Algeria
145 Angola
146 Argentina
147 Benin
148 Brunei
149 Bulgaria
150 Burma
151 Burundi
152 Cambodia
153 Cameroon
154 Cape Verde
    Islands
155 Central African
    Republic
156 Chad
157 Chile
158 China (Com.)
159 Cuba
160 Czechoslovakia
161 Equatorial Guinea
162 Ethiopia
163 Gabon
164 Germany (E)
165 Ghana
166 Guinea
167 Guinea-Bissau
168 Haiti
169 Hungary
170 Iran
171 Iraq
172 Ivory Coast
173 Jordan
174 Korea (N)
175 Kuwait
176 Laos
177 Libya
178 Malagasy
    Republic
179 Malawi
180 Mali
181 Mauritania
182 Mongolia
183 Mozambique
184 Niger
185 Nepal
186 Oman
187 Panama
188 Paraguay
189 Poland
190 Rhodesia
191 Rumania
192 Rwanda
193 Saudi Arabia
194 Somalia
195 Sudan
196 Syria
197 Tanzania
198 Thailand
199 Togo
200 Transkei
201 Tunisia
202 Uganda
203 USSR
204 Uruguay
205 Vietnam
206 Yemen (N)
207 Yemen (S)
208 Yugoslavia
209 Zaire

**Territories &
Dependencies**

Chile:
210 Easter Island
211 Juan Fernandez
South Africa
212 South West Africa
    (Namibia)

The Map of Freedom*

* Courtesy of Freedom House.

the simultaneous growth of inventions and manufactures and the expansion of markets. Machine building and maintenance created opportunities for small, artisanal enterprises as well as encouraging the factory system. The first result was not large-scale enterprise but subcontracted enterprises which dispersed manufactures, increased productivity, and rendered industrial innovation into an intimate social experience. These brought factory work and home work together.[7] A century after the first stir of industrial manufacturers (or roughly 1850), however, the overwhelming bulk of the occupational workforce in Britain was still in agriculture, domestic service, or crafts. Since industrial methods did not come all at once, there was no "new" reality imposed suddenly on the "old," as is true in many developing countries today. Indeed, inventions and technological innovations occurred in practical areas closely related to the hand work with which everyone was familiar. The Industrial Revolution was not made by theoreticians.

Once the Industrial Revolution had taken hold, helped in part by colonialism and imperialism, the Western view was that both economic and political expansion were "uplifting" and progressive. Even Marx, who regarded industrialization as a necessary evil, believed in its progressive consequences. Not only would it generate the possibility for a new kind of life of abundance and freedom in advanced societies, but in countries like India, China, and Turkey, which he regarded as static, despotic, and barbaric, colonalism would serve to innovate and stir things up. Colonialism, then, for Marx was a progressive force insofar as it was the instrument of advanced capitalist societies breaking through what he called the "Asiatic mode of production." This would introduce conflict and change in backward countries, while producing war, depression, and intensification of crisis in the "metropole" or mother country. Hence colonialism and imperialism would in the long run both introduce dynamic changes in the "periphery" and hasten the emergence of socialism in the "metropole."[8]

The countries that came early to the industrial process more or less eased into it. We know how much suffering the Industrial Revolution engendered. Even so the shocks and problems of transition were far less radical than those experienced by latecomers.[9] To create something new without being fully aware of its novelty is, after all, quite different

7. See David S. Landes, *The Unbound Prometheus* (Cambridge: Cambridge University Press, 1969), p. 118.
8. See Karl Marx, "The British Rule in India," in *Karl Marx on Colonialism and Modernization,* ed. Avineri, op. cit., pp. 88–95.
9. See Marion J. Levy, Jr. *Modernization: Latecomers and Survivors* (New York: Basic Books, 1972).

from trying to play catch-up. One-party states, vanguard parties, military regimes, and repressive governments are the results of uneven growth and social conflicts generated in the catch-up process. Hence today the concept of political development no longer implies democracy as much as a stable system of authority promoting a favorable climate for investment, and infrastructure growth. Along with the modern idea of development goes an ideology of economic growth which legitimizes the political instruments capable of inducing growth. This capability gives political leaders both a "Promethean" and "Protean" quality; they wrestle with underdevelopment like those heroes wrestled with the gods and they change their characters without warning. Because modernization requires reshaping both physical and human materials, leaders of developing countries largely believe that all social life and material existence is plastic, and therefore subject to continuous change. The results of this philosophy vary.

Such a view also requires that leaders endorse the idea that development policy follows the logic of science, inducing growth and change by the most efficient means possible. The process requires only power plus judgment plus technology plus disciplined political cadres. Different people may subscribe to different cultures, after all, but all utilize the same mathematics and science, the same or similar technologies. Hence political leaders are the doers and shakers of the developing world. (Nor are such ideas limited to leaders of developing countries. A US aid official with a briefcase packed with proposals and plans, or a Soviet aid official, despite obvious differences in background, language, and ideologies, will follow much the same line of thinking.)

Does this imply that development will eventually produce a unified world in the sense that the strategic and central institutions and the relationships among people will be profoundly affected by the insistence of the industrial process? That they will draw closer to each other in conduct and behavior? Those who, following a unilinear pattern of development, believe that the main processes of modernity are the same everywhere and have the same basic consequences, argue thus. But not even a unilinear theory of modernization implies that all social institutions, norms, and values will be identical, but only certain crucial ones.

For two centuries (at least) the belief that economic growth was one of those self-evident "truths" along with liberty and equality, one aspect of the pursuit of happiness, has persisted. Today, however, people are beginning to doubt. Seemingly self-evident and optimistic notions of unilinear accomplishment have been shaken. The morphology that shows how people's belief constructs turned from the magical to the scientific, the sacred to the secular, the agricultural to the industrial, the rural to the urban, the community of *Gemeinschaft* to the atomistic and bureaucratic *Gesellschaft,* is no longer regarded as good or necessarily even true. While there always were warnings against the distintegrating effects of developmentalism, not until recently have such warnings been taken seriously. Any one person or society stands against development like King Canute against the tides. (Only China and Tanzania have, in their different ways, proceeded more cautiously, doubtful of the self-evident benefits of the most rapid rate of growth.)

Nostalgia versus inevitability: Development as an ideology: Today the difficulties crowd in on us, for clearly development has a many-sided nature. It affects even the functional needs of individuals and societies. For example, a member of a tribal group living on an island in Melanesia does not have the same needs, and does not function in the same way, as a New Yorker on Manhattan Island. The New Yorker may regard the Melanesians as being richly endowed with secure cultural verities, may even envy their closeness to nature, and a style of life directed along a highly prescribed route of ritual cycles attending birth, puberty, work, and marriage, and rewarding age with honor. But no matter how harried, frightened, or insecure, how pressured by careers or infuriated by tax forms, bureaucrats, and IBM machine-made mistakes, not to speak of the absence of elemental safety, the flight of New Yorkers to Melanesia is remarkably small!

So if the developmental idea is not exactly arcadian, even its critics are not prone to renounce it. In the United States there may be a strong nostalgia for a rural tradition, but it is a nostalgia of the intellectuals, particularly those inheritors of Rousseau, Tocqueville, and Crèvecoeur. What Hofstadter has called the "agrarian myth" remains but as an ideal.

Its hero was the yeoman farmer, its central conception the notion that he is the ideal man and the ideal citizen. Unstinted praise of the special virtues of the farmer and the special values of rural life was coupled with the assertion that agriculture as a calling uniquely productive and uniquely important to society, had a special right to the concern and protection of government. The yeoman, who owned a small farm and worked it with the aid of his family, was the incarnation of the simple, honest, independent, healthy, happy human being. Because he lived in

*close communion with the beneficent nature, his life was believed to
have a wholesomeness and integrity impossible for the depraved populations of cities. His well-being was not merely physical, it was moral;
it was not merely personal, it was the central source of civic virtue; it
was not merely secular but religious, for God had made the land and
called man to cultivate it. Since the yeoman was believed to be both
happy and honest, and since he had a secure propertied stake in society
in the form of his own land, he was held to be the best and most reliable
sort of citizen.*[10]

Similar arcadian ideals were to be found in England and France.
In England they were associated with the writings of Wordsworth,
Ruskin, and William Morris.[11] In France they were idealized by the
Physiocrats, who saw rural gentry as the foundation of a stable and
commercial agriculture.

Nostalgic as such arcadian myths were (and are), they did not
stop for a minute the desire for development or belief in its virtues.
In the United States developmentalism early became progressive, nostalgia reactionary—in a Jacksonian rather than Jeffersonian context—
and, generally speaking, liberal in the sense of favoring competition,
hard work, accumulation, investment, and growth. In Britain developmentalists took an anticonservative, antiaristocratic tack, favoring Whig
rather than Tory politics. When the effects of developmentalism produced obvious inequities and social conditions of which even the most
arcadian critics of development had not dreamed (in terms of the
brutalization of workers, substandard and slum housing in cities, and
other now familiar conditions under which nineteenth century industrialization thrived), the response was to reform, not to reassert the
virtues of the simple life. Socialists who acquiesced to developmentalism sought to provide new, more equitable political and social arrangements. They believed that removing control of economic power from
private hands would ultimately enable all citizens to realize the

10. Richard Hofstadter, *The Age of Reform* (New York: Vintage Books, 1955),
pp. 24–25. Hofstadter quotes the following poem as illustration.

"How happy in his low degree/How rich in humble poverty, is he,/Who leads a
quiet country life,/Discharged of business, void of strife,/And from the griping
scrivener free?"

11. See Herbert L. Sussman, *The Victorians and the Machine* (Cambridge, Mass.:
Harvard University Press, 1968).

potentialities of industrial life. Arcadianism was backward looking. Socialism and liberalism were forward looking. For those imbued with the spirit of socialism, then, development offered the condition of fulfillment. The Marxist ideal of nonalienation became a kind of romantic conception for the future in much the same way the "happy yeoman" was a romanticized conception of the past.[12]

However conceived, the actual achievements of science, technology, and the dynamism these affected in some parts of the globe—generating power, empire, markets, glory—knocked nostalgia on the head. As Hobsbawm put it,

> . . . *some time in the 1780's, and for the first time in human history, the shackles were taken off the productive power of human societies, which henceforth became capable of the constant, rapid, and up to the present limitless multiplication of men, goods, and services. This is now technically known to the economists as the "take-off" into self-sustained growth. No previous society had been able to break through the ceiling which a pre-industrial social structure, defective science and technology, and consequently periodic breakdown, famine and death, imposed on production.*[13]

The Idea of Modernization

The premise of developmentalism (as well as its promise—the teleology of growth) represents an ideology: that growth is itself history acted out as a set of stages. Each stage has its own predicaments. The unilinear theory considers development inevitable. In the unilinear model, mod-

12. For Marx, development was a complex process. The subject is "man as a species being. In essence it is a theory of mankind's historical growth process and final self-realization in a post-historical society that Marx treats under the heading of 'socialism' or 'communism'." See Robert C. Tucker, *The Marxian Revolutionary Idea* (New York: Norton, 1969), p. 94.
13. Eric J. Hobsbawm, *The Age of Revolution* (New York: Mentor Books, 1962), p. 54. Hobsbawm also points out that if the Industrial Revolution was at first British, it was not because of a superior science, for in science and technology the French were ahead. What the British had was a practical and innovative shrewdness appropriate to a relatively primitive set of technological needs (like the steam engine and its use in the coal mines). And what they designed could be built by artisans using available know-how. See also Landes, op. cit., p. 61. Landes calls the question of British mechanical skill "mysterious." England was not the only country with gifted artisans, but nowhere else was there reaped a "harvest of inventions."

ernization is a process. Like the flow of goods and services in economic life (business goes where profit is to be had), modernization takes place where it is most easily accepted or wanted. We will call modernization the transfer of roles from metropole to periphery.

Stage one: In the early stages modernization begins with a few hardy, enterprising individuals with a particularly strong sense of mission—or greed, or zeal, or desire for adventure. They are the pioneers. Historically they paved the way for institutions of innovation within the context of colonialism. The conquistadores, and the entrepreneurial adventurers who formed the first charter companies for trade in Africa and the Indies, were followed by colonialism.[14] The Portuguese went to Africa in the fifteenth century, the Spaniards to the Americas in the year of the Inquisition, 1492. The Dutch went to Java and Bali late in the sixteenth century.[15] Similarly, the British colonized North America and India. All settled in exotic, underdeveloped foreign parts where native populations lived a "traditional" mode of life. Hence the first stage of development represented a process by means of which the then new wealth of Europe and new technologies, by creating opportunities for trade, effected not only the settlement of trade centers but the acquisition of territory. It was accompanied by the belief that the condition of dependent peoples must be changed. Colonized nations were expected to become Christian, to live in "civilized" Western fashion.

In the first stage, then, there was contact between colonial (and missionary) and indigenous populations. But as local elites formed, new social formations arose.

Stage two: The second stage of development shows the effects of colonialism. Innovative foreign elites—mercantile, bureaucratic and governmental, religious and evangelical—created urban centers where there had been none, or transformed those that were. Native peoples drew into closer contact with foreigners. Rules and regulations required *local* authorities to aid and assist in carrying out the dictates and mandates of the colonial regimes. The mystique of empire was that if the "civilized" nations would bring the benefits of the markets, edu-

14. See George Masselman, *The Cradle of Colonialism* (New Haven, Conn.: Yale University Press, 1963).
15. See Clive Day, *The Dutch in Java* (New York: Oxford University Press, 1966). See also Carl Polanyi, Conrad M. Arensberg and Harry W. Pearson, eds., *Trade and Markets in the Early Empires* (Glencoe, Ill.: The Free Press, 1957).

cation, and Christianity to the "savages," the latter would prosper. What prospered even more were the cultural and racial notions of superiority used to justify domination. So "primitive" countries were opened up to the benefits of civilization, trade, and commerce, not always to their enhancement. In Africa, to cite the extreme example, colonialism followed hard on the heels of the slave trade. Thus colonialism was both stimulated by the traffic in human beings, and later justified on the grounds that it would eliminate that traffic. Local authorities were established in remote areas where medical, commercial, educational, and other facilities followed. In this way development spread from metropolis to periphery, creating towns, markets, schools, all of which offered alternatives to lives which in European standards were regarded for the most part as dull, nasty, brutish, and short.

The mixture of benefits and costs brought by European colonialism will be the subject of debate for decades.[16] No one knows how many Africans were removed from the African subcontinent by such "beneficial enterprises" as the slave trade, whose cost in lives, talent, and suffering was incalculable.[17]

Stage three: As new elites emerged (often products of intermarriage between foreigners and indigenous people) more complex associations in politics arose. Local elites demanded more participation for educated people. (In India Mahatma Gandhi was a prototype. A lawyer, a nationalist, a member of the new elite, he rallied the educated, the mercantile class, the residents of towns, and the people of urban areas. Eventually, however, he turned his crusade to the benefit of the peasantry, the poor, the untouchables, and then became a powerful force.)

So the picture changed. Those engaged in modern sectors of society, having grown to large proportions, directed their activity to creating mass movements. Attacks on colonial authorities combined with the demand for sharing power. Often the inspiration was the American Revolution, the first revolution for "decolonization".[18]

16. See Stanislav Andreski, *The African Predicament* (New York: Atherton Press, 1968).
17. See Daniel P. Mannix and Malcolm Cowley, *Black Cargoes* (New York: The Viking Press, 1962); see also Sir Reginald Coupland, *The British Anti-Slavery Movement* (London: Frank Cass, 1933), and Basil Davidson, *The African Slave Trade* (Boston: Little, Brown, 1961).
18. See Seymour Martin Lipset, *The First New Nation* (New York: Basic Books, 1963).

Stage four: The fourth stage of modernization is characterized by political rather than economic development. Cries for participation turned into demands for independence, or at least freedom from overseas domination. Today the problem is for developing nations to use political independence to produce more viable and effective communities without becoming ensnared in "neocolonialism." This is partly a matter of promoting economic growth, partly an awakening to the predicaments of uneven change. To avoid such predicaments of modernization some political leaders opt for *developmental socialist* solutions. Each proposed solution, however, and each type of political system soon generates its own problems and difficulties. Some rely on force at the expense of liberty. These spend large sums on police and army fire power. Others which emphasize liberty soon find themselves at the mercy of the rich or middle sectors of the population who claim access to politics (and supply a good many of the politicians) at the expense of the poor.

Figure 14-1 describes the processes and stages of modernization. Typically *A* represents the first stage of modernization (the agency of modernization is external). The original impetus can be the establishment of a charter company or an evangelical mission. (Examples are Latin America under Spanish rule, or the African territories under

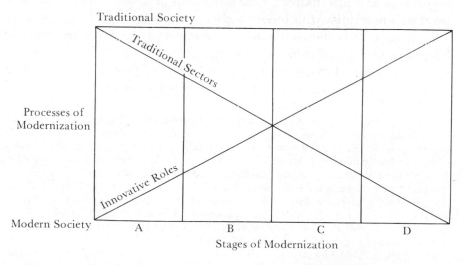

Figure 14-1. The Unilinear Model of Political Modernization

European dominion.[19]) The consolidation of alien rule, the erection of a stable system of authority, and the beginnings of urbanization, health, and schooling for an elite occur at the end of stage *A*.

Stage *B* is much more mixed. The proportion of innovative roles is larger and the innovators develop institutions. Instead of a single official representative of colonial authority there is a bureaucracy. Instead of the missionary *cum* teacher there is a school system. Instead of the trader there is a commercial network. Locals and foreigners interact. New forms of association occur and new interests arise. A banking and credit structure forms. So does the embryo of elite nationalism. Local representatives demand more participation and greater shares of responsibility. Typically the initial reaction of the colonial authorities to such political vigor is negative. Unrest, conflict, and confrontation follow, involving more and more people. Usually some concessions are made by government, some nationalist militants are jailed.

By stage *C* the process is more advanced. Colonial governments tend to become highly participant, favoring local political moderates and modeling political development after the imperialist's example. (French African political institutions, for example, were very French, those in English possessions were English.[20]) Such responses, in turn, stimulate political organizations, mass movements, demands for greater independence, and other forerunners of the impending break with the colonizing power. Intellectuals foment rebellion, providing ideological arguments and alternatives. Charismatic or near charismatic leaders promise a new unity with independence.

In stage *D* is the conversion to independence. Then the process begins all over again in political terms. An advantage of the model is that it can be used to document a morphology of post-independence as well as colonial stages. The initial phase is one of enthusiasm and sup-

19. See C.H. Haring, *The Spanish Empire in America* (New York: Harcourt, Brace and World, 1947) ; Richard Morse, "The Heritage of Latin America," *The Founding of New Societies,* ed. Louis Hartz (New York: Harcourt, Brace and World, 1964) ; and Magali Sarfatti, *Spanish Bureaucratic-Patrimonialism in America* (Berkeley, Ca.: Institute of International Studies, University of California, 1966) .
20. See Robert Delavignette, *Freedom and Authority in French West Africa* (London: Oxford University Press, 1950) ; Virginia Thompson and Richard Adloff, *French West Africa* (Stanford, Ca.: Stanford University Press, 1957) ; Ruth Schachter Morgenthau, *Political Parties in French-Speaking West Africa* (Oxford: The Clarendon Press, 1964) ; William H. Lewis, ed., *French-Speaking Africa* (New York: Walker, 1965) . See also George Bennett, ed., *The Concept of Empire* (London: Adam and Charles Black, 1953) : Donald Winch, *Classical Political Economy and Colonies* (London: G. Bell and Sons, 1965) .

port for the nationalist leadership. The next is disaffection, and conflict at the top of the hierarchy. The winner creates a one-party state. The third stage is a period during which the authority is liable to overthrow by military coups. The final stage elicits attempts to enfranchise alternatives to the military.[21] At this point in the cyclical nature of development the whole process is renewed again, on a new level of sophistication, perhaps, but nevertheless following the same basic model.

Unilinear stages and political predicaments: The idea embodied in the unilinear notion of political development is that economic and technological change stimulates development that filters down from the more advanced to the less. Then the less advanced proceed in stages to join the ranks of the more advanced. Contact between innovators and "traditionals" is followed by colonialism and imperialism, which in turn break up when nationalist elites become independence-minded. Again, the urge toward independence is followed by a post-independence cycle during which internal opposition to the home rule of nationalist leaders compounds conflicts between primordial separatists, between classes, between the urban and rural populations, and between rich and poor. All such conflict jeopardizes the stability of the society. Then there is a scramble for new political solutions, the growth of single-party systems, vanguard parties, military regimes, and other phenomena of political disintegration. (Some argue that the idea of developmental stages is in reality one of those grand fictions of developmental theory; the "beginning" is oversimplified and the "end" is without end, as any inhabitant of a modern industrial society can testify.) [22]

We can now review our discussion by identifying typical predicaments. The first is the set of incongruities or contradictions that appear when a dominant colonial system is imposed on an indigenous society or societies which are then made to conform to alien rule. Conflicts in belief, roles, government, and virtually all the activities of life arise and are mediated or controlled by external rulers.

Second, an elite forms which, no longer part of traditional society,

---

21. See A.F.K. Organski, *The Stages of Political Development* (New York: Knopf, 1965). See also W.W. Rostow, *The Stages of Economic Growth* (Cambridge: Cambridge University Press, 1964).
22. See S.N. Eisenstadt, *Tradition, Change and Modernity* (New York: Wiley, 1973), pp. 98–115.

is nevertheless excluded from effective participation in the colonial system. Such an elite forms coalitions with factions, bands, and other groupings to form an ideology of nationalism. In turn, popular leaders, becoming ever more daring and explicit in their demands, displace the elites with mass movements. This ends with independence.

Next there is conflict between remnants of the old elite, the survivors of old colonial forms, and those who wish to purge the society of the past and start fresh. The conditions of rule are precarious. Either the new government succumbs to other contenders, or it becomes highly coercive, and possibly imprisons or eradicates its opposition. This is the period of single-party jurisdiction. Then, as the use of the police and military as peacekeepers draws the armies into politics, the extant government becomes vulnerable to overthrow.

Finally, there is the search for a solution among various alternatives to military rule: corporatist, radical socialist, liberal capitalist, or some other combination. One is the period of contact and control; two of reaction and emancipation; three of contradiction; and four represents a search for a new generative solution.

Crisis Analysis in Political Development

There is an alternative to the unilinear model: the *crisis model*. The crisis model offers the advantage of focusing on concrete issues and problems in order to evaluate both immediate and general significances. By emphasizing typical or universal problems (crises), the more firmly anchored concrete problems which everyone recognizes out of experience are seen in larger perspective. The crisis model answers to one problem of developing countries: the issue of whether political development must precede economic development. To deal with this problem calls for a knowledge of what kinds of politics facilitate what kinds of growth.

Marxists have particular difficulty solving the equation. Marx argued that each society would go through the bourgeois phases of development preliminary to the socialist state. But even in the first stage of a socialist society, the dictatorship of the proletariat exists in a "dying" state. Well, reverse the order of development and the dictatorship becomes a dictatorship in earnest, one (like Stalinism or neo-Stalinism) relying on forced methods of economic growth, heavy industrialization, and peasant collectivization as the way to accumulate funds for investment. In all fairness, however, proponents of democracy confront problems equally dogged because the democratic state is, under similar circumstances, prone to corruption, payoffs from foreign investors, disorganization, inefficiency, instability, and short-run solutions designed to placate the demands of the marketplace rather than instill in the society the discipline for sacrifice which today's developmental needs require. Between the dilemmas posed by these two alternatives, most of the world's developmental systems seek compromise solutions.[23]

Developmental models: We have already raised the question about the extent to which industrial societies really represent models. In a certain sense both the democratic and the Soviet solutions are hard to emulate, although for different reasons. The democratic solution in the West represents the mutual interaction and growth of both the economy *and* political democracy. These are mutually reinforcing, even if the relationship is bumpy and difficult. In most developing countries, however, this socioeconomic synthesis is not possible. On the opposite pole, the *cost* of the Stalinist model of development, its rigid bureaucracy, the purging of cadres, and the other human losses, are too great.

If the two industrial alternatives are not models, then, where does this leave developing countries? For the most part they are neither fish nor fowl. They seek *partial* (largely remedial) solutions. They experience a high degree of instability, failure, and quite often the decay rather than the enhancement of political institutions.[24]

So back to the question, what criteria define what types of political development? If one accepts the view that modernization is the process of moving economically and socially from a state of underdevelopment toward industrial status, then does it necessarily follow that the political system develops concurrently? Or put the matter differently: Is political development independent of the syndrome of modernization? Political criteria for modernization include the assertion of the ideology of nationalism to the extent that groups begin to act on their own behalf to mobilize toward independence. Political development, then, is reflected in a growth rate of successful transactions—flows of exchange: economic,

23. See René Dumont, *Socialisms and Development* (New York: Praeger, 1973). See also Helen Desfosses and Jacques Levesque, eds., *Socialism in the Third World* (New York: Praeger, 1975).
24. See Samuel P. Huntington, *Political Order in Changing Societies* (New Haven, Conn.: Yale University Press, 1968). See also Samuel P. Huntington and Joan M. Nelson, *No Easy Choice* (Cambridge, Mass.: Harvard University Press, 1976).

social, cultural—both within and between nations.[25] Therefore developmentalists emphasize the operation of public institutions within the framework of the nation-state (thus associating political development not with stages but with *institutions* of government) , and the evolution of the infrastructure of governmental bodies designed to *do* things, from running the posts and telegraph to the organizing of international meetings for the heads of the Third World countries.[26]

Strategic institutions: So we shift our attention to the strategic institutions within government. One commonly considered to be crucial is the structure of law and its administration. Another is the civil service, or bureaucracy. A public service is quite often the most critical inheritance of a new government, particularly when nationalist leaders have little experience in government (their politics having theretofore consisted mainly of organizing the opposition) . Some leaders come from the relatively restricted environment of the military; hence the tendency to rely heavily on the civil servants (or on the army or secret police) . Nothing is more paralyzing than a corrupt or inflated bureaucracy, but a good public service is essential for effective government.[27]

Another problem is to involve citizens in the goals of the state, to mobilize them, and to arouse their interest and participation. Apter suggests ten conditions of nationalism composed of the following demands: *political equality,* between and within nations; *democratic government,* either as an immediate demand (against colonialists for example) or for the future (as a goal) ; *rapid social mobility; equal opportunity; racial tolerance; the responsibility of the individual to the group* (state) ; *technological development; government enterprise* (or mixed enterprises) ; *a satisfactory explanation of imperialism;* and *political discipline* (the search for a new puritanism being its most austere form) .[28] Whatever the particular form of an ideology, it should aim at using the population as a resource and simultaneously advancing both social and economic development.

25. See Karl W. Deutsch, "Social Mobilization and Political Development," *American Political Science Review,* Vol. LV, No. 3 (September 1961) : 493–514.
26. See Kalman H. Silvert, *Expectant Peoples: Nationalism and Development* (New York: Random House, 1964) .
27. See Fred W. Riggs, *Administration in Developing Countries* (Boston: Houghton Mifflin, 1964) . See also J.P. Nettl, *Political Mobilization* (London: Faber and Faber, 1957) .
28. See Moore and Feldman, op. cit., D.E. Apter, "Political Organization and Ideology," pp. 329–31.

More specifically, a concern of the West is to build democracy, or representative government. If this is held to be the sole indicator of political development, then by that criterion the picture is not very happy. There are, as we have seen, far fewer "democratic" societies among the developing countries today than when the so-called "development decade" (1960–1970) began.

Perhaps as a result many assert that there is incompatibility between political democracy and economic growth where political stability is the preferred criterion. However, stability needs to be measured by more than the sheer political survival of a regime. (A sufficiently brutal government can maintain its rule with bayonets.) Stability must be accompanied by effective planning, with economic growth leading to social improvement. Many who support military rule in Brazil, for example, or Turkey, or other "corporatist"-type systems despite their implicit authoritarianism, argue that these governments have been both politically stable and economically successful. Are these preconditions of a transition to democracy (Greece being a case in point)?[29] No one knows the answer.

To what extent should political development be regarded from the standpoint of successful mobilization, both of resources and manpower, above other developmental goals? In this regard both Brazil and the USSR under Stalin would be considered successful, despite their brutality. Such a view ignores human costs.

Finally, there is the question of multidimensional change itself. Since political development has so many aspects, and because no single factor, such as economic growth, is a sufficient indicator, what criteria tell us which functions are most significant, and how the multiplicity of factors should best be examined? This problem is perhaps the most fundamental one.[30]

To deal with the questions thus posed, political scientists propose certain universal measurable *crises*. The crisis hypothesis differs from the unilinear progression of modernization in that there is no modernization spectrum. A society can suffer crises at any stage. The important thing is universality. The fundamental political crises are as follows:

29. See Alfred Stepan, *The Military in Politics: Changing Patterns in Brazil* (Princeton: Princeton University Press, 1971); see also his *The State and Society: Peru in Comparative Perspective* (Princeton: Princeton University Press, forthcoming).
30. See Lucian W. Pye, *Aspects of Political Development* (Boston: Little, Brown, 1966), pp. 33–45.

Identity—The individual seeks to develop an authentic personality, and the state its own political culture.

Legitimacy—There is a validation of the exercise of government and power by means of ideologically effective public support.

Participation—The conversion of a passive population into an active one takes place through voting, representation, mass parties, or mobilized populations.

Distribution—There is greater equality of opportunity and social mobility.

Penetration—There is an equalization of obligation and the breaking down of parochialism and separatism of any kind.

Each of these crises represents a problem for all developing countries. Politics continuously undertakes to resolve them.[31]

The crisis model, unlike the unilinear model, assumes that different political systems evolve strategies particular to the case. The latter tries to account for change cumulatively, in terms of the impacting of one stage on another. The unilinear model is *comparative,* although it can be used with cases. The crisis model is *configurational.*

Methods of Developmental Analysis

Comparative cases: We have tried to show how political development and economic growth are intertwined. We suggested that latecomers to independence suffer from having to recapitulate all the innovations of the past by political means, a problem not confronted by the first industrializers who, no matter what difficulties they experienced, at least did not have the additional handicap of being victimized by externally induced changes. We suggested a model for stages of modernization. We also contrasted stage analysis with crisis analysis, a nonunilinear model. We now want to discuss some of the ways both models have been used in comparative research.

The unilinear model illustrates a certain pattern, more or less an historical evolution, but not strictly historical. One could compare the different systems of colonization which occurred at stages *A* and *B* without reference to time. For example, it is extremely interesting, in

---

31. See Leonard Binder et al., *Crises and Sequences in Political Development* Princeton, N.J.: Princeton University Press, 1971) , p. 65.

light of subsequent developments, to compare the pattern of Spanish colonialism, its highly centralized and bureaucratic structure and its mixture of sacred-religious and secular-imperial aims operating under a system of mercantilism, with, say, British colonialism in Africa. This was more capitalist, more local, aimed at building up local elites. But in terms of history the Spanish empire spans from the fifteenth century to the beginning of the nineteenth century, while for all intents and purposes British rule in Africa only began in the latter part of the nineteenth century. Despite vast differences between the two systems and the worlds they represent, it is possible to make such comparisons for certain purposes, just as it is possible to compare British colonialism in Africa and in India, regions so culturally different that it would seem unwise to make any kind of generalization between them whatsoever.[32]

We find that comparisons made between systems rather than across time often illustrate certain common features, typical consequences. For example, the Latin American struggle for independence from Spain grew out of nationalist movements of volunteer forces, patriot armies made up of diverse elements. There was one charismatic leader in the person of Simón Bolívar, the "great liberator," a native of Caracas who joined in cultural associations, held secret meetings, and formed a revolutionary junta. His supporters consisted of creoles, foreign volunteers, *mestizos*, mulattoes, Indians, and freed Negroes. Another such figure was the Argentinian hero José de San Martin. Both were founders of new societies. Both confronted the problem of how to organize ill-defined, ex-colonial territories into effective political units. After independence both faced deteriorating economies, threatening parochial or regional bands, localism, and growing uncertainty and disaffection among the people. Both leaders suffered reverses in their fortunes and lost power shortly after independence (Bolívar within six months).[33]

The growth of loosely formed bands around romantic and attractive leaders, and the problems attending independence have their counterparts in modernizing countries emerging in the past few decades. The problems of leadership, deteriorating internal conditions, the emergence of local ethnic or parochial separatist movements, and the problem of military takeovers (once thought to be somehow uniquely

32. See, for example, D. A. Low, *Lion Rampant* (London: Frank Cass, 1973).
33. See Donald Marquand Dozer, *Latin America: An Interpretive History* (New York: McGraw-Hill, 1962), pp. 190–247. See also, Richard Rojas, *San Martin* (New York: Cooper Square Publishers, Inc., 1967).

Latin American) have become the common lot in many countries. Some African states follow much the same pattern, as have Indonesia, Thailand, and other countries. If the degree of modernization can be roughly correlated with the increase in internal difficulties, incongruities, and contradictions, then comparison between *stages* rather than over time—that is, synchronic comparison—is valid in modernization studies.[34]

What sort of developmental comparisons have been made? Some scholars have compared traditional societies, or types of traditional systems. Then too, traditional societies have been subdivided into types: tribal, centralized, bureaucratic, segmented, and so forth. One monumental comparison of many cases of a single type juxtaposed bureaucratic traditional societies.[35] Although the cases consisted of historical examples, the comparison itself was not historical, but synchronic. Its purpose was to examine how different forms of centralized bureaucracies worked. Ancient empires, like those of Egypt, Babylonia, the Inca, and the Aztec, were compared with the Chinese, Persian, Roman, Hellenistic, Byzantine, and Hindu, and with the Arab Caliphate, feudal systems in Europe, and others in terms of characteristics of rule, methods of policy making, modes of political participation, patterns of social organization, and so on.

Other forms of comparison concentrate on discovering certain characteristics of each stage. For example, C.E. Black, an historian concerned with modernization, names four stages, or phases, of modernization: (1) *the challenge to modernity,* which represents the initial confrontation with an advanced technology, modern ideas, and institutions of a society with a traditional framework of knowledge; (2) *the consolidation of a modernizing leadership,* including the transfer of power from traditional to modernizing leaders; (3) *a transformation* phase in which economic and social changes turn societies from their predominantly agrarian ways to urban and industrial ones; and (4) *the integration of society,* during which time the transformation of the entire society is completed.[36] Black compares these phases of modernization with seven historical patterns abstracted from studies of 175 coun-

34. See Robert T. Holt and John E. Turner, *The Methodology of Comparative Research* (New York: The Free Press, 1970).
35. See S.N. Eisenstadt, *The Political Systems of Empires* (New York: The Free Press, 1963).
36. See C.E. Black, *The Dynamics of Modernization* (New York: Harper & Row, 1966), pp. 67–89.

tries. The resulting comparisons led him to formulate theories about democracy, the effects of outside intervention, the effects of colonialism, and other developmental issues.[37]

Some comparativists are concerned with the properties of alternative political solutions that do not follow in a particular sequence. Apter has developed a typology or set of characteristic properties based on alternative combinations of legitimacy and organization, *bureaucratic*, based on the principle of order, *theocratic* based on the principle of belief, *mobilization* based on the principle of *potentiality*, and *reconciliation* based on the principle of mediation.[38]

Edward Shils suggests a more elaborate typology of *political democracy, tutelary democracy, modernizing oligarchies, totalitarian oligarchies, and traditional oligarchies,* each having different components and characteristics.[39] Each also responds differently to public opinion, use of the media, educated elites, and so on. While a cultural predisposition toward a certain type of political system depends to some extent on the level of societal development, there is no direct correlation between stages of political modernization and specific forms of political systems. Only by comparing traditional bureaucratic systems or political regimes does Shils propose patterns and typologies that provide better understanding of how different systems operate.[40]

Case studies: Case studies normally follow a single example through time, or through successive stages. So, for example, in examining the development of modern nationalist politics in Ghana, Apter examined a single territory which originally consisted of a number of ethnic groups clustered by the British into a single colony, the Gold Coast. When Ghana became an independent country, it helped spearhead the emergence of pan-African nationalism in Africa as a whole. Apter traces some of the characteristics of traditional ethnic systems, how elite nationalism occurred during the period of colonialism, how this gave way to mass nationalist politics under Kwame Nkrumah (within the context of a system of British-style parliamentary democracy), and

37. Ibid., pp. 106–128.
38. See David E. Apter, *Choice and the Politics of Allocation* (New Haven, Conn.: Yale University Press, 1971).
39. See Edward Shils, *Political Development in New States* (s'Gravenhage: Mounton & Co., 1962), pp. 47–84.
40. For a critical review of such typologies see Robert T. Golembiewski, William A. Welsh and William C. Crotty, *A Methodological Primer for Political Scientists* (Chicago: Rand McNally, 1969).

how after independence the country was transformed into a single-party mobilizing state later swept away in a coup.[41]

Some case studies have dealt with the responsiveness of traditional societies (bureaucratic or religious systems) to modernization.[42] These focus on the problem of building national states out of diverse groupings with sectarian interests and loyalties. Such case studies represent a kind of political anthropology or political ethnography. Their purpose is to show how the traditional societies and internal organization affect the response to innovation, and how new problems arise with which governments have to deal. Several such *configurational* studies have had wide theoretical significance. Ronald Dore's *Education in Tokugawa Japan*,[43] which deals with the effect of early education in Tokugawa Japan, is important precisely because it shows how the emphasis on knowledge helped to create a condition of literacy, an awareness of books, postal communications, and other characteristics associated with highly modernized societies, *before* Western contact with Japan. Hence, when such contact did occur in 1853, the Japanese were able to make use of Western technology and adapt rapidly to innovation while controlling the results. An emphasis on merit appointments of administrators had also established objective standards of excellence, which facilitated the transition to modern institutions as well.

Another case study of great significance is Franz Schurmann's *Ideology and Organization in Communist China*.[44] Not only does this work deal with the relationships between norms and structure, with how the Chinese Communists instilled sufficient militancy and a belief in the transforming ideology of Maoism to affect the behavior of the population, but also with how they transformed the structure of social and economic life. Ideology in practice is examined in the roles of the party, the government, bureaucracy and management; in methods of control in villages, towns, and people's communes; in factories, production brigades, and other organizations.

Such studies inform comparisons of other areas. For example, it is

41. See D.E. Apter, *Ghana in Transition,* 2nd rev. ed. (Princeton, N.J.: Princeton University Press, 1973) .
42. See Lloyd A. Fallers, *Bantu Bureaucracy* (Cambridge: Heffers, 1956) ; Clifford Geertz, *Religion in Java* (New York: The Free Press, 1960) ; Robert N. Bellah, *Tokugawa Religion* (Glencoe, Ill.: The Free Press, 1957) .
43. See Ronald Dore, *Education in Tokugawa Japan* (Berkeley, Ca.: University of California Press, 1965) , pp. 291–316.
44. See Franz Schurmann, *Ideology and Organization in Communist China* (Berkeley, Ca.: University of California Press, 1966) .

useful to consider the problems which Chinese Communism has confronted in contrast to Soviet Communism, from which it differs in important respects. Also, case studies of other Third World countries influenced by the Chinese can be evaluated in terms of their own local variants. A good example is Tanzania, where the emphasis on the formation of village communities and the role of the single party, not to speak of the emphasis on the leader as a teacher, *Malimu,* all show the influence of the Chinese, especially their emphasis on self-reliance.[45]

Still other configurational studies deal with the problems of localization and fragmentation, and most particularly with the role of political parties in holding the nation together. One such model is India which, following the British tradition, has, until recently, tried to deal with intractable problems of separatism, poverty, and the population explosion essentially by democratic means. One of the most important studies of India, which enables comparisons with Western practice (and also Chinese), is Rajni Kothari's *India.*[46] Kothari uses a consociational pluralist model to examine such problems as linguistic conflict and its mediation, the assertion of an Indian culture above more parochial ones, and the role of various grass-roots movements in promoting modernization.

Other case studies which apply class analysis to development include James Petras, *Politics and Social Forces in Chilean Development,* and Alfred Stepan, *The Military in Politics, Changing Patterns in Brazil* (the latter focuses on the relations between society as a whole and the military in particular).[47] Still another, which deals more directly with themes of colonialism, underdevelopment, and neo-colonialism, is the study done by Colin Leys in Kenya. Leys' approach stresses the method of contradiction and illustrates how the problems named confront the government with grave difficulties.[48]

All of the works cited (and there are many others as well) represent ways of handling the single case through time. Each tries to show

45. See Henry Bienen, *Tanzania, Party Transformation and Economic Development* (Princeton, N.J.: Princeton University Press, 1970). See also Cranford Pratt, *The Critical Phase in Tanzania 1945–1968* (Cambridge: Cambridge University Press, 1976).
46. See Rajni Kothari, *India* (Boston: Little, Brown, 1970).
47. See James Petras, *Politics and Social Forces in Chilean Development* (Berkeley, Ca.: University of California Press, 1969); Alfred Stepan, *The Military in Politics, Changing Patterns in Brazil* (Princeton, N.J.: Princeton University Press, 1971).
48. See Colin Leys, *Underdevelopment in Kenya, The Political Economy of Neo-Colonialism* (Berkeley, Ca.: University of California Press, 1974).

how a particular legacy—colonialism, say, or class—creates and responds to urgent political problems. Each discusses attempts to resolve these in detail.

In terms of political modernization the good case study does several things. First it digs deeper than simple historical fact. It identifies basic characteristics, either systemically or typologically. Second it compares change from system-type to system-type, showing events that essentially illustrate the key variables of transformation. Third it shows how, in the movement from stage to stage, the case confronts new problems even while resolving others. Finally it deals with the effects of societal-level change on government-level change. The stability of political regimes is thus seen in *interaction* with the problems each society confronts. In this respect the good case study is valuable not only because it details how political systems work, but because the results can be used for comparative purposes, for the framing of new hypotheses, models, and propositions. Like good comparison studies, then, case studies add a cumulative body of theory to the analysis of developmental politics.

Combined research strategies: We can combine the elements of the discussion so far in the diagram in Figure 14-2. Each of the four boxes represents a different approach to developmentalism. Either stage or crisis analysis can be used with each approach.

The Single Case Through Time. Most examples of this kind approximate studies of political anthropology. They require detailed field work,

	Diachronic	Synchronic
Configurational Analysis	The single case through time	System in relation to sub-system(s)
Comparative Analysis	Sample of cases through time	Multiple cases using Cross-National Data

Figure 14-2. Types of Developmental Analysis

facility with local languages, and a knowledge of the specifics of social and political organization. Time is actually used to demarcate different systems at points of transformation. For example, Apter's work on Uganda dealt with the particular case of Buganda and its implications for the development of a viable national state. Ethnic separation was the key problem confronting the nationalist movement; ethnicity was used to blunt innovation, presenting the "modernizing autocracy" with a unique problem.[49] Similarly, studies of Russia can stress the continuity of Tsarist absolutism in Stalinism, the role of the bureaucracy, and other factors like the differences between the rural agricultural system and the industrial system under socialism, use the case study approach to compare specific institutions from system to system.[50] Others mark the changes in the political system of the USSR at different stages of development.[51]

A Sample of Cases Through Time. Studies using this strategy tend to employ a limited number of cases, which are compared at different stages of development. We have already discussed the work of Barrington Moore (Chapter Twelve). Another good example is Reinhard Bendix's comparison of premodern structures and transformations that occurred in Western European society (both medieval and post-eighteenth century), and the effects of these on the emerging nation-states. This work prepares the ground for comparative analysis of Western Europe with Russia, Japan, Germany, and finally India.[52]

On the whole, studies that compare cases through time concentrate on how national institutions evolve, the character of authority, the relationship of societal development to political development, the role of specialized agencies of government, and so forth. They do not generally require much quantitative data or survey or other techniques of analysis. Rather the approach is essentially typological or structural.

Systems in Relation to Subsystems. Studies based on systems relations tend to focus on some particularly crucial and dynamic subsys-

49. See D.E. Apter, *The Political Kingdom in Uganda* (Princeton, N.J.: Princeton University Press, 1961).

50. See, for example, Cyril E. Black, ed., *The Transformation of Russian Society* (Cambridge, Mass.: Harvard University Press, 1960).

51. See Moshe Lewin, *Political Undercurrents in Soviet Economic Debates* (Princeton, N.J.: Princeton University Press, 1974).

52. See Reinhard Bendix, *Nation Building and Citizenship* (New York: Wiley, 1964).

tem of the political whole. For example, in the study of development
there have been specialized examinations of a number of critical agencies that produce change. Many useful contributions have been made
in a series of publications under the auspices of the Committee on Comparative Politics of the Social Science Research Council.[53] One deals
with bureaucracy, its role and function in new societies. A sound
bureaucracy may be the frame which cements a country in the face of
fragmentation, opposing political parties, primordial conflicts, and
other separatist tendencies which might intensify with development.
The comparative study of bureaucracy's effect on political development is thus of exceptional importance because a bureaucracy can become the critical instrument of growth or its hindrance.[54]

Other specialized subsystems are the mass media, its role in promoting cultural and political change, and its effects on communications,[55]
and education. Schools, universities, training centers, and research
institutes are among the more critical subsystems.[56]

Other "carriers" of modernization with almost as great an impact
on society as knowledge, are multinational corporations. These have
the capacity to innovate for the sake of economic expediency, without
regard for political or social consequences. Their organizational power
permits them to interfere in the social and political life of developing
countries. They may create false expectations and generate class conflict
and the like, but they also enable the transfer of new technologies from
industrial metropoles to developing areas. They create markets, and
provide both new opportunities for development and headaches for
host governments. A great deal of work has been undertaken on multi-
nationals as these affect the workings of the economy and politics in
developing areas.[57]

53. See Leonard Binder et al., *Crises and Sequences in Political Development*
(Princeton, N.J.: Princeton University Press, 1971).
54. See Joseph LaPalombara, ed., *Bureaucracy and Political Development* (Princeton, N.J.: Princeton University Press, 1963). See also J.P. Nettl, *Political Mobilization* (London: Faber and Faber, 1957).
55. See Daniel Lerner, *The Passing of Traditional Society* (New York: The Free
Press, 1958). See also Lucian Pye, ed., *Communications and Political Development* (Princeton, N.J.: Princeton University Press, 1963).
56. See James S. Coleman, *Education and Political Development* (Princeton, N.J.:
Princeton University Press, 1965).
57. See David E. Apter and Louis Wolf Goodman, eds., *The Multinational Corporation and Social Change* (New York: Praeger, 1976). See also John H. Dun-
ning, ed., *The Multinational Enterprise* (New York: Praeger, 1971), pp. 221–88,
and Raymond Vernon, *Sovereignty at Bay* (New York: Basic Books, 1971).

These and similar specialized and innovative subsystems require mediating agencies. Hence one of the more interesting aspects of such system–subsystem comparisons is the generation of *lead-and-lag effects*.[58]

Multiple Cases Using Cross-National Data. Studies using this strategy rely heavily on statistical and survey analyses, crosscultural data, and other quantitative materials. Some specify a small sample of cases (for example, the Almond and Verba five-nation study[59]). Others detail many cases (say all countries which are members of the United Nations[60]). The most elaborate research on cross-national data for comparative purposes is the work of Bruce M. Russett and associates. Distribution profiles were developed for human resources; wages and salaries; deaths and births; population rates; urbanization; social welfare and security expenditures; revenues tagged for government, military, and defense spending; party organization and voting; violence; and so forth. All these indicators were used to examine rates of growth. Problems attending development were evaluated in conjunction with the other strategies we have discussed.[61]

Some research strategies favor the use of computer analysis because cross-cultural data can be brought to bear on the analysis of some problems. One good example of the use of such data which treats the single case as a universe for diverse comparison, is the study of Venezuela undertaken jointly by Frank Bonilla and José A. Silva Michelena. Their study covers all the approaches discussed in this section—examining such subsystems as public opinion and the media, innovative forms, elites and elite subsystems—within a framework of statistical analysis.[62]

58. See Marius B. Jansen, ed., *Changing Japanese Attitudes Toward Modernization* (Princeton, N.J.: Princeton University Press, 1965).
59. See Gabriel A. Almond and Sidney Verba, *The Civic Culture* (Princeton, N.J.: Princeton University Press, 1963).
60. See Frederick W. Frey, *Survey Research on Comparative Change: A Bibliography* (Cambridge, Mass.: The M.I.T. Press, 1969).
61. See Bruce M. Russett, Hayward R. Alker, Jr., Karl W. Deutsch, Harold D. Lasswell, *World Handbook of Political and Social Indicators* (New Haven, Conn.: Yale University Press, 1964). See also Charles L. Taylor and Michael C. Hudson, *World Handbook of Political and Social Indicators,* 2nd. ed. (New Haven, Conn.: Yale University Press, 1972); Richard L. Merritt and Stein Rokkan, *Comparing Nations* (New Haven, Conn.: Yale University Press, 1966); and Raymond A. Bauer, *Social Indicators* (Cambridge, Mass.: The M.I.T. Press, 1966).
62. See Frank Bonilla and José A. Silva Michelena, *The Politics of Change in Venezuela,* 3 vols. (Cambridge, Mass.: The M.I.T. Press, 1967, 1970, 1971).

Similar other efforts to use quantitative techniques increasingly make use of set theory and computer analysis.[63]

Any or all of these strategies can be used in conjunction. Mainly the choice of a strategy will depend on the problem being examined, the kind of theory applied to the study of development, and the particular operations to which it is susceptible.

Conclusion

We have tried to give a brief overview of some of the ways analysts consider the connection between development at the economic and social levels and political development.[64] We have contrasted stage analysis and crisis analysis. A good deal of the work being done on development represents a search for appropriate strategies by means of which all types of development can be applied in configurational and comparative studies. Varieties of combinations are available, and various alternatives open to the researcher in anthropology, for example, would also apply to the political scientist interested in development. According to Nash:

The first mode is the index method: *the general features of a developed economy are abstracted as an ideal type and then contrasted with equally ideal typical features of a poor economy and society. In this mode, development is viewed as the transformation of one type into another.*

The second mode is the acculturation view *of the process of development. The West (taken here as the Atlantic community of developed nations and their overseas outliers) diffuse knowledge, skills, organizations, values, technology and capital to a poor nation, until*

63. See James M. Beshers, ed. *Computer Methods in the Analysis of Large-Scale Social Systems* (Cambridge, Mass.: The M.I.T. Press, 1968). See also Ronald D. Brunner and Garry D. Brewer, *Organized Complexity: Empirical Theories of Political Development* (New York: The Free Press, 1971).
64. For further reading see Samuel P. Huntington, "The Change to Change," *Comparative Politics*, Vol. 3, No. 3 (April 1971): 283–322. See also D.E. Apter and Charles Andrain, "Comparative Government: Developing New Nations," *Political Change*, ed. D.E. Apter (London: Frank Cass, 1973), pp. 180–238. See also John Brode, *The Process of Modernization, An Annotated Bibliography of the Sociocultural Aspects of Development* (Cambridge, Mass.: Harvard University Press, 1969).

over time, its society, culture and personnel become variants of that which made the Atlantic community economically successful.

The third mode . . . is the analysis of the process *as it is now going on in the so-called underdeveloped nations. This approach leads to smaller-scale hypotheses, to a prospective rather than a retrospective view of social change, to a full accounting of the political, social, and cutural context of development.*[65]

All these modes of analysis have been used extensively. They afford quite different criteria both for the examination of modernization as a process of cumulative growth and qualitative change, and as a set of strategies for research on the flow of exchange from metropole to periphery and back again. If at one time modernization was considered a one-way process, this is getting increasingly less true. (One has only to note the visible effects on British economic and social life of the "recycling" of Arab petro-dollars in the British economy.) As new situations arise, the assumptions of the unilinear model are challenged. As the problems of postindustrial society grow in magnitude, the notion that industrial societies have all the answers, or represent an integrated "end-point" for development, becomes less true. Many of the teleological assumptions built into the idea of development itself, whether economic or political, no longer hold. How we shall live in a world without belief in development is perhaps the key developmental question.

65. See Manning Nash, "Approaches to the Study of Economic Growth," *Journal of Social Issues,* Vol. 29, No. 1 (1963) : 5. Emphasis mine.

chapter fifteen
Theories of Development

In Chapter Fourteen our intention was to give a background for developmental analysis. We pointed out some of the assumptions and methods characteristic of the approach. Now we turn to some of the more important theoretical concerns which have become central to research. Of course, the literature is huge. A wide variety of studies apply many different strategies to many different parts of the world. We shall single out for amplification only those theories that illustrate the five analytical approaches we examined in previous units. We want particularly to discuss the connection between one's orientation toward developmental possibilities and policy. We have already indicated how bumpy a process is development. Some advocate controlling it by means of policy aimed at *balanced* growth; others follow a more pragmatic line. But taking the broad view, one's stance on development at home or on developmental assistance abroad and overseas aid is a matter of how one analyzes the problems and, more pragmatically, what makes sense. The American attitude has been articulated very well by the Committee for Economic Development.

More rapid growth and rising incomes will not necessarily win friends and allies or ensure peace and stability in the less developed countries. On the contrary, real progress involves a break with the past and may induce highly destabilizing political and social change. But profound changes are already under way in the less developed world regardless of what the United States does or does not do. The long term political rationale for aid, therefore, rests on the calculated risk that accelerating the modernization process, and reducing the sacrifice required to achieve it, will enhance the odds in favor of an earlier evolution of responsible and independent states in the low-income regions of the world. By the same token, the risk of involvement by the great powers in crises and power vacuums abroad will thereby be reduced.[1]

In other words, development will not necessarily produce a world in which people feel comfortable, safe, and secure, but neither are we likely to experience less development in the future. Taking the Committee for Economic Development's statement as our premise, we shall now proceed to examine just how development can best be geared to realize attainable political goals. We'll work backward in our analysis; that is, back through structural, pluralist, and behavioral models, all the way to institutional and philosophical topics. If development is the way of the future, we had better bring all our knowledge of the past to bear in facing its challenges.

Structural Concerns

The preceding extract from the Committee for Economic Development's policy statement assumes that development produces structural incongruities. Therefore, if developmental processes are basically malintegrative, then what is required to maintain structural integrity is remedial action which reduces the strain of social transformation. A Marxist would go much further: Developmentalism produces a fundamental (though ironic) contradiction, namely, its converse, *underdevelopment*. This phenomenon (which we shall discuss in more detail) results in the growing dependency of recently independent nations on externally induced innovations. While a liberal analyst would argue for more aid to developing nations to generate new structural solutions, the Marxist would suggest that the more aid given, the greater the dependency becomes. The former argues for a world of interdependent nations; the later flatly denies this as a possibility. Marxists see overseas aid as a way to promote the hegemony of the powerful industrial metropole over the weak periphery, maintaining dependence rather than encouraging interdependence. To see how similar facts of life can produce such different interpretations, let us apply equilibrium and contradiction theories to development itself.

The method of equilibrium: In Chapter Twelve on Structuralism we showed how the method of equilibrium followed two main theoretical

1. Research and Policy Committee, *Assisting Development in Low-Income Countries* (New York: Committee for Economic Development, 1969), p. 2.

lines: functionalist and structural functionalist. Functional analysis begins with the assumption that all societies have a political structure.
The structure may be centralized or decentralized. It may be specialized, with a well-defined governmental apparatus, or it may be diffused
among institutions such as kinship or religion. But no matter how it
performs, every society has a *legitimate machinery of control* to maintain order and to govern.[2] Perhaps the most widely used functional
scheme for the analysis of the politics of developing countries suggests
that all governments have four input functions and three output functions.

1. Political socialization and recruitment. The socialization process fosters appropriate conduct by instilling proper motivation. In
turn, its efficiency depends on how well the values of a modern political
culture are internalized and on the effective recruitment of the young
into the modern sector of political activities in a nondisruptive manner.

2. Interest articulation. The different interests in the society,
whether based on kinship, patron–client relations, or urban business,
are identified so that those in positions of political authority can understand the problems each group in society faces. Interests may be articulated by a band of warriors, a clique, a faction, a palace guard, a political party, an interest group or any other aggregate or individual unit.

3. Interest aggregation. Except for very powerful interest groups
(for example, an army), interests that overlap are those most likely to
become salient and to stimulate responsive government action. One
typical way interests aggregate is by means of a nationalist movement
which scoops up a variety of diverse interests and clusters them around
an overriding concern for freedom, or independence, or greater economic growth.

4. Political communication. Articulated and aggregated interests
must be communicated, both between groups and to those in authority.
The communication process may operate through influence peddling,
intrigue, family connections, public demonstrations, agitation, party
organization, the press and mass media generally, or any one or a combination of other modes of information distribution.

The result of these inputs is a set of output responses made by
authorities.

2. See Gabriel A. Almond, "Introduction," *The Politics of Developing Areas,* eds.
Gabriel A. Almond and James S. Coleman (Princeton, N.J.: Princeton University
Press, 1960), pp 3–64.

1. *Rule making*. Rule making establishes principles of order which prescribe the activities of social life. A chief's council, or a military junta, or an elaborate democratic procedure may be responsible for rule making.

2. *Rule application*. Essentially, carrying out rules is a function detailed to a bureaucracy or civil service, a police or security body, a network of elders ordained by kinship or merit, or a system of local government.

3. *Rule adjudication*. Since disputes arise about the proper application of rules, even in the most autocratic systems, some method of redress is necessary for those who feel aggrieved. The role of adjudicator may be performed by a chief holding court, by a priest using divination procedures, or by magistrates, courts, and all the paraphernalia of a modern legal system.

These functions (like Malinowski's) provide universalized categories that describe how societies govern themselves. Data gathered show differences between societies regarding how such activities are performed. Different functions interact, and they also suggest an evolution from more diffuse to more specific political forms as well. Useful for comparing political-system change, the functions enable intercultural (or inter-regional) comparison, and within each culture region they allow both synchronic and diachronic analysis using comparative or configurational methods. (For example, comparing politics in Southeast Asia, South Asia, Sub-Saharan Africa, the Near East, and Latin America results in a set of syndromes indicating how competitive or authoritarian different modernizing regimes are, how modernized the societies are, degrees of conflict and integration, and other pertinent factors.) It is also possible to correlate indices of development—such as per capita GNP, the ratio of doctors to population units, degree of industrialization measured by per capita energy consumption, trade unionization, or urbanization and education variables—with type of political system and by major regional area.[3]

Thus functional analysis enables an observer to describe in greater detail the main points raised in the Committee on Economic Development policy statement. It allows the elaboration of various *syndromes* of uneven modernity, and the degree to which tribal, communal, or racial interests can be absorbed into a legacy of nationalism. But if the aim is to realize this in a democratic way, the functional study of change suggests how difficult it will be.

3. Ibid., Table 2, p. 540.

Pattern Variables. Almond's functional set refers to the political system. The equilibrium method of defining structure for whole societies includes the work of Parsons, Levy, Moore, Smelser, and others (see pp. 398–410). Adapting Talcott Parsons' pattern variables, for example, to the problems of developing countries, Francis Sutton distinguished two types of societies, agricultural and industrial. The agricultural type has the following characteristics:

1. *Predominance of ascriptive, particularistic, diffuse patterns.*
2. *Stable local groups and limited spatial mobility.*
3. *Relatively simple and stable "occupational" differentiation.*
4. *A "deferential" stratification system of diffuse impact.*[4]

The contrast between agricultural and industrial societies is that in the latter the following features prevail:

1. *Predominance of universalistic, specific, and achievement norms.*
2. *High degree of social mobility (in a general—not necessarily "vertical"—sense).*
3. *Well-developed occupational system, insulated from other social structures.*
4. *"Egalitarian" class system based on generalized patterns of occupational achievement.*
5. *Prevalence of "association," i.e., functionally specific, non-ascriptive structures.*

Together these two sets represent alternative conditions of equilibrium; but under the impact of modernization, patterns of the first type begin to change into the second.[5] Where ascription might have been based on a certain quality (such as belonging to a particular ethnic or language group), or may have been particularistic (as regarding, say, social rank), with modernization, perhaps recruitment to office or an influential position will depend on achievement or merit. This shift in influence can cause terrible conflicts between traditionalists and modernists. Each side may mobilize forces and followers and

4. Francis Sutton, "Social Theory and Comparative Politics," *Comparative Politics,* ed. Harry Eckstein and David E. Apter (New York: The Free Press, 1963), p. 1.
5. See Neil J. Smelser, "Toward a Theory of Modernization," *Social Change,* ed. Amitai and Eva Etzioni (New York: Basic Books, 1964), pp 258–74.

thus aggravate the tension. Then stable local groups, usually conservative in outlook, may lose their predominance to growing urban industrial (modern) populations. New hierarchies are established during the process, and new forms of class differentiation. Often the rise of industrialism creates a burgeoning middle class whose growth maximizes the tension between traditional aspirations and new. As this occurs, the deferential patterns of the old system are eroded, leading to anger, violence, and at times terrorism. More often than not political regimes facing such a structural/developmental crisis respond with ruthlessness and brutality.[6]

Both political and societal models lead an observer to favor policies designed to stimulate the growth of a modern industrial society in which conflicts would subside as universalistic, specific, and high-achievement norms became predominant. A new equilibrium would be established as such changes transpired. There would be a high degree of social mobility; a well-developed occupational system insulated from other social structures; an egalitarian class system based on occupational achievement; and a functionally specific network of non-ascriptive associations. Patterns of representation would become more diverse and pluralistic, patterns of stratification more open. Then, as the society became more integrated, social institutions other than government could take the primary responsibility for controlling deviance (unsocialized behavior) and coordinating groups imperfectly integrated in the social system. As societies move toward the industrial, integration becomes less authoritarian and more democratic.[7] Political functions would be handled in a more participatory way.

The method of contradiction: Advocates of the method of contradiction disagree. Their emphasis is on the growing conflicts accompanying development. These are both internal and external. For example, capitalist crises exported to developing countries produce imperialism. Marx described this process at work in advanced capitalist countries in the *Communist Manifesto:*

6. In Argentina, Chile, Uruguay, Brazil, Paraguay, and Bolivia, for example, terrorism and police and army brutality go hand in hand. Roman Catholic Church sources have estimated that one thousand people were tortured to death in Chile between 1973, when President Salvador Allende was overthrown in a military coup, and 1976. One out of five hundred of Uruguay's three million people are said to be either political prisoners or refugees (*The New York Times,* October 31, 1976).
7. See Sutton, op. cit., pp. 78–79.

*The bourgeoisie, during its rule of scarce one hundred years, has
created more massive and more colossal productive forces than have
all preceding generations together. Subjection of Nature's forces to
man, machinery, application of chemistry to industry and agriculture,
steam navigation, railways, electric telegraphs, clearing of whole
continents for cultivation, canalization of rivers, whole populations
conjured out of the ground—what earlier century had even a presenti-
ment that such productive forces slumbered in the lap of social labor?*

*We see then: the means of production and of exchange, on whose
foundation the bourgeoisie built itself up, were generated in feudal
society. At a certain stage in the development of these means of production and of exchange, the conditions under which feudal society produced and exchanged, the feudal organization of agriculture and
manufacturing industry, in one word, the feudal relations of property
became no longer compatible with the already developed productive
forces; they became so many fetters .They had to be burst asunder;
they were burst asunder.*

*Into their place stepped free competition, accompanied by a social
and political constitution adapted to it, and by the economical and political sway of the bourgeois class.*

*A similar movement is going on before our own eyes. Modern
bourgeois society with its relations of production, of exchange and of
property, a society that has conjured up such gigantic means of production and of exchange, is like the sorcerer, who is no longer able to
control the powers of the nether world whom he has called up by his
spells. . . .*

*The weapons with which the bourgeoisie felled feudalism to the
ground are now turned against the bourgeoisie itself.*[8]

Development, for Marx, proceeds in stages, capitalism being the
great transformational stage which opens up undreamed of new opportunities. Capitalism also creates, however, the greatest contradictions.[9]

According to the conflict model, then, development is a process of

8. Karl Marx and Frederick Engels, "The Communist Manifesto," *Selected Works*
(Moscow: Foreign Languages Publishing House, 1962), pp. 39–40. For an interest-
ing discussion of Hegel's views, prior to Marx, see Albert O. Hirschman, "On Hegel,
Imperialism, and Structural Stagnation," in *Journal of Developmental Economics*,
No. 3, 1976, pp. 1–8.
9. The exception is the "Asiatic mode of production." See George Lichtheim,
"Marx and the Asiatic Mode of Production," *Karl Marx*, ed. Tom Bottomore
(Englewood Cliffs, N.J.: Prentice-Hall, 1973), pp. 151–71.

continuous contradiction, continuous struggle. The end is not simply a happy-stateless society, but an expanded rationality, an ability to transcend the limitations of the world as it is, to consider the world as it can be. Marx thought the developmental process would occur in the most highly industrial societies, for no society emerges into a new stage until the productive relations of the previous stage have exhausted themselves. But what happened was that socialism became the ideal of the developing countries, not the advanced industrial societies. As a result of this surprising situation Marxists argue about how to proceed with developmental strategies—whether to develop the capitalist phase first, what to do about the state.

The most important controversy is over superstructure. Should the Marxist state promulgate an ideology of development to legitimize forced methods and generate an industrial base? Should a government speeding up the process of economic growth eliminate the rural peasantry to create instead an industrial infrastructure and a proletariat? Revisionist Marxists challenge this approach, warning that industrialization by forced means results in a superstate, or a state-capitalist bureaucratic and totalitarian regime. The first great developmental debate among Marxists over the role of the state involved the German Marxist Karl Kautsky and Lenin.[10] A more radical attack came from the Polish Marxist Rosa Luxemburg, who disbelieved the solutions Lenin and Trotsky had found in Russia.

The elimination of democracy as such, is worse than the disease it is supposed to cure; for it stops up the very living source from which alone can come the correction of all the innate shortcomings of social institutions. That source is the active, untrammeled, energetic political life of the broadest masses of the people.[11]

Later the argument would recur, especially between Joseph Stalin, who wanted to use the superstructure to intensify the class struggle and to accumulate funds by expropriating lands from the "kulaks" (Rus-

10. See Karl Kautsky, *The Dictatorship of the Proletariat* (Ann Arbor, Mich.: University of Michigan Press, 1962) ; V.I. Lenin, *The Proletarian Revolution and the Renegade Kautsky* (Moscow: Foreign Languages Publishing Co., 1962) ; Rosa Luxemburg, *Leninism or Marxism?* (Ann Arbor, Mich.: University of Michigan Press, 1961) ; and Leon Trotsky, *The Revolution Betrayed* (New York: Doubleday, Doran, 1937).
11. Rosa Luxemburg, *The Russian Revolution and Leninism or Marxism* (Ann Arbor, Mich.: University of Michigan Press, 1961) , p. 62.

sian middle-sized peasant land holders), and Nikolai Bukharin, who wanted to organize a Marxist version of a market in which public wants could be manifested and priorities established. Stalin won, but the issues remain.

Stalin argued that Russia, before the Revolution, had been the most backward of the powers. It had had a core of industrial development within its feudal-peasant structure that resembled an imperialist capitalist base. The combination of imperialism, capitalism, and feudalism had initiated severe contradictions between peasants and aristocrats, workers and owners, and Russia was therefore the "weak link" in the chain of imperialism. Although this weakness was precisely what made it from the Marxist viewpoint an unlikely target for revolution, it was ironically also the very seed of revolution.[12]

Since the revolution had not occurred in a Western industrial center, Stalin saw that it was necessary to cultivate beliefs in socialist principles in Russia by political means: The state would have to transform the base, rather than the reverse proposed by Marx. The stage had not been properly set, but the "dictatorship of the proletariat" would intensify the class struggle against *farmers*. From there, expropriating their land and money would provide the capital to build up heavy industry, and especially to build up the armed forces necessary to break out of "capitalist encirclement."

Here then are the structural problems confronted by developmental Marxists: Is it possible to establish socialism by state means *without* the formation of a bureaucratic apparatus which itself becomes the basis of a new exploiting class? Can democracy work under state socialism in a society where the instruments of production are not developed sufficiently to produce material abundance? What should be the role of a communist party? Can it stand as a vanguard for change without becoming an instrument of oppression?

The Soviet experience represents an extreme case of developmental engineering. Few countries are willing to pay the human price asked by Stalin. Moreover, as the character of capitalism changes, metropolitan countries, far from acquiring new colonies, have divested themselves of them. Similarly Marxists have renounced Stalinist solutions to pursue alternative possibilities in developing countries. They recognize, however, that as colonialism declines, it leaves behind institutions linked to the former metropole—including the banking system,

12. For the conflict between Stalin and Bukharin, see Moshe Lewin, *Political Undercurrents in Soviet Economic Debates* (Princeton, N.J.: Princeton University Press, 1974).

private enterprise, a class structure, and an elite educational system—all of which sustain transactions between capitalist countries and developing ones. To Marxists, even if the formal domination of colonialism goes, *neocolonialism* remains.[13]

Neocolonialism and underdevelopment: The typical consequence of neocolonialism is the emergence of high development *sectors* stimulated by external investments. Within these sectors capital-intensive enterprises (those requiring little local unskilled or semi-skilled labor) attract people who leave their farms in search of jobs. The resulting flood of poor migrant workers forms into an "industrial reserve army," that is, an army of cheap labor easily exploited, existing in a "marginal" condition. The creation of marginals, deprived of their traditional means of livelihood on the farms, and with little prospect for employment in urban areas, represents a condition of *underdevelopment*. The people who form this group, and live as squatters, or in squalid slum areas which fester around most urban centers in developing countries, are in a worse condition than before. Their traditional methods of social security, their family system, their tenure on the land, the continuity and pattern of life are all broken down. Poverty, disease, despair, and degradation is their common condition.

This theory of underdevelopment derives from Marx who argued that in the long run it would have a detrimental effect on the industrial metropole as well as the underdeveloped periphery. Lenin developed the idea further. He considered imperialism the highest stage in the evolution of capitalism. Capitalist countries would "export" to their colonies not only innovation but their own internal crises as well. Therefore, where capitalism had created gross inequalities at home, it could also do so abroad.[14] Modern theorists of underdevelopment agree:

Far from serving as an engine of economic expansion, of technological progress and of social change, the capitalist order in these countries has represented a framework for economic stagnation, for archaic technology, and for social backwardness. Thus, to the extent to which it

13. See Charles Bettelheim, *Planification et croissance accélérée* (Paris: Maspero, 1954).
14. V.I. Lenin, *Imperialism: The Highest Stage of Capitalism* (New York: International Publishers, 1939). See also Maurice Dobb, *Studies in the Development of Capitalism* (New York: International Publishers, 1947); and *Capitalism, Development and Planning* (London: Routledge and Kegan Paul, 1967).

depends on the volume of aggregate output and income, the economic surplus in backward capitalist countries has necessarily been small. Not that it has constituted a small proportion of total income. On the contrary . . . the consumption of the productive population has been depressed to the lowest possible level, with "lowest possible" corresponding in this case closely to a subsistence minimum or to what in many underdeveloped countries falls notably below that benchmark. The economic surplus therefore, while by comparison with the advanced countries small in absolute *terms, has accounted for a large share of total output—as large as, if not larger than, in advanced capitalist countries.*[15]

As the bourgeoisie is integrated into the cultural and economic life of the capitalist advanced countries, it acts as the agent of Western imperialism, enabling Western ideas and innovations to dominate the political and economic life of the developing countries. Together the foreign and domestic bourgeoisie exploit the rest of the population, much of which lives in squalor in the cities (*villas miserias*) or in the outlying squatter areas, victims of disease, unemployment, and "marginality."

One comparative study applying these attributes to Chile and Brazil sees the connection of these countries to Western capitalism in terms of "satellite colonization." Feudalism and capitalism form a combined system in Latin America, where feudalism in the rural areas sustains landed aristocracy alongside a capitalist bourgeoisie which exploits the proletariat. The result is double exploitation: the aristocracy exploits the peasants, the bourgeoisie exploits the workers and the marginals.[16]

Recent case studies have followed up this general line of argument, saying that the institutions of an "imitation" bourgeois state remain in newly independent states. The party as a mass movement is only a shell within which *compradors,* or a local bourgeoisie, manipulate power. Inequality and unemployment flourish, with the result being agricultural stagnation, urban immigration, food shortages, inflation, balance of payments crises, further dependence on foreign finance, and a noncompetitive domestic industrial sector.[17]

15. See Paul A. Baran, *The Political Economy of Growth* (New York: Monthly Review Press, 1962) , pp. 163–64.
16. See Andre Gundar Frank, *Capitalism and Underdevelopment in Latin America* (New York: Monthly Review Press, 1969) .
17. See Colin Leys, *Underdevelopment in Kenya* (Berkeley, Ca.: University of California Press, 1975) , pp. 271–73.

Social dependency: Underdevelopment goes hand in hand with economic dependency. Some of the best work on this condition has been done by Latin American scholars. Some have specialized in marginality as an equivalent for Marx's idea of an industrial army (a pool of the unemployed competing for jobs) .[18] Others have been concerned with the dynamics of interethnic, class, and cultural conflicts in a neo-colonial setting.[19] Fernando Henrique Cardoso, for example, has put forward a model of "associated-dependent" development which combines the idea of development with that of dependence. Changes in international capitalist organization, says Cardoso, have produced a new international division of labor, the key to which is the multinational corporation. The interests of foreign corporations become essential to the internal prosperity and growth of dependent countries. On the one hand they help to produce growth. On the other hand, countries that host multinational development are dependent on their decisions and activities.[20]

The literature dealing with these themes of development links the structural changes of capitalism to the structure of developing areas.[21] This linkage is, in turn, associated with the intensification of crises.[22] Crises are accompanied by the growth of terrorism. The use of violence to induce structural change has also been analyzed. The psychological value of violent confrontation is that it eliminates the emotional burden of dependency. The work of Regis Debray, Frantz Fanon, and others in this area is extremely important because they emphasize not only capitalist contradictions in developing areas, but the inversion of the dominated and the dominating.[23]

18. See José Nun, ed., Special Issue on Marginality, *Revista Latinoamericana de Sociologia* (Buenos Aires, Vol. 5, No. 2, July 1969).
19. See Pablo Gonzales Casanova, "Sociedad plural, colonialism interno y desarrollo," and Rodolfo Stavenhagen, "La dinamica de las relaciones interethnicas: clases, colonialismo y aculturacion" in Fernando H. Cardoso, Anibal Pinto, and Osvaldo Sunkel, eds., *America Latina* (Santiago: Editoral Universitaria, S.A., 1970), pp. 141–64. See also Guillermo O'Donnell and Delfina Linck, *Dependencia y autonomia* (Buenos Aires: Amorrortu editores, 1973).
20. See Fernando Henrique Cardoso, "Associated-Dependent Development: Theoretical and Practical Implications," *Authoritarian Brazil*, ed. Alfred Stepan (New Haven, Conn.: Yale University Press, 1973), pp. 142–76; and *Estado y sociedad en America Latina* (Buenos Aires: Ediciones Nueva Vision, 1962).
21. See, for example, James O. Connor, "The Fiscal Crisis of the State, Part I," *Socialist Revolution,* Vol. 1, No. 1 (January–February 1970) : 12–54.
22. See Manza Alavi, "The State in Post-Colonial Societies—Pakistan and Bangladesh," *New Left Review,* 74 (July–August 1972) : 59–81.
23. See Leo Huberman and Paul M. Sweezy, eds., *Regis Debray and the Latin American Revolution* (New York: Monthly Review Press, 1968). See also G.K.

While the study of colonialism and developing countries has been going on for a long time, socialist states in developing areas are young. And, if one excludes the Soviet Union, China, and Cuba from the analysis, one finds that the global experience of socialist development has been mixed. Today more and more studies are concerned with class formation and bureaucracy under socialism.[24] Studies have been done regarding moderate socialist experiments;[25] so has comparative work on the impact of modern imperialism seen from a Marxist perspective.[26]

Indeed, socialists are beginning to address the question of contradictions in socialist development itself.[27] The modern left's criticisms of socialism have to date had much in common with Trotsky's arguments against Stalin's bureaucracy or Rosa Luxemburg's criticism of Lenin. In fact, Dumont argues that most developing countries have created a system of *proto-socialism,* a form of bureaucracy which elevates to power a new, and essentially corrupt, repressive class.[28] In more sweeping terms, Leszek Kolakowski has said,

[Socialist systems] solved at incalculable human cost, the problems of industrialization in some underdeveloped countries and so they assumed the role of organizers of primitive accumulation, but they have been unable to cope with a single task which, according to the tradition of socialist thought, was supposed to fall to the specifically socialist *form of social organization.*[29]

Whether existing socialist societies can be considered as poor preliminary systems working toward the socialist ideal as defined by Marxist tradition, or simply as instruments of rapid industrialization in

Grohs, "Frantz Fanon and the African Revolution," *Journal of Modern African Studies,* Vol. 6, No. 4 (December 1968) : 543–56
24. See Claude Meillassoux, "A Class Analysis of the Bureaucratic Process in Mali," *The Journal of Developmental Studies* (January, 1970) .
25. See G. Arrighi and John S. Saul, *Essays on the Political Economy of Africa* (New York: Monthly Review Press, 1973) . See also John S. Saul, "The State in Post-Colonial Societies: Tanzania," *The Socialist Register* (1974) : 349–72.
26. See Samir Amin, *Neo-Colonialism in West Africa* (London: Penguin Books, 1973) ; Nicos Poulantzas, *Political Power and Social Classes* (London: Sheed and Ward, 1973) ; and Jozsef Bognar, *Economic Policy and Planning in Developing Countries* (Budapest: Akademiai Kiado, 1969) .
27. See Charles Bettelheim, "State Property and Socialism," *Economy and Society,* Vol. 2, No. 4 (November 1973) : 395–420.
28. See René Dumont, *Socialisms and Development* (New York: Praeger, 1973) , pp. 110–11.
29. See Leszek Kolakowski and Stuart Hampshire, eds., *The Socialist Idea* (London: Widenfield and Nicolson, 1974) , p. 9.

countries on the peripheries of capitalist development is a matter of continuous debate. Most of the single-party, leftist regimes in developing countries have little resemblance to true socialist states. For example, Guinea under President Sekou Touré has become a "proto-Stalinist" African state, where the President is the supreme arbiter of the economic and cultural life of the people.[30]

All modern socialist states are a rather far cry from Lenin's ideal dictatorship of the proletariat which he believed would start withering away the moment it came to power. Lenin reckoned without the singular role that the state plays in development and the absolute power provided the leader. In political terms, this power derives from a highly centralized authority (see Chapter Fourteen) which holds the goals of the state sacred. The party becomes the sole interpreter of political matters. The party leadership determines the party's interpretation. To use Guinea as an example again, even folk stories and cultural traditions have been converted to the service of the state.

Old epics and tunes have been readapted to sing the P.D.G.'s (Democratic Party of Guinea, the only party permitted) revolutionary role and Touré's enlightened leadership; and new compositions must deal with these themes. This policy has brought about a rigid control over creativity. . . . No major works have recently been published in Conakry except the President's books and poems, and these must be abundantly quoted by members of the elite to secure their positions. Thus, Guineans have been . . . reduced to be pupils of Touré.[31]

Nor is Guinea the extreme case. The point is that in an underdeveloped country, developmental change in a socialist direction produces its own forms of structural contradiction.[32]

To most structuralists interested in development, the scientists, agronomists, the new *technocrats*, or technical specialists, are the dynamic factors in introducing change. Each innovator generates a network of new roles—educational, scientific, bureaucratic—distributed

30. See Lansine Kaba, "Cultural Revolution, Artistic Creativity, and Freedom of Expression in Guinea," *The Journal of African Studies*, Vol. 14, No. 2 (1976) : 201–18. See also Helen Desfosses and Jacques Levesque, eds., *Socialism in the Third World* (New York: Praeger, 1975) .
31. Kaba, ibid., pp. 214–15.
32. For a good discussion of Marxist approaches see Szymon Chodak, *Societal Development* (New York: Oxford University Press, 1973) , pp. 18–41.

throughout civic and cultural institutions, schools and universities, laboratories and research facilities, the civil service, and business. Knowledge by these means is today internationally available. Universities have become part of an international network. So, too, have multinational corporations which establish high technology networks supporting a technical managerial elite and a mediated middle class.[33] In part the job of technical elites, therefore, is to deal with incongruities arising out of the process of development. Partly, it is to speed up the process of change itself. Ironic though it may seem, quite often it is the intellectuals and the new technical elites who, anxious to promote innovation, propose radical political solutions.[34]

Innovative change may well result in an expanded middle class, in much the same way as did the Industrial Revolution. For liberals the invigorating force will be the search for equilibrium which would gradually incorporate the marginals, the poor, the displaced into the mainstream of modern life. Conversely, the aristocracy would be *expropriated* as it becomes functionally superfluous; and political democracy should evolve.

For Marxists the scenario is quite different. Through the method of contradiction they downgrade the emphasis on elites and new technocrats because this ignores the impact of change on other sectors of society.[35] Above all, Marxists are concerned with how contradiction affects the level of self-awareness or consciousness of the people.[36]

Pluralism and Development

Pluralist approaches to development emphasize the experimental and tentative nature of all proposed solutions. Precisely because develop-

33. See Raymond Vernon, *Sovereignty at Bay* (New York: Basic Books, 1971); Richard J. Barnet and Ronald E. Müller, *Global Reach* (New York: Simon and Schuster, 1974); and D. Apter and Louis W. Goodman, *The Multinational Corporation and Social Change* (New York: Praeger, 1976).
34. See Edward Shils, "The Intellectuals in the Political Development of the New States," *Political Change in Underdeveloped Countries*, ed. John Kautsky (New York: Wiley, 1962), pp. 195–234. See also John Friedmann, "Intellectuals in Developing Societies," *Kylos*, 13 (1960): 524–40.
35. See John Saul, "Africa," *Populism*, Ghita Ionescu and Ernest Gellner, eds. (London: Widenfeld and Nicolson, 1969), pp. 139–40.
36. Louis Althusser, *For Marx* (New York: Vintage Books, 1970), pp. 89–128; See also Stanislaw Ossowski, *Class Structure in the Social Consciousness* (London: Routledge and Kegan Paul, 1963).

ment is so complex a process, they say, the best-laid plans are likely to go awry. But pluralists are not necessarily against planning. Rather they assume that the more a society develops, and the more complex it becomes, the more difficult it is to fit the needs of the people to the needs of the developers. Hence there is bound to be a certain fluidity and open-endedness to the process.

Pluralists oppose those theorists who try to oversimplify society, or to describe it as "undifferentiated." And since the basic thrust of development is to make the simple complex, they see development as integral to a pluralistic give-and-take model.

Pluralist approaches to development are pragmatic. The pluralist will say that the Marxist ideology doesn't fit the case. Nor does any other. In fact, ideologies of any sort destroy realistic perceptions, so that people cannot see what is in front of their noses. Albert O. Hirschman tells a story which illustrates the point:

A man approaches another exclaiming: "Hello, Paul. It's good to see you after so many years, but you have changed so much! You used to be fat, now you are quite thin; you used to be tall, now you are rather short. What happened, Paul?" Paul rather timidly replies: "But my name is not Paul." Whereupon the other retorts, quite pleased with his interpretation of reality: "You see how much you have changed! Even your name has changed."[37]

Pluralists are against fancy labels or obfuscating ideologies. They want to remain close to realities. They favor utilizing lots of *different* developmental strategies at once. Suspicious of putting all their eggs into one basket, they propose planning modestly by increments that will enable continuous review of the priorities. While they recognize the value of planning and the need of governments to put down in writing their dedication to the improvement of living standards, they are not too hopeful about the effectiveness of such a plan.

The development program is therefore a convenient restraint on the central government which permits it to push through high-priority projects without being sidetracked. This function of a development program is usually not the principal motive for adopting it in the first

37. Albert O. Hirschman, *A Bias for Hope* (New Haven, Conn.: Yale University Press, 1971), p. 337.

*place, but the realization of its usefulness becomes often a major reason
for continuing the experience. On the other hand, this very freedom-of-
choice-limiting property of development programs can be felt as excessive, and then results in the frequently observed spectacle of a
government acting in contradiction to the course of action which it
had laid down for itself.*[38]

Pluralists are concerned that what looks like innovation on the
drawing board will run into all sorts of practical obstacles. Innovations
may have hidden social costs; changes in the mode of production may
be resisted by people who might otherwise benefit economically.

*Innovations are not therefore easily introduced in communities where
there is tenderness towards established expectations; it flourishes better
in places where competition is well regarded, and where attempts to
create or preserve monopoly positions are ruthlessly suppressed.*[39]

More specifically pluralists favor *budgetary accountability* over planning. Where planners constitute a pressure group for increased investments, budgeters do just the reverse. They are likely to want to cut
down expenditures. As a consequence a kind of competition may
evolve between the two, a face-off between short-term decision making
and long-term planning, crisis action versus programs. What most
pluralists would agree on, however, is the need to keep the solution
simple.

*The keynote in poor countries should be simplicity. Designs for de-
cisions should be as simple as anyone knows how to make them. The
more complicated they are, the less likely they are to work. On this
basis there seems little reason to have several organizations dealing with
the same expenditure policies. One good organization would represent an enormous advance.*[40]

Unfortunately most countries have attempted what pluralists regard as the worst possible combination—bureaucratic planning plus
ideology—thus inaugurating a program essentially for wasting resources.

38. Ibid.
39. W. Arthur Lewis, *The Theory of Economic Growth* (London: Allen and Unwin,
1957), p. 179.
40. Naomi Caiden and Aaron Wildavsky, *Planning and Budgeting in Poor Countries* (New York: Wiley, Interscience, 1974), p. 300.

The promotion of economic development by deliberate economic policy has throughout history been associated with the political objective of building a nation-state or strengthening a nation-state in rivalry with others; this is almost universally the case with the less developed countries of the present time. The nationalist objective, with its overtones of possible military conflict, provides the motivation for bearing the costs of establishing a "modern" national economy and polity, and may well be the only force capable of mobilizing a society for economic development. On the other hand, nationalist motivations inevitably lead to economic policies that waste economic resources and inhibit the economic development they aim to stimulate.

The main reasons for this are, first, that nationalism generally derives its economic objectives by imitation and emulation of the economic structure of established nation-states, and second that it envisages economic development as consisting in the ownership and control by nationals (individually or collectively) of desirable types of "modern" property—industrial factories, professional and managerial jobs—rather than as consisting in the development of a system of economic organization that efficiently exploits the country's available human and material resources and improves its own efficiency.[41]

The administrators of a government emphasing a nationalist ideology have special access to both property and power. Both easily corrupt, and where there is corruption the bureaucracy represents a self-serving elite. A more practical approach to rule would be to use incremental decision making for policies which differ only slightly from the status quo. Limited or incremental change would thus have restricted consequences. As developmental processes would be predominantly remedial, they would enable continuous reevaluation. As more and more sectors of the society are involved in the process the costs can be realistically assessed.[42] Some countries have tried to mix incremental policy making with planning. Tanzania, for example, has tried a system of "open" planning within a context of manageable goals and public involvement, while severely limiting the role of the bureaucracy. It is too soon to tell how well that is working.[43]

41. Harry G. Johnson, *Economic Policies Toward Less Developed Countries* (Washington, D.C.: The Brookings Institution, 1967) , p. 67.
42. See Charles E. Lindblom and D.A. Braybrooke, *A Strategy of Decision* (New York: The Free Press, 1963) . See also Charles E. Lindblom, "The Science of Muddling Through," *Public Administrative Review*, 19 (1959) : 252.
43. See Colin Leys, ed., "The Analysis of Planning," *Politics and Change in Developing Countries* (Cambridge: Cambridge University Press, 1969) , pp. 247–75.

Pluralists also consider the different kinds of ethnic and other groupings which may fragment a society as possible sources for healthy growth. Under the right circumstances ethnicity can lead to a lively competition between communities rather than to explosive and dangerous conflict. A useful study of ethnic competition within a single-party framework has been done by Aristide Zolberg in the Ivory Coast. Zolberg shows how, within the context of a single party, different ethnic groups and classes are represented within both party and government. But there is a hitch.

Although Ivoireiens admit that democracy of the Western type has been restricted because it is undesirable at this stage of the country's development, the outside observer is told to look for a substitute form of democracy inside the party. Spokesmen for the regime maintain that there he will find genuine responsiveness on the part of the leadership, extensive consultation, and mass participation in decision-making.[44]

Zolberg is doubtful that such is the case. Yet in one sense factionalism and conflict do counterbalance centralized control. Moreover, as if to prove the contention of the pluralists, the Ivory Coast is one of the few economic success stories in Africa.

Despite arguments against the outcomes of nationalism and bureaucracy in developing nations there are reasons why both are important. The need to coordinate and manage a society in which skills and resources are scarce produces a tendency toward centralized management. Also, countries with few raw industrial materials usually lack investment funds for their own development. Nationalism and political bureaucracy enable poor countries to manipulate the conflict between capitalist and socialist countries and get support and aid.[45]

Hence governments anxious to stimulate developmental aid want greater freedom of action than democracy allows. This is why at the end of the so-called development decade, 1960–1970, there were more authoritarian regimes among the nations of the world than ever before. The assumption that developing areas (even like Europe under the Marshall Plan) need mainly technical assistance to free up local innovative talent has been proven wrong. President Truman's Point Four

44. See Aristide Zolberg, *One-Party Government in the Ivory Coast* (Princeton, N.J.: Princeton University Press, 1964), p. 314.
45. See Albert O. Hirschman, *The Strategy of Economic Development* (New Haven, Conn.: Yale University Press, 1958), p. 198.

doctrine, for example, a plan which offered technical and financial assistance to stimulate and to aid both the host and the donor countries paid too little attention to social factors and too much to political factors.[46]

Later, particularly during the Kennedy Administration it was widely believed in the United States that small injections of developmental aid plus American technical know-how would "win" the Cold War with the Soviet Union; promote American security; contribute to economic development abroad; and promote stability, democracy, and pro-American attitudes in a world system to be based upon constitutionalism and pluralistic democracy.[47]

Figure 15-1 shows that since the "development" decade the American proportion of foreign aid disbursements have dropped considerably. Today it has become clear to Americans that the picture is far more complex than anyone anticipated. Certainly the pluralist assumptions that were built into the Foreign Assistance Act of 1961 (which, although much amended, remains the basic enabling legislation for U.S. overseas assistance) have fallen far short of their objectives. Certainly too the political questions of the moment—What motivates and stimulates growth? How can growth be managed? What political systems manage best?—show not a correlation between growth and political democracy, but an inverse relation. But it is also true that so-called monolithic regimes can change without notice. The Egypt of today is more pluralistic than during Nasser's time.[48] And India has dashed some pluralists' hope that it would become a model for a developing pluralist democracy,[49] while Portugal, since 1976, has become exemplary as such.

Behavioralism

The effectiveness of the political machinery which pluralists are anxious to set in motion depends a great deal on finding precise and clear

46. See Robert A. Packenham, *Liberal America and the Third World* (Princeton, N.J.: Princeton University Press, 1973).

47. Ibid., pp. 108–110. See also Robert Hunter, *The United States and the Developing World* (Washington, D.C.: The Overseas Development Council, 1973).

48. See Nadav Safran, "Egypt's Search for Ideology: The Nasser Era," *New States in the Modern World,* ed. Martin Kilson (Cambridge, Mass.: Harvard University Press, 1975), pp. 37–56.

49. See Robert E. Hunter and John E. Rielly, *Development Today* (New York: Praeger, 1972).

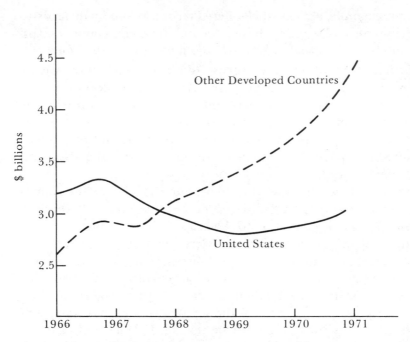

Figure 15-1. Official Development Assistance Disbursements: United States in Comparison to Other Developed Countries, 1966–1971

Source: Reprinted, with permission, from Robert E. Hunter, *The United States and the Developing World: Agenda for Action* (Washington, D.C.: Overseas Development Council), p. 155. Based on data from Report by the Chairman of the Development Assistance Committee, *Development Co-operation, 1972 Review* (Paris: OECD, 1972).

indicators of how the processes of modernization actually affect behavior. The behavioral perspective in developmental politics focuses on factors that induce behavioral change away from traditional ways, and the ability of a society to make adaptive use of new opportunities. The study of behavior in developing countries is new, largely because it is extremely difficult to study societies in which a large or significant proportion of the population may be preliterate and where a full catalogue of cultural and social patterns is unavailable. Of the many significant behavioral emphases, we shall concentrate on two. The first deals with the formation of a *dependency complex* resulting from colonialism. The oppressive and often exploitative rule of an imperialist nation generates feelings of inferiority in a colonial population. This in turn leads to the repression of the people by representatives (native

elites) of their own society, a situation which can produce powerful reactions which aim at a total transformation, perhaps even revolution.[50]

Similar materials have also been applied to the formation of national and cultural personality, and to the problem of mixed identities
experienced by people living in mixed cultures.

The second main emphasis deals with the *process* of becoming
modern: (1) studies of the extent to which people are predisposed
toward achievement, adaptation, and innovation; and (2) studies of the
extent to which a *multiplicity* of factors can be mobilized in different
settings to stimulate modern behavior.

The theory of identity: Before applying the concept of identity to
developing societies we need to review the main characteristics of
identity formation. The theory of identity is based on Erikson's theory
of the evolution of the human personality across certain developmental stages defined by paired opposites. Each stage contributes something to the identity of the person. Beginning in infancy, the way a
child is handled and the nature of the child's immediate intimate universe determine whether the child becomes *trusting* of the environment
or *distrusting*. Later, as the child develops, he or she experiences either
a sense of *autonomy* or some private *shame*. The third stage, building
on the second, is reached when a child begins to act from *initiative* or
out of a sense of *guilt*. By the time the child begins to deal with others—
in the classroom, for example—he or she will be motivated by a sense
of *industry* or a sense of *inferiority* for which the child feels he or she
needs to compensate. With the advent of puberty these initial stages
come to a head in a clear sense of either *identity* or *role confusion*.
Then, in later life, people who have a clear identity tend to be able to
communicate with others and to be capable of *intimacy*. Those who
have unclear roles tend toward *isolation*. In the adult world the former
develop a sense of *generativity*, a responsibility for guiding the next
generation as well as being productive and creative. The latter experience personality *stagnation*. Finally, as a result of the choices made in
previous stages, personality becomes shaped in terms of *ego integrity* or
despair.[51]

Each stage is a point of crisis in the formation of the personality.

50. See O. Mannoni, *Prospero and Caliban, The Psychology of Colonization* (New
York: Praeger, 1964) ; Frantz Fanon, *Les damnés de la terre* (Paris: Maspero, 1961) ;
and Wulf Sachs, *Black Anger* (New York: Grove Press, 1947) .
51. See Erik H. Erikson, *Childhood and Society* (New York: Norton, 1963) , pp.
247–71.

It is possible, however, for a distrustful child to develop a sense of autonomy given the right circumstances, or for a stagnant person to develop a sense of generativity. The personality is open and identity can be altered. Development, in a sociopolitical, cultural, or economic context, alters personality by making ambiguous the situation or environment within which these stages are encountered. A child who cannot trust the environment learns shame, guilt, and so on, at the hands of foreign or expatriate teachers or parents alienated from their traditional cultures.

There are many ways to examine the effects of identity and change in developing countries. One may study the personality of political leaders. How are their identities formed? How, at each stage, do they either reverse the combination to rectify a previous stage, or cement the pattern? The most exceptional leaders are those with a particular drive to develop their ego integrity. Often they see themselves as messianic. Luther, for example, or Darwin, or Freud were all figures who made their most decisive contributions after undergoing severe identity crises, breaking with the intimacy of the family, and becoming highly autonomous. Only after Freud believed that he understood his own relationship to his father could he "establish the existence of the universal father image in man, break through to the mother image as well, and finally arrive at the Oedipus complex, the formulation of which made him one of the most controversial figures in the history of ideas."[52] Similarly, Mahatma Gandhi foresook his caste, his father, his family, and all other ancestral obligations to search for a "Great Soul." The search went unrequited, says Erikson, and so Gandhi undertook to become the "Great Soul" himself, the true leader to a new way.[53] Thus the concept of identity is useful in studying leadership formation using biographical and psychoanalytical materials. Indeed, the founder-leaders of new nations are said to project their own personalities onto society; that is, through a mutual identity the "creator" of the society takes on God-like properties to create a society in his or her own image.[54]

Some questions with which the theory of identity enables us to

52. Erik H. Erikson, *Young Man Luther* (London: Faber and Faber, 1958), pp. 43–44.
53. See Erik H. Erikson, "In Search of Gandhi," *Philosophers and Kings: Studies in Leadership*, ed. Dankwart A. Rustow (New York: George Braziller, 1970), p. 44.
54. See Robert C. Tucker, "The Theory of Charismatic Leadership," ed. Rustow, ibid., pp. 69–94.

deal are these: What are the traits or characteristics of leadership that generate the desire for autonomy in the society, and for self-reliance and control in contrast to self-appraisals more susceptible to negotiation, support, external assistance?

The second way the concept of identity has been used is in the analysis of political change. Theorists have argued that the traditional world is essentially a fragile one, and that the impact of innovative, Western modernization patterns is destructive. For example, when traditional ways of bringing up children change, the impact on the human personality is tremendous. People brought up under one way of life establish their identities on that basis. Innovation is a process of identity smashing. But how should society renovate its identity? When nationalism and other ideologies replace the old identities with new ones, shattered personalities must rebuild new human associations. This is why leaders with highly autonomous and messianic identities are so influential during times of great innovation (whereas they may appear absurd in more stable times). Hence the fervor of symbolic notions of rebirth which attend the formation of newly independent countries. This is why George Washington is the "father of our country," Lenin the "father of the revolution," and Mao, even in death, a legacy to the new Chinese personality.[55]

One case study involving the concept of identity on a national scale is Lucian Pye's analysis of Burma.[56] Pye sees the characteristics of transitional societies as blurred—with political institutions not separated from other social institutions; political parties representing an outside, or global, view rather than the parochial views of the people; widespread use of manipulative power by cliques which operate behind the scenes; and the elevation of political leaders to exceptional degrees of authority. As a result of this confusion Pye hypothesizes the importance of new and old symbols of attachment. A confused public looks to these for security. Lacking a single system or medium of communication and information, gossip and rumor abound. Not surprisingly there is little governmental trust. New elites seek exceptional access to power. Deep cleavages and suspicions are aroused. There is a sense of betrayal between generations.

Because *all* the institutions of Burmese life are affected by these

55. See Everett E. Hagen, *On the Theory of Social Change* (Homewood, Ill.: The Dorsey Press, 1962), pp. 161–99.
56. See Lucian W. Pye, *Politics, Personality, and Nation Building: Burma's Search for Identity* (New Haven, Conn.: Yale University Press, 1962).

considerations, none, not even the most modernized ones like the civil service, function as do their counterparts in Western society. The Burmese people's conception of development therefore remains very different from those of Westerners. In addition, traditional patterns of socialization may continue to exist even into the modernization period so that the behavior of the business community, civil servants, government officials, and so forth only superficially resembles Western counterparts. The problem is to establish a new national identity and a new culture using appropriate modes of socialization and institutionalizing roles functional to a modern society. Unless efforts to shape a new social order are successful, it remains impossible to build anew the individual order and the stable personality.

Innovative behavior: One question posed originally by Max Weber is: Why did capitalism arise when it did and where it did? Why was it not born, for example, in China, which had an elaborate mandarin class elite, a civil service, a commercial establishment, large-scale urbanization, and other attributes of "modern" culture. Or why not in India, or among the ancient Hebrews? Instead it began in England and spread to other essentially Protestant countries. It was an outgrowth, said Weber, of Calvinism, with its doctrine of the autonomy of the individual, its emphasis on predestination and the associated virtues of good works, abstinence (which took the form of savings and accumulation), and the coincidence of wealth with godliness (see p. 390). Calvinism was a religion that motivated people to act in a way which foreshadowed capitalism, the autonomy of the entrepreneur, financial risk taking (a way to reveal God's grace), and the bond of integrity among all those engaged in the enterprise. (One only needs to recall the grim, dour portraits of the Puritans to remember how important Calvinism was.[57])

One problem for the behavioralists is how to make Weber's theory more generally applicable. What themes can be found in societies which, if they do not actually *produce* capitalism, make some systems more innovative than others? Asking this question in an experimental and comparative way the psychologist David C. McClelland began early to develop tests which would reveal tendencies toward innovativeness. McClelland asked whether daydreaming correlated in any way with the achievements of an individual. Are our childhood fantasies

57. See Michael Walzer, "Puritanism as a Revolutionary Ideology," *The Protestant Ethic and Modernization,* ed. S.N. Eisenstadt (New York: Basic Books, 1968), pp. 109–34.

indicative of what we want to achieve? Are the values of Protestantism, which emphasized self-reliance and which found expression in the spirit of modern capitalism, so different from the values of people all over the world? More important, can the *desire* to achieve actually lead to achievement?

It is the theme rather than the dream which is important. McClelland located themes which characterize certain cultures to a markedly greater extent than others. He found a correlation between actual achievement and the *striving* character of the folk tales of a particular society. What McClelland calls *n* (need) -Achievement is highly correlated with cultures whose folk tales emphasize the triumphs of gamblers, hunters, and athletes, and other heroes. So folk tales and children's stories serve as important clues to the general level of receptivity to change and innovativeness in different traditional societies.

Clearly, *n*-Achievement can be measured in many ways. McClelland correlates themes in literature with actual indices of growth. These he connects cross-culturally to family structure, in Germany, for example, and Turkey. Religion, school, and other factors are correlated with some of Parsons' pattern variables like achieved versus status. But how does all this relate to politics? The problem for government in a new or emerging society is to stimulate *n*-Achievement. It is possible to promote achieving behavior by government stimulation. In societies where *n*-Achievement is low it is necessary to promote it through a highly centralized authority, perhaps concentrating on controls over production. (This is precisely what the Communists did in Russia, a country that had at the time a low *n*-Achievement.) On the other hand, where there is low *n*-Achievement such centralized institutions indeed are likely to prove inefficient.[58]

The McClelland study has had many implications for modernization because developmental strategies depend on the supply and distribution of *n*-Achievement. One of the problems in Nigeria, for example, is that there are different distributions of *n*-Achievement among different ethnic groups. Some of the most populous groups, which are among the least achievement oriented, have the greatest political power. Other powerful groupings have high *n*-Achievement and resent being dominated by low achievers for whom they have contempt.[59]

58. See David C. McClelland, *The Achieving Society* (Princeton, N.J.: Van Nostrand, 1961), pp. 418–21.
59. See Robert A. LeVine, *Dreams and Deeds, Achievement Motivation in Nigeria* (Chicago: University of Chicago Press, 1966).

Complex factors are associated with innovative behavior. To study individual change in six developing countries—Argentina, Chile, East Pakistan, India, Israel, and Nigeria—Alex Inkeles of Stanford University developed an index of modernization composed of three main *perspectives:* analytical, topical, and behavioral. These Inkeles subdivided into themes which were coded on computers. The analytical perspective included themes of aspiration, calculability, change orientation, dignity, efficacy, growth of opinion, optimism, particularism, technical skill, and understanding. The topical perspective included evaluation of modes of participation, aging, citizenship, attitudes toward consumption, family size, patriotism, kinship obligations, religious attitudes, work commitment, and so forth. The behavioral perspective included tests of political activity, consumption behavior, arithmetic, and so forth.

Within each country, Inkeles sampled four basic groups: cultivators, new workers, urban nonindustrial workers, and experienced workers. Workers, in turn, were subdivided according to whether the employing firms were modern or not.

Many indicators were used to measure degree of economic development, among them per capita incomes, economic growth rates, industrial employment, percent of wage and salary earners, percentage of manufacturing, percentage of labor force in agriculture, population increases, birth rates, infant mortality, literacy, and so on. The independent variables were personal and family characteristics, origin, residence, socioeconomic level, education, intelligence, skill, occupational characteristics, factory characteristics, level of information-media exposure, and work-behavior scales. The variables together compose an *overall modernization (OM) scale* that was applied by means of cross-cultural survey and questionnaire analysis in the six countries. Without going into the details of the study, we shall note several important findings.

Some theorists find it almost impossible for people to be "resocialized" in later life. However, others suggest that it is possible to change one's identity and adapt at different points all through life. Inkeles discovered that not only can people shift from a traditional to a modern way of life, but also that late socialization can play an even more important part in determining people's modernity than their early socialization. The theory of "fixed" initial or early socialization and identity is thus open to question.[60]

What makes people modern, therefore, are modern institutions.

60. See Alex Inkeles and David H. Smith, *Becoming Modern* (Cambridge, Mass.: Harvard University Press, 1974) , p. 303.

Inkeles also confirms the findings of Lerner's study[61] which stressed the importance of the mass media. Some of his findings are surprising. For instance, urbanization, often regarded both as an indicator of modernization and as a cause of it, was found to be unimportant. The city, even the most cosmopolitan one, does not necessarily have a modernizing impact. One can retain a traditional way of life while living in an urban ghetto area. Nor are the consequences of ethnic origin or religion particularly important to modernization. Perhaps most important, Inkeles felt, was the education of fathers. "The father's education played a major role in determining the level of the son's education, and that, in turn, had a very powerful direct effect on individual modernity scores."[62]

More generally, the study establishes that people change when and if they incorporate the norms of modernizing institutions into their own personality and express them in their attitudes, values, and behavior in general. This is true cross-culturally. The implication is that if a government desires modernization, then it had better get on with the job of building factories and educating parents. In other words, it should consider modernizing its institutions.

Institutionalism and Development

Institutionalists would agree with Inkeles' assumption, but would apply it to *political* as well as social institutions. The institutionalist's thrust toward building up educational facilities, commercial networks, and the public service is part of the design for erecting the key infrastructures for development. These would, in turn, form the foundation for constitutional governments. Representative institutions mediate, and so diffuse, the conflicts arising during modernization.

Institutionalists answer the charge that their belief in the power of democratic governments in periods of major development has been unrealistic by arguing that the requisite time has never been available to make the institutions of emerging democracies work. Most new countries have become independent too soon and without the necessary socioeconomic base.

The institutionalists assumed that commercial activity and local enterprise had to expand along with local government. These would

61. See Daniel Lerner, *The Passing of Traditional Society* (New York: The Free Press of Glencoe, 1958).
62. Inkeles and Smith, op. cit., p. 304.

form the basis for a national state under the tutelage of a colonial power which could keep armed forces from being politicized. A progressive colonialism could undertake institution-building from the bottom up, from local levels to the national level. Once this was accomplished and people had learned to use the institutions, then a transfer of power would occur.[63] The problem was that, in practice, even in their fledgling states nationalist movements demanded a widening franchise and greater responsibility than colonial governments were willing to grant. The discrepancy between these points of view led almost invariably to protracted struggle. So most institutionalists were caught by surprise by the speed with which nationalist movements gained momentum after World War II. What began in Ceylon, India, and Pakistan, Burma, and Indonesia, quickly spread to Africa and elsewhere. The reason efforts to promote representative government in the emerging states proved abortive was that independence came too soon and too suddenly. Democratic government needed a longer gestation period in which to become institutionalized.

Despite the short reign of representative governments in most developing countries, there is a large literature which deals with its different aspects. Some researchers concentrate on political parties, others on class formations.[64] Some show how national politics and national political institutions evolve together.[65]

Many studies examine how interest group conflict leads to violence and the intrusion of the military into government.[66] Others have described the role of the military in the politics of new nations.[67] In some,

63. See Kenneth Robinson and Frederick Madden, eds., *Essays in Imperial Government* (Oxford: Basil Blackwell, 1963). See also Sir Charles Jeffries, *Transfer of Power* (London: Pall Mall Press, 1960).
64. See, for example, Thomas Hodgkin, *African Political Parties* (London: Penguin Books, 1961). See also Richard Sklar, *Nigerian Political Parties* (Princeton, N.J.: Princeton University Press, 1963).
65. See Keith Callard, *Pakistan* (London: Allen and Unwin, 1957). See also James S. Coleman, *Nigeria, Background to Nationalism* (Berkeley, Ca.: University of California Press, 1958).
66. See Philippe C. Schmitter, *Interest Conflict and Political Change in Brazil* (Stanford, Ca.: Stanford University Press, 1971). See also Francisco José Moreno and Barbara Mitrani, eds., *Conflict and Violence in Latin American Politics* (New York: Crowell, 1971).
67. See John Johnson, ed., *The Role of the Military in Underdeveloped Countries* (Princeton, N.J.: Princeton University Press, 1962). See also Morris Janowitz, *The Military in the Political Development of New Nations* (Chicago: University of Chicago Press, 1964). Other useful studies include Edward Feit, *The Armed Bureaucrats* (Boston: Houghton Mifflin, 1973); W.F. Gutteridge, *The Military in African Politics* (London: Methuen, 1969); and Robin Luckham, *The Nigerian Military* (Cambridge: Cambridge University Press, 1971).

as, for example, in Peru, the military takes the role of a vanguard army. In Peru a modern military elite which is antiaristocratic is anxious to promote land reform and improve the economic condition of the society. It is angered at the corruption of politicians and the *immobilisme* produced by democratic institutions. Elsewhere too, new military regimes may replace colonial authority although, in effect, retaining its characteristics and trappings. It remains, that is, a managerial body concerned with law, order, and improving local conditions.[68] This resemblance between pre- and past colonial rule is particularly noteworthy in countries formerly under British control.

The "new military" is efficiency minded. When involved in politics it tries to stand above the various factions—tribal, ethnic, regional, or other. It is concerned with *social engineering*. Sometimes the rule of the military is referred to as *Kemalism,* after Kemal Ataturk, the officer who overthrew the old Turkish monarchy right after World War I and established a modernizing military regime. He was the first to centralize power in the hands of the military leader, while at the same time promoting broad appeal among a peasantry that had hitherto been unchampioned. Kemal deposed the religious elements in Turkish politics, instituted reforms, secularized the religious institutions, quelled separatist rebellions, removed the veil from Turkish women, reformed the land, and performed other feats of social reorganization.[69] Ataturk, however, was a far cry from the conservative *caudillos,* the "men on horseback," who led most Latin American so-called military coups. Now the military concentrates its power for developmental change. It holds on to rule, but the ruler stops acting like an army officer and speaks for the nation.[70] (Egypt's Nasser was a good example.) In Brazil, the military, intent on transforming the institutions of the country, uses terror to suppress opposition, and concentrates on conducting a technocratic revolution—that is, on the use of technically trained elites to operate the machinery of government—while relying on outside invest-

68. See Wilson C. McWilliams, ed., *Garrisons and Government* (San Francisco: Chandler, 1967), pp. 31–32. See also William F. Gutteridge, *Military Institutions and Power in the New States* (London: Pall Mall Press, 1964); Ernest W. Lefever, *Spear and Scepter* (Washington, D.C.: The Brookings Institution, 1970); and Samuel P. Huntington, *The Soldier and the State* (New York: Vintage Books, 1964), pp. 7–97.
69. See Bernard Lewis, *The Emergence of Modern Turkey* (London: Oxford University Press, 1961), pp. 234–87.
70. Marx originally called this syndrome *Bonapartism,* and Antonio Gramsci called it *Caesarism.* See Antonio Gramsci, *Selections from the Prison Notebooks* (London: Lawrence and Wishart, 1971).

ment from multinational corporations to build up the industrial base of the society.[71]

Institutionalists were originally interested in how democratic institutions could be grafted onto societies that had not developed them indigenously. The idea was to capitalize on the beneficial consequences of both economic and political development in new nations to spread democracy. Hence virtually all technically superior democratic countries have implemented aid programs designed to facilitate growth abroad while at the same time fostering democratic public administration and assisting in rural development, population control, and the development of educational institutions through exchange and training programs and the like.

One of the problems with this approach, however, is that one of the effects of modernization is the growth of populist demands for benefits which a government often cannot provide without going bankrupt. Respect for the institutions of democracy does not grow in proportion to the demands made of it. As Samuel Huntington puts it,

The level of political institutionalization in a society with a low level of political participation may be much lower than it is in a society with a much higher level of participation, and yet the society with lower levels of both may be more stable than the society having a higher level of institutionalization and a still higher level of participation. Political stability . . . depends upon the ratio of institutionalization to participation. As political participation increases, the complexity, autonomy, adaptability, and coherence of the society's political institutions must also increase if political stability is to be maintained.[72]

Otherwise the result will be the decay of democratic institutions and the rise of what Huntington calls *praetorianism,* or the growth of modernizing military regimes. The problem, from an institutionalist point of view, is outlined in Figure 15-2.

The mobilization of society leads to frustration and aggression, the levels of which depend on the demand for participation and the presence or absence of regulating and mediating institutions. Mobilization without a high degree of institutionalization leads to the following

71. See Alfred Stepan, *The Military in Politics* (Princeton: Princeton University Press, 1971).
72. See Samuel P. Huntington, *Political Order in Changing Societies* (New Haven, Conn.: University Press, 1968), p. 79.

(1) $\dfrac{\textit{Social mobilization}}{\text{Economic development}}$ = Social frustration

(2) $\dfrac{\textit{Social frustration}}{\text{Mobility opportunities}}$ = Political participation

(3) $\dfrac{\textit{Political participation}}{\text{Political institutionalization}}$ = Political instability

Figure 15-2. Huntington's Mobilization-Institutionalization Hypothesis

Source: Huntington, *Political Order in Changing Societies.* Reprinted with permission of Yale University Press.

paradox: The greater the modernization of society, the greater the likelihood of decay among political institutions. Hence the importance of the military, which steps into the breach. More and more the entrance of the military represents not the praetorianism of an old elite, but rather middle-class or radical praetorianism anxious to produce widespread reform.

Some institutionalists argue that, given the facts of modernization in most societies and the predicaments Huntington describes, a modernizing military regime will at least inaugurate the basic reforms no democratic government can undertake, thus paving the way for the return of a more effective democracy. The primary alternative is socialism, with all its implications of bureaucratic, state-capitalist regimes and few prospects for the growth of democracy.

Philosophical Implications

We now confront the larger questions of development. If we consider development to be an open-ended process, we then need to ask ourselves the following questions about the future of highly industrial societies. What is the future of democracy? What is the future of capitalism? What will be the impact of the future on less developed countries? To what extent will the transformation of the less developed countries change the character of international relations? Will the big industrial countries dependent on raw materials become dinosaurs, too big and clumsy to last in an environment which no longer supports them? Is the nation-state becoming obsolete? Will new forms of jurisdiction arise

—regional associations designed to control population growth, the movement of populations, the multinational corporations, fiscal policies and monetary systems, higher education, and the like? Such questions are as philosophical as they are technical. They imply ends rather than means, values rather than consequences.

Radical views of developmentalism: The radical interpretations of developmentalism can be put in terms of five major tendencies or schools of thought. First there is the *socialism of the workplace,* represented by the philosophies of the utopian socialists who, by and large, pre-date Marx. Their beliefs were almost entirely dismissed by Marx, yet they are returning to vogue, often in countries claiming to be Marxist. The most important resurgence of the socialism of the workplace is in the area of worker participation. More and more the emphasis is on the factory as the place where people spend their working time yet have little or no control. Perhaps the most important emphasis on workplace socialism has been in Yugoslavia, which has modified the institutions of national government to fit with worker participation.[73] Yugoslavia has a constitution based on worker participation rather than party competition. To structure the idea of workplace socialism into the system involved both a decentralization of decision making and the fostering of worker-management councils which make the key decisions for the operation of a specific plant or industry.

The Yugoslavian experiment has been attractive to other countries. Chile, under its short-lived (1970–1973) democratic socialist regime headed by Allende, nationalized many enterprises and established worker councils to manage them. In Sweden and other highly industrial countries (including the United States) similar experiments are proceeding. Workplace socialism is attractive to people in underdeveloped countries because it is a way of increasing participation without increasing the proportion of unrealistic demands made on government. People participate in terms of their knowledge and experience rather than their hopes and sentiments.[74]

Workplace socialism is increasingly considered a viable alternative to the Stalinist mode of development, *the socialism of the command economy.* Under this method, forced draft procedures outlined by the

73. See Ichak Adizes, *Industrial Democracy: Yugoslav Style* (New York: The Free Press, 1971).
74. See Alvin Z. Rubinstein, *Yugoslavia and the Nonaligned World* (Princeton, N.J.: Princeton University Press, 1970).

superstructure of the Communist Party and the bureaucratic state create the base or the infrastructure of development by exerting coercive controls, building up heavy industry and the military, holding down consumption, and nationalizing everything under a system of highly centralized planning known as a *command economy*. Such a system is costly in terms of human resources, but it is also beyond the reach of most societies which lack the material resources to undertake the job.[75]

Secondly there is China, which is, of course, the main alternative to Stalinist Russia. It has accepted the concept of centralized planning and relies on centralized control, yet Maoism is a doctrine of mediation rather than a vehicle for the intensification of struggles. The difference is important. The Chinese have placed high emphasis on education and discussion. Under their system contradictions are identified and, when understood, turned to productive action.[76]

A third alternative is the socialism of the highly developed countries (particularly Italy and France), including *the socialism of the intellectuals*. The idea of the Soviet Union as the center of the communist world, and the notion of the transformation of backward countries, is counter to the main thrust of Marx, who argued that capitalism had to run its course before socialism could be effective. Marx believed this because he foresaw that during the later stages of capitalism a working class would appear which could displace the bourgeoisie and become a universal class. Thereafter the state would not be used as an instrument of oppression and hegemony. A new and higher form of understanding, or consciousness, would be available to all.

Two Marxists interested in the consciousness of the proletariat, Georg Lukacs and Antonio Gramsci, helped to revive the original Marxist concern with such matters. Lukacs saw the potentiality for an evolution of consciousness as equivalent to the evolution of the working class. Gramsci was more concerned with how intellectuals would participate in the state and give voice to new forms of social life.[77]

Finally we come to the social democratic alternative, *evolutionary*

75. See David and Marina Ottaway, *Algeria, The Politics of a Socialist Revolution* (Berkeley, Ca.: University of California Press, 1970).
76. See James R. Townsend, *Political Participation in Communist China* (Berkeley, Ca.: University of California Press, 1967). See also Franz Schurmann, *Ideology and Organization in Communist China* (Berkeley, Ca.: University of California Press, 1966).
77. See Georg Lukacs, *History and Class Consciousness* (London: Merlin Press, 1971); and Antonio Gramsci, op. cit.

Marxism, which is the basis of modern social democratic parties and regimes in Scandinavia, Germany, and elsewhere.[78] The central concern of evolutionary Marxism is the *embourgeoisement* of the workers; that is, the assimilation of the workers into the middle class rather than their radicalization. Social democrats have been relatively generous in overseas aid. They seek to strengthen the links between the Third and First Worlds.

Enlightenment views of development: From the standpoint of Enlightenment philosophy, the question is: Should developmentalism be a respecter of institutions or a destroyer of them? The assumption of the Enlightenment was that rules govern the universe of human beings just as rules govern the universe of nature. These rules can be found documented in classical economics and in the social contract, or the utilitarian measure of benefits. The modern emphasis, however, is on *interests.* Therefore, with morality so trivialized, there has been a renewed concern with principles of justice and equitable distribution, and with the modes and methods which best allow the practical fulfillment of these principles. There is no purely utilitarian calculus today, but the race is on to clarify and realize those values pertaining to principles of fair justice in democratic institutions. This has been the main contribution of the philosopher John Rawls, whose objective is not to define some actual equality but rather to describe the conditions of inequity which exist.

> *. . . the plurality of associations in a well-ordered society, each with its secure internal life, tends to reduce the visibility, or at least the painful visibility, of variations in men's prospects. For we tend to compare our circumstances with others in the same or in a similar group as ourselves, or in positions that we regard as relevant to our aspirations. The various associations in society tend to divide into so many noncomparing groups, the discrepancies between these divisions not attracting the kind of attention which unsettles the lives of those well placed. And this ignoring of differences in wealth and circumstance is made easier by the fact that when citizens do meet one another, as they must in public affairs at least, the principles of equal justice are acknowledged.*[79]

78. See Eduard Bernstein, *Evolutionary Socialism* (New York: Schocken Books, 1961).
79. See John Rawls, *A Theory of Justice* (Cambridge, Mass.: Harvard University Press, 1971), pp. 536–37.

Modern "Enlightenment" theorists study how to promote equity. What is the preferred character of group life? What rules need to apply in order to promote justice?[80] Which brings us back to behavior—not behavior of the individualistic kind, but organizational behavior, the application of decision-making rules to complex organizations. Shall we learn how to gain compliance, establish goals, maximize effectiveness, and establish cohesion, both with respect to modernizing and highly industrialized institutions? In the context of modern institutions the Enlightenment tradition has been downgraded into an examination of the rules of organized life.[81] As a consequence *implementation* has become the critical focus for study. Developmental change may require new principles of fair justice, but no matter how widely understood and accepted, these in their turn require appropriate mechanisms of application. So the search for appropriate modes of leadership and organization is the modern substitute for institutionalism.

The development of rationality: The Greeks perceived the rationality of the world as well as the paradoxes of rationality. (When demand is stimulated more becomes less. Participation creates political instability. The mobilization of the public produces authoritarian leaders who speak in the name of the people but do not let the people speak for themselves.) So now we have come full circle. We must still ask ourselves, how can we enable rationality to rule our politics? How can our understanding of the universe help us to control it, manage it, and make it serve our purposes?

Let us return for a moment to the findings of McClelland which we discussed in the previous section. He suggested that in countries that exhibit a low need for achievement quotient there are advantages in concentrating authority in a centralized way, in order to combine managerial talent with the rationality of planned achievement measured in growth or output. By one standard then, rationality represents a plan, an organized set of priorities, with scarce talent organized around its implementation.

Inkeles argued that two other factors besides *n*-Achievement affect

80. See Brian Barry, *Political Argument* (London: Routledge and Kegan Paul, 1965).

81. See Victor H. Vroom and Philip W. Yetton, *Leadership and Decision-Making* (Pittsburgh, Pa.: University of Pittsburgh Press, 1973); Amitai Etzioni, *A Comparative Analysis of Complex Organizations* (New York: The Free Press, 1962); Anthony Downs, *Inside Bureaucracy* (Boston: Little, Brown, 1967); and Philip Selznick, *Leadership in Administration* (Evanston, Ill.: Row, Peterson, 1957).

modernization most: the educational level of fathers, and the actual institutions of modern production such as schools and factories.

Taken together these two findings make a powerful argument for a developmental rationality of the following kind. *A highly centralized, mobilized, hierarchical system of rule, concentrating on planned productive priorities and investing in an educational infrastructure and the construction of productive enterprises, offers the most rational means for maximizing modernization.* This has been precisely the course followed by the Soviet Union, Communist China, and Cuba.

But another kind of rationality argues that the cultural, moral, personal, and psychological costs of forced draft modernization are precisely what is most objectionable about modernity itself. The result has been that modern people of those countries where forced draft procedures have been implemented live lives that are more narrow, confined, fearful, restricted, provincial, and hopeless than ever before.

The Greeks, inheritors of a belief paradigm in which humans were the playthings of the gods, posed the problem of rationality versus religion. Today we are concerned with the kind of world in which some people try to play god and treat other human beings as their playthings. The Greeks sought to solve the problem by assuming and subscribing to some higher rationality. Nowadays we have come to doubt that such a higher authority exists. As we stated in the early pages of this text, rationality is a political concept that cannot be limited to singular judgments regarding one specific case, or one point in time, or even one function or jurisdiction. Rather it must be applied in a plural fashion, to *all* aspects of government or rule. And it is this condition with which developmental politics must come to grips.

Developmentalism brings us back to the fundamentals—to first principles and questions. But the answers still elude us. Development fosters concerns for the here and now. It exacerbates demands. It stimulates what Aristotle called practical (and which we might refer to as instrumental) wisdom. It is a kind of common sense, the difficulty of which is that it produces irrationalities when the practical wisdom of individuals fails to coincide with that of the larger group. The problem is that when people want too much they consider their own ends to the exclusion of the larger purpose. Yet it is only through the realization of larger purposes that people can give the right aim and direction to their practical wisdom and achieve a more rational community. When that begins to happen then the term *public interest* begins to mean something and the whole of society is better for it.

In turn, appreciation of the larger end requires both education and a mature judgment which comprehends the virtue of understanding beyond practical wisdom. Such understanding comes through reasoning. It dignifies the power of discretion that all people must exercise for themselves. The real question is not whether human beings are capable of an improved reasoning, but whether individual virtue, social excellence, and political rationality can come together in the modern world. The political philosophy of the Greeks went far beyond matters of practical wisdom in politics to a consideration of what makes virtue excellent and excellence virtuous. Both, when combined with justice, represent the ingredients of political rationality. This remains true of political science today.

Epilogue

chapter sixteen
The Future of Political Science

At the beginning of this book we assumed that, despite the diversity of interests and range of queries of political scientists, a *corpus*—a body of interrelated ideas—binds the field together. In keeping with this assumption, we began with a discussion of political theory and concluded with one as well. Questions of theory are revitalizing the center of inquiry today. If, for a time, specialization shifted interest away from larger questions, this is no longer the case. Indeed, now there is even a new relationship among the politician, the intellectual, and the political scientist. More and more the intellectual and professional are moving closer together, and the fear that the professional and the politician would associate at the expense of the intellectual has proven unfounded. Politics has become the focus for larger questions of social purpose. And the search for novel solutions and alternatives to our condition is being heightened. The danger that finely honed professionals will direct attention away from political *facts of life* toward technical puzzles or model building is declining. As professionality grows, so does the scope of research. Today's behavioralists are concerned with freedom, equality, and revolution. Modern structuralists puzzle over the developmental future. Both, however, pose questions in a philosophical manner. Moreover, a new generation is awakening an interest in broad philosophical questions as well as direct solutions, asking why and wherefore.

If political science began in political philosophy, it is also true that it shifted away from it. The shift took place partly because political philosophy had become too dull and metaphysical. It assumed too much. Self-evident purposes dwindled into mere banalities. Indeed, once political philosophers stopped adding new values and political norms and simply repeated old civilities, philosophy became little more than a noteworthy but not very dynamic set of abstractions. Hence we saw the wholesale rejection of it, especially by the behavioralists during the 1950s. Yet by ignoring political philosophy political science trivialized itself. So its renaissance revitalizes all our approaches. Not only do we see the contributions of the classical, Enlightenment, and radical traditions with a fresh relevance. They serve also as an antidote to narrow professionalization in the field and the here-and-now orientation of politicians. Moreover, political philosophy has come back on its own terms as a fresh force.

1. There is a renewed interest in the link between base, superstructure, and consciousness, to phrase the issue from the Marxist point of view; or to put it another way, between structure, beliefs, and behavior. Marxist theory has come alive through the work of Louis Althusser and others in France and Italy who have helped to return Marxist political thought to the mainstream of both political life and political theory.

2. There is growing concern with psychoanalytical contributions and how they fit into structural analysis and behavioralism. This has revived interest in philosophy, especially the work of phenomenologists like Edmund Husserl and early psychologists like Wilhelm Dilthey. One merger of Marxism, phenomenology, and psychoanalysis is represented by the Frankfurt School of critical theory, which began in Germany in 1923 and whose outstanding representative was Max Horkheimer. Today Jürgen Habermas has confronted the problem of how the old political theory contrasts with new approaches to politics, and emphasizes the return to history as a method. Too much emphasis on politics as a science drives out history. Too much positivism results in the exclusion of other questions.[1]

3. Another main line of inquiry closely related to the first is with language as it affects meaning; that is, as the conceptual basis of our thinking about politics. Issues in structural linguistics are becoming important. Some derive from the work of philosophers like Ludwig Wittgenstein. Others, like Peter Winch, are more directly concerned with structure—with social science as a science of rules. Obviously rules of thinking and rules of behavior are related, but all the connections have not yet been made in a political context.[2]

4. Institutional analysis is also being revived. No longer preoccu-

1. For a general discussion of the Frankfurt School see Martin Jay, *The Dialectical Imagination* (Boston: Little, Brown, 1973).
2. See Richard J. Bernstein, *The Restructuring of Social and Political Theory* (New York: Harcourt Brace Jovanovich, 1976).

pied with building a better parliamentary or presidential system, institutionalists are reconsidering other models of politics, examining institutions of government in socialist countries and developing countries in fresh terms. In France a group of institutionalists has developed a *theory of institutions*. Scholars like Maurice Hauriou, Georges Renard, and others are renewing attention to the effects of institutions on the social order, the mediation of institutions which affect the pace of change at the political level, and the connections between modern law and institutions.[3]

5. Behavioralism and pluralism are combining in a context of enlightened philosophical concerns. Some scholars have been particularly stimulated by the study of justice and fairness, employing the "new social contract" of John Rawls as a standard for modern utility theory. Their emphasis shifts away from simple maximization and the role of coalitions and group behavior to focus on ways to distribute satisfactions and to the fundamental rules that, when applied, contribute to perceptions of fairness. The work of Douglas Rae, Brian Barry, and others is designed to specify the connection between larger goals of equity and appropriate conditions of choice. This area of concern, *choice analysis*, is also attracting those interested in more technical forms of modeling such as mathematical and statistical analysis.[4]

6. Structuralism is also connected to other new tendencies. It emerged as an issue in political science when scholars became interested in the analysis of social change. While once it was based on functional comparisons and case studies, it is now becoming more theoretically comparative, looking at how systems of policies affect or limit choice. Drawing on both the contributions of Marxism and the Frankfurt School, modern structuralism confronts philosophical questions about deduction and valid inference. Marxists and structural functionalists both note broad patterns of change which frame, contain, and limit behavior at the center of their approaches. Yet the two schools represent quite different interpretations of developmental politics. Some efforts are being made to combine the two by, for example, applying the method of contradiction to the societal level and the method of equilibrium to the governmental.[5]

---

3. See Albert Broderick, ed., *The French Institutionalists* (Cambridge, Mass.: Harvard University Press, 1970).
4. See Brian Barry, *The Liberal Theory of Justice* (Oxford: The Clarendon Press, 1973).
5. See D.E. Apter, *Choice and the Politics of Allocation* (New Haven, Conn.: Yale University Press, 1971).

7. Modern pluralism has also shifted its focus to new modes of participation, particularly workplace socialism and joint management schemes. There is now a considerable literature on self-management, and if self-management experiments continue to be successful, the scheme may well supplant conventional representative institutions. Thus modern pluralism is slowly turning back to questions of an institutional nature, even to examine jurisdictions, regionalism, multiple centers of power, planning, implementation of plans and decisions, and new forms of accountability. New attention is also turning to case studies of worker participation in many countries—old industrial as well as new nations moving in a socialist direction.[6]

8. Developmentalism has produced a large literature, using what Huntington calls the *systems function* approach, which relies heavily on the dichotomy between tradition and modernity. But this dichotomy is no longer very satisfactory. Scholars are moving more and more toward the study of political economy as a search for parameters imposed by economic growth on political possibilities. This present-day concern of such widely divergent theorists as neo-Marxists and quantitative comparativists also turns developmentalists toward behavioral models. The question is posed: What are the limits of our economic lives?[7]

Alongside the "new" behavioralists there are also those who favor a return to more historical forms of analysis. The problems of developing countries are no longer regarded as exotic or unique or different, but as part of the mainstream of economic and social evolution on a worldwide scale. This new feeling of identity has prompted a good deal of soul searching about the conditions under which representative democracy might prosper in developing countries.[8]

9. Finally, there is a new tendency towards the use of mathematics and statistics in political science, particularly regarding set theory and computer analysis which emphasize formal modeling and causal theo-

6. See, for example, Alvin Z. Rubinstein, *Yugoslavia and the Nonaligned World* (Princeton, N.J.: Princeton University Press, 1970).
7. See Ronald Cohen, "Anthropology and Political Science," in Seymour Martin Lipset, ed., *Politics and the Social Sciences* (New York: Oxford University Press, 1969), pp 29–64. See also Ronald D. Brunner and Garry D. Brewer, *Organized Complexity: Empirical Theories of Political Development* (New York: The Free Press, 1971).
8. See Samuel P. Huntington and Joan M. Nelson, *No Easy Choice: Political Participation in Developing Countries* (Cambridge, Mass.: Harvard University Press, 1976). See also D.E. Apter, *The Politics of Modernization* (Chicago: University of Chicago Press, 1965).

ries. The reorganization of political thinking around quantitative categories will in the future differ from the more conventional quantitative study of aggregate data useful for statistical correlations and factoring. For the language of mathematics to be effectively applied to problems of politics, however, new models are required which are both highly formalized, yet capable of empirical application. Professional knowledge in quantitative political science may well make a quantum jump in the next generation.

Political science, no matter how scientific it becomes in the technical sense, will nevertheless in certain respects always remain an interpretive discipline, for unlike physical scientists, political scientists must continually ground their ideas in fundamental principles. Politics and governments exist to serve human interests and needs.

If we sum up the most important general trends of political analysis over the past few years, two stand out. First, as the concerns of the discipline multiply it becomes less and less a United States or Europe-oriented field of study. It has become much more genuinely international in scope. Indeed, recent contributions to political theory come from scholars all over the world. Contributions are being made to research by people in developing countries who are able to probe deeply into the affairs of their compatriots from a fresh perspective, as well as casting a cold eye on our own cherished institutions.

Second, we cannot overlook the importance of the growing debate between empiricists and rationalists or better, the behavioralists and paradigmists. In the 1950s and 1960s the rationalists, theorists who search to establish the contexts within which a subject matter can be meaningfully defined, attacked old political conventionalities and applied new theories to broad problems of change, mainly in regard to developing countries. Empiricists largely agreed with the attacks but were more concerned with finding specific attributes of political life in as precise a manner possible than with writing broad theories. While the two schools had been uneasy partners, they now have come to represent alternative tendencies in contemporary political thinking. We will conclude our discussion with some observations on the tension between advocates of "paradigmatic" (or rational) and behavioral (or empiricist) analysis in political science, something which is likely to intensify with time.

Paradigmatic versus Behavioral Thinking

Some years ago Princeton professor Sheldon Wolin wrote a book called *Politics and Vision*.[9] Wolin reviewed the field of political philosophy as a network of interrelated arguments about the nature and purpose of social life, and showed how political argument was not only a means to an end, offering some practical and working solutions, but a complete vision of an ethical and moral world in which political knowledge is necessary in and of itself.

Take each of the various approaches discussed in this book. Each is itself a form of political thinking. Each engages a special dimension of argument. Each implies not one but many visions of the future as well as ways to interpret and review the past. But the important thing is not simply the diversity of the political dialogue. The significance of these forms of discourse is that each expresses a way of thinking about the virtuous distribution of power. Each represents a *language* of politics that offers us social insights into ourselves through a unique *line of moral vision*. Each helps locate and identify a context of equity, a sense of proportion in different aspects of political life so that societies can be evaluated on several conceptual planes.

But there are differences in the way one directs the enterprise. The professional emphasis is on testing for manageable, narrow truths to instruct the conduct of political affairs. The behavioralists and pluralists prefer to break wholes into parts and to dissect, examine, and experiment individually with each component unit. On the other hand, structuralists regard the full-blown systems model itself as a generative idea.

To realize the ideal *politics of vision*, then, is a complex affair. Just as no one person's vision is likely to be inclusive and convincing, so no one approach to political analysis is pertinent to all cases. Each reveals a different aspect of our political lives. The problem is to keep overlapping perspectives from blurring the vision altogether. In considering the different questions and answers within the field, we need to see beyond the microscopic or the macroscopic view. Each approach opens the door to a whole literature, a set of ideas, an intellectual culture, all of which are a basis for communicating, for thinking, and for identifying those issues of priority across schools of thought as well as national boundaries. Understanding the issues will require more and more effort as the field becomes more international and the world more complex. The solutions offered will always be transitory.

9. See Sheldon Wolin, *Politics and Vision* (Boston: Little, Brown, 1960).

However, underlying all six approaches, and despite their complementarity, is a fundamental dualism between behavioral and rational or "paradigmatic" thinking.[10] (Plato was a paradigmatic thinker, as was Marx. So too are modern structuralists.) Behavioral thinking is operationally oriented. It starts from the assumption that people, perceiving themselves at work in the practical world, are able to adapt, learn, and innovate. Behavioral thinking is therefore pragmatic, scientific in the experimental sense, and very Anglo-American in conception. Behavioralists are suspicious of broad, general theories not so much because they might be wrong but because they can never be proved wrong. To behavioralists paradigm thinkers sometimes appear to be opinionated fellows who present their prejudices and preferences in the form of science but whose theories on close inspection lack substance. The behavioralists prefer good proofs of validity about propositions. For the behavioralist science is piecemeal and doing that obligates one to greater modesty. Theory which consists of building up *cumulative laws* requires first the acquisition of a great deal of valid evidence. Hence science in politics depends on effective techniques, careful empirical observation and correlation.

For the paradigmist on the other hand, science is different. It consists of formulating *systematic ideas* which encourage interpretive leaps beyond the boundaries of the known. Its object is to anticipate the next set of paradoxes, issues, important events. Most of the innovative thinkers were paradigmists. Even a behavioralist who regards Marx or Freud as "myth-makers" of science would have to concede, however, that their impact on social science's thought has been tremendous.

There is, of course, a third position, one not often proposed in political science textbooks, but one to which this author subscribes. I prefer the *hermeneutic,* or interpretive, point of view over strict notions of science. In my view the danger of the behavioral position, with its emphasis on quantitative detail, specialization, and fine applications, is that it will engage small minds on small issues, while the paradigmist position with its emphasis on grand solutions will engineer empty architectural plans for buildings that can never be built.

Basic to the hermeneutic position is the idea that in social science one does not simply review research findings but considers them in an ever-changing moral and intellectual context. This is particularly the case with political science. One reads both theories and data, using

10. Ernest Gellner, *Legitimation of Belief* (Cambridge: Cambridge University Press, 1974), pp. 168–84.

paradigms and empirical facts in a world of shifting emphases and circumstances. All of us seek to unlock both the secret of the moment and its meaning in the larger perspective of change. One thus goes back as well as forward. It is important to know the extent to which what one may have considered to be new, different, surprising, or shocking, has its past equivalent. It is also necessary to consider what is genuinely new or qualitatively different and when old solutions, no matter how venerable, are inadequate no matter how sentimental our attachments to them.

The proper way to think back on this book is as a resource for the multiple interpretation of politics. The approaches we have reviewed—political philosophy, institutionalism, behavioralism, pluralism, structuralism, and developmentalism—all have been the subject of analysis. But each provides a different perspective for the analysis of political things. If interpretation requires us to see political science as a whole, as a corpus of thought, it is also a way of breaking up and making manageable its various parts. It is hoped that the result will be a more humane perspective to accompany the scientific one. What will be required is a little intelligence, greater patience, and above all, a touch of humor.

Subject Index

Name Index